Writing Software Documentation

THE ALLYN AND BACON SERIES
IN TECHNICAL COMMUNICATION

Series Editor: Sam Dragga, Texas Tech University

Thomas T. Barker

*Writing Software Documentation:
A Task-Oriented Approach*

Dan Jones

Technical Writing Style

Charles Kostelnick and David D. Roberts

*Designing Visual Language: Strategies for
Professional Communicators*

Carolyn Rude

Technical Editing, Second Edition

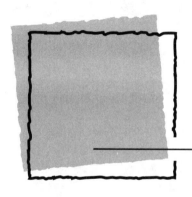

Writing Software Documentation

A Task-Oriented Approach

Thomas T. Barker
Texas Tech University

Allyn and Bacon

Boston   London   Toronto   Sydney   Tokyo   Singapore

Vice President, Humanities: Joseph Opiela
Editorial Assistant: Rebecca Ritchey
Executive Marketing Manager: Lisa Kimball
Editorial-Production Administrator: Donna Simons
Editorial-Production Service: Omegatype Typography, Inc.
Composition and Prepress Buyer: Linda Cox
Manufacturing Buyer: Megan Cochran
Cover Administrator: Jenny Hart
Text Designer: Carol Somberg/Omegatype Typography, Inc.

Copyright © 1998 by Allyn & Bacon
A Viacom Company
160 Gould Street
Needham Heights, MA 02194

Internet: www.abacon.com
America Online: keyword: College Online

Library of Congress Cataloging-in-Publication Data

Barker, Thomas T.
    Writing software documentation : a task-oriented approach / Thomas
T. Barker
      p. cm.
    Includes bibliographical references and index.
    ISBN 0-205-19576-8
    1. Software documentation.   I. Title.
QA76.76.D63B37   1998
005.1'5—dc21   97-22198
                                                  CIP

Printed in the United States of America

10 9 8 7 6 5 4 3 2 1   02 01 00 99 98 97

For Emily and John

Contents

chapter **3**   Constructing a Task List   87

chapter **4** Planning and Writing Your Documents   129

chapter **5** Getting Useful Reviews   173

chapter 6   Conducting Usability Tests   196

chapter 7   Editing and Fine Tuning   222

chapter 8   Designing for Task Orientation   248

chapter **11**   Using Graphics Effectively   352

chapter **12**   Writing to Teach—Tutorials   394

chapter 15   Designing Indexes   462

Foreword by the Series Editor

The Allyn & Bacon Series in Technical Communication is designed for the growing number of students enrolled in undergraduate and graduate programs in technical communication. Such programs offer a wide variety of courses beyond the introductory technical writing course—advanced courses for which fully satisfactory and appropriately focused textbooks have often been impossible to locate. This series will also serve the continuing education needs of professional technical communicators, both those who desire to upgrade or update their own communication abilities as well as those who train or supervise writers, editors, and artists within their organization.

The chief characteristic of the books in this series is their consistent effort to integrate theory and practice. The books offer both research-based and experienced-based instruction, describing not only what to do and how to do it but explaining why. The instructors who teach advanced courses and the students who enroll in these courses are looking for more than rigid rules and ad hoc guidelines. They want books that demonstrate theoretical sophistication and a solid foundation in the research of the field as well as pragmatic advice and perceptive applications. Instructors and students will also find these books filled with activities and assignments adaptable to the classroom and to the self-guided learning processes of professional technical communication.

To operate effectively in the field of technical communication, today's students require extensive training in the creation, analysis, and design of information for both domestic and international audiences, for both paper and electronic environments. The books in the Allyn & Bacon Series address those subjects that are most frequently taught at the undergraduate and graduate levels as a direct response to both the educational needs of students and the practical demands of business and industry. Additional books will be developed for the series in order to satisfy or anticipate changes in writing technologies, academic curricula, and the profession of technical communication.

Sam Dragga
Texas Tech University

Preface

This textbook covers the subject of software documentation, which comes in many forms—from the familiar print *User's Manual* or *Installation Guide* to the increasingly familiar online help program. I focus exclusively on creating documents (or *information products*) that help software users learn program features and use them to work productively. Most manuals and help documents that accompany software programs are written by technical writers in the software industry. Students or professionals interested in doing this interesting and challenging work will find in this book a basic foundation in the principles of writing these kinds of documents.

Two words sum up my approach in this book: *task orientation*. The software instructions, procedures, manuals, and help programs that users find useful in their work reflect the organization of the user's tasks. For example, if you organize the features of a word processing program alphabetically, the user must know a great deal about the software to find the right command. But if you organize the features of the same word processing program around the usual tasks the office worker performs, then the person already has some knowledge about how to apply the software productively. In this book I show you how to apply this simple principle to all the elements of documentation. Using this principle will help you design successful projects.

What Can This Book Do for You?

The following list covers some of the ways this book can help students and professionals learn to write successful, task-oriented manuals and help.

- *Give you a place to start if you don't already have one.*   Chapters 1 through 7 follow a complete step-by-step process for analyzing users, learning a software program, and designing task-oriented documents.

- *Teach you the basics about page and screen design.*   Chapters 8 through 15 provide you with the right background in designing useful information, laying out pages and screens, and designing various forms of manuals and online help.

- *Provide useful tools for writing manuals and online help.*   Each chapter has a checklist of the main points you want to remember in preparing your documents. These checklists can keep you organized and on track.

- *Provide practice in writing.*   The chapters all have useful and interesting exercises you can use to build useful skill sets that are valuable in the technical communication job market.

- *Help you understand software users.*   All chapters relate in important ways to one guiding idea: Understand your users' information-oriented tasks above all, and you'll have the key to helping that person use software productively in the workplace.

Why Should You Read This Book?

This book meets the needs of two types of people: those interested in finding practical steps to help them start and complete a project successfully, and those interested in exploring the ideas behind software documentation as a discipline and as a profession.

■ If you're a project-oriented reader facing a manual or help project and needing assistance, this book can guide you through an entire successful documentation project sequence.

■ If you're relatively experienced with writing but new to software documentation and you want to broaden your understanding of the ideas behind designing product-support documents for software programs, you will find a comprehensive discussion of the ideas and research behind the idea of task orientation.

Perhaps your motivation contains a combination of these two situations. Both of these activities can be relevant to the education and training of a professional technical writer in the software industry. To help you meet these goals in reading, the chapters have two tracks, represented by the two main expository sections of each chapter: the reading-to-do track (the Guidelines section) and the reading-to-understand track (the Discussion section). These two tracks complement one another, meeting the needs of the project-oriented reader, the understanding-oriented reader, and the needs of the reader who is reading for both of these purposes.

The Reading-to-Do Track

The ideas in the Guidelines section of the chapter give the person facing a project immediate, practical help and advice on how to proceed. Guidelines use the command form of the verb in order to suggest action and doing. Often Guidelines will focus on the steps for achieving some documentation objective, such as getting useful review information after you've written a draft, or finding out if your procedures work right. At other times Guidelines function as general advice, not given in a definite step-by-step order.

Readers who are interested in getting a jump start on a project will also find inspiration by browsing the Discussion section of each chapter, where I've tried to include as many useful examples and models as possible. Similarly, when you're in the midst of a project, you'll find the Checklists at the end of each chapter very useful as reminders of the principles in the chapter.

The Reading-to-Understand Track

The Discussion section of each chapter looks at key issues related to the chapter topic. For instance, in Chapter 12, "Writing to Teach—Tutorials," the Discussion section explores the background in cognitive psychology that informs much tutorial design in the profession today, contrasting the elaborative approach and the minimalist approach.

The reader interested in deepening his or her understanding of the principles behind task-oriented documentation will appreciate the Practice/Problem Solving suggestions at the end of each chapter. Also, where relevant, I have tried to include cross references to material in the Guidelines sections.

What Is Software Documentation?

Here is an important definition:

> *Software documentation* is a form of writing for both print and online media that supports the efficient and effective use of software in its intended environment.

In its purest sense, the term refers to the documentation of what's on a screen, as if the manual and help were a "documentary" of interaction events. This makes sense on one level, because technical writers in the software industry do a lot of recording of what happens as a way of presenting material to the software users in manuals and online help.

But software documentation, as many researchers have shown and as technical writers and software documenters know from their work in the business, contributes significantly to the value of the software product. So in this sense the documentation contributes to the user's efficiency in the workplace and thus has an important role to play in modern business. Think of how often you hear people complain about manuals and online help. To me, this speaks for a need for documentation—more useful and practical documentation than has characterized the software industry in the past.

Over its evolution, software documentation has expanded to take on the challenge of providing useful and practical information products for users. Whereas documentation once aimed to satisfy the support needs of the experienced user, documentation in the 1990s aims also to make software useful. This means not just teaching features but supporting workplace tasks with step-by-step accuracy.

In changing from the goal of supporting experts to guiding and teaching beginning and intermediate users, writers looked to a number of resource disciplines, including document design, instructional psychology, cognitive psychology, ergonomics and human factors, and traditional rhetoric. These explorations created a great number of design innovations that, coupled with technological advances in page design and functionality, have given us the exciting world of HTML documents (online documents with automatic links among topics) and help files (online documents that teach, guide, and support the user through text and graphics provided with the program).

But of all the innovations that sprang from the rapid rise of computer and software technology during the 1980s and 1990s, task orientation has provided the most dependable and useful tool for manual design. Task orientation, as an organizing principle in manuals and online help and as a goal in their design and writing, informs the approach I take in this book.

Consider another important definition:

> *Task orientation* is an approach to software documentation that presents of information in chronological order based on the user's workplace sequences.

Task orientation encourages the successful application of software to workplace objectives. Other terms used for task orientation include how-to, step-by-step, procedures, walk-throughs, and tutorials. This approach to documentation is shown in a variety of print and online forms: tutorials, "getting started" booklets, instruction steps, job performance aids, and online help procedures.

In this book I take task orientation seriously and show you the benefits of using this strategy in every part of the design of your information product. In so doing you will leverage the user's interest in performing the job successfully, not just learning a new piece of software. The next section illustrates some of the benefits of the task-orientation design strategy.

Who Can Benefit from Reading This Book?

Those who can benefit from this book include any students or professionals associated with writing for the software industry. The section below describes characteristics of some of these people and points out how the information in *Writing Software Documentation* can help them in their learning and work.

Students Preparing for Careers in the Computer Industry

If you want to succeed as a writer in the computer industry you need to know how to design user documentation from a task-orientation point of view. Consider this scenario: A medical management software company keeps incurring high support costs from a client who still has an old version of their manual. That manual contains screen shots of the menus with explanations, in arcane computer terms, of what each of the menu functions does. Other clients using the same system log only half the support calls of this client, but they have received and used the newer step-by-step version of the manual. They can find, by skimming the table of contents, tasks that relate to their work and that have practical value in the workplace. They see listed there things they get paid to do, like "Print a Patient-Tracking Report" or "Create a Sales Analysis Graph." When they turn to these procedures they find steps leading them logically through the task, whether it's printing a document in a special way or converting a document from Microsoft Word to HTML format.

Which manual would you want to have produced? The one that doubles the support calls (at an average cost of $75 each) from perplexed users who need to know how to edit their *config.sys* file, or the manual that lowers the number of support calls or otherwise shows an improvement in user productivity—productivity you can measure convincingly and repeat in other projects?

Engineers, Computer Scientists, Managers, Trainers, Usability Specialists

This book has also something to offer readers from the technical side of the computer industry who have a great deal of technical expertise in software programming, system design, and hardware training but may not have a full range of documentation resources at their fingertips. For these readers this book can offer a number of benefits:

- ■ *Current examples.*   The examples, many of which won awards or represent current page or screen designs, can help the software engineer keep up with current designs.

- ■ *Overview of the standard documentation process.*   The reader accustomed to engineering processes will feel right at home following the standard documentation procedure outlined in Chapter 4, "Planning and Writing Your Documents." This procedure has helped me and many others see ways to keep development costs down.

- ■ *Insight into making their products useful.*   The ideas of task orientation have a broad application in many areas. Technical employees and designers need to understand the approach used by writers interested in building a bridge between users and technologies.

■ *Useful tips and techniques.*   The programmer who wants to document his or her new application may appreciate helpful hints on structuring a help file for maximum usability or efficiently using information in the manual and the online help.

What Topic Areas Does the Book Cover?

Chapters 1 through 7: The Document Development Process

Chapters 1 through 7 present information in the sequence a writer would need while writing a manual or help system. Although the phases of the process overlap considerably and some require more time than others, the process roughly follows that used by writers in the software industry.

Chapter 1, "Understanding Task Orientation," describes the nature of software-mediated work and analyzes ways to design task orientation into manuals and online help. It offers a set of guidelines to direct the document development process.

Chapter 2, "Analyzing Your Users," shows how to conduct a thorough user analysis, thus forming the basis for the design work on the documents that will follow. Because task orientation implies a thorough knowledge of the user's workplace, the chapter focuses on special techniques for getting the right information.

Chapter 3, "Constructing a Task List," demonstrates how to convert the features of a program into a useful task list containing the basic information you will need in order to build pages and topics.

Chapter 4, "Planning and Writing Your Documents," guides you through the stages of writing a manual or help document and covers how to organize people and resources and design a document with maximum usability.

Chapter 5, "Getting Useful Reviews," covers the process of sending out a draft for review by team members and users. This crucial process helps insure usability and task orientation, but you need to handle it carefully to make it anything but a waste of your time and the client's time.

Chapter 6, "Conducting Usability Tests," discusses types of usability tests you can perform to measure how well your manual supports user tasks. It offers an easy-to-follow ten-step process for planning and conducting valuable usability tests.

Chapter 7, "Editing and Fine Tuning," covers the basics of switching from the writer mode to the editor mode. It looks at the industry standard method of editing and shows how that method can contribute to the overall task orientation of the final product. In fact, much of the polishing of a task-oriented approach occurs during editing.

Chapters 8 through 15: The Document Design Handbook

Chapters 8 through 15 present information by topics selected for their importance in designing task-oriented manuals and online help. These chapters function as a reference for the writer, a place to read about design techniques and ways to apply them to real-world writing problems. The reader moving through the progression of the first seven chapters will want to consult these chapters as necessary to fill in the background.

Chapter 8, "Designing for Task Orientation," presents techniques for structuring documents in a way that allows for ease of use and productivity. It ties in with Chapter 2, "Analyzing Your Users," by showing how each of the seven information areas relevant to the user analysis can get converted into useful and productive document designs.

Chapter 9, "Laying Out Pages and Screens," tackles the basic elements you need to know about pages: layout and words. It focuses on how to arrange text on pages and screens (layout) and how to pick the right fonts for the right job (words). It contains a number of examples of common formats and provides a methodology for designing pages and screens.

Chapter 10, "Getting the Language Right," contains guidelines that show you how to maintain a high degree of task orientation by selecting language related to task work and by structuring sentences and paragraphs for easy comprehension and job performance.

Chapter 11, "Using Graphics Effectively," puts graphics—screens, drawings, diagrams, and icons—into the context of the user's questions about a software product and shows ways to answer those questions using images. It elaborates on seven ways to use graphics and gives descriptions of the most popular forms in manuals and help.

Chapter 12, "Writing to Teach—Tutorials," focuses on how to write to help users memorize basic program features in order to guide them from being novices to being experienced users, or from being experienced with a program, to being *expert*. The chapter shows how to organize the two main types of print tutorials in use today: direct instruction and minimalist. The principles of skill selection and tutorial structure apply to teaching documentation in online and multi-media formats as well as print.

Chapter 13, "Writing to Guide—Procedures," focuses on how to write procedures: step-by-step tasks that form the heart of the task-orientated approach. This chapter discusses various formats for presenting procedural information and the elements of a typical task.

Chapter 14, "Writing to Support—Reference," focuses on how to create technical support pages and screens for expert users, using the strategy of the structured reference entry. The chapter also looks at methods of organizing reference information and the psychology behind reference support.

Chapter 15, "Designing Indexes," examines one of the most important elements of software documentation: the index, or, if online, the keyword search. This chapter shows how to increase the usability of a manual or online help system through indexes.

How Are the Chapters Organized?

Each chapter contains the following sections:

- *How to Read This Chapter.*   The introductory section helps you identify which topics you can use for particular documentation tasks or problems. It also includes specific advice for reading the chapter, whether you're new to software documentation or have some experience.

- *Examples.*   The examples section of the chapter presents a page or other element relevant to the chapter topic. The examples serve to set the stage for the subsequent guidelines and discussion.

- *Guidelines.*   The guidelines section breaks the work presented in the chapter into discrete steps, a set of wise maxims to follow. The guidelines often contain many examples and practical tips for putting documentation features to work or preparing to write documentation.

- *Discussion.*   The discussion section steps back from the process and looks at the underlying principles of the chapter topic.

- *Checklist.*   The checklist section summarizes the chapter's contents in checklist format to aid the reader who's actively working on a documentation project.

- *Glossary.*   The chapter glossary collects all the terms of a specific chapter that relate to the topic and warrant definition. (These terms are shown in bold italic in the text.) Terms also are represented in the book's index.

- *Practice / Problem Solving.*   The practice / problem solving section of each chapter poses cases for applying the chapter ideas or starting interesting discussions of the chapter topics.

Acknowledgments

I would like to thank the many people who directly and indirectly contributed to this book.

At Allyn & Bacon: Joe Opiela, who made all the right executive decisions and believed in this book; Donna Simons, for following through with the production; Kate Tolini and Carol Alper for help in preparing the manuscript for production. And for their thoughtful reviews, Johndan Johnson-Eiola at Purdue University and Ron Fortune at Illinois State University.

At Omegatype Typography: Tom Schaefges, for his tasteful graphics work, and Kathy Robinson, for her caring, thoughtful, and thoroughly professional editing.

At Texas Tech University: Sam Dragga, series editor, for his encouragement from the very beginning of my ideas for the book and his editorial advice as the book progressed; Carolyn Rude, for scheduling me to teach the manuals class regularly and often (and for all-around support and professionalism); Patricia Goubil-Gambrell, for helping me understand user behaviors and how to study them; Stuart Selber, for testing the book in the classroom and for good advice on its form and content; David Dayton, for help in preparing the manuscript for production; Joseph Unger, for answering many technical questions and sending me good examples of manuals and help when he found them; Wendell Aycock, for supplying me with two really good computers to work with, and for helping me get development leave to write.

For inspiration to study task orientation and manual writing: John Brockman, for helping me understand issues in software documentation through his seminars; Dave Farkas, for encouragement in the book business; Mac Katzin, for ideas too numerous to mention in our many talks about document testing and documentation management; Roger Grice, for helping me learn about task orientation back when nobody cared about it; Herb Michaelson, a famous TTU graduate, who is a continuing inspiration in writing and promoting my writing; and Edmund Weiss, who inspired me to take software documentation seriously.

For inspiration in audience analysis and user-oriented design: Shoshanna Zuboff, for her pioneering work in the application of computers to workplace tasks in organizations; Donald Norman, whose work helped me understand task-oriented design; Saul Wurman, for original and inspiring thinking about information anxiety; and Ted Daniels, who gave me an opportunity to study computer users in an R & D organization.

For teaching me editing: Carolyn Rude, whose work I trust and turn to often, and Judith Tarutz, who writes in a lively and realistic way about the work of editing.

To my clients and students: To the many clients who gave me the opportunity to learn the realities of software documentation and the chance to practice what I preached. To the many, many students at Texas Tech University in my courses in *Writing Instructional Materials* and *Writing for the Computer Industry,* who suffered through the early manuscript versions of this book and who worked with me through many of the ideas I present here.

For encouragement and personal support: Sherry Ceniza, author and Associate Professor of English, Texas Tech University, who discussed many aspects of the book with me and gave me inspiration and encouragement throughout the entire process. In many ways I owe Sherry the largest debt of thanks.

Writing Software Documentation

chapter

1

Understanding
Task Orientation

This chapter helps software documentation writers achieve two goals: encourage knowledge of the program (proficiency) and encourage application of the program to the user's job (efficiency). This chapter defines *task orientation* and gives two examples. It describes and explains ten characteristics of manuals that provide workplace answers for users. It explains the five characteristics of the **computer-mediated** user and explains five characteristics of the **task-oriented** user.

How to Read This Chapter

- If you're unfamiliar with software documentation, read the Example, then the Discussion section, then the Guidelines.

- If you have some experience in software documentation, read the Guidelines, then compare your work to Figures 1.1 and 1.2 in the Examples section. Then ponder the Discussion.

xamples

A number of things determine the success of software documentation; put another way, you can easily find a number of ways to mess up a documentation project. This book examines as many dos and don'ts as possible in software documentation, but focuses on one overriding principle: Make the software easy to use and usable. A manual that does this adapts the software to the user's job, rather than making the user adapt to the software. What kind of manual encourages adaptation to the user's job? We can begin our exploration with an example.

The PV-Wave Manual Encourages Decision Making and Creativity

This example comes from a tutorial manual for a program called PV-WAVE P&C. This program enables scientists and engineers to manipulate research data and view it in charts and graphs. These highly technical users may have used other programs or methods to manipulate their data, and may not easily see how this program can make a difference to them. To accommodate such users, the writers went to considerable lengths to make the integration of the program easier. A number of features, indicated in Figure 1.1, encourage such use. Don't get the wrong idea—that this manual doesn't offer procedural information. These introductory pages help new users understand how the following procedures apply to their work.

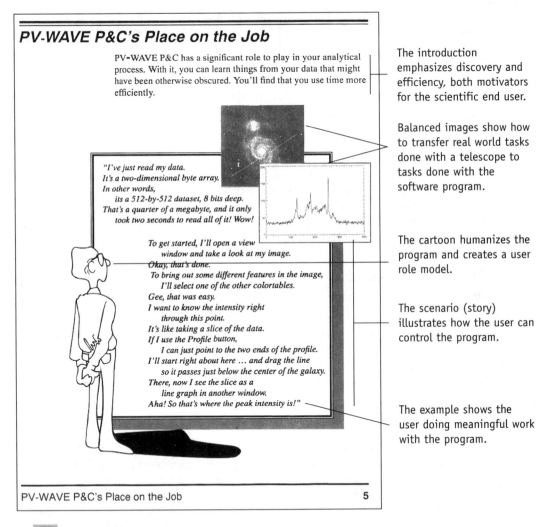

PV-WAVE P&C's Place on the Job

PV-WAVE P&C has a significant role to play in your analytical process. With it, you can learn things from your data that might have been otherwise obscured. You'll find that you use time more efficiently.

The introduction emphasizes discovery and efficiency, both motivators for the scientific end user.

Balanced images show how to transfer real world tasks done with a telescope to tasks done with the software program.

"I've just read my data.
It's a two-dimensional byte array.
In other words,
    its a 512-by-512 dataset, 8 bits deep.
That's a quarter of a megabyte, and it only
    took two seconds to read all of it! Wow!

To get started, I'll open a view
    window and take a look at my image.
Okay, that's done.
    To bring out some different features in the image,
    I'll select one of the other colortables.
Gee, that was easy.
I want to know the intensity right
    through this point.
It's like taking a slice of the data.
If I use the Profile button,
    I can just point to the two ends of the profile.
I'll start right about here ... and drag the line
    so it passes just below the center of the galaxy.
There, now I see the slice as a
    line graph in another window.
Aha! So that's where the peak intensity is!"

The cartoon humanizes the program and creates a user role model.

The scenario (story) illustrates how the user can control the program.

The example shows the user doing meaningful work with the program.

PV-WAVE P&C's Place on the Job   5

Figure 1.1

Getting Started with PV-WAVE

This software encourages user control through a scenario that suggests efficient application of the software to work.

Microsoft Help Files Encourage Multiple Access to Information Work

Software users often need how-to information while working with a program. In the example in Figure 1.2, the electronic controls over the presentation of information allow the user to choose the correct level of detail of information needed. Users like how-to information because it relates the program to their workplace, instead of dryly cataloging the system features. The electronic controls make it possible for users to get to the correct steps to follow quickly.

Guidelines

All software documentation should do what the page shown in Figure 1.2 does: Explain and show the connections between the user's professional work and the computer program. *Scenarios,* certain user-oriented examples, and page layout can all contribute to this explanation. A manual that does this can be described as "task oriented," because it helps

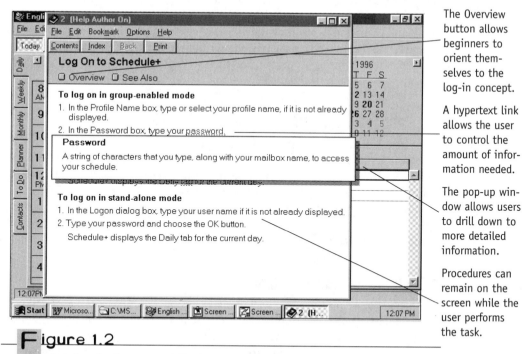

The Overview button allows beginners to orient themselves to the log-in concept.

A hypertext link allows the user to control the amount of information needed.

The pop-up window allows users to drill down to more detailed information.

Procedures can remain on the screen while the user performs the task.

Figure 1.2

Getting Assistance While You Work

This help screen encourages task-oriented software use by highlighting step-by-step information and by providing background information to uninitiated users. It suggests the use of "Tips" as an efficient way to get work done.

1. Emphasize problem-solving.

2. Provide task-oriented organization.

3. Support user control of information.

4. Orient pages semantically.

5. Facilitate information tasks.

6. Use multi-document support.

7. Design for users.

8. Facilitate communication tasks.

9. Encourage user communities.

10. Support cognitive processing.

Figure 1.3

Guidelines for a Successful Software Manual

the user manage and communicate information related to his or her task. This book contains many strategies for encouraging task-oriented, integrated software use. Figure 1.3 presents a summary of the main strategies.

As this book progresses we will explore these and other techniques that can help you create a manual or help system that focuses on user tasks, one that helps your users clearly see the relation between this new program and their workplace. The following paragraphs briefly explain some of these techniques.

1   EMPHASIZE PROBLEM SOLVING

A manual or help system should help users solve problems in the workplace. Some problems might include: "How can I organize this project?" "Where should our company invest development time?" or "Where can I find the peak intensity of data?" You can help the user through introductory paragraphs that preview not only the steps to follow, but the goals and objectives of the procedures. As you will see in Chapter 12, "Writing to Teach," you have opportunities to encourage creative solutions to exercises, thus increasing the users' task orientation.

2   PROVIDE TASK-ORIENTED ORGANIZATION

Organize a manual or help system in a way that matches the kinds of tasks a user will perform. For example, a word processing manual that follows the "open a file, type in words, save the file, exit the program" sequence would seem more logical than one organized alphabetically, for example, or according to the menus of the program. A task-oriented arrangement begins in the table of contents (of your manual) or the introductory screen (of your help system). As the following chapters will show, a task orientation should pervade the design of your manual or help system so that even the seemingly mechanical forms of reference have the right touch to make them very functional in the workplace.

3   ENCOURAGE USER CONTROL OF INFORMATION

"User control of information" means the feeling, among software users, that *they* decide what the program does for them. To encourage this, the manual should show users how to make key decisions, supply key information, or determine key program outputs. Examples include: specifying what a database program will search for and identifying which data the program will process (as in Figure 1.1, which shows the scientist selecting just the right "slice" of data to use). Users need to feel in control of the program. Cross-references in manuals and hypertext links in online systems can help maintain the user's sense of control over the documentation because these document design elements allow users to choose where they go for additional information, or where to proceed after they have finished a section. Chapter 13, "Writing to Guide," explores the importance of emphasizing the actions the user takes.

4   ORIENT PAGES SEMANTICALLY

Semantic orientation in page design means you arrange the elements of the page meaningfully, according to elements of the job the user needs to perform. Figure 1.1, showing the non-computerized image of the galaxy and the computerized chart of the peak intensity, illustrates a semantic orientation. The juxtaposition of the two items mirrors the user's work progress from the telescope to the graph. Other examples of semantic organization include putting important elements first and making important elements larger to help users see the application of the program to their work.

One of the best way to orient pages semantically employs visuals and graphics to balance text in a complementary way. Chapter 9, "Laying Out Pages and Screens," discusses ways to balance graphics and text and also to maintain the appropriate density of print and legibility of letters. These basic elements can contribute to the usability of information in the workplace.

5   FACILITATE INFORMATION TASKS

All programs require information or help users create information they can use in their jobs. For professionals, this information may include account data, analysis data from field studies, or data collected from electronic measuring equipment. Knowing how and where your user gets, stores, and shares information can help you find those functions of the program that support these tasks. If you emphasize the ways your program does these information tasks, you can catch the users' attention and tap into their professional motivation. You learn about a user's information tasks during the user analysis, covered in Chapter 4, "Analyzing Your Users."

6   USE MULTI-DOCUMENT SUPPORT

We no longer need to put all the information into one manual. In fact, users like their manuals sectioned and divided according to tasks, such as the operator's manual, installer's manual, or executive's manual. Such sectioning can encourage the users' putting the software to work. Increasingly too, users look for information online, in help screens, online references, and online tutorials. Finding the right document types for your users can facilitate their use of the software.

Packages exist today that allow you to create a text file containing text and graphics, then convert that file into suitable help files—*html* help files (documents that carry information over networks)—and link the files to multimedia presentation tools. The technological possibilities offer the writer or document author sophisticated tools. These tools enable you to vary your information design in lots of ways. Chapter 8, "Designing for Task Orientation," explores some of the ways you can vary your information design.

7   DESIGN FOR USERS

The concept of user-driven design means that the organization of a manual comes from the user's needs rather than from models or templates of what a user's guide *should* look like or from schemes based on giving some users one kind of information and other users other information. User-driven design requires the kind of extensive user analysis discussed later in the book. It means that each manual or help system presents you with new design challenges requiring you to consider the user's job needs in regard to your program.

When you study your users following the seven suggestions in Chapter 2, "Analyzing Your Users," you will find that each of the topic areas discussed in that chapter ties in to specific techniques, such as using icons to suggest key points or tables to show how features and their uses can add to the task orientation, and thus the value, of your documents.

8   FACILITATE COMMUNICATION TASKS

Users of software programs work in environments that require them to communicate about their work. Document designers can help them do this by analyzing what kinds of information they communicate and to whom, and then identifying those program functions—for example, print functions, report functions, or disk output functions—that can help the users become effective communicators.

Learning about the user's communication tasks presents a great opportunity to record the common terminology for procedures and tasks, "jargon" that you can use in glossaries and for writing steps and explanations. The specifics of using communication-oriented language are discussed in Chapter 10, "Getting the Language Right."

9   ENCOURAGE USER COMMUNITIES

Often, software use occurs in environments where users find themselves isolated with a new program. Task-oriented manuals recognize that users often need encouragement to rely on other users of the program, their **user community;** task-oriented documentation encourages users to identify and get help from others. Other users of the program, while not exactly experts in the software, can render valuable help because they understand the user's job demands. Companies like Apple Computer, Inc. list addresses and phone numbers of user groups of their products. Some software contains specific features that encourage group use or work done by teams. These users can get help in using the program from others on their team.

User communities, discussed in detail in Chapter 2, "Analyzing Your Users," can provide a wealth of information about user tasks. Users can also help support your development effort. Chapter 4, "Planning and Writing Your Documents," discusses the idea of including users in the development process through interviews and client reviews. User communities can help provide candidates for this kind of user-involved document development.

10 SUPPORT COGNITIVE PROCESSING

Since the advent of computerized work in business and industry, we have learned much about how users process information. We have learned that people use mental models, called *cognitive schema,* that help them learn new information, process the information, and apply the information that comes at them at an alarmingly faster and faster rate. The task-oriented manual uses principles of knowledge representation, parallelism, and analogy to convey software features and applications to workplace tasks. These techniques, described in Chapter 14, "Writing to Support," allow users to absorb what your manual or help system has to say with as little effort as possible.

For the modern professional in business and industry, the software program lies at the heart of the information management problem because computers both represent the cause and the solution to the problem. Computers generate complex information, and computer software allows the user to store, transfer, and present it. Our understanding of how computers affect work grows through research on the impact of computers on people's work and workplace roles. If we explore software use from the point of view of the user's information environment, we see a strong need for good software documentation.

A Note about the Guidelines

Inevitably, the documentation designer will find that the guidelines conflict with one another. You are bound to encounter a situation where you simply can't afford to elaborate on a key point and you know your user will have to "fly" on what you are able to include. Or you'll find that encouraging user communities doesn't work in modern "intranetted" business environments. Some of the tradeoffs you inevitably have to make among competing guidelines are discussed in a later chapter.

iscussion

The principles that underlie the guidelines above derive from studies of the use of software to perform productive work. A good manual or help system has many features that make it succeed, but the bottom line is this: *the more a manual can support productive work, the greater the chance of acceptance and satisfaction by a user.* First, consider the overall goals of software documentation and examine some problems inherent in doing software work, then examine some ways a good online or hard-copy manual can help users overcome these problems.

The Goal of Software Documentation

This book addresses an important need in the business and professional workplace today to help people use software efficiently and effectively. What grew to a $45-billion computer service industry in 1985 subsequently almost doubled to an $80-billion industry by 1990. Like it or not, those technical communicators who choose to write software documentation—manuals, help systems, and other information products that accompany software programs—find themselves confronted with no less of a challenge: make users *proficient* with software and *efficient* in their jobs. While such factors as training, individual motivation, peer pressure, the boss's dictate, or fear of falling behind in a career can certainly contribute to people using their software (and thus their computer) efficiently, the computer manual (print or online) remains the single most common form of support. When in doubt, most users do, in fact, turn to the manual.

One researcher, Donald Norman, looks at the challenge to manual designers from a cognitive perspective. According to Norman, the job of the manual writer or designer consists of constructing manuals, maps, and other items that help users make the most of technological devices. He articulates his challenge in this way: "The result . . . is that we are ever more dependent upon the design of our devices to make the information visible and to make the artifact usable."[1] In terms of our discussion of the goals of the software manual, *making the information visible* requires making the features of the program available and accessible to the software user.

Table 1.1 refers to this as the user wanting to "learn to use the program." The documenter has to convey the correct information on how to make programs work, helping the user to understand opening screens, learn commands and icon definitions, and navigate menu systems. Documentation focuses on the interface elements. But good documentation also has a second goal: applying the program—making "the artifact usable," in Norman's phrase.

Making the artifact usable requires helping the user apply the software to a specific task. It often comes in the form of "how-to" procedures or tutorials. With this task-oriented approach you couch information in easy-to-follow procedures, or link procedures to overview screens in the help facility. You suggest how the user can adapt the program to particular work scenarios.

This chapter offers a strategy for addressing the needs of software users when they turn to the manual. First you will look at a definition of a design strategy for manuals that

Table 1.1

Goals of the Software User and Manual

Goals of the Software User	Goals of the Manual or Help
Learn to use the program	Support for the features of the program
Apply the program to useful work	Tell how to apply the program to the user's job

attempts to address the user's needs productively to encourage efficient use of word processors and database programs. Then you will examine examples of manuals that exhibit some of the features that contribute to efficient software use. To understand how these manuals work, you need to look at changes that have taken place in the modern workplace since computers and computer software arrived. You will see that working with software requires a significant shift in thinking and learning, a shift that requires users to develop new skills and job roles and documentation writers to adjust their approach to writing manuals and online help.

A Definition of Task Orientation

This book uses the term *task orientation* to indicate the writer's purpose. The following definition expresses how task orientation helps articulate this purpose.

> *Task orientation*: A design strategy for software documentation that attempts to increase user knowledge of and application of a program by integrating the software with the user's work environment.

This definition embodies a number of premises that underlie the approach in this book. For example, it suggests a user-driven strategy—meaning that the form, language, and organization of the software manual should depend on the user's job needs. The approach contrasts with a very similar market-driven approach that suggests the software manual should meet the needs of the software buying market. Much of the current debate on whether marketing information has a place in manuals stems from this market-driven approach. A user-driven approach differs, however, because you look to the user's job-related needs rather than the user's software buying trends.

This definition also suggests that the task-orientation approach contrasts with the template approach. This approach, used, for example, in Bell and Evans's *Mastering Documentation,*[2] provides templates or masters of documents that the writer can follow. These masters provide easy, almost "cookie-cutter," models for user's guides and other document types. Document Wizards in some desktop publishing programs embody the template approach. But as anyone who has used these template wizards knows, they often hit wide of the mark of genuine usability. While the template approach can lead to greater uniformity of documents within a company, it does not lead to adapting the manual to the user's individual needs. It does little to relate the software program to the job the user has to do.

When confronted with a new piece of software, most users have one question to ask: "How will this program help me in my job?" An informed answer to that question, one that points out exactly the greater job efficiency, or the savings in time, or the greater accuracy of production, can provide just the motivation a new user needs. Those who reject a software program often do so with a parallel observation: "This program did not help me in my job." Often the complaint gets worse: "This program slowed my production time down," or "This program alienates my employees and makes them feel like subordinates to a machine." But when a user sees that learning and using a program can *increase* job efficiency, most will take the time to read the manual and learn the program. Clearly, the manual that encourages this kind of integration with job goals will also increase job efficiency. Table 1.2 matches programs and types of information they produce.

The Theory behind Task Orientation

While the idea that software should help people do meaningful work may seem obvious, it is nonetheless helpful to explore the theory behind the approach. Exploring the theory may help you understand the principles that can guide your design of manuals and online help, and provide the foundation for techniques you will find in the chapters that follow.[3]

The Computer-Mediated User

The concept of focusing on the user's work environment began in the work of Shoshanna Zuboff, who observed that computers not only do work for us, they also record information about that work. For example, when the checker at the grocery store scans your purchases with a laser beam, more gets recorded than just the price and description of the item. The computer that reads the universal product code also records the frequency of sales and deducts the item from inventory stocks. It does the job and keeps track of the job at the same time. The same is true for, say, stock broking. The computer brings information about stock and bond prices, but also records the broker's sales figures, client list, and other information that allows for advance planning and tracking of sales progress. This extra information complicates the task and—in subtle ways—a person' relationship to the computer and the job. See Table 1.3 for typical user characteristics.

Zuboff calls the recording of information about a task *informating,* which contrasts to simple *automating.* Persons who do informated work, work that involves computers and also involves keeping and managing information, face difficulties that other persons do not. Often, people resist using computers and software because of the inherent complexities of abstraction and information overload. In fact, the difficulties in using com-

Table 1.2

Kinds of Information Generated by Programs

Program	Use	Kind of Information Generated
Database	Look up customer addresses	Frequency of look-ups
		Records of look-ups by region, date, etc.
Email Editor	Write electronic messages	Numbers of documents written
		Most frequent addresses
		Most frequently used program functions
Word Processor	Write letters and reports	Average letter/report size
		Most common styles used
Engineering Design/Drawing	Draw plans for machinery	Average drawing size
		Amount of yearly use of the program

Table 1.3

The Computer-Mediated User

- Decreased importance of job skills
- Increasingly abstract tasks
- Increasingly isolated from other employees
- Remotely supervised
- Overloaded with information

puters and software fall into roughly five categories: deskilling, increased abstraction, increased isolation, remote supervision, and information overload. A brief overview of these areas can demonstrate the challenges facing software documenters who are determined to help software users be efficient in their jobs.

DECREASED IMPORTANCE OF JOB SKILLS: "MY EXPERIENCE ISN'T ANY GOOD ANY MORE."
When we speak of workers' skills losing their importance we often speak of it as *job deskilling,* which means that the computer program can perform many of the tasks a person used to perform so the job requires less skilled people. Consider the example of the maintenance worker in a plant. Before the advent of the computerized inventory control system, keeping track of parts for machines required experience acquired over years of repairing motors. With the computer system in place, parts are reordered automatically once the levels of inventory fall to predetermined levels. The decision to order new parts, for example, has gone into the computer, so the company can now afford to hire persons with less job experience, with fewer special skills.

Much resistance to computers derives from the realization by professional persons that the computer, often in company-wide systems, has begun to appropriate skills, to take over some tasks that employees used to do. It may even appear to do the thinking for some people. Some managers and professional workers report in research studies that they perceive their jobs as less meaningful than before.[4] Software programs, because they can handle many routine tasks, often pose a challenge to users: Will I use my judgment and discretion in performing this task, or will I let the program take care of it? Whatever the answer, the decision itself begs for attention from the software documenter. How can the writer help the software user decide on what skills to use to perform the task best?

Another problem lies in the way people learn new skills. As you will see in subsequent chapters in this book, much learning of new skills comes from building on old skills. A person who carves well probably can also whittle or sculpt, because carving skills carry over to the new skill areas. Researchers in training call this phenomenon *skill transfer.* Much research seeks to learn how software affects skill transfer, how job skills transfer into software skills, and how beginner skills transfer into advanced skills. The software manual should encourage advanced skills. The manual or online help writer must realize that many users have trouble seeing the connection between doing things by hand and doing things with a computer.

INCREASINGLY ABSTRACT TASKS: "I JUST CAN'T UNDERSTAND HOW THIS THING WORKS."
Part of the reason people have trouble seeing the link between doing by hand and doing with a computer lies in the abstract nature of computer work. Anyone who has tried to learn a computer programming language has experienced the abstractness of the way computers do things. Compare by-hand work and computer work to playing the violin and playing the piano. Both instruments make music, but in very different ways. The violin creates sound directly when the bow causes the string to vibrate. You can see the sound being produced. But piano keys activate a complex system of levers, rockers, and hammers that finally produce the sound. You can't see it; it all happens inside the wooden box.

By-hand work (writing your name with a pencil) and computer work (writing your name with a word processor) embody a similar contrast as in the example of the violin and the piano. The pencil creates marks simply, when a piece of graphite is dragged across a page leaving a visible trail. The computer uses a highly complex, electronic system of buffers, wires, computer chips, and circuits to leave its visible phosphorescent trail on the screen. How does it happen? The computer does things in a very abstract way. You can't touch it; it's not concrete.

How does the worker or professional person respond to using this abstract tool? Partly, the answer lies in the loss of control. People often feel good about their work because they develop a tactile sense of their tools. With writing, for example, some teachers report that college writing students have been known to resist using word processing software because they enjoy the tactile feel of the page under their hand or writing with a favorite kind of yellow pencil. The very first word processing program was called "The Electronic Pencil," but its methods differed greatly from the pencil's. No more soft feel of vellum paper under your palm as you write. You can't sharpen a computer "pencil." Now, writing demands a keyboard and a computer and software that all work easily—or fail completely. This apparent loss of control over the tool creates difficulties for some writers.

The same feeling of loss of control faces all computer users. Without a feeling of control over their work, workers feel that it loses most of its simplicity. And this apparent loss creates resistance to software and threatens efficient use. Writers of manuals and help systems need to develop techniques—such as decision trees, lists of suggested uses, examples in different disciplines—to re-awaken the computer user to a confident awareness of the computer as a flexible tool.

Whereas increased abstraction relates to how people see their jobs through their tools—computerized or not—work also takes place in a social domain. And that, too, appears threatened by computer-mediated work.

INCREASINGLY ISOLATED FROM OTHER EMPLOYEES: "I'M STUCK IN FRONT OF THIS COMPUTER." Business organizations embody a complex web of social structures that have evolved over history and often have to change because of work done at a terminal. Social structures—the people we relate to at work, the work communities we inhabit, the coalitions we form—play a major role in our job satisfaction. In some companies, social groups take on names: the front office, the back office, the first floor, and so on. But now, Zuboff asserts that the terminal has now become the primary focus of a person's interaction with a company, and with others in the company. No more chatting over the cubicle walls, no more friendly errands to run to different parts of the building. One person, a benefits analyst at an insurance company, put it this way: "No talking, no looking, no walking. I have a cork in my mouth, blinders for my eyes, chains on my arms. With the radiation [from the computer terminal, supposedly] I have lost my hair. The only way you can make your production goals is to give up your freedom."[5]

People need others to communicate with, to get feedback from, and to get rewards and other incentives that make work enjoyable. They create useful dialogs with others to help share and solve problems. But people using computers risk a diminished importance of their co-workers in their job. One researcher noted that responses of computer users to surveys about their dealings with others showed that regular computer users may suffer from a lack of strong interpersonal relationships, partly because of their focus on computerizing their work.[6] Many potential software users, understandably, resist this isolation. They lose their social contact, even if, before, they may not have realized the social aspect of their work. The software documenter, as we will see below, faces a challenge to introduce the isolated user to new possibilities of interaction with co-workers *through* the computer.

REMOTELY SUPERVISED: "MY BOSS HAS AN ELECTRONIC LEASH ON ME." Ironically, the computer-mediated user will feel both increased isolation because he or she seems chained to a terminal, but can also feel increasingly exposed to the manager or supervisor. For example, before the secretary had a computer to work on the boss had to physically walk to the secretary's desk to check on the status of a typing job. Now the boss can check on the secretary by looking up the file on the network. Before, the manager had to catch you loafing or had to come to your desk and pull files to make sure you kept up with your work. Now the manager can access your files electronically, check on your productivity, even organize your work day for you without ever showing up physically (Figure 1.4).

You're all plugged in. You can never miss a call, forget an appointment, lose a document or be out of touch again. God help you.

edStein '92
Rocky Mtn.
News-Nea

© Ed Stein, reprinted by permission of Newspaper Enterprise Association, Inc.

Figure 1.4

Remote Supervision Doesn't Work For Everyone

Workers in computerized environments often feel a sense of lacking a place of their own away from the boss and co-workers. Often our best creative work occurs in such spaces.

This kind of remote supervision through the computer system can result in a number of detrimental effects. Some computer users may feel that they can't think up new ways of doing things because the computer "has it already figured out." Others may get an ambiguous sense of their actual boss, and may attribute authority to the computer system itself. They may lose their sense of control over their work because of the increased supervision exercised *through* the computer system. Whatever the effect, computer users often resist using software because of the control they perceive it has over their work.

OVERLOADED WITH INFORMATION: "WHY DO I NEED TO KNOW THAT?" Another reason for resistance to software use concerns the nature of information generated by software. Computers produce lots of information very quickly. Anyone who has used a word processing program knows that it can count words in a document more quickly than a person can. An oil well analysis program can calculate flow rates much faster than a person working with a pencil or a calculator. Aside from their speed, computers can also produce astounding amounts of information. A statistical analysis program like StatView can calculate huge quantities of descriptive statistics about research data: means, medians, standard deviations, and so on. Network listservers send huge volumes of messages from all around the world to an individual user's email account. Finally, computers can produce highly organized information. Doctor's office management programs, for example, can arrange patient information into categories of treatment, referrals, payment history, and many others. For many users, this speed, volume, and organization of information provides a very useful and efficient justification for using software to perform tasks. For others, these advantages can provide a reason to resist.

Some users resist computer use because they feel overloaded by information. (It's not uncommon for a frequent email user to accumulate hundreds of unread messages while away from the computer on vacation.) Consider the writing student who can't decide which of the suggestions made by a grammatical analysis program to follow up on. Or consider the researcher faced with volumes of descriptive statistics but little idea as to which ones to regard as significant. Similarly, a computer network management program can provide a supervisor with a full screen of information about network use, but such a screen can also intimidate the supervisor who can't tell which statistics mean more than others. Having volumes of information does not always solve problems for users. In fact, according to author Richard Wurman, having too much information without the ability to understand its significance can cause *information anxiety*.[7] This anxiety can afflict computer users who find themselves flooded by information without knowing which they should try to understand.

Computer users face many problems with information overload. On the one hand, they need ways to filter, to sift through and make sense of the information that floods them. Software manual writers can certainly help here by providing ways to reorganize information around categories relevant to users. But computer users face an even more subtle problem. As problem solvers, computer users need to have a sense of the unknown, of the ambiguity of their work, in order to respond in a human way. Take a coach who uses a program to track the progress of athletes: What could cause such a user to reject a program that seems to provide all the answers? In fact, users reject programs specifically because of this: They want to use their experience, to explore the ambiguity of experience, to rely on the unknown in order to feel in control of a task. The coach faced with

Table 1.4

The Computer-Mediated User versus the Task-Oriented User

Computer-Mediated User	Task-Oriented User
Decreased importance of job skills	Challenged by skill demands
Increasingly abstract tasks	Conceptually oriented
Increasingly isolated from other employees	Aware of user communities
Remotely supervised	Self-managing
Overloaded with information	Information-rich

a screen of statistics still needs to call on experience to determine the best training plan for his or her athletes. The danger of information overload lies in the way software can rob users of their sense of creativity, their sense that all is *not* known. Table 1.4 contrasts computer-mediated and task-oriented users.

The Task-Oriented User

As indicated earlier, software documenters face the challenge of making programs easy to use and applicable to workplace objectives. This book will help you meet that challenge. As a beginning, we can examine the difficulties that face the users of computer software, and see how we can address them through documentation design. The following discussion of the characteristics of the task-oriented user, whose software use fits with his or her work environment, can help you build a model of efficient and productive software work.

CHALLENGED BY SKILL DEMANDS: "THIS PROGRAM MAKES ME A BETTER MANAGER." While software can perform some of the skills of trained employees, most of the time the higher-level skills require the human mind. A computer can sort and categorize but it cannot handle ideas. When grammatical analysis programs first became popular, some people mistakenly thought that programs like Grammatik would take over the editing of reports and put editors out of work. But the user still had to determine when to implement editing suggestions made by the program. This required consideration of the audience and the writer's purpose—something the computer program could not handle. People held the same mistaken impressions about language translation programs. But in fact, these programs only perform routine skills, leaving more sophisticated reasoning tasks up to the user.

The software documenter needs to find ways to reinforce the skill challenges inherent in efficient computer work. Making the program functions easy to use can help, because it allows the writer to focus on higher-level, advanced skills that challenge the user. In this way, users begin to see computer work as more than mere keyboarding. Users need to see their work as significant: to see that what they do with a software program can have an impact on their work, their organization, and others within their organization.[8] Challenging the user often requires teaching computer skills in the context of a person's job so that the user can see the benefit of the software (Table 1.5). Training materials

Table 1.5

Statements That Reinforce User Skills

"The LOGDAT file contains oil well information organized according to geographical areas familiar to well analysts."

"[Owners of printshops] can give you valuable advice that will affect how you create the publication—for example, which printer to compose the publication for. (There's more about this in "Using an Outside Printing Service" on page 197.)"

should consider the need for skill transfer from a person's non-automated job to his or her computer-mediated job. Additionally, software support should reinforce decision making and problem solving as important computer skills.

CONCEPTUALLY ORIENTED: "THIS GIVES ME SOMETHING NEW TO THINK ABOUT." Work with software requires handling abstract concepts such as data types and processing instructions that make computer work difficult and can cause users to reject programs. Technical writers have always faced the challenge of explaining abstract and highly technical information to novice readers. Fortunately, researchers in instructional design have found ways to help explain abstract concepts. The paragraphs below present some of the new approaches available to the software documenter.

Part of the difficulty users have with learning abstract concepts lies in their learning preferences. Some users have an easier time learning abstract concepts; others have an easier time learning analogically, with concrete examples. Researchers have determined that using the right *training method* (one based on the program, or one based on the application of the program) can facilitate learning of software programs.[9] Using the right learning preference, explored later in this book, can help those with difficulty learning abstract concepts to overcome some of the confusion they find inherent when learning something mostly symbolic, such as computer languages or how to write formulas for spreadsheets.

Documentation that uses the appropriate training method is *conceptually oriented.* Conceptually oriented documentation concentrates on the ideas the user needs to operate and handle the information generated by a software program. Research in cognitive science also provides ways of teaching abstract concepts to users. Writers can set up categories of information for users that match the user's expectations and present them in overviews called *advance organizers*. Advance organizers help users understand instructions by providing a context for each step. When users perform the step, they have a clearer idea of the outcome and relevance of their actions. On the other hand, some researchers have had success teaching computer concepts by making the learning *experiential,* so that users can explore and take charge of their learning. Allowing users to manipulate programs in this way decreases the anxiety they might feel in a world of abstract concepts. Finally, computer technology allows graphics to be used much more freely and with greater effectiveness than before, both in manuals and online help. Graphics (icons, process diagrams, structure charts, flow charts, cartoons, pictures) embody metaphors which clarify abstract concepts and help users navigate this difficult aspect of computer software. Fortunately, draw programs and desktop publishing programs can help documenters easily use graphics to portray abstract concepts for computer users (Figure 1.5).

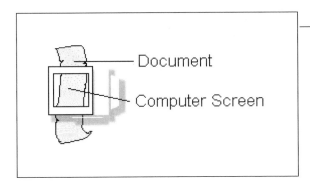

AWARE OF USER COMMUNITIES: "SHAKESPEARE WOULD USE EMAIL ... NOW." The inherent communicative nature of computing provides numerous ways for the documenter to help users overcome the isolation they experience when converting their work to a computer. For one thing, computer users automatically become part of a ***user community***. The term refers loosely to those who use the same program within an organization, but it can also refer to others who use computers in their work. Computer support divisions in large corporations have discovered an increase in user acceptance of software when they encourage the formation of user groups. The term *user groups* refers to groups that meet to discuss issues with their computing and exchange ideas to increase efficiency and productivity. In an R & D organization, for example, you might find UNIX operating system user's groups or WordPerfect user's groups. Meeting with these groups allows users to increase their social contacts within an organization and overcome any sense of isolation they may feel.

Computers also can fit well into existing social groups within a business. Most employees work in groups and as a result have to coordinate their activities, share work in progress, and store the results. This collaboration often creates situations in which managers must produce group reports or engineers must contribute designs of parts to an overall project. Documentation can play a key role in supporting collaborative work by indicating ways that users can convert output files (reports, designs, spreadsheets, etc.) into formats that other team members can use. In fact, given the prevalence of computer networks in companies, many users have come to prefer this method of coordinating activities and sharing information.

In these ways and others, documentation can support what we call an individual's ***organizational existence:*** the *persona* a person creates as an employee in an organization.[10] By using software's communicative functions strategically, the computer can become an important tool to enhance the user's social arena.

SELF-MANAGING: "MY SOFTWARE HELPS ME SORT OUT MY WORK." Computers connect workers to managers and supervisors in ways that may make users feel overly supervised. On the other hand, software opens up many opportunities for self-management. To emphasize self-management the documenter should clarify the position of authority that the user has over the program. Statements like "The program will do this ... " or "The program decides ... " can mistakenly contribute to the user's feeling that the software controls the interaction. In fact, statements like "You can do this with the program ... " or "After the

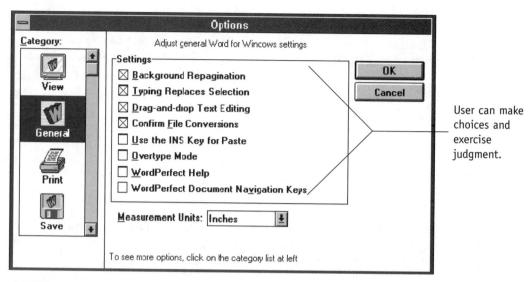

User can make
choices and
exercise
judgment.

Figure 1.6

Microsoft Word General Options Dialog Box

Show users areas of discretion to help put them in control of programs.

program calculates the coefficient you can then . . . " help the user maintain an appropriate attitude of *instrumentality* and self-management with regard to the program.

A thorough analysis of the user's job situation will help the documenter see areas where the user has discretion in a job. Even the most menial jobs allow a measure of choice for employees, and often the manual can point up the connection between the software and these important self-management tasks. For example, a person setting up a word processing system such as Microsoft Word can make a number of decisions regarding the screen or the kinds of capabilities the program will use. A truly usable manual will emphasize these and other discretionary elements of the program as a way of assuring the user of the control he or she has over it. Certainly users may resist the intrusion of the computerized supervisor into their work, but knowing that they can control the program can help them see opportunities for independence and self-management.

INFORMATION RICH: "MY SOFTWARE GIVES ME A BETTER VIEW OF MY TASKS." Software gives users new opportunities to manage information. Helping users realize the value of accumulated information and the importance of managing it relates to its political dimension. In organizations today, information has become *the* currency. Those who control information—about production statistics, about deadline histories, about efficiency ratings—can use it to acquire important resources or plan effectively. Consider the manager who keeps track of production times through automated tracking of past projects. Such a person can plan future projects much more accurately than before, saving time and money for the organization. Such a person gains the power to speak with authority at meetings because of the soundness of the support for projected dates of completion and resource needs. In modern corporations, information represents the source of power and authority. But for users to realize this fact they need help in managing information and in putting it to productive use. Good software documenters should find ways to reinforce managerial skills by showing users the potential use for information that programs generate. For example, a phone utility program that records time spent on the phone can generate valuable information for sales reps about time of contact with clients. But just how to apply this information may elude the novice user. Pointing out how to use phone tracking time in progress reports to supervisors can help salespersons understand the value of this program feature. Support materials should help users find innovative ways to use, store, and re-use information so it makes sense to them and helps them overcome some of the problems associated with information overload.

Not only does software increase the ways employees can manipulate information, it can open them up to new kinds of tasks. Table 1.6 below lists and describes a number of new kinds of tasks facing the task-oriented software user.[11]

Table 1.6

New Types of User Tasks

Type of User Task	What the Person Does	Example
Planning Tasks	Identifying goals and manipulating time and resources in the abstract, to find ways to meet the goal. Articulating future events using various computer programs.	"What's the best way to organize the shop inventory?"
Decision-Making Tasks	Assembling rich alternatives without giving in to one solution for doing something. Clarity of evaluation of alternatives in settling on an action or stance.	"Which supplier provides the most efficient delivery times?"
Problem-Solving Tasks	Identifying elements that block progress in business or organizations and identifying and evaluating ways to accommodate the unexpected.	"How many strawberries can we ship in each box?"
Operating Tasks	Keypunching and inputting of information and using menu items to manipulate the program and the data. Essential work in information processing, involving questions of transfer and storage.	"How do I translate my design into transferable format?"
Knowledge Work Tasks	Identifying information of value to an organization or department, with the intention of accumulating valuable wisdom.	"I would like to open this meeting with figures showing last quarter's increase in productivity in our department."

Glossary

advance organizer: a design tool for writers that explains the organization of a section to the reader. Often these occur in the chapter introductions, and may appear graphically. They function to help the reader expect certain information and therefore process it more efficiently. Advance organizers work in introductions as explanations of concepts, as well as introductions to procedures (step-by-step information).

automating: a process of converting a manufacturing or business task from one done by human action to one done through a machine such as a robot or a computer. Tasks such as calculation, writing, and analysis are automated by computers. Contrast the process of automating to *informating,* where the machine performs the task and also records information about the performance of the task.

cognitive schema: in cognitive psychology, this term refers to mental models of people, things, organizations, and so forth that people form as a way of interpreting their world. For example: the schemata for a kitchen would include a room with a stove, refrigerator, counter, sink, and appropriate cooking tools and materials. Knowing a user's schemata can help documenters understand thought processes users employ when they approach work problems.

computer-mediated: a kind of task accomplished through the medium of a computer or information system rather than direct involvement with the task. Computer mediation of tasks puts the performer of the task a step away from actual physical contact with objects in performing a task.

conceptually oriented: a type of page layout that organizes paragraphs around *ideas* that underlie software use. Researchers tell us that users with the right conceptual understanding of a task perform that task more effectively.

informating: introduced by Shoshanna Zuboff, this term refers to the process of a computer performing a task but also providing information about the nature of the task's performance, such as frequency of performance and success rates. Informating adds to the complexity of the task from the user's point of view, because it often requires the user to manage the additional information.

information anxiety: a problem experienced by computer users and others that relates to our ability to make use of information. The feeling of information anxiety comes from experiencing an overload of data but not understanding how to use it.

instrumentality: a phrase used by researchers in end-use computing that refers to the user's feeling of control over a program and feeling that the program functions as an effective tool in productive work.

job deskilling: in management terminology, this term indicates what happens to a job when thinking and analytical skills get taken over by a computer. A certain job is deskilled when the skills formerly needed to perform it are no longer needed and a person possessing lesser skills can be hired, usually for less money, to perform the job.

organizational existence: in end-use computing, this term refers to a person's understanding of his or her role within a corporation as part of a network of information, knowing where information comes from and where information goes. Users who understand their place in this network have a strong sense of the context of their computer work and learn to apply software to their work effectively.

scenario: a kind of narrative of events that describes what a person does to perform a specific task. Often taking on the form of a story or play, a scenario tells the rich details of a person's work. Documenters use scenarios to help understand the complexities of a user's work in order to provide well-designed support. A scenario for an advertising account representative who decides on a kind of media for a client would include a description of the client and the problem and the steps the representative took to research, solve, and present the solution to the client. A documenter writing online and print manuals for the advertising representative would be greatly aided by having such a scenario—both for understanding the context of the user's job, and for creating realistic examples.

semantic orientation: a type of page layout that orders or creates patterns of information on the page according to the user's task needs. Example: headings for skimming the page to find topics, and paragraphs to help the user understand concepts.

skill transfer: refers to the way skills used in one activity can also apply to the learning of a new activity. For example: a person with the basic knowledge of how to fry can learn to fry green tomatoes more quickly than the person without the basic knowledge in this area. In software work, skill transfer often refers to a person's ability to learn a new program more readily if the basics are already understood through the use of a similar program. The skills from one program transfer to the learning of the second.

task-oriented: a method of organizing online and hard-copy documentation that follows the typical tasks and task sequences of the software user.

training method: in training literature, this term relates to kinds of structures of training for computer users. Training methods include: applications based (which teaches the user to apply the program to work) and construct based (which teaches the user the features of the program.) Good documentation should include both kinds of teaching for appropriate user tasks.

user community: a group of users who use the same program. They may exist within the user's organization or within the larger community, and may be organized according to various degrees of formality. Some user communities meet on a regular basis and exchange information, others exchange information only informally. Examples: WordPerfect users in a college department, UNIX users in an R & D organization, "NUGies," The Netscape Users Group, http://help.netscape.com/nuggies/.

Checklist ✔

A manual that integrates a software program into the user's information environment has a better chance of getting used than a manual that only documents the features of the program. Often users subconsciously perform a cost/benefit analysis when considering a program: "Will this program help me do enough productive work to offset and compensate me for the time it takes to learn and operate it?"[12]

Cost/Benefit Analysis Checklist

If we translate the characteristics of the task-oriented manual presented above into a cost/benefit analysis for the user it might look something like this:

Cost/Benefit Analysis Checklist

- ☐ Will the manual help me use the software to solve problems?
- ☐ Does the manual reflect tasks that I perform in my job?
- ☐ Does the manual tell me how I can control the program?
- ☐ Do the pages follow a logical design that emphasizes what I need to know?
- ☐ Will this manual help me understand and manage the information the program generates?
- ☐ Is the manual clearly segmented into useful activities?
- ☐ Is the manual designed for use rather than to describe the system?
- ☐ Will the manual help me communicate the information I generate with the program?
- ☐ Does the manual help me connect with other users of this software?
- ☐ Does the manual answer my questions about the software?

A user who can answer yes to these questions might find the manual and the program useful, and might use it. Most importantly, your manual should function to provide access for the user to the thinking and working capabilities of the program.

Practice/Problem Solving

1. Examine a Manual or Help System for Task Orientation

Examine a copy of a manual for a software program such as a word processor, spreadsheet, or database, or examine a help system for a program you use regularly. Study the table of contents, looking at all the elements in the documents (there may be more than one document included in the printed set). Find instances where you think the manual or help reinforces the user's workplace and workplace tasks. How much of the document is in "how-to" format?

2. Examine a Computer User for Work Characteristics and Software Use Habits

Interview one or more people who use computers in their work. Find out how they use computers and what job goals computers help them achieve. Compile a short report covering the following topics:

- ■ description of the job: duties, co-workers, decisions, types of computers used, kinds of information encountered
- ■ description of the level of computer expertise required

■ description of their methods of learning software skills: user community, manuals, training sessions, and so forth

■ suggestions they have for making the software manuals they use more useful

If you were writing a word processing manual for this person, which tasks would you address? What about a manual for a spreadsheet or database program? A business statistics program?

3. Link Program Features with Work Tasks

Find an example of a software program that has no documentation (or for which you currently have no manual). You can often purchase low-cost software at bookstores or computer stores. Often you can get inexpensive software for both the Macintosh and PC computers through shareware distributors, or through the Internet (http://wuarchive. wustl.edu). If you want, you can use the undocumented software that accompanies this textbook for this practice exercise.

Familiarize yourself with the software program until you gain a basic understanding of it and can list some of its features. Then, think of who might use the software, and complete the form below. You can add to the list of features if you like. The point is to think not only of things a program can do but how to apply the program.

PROGRAM NAME:	
USER:	
Program Feature	Use in the Workplace
1.	
2.	
3.	
4.	
5.	

4. List the User and Tasks for a Program

Here is a quotation from a product information brochure about a program called *IT'S LEGAL*.

Protect your family and your assets! Want your wishes respected? They will be, but only if you act now. In case after case, the U. S. Supreme Court has sent down the same message: Get your wishes in writing before you get into court. Designed by a team of attorneys, our *IT'S LEGAL* software allows you to prepare your own wills, leases, power of attorney documents, and promissory notes saving you money on legal fees. Customized by state, *IT'S LEGAL* documents are valid in 49 states and the District of Columbia, but may not be valid in Louisiana. Written in plain English, not legalese . . .

What specific tasks might the following users find for this program?

- Accountant
- Engineering consultant
- Business owner
- High school teacher

2 Analyzing Your Users

The user analysis makes up the basic research phase of the documentation process. In preparing a user analysis you use interviews, questionnaires, and surveys to gather information about users. The analysis itself consists of inquiry into eight areas:

1. Tasks the user will perform
2. User's informational needs
3. User's work motivations
4. Range of the user's computer experience
5. User's knowledge of the program's subject matter
6. User community
7. User's learning preference
8. User's usage pattern

Information gathered during the user analysis informs the goals you set for the documents and the features included in them. You will use information from your user analysis later in the development process when you design documents.

How to Read This Chapter

- If you're reading this chapter to *understand,* read the Example, then the Discussion section, then the Guidelines.
- If you're reading this chapter to *do,* read the Example section, then the Guidelines section to find some techniques for forming focus groups, creating questionnaires, and conducting interviews. Also check out the section "How to Design Documentation for Intermittent Usage" in Chapter 8, "Designing for Task Orientation."

Example

User analyses can get very detailed because the more you can immerse yourself into the workplace world of your users, the more you will learn how to help them integrate your software into it. The example in Figure 2.1 illustrates how you can summarize information from interviews, observations, and surveys using the analysis checklist provided at the end of this chapter.

User Analysis Checklist

Program: ***DeskTop Set: Professional Organizer for Windows***   *A personal information management program that includes a calendar, phone dialer, and address book. Features include calendar and schedule printing, to-do lists, interfaces with numerous other programs, and monthly and yearly schedule views.*

Possible Users of the Program

- What recognizable groups (teacher/student, system administrator/end user) will your users compose? Describe each group briefly.

    End users: *Most users would install the program and enter their own personal and business information*

    Data clerks: *Some users might import and export data from another system maintained by a secretary. The secretary might need special support, like a command summary card, to a) input information for the executive, b) transfer information to the executive.*

- Provide a brief scenario of use by representative professions that would provide a role model of how the program will serve different professional user groups.

    Executive: *Corporate executives and business owners would use the program to keep in phone touch with managers, organize their schedules of meetings, travel, appointments, court dates, and create reports, schedules, and calendars.*

    Sales Representative: *Keep track of appointments, clients, suppliers, other sales persons, manage product information in a pc, prepare sales packets with labels and addresses, make phone calls, print reports, schedules, and calendars.*

    Documentation should include examples from these kinds of personal (family, etc.) and professional activities.

Figure 2.1

A Completed User Analysis

This user analysis (shown in italics) demonstrates how you might organize information about users for use in design decisions as you plan your documentation.

Example   27

Primary Issues Raised by the Program

- What learning difficulties, motivational problems, technical difficulties will your users face?

    Ease of Use: *Users want the program to work effortlessly, with little or no investment of time in learning.*

    Integrating with Other Programs: *Users employ other business-oriented programs like Lotus 1-2-3, Excel, and others. Using this program should not isolate them from the data in these programs.*

The User's Tasks

- What workplace jobs will the user do with the program?

    Schedule meetings, appointments, phone colleagues/clients, send faxes, take notes on phones, log phone use, create envelopes, create reports, arrange other people's schedules, send email.

- What important sequences will the user follow that can help you organize your program tasks?

    Sample Calendar sequence: *Open the calendar, update the day's activities, consult the daily to-do list, print the daily to-do list.*

    Sample Address Book sequence: *Open the address book, open the dialer, search for a number, call a number, log the call.*

- What tasks can you use as examples in your online and hard-copy manuals?

    Set up a staff meeting, schedule lunch with attorneys, remember to pick up son from ski trip, prepare/transfer monthly sales report.

The User's Informational Needs

- What important kinds and forms of information does the user need?

    Addresses and phone numbers of businesses and individuals; employee, colleague, secretary, and personal schedules; communication settings.

- With whom does the user communicate, and in what forms and media?

    The user will communicate with colleagues, airlines, lawyers, press contacts, advertising agencies, car rental agencies, doctors, clients, vendors, accountants. These audiences will have phones, fax machines, printers, and digital pagers.

Continued

Figure 2.1

(Continued)

The User's Work Motivations

- What internal and external motivations affect the user?

  Efficiency: The user will want fast and efficient access to information.

  Productivity: The user will see the connection between being organized and doing a good job, and will not invest time in a time manager that will not make her or him more productive.

The User's Range of Computer Experience

- Describe the kinds of novice, experienced, and expert behavior exhibited by the user. Pay attention to the numbers and different kinds of programs, degree of technical knowledge, user attitudes towards computing, and the learning behavior of the user.

  *Users will range from novice to expert, but most will fall in the **experienced** range. The user will use spreadsheets, database, and word processing programs regularly. The user will have moderate technical knowledge for installation and modem setting up, and will see the computer as a tool to increase productivity. The user will take the manual and online system seriously and expect guidance and support for the program's features.*

The User's Knowledge of the Subject Matter of the Program

- What kinds of vocabulary reinforcement and subject/matter background will the documentation need to provide?

  Users may need some background in ways to organize information according to multiple categories, groups, and so on. Otherwise they will need little support here.

The User's Workplace

- What other computer programs are found at the user's job site?

  Lotus 1-2-3 (all versions), DBASE, (all versions), Excel (all versions), Microsoft Cardfile, Address Book Plus, Tandy Deskmate, Casio BOSS, Sharp Wizard, WordPerfect (all versions), Microsoft Word (all versions), Mosaic, Borland Quatro, Hayes-compatible modems, WinFax Pro.

- What user's groups does the user belong to or have available?

  Windows for Workgroups, word processing groups, and other members of office work groups, production teams, sales teams, executive boards.

- Describe the degree of organizational support for computers and software in your user's organization.

  Most users work in corporations and have access to some informal technical support for individual programs. Such support may be counted on for network and communication areas.

Figure 2.1

(Continued)

The User's Learning Preferences

▪ Describe the user's preferences for instructor, manual, or computer-based learning.

Most users would prefer computer-based learning. They explore programs readily and rely on online help more than manuals. These users expect to figure out something they need at the time they need it. They rely on other users to some extent.

The User's Usage Pattern

▪ Describe the patterns users will exhibit in terms of regular, intermittent, and casual usage.

Users will follow a regular or intermittent usage pattern. Most who use the program will do so on a daily basis, and although they will not perform work with the program, they will use it regularly to organize their work. They may need to explore new features and, when doing so, will need good online support.

Document Goals

▪ What goals in the areas of meeting user needs do you envision for the documentation set you plan to write for the users you have described above?

The installation guidance should have the program installed and usable within ½ hour. Online help should provide command explanations as well as procedures for intermittent users.

Suggested Documentation Features

▪ Describe the documentation features that your user analysis suggests. Pay particular attention to areas of organization, emphases for motivation, separate sections or other elements you want to provide to meet special needs and characteristics you discover.

The documentation should emphasize creativity and productivity; exercises and examples should reflect workplace situations; goal statements in procedures can help motivate toward effective use; the emphasis should fall on the program as an efficient, organized assistant. The document should include tips for efficient use and invitations to explore new features.

Figure 2.1

(Continued)

Guidelines

Figure 2.2 lists the steps involved in a user analysis. Each step is explored in the paragraphs that follow.

1   Choose Users Carefully

You may have to use your imagination in identifying possible users. In the early stages of user analysis you should list every possible user group, no matter how improbable a user

1. Choose users carefully.

2. Anticipate transfer of learning by studying noncomputer-mediated tasks.

3. Mock-up hard-to-contact users.

4. Write user scenarios.

5. Plan interviews carefully.

6. Involve users in all phases of the project.

7. Identify document goals.

8. Tie the user analysis to document features.

Figure 2.2

Guidelines for Conducting a User Analysis

might sound at first. Study the list of possible users you have brainstormed and ask yourself: "Which users would most probably use the program and which users can I interview most easily?" The answers to these questions will help you narrow your search. Look for users with whom you can develop a working relationship that will last through the project. You should try to find the most typical users, the ones who represent the most probable intended users of the program. Table 2.1 shows some examples of user groups for programs.

Table 2.1

Examples of User Groups for Programs

Program	User Group	Tasks
Network Program	System Administrator	Set up user accounts and passwords.
	User	Log in, run programs, store files.
Jogging Log	Coach	Enter data about athletes, create reports, track progress.
	Athlete	Enter data about workouts, create reports, track progress.
Math Tutor	Teacher	Set up tutorials, track progress.
	Student	Run tutorials, score tests, record progress.
Family Financial Planner	Financial Consultant	Create customer profiles, reports for customers.
	Head of Household	Enter data about assets, income, investments, create tax reports.

Once you have narrowed the list you can conduct user interviews. If you don't work with the users, locate some people with similar jobs in your own organization. Call them, explain your documentation project, and ask if they would let you discuss their work with them. As you build your list of job tasks, pay particular attention to information-related tasks: communicating, storing, sharing. Identify users with these concerns; they should be able to tell you a lot about how your software could be implemented in task-relevant ways.

During the first part of the research process, identify users according to the types of task they perform: installation, *configuration,* and end use. In large organizations you may have users that just install and configure software, but most of your users will need to perform end-use tasks. In smaller organizations you will probably have one user, or the owner of the program, performing all tasks.

2   Anticipate Transfer of Learning: Study Non-Computer-Mediated Tasks

The user interview should provide you with a wealth of information about a particular user. But remember, when it comes to job duties, you want to describe the non-automated situation, meaning the things the user does and the way the user does them, *without the benefit of your program.* For example, talk to a club president about the kinds of documents he or she writes, as well as about how he or she would use your word processor. On the other hand, if your user conducts mathematical research, find out what computational tasks he or she performs, as well as more hypothetical information about what he or she *might* do with your graphing software. Eventually you will match the software functions with the user's tasks, but at first the focus should fall on compiling a complete inventory of nonautomated and automated tasks.

Study the example in Figure 2.3. This description of user tasks was prepared during the documentation planning phase for some database management software (DBMS).

Every Friday, Charlie had to do the weekly sales summary for his boss, Adam. He downloaded raw data from the mainframe into a comma-delimited ASCII file his spreadsheet could read. Next, he used the spreadsheet's database functions to extract the information for each salesperson, one person at a time, summed the figures, and manually transferred the total to another part of the spreadsheet. He manually maintained weekly totals since January 1, and adjusted the line chart to include another week.

Describes the user before using the program

With his new DBMS, he creates a single query that requests the sales figures since January 1 from the mainframe, cross-tabulates them by salesperson by week. A one-page report with a 3-D line graph is automatically updated.

Describes the user after using the program

Figure 2.3

An Example of Users Before and After Using a Program

A description of a user task should describe the noncomputerized work. This will help the documentation designer find ways to promote transfer learning.

Research shows that skills learned in the workplace can transfer to skills using software. The more you understand these skills in your user, the better you can transfer this valuable learning to the use of your software.

Notice even small facts about users, such as their attitudes toward computer programs or their habits when developing computer skills. Look for artifacts like notes stuck on bulletin boards, diaries of skills, or third-party computer manuals that users employ in their daily struggle to get the most out of their existing technology. Learn what other types of employees the user interacts with. Find out what values—efficiency, team orientation, environmental concerns, ethical issues—confront your user, and how he or she responds to them. Such information can help you understand the motivation your users have: motivation that leads to striving in job performance, that can provide the energy to get them through a tutorial or direct them to a procedure.

3   ## Mock Up Hard-to-Contact Users

In some instances you don't have actual users at your disposal. You may find yourself without actual users to interview and only limited information about the tasks the software supports. In the absence of actual users, you can construct a mock-up of the user, a kind of model to use as a resource in making design decisions. Do this by focusing on the user's occupation as described in easy-to-find library materials.

Occupations tend to have a degree of generality about them. You can find out about them by consulting guides such as *Career Occupational Briefs, The Dictionary of Occupational Titles,* or *The Encyclopedia of Careers and Vocational Guidance.* These guides—intended to assist job searchers—contain specific information about just about every kind of job you can imagine. Table 2.2 lists some of these printed guides and some software programs. In addition, placement services at your local college or university often have computerized career information systems containing descriptions of job titles.

Beyond this, you can look over some of the job descriptions found in publications put out by companies (usually found in placement services, personnel agencies, or from the companies themselves). Haliburton, Inc., for example, employs numerous engineers, researchers, managers, account executives, and writers in its work in oil field services. The descriptions you find in these kinds of publications may provide the best information about jobs and tasks, because they show how different organizations define different jobs. A systems analyst, for example, gets mentioned in just about every guide to job titles, but the definition of a systems analyst varies greatly from company to company. To find out what a systems analyst would do in a bank as opposed to a communications firm, you can consult the literature produced by each company.

4   ## Write User Scenarios

Why bother writing *user scenarios*? User scenarios depict the tasks that users of the software would perform, based on your interview notes. Doing this takes time, but it helps you visualize users and creates a useful document that you can share with clients, potential users, or other members of the writing team. You can use scenarios in your documentation to

Table 2.2

Sources of Job Descriptions

Sources	Titles
Guides	*Occupation Outlook Handbook*
	Dictionary of Occupational Titles
	Encyclopedia of Careers and Vocational Guidance
Software programs	*Sigiplus*
	Discover
WEB SITES	
Online Career Center	http://occ.com
Yahoo! Business and Economy	http://www.yahoo.com/Business/Employment/Jobs
America's Job Bank	http://www.ajb.dni.us/

provide role models for users. You can also use scenarios in your ***documentation plan,*** to justify the documentation set you plan to produce.

Start with the notes you took during user interviews. Scenarios should describe how the program gets used. They identify what tasks the user will need information about, and what manuals you need to write. You should prepare one or more scenarios for each user type that you envision for the software you are documenting. The documentation needed for each user may vary: you may have special sections for each type of user or, if their needs differ greatly, each type of user may require a separate document. The major sections of the user scenario illustrated in Table 2.3 should provide you with enough general guidance to prepare one easily.

In your user scenarios, some of the elements will overlap with documentation needed for other users or will be used by other users. For example, some novice users will require a ***procedures manual,*** as may your experienced users. In many cases, you can incorporate features into your documents that will make them usable by more than one user at the same time, such as special ***cuing, layering,*** or ***navigational devices.***

When you decide what documentation is needed, you should study the chapters on documentation forms—Chapters 12 (tutorials), 13 (procedures) and 14 (references)—and document design, Chapter 8. When you describe a form, whether as a section or an entire manual, think of it as a commitment to creating that form. Also, consider that you want to provide the minimum documentation you can. Don't think up an array of many different document forms if you only have the resources to produce a limited number.

Review your user scenarios carefully. Ask your potential users to read them and comment on how correctly you have described the overall and typical-use descriptions. How easily can your users identify with the role model they find in your scenarios?

Table 2.3

Elements of a User Scenario

Topic Area	Writer's Question	How to Write It
Professional Role	How do my users function in their work environment? What objectives must the users achieve to perform their jobs successfully?	State the job title of the person who would actually use the program. For example "Manager in charge of scheduling a fleet of school buses," or "Temporary secretary needed to fill in for vacationing employees."
Profile	How much do my users know about the subject matter of the program and about computers in general?	Describe how the user would use the program on the job, and how much the user knows about computers in general. List the user type.
Overall Use of the Program	How will my users integrate the program into their work environment? Which program tasks relate to which professional goals?	Describe the series of actions the user would take in integrating the program into a work situation. Give realistic life examples of what a person would do with a program.
Typical Use of the Program	What tasks will the user perform most typically?	Describe the **most typical** use (no more than 5 or 6 tasks.) This will be a subset of the tasks in the program task list.

5   Plan Interviews Carefully

Known as *research* or *background research,* your interviews with users provide the most important source of information for planning your documentation project. In an interview, you encounter potential users of the program and, often in one or two settings, learn enough to design a documentation system that will satisfy your goals as a writer: to encourage them to learn the features of the program and put the program to useful work. The advice under this guideline pertains to the process of interviewing users: making site visits, spending an hour or two with a potential user, and getting potential users to fill out questionnaires. A full user analysis should not only study users in one or two episodes, but should involve users in the whole documentation cycle, so see the activities described below in that larger context of user involvement.

What Support Issues Does Your Program Raise?

Not all documentation projects require the same kinds of questions of users, or pose the same set of challenges to the writer. For example, with a customized messaging system like Pegasus Mail, users in a research and development environment would have used similar systems in the past. So the issue involves their messaging behavior, and trying to find out how much they know about messaging in general. Trying to determine their knowledge of engineering design principles would put you and the users on the wrong track. Save those questions for your next project, the Probe circuit design software package.

Your familiarity with the program and the developers of the program will help you identify what issues to try to resolve in your interviews. Consider how the programs indicated in Table 2.4 raise different issues for user analysis.

How to Plan an Interview

An interview *plan* may seem like an extra way to waste your time rather than just getting down to the job of learning about your users, and a sketchy one will, in fact, waste your

Table 2.4

Kinds of Issues Raised in User Interviews

Program	Users	Issues
Microsoft Word (word processing)	All levels, very general	What tasks do most users do most regularly?
		What other word processing programs have users used?
RunLog (jogging records)	Novice	What motivates use?
		How do coaches and runners work together?
Network program (sets up email and file sharing)	All levels	What kinds of security do users need?
		How do users store and transfer information?
		What email behaviors do users have?
		What technical problems face users?
Pat's Food Shopper (organizes grocery store visits)	Novice	What shopping patterns does the user have?
Color Time (elementary school coloring book maker)	Experienced (teacher)	What goals do teachers have for elementary art students?
		What kinds of illustrations do teachers use for math, history, and spelling pages?
Phone Book Plus (manages client addresses/phone numbers, automatic dialing)	Experienced	What equipment does the user have to handle phone calls?
		How well does the user understand complex communication protocols?

time. But unless you have a lot of time for your project and abundant users available, investing time in an interview strategy can pay off in forestalling repeat visits or unproductive interviews. To plan for productive user interviews, follow these general steps:

1. Do preliminary research into the user's job and the programs already in use.
2. Review the software program and identify the issues.
3. Establish the scope of your interviews (how many, with whom, etc.).
4. Make a list of interview questions.
5. Get permission (from bosses, from users, from security).
6. Decide how you want to collect information (interviews, observations, questionnaires).
7. Set up an interview schedule (dates, times, places).
8. Plan a follow-up (thank you letters, reviews, testing).

How to Conduct an Interview

As indicated above, a successful interview with a user often results from careful planning. Below you will find a brief discussion of some of the aspects of interviews you should consider as you prepare for the interview itself.

KNOW YOUR USERS. Clearly, you want to learn about your users during an interview, but the more background you accumulate about the users beforehand, the more you can focus your questions. If you're interviewing an accountant, for example, you don't want to waste your time and your user's time asking questions about elementary accounting principles. Similarly, you don't want to get sidetracked into a discussion about the other kinds of software they use. You can learn about these areas by doing a little preliminary research into company literature or going over computer sales literature. Gain points and show respect for your users by demonstrating a working knowledge of their field and their computer use.

KNOW YOUR PROGRAM. You should have started to work on your task list for the program *and have used the software you're writing about* before you present it to your users. After all, it's your job to act as a go-between for the software and the user, so you have to know both. If you have product literature about the program, sample screens and menus, descriptions of functions, and other information about the program, be familiar with it and take it with you to the interview.

GET AUTHORIZATION. Most of the time you can just call a potential user and set up an interview time. However, larger companies often have policies regarding interviews with employees. In such cases you should, through a phone call or letter, obtain authorization to interview employees.

PREPARE A LIST OF QUESTIONS. Having a list of questions adds a lot to your interview outcome: it adds structure to your interview, allows for consistency over multiple interviews, helps you focus on the issues, and makes you look professional. Probably during a one-hour interview you will only have time to ask eight to ten questions, so you will want to give some thought to their wording. Remember to make your questions open-ended, so they get your user talking and you listening.

Follow the sample questions in Table 2.5 to start writing interview questions.

Table 2.5

Sample Interview Questions

To find out about this...	Ask something like this . . .
What tasks will the user perform with the program?	Tell me about your job. What tasks do you do over and over? Can you describe your key job responsibilities? What sequence do you follow in performing [task]? How can you tell that [task] has been done well?
What are the user's informational needs?	Whom do you communicate with in your job? What kinds of reports or documents do you produce on your job? Where do you get information to use in [task]?
What are the user's work motivations?	How long have you worked as an accountant? How do you tell a good report/design from a bad one? How much time did you spend on this report/design?
What's the user's range of computer experience?	How do you use computers in your job? Do you think computers help you in your job? What other programs have you used? What kinds of formal or informal computer training have you had?
How much does the user know of the subject matter of the program?	How long have you been working as a [professional role]? What has been your experience with [subject matter]? How did you learn about [subject matter]?
What's the user's workplace environment—the user community?	What kinds of equipment do you have in your office? What kinds of computers do you use? What kinds of software does your work group use?
What's the user's learning preference?	How did you learn to use your current software? Which would you prefer: a teacher or a book? What motivates you to learn a new software program? What do you do when you can't figure out how to do something with a program?
What's the user's usage pattern?	When you get a new software program, what do you do first? Do you ever forget how to use a program feature? How often do you use online help systems?

WRITE AND LISTEN A LOT. When interviewing, you should use a pen or a recorder (after asking permission from the user) to record as much as possible of what gets said. As a rule of thumb, you know an interview is becoming unproductive when you find yourself talking more than the user. Sure, you'll have to explain your questions, but the user should do most of the talking. You may find it useful to concentrate on your writing (on a pad) and take your eyes off the interviewees during interviews. That way the speakers tend to talk more. If you look at them, they shut up.

COLLECT SAMPLES. When you interview a potential user, you have the opportunity to collect samples of work that you can later use in your manual. These samples contribute to the goal of making the documentation reflect workplace usage. You can use them in user scenarios, examples that introduce procedures, in mocked up screens, as tutorial lessons, and many other ways. Make it clear to the user how you intend to use these samples, and do not use them without permission. If the user seems skittish about his or her name or company's name appearing in the document, you might offer to use the data but change the important, identifying elements such as names, names of vendors and clients and such. During an interview, stay on the lookout for the kinds of samples described in Table 2.6.

How to Observe

Instead of (or in addition to) interviewing your potential users, you may wish to *observe* them. Observation consists of your spending time at the workplace watching users perform their jobs, recording the sequences of tasks, and also taking in the atmosphere of the workplace. You should use observation when you have a variety of users at one site or when you want to correlate your interview information with observed information. Certainly you will do some observing during all interviews, keeping your eyes open for telling details of the user's surroundings to add to your overall picture of the user. But a structured observation of users requires that you put some thought into the process ahead of time, that you understand some of the limitations of observation as a research technique, and that you follow some guidelines for maintaining your objectivity.

Table 2.6

Kinds of Samples to Look for during an Interview

Sample Type	Specific Forms
Reports	Financial reports, progress reports, activity reports, earnings statements
Documents	Letters, reports, newsletters, sample printouts, drafts of documents, research reports, parts lists, designs and drawings, resumes, procedures, policy documents
Forms	Invoices, order forms, job application forms, ledger sheets

Above all, you should try to avoid the following two main types of distortion:

- **Getting Too Involved.** You can easily distort what a user does by allowing your presence to affect the sequence of the task. If you let the user know what you want to happen ahead of time you risk the chance of it happening whether or not it is "natural," because users generally want (even subconsciously) to satisfy the expectations of the person who has taken an interest in their work. And too, your heightened expectancy of a certain outcome can cause you to miss some details, or even supply steps that didn't occur. When you observe, make sure your very presence doesn't change what happens.

- **Not Getting Involved Enough.** By not asking questions of your user, you risk focusing on the wrong details. You may take notes on a user's gathering of electronic information to prepare for a meeting, when in fact this particular meeting happens only rarely. You should also make sure you cross-check your information. Distortions can occur in unexpected and unintended ways. If the user describes a report's contents, ask to see the report and double-check to see that it contains the contents the user said it would.

How to Write a Questionnaire

Like an interview, the questionnaire enables you to get information from a variety of users. It increases your chances of getting a unique and very valuable piece of information, but more important, it can show a reliable pattern of use that you can't get from one user.

MAKE IT OPEN-ENDED. Some kinds of questionnaires, such as those you provide the user to help evaluate a manual or a help system, carefully guide the user's responses so you get specific information about the documents' design. These are called *product insert questionnaires*. However, for user analysis, *open-ended questionnaires* (that ask essay-type questions instead of yes/no or multiple choice questions) usually work best. Open-ended questionnaires enable you to question users when you can't imagine all the possible answers to your questions. They allow your respondents to provide in-depth answers, and to reveal what they think is important about their use of a software program.

GUIDELINES FOR WRITING QUESTIONNAIRES. Questionnaires can provide you with a wealth of information about users if you follow these guidelines for preparing them.

- **Get it right the first time.** You probably can't expect users to re-answer a questionnaire that takes thirty or more minutes to fill out, so you need to get it right the first time. To ensure you have the right questions, try a sample set of questions on one or two users, refine the questions, then prepare the final questionnaire.

- **Provide clear instructions on how to fill out the questions.** Leave enough room for users to provide complete answers, and remember that it's rare for a user to write beyond the limits set by the space allotted.

- **Focus on a topic, but leave the question unstructured.** Indicate the area of your question, such as "What has been your experience using online help systems?" but avoid giving too much guidance, as in "Name the three best online help systems you've used in the past year." Questions that assume certain conditions (such as the person has used three programs in the past year) are sometimes called "double-barreled" questions. Avoid them.

■ **Phrase questions affirmatively.** Avoid the negativity of questions like "You wouldn't want to read a Reference Guide, would you?" or "What don't you like about tutorials?" Better phrasing would be "Have you used reference guides in the past?" or "Describe your experiences (if any) using tutorials."

■ **Stimulate responses by including sample passages.** You can use mocked-up examples from manuals to test users' responses to certain design ideas you may have. You may want to show the user a sample layout of a tool description for a drawing program, or ask for their responses to a variety of ways of describing *command syntax*.

6   Involve Users in All Phases of the Project

A full user analysis should not only study users in one or two episodes, but should involve users in the entire documentation cycle. So you should see the activities described here in the larger context of user involvement in your entire project. Subsequent chapters in this book rely on your establishing good relationships with your users early in the project. For example, where do you think you will find good user reviewers when you're sending your draft out (Chapter 5, "Getting Useful Reviews")? Similarly, your testing will require real persons from the user population to help ensure productive results (Chapter 6, "Conducting Usability Tests").

Researchers have assessed both the benefits and drawbacks of involving users in the writing process. Usually, involving the users in the process can have the following benefits:

■ **Increased accuracy.** Users can indicate mistakes or lack of clarity in manuals.

■ **More appropriate information.** Users can identify information that is not useful to workplace tasks.

■ **Increased usability.** Users can advise on the most useful design techniques for information.

■ **Empowered readers.** Users can help plan the documents they need most.

■ **Improved politics.** Users are flattered to be consulted.[1]

In instances where the development of documents parallels the development of the system, user involvement in the entire project becomes critical. Companies like Technical Information Associates, based in Denver, Colorado, create systems for office automation that involve databases, decision support, and information management as well as standard applications like word processing, spreadsheets, and communications. Developers, programmers, and documentation specialists working on projects for this company would want, and *need,* to involve users because of the complexity of the total product. Table 2.7 examines the standard stages of the document design process and ways you can involve users.[2] The idea of involving users in the documentation process relates to two other key ideas: usability (making sure of the readability of the documentation and its suitability to the task) and collaborative writing (users and documentation specialists collaborating to produce the documentation product).

Table 2.7

Involving Users in the Phases in the Manual Production Process

Production Phase	Ways to Involve the User
1. Perform the User Analysis	Interview, observe, survey potential users.
	Provide examples/sample data.
2. Create the Program Task List	Double-check for clear wording.
	Check for sensible grouping of tasks.
3. Design the Documents	Check document objectives for suitability to users' needs.
	Get user feedback/reality check on design prototypes.
4. Write the Project Plan	Check outlines for appropriate task organization.
	Check list of hypertext links for online structures.
	Check outlines for completeness of information.
5. Write the Alpha Draft	Test prototype designs with users.
6. Conduct Reviews and Tests	Get user reviews for suitability, accuracy, completeness.
	Use users in usability testing of users guides and tutorials.
7. Revise and Edit	Reconfirm changes with users.
	Review graphics/tables/figures for accuracy.
8. Write a Final Draft	Confirm vocabulary decisions with users.
	Elicit user input on terminology used for indexing.
	Review definitions with users.
9. Conduct a Field Evaluation	Survey actual users for reactions, needed improvements.

Cultivate Relationships with Users

When you make your initial contact with users, plan to include them in as much of the documentation work as you can. Their perspective can inform your work and give you a reality check on the many design decisions you have to make as the project moves forward. You will even find that what you learn about users on one project will be useful on subsequent projects, as your knowledge of user categories and the cognitive demands on users grows.

As a writer, you often take on the role of *user advocate*.[3] Make the most of the relationships you form with your users as a useful counterbalance to the relationships you form with members of your development team: programmers, managers, testing specialists, and so on. This relationship can help you maintain a clear focus on your professional role.

Do a Focus Group

To study users and to lock them into your plan throughout your project, consider conducting a focus group. Focus groups consist of groups of seven to ten participants who either have experience with previous releases of your documentation or whom you have identified as potential users. Focus groups can provide a rich wealth of information about how your product fits into a workplace. Focus groups typically meet for one to two hours and attempt to come up with a variety of opinions about a product and its use. While the moderator—the writer or a hired consultant—structures the group's work around specific questions pertaining to the use of software and the features of documentation that would support the use, the group aims primarily to spark new ideas rather than come to a consensus.[4]

As with all research methods, focus groups require some planning. To plan a successful focus group, follow these steps:

1. Locate potential participants.
2. Develop and administer a telephone screening questionnaire.
3. Confirm invitations in writing.
4. Draft open-ended questions and follow up questions, then revise.
5. Plan any hands-on activities (demos, dry runs, walkthroughs of procedures).
6. Make reminder calls.
7. Pilot-test the questions with one or two group members.[5]

Typically, your focus group will meet in a conference room or room with separate tables for smaller groups. Depending on the topics you want to explore, you can work with the entire group or, at times, break into smaller groups and then return to a whole-group format. On the simplest level, you would provide each member of the group with written questions, then discuss them one by one. Table 2.8 illustrates some questions you might use.

One procedure that focus group moderators sometimes follow involves asking group members to do a group brainstorm of the ideal characteristics for the support of a given program. The support could include manuals, training, online support, phone support, consultants—the works. After the moderator has collected (without commenting on their validity or feasibility) a list of characteristics, he or she breaks the group into smaller groups to come up with some suggestions as to what the writers could do to provide this support. After that the groups can come back together as a whole, with each group sharing their ideas. The moderator then records these and a general discussion follows. This procedure has the advantage of involving all members in the design process. Users who

Table 2.8

Sample Focus Group Questions

- In general, where is the first place you turn to find answers to your questions?

- In general, what usually drives you to consult a manual?

- When you do consult a manual, how do you locate the information you're looking for?

- If you could design an ideal set of manuals or an ideal help system for [program x] what features would it contain?

- What things in your existing manuals do you wish the writers had done better?

- How would [program x] fit in with the other programs you use at work?

- [Show a prototype and explain the proposed manual set. Make sure to say that this is very preliminary.] Overall, do you think the proposed set will be easier to use? Why? Why not?

- What support at your workplace do you think can help you use this program?

---

show enthusiasm for a program might even find themselves motivated to contribute to the support of a program by forming a special user's group.

Focus groups can go a long way towards giving your users the sense of involvement in the process of document production. By encouraging them in this way, you extend the possibilities of user-centered design.

7 Identify Document Goals

All human activities should have goals: They keep people on track and give them something to measure their performance by. For a documentation project, you can communicate the goals to other writers, managers, and clients. If you don't have time to explain to another writer how to do something, you may be able to get what you want if you have well-defined goal statements. Goals can come in very handy. Documentation goals consist of statements of purpose that articulate what you expect to do for the user. Of course, they should reflect the goals of all software documentation—to encourage users to learn features of the program and to put those features to work—but they should state how you hope to do that for this particular set of users and this particular program.

You may not have the writing-goals habit, being instead the kind of person who dives in, stays flexible, and adjusts along the way. Fine, but writing effective manuals isn't the same as playing a basketball game. The clearer your objectives, the better the chance that you will achieve them. Consider, too, that goals drive many parts of the documentation process. You use them in document design as a way to guide decisions about page layout and text design (see Chapter 9). You use them in testing at various stages of the writing and editing (see Chapter 7).

It may help if you examine some examples of goals statements and consider the elements of a good one. The examples in Table 2.9 helped writers of those documents keep

Table 2.9

Typical Goals Statements

Document Type	Goal Statement
Section of a document	The "Setting Parameters" section of the BitCom User's Guide will provide procedures for novice users in education and business to perform tasks associated with using the DOS mode command and the online setup utility.
Booklet	The BitCom Getting Started booklet will provide tutorial support for novice users in education and business to perform routine logons and logoffs.
Chapter	Chapter 5 of the PhoneNET Talk User's Guide will provide reference support for novice users in general professions to use all twenty of the ANET commands available through the command interpreter.

their projects on track. Goals statements can get very involved and you may need to take them to a fine level of detail, especially if you have a very narrowly defined spectrum of users. But the illustrations in Table 2.9 will work as models for most goals statements. They contain the name of the document or section, refer to the user type—novice, experienced, expert—and the kind of support you intend to provide: tutorial, procedures, or reference.

8   Tie the User Analysis to Documentation Features

The checklist in this chapter will help you organize your user analysis so you focus on, and gather, the information that will allow you the greatest success in designing your documents. But all the analysis you do will not help unless you tie the user analysis to documentation features: aspects of the documents that tailor information to specific users. You cannot, at the stage of user analysis, state the details of your document design: the page layout, choice of type size, style, fonts, or stylistic choices. That level of design results from considering the many design tools available to the writer. You should base all your design decisions on the user task needs that you discover in your user analysis. As you interview, observe, or survey your users, you should try to see how you can tailor the documents to the user's needs. Ideas that you get during your analysis can help to guide your later, more detailed, document design.

In Table 2.10 you will find a preliminary summary of some of the document features that you can use to meet some user needs. The list contains lots of good ideas to use as guidelines, but it by no means contains all the ideas that exist, or that you will come up with on your own. Use the list to keep yourself pointed in the direction of meeting user needs.

Table 2.10

Match Document Features with the User Analysis Results

Analysis Results	Features to Meet User Needs
POSSIBLE USERS OF THE SOFTWARE	
What recognizable groups (teacher, student, system administrator, end user) will your users comprise? Describe each group briefly.	Documents/sections for separate groups
	Illustrations targeting different groups
Provide a brief scenario of use by representative professions to act as a model of how the program will serve different professional user groups.	Brief scenarios included for different groups
	Special glossaries for individual groups
	Group-specific organizational schemes for different groups
PRIMARY ISSUES RAISED BY THE SOFTWARE	
What learning difficulties, motivational problems, technical difficulties will your users face?	Focused tutorials for technical difficulties
	Explanations of workplace applications
	Suggestions for contact with user's groups
	Encouragement of use of online support
THE USER'S TASKS	
What workplace jobs will the user do with the program?	Organization of sections, chapters, manuals around user-defined tasks
What important sequences will the user follow that can help you organize your program tasks?	Suggested sequences for difficult tasks
	Examples of tasks in procedural elaborations
What tasks can you use as examples in your online and hard-copy manuals?	Special job performance aids for difficult tasks
THE USER'S INFORMATIONAL NEEDS	
What important kinds and forms of information does the user need in order to use the program?	Lists of sources of information for input to the program
Whom does the user communicate with, and in what forms and media?	Suggestions for importing and exporting data to and from other programs
	Emphasis of reports and documents the program produces
THE USER'S WORK MOTIVATION	
What internal and external motivations affect the user?	Illustrations of efficient, creative, productive use of the program
	Emphasize the value of program output
	Reward accurate response to help screens
	Encourage independent thinking and problem solving

Continued

Table 2.10

(Continued)

Analysis Results	Features to Meet User Needs
THE USER'S RANGE OF COMPUTER EXPERIENCE	
Describe the kinds of novice, experienced, and expert behavior exhibited by the user. Pay attention to the numbers and kinds of programs, degree of technical knowledge, user attitudes towards computing, and the learning behavior of the user.	Analogies to other programs Types of documentation: tutorial, user's guide, command summaries Media of documentation: online, hard copy Support for technical background Full index of terms for novice users
THE USER'S KNOWLEDGE OF THE SUBJECT MATTER OF THE PROGRAM	
What kinds of vocabulary reinforcement and subject/matter background will the documentation have to provide?	Glossary to reinforce terminology Encyclopedic overview of key concepts Suggestions for further reading Illustrations of application to workplace tasks
THE USER'S WORKPLACE	
What other computer programs are used at the user's job site? What user's groups does the user belong to or have available? Describe the degree of organizational support for computer use in your user's organization.	References to other programs Background information on user groups Encouragement/guidelines for group learning and use Suggestions of organizational support Encouragement of networked/integrated use
THE USER'S LEARNING PREFERENCES	
Describe the users preferences for instructor, manual, or computer-based learning.	Choice of manual, instructor-based, or computer-based tutorial Creation of workplace scenarios for training Suggestions for group learning
THE USER'S USAGE PATTERN	
Describe the usage patterns users will exhibit in using the software in terms of regular, intermittent, and casual usage.	Organization of sections, documents, chapters around sets of features Emphasis on online support for intermittent users Quick overview cards for casual users

The user analysis constitutes a major element in the design of task-oriented documentation. The user analysis allows you to study the user's personal needs and the organizational goals in which the software, the manual, and the help system must function. The user analysis document that results from your user analysis models the user, just as the program task list models the computer program. As a model of the user, the user analysis allows you to experiment with design elements associated with the three levels of support to find those that will work best. The user analysis also helps you determine goals for your documents. With these design elements completed, you have the basis for making decisions on the kinds and nature of documents and task user required. The user analysis, in other words, culminates your research work for a software documentation project. After the user analysis, you can confidently write a plan, called a *documentation plan,* outlining your manuals and showing the tasks needed to complete them.

The Importance of a Thorough User Analysis

The user analysis can help you in many ways. It allows you to determine what tasks the user needs to perform with the software. In addition, it gives you the occasion to apply other documenter's tools, such as user types and user scenarios, to the design problem. It also gives you a first contact with your actual users, through interviews and other forms of research. From this contact you may identify potential topics for testing and persons to serve as test subjects.

Your user analysis will provide you with examples to use in your tutorials, but the user analysis does not just apply to the *teaching* level of task support. It applies to all levels of task support—tutorial, guidance, and reference—and to the document forms you design to operate on those levels. The user analysis helps you organize and write your table of contents by providing a task-oriented sequence for procedures. It applies to "getting started" sections by implying what kind of computer system, printer, and other hardware the user has. In tutorial documentation, the user analysis provides the scenario that the lessons teach. Examples generated by the user analysis also show up in procedures and in reference documents. The user analysis guides you in your index preparation by suggesting vocabulary to cross-reference. Additionally, the user analysis helps you design the look of your manuals. It informs your choice of page layout, type design, and organization. It helps you decide what kinds of graphics to use and for what purpose. Table 2.11 illustrates some ways that manuals and online help reflect your user analysis.

Thus, your user analysis, if done well, can unify your documentation set. If poorly done, it can contribute to the fragmentation of the documentation set and the consequent frustration of the user who does not see his or her professional role reflected in the descriptions and applications of the program.

What Does *Use* Mean?

What exactly is meant by *use* of the program? The answer lies partly in the general nature of computer programs: the way they act as tools to accomplish personal and professional

Table 2.11

Some Ways Manuals Reflect User Analysis

Element	Reflects this Aspect of the User Analysis
Installation	Kinds of hardware/operating systems used
Getting Started	User's subject matter background knowledge
	User's computer experience
Tutorial	Examples for lessons
	Background knowledge of subject matter and computer experience for transfer learning
User's Guide	Examples
	User goal statements
	Organization of tasks
Reference	Vocabulary
	Sequences for **hypertext links** in online help
Job Performance Aids	Needs for specialized support
Index	Terms for cross referencing
	User questions and problems

goals in various corporate, industrial, educational, and domestic environments. Behind the idea of user analysis are the documenter's two motivations: to encourage efficient use of the software (knowledge of the program features) and effective use of the software (application of the program features to useful work). If you know what features the user needs to apply in the overall task and information environment, you can design your manuals to encourage that application.

Things You Want to Know about Users

In preparing a user analysis, you basically ask the following eight questions:

1. What tasks will the user perform with the program?
2. What are the user's informational needs?
   - What information does the user need?
   - How does the user communicate?
   - What work motivations affect the software user?
3. What are the user's work motivations?

4. What's the user's range of computer experience: novice, experienced, expert?

5. How much does the user know of the subject matter of the program (e.g. accounting, writing, designing)?

6. What's the user's workplace environment: the user community (e.g. organizational structures/other software users)?

7. What's the user's preferred learning preference (instructor/manual/online)?

8. What's the user's usage pattern (learning curve regular, casual, intermittent)?

You may not *gather* information about all of these questions for a specific project. But you will need to *know* all of this information—either from past experience or the interviews, observations, and surveys discussed above. The questions you ask in investigating your users in these areas, as Table 2.12 shows, have a significant effect on your project.

If you look ahead to Chapter 8, "Designing for Task Orientation," you will see that the decisions you make for design of your document use the information you gather for these eight areas. So you can also see the importance of using them and adapting them as carefully as you can, to save time and ensure a successful project later.

This discussion will focus on each of these areas in turn, explaining the rationale for each and giving examples of the kinds of information each provides and how you can use that information in your manual project.

Tasks the User Will Perform with the Program

Of all the work you do in your document-development process, identifying user tasks probably ranks the highest. Consult Chapter 6, "Conducting Usability Tests," for example, and you will see that tasks form the starting place for your testing activities. In Chapter 13,

Table 2.12

Topic Areas of Your User Analysis, Related to Your Documents

Topic Area	Effect on Documentation
Tasks	Organization of procedures
Informational Needs	Choice of emphasis in job performance aids, choice of examples
Work Motivations	Choice of tone, choice of examples
Computer Experience	Tutorial design, vocabulary, organization of procedures
Subject Matter	Choice of background information, vocabulary, special reference, aids/templates, configuration preferences
User Community	References to organizational support, choice of examples, reference design, patterns of integration of computers and help
Learning Preference	Tutorial design, choice of examples, choice of teaching media
Usage Pattern	Structure, page layout, documentation set design

"Writing to Guide," (as well as Chapter 12, "Writing to Teach," and Chapter 14, "Writing to Support"), the task forms the significant unit of information in your manual or help system. So as you identify tasks here, keep in mind that you're shaping the information units of your document.

Begin your identification of users at the level of job titles. On some smaller programs, these roles may all refer to the same person: the end user. On the other hand, each of these roles, especially with larger programs, could themselves break further into categories. End users can come in various types. Consider an office system: managers, sales personnel, clerks, executives—all these fall into the group known as end users.

Knowing about these job roles gives you somewhere to start in determining user tasks. User tasks form the basis of your task-oriented information product. If you learn nothing else about your user, learn the usual tasks associated with his or her type of work. Chapter 3, "Constructing a Task List," will suggest that you can use these tasks to help assemble and organize the information in your manual or help, so it's a good idea to do a thorough job of investigating here. Table 2.13 illustrates some of these kinds of end users. Above all, you want to reinforce your task orientation with your selection of users. Using job titles as categories can help, by emphasizing what the user does with the program. In other words, for a specific program, identify the users by job title.

Example: How a Field Engineer Uses Software

Consider an example taken from a job description of field engineers with Haliburton, Inc., which performs oil-field support for clients. They test wells using sophisticated pressure sensing equipment; they also install and operate pumps or oil treatment equipment. According to information from the Haliburton Services brochure, field engineers do a number of jobs:

- Evaluate customer needs.
- Design treatments to fill those needs.
- Sell the job and equipment to the customer.
- Coordinate and manage the equipment to carry out the job.

Your interview with field engineers might uncover the sequences of tasks described in Table 2.14. Depending on the type of work your program does, these sequences will help you organize tasks from your task list. But the brochure goes into even further detail about the field engineers' work. Field engineers, for example, need to establish and maintain "effective communications with customers, co-workers in the field, and . . . research personnel." To do this, field engineers will undoubtedly use a number of communication technologies and, in the process, encounter a number of communication-related computer programs. These computer programs might include a word processor for writing, software for transferring data, and electronic mail for sending and receiving messages.

In addition, the field engineer for Haliburton Services needs to have access to information. The brochure points out that "The vast network of knowledge and support that

Table 2.13

Typical Kinds of Computer End Users

	Word Processing	Spreadsheet	Database	Communications (Email/Modem)	Draw/Design	Specialized Analysis	Accounting/Inventory
Retail Manager	■	■	■	■			■
Grocery Clerk							■
Land Buyer	■	■	■	■		■	
Engineering Designer	■	■		■	■		
Scientist/Researcher	■		■	■		■	
Teacher	■		■				
Student	■			■			
Banking Executive	■	■	■	■			
Engineering Consultant	■	■	■	■	■	■	
Receptionist				■			
Financial Planner	■		■			■	
Securities Auditor	■	■		■		■	■
Legal Secretary	■		■	■			

Haliburton has established to aid . . . decision-making is a definite plus for the field engineer." In this need—having access to information—the user will again use computer programs. These might include database programs of many types, research data search programs, and programs that allow access to histories, lists of files, and other valuable information to support decision making. The documenter should pay special attention to these kinds of programs, because, for the professional person to excel in a job requires access to the necessary information.

In both the examples above, the most important elements lie in the professional's need for communication and information. Most professionals—engineers, attorneys, and so on—will use a program well only if they see how it fosters these goals. To the extent

Table 2.14

Task Sequences for Field Engineers

Responsibility	Task Sequence
Communication	1. Open a new file in the word processor program. 2. Enter the text of the document. 3. Edit the document. 4. Format the document. 5. Print the document. 6. Exit the word processor program.
Pump Analysis	1. Open the analysis program. 2. Import the pump data from measuring instruments. 3. Run analysis routines. 4. Format analysis report. 5. Print analysis results.
Gauge Calibration	1. Open calibration program. 2. Login to central calibration data server. 3. Enter calibration information from depth-measuring equipment. 4. Receive calibration data from server. 5. Re-calibrate equipment. 6. Logout from central calibration data server. 7. Print error log from calibration program. 8. Close calibration program.
Manage Removal and Repair of Equipment	1. Open project management software. 2. Enter personnel and resources data. 3. Graph planning chart. 4. Edit planning chart. 5. Print preliminary planning chart for approval. 6. Close project management software.

that it does not, you will find very little energy expended on using the documentation for these programs. Documentation that truly supports professionals should make up a part of the toolkit those professionals use to further their acquisition of information and their communication with other employees.

The User's Informational Needs

People use computers primarily as tools. Whereas users formerly viewed computers as machines that do work, users now see computers as tools—that they control—to help them perform their jobs more efficiently. The thesis of this book states that good documentation should reflect this fact and should show, in all its elements, a design that supports the view of the computer as an instrument of the human operator, making the technology adapt to the person and not the person adapt to the technology. To do that, we need to design for the way people do their jobs.

Increasingly, today's employees take on a more important role in their workplace than that of mere workers. Because of economic trends, increased availability of information technology, and new management strategies, many employees manage their own work, make independent decisions, and set their own production goals. This phenomenon sees each employee as more independent than before while also a part of a production team, and as needing the appropriate resources. For this reason, job motivation (independence), communication (being part of a production team), and information (having the appropriate resources) have become major priorities of computer end users.

Research into how computer users apply their programs to their expanded roles in the workplace focuses on three areas:

- Information needs
- Communication needs
- Work/professional motivation

These areas have received considerable research attention because they make up variables that affect software use. As you can see, they reflect the employee's need for information, the employee's need to communicate with a group, and the employee's needs for appropriate motivation. Information about each of these three areas can help the software documenter make accurate design decisions about what levels of support and what forms of documents to produce.

What Information Does the User Need?

Users need to know what's going on in their sphere of influence. For example, the winery manager needs to see lists of grape suppliers and the quality of their crop in order to decide which suppliers to use for the next quarter. Access to this kind of information often comes through computers, or gets generated by saving and tracking functions of software. Program tasks such as those listed in Table 2.15 help users access and use this information. These kinds of tasks should receive special attention in manuals and online help because of their strategic importance. These tasks might include importing information from other files or downloading information from network sources. Additionally, they might include tasks that allow for browsing, searching, and extracting information from databases. Knowing this information allows the user not only to see what's going on, but to expand it.

To analyze this area of use, we need to know the user's main sources of information. We know that people need information to do their work well, but where does it come from? Educators require conferences or regular in-service meetings to keep up with

Table 2.15

Tasks That Foster Getting and Using Information

- Importing data from other programs
- Storing data in files
- Setting up file names
- Exporting data to other programs
- Importing information from electronic sources

changes in curriculum. Engineers study production reports and gather data from measuring instruments. In the example above, the winery manager probably reads trade publications, keeps up with scientific literature, and consults with other managers at other wineries. Without these sources the winery manager would not know what kinds of suppliers to use. Professionals read a wide variety of reports produced by their organizations and they keep up with a wide variety of journals, trade magazines, trade papers, and newsletters to get essential information to do their jobs.

Know the Direction of Information Flow

You should also gauge whether the information flows to your user follow a vertical pattern or a horizontal pattern, or both. Vertical patterns of information flow indicate information coming from the top (management, executives, etc.) to the employees. Often, vertical information flow follows lines of authority set up within a company and reflects the existing company structure. On the other hand, horizontal information flow refers to information shared among members of a user's primary work group, department, or team. Task-oriented software use often reflects horizontal flows of information because it represents decision making at the level of the end user, the person at the counter, or the person on the production floor. Whatever the pattern, you should try to assess how information flows to your user.

Where Does Information Come From?

Information, from whatever source, bombards today's user as it never has before. Consider the winery manager described above. Her information about suppliers comes from personal experience, trade magazine reports, information about research on grapes, and other raw materials. When she uses her spreadsheet and database programs, she needs to know how this information affects the data it produces. She needs to know how to get this information into her program, and how to manipulate the program to show her the angle on the data that she needs to make ordering plans. Documentation for this user should show how the program tasks—data input, tracking, sorting, categorizing, analyzing, printing—help to manipulate this crucial information to reflect her business goals.

Increasingly, professionals get their information electronically. Sources of electronic information include the following:

- The Internet: a vast and growing network of information sources. With such areas as the World Wide Web and FTP sites (sites for transferring files and programs) the professional can find information on just about every topic. Many companies include company information on their home pages, and the Internet gives users a connection to others with their motivations and concerns.

- Databases and data files kept on customers, vendors, production levels, sales, commissions, inventory, and many other topics.

- Commercial databases such as ProQuest and WestLaw that provide software and hardware reviews, industry news, government policy, regulatory changes, and other national and international business information.

- Organizational databases and networks created specifically for the organization, containing investment statistics, stock information, production guidelines, design specifications, and specialized libraries.

You should not only know what kinds of information the user needs, but also what forms it comes in, because when it comes to *strategic use*—use for the most important job duties—the user will exhibit definite preferences. This stands to reason, because strategic use demands information in relevant and usable forms. We looked at some forms of electronic information above, but you should also examine the other kinds of documents the user relies on—manuals, printed reports, faxes, and such—to help gauge the user's preferences. What you know about information needs can help you point software users to information that can help them in using your program.

How Does the User Communicate?

You can distinguish communication needs from information needs by looking for tasks that require storage and sharing of work in progress (*information* tasks) and tasks that require sharing of finished work (*communication* tasks). In the example above, after the winery manager has decided on a grape supplier for the next quarter, she needs to communicate that information to a number of other people: the supplier, the bookkeeper, the purchasing agent, other managers, and, finally, a boss or other executive. Employees require not only information to assert their professional presence, they also require tools for communication. For this reason, program tasks that foster communication should get special attention in your documentation. Among these tasks you might find report generating tasks, printing tasks, faxing, and storing for future use. Table 2.16 describes some kinds of communication tasks users engage in. You should do your best in the documentation to point out—through examples, notes, and suggestions—how the user can put these tasks to work.

You can examine communication needs by looking at the persons with whom your user communicates. On the nearest level, professionals need to communicate with others in their work group, development team, sales team, or research team. Increasingly, the work group makes up the primary unit of work in organizations. But while people need to share among team members, they also need to communicate with employees outside their immediate group: supervisors, clients, suppliers, government agencies. Ask any professional to rank "communication" on the list of essential tasks. Studies have shown that professionals in engineering, for example, report engaging in communication, especially

Table 2.16

Tasks that Foster Communication

- Choosing types of reports (document files, drawings, images, spreadsheets)
- Printing reports (document files, drawings, images, spreadsheets)
- Storing reports on hard disks, floppy disks, network disks
- Importing information (documents, designs, and spreadsheets created by other programs translated into the format of the current programs)
- Scanning (images and text)

writing, approximately 20 percent of the time. That's one day each work week spent communicating.

Users also like to identify types of documents they know. Users know FAQs (Frequently Asked Questions) and they know the short, informative "article" one sees so often on the Internet. It's a lesson in adaptation to notice that the Windows 95 Companion contains not chapters but "Articles" on various user-related, efficiency topics. This shows that the user's preferences for certain types of communication can affect the design of the document.

How does your user communicate? What forms does he or she prefer? Table 2.17 presents some typical forms of communication:

Table 2.17

Typical Forms of Communication

Presentations	
Meetings	Articles
Interviews	
Conversations	
Documents	
Reports	Memos
Letters	Proposals
Agendas	
Papers	
Teleconferencing	Conferences
Internet information	Web pages
Sources	
Messages	
Local area	Email
Wide area	Newsletters
Commercial	Distribution lists

Whatever forms of communication your user prefers, you should have a clear idea of them. They represent the ways users keep up with each other so their instructions get followed, their recommendations and suggestions get made, and their work gets appreciated. You should know what forms of communication your user needs and how your software fits into the picture through its report generating and other output functions. Think how much the winery manager appreciates support for her electronic faxing of reports to colleagues, or of printing multiple copies for training sessions.

Becoming familiar with the kinds of documents your users employ can help in another way. It's a key to the user's language: Using the terminology familiar to the user can trigger, in a psychological sense, a recognition of something familiar. Thus, when you are making up lists of terms to include in your index or keyword search list (Chapter 15, "Indexing and Keyword Searching"), you should spend some time looking over sample documents for important terminology.

The User's Work Motivations

What software documenter would not like to have an answer to this question: What motivates efficient and effective task-oriented software use? Part of the answer lies in the issues discussed above: awareness of the users' information and communication needs. We now turn to the user's personal and professional motivation. When it comes to what motivates users, follow this simple principle: What motivates users professionally will also motivate them to do well with software. In fact, if we can tap into a person's desire to do well professionally, we can channel that energy into the use of software. Documenters can't become experts in human motivation, but an awareness of some basic ideas can help you design for effective use.

In general, people respond to different kinds of motivation. We refer to these motivations as needs. What motivates specific individuals can vary considerably. But psychologists have nevertheless attempted to classify people's needs as a way of understanding human behavior. They show us that not only do persons have multiple needs, but that these needs fall into categories depending on their importance. Thus, we speak of basic needs such as "food" and "shelter." We also have higher-level needs such as recognition by our peers and self-esteem.

The motivation of people in jobs has received a great deal of research attention because of its importance in enhancing employee productivity. Researchers have identified some motivations, specific to the work environment, called *work motivations*. Work motivations come from two sources, as shown in Table 2.18. They include such things as achievement, the use of one's abilities, and one's desire for status. Motivation by these needs relates directly to the idea of task orientation; the concept of task orientation means that the person operates out of his or her individual job initiative. People like to think of themselves as contributing, as important, as goal oriented. Some companies consider this motivation as a resource.

The writer of task-oriented software documentation thus is faced with the following question: what part does software use play in satisfying these work motivations? How can I design manuals and online help that tap into the user's motivational construct to channel job energies into the use of software?

Table 2.18

Sources of Work Motivation among High-Tech Workers[6]

Internal Motivations	Environmental Motivations
Achievement	Independence
Use of Abilities	Job Security
Autonomy	Physical Conditions
Responsibility	Compensation
Creativity	Variety
Status	Activity Level
Authority	Upper Management
Recognition	Technical Management
Advancement	Company Policies

What Internal Motivations Affect Software Users?

Internal motivation, as shown in Table 2.18, derives primarily from the individual's personality, personal background, and training. Ask yourself, what needs underlie the behavior of doctors? Do doctors commit themselves to serving humanity? To recognition by their peers? To status in their community? The keys to this motivation lie primarily in a person's background—religious training, family background, education, and so forth—but studies have shown that the members of some professions exhibit, in general, different internal motivations than others. What generally motivates auditors, for instance, may not motivate engineers. High-tech workers, persons who work with computers daily, when compared to non-high-tech workers, exhibit a greater need for *achievement* and *growth* and a high degree of need for *social interaction* in the workplace.

Knowing internal motivations can help you design for task-oriented use by allowing you to glimpse important needs in users—needs that you can channel into success with a piece of software. Consider the following example. A student once wrote a manual for a piece of instructional software that trained students to identify musical intervals (thirds, fifths, etc.). The writer, after studying the user's internal motivations, determined that motivations like using one's skills and abilities and creativity topped the list. Instead of simply outlining the uses of the program, the writer constructed a special section showing the user how to combine the exercises *creatively*. The result helped channel the user's needs for creativity into the use of the program and helped make the manual more successful.

What External Motivations Affect Software Users?

As the term implies, external motivation comes from the employee's environment. External motivations result from the kind of job situation in which a person works. Of course, the motivation to follow the dictates of upper management and supervisors seems obvious. Other motivations relate to how one sees the work environment. The activity level of an office, for example, can have subtle effects on a worker. The security of a job, especially in times of recession, can motivate a person to do well in order to keep the job. On the other hand, the physical surroundings—drab cubicles or spacious offices—can also affect a user. The documenter should study the user's work surroundings to see what elements can motivate efficient and effective software use. A manual can help a user operate in high-stress environments by making information easy to find and use, by helping ensure data security. Manuals can also help users succeed in environments where efficiency or technical accuracy take top priority. The more you know what environmental motivations affect your user, the more you can help by showing that user how the software fits in.

You may wonder how the writer connects user's motivations and the design problems inherent in manuals and online help. In fact, you can evoke motivations in the manual elements listed on the left-hand column of Table 2.19: the background information section, the examples throughout the book or help system, the demos, and so on. The list on the right gives an example of how you might write these elements when you know what motivations you want to focus on.

Range of Computer Experience: Novice, Experienced, Expert

Some users may bring a different level of computer expertise to each new program they learn. Some will learn the program faster than others because they have a broader range of computer experience. And because they have more experience, they will learn the program in different ways, using more guidance and support documentation, less tutorial. The range of computer experience they have, coupled with their strategic uses of the program, determines, in part, the level of task support they require.

The following discussion looks at a couple of important variables that distinguish users with a broad range of experience from those with a more limited range, though it is not meant to prescribe or stereotype these users. Also, the expert user might look and behave like a novice user in some instances. Imagine the UNIX guru struggling to use a

Table 2.19

Ways to Use Motivational Information in Manuals

Motivation	Manual Element
Achievement, efficiency	Online help, tips, layered page layout
Social needs	Examples involving realistic scenarios
Production	Tips for shortcuts
Creativity	Tips for customizing steps
Speed of use	Online help, quick-reference card

Mac in a documentation class, or Mac experts struggling to learn how to set command flags or find process IDs in UNIX shell accounts. Making distinctions about *experience* can get complicated.

Attitude Can Make a Difference

A number of researchers have studied how anxiety (feelings of stress, fear, apprehension about computers) affects users' performance. Honeyman and White, citing other sources, note that computer anxiety relates to the feeling that the computer controls the events, not the user.[7] Also, many persons may feel a general fear of technology, and this can frustrate them in learning a program. Bracey, in another study, confirms what many researchers have noticed, that the more experienced the user, the less likely the user will feel computer anxiety.[8] Honeyman and White support this observation, noting that exposure to a positive experience with a computer can reduce anxiety. Users who once feared the "intelligence" of the computer begin to see it as a tool to help them reach their professional goals.

The Ability to Transfer Learning Can Make a Difference

Experience with computers creates a pattern of knowledge, what psychologists call a cognitive schema, that helps users transfer their knowledge from past experiences to current experiences. The underlying differences between the novice computer user and the experienced one pervade the research about learning computer programs. As one researcher puts it, you can see "a world of difference between the person for whom use of a computer-based system is routine and the novice or occasional user."[9] The novice basically exhibits very different degrees of anxiety and receptivity to different interface and media types than does the experienced user. Users with very little computer experience tend to take more time to learn functions, so the pitch of their learning curve remains gradual when compared to that of users with a lot of computer experience. They can transfer less of their previous experience into the mastery of their new experience.

Let's look at a discussion of three common user types based on their range of expertise: the novice user, the experienced user, and the expert user.

Novice Computer User: Emmet

Emmet teaches courses in psychology at a university in Arkansas. He uses a word processor to write professional journal articles. He has a computer at home and one in his office. He also has access to a building-wide and campus-wide computer network, with email and online research services.

Emmet began using PC-Write about five years ago, and now has graduated to Microsoft Word for Windows. Beyond Word, Emmet has little computer experience. He uses few other programs, either on his computer at home or in his office. Emmet has little need for the technical elements of his computers and their programs. When he first tried to learn to send email messages, he became frustrated with the complexity of the system and had a hard time keeping the different programs and commands straight. Besides, in his work he saw little need at that time for these programs. Learning email took four or five sessions. He preferred to watch someone demonstrate the program to reading the manual. A friend changed a program for him once, trying to make the interface more usable. He tried out the change and asked me to "fix the program back the way it was before."

Emmet keeps up with technology and computers, and readily acknowledges the value of computerized work, but doesn't need more than two or three programs.

NUMBER OF PROGRAMS. What kinds of behaviors in this example characterize Emmet as a novice computer user? For one thing, novice users like Emmet have used few computer programs. Many novice computer users have *never* used a computer. Often they may know one program well, such as a word processor or a mail program, but in learning new programs they do not have the benefit of knowing a variety of interfaces or computer types. This lack of experience makes learning difficult. The same principle holds true for learning in other situations. Many cars have similar dashboards. Thus, a person who has operated one or two late-model cars has an easier time dealing with the dashboard of a rental car than a person who does not have this experience. Such an experienced person would know where to expect to find the light switch, horn, and so on.

DEGREE OF TECHNICAL KNOWLEDGE. Furthermore, novice users have little or no technical knowledge (beyond the identification of drives and displays, etc.) of the computers they use. In terms of cognitive schemas, you could say that they do not have elaborate, highly differentiated models of how computers work. Thus, their learning takes more time. Adding a command to their repertoire often means that they have to build the mental model, or adjust an existing one, to accommodate the new information. In a sense, they have to learn and assimilate information at the same time, instead of just learning it. Because they feel uncertain of their computer skills, novice users generally resist invitations to "explore" the software. They like you to tell them what keys to press, almost mechanically.

ATTITUDE. Novice users often do not see a clear relationship between the program and their work. For novice users, inability to see the benefits of a program impedes their willingness to spend time learning it. And because they don't see the value of using a program they often form negative attitude toward new software. Writer Donald Norman refers to one typical novice attitude called *false causality;* this occurs when the computer coincidentally does something immediately after a user action and the user thinks he or she caused the effect. "Many of the peculiar behaviors of people using computer systems or complex household appliances result from such false coincidences," asserts Norman.[10] When the result is *not* what the user expected, the effect on the user's attitude is negative. These negative attitudes get expressed in a variety of ways, as Table 2.20 shows.

LEARNING BEHAVIOR. Another characteristic we see in Emmet tells us something about difficulties novices have in learning new programs. Because Emmet had used few programs, he lacked the experience of learning programs. Learning programs requires understanding principles that may be very abstract, and often users have to chart a learning course that suits them. Some use tutorials. Some dive in and "follow the bouncing cursor." Some rely on friends. Whatever the pattern, novices users don't have one. They distrust manuals, feeling overwhelmed by their usually technical nature and arid prose.

Table 2.20

Beliefs and Attitudes of Novice Computer Users

Belief	Attitude	Reality
The computer is a magic black box.	Awe	The computer follows understandable logic.
The computer "thinks."	Fear	The computer makes rough predictions based on mathematical formulas.
The computer is a machine that does all a human's work.	Competition	Computers are tools that people use to do some work.
Learning computers requires learning programming and other technical things.	Defeatism	Computer interfaces allow for use without learning technical details.
I broke the computer.	Disappointment	The computer does something after an action, but the first action didn't really cause the second action.

Experienced Computer User: Smitty

Smitty works as an engineer at an Air Force base in Florida. He has a computer at home and at the office, and his wife uses computers in her teaching at a university. He communicates using a modem with the network at the base. He also has access to and uses the base mainframe computer.

Smitty uses the MS-DOS operating system, Windows, WordPerfect (for word processing) and Freelance (for graphics). He also uses WordPerfect on the mainframe computer. In college, Smitty learned to program in BASIC, FORTRAN, and Pascal, as well as learning to program engineering graphics. When a virus scare occurred, Smitty obtained and used some protection programs (with only online readme files as documentation) from a friend who managed the computer system for a local hospital. Smitty also used his computer for freelance work, writing software documentation for the county administrator's office.

NUMBER OF PROGRAMS. What characteristics of the experienced user does Smitty have? He uses many programs in his work. Additionally, he uses more open-ended programs (like computer languages) than does the novice. It takes an advanced degree of understanding of computer processing rules and methods to construct programs from computer languages. For Smitty, and for other experienced users, program use ranges beyond just knowing one program well: they use utility programs (like the virus protector), analysis programs, and drawing programs, among others. Computer programs, for the experienced user, work together as part of a system.

DEGREE OF TECHNICAL KNOWLEDGE. Smitty, like other experienced users, has some technical knowledge of computers. He knows how to install special components (such as phone modems and mouse boards) in his personal computer. This technical knowledge gives him a broader base of understanding of the computer—a more highly differentiated mental picture of how things work. Besides, he uses more than one computer. This understanding affects both attitude and learning behavior. Also, you can count on experienced users to have less trouble understanding installation procedures for software programs that require hardware installation, such as scanners, tape backup systems, and modems.

ATTITUDE. Perhaps the major difference between experienced users and novices lies in attitude and the way they relate programs to their work environment. Experienced users have moved beyond seeing the computer as an awesome thinking machine, to seeing it as a tool in their work. You can see evidence for this in the way Smitty integrates a number of programs to do a single task or perform a single job role. As an engineer, he uses word processing and draw programs together to create drawings. Experienced users see themselves as the most important element of the computer/job/person configuration. The computer serves the purposes they decide on, and if one program won't work, they try another. They exercise critical judgment over what software can do for them.

LEARNING BEHAVIOR. Experienced users, finally, have a more patterned learning behavior than novices while remaining open to learning in new ways. Because of their familiarity with programs, experienced users have begun to form definite likes and dislikes as to how they want to learn new skills and new programs, so we can see more of a pattern in their learning. On the other hand, they are less skeptical of manuals and documentation than novices, because they have begun to see the value of manuals and help in opening up programs for them. They accept online help systems more readily.

Expert User: Sharon

Sharon studies computer science at the university, and also writes computer programs for Market Master Data and Design, a spin-off company of a large agricultural radio marketing service. Her work gained her such respect from the parent company, the manager literally created the programming department around her expertise. She uses mostly IBM-type computers, and has a favorite keyboard or "deck" that she often carries back and forth between her apartment and work. She often spends late nights programming.

Sharon gets programs from many sources: from Internet FTP (file transfer protocol) sites, bulletin boards, commercial computer networks, and shareware distribution catalogs. Additionally, she orders software for the office from software catalogs. The small office where Sharon and the two ther programmers work literally overflows with programs. Manuals litter the floor, along with computer parts, disks, cables, disk drives, printers, modems, and various other hardware. The programmers use these programs to run the office and do other chores in the programming shop.

In the programming work, Sharon handles large databases of information from the farm census, the USDA, and other research organizations. She creates programs that translate this database information into forms usable by marketing executives and sales personnel. Her work involves file encryption and compression, which can get very technical. She also sets up the computer network for the entire, extended company office and maintains the electronic fax system and the secretaries' computer systems.

NUMBER OF PROGRAMS. What characteristics of the expert user does Sharon have? She not only works with many programs, she works with an extraordinarily rich selection of programs: word processors, language compilers, and programmer's utility programs she can find. Like other expert users, Sharon works in the computer industry. That industry encompasses the fields of programming, information science and systems, network services, and hardware maintenance. Professionals in the computer industry work with an extraordinary large number of programs and systems. In fact, most of these could be called open-ended programs, having a broad applicability. In contrast to *experienced* users, the *expert* user's familiarity with programs spans different operating systems and computer types.

DEGREE OF TECHNICAL KNOWLEDGE. Sharon's knowledge spans technologies, from communication to CD-ROM to network systems. Her expertise allows her to dismantle computers with confidence, and trouble-shoot highly complex hardware configuration problems. She uses this knowledge to set up systems and create software and hardware products. This technical knowledge creates a willingness and ability to learn technical details, and a well defined background in programming languages and circuit board design.

ATTITUDE. Unlike the novice and the experienced users, the expert user like Sharon sees software for itself. While she uses many programs as tools—programming languages, for example—she goes a step beyond that level and sees them as ends in themselves. She cares about how a program works, how it's assembled, and what kind of interface it has. She knows the limitations of much of the software she uses, and from that awareness derives principles to apply to her own programs.

LEARNING BEHAVIOR. Usually computer professionals like Sharon learn programs very easily. She will quickly get the general idea of how a program works, apply the program to her specific use, and go on to another program. This stands to reason because of her work as a software designer. She knows how many programs work, and she uses this knowledge to operate them and create new ones. Like other professionals, Sharon uses manuals occasionally and online help a lot, because she likes screen accessibility. She likes online help because it doesn't take her away from the computer screen and it's sometimes easier to get to than a manual. In many ways, the expert's learning patterns have become very differentiated because they get repeated so often.

How to Design Documentation for Specific User Types

Researchers have found that learners have different methods of learning or recalling information. In particular, Barfield and others studied expert and novice users with an eye to their methods of solving problems. They found that the problem-solving characteristics of experts and nonexperts differed greatly. Expert users tend to recognize commands more easily and also to string them together more easily than nonexpert users. In fact, one may argue that rather than the degree of information, the arrangement of information in the user's mind distinguishes the expert from the novice.[11] Research by Marchionini seems to corroborate this observation. He notes that novices make few plans when they learn a computer program, instead reacting to program responses one at a time.[12]

In structured reference entries, command summaries, and keyboard shortcuts, you are writing for expert users. You will find these observations about the way expert users learn and apply software valuable when you're designing reference documentation for expert users (Chapter 14, "Writing to Support").

Table 2.21 summarizes the descriptions of the three types of software users. It also includes some generalizations about the kinds of documentation each prefers. Use the table carefully to remind you of the differences among users, remembering that user types represent generalizations rather than fact, and that documentation preferences will, of course, depend on your user's individual characteristics and needs.

Extent of Knowledge of Subject Matter of the Program

How much users know about the subject matter of a program can determine their ability to see the relationship between the program and the work they do. A high degree of subject matter knowledge can affect the amount of background knowledge you need to supply in your program. Take, for example, the lesson the producers of desktop publishing software learned about the amount of background subject matter to supply with their software. When the new software became popular, many computer users discovered a tool to re-do their newsletters, brochures and other documents, using powerful page layout, type fonts, and graphic placement features. These users generally had little knowledge of page layout; the result was newsletters with a jumble of fonts and pages cluttered with unneeded clip art. Subsequently, some desktop publishing software producers published a separate booklet

Table 2.21

Characteristics of User Types

Characteristic	Novice	Experienced	Expert
Number of Programs Used	Few	Low	Many kinds
Degree of Technical Knowledge	Low	Some	High
Attitude	Vague, illogical, negative	Computer as tool; open	Programs as programs, not tools; for their own sake
Learning Behavior	Undifferentiated, resistant	Patterned, open, flexible	Highly differentiated
Documentation Preferences	Tutorials, index and table of contents, visuals, guided tours	User guide, job aids, online help, "Getting Started"	Command and task reference; online help; user guide

with their program that covered the basics of page layout vocabulary, how to design a page, and many examples of layouts and their uses.

In a similar way, if you write a manual that automates accounting procedures and your user lacks a background in accounting—does not know the function of a general ledger or the meaning of terms like *accounts receivable* and *accounts payable*—then you can expect a more limited learning and use of the program. Table 2.22 shows some of the various kinds of subject matter knowledge needed for software use. You can find a number of ways to support subject matter knowledge in your manual. Depending on your design, you can use subject matter knowledge in introductions, examples, background sections, and elsewhere. Figure 2.4 shows how you can support subject matter knowledge in a glossary.

The Workplace Environment: User Communities

In an article entitled "Usage Pattern and Sources of Assistance for Personal Computer Users," Denis Lee asserts that, overall, users expressed dissatisfaction with the written information that accompanied their software, including manuals and documents. As the best source of information, Lee discovered that users relied on their own colleagues and their organization's information systems staff.[13] This testifies to the importance of these sources of information in encouraging efficient and effective software use. The documenter does well to leverage these sources in the use of a specific software product.

User Communities Provide Software Support

Like it or not, most computer programs require a person to work individually with a terminal and a keyboard. But as many researchers have shown, not all users enjoy feeling

Table 2.22

Kinds of Subject-Matter Knowledge Needed for Software

Program Example	Kind Of Subject-Matter Knowledge Needed
Microsoft Paint	Composition, color mixing, art terminology (e.g., *brush, feather, polygon*)
DAK Accounting	Bookkeeping, accounting
Microsoft Word	Writing techniques, formatting techniques, use of fonts
AutoCad	Engineering design, terminology (e.g., *layers, ikk lines, projection*)
HomeInventory	Financial planning, investment strategies
Probe (electronic circuit analysis)	Electronic circuit design, circuit terminology (e.g., *capacitors, inductors, diodes*)
Excel (spreadsheet)	Statistical functions, mathematics

APPENDIX E: NETWORK TERMINOLOGY

NOTE: Not all of these terms were used in the text of this guide; however, you may find them helpful as you get started on the Internet.

archie	a system for locating files that are stored on FTP servers
ASCII	(American Standard Code for Information Interchange) default file transfer mode
asynchronous	transmission by individual bytes, not related to specific timing on the transmitting end
backbone	high-speed connection within a network which connects shorter (usually slower) branch circuits
bandwidth	the difference, in Hertz (Hz), between the highest and lowest frequencies of a transmission channel; the greater the bandwidth the "faster" the line
baud	unit of measure of data transmission speed; usually bits/second; may differ from the number of data bits transmitted per second by the use of techniques that encode two or more bits on a single cycle (i.e., 1200bps and 2400bps modems actually transmit at 600 baud)
binary	refers to a condition that has two possible different values; a number system having a base of two (0 and 1)
bps	(bits per second) measure of the rate at which data is transmitted
bridge	a device that acts as a connector between similar local area networks
broadcast	a packet delivery system that delivers a copy of a given packet to all hosts attached to it
client	the user of a network service
coaxial	cable comprised of a central wire surrounded by dielectric insulator, all encased in a protective sheathing

Figure 2.4

A Glossary Supports the User's Need for Subject-Matter Knowledge

Glossaries like this one from the Texas Tech University's *Network and E-Mail Reference Guide* support the user's subject matter knowledge and can help the user see the relevance to workplace tasks.

chained to the keyboard. They like the social contact with other users and the support they get from them. Documentation can help mitigate the isolation that often comes with computer-mediated work by encouraging users to make contact with other users of the same or related programs in their organization (Figure 2.5).

You can easily imagine the difference that belonging to a user community can make. If you have ever started using a new program, you know how you need to rely on other users of that program. Until you gain experience with it, you need someone to call on for help. VAX users support other VAX users; the same is true for UNIX users and DOS users. Users provide an informal level of support that manuals are hard-pressed to match. Before a user opens your user guide, he or she may very likely have tried consulting a fellow user.

Apple user groups

No matter what your level of computer experience, you can get lots of support by joining an Apple user group. Apple user groups are composed of people who work with Apple computers and who enjoy sharing what they know with others. Activities may include new product demonstrations, informal question-and-answer sessions, and regular classes on using popular software applications or learning to write your own programs. Many user groups have special beginners' nights.

Ask your authorized Apple dealer for the name of the Macintosh user group nearest you, or call (800) 538-9696. For information about starting your own user group, contact one of the following.

- The Boston Computer Society
  One Center Plaza
  Boston, MA 02108
  USA
  (617) 367-8080

- Berkeley Macintosh User's Group
  1442-A Walnut Street #62
  Berkeley, CA 94709
  USA
  (415) 549-BMUG (415-549-2684)

Figure 2.5

A Manual That Suggests Help from User Groups

Research into user groups, as illustrated by these references to user groups (the first of which is now defunct), can help you plan extra help for users. This example comes from the Macintosh IIci *Owner's Guide*.

Ways to Find User Groups

Persons in organizations often form communities of users who each use the same program. When you can identify a group of people who use a certain program, you have identified a *user group*. One way to identify user groups parallels the office organization. For instance, consider a communications company dealing in long distance service. The accounting system the employees use has many menus, but the system only lets them see the menus relevant to their jobs. The front office has its set of menus, the sales office has its set of menus, technical support has its set, and so on. Each of these groups is a user community because each one uses the program differently. Managers in the front office need functions to help them track performance; technical support people need functions to diagnose system performance.

You can also find user groups by identifying those who use the same programs. For instance, one group will favor WordPerfect; others will favor Microsoft Word. These people make up user communities based on their use of the different programs, even though they may all work on the same network and thus share logon procedures, disk storage requirements, and data sharing methods. This difference among otherwise similar computing circumstances shows that user groups don't always flow along easily recognizable corporate lines such as departmental reporting structures.

Some software companies sponsor user groups among their customers to support their products. In one example, ProfitKey, Inc. sponsored user groups throughout the country for its productivity software. According to Richard Lilly, president, members of the user groups gave presentations on what they did uniquely with the software.[14] This format allowed members to see each others' effective use. In some cases, organizations will establish meetings of these users for the expressed purpose of sharing technical and other use information.

User groups can also help your user in more subtle ways than telling what keys to press: They can provide encouragement and motivation. Some users in the group will provide examples of how to apply the program, and encourage the effective use of a program. This kind of sharing of efficiency can really help new users of programs. And it makes up one of the most important elements of your manual.

Tip Your User to Help from Others

You should try to learn what user groups your user belongs to. If you're writing about a large program with established user groups, then you should pass along information about the group to your users. Often these groups have meetings and produce newsletters. If your software has other user categories, consider encouraging your users to consult them: Student users can consult with teacher users, data entry clerks can consult with analysis types. Suggest that these users ask others and, in your explanations and elaborations of procedures (Chapter 13, "Writing to Guide" can show you how to do this), acknowledge that the user doesn't work in a vacuum—that other persons use the program for related tasks.

How Do the User's Organizational Structures Support Software Use?

Most large and medium-sized companies have divisions, departments, areas, or other organizational units. *Organizational structure* refers to how these units relate to one another.

Organizational structure also relates to how individuals relate to one another. Some units have managers or supervisors, and workers. Others have work teams or development groups. Increasingly, employees find themselves working in development groups or teams. Such units, on the group or individual level, help companies arrange and control patterns of authority. Some companies delegate authority to individuals (managers and supervisors); others delegate authority to groups.

The structures—patterns of authority—in a company can express that company's commitment to computer use. For example, one researcher who studied the attitudes and behaviors of computer users found that of all the variables that affect successful computer use, three stand out: job involvement, current usage, and *organizational commitment*.[15] Job involvement—a person's overall interest in and motivation in their job—encourages efficient computer use because the person sees how to apply the program to the job. Current usage—how much a person currently uses computers—also contributes, because the higher the current usage, the more likely the person will be to use subsequent new programs effectively. Organizational commitment—the company's promotion (through training and support) of computer use—also helps an employee use computers effectively, because the employee can see how using the computer can foster organizational goals.

How does this relate to the work of software documenters? For one thing, these findings suggest that we can encourage employees to accept new software if their organization (company, institution, facility) actively promotes the goal of computerization.[16] Documenters should know what attitude a company takes toward the computerization of its operations. If the company takes an active role in supporting computers (in ways we will examine below), then the documentation should acknowledge this fact and use it to help motivate the user.

You may find that many organizations do not actively promote computer use, or they take a neutral stance. Some smaller companies, for example, may lack the resources of larger ones for training and support. Let's examine an example of the difficulties involved in organizational structures and their support for computer use. This example comes from research done on the use—or lack of it—of computer-assisted design software in an engineering firm.[17]

Example: Computer Use Follows Lines of Authority

In many engineering firms, design of products falls to more than one team. One team will design the product, another team will test it, and a third will produce it. In such an environment, each team should work from the same drawings so they can minimize overlapping (or conflicting) efforts. The traditional method for communicating design information consisted of passing hand-drafted drawings from one group to another. With new computer-assisted design (CAD) programs came the opportunity to communicate information electronically from department to department. This meant that the design team, by preparing drawings on a computer with CAD software, could communicate those drawings electronically to the testing team, and so on to the manufacturing or production team. A study by Liqueur and others tried to determine whether companies actually took advantage of these cost efficiencies. They asked the following question: Did the companies studied reap the benefits of this enhanced, faster, and almost fool-proof method of design communication?

The researchers found that, in fact, design information did not get communicated in this efficient manner. The problem, it turned out, lay in the organizational structure of the engineering firm. Engineering firms often have a hierarchical structure: one that delegates authority in a top-down manner through systems of supervisors and managers. This kind of structure—followed by many companies today—encourages individualistic attitudes toward work groups and teams. This discourages information sharing among design, testing, and production groups. According to the structure of the company, individual groups worked alone, had an individualistic idea. In this situation, the company's structure could not take advantage of the integration of design ideas that the computerized methods made possible.

This example shows an organizational structure that would not support effective and efficient software use. Because individual groups did not share design information, employees had to needlessly copy designs back into the computer and drafters had to re-do work. The features of the software (menu items) that supported an integrated design—communication of data, tracking of production statistics, shared storing of designs—got little attention from users. When companies show their support for integrating these functions, employees will learn and use these functions more readily. If you know what kinds of organizational support exists, you may find ways to channel that support (through manuals and help) into effective software use. Chapter 8, "Designing for Task Orientation," and Chapter 9, "Laying Out Pages and Screens," contain suggestions for how to do this.

Ways Organizations Can Support Software Use

The preceding discussion of information resources that are available to your users should suggest some ways you can tap into these learning resources in your documentation. Not surprisingly, it sometimes takes a lot of research to uncover such information, and the amount of information grows steadily with increased access of users to Internet sources. So, in examining organizational structures to leverage in your manuals and help, look for the following kinds of opportunities.

- **Allowance for input in hardware and software decisions.** Some companies allow end users to have a say in the kinds of computer systems they employ. They find that by allowing for user input they can save money and increase acceptance of new technologies. You might point out uses that might require the user obtaining other, related software.

- **Integrated computers through networks.** Networks (members of different groups to share information), especially Intranets (local networks within a company that allow users to use Internet software like browsers to do company business), encourage use of shared help by including support addresses in manuals and help.

- **Organizational support for training, help, user groups.** Many organizations find that they can make software use more efficient by well-planned training sessions, employing help and other support persons, and by encouraging users of similar programs to share their information. If you are designing online documentation, if the company has an *intranet* (a distributed computer network within a company) you might include a link to their home page in your help file.

- **Decentralized computing systems.** Many companies find that their organizational units (departments, divisions, etc.) work more efficiently if they have their own computing resources instead of having all the computing resources located in one building or location. Standalone or networked personal computers—rather than larger, centralized mainframe computers—represent this kind of decentralized or *distributed computing*. How much autonomy does this give your user in configuring and applying software?

- **Information systems.** Many companies employ information systems professionals who help supply employees with the right equipment and training to get the kinds of hardware and software they need. Such professionals represent the documenter's silent partners, because they share the goal of efficient computer and software use. Can you include their phone numbers and email addresses in your manual or help?

The example in Figure 2.6, from the pages of an inhouse online document, demonstrates a way to incorporate information about organizational support into a newsletter.

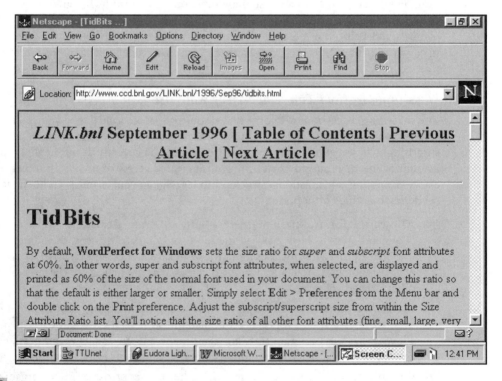

Figure 2.6

A Document Emphasizing Organizational Support

This online newsletter, *LINK.bnl,* published on the World Wide Web by Brookhaven National Laboratory, is an example of organizational support for software use.

Users' Learning Preferences

You may find that the organizational influences on the user also pattern another important element of user characteristics: the user's learning preferences. People who did not grow up with computers bear the imprint of their earliest successful learning, and they continue to want to learn in that way.

Learning preferences means the way your user likes to accumulate expertise in working with software. As many researchers have shown, no single method of training or presenting information for users works for all levels of expertise or job roles. Fortunately, researchers have extensively examined learning preferences among software users over the past twenty years and we documenters can benefit from their discoveries. Knowing about the kinds of learning preferences users have and how to identify them can take you a long way toward designing useful print and online documentation for them. In particular, if you find the need to teach your user a subset of the overall tasks of a program—as discussed in Chapter 12, "Writing to Teach"—then what you learn in this phase of your user analysis will contribute greatly to the success of your information product. Software learning falls roughly into three categories: learning with an instructor, learning with a manual, and learning through a computer.[18]

Learning from an Instructor

Learning from an instructor means you have a person who teaches users how to execute the features of the software and how to use them a workplace.

SETTING. Often, instructor-based learning can occur in a classroom or training room or on the user's job site. Even if it occurs on the job site, more than one person can learn at a time.

SOURCE. Usually, organizations will sponsor instructor-based training, either by hiring consultants trained by a software company to come in and do classes, or using inhouse training experts. The advantage of the inhouse training expert lies in the fact that, in knowing a user's specific job demands and responsibilities, the instructor can tailor the instruction to very specific user.

VARIATIONS. You will find that your users will report many variations of instructor-based training. Users may report having the attention of a single professional teacher, or having learned from a friend who knew the program. Some organizations even promote an "each one teach one" plan to encourage the spread of software learning. Other companies use the technique of putting a computer-automated employee in an adjacent cubicle to a non-computer automated employee and letting a natural sharing of expertise take place. Users like this method because of the immediacy of the learning. Their instructors can tailor their message to workplace goals.

MEDIA. Instructor-based training can occur in two forms: video or multimedia, and live. Video taped instruction—or better, multimedia instruction—can be produced by inhouse sources or by documentation specialists. Multimedia instruction has the advantage of using sight, sound, motion, and other effects to involve the user. The more common form of video learning is the tape, often supplied by the software company, showing an instructor and screens. Often, users will watch while sitting at workstations (in their offices or in a training room), pausing the tape when they want. Live instruction, on the other hand, requires a set time, preparation by the instructor, and often overhead transparencies or workbooks. Usually, the instructor will demonstrate a procedure, then help the users perform the procedure on their workstations.

ADVANTAGES. The advantages of instructor-based learning include the ability to ask questions, and the close relationship of the instruction to one's workplace tasks. It also offers the security of having an expert at hand in case the learners get stuck or need extra help.

DISADVANTAGES. Instructor-based learning requires a degree of structure: someone has to set it up, plan it, and take time out of the usual workday to attend the classes. Often, too, users can feel intimidated by a class and an instructor, feeling that, as adults in a profession, they don't need an outsider to tell them how to do their job.

USER TYPES. Novices like instructor-led software learning because of the handholding it provides. Experienced users like this method for larger programs because it gets them started and they can take advantage of the instructor to help them realize workplace applications of a software program.

Learning with a Manual

Learning with a manual involves the user having some form of book, usually called a *tutorial,* containing lessons oriented toward learning and applying program features. The point with manual-based training is that the information on how to use and apply the program comes primarily through reading, not listening to an instructor.

SETTING. Manual or text-based learning often occurs on the job site, where the user has access to real-world tasks to perform. It requires some time taken away form the job. On the other hand, some companies have libraries of manuals and encourage users to check out manuals for new programs so they can study at home. Manual-based training can also occur in a training or class room, with or without an instructor or monitor present.

SOURCE. Manuals usually are produced inhouse by documentation departments, by the software companies themselves, as was the *Microsoft Windows User's Guide,* or by third-party commercial companies, such as Que books' *DOS for Dummies.* In some cases, manuals take the form of instructions written by a former employee about how to use a system.

VARIATIONS. Manual-based learning takes three basic forms: *tutorials* created to teach a specific set of lessons; *user's guides,* sets of procedures organized in various ways from alphabetical to task-sequenced; and *reference documentation,* lists and explanations of commands. The degree of structure and the degree of design with the clear intent to teach decreases from tutorials to reference documentation. Clearly, the greater the design to teach in these manuals, the better the chance that the user will have a successful learning experience.

MEDIA. The usual media for manuals is the book; however the booklet or quick overview can often do the job of teaching a specific task. Some manuals include workbooks for the users to calculate or record information.

ADVANTAGES. Many users like learning from manuals because they can do it alone, avoiding making any embarrassing errors in the presence of colleagues. Users also like the flexibility of the book: They can pace their own instruction and take the book to various settings, such as on a coffee break or overnight at home. Manuals also offer point-of-need support and teaching, which means that the user can consult the book when he or she has a problem. Too often, with more structured learning, such as in a classroom, the user will not think of a question until back at the desk confronted by workplace problems.

DISADVANTAGES. Often, manuals isolate the user from expert help; if a problem arises, the user can get stuck. Also, even though practically everyone has experience using books and print, some users may not have much experience learning highly abstract computer concepts using a manual. Studies have shown that manuals work best for users with a history of using them.

USER TYPES. Experienced and expert users like manuals because they have had enough experience to make it over hurdles by themselves and they like the independence manuals provide.

Learning with a Computer

Learning with a computer differs from the two previous learning methods in that the information comes to the user primarily through the computer. Usually, such training takes the form of a computer-based tutorial on a disk, or a multimedia training package.

SETTING. Computer-based learning can occur on the job site or in a classroom. Often, users will have an instructor or monitor present, but the computer acts as the primary teacher, pacing the delivery of instructional information.

SOURCE. Computer-based training software often is packaged with a program. Commercial companies that do specialized training also create computer-based training programs for clients.

VARIATIONS. Computer-based training appears in many variations, as indicated in the table below.

Variation Type	Description
Computer-Based Training Programs	Lessons followed through choices on a menu
Manuals with Online Components	Lessons that the user performs using the program on sample data
Online Help and Reference	Procedures and descriptions of commands
Guided Explorations	Hands-on exploration of the program while supporting recovery from errors
Trial and Error	Users make menu choices on their own and try to figure out the program, taking cues from dialog boxes and relying on their overall knowledge of software

MEDIA. The primary media used in computer-based training is the computer itself, although some computer-based methods contain text components.

ADVANTAGES. The main advantage of the computer-based tutorial, from the user's standpoint, lies in the hands-on experience the computer can give. Also, users enjoy the sense of accomplishment they get from using a computer to learn *about* computers.

DISADVANTAGES. Computer-based instruction assumes some sophistication of users before they can succeed with it. They have to at least get the computer and the program started. And if the computer messes up, crashes, or can't find a needed information file, then the user can't proceed.

USER TYPES. Most users like this form of training because of its reliance on the computer. Novices tend to learn less from it, according to Czaja.[19]

Users have definite choices among kinds of learning, and often they base their preferences on past experiences. If they had success learning with a manual, then they will gravitate toward that method again, and so on. Often they will combine methods. As part of your user analysis, you should find out what experiences they have had with learning software and use it as a guide to design.

Usage Patterns: Regular, Casual, Intermittent

The term *usage pattern* refers to the interaction of users with programs over time. Users don't learn and use all the features of a program the first time they use it. Instead, they learn a few, then more, and so on, accumulating those features that apply. We call this their usage pattern. You can easily conceive of a usage pattern by viewing it as a learning curve, which measures the number of features a user learns or uses regularly on the x axis and the time span of their use on the y axis. In Figure 2.7, use of a word processing program grows from

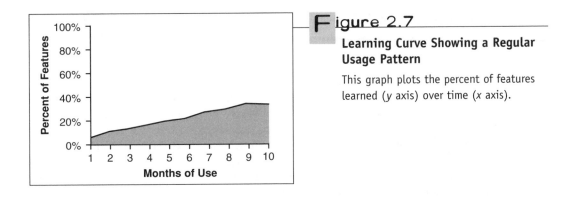

Figure 2.7

Learning Curve Showing a Regular Usage Pattern

This graph plots the percent of features learned (*y* axis) over time (*x* axis).

the user knowing 5 percent of the features in month 1 to the user knowing 30 percent of the features after 10 months. (Actually, use would level off at about 10 percent—the estimated number of program functions that about 90 percent of the users employ.)

No ideal usage pattern exists, because of the uniqueness of each user's experience with a program. The learning curve provides us with a way to track how learning may or may not progress with a program. After users have been using a program for a while, their learning slows down because they tend to use only a subset of all the functions. They add to this store of knowledge less frequently than they did when they started.

Use the Task List to Measure Learning Curves

You can measure learning curves by presenting users with a task list (Chapter 3, "Constructing a Task List") and asking them to identify the tasks they perform more frequently than others. Done over time, this simple inquiry will tell you how their learning changes, or how they vary the number and kinds of tasks they perform.

What Causes Usage Patterns to Vary?

Usage patterns vary for a number of reasons. Users' motivation to learn new functions changes over time because the initial excitement and anticipation naturally decrease with familiarity. Also, users ordinarily undergo some sort of initial training that instills in them a basic competency. Without further training, their learning of new skills naturally levels off. But perhaps the main reason for variations in usage patterns lies in the nature of the features. Programs have subsets of basic and advanced features, resulting in users learning and using some on a more regular basis than others. A user's learning curve rises over time because some features get learned later. Researcher Michael Cooper, for example, found that the mail task of "review in-basket," which entails checking to see what electronic mail a user has, was used in 93 percent of cases within the first 6 to 12 months of use. However, the task "manage personal directory," which entails deleting and rearranging files in an electronic mail system, was only used in 45 percent of cases during the same time period.[20] Clearly some features are used more than others and at different times.

Your user analysis should include some investigation of the usage pattern you expect with your software. In general, you can expect three main types of usage patterns: regular usage, intermittent usage, and casual usage. The following paragraphs describe these kinds of usage.

Regular Usage

Regular usage refers to the pattern a user would follow in using the program daily. Regular usage happens with people who use one or two programs all day as an integral part of their work. You find regular usage among secretaries and design engineers who use word processing and computer-assisted design software every day as the main way they do their jobs. Regular users become experts with one or two specific programs. Regular usage does not require frequent reference to manuals or help systems, and regular users do not make frequent errors. They become experts in the use of one program.

This pattern assumes **incremental learning,** meaning that a user learns some features before others, and that the learning of advanced features assumes knowledge of the basics. It refers to the pattern that a user would follow to get started. The most usual pattern goes something like the one illustrated in Table 2.23.

Knowing the usage pattern can help you design better manuals and help. Often, documents express the usual pattern in the *About This Manual* section in the front. The *About This Manual* section in Figure 2.8 shows you how to build information gathered about usage patterns into the documentation set, and how usage patterns can help you model the user's behavior. Clearly, the more accurate the model of the user's behavior, the more readily the user can identify with the usage pattern presented.

Intermittent Usage

Intermittent usage refers to usage by persons who know the software well enough to perform basic tasks but do not use the program as the primary software in their work. They use the software frequently and voluntarily, but at irregular intervals. Because of their in-

Table 2.23

The Pattern of Regular Usage

Number of Features Learned	Activity	Documentation Needed
One or two	Taking a tour	*Guided Tour/Getting Started*
Several to many	Learning the basic functions	*Tutorial*
Some to few	Learning some advanced functions	*User's Guide* or *Online Help*
Few	Looking up advanced information/commands	*Online* or *Printed Reference*

About This Manual

3

The explanations, examples, and illustrations in this manual will help you take full advantage of Microsoft Word's many features. This manual is divided into three parts, "Learning Word," "Using Word," and "Word Reference."

Learning Word will teach yhou how to create, edit, format and print a short document. When you're finished, you'll understand how to use Word and you can build more complex documents to fit your needs.

Using Word is a guide to word processing with Microsoft Word. This part is organized into five general categories: Editing with Word, Formatting Your Work, Working with Complex Documents, Printing Documents, and Handling Documents. The hold heads in the margin show you where to find the step by step instructions for each task. "Using Word" also describes how you can use document windows to simplify complicated editing tasks, such as moving text between documents and how you can use the glossary window for inserting frequently using text into documents automatically.

Word Reference contains a directory of Word commands, a list of terms used in this manual and appendices that cover key sequences, preset page options, disk and memory management, the use of other Macintosh applications with Word, and daisywheel printers.

Figure 2.8

An *About This Manual* Section

This section from a Microsoft Word *User's Guide* incorporates information about the regular usage pattern into the design of a document, providing a role for the user.

termittent pattern of usage, they make more mistakes than regular users. Making mistakes leads to frequent consultation of user's guides and online help systems. Intermittent usage occurs where software provides an important tool in a person's work, but their work does not require them to use the program all the time. Thus, their learning curve tends to plateau (indicating that they have learned a set of basic skills) at around 10 or 15 percent of the total functions of a program. In fact, where you find intermittent usage you will often find that users have learned and forgotten program features. For more information on how to design documents for intermittent usage, see Chapter 13, "Writing to Guide," Procedures section.

INTERMITTENT USAGE REQUIRES ONLINE HELP. According to researchers Santhanam and Weidenbeck, the irregular behavior and frequent use of support documentation by intermittent users makes the intermittent usage pattern perhaps the most frequently encountered usage pattern among computer users, and the most likely pattern of usage to need support by online systems. Online help systems are particularly useful when you have an intermittent usage pattern. When users have forgotten a command, they can consult a help system to find answers (steps or explanations of functions) easily and quickly. Online systems work well where you find intermittent usage because the pattern reflects the behavior of experts as well as novices. Like that of expert usage, the intermittent usage pattern assumes a basic knowledge of the software and the online system so users posses the skills needed to use the online help effectively. However, like that for novice usage, the pattern assumes that users will progress more slowly, make more errors, and require support.[21]

HOW TO DESIGN DOCUMENTATION FOR INTERMITTENT USAGE. Despite the number of errors intermittent users make, their behavior has received wide attention among researchers because of its prevalence. Intermittent users display two main kinds of behaviors that affect the design of support for them: a *production bias* and the *suboptimal usage.*

The production bias means, according to Santhanam and Weidenbeck, that intermittent users do not feel a need to learn a new command as long as they can get their normal work done without too much difficulty. Thus, they consult online help and manuals but don't really learn from them. They use them as guidance to overcome a problem in their work, but don't retain the information as learners would. Intermittent usage also reflects suboptimal usage: using more steps to perform a task when a more powerful command would do the task in fewer. For example, a user might change the configuration of a program by exiting the program and editing the initialization file rather than using the easier method of selecting the "Preferences . . ." command from a menu. Users may do this because they are more familiar with the time-consuming method or because they feel more secure about the results; as long as the suboptimal method works, they will willingly put out the extra effort rather than learn a new function.

The existence of a production bias and of suboptimal usage among intermittent users affects our view of users guides, indicating a main purpose of guidance documentation (Chapter 13, "Writing to Guide"): to lead to a solution to a problem rather than teach skills. In fact, researchers have noted goal orientation and problem solving behavior as characteristic of users of procedural documentation. They have also mentioned that online systems should follow an organization around command types and user actions.[22] To find out more about intermittent usage and the kinds of tasks (e.g. configuration tasks) that these users perform, see Chapter 3, "Constructing a Task List," Guideline 2: Categorize the Program Tasks.

Casual Usage

Casual usage refers to usage by persons with little or no formal training with the software system who need to use it immediately. In effect, they have no learning curve, because they never "learn" the system. They need to use it on the spot. Examples of this kind of usage occurs in library searches, searches for information in encyclopedias, electronic bulletin boards, and any variety of information systems. This kind of usage presents a problem to documenters because casual users rarely make use of *any* online documentation or hard copy, but prefer to peck at the keyboard or click with the mouse until the system coughs up what they need.

Casual users make up a distinct group of users among other users of software. You may have regular users who undergo training or use manuals, for whom you provide the usual kinds of support, patterned on incremental learning. But you may also need to provide some support for users who lack any prior familiarity with the system. Take a college library's catalog system, for example. The manuals for the librarian staff contain explanations of tasks; librarians can refer to these for details. But most students step up to the terminal and need to use it to find titles with no training at all. If your system has a group of users like this, you should carefully identify them and try to get a feel for the difficulties they will face.

According to Marchionini, casual users face the difficulty of not having an adequate *mental model* of the system they face.[23] A mental model refers to the users' prior understanding of the problems they need to solve and their understanding of the mechanism that the software provides for meeting these problems. Using the library example, casual users of such a system would probably have the hard-copy version of a card catalog (with drawers arranged according to author, subject, and title) as their mental model. Support for the casual user of the library system might require that you provide some link for the user showing how the menu system allows for searches by subject, title, and author, much like the traditional divisions of the hard-copy card catalog.

Searchers of an encyclopedia would probably conceive of their problem as needing to locate a subject term; they would perform their search based on the alphabet. For these users, you need to point out not only that searches can use alphabetical sequences much like a printed encyclopedia, but that searches can also follow hypertext links. In the case of hypertext links, your task as documenter becomes more complicated because you have to create the mental model for the casual user and present it in terms that can he or she can grasp immediately.

Glossary

cognitive schema: the "mental" pattern or structure of ideas or objects that a person uses to interpret future experience, such as the experience of using a program or reading a manual. Knowing that users interpret computer events using these thought patterns can help documenters design better manuals and online help.

command syntax: in software, the order of elements in a command that the user types to make the computer perform a certain function. Often the reference manual for a program has to describe how to enter these commands.

configuration: the task or tasks of customizing a software program to fit a user's needs. Often users do this by setting "Preferences" or "Options." Some programs keep the user's configuration details in a separate file called an initialization file.

cuing: the technique of setting off in a manual or help system certain elements of a program interface with special text styles, such as bold or italics.

distributed computing: a system or network of computing within an organization where the processing capabilities reside at the terminal or individual workstation. The opposite of distributed computing, *centralized* computing, concentrates the computing power in a main computer, and uses terminals that only allow you to communicate with the main computer. Distributed computing usually involves a network of personal computers. To the user, distributed computing means that she or he must organize a hard drive, install programs (often), and perform other software maintenance skills.

documentation plan: a document that lays out for the members of the documentation team the goals and plans for the documentation set. It consists of a summary of the user analysis, outlines of documents, and schedules for writing, testing, and editing.

false causality: the belief that an action causes a result (as when a key is pressed and a computer error occurs), when actually the result occurs only as a coincidence. False causality is common with poorly designed computer interfaces. Novices are most susceptible.

hypertext links: electronic connections between topics in an online help system. Sometimes called *hot buttons,* these links allow users to move from one topic to another by clicking with a mouse.

incremental learning: a kind of learning where you build one lesson on another, and you cannot perform advanced skills until you have mastered the basics.

intranet: a network of computers, limited to a specific company and run by that company, that allows users to employ their Internet software (e.g., browsers like Netscape Navigator) to conduct company business and share information. Usually, Intranet users have access to the Internet as well.

layering: the technique of putting two levels of information (by using separate columns) on the same page to accommodate different users.

mental model: the idea that a user has of a problem or software program before he or she actually uses it.

navigational device: a technique used in a manual or help system that indicates where users should go for certain kinds of information pertaining to their needs. Sometimes you do this with a "How to Use This Manual" section.

open-ended questionnaires: questionnaires that don't give multiple choices to questions, but instead ask a user to write thoughts in a space provided. These work best because they don't prescribe a reaction for the user, but instead gather the user's actual thoughts.

procedures manual: usually entitled User's Guide, this is a manual containing step-by-step tasks for using a software program.

product insert questionnaires: short questionnaires packaged with the software program that ask questions of the user. They help you analyze the user's needs and probable uses for the document.

research: background investigation into the user of the program. It can also refer to interviews with subject matter experts and programmers who created the program or worked on its development.

strategic use: the use of software to share, communicate, or store information. Strategic use differs from operational use; strategic use refers to work with the information the program creates, rather than the actual creation of the information. In business, strategic tasks often embody an individual's coordination of work with other employees or the expression of organizational goals. Task-oriented software documentation makes an attempt to support strategic use.

user scenario: a formal description of a model user, someone you can envision using the software. While not the *only* user, the user described in the user scenario embodies many of the qualities of the most *general* user so you can use it as a planning tool and in the documentation as a model of your typical user.

work motivations: a group of psychological characteristics of people in their jobs. Work motivations meet needs that are internal (imposed by personality) and external (imposed by the job). Effective software and documentation taps into these needs, so showing the user how to integrate software into his or her work can be a way to encourage software and manual use.

Checklist ✔

After identifying your users, you should conduct research in the form of interviews, observations, and surveys to collect information usable in determining the documentation needed for your project. Use the following checklist as a way to remind yourself of the important elements.

User Analysis Checklist

Possible Users of the Program

☐ What recognizable groups (teacher/student, system administrator/end user) will your users comprise? Describe each group briefly.

☐ Provide a brief scenario of use by representative professions to provide a role model of how the program will serve different professional user groups.

Primary Issues Raised by the Program

☐ What learning difficulties, motivational problems, and technical difficulties will your users face?

The User's Tasks

☐ What workplace jobs will the user do with the program?

☐ What important sequences will the user follow that can help you organize your program tasks?

☐ What tasks can you use as examples in your manuals and online help?

The User's Informational Needs

☐   What important kinds and forms of information does the user need in order to put the program to work?

☐   With whom does the user communicate, and in what forms and media?

The User's Work Motivation

☐   What internal and external motivations affect the user?

The User's Range of Computer Experience

☐   Describe the kinds of novice, experienced, and expert behavior exhibited by the user. Pay attention to the numbers and kinds of programs, degree of technical knowledge, user attitudes toward computing, and the user's learning behavior.

The User's Knowledge of the Subject Matter of the Program

☐   What kinds of vocabulary reinforcement and subject/matter background will the documentation have to provide?

The User's Workplace

☐   What other computer programs are found at the user's job site?

☐   What user groups does the user belong to or have available?

☐   Describe the degree of organizational support for computers and software in your user's organization.

The User's Learning Preferences

☐   Describe the user's preferences for instructor, manual, or computer-based learning.

Usage Pattern

☐   Describe the patterns users will exhibit in terms of regular, intermittent, and casual usage.

Document Goals

☐   What goals in the area of meeting user needs do you envision for the documentation set you plan to write for the users you have described above?

Suggested Documentation Features

☐   Describe the documentation features that your user analysis suggests. Pay particular attention to areas of organization, emphases for motivation, separate sections, or other elements you want to provide to meet special needs and characteristics you discovered.

Practice/Problem Solving

1. ## Use the checklist to analyze professionals for their computer usage.

   Francis works as a graphic artist for a publishing and printing firm. She gets designs from clients, or comes up with her own, for book covers, spot art, technical art, drawings, photographs, and other visual elements of books, pamphlets, and posters.

   Ray does reception, clerking, and other office work in a multiple-practice doctor's office. He welcomes patients, checks their appointments, and prints a daily routing sheet for each one. He sets up new appointments and processes checks and other payments.

   Use the user analysis checklist to analyze the two professionals described in the scenarios above. Describe ways in which you think software could address their task needs. If you know what software programs they use, you might want to address some of the informational deficiencies of the documentation they use—where they may wish a manual would help them, but does not.

2. ## Practice writing about professional roles you know little about.

   Pick an "obscure" professional role from the following list (or find an equally arcane profession on your own).

   - Hazardous waste/nuclear waste management-environmental compliance specialist
   - Business process reengineering, project management
   - Research scientist (at a nationally sponsored R & D lab)
   - Quality-Assurance Specialist (hybrid microcircuit manufacturing)
   - Retail Farm Radio Marketing Account Executive.

   Find resources about this profession in your local job placement service, by contacting or visiting the company (calling the personnel director), or from a private or public employment agency. After studying the materials you find, answer the questions on the user analysis checklist about a person working in this profession. You may have to use your common sense to fill in any information gaps.

3. ## Plan an interview.

   Select a program you know fairly well, such as a popular word processor or an Internet browser, and construct a plan for interviewing a user of a new version of that program. Follow the guidelines earlier in the chapter for identifying issues, questions, and methods of gathering information from the user. Write the questions and set up a schedule for the interview and a follow-up interview for that particular program.

   Write a memo to the publications manager suggesting procedures for interview planning for your department. Assume that your memo will inform the department's style and procedures guide.

4. Do a survey of software learning preferences.

Identify a group of users to which you have access: office workers, service representatives, students. Survey them for the kinds of learning preferences outlined briefly in Chapter 2. In particular, focus on learning from an instructor, with a manual, or with a computer. Which method does this group employ primarily? Do they use a combination? How will knowing about their learning patterns help improve your documentation products?

3

Constructing a Task List

This chapter is about software programs and how to look at them from the user's point of view. It will help you analyze the tasks the program can perform and put those tasks in the form of an outline of the program called a *task list*. When you create a task list, you create a descriptive model of the program features. Depending on your specific project, you should create the list so that another writer can rely on it. Task lists may contain bare bones information—just the task names—or contain rich detail—who performs the task, starting and goal states, steps, options, and screens. You know you have completed the task list when you have recorded and tested all the features of the program in a way that indicates their usefulness to a user.

How to Read This Chapter

- If you've never written a task list before and you're planning a project, read the Examples section, then read the Discussion section, followed by the Guidelines. The Discussion section tells you how to use the task list as a development tool, not as a document template.

- If you need tips on how to refine a task list or how to test a task list, look for the information you need in the Guidelines section—but read the Examples section first.

Examples

Something to remember about task lists: The individual tasks look like procedures. In fact, they record procedures, but they do so as an outline of tasks rather than something users could follow. The real audience for the task list is you and the members of your writing team. Keep this in mind when preparing the list: It's a planning tool.

Another point about task lists: Manuals include more than tasks. Examine an example of a manual or help system and you will find task names (look under "procedure information" in a help system) and steps; you will also find introductory information, *interface descriptions, command summaries,* user scenarios and any number of other im-

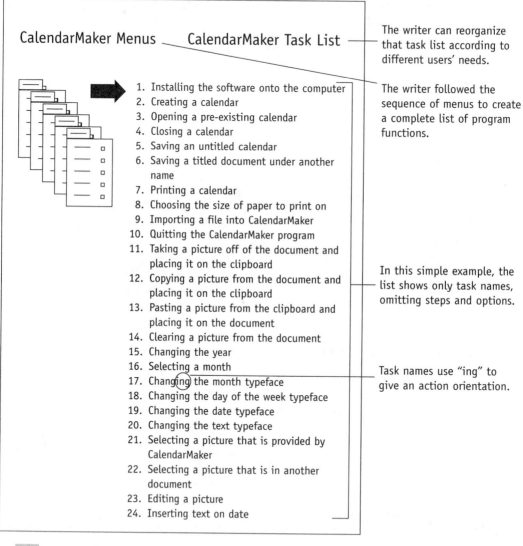

CalendarMaker Menus ___ **CalendarMaker Task List** ___

The writer can reorganize that task list according to different users' needs.

1. Installing the software onto the computer
2. Creating a calendar
3. Opening a pre-existing calendar
4. Closing a calendar
5. Saving an untitled calendar
6. Saving a titled document under another name
7. Printing a calendar
8. Choosing the size of paper to print on
9. Importing a file into CalendarMaker
10. Quitting the CalendarMaker program
11. Taking a picture off of the document and placing it on the clipboard
12. Copying a picture from the document and placing it on the clipboard
13. Pasting a picture from the clipboard and placing it on the document
14. Clearing a picture from the document
15. Changing the year
16. Selecting a month
17. Changing the month typeface
18. Changing the day of the week typeface
19. Changing the date typeface
20. Changing the text typeface
21. Selecting a picture that is provided by CalendarMaker
22. Selecting a picture that is in another document
23. Editing a picture
24. Inserting text on date

The writer followed the sequence of menus to create a complete list of program functions.

In this simple example, the list shows only task names, omitting steps and options.

Task names use "ing" to give an action orientation.

Figure 3.1

CalendarMaker Task List

The task list for the program CalendarMaker follows the menu closely, translating the program features into workplace tasks.

portant elements. But the key to the program lies in its features: what it can do. We focus on the task list because it embodies those features. It records, analyzes, groups, and otherwise allows us to begin to adapt the program to the user and the user's job. This chapter has two example task lists—the first one fairly simple, and the second more elaborate.

CalendarMaker Task List

CalendarMaker does what the program says: it lets you construct custom calendars with icons and memos for daily activities. A small program, it has gained wide acceptance among Macintosh users. Students constructed the task list of the program shown in Figure 3.1.

"Save" Command Task

The example in Figure 3.2 shows only one task, but a very elaborate one. This task describes the Save function in Microsoft Word for the Macintosh. It covers the steps from selecting the function on the file menu, through naming the file, choosing its format, and finally saving it. You will notice that the steps represent a path that covers *the most likely things a user would do* when performing this task. As such, it represents a version of the logical and typical use of the feature.

While it takes time to write, an elaborate task description of each task you will document can unify your project and keep it on track. This one represents an elaborate version so you can see the various parts it could contain. Table 3.1 describes the elements of a task, indicating their usefulness to the writer and project planner.

Table 3.1

Elements of a Task Description

Element	What it Does
Task Name	Describes the feature in performance-oriented language.
Starting and Goal State	These elements of the task description help identify the state of the program before and after the user performs the task. Example: users have to have a network account before they can perform the task "Setting a new password." Task names help you identify the boundaries of a task.
Options	Options record settings and other choices the user makes during task performance. Recording them in the task description helps you design tables in your documentation. Options include keyboard shortcuts, file types, *processing parameters,* format choices, and **output devices.**
Screens	Screens (electronically captured menus and dialog boxes) help orient the writer to the program interface during composition. Screen types include menus, *dialog boxes,* buttons, fields, and help screens.

Task Name: Saving an untitled document

User: *end-user*
Starting state: *Untitled (or new) document has been opened*
Goal state: *Untitled document has been titled and saved in the user specified folder*

Steps:

1. Choose Save... from the File menu (⌘ **S** or 🖫)
2. Type in name of file in "Save Current Document as:" field
3. Select drive and folder for saving
        Options:
        Drive bar: selects drive or path
        Double click on folder: opens selected folder
        Horizontal scroll bar: scrolls through folders in selected drive
        Double click on drv. icon: displays desktop in selection box
        Open button: opens selected folder or drive
        Desktop botton: displays desktop in selection box
        Cancel button: cancels save and returns to editing display
        New folder button: creates new folder
        Eject button: ejects selected disk
4. Set backup and save methods
        Options:
        Make backup switch: creates "Backup of [document name]"
        Fast Save switch: saves document faster but uses more disk space
5. Select file type in "Save File as Type" field
        Options:

Normal	MacWrite II 1.x
Text only	Word for MS Dos
Text only with line breaks	Word for Windows 1
Microsoft Mac Word 3.x	Word Perfect 5.0
Interchange format (RTF)	Word for Windows 2.0
Stationery	Word Perfect 5.1
MacWrite	

        Default for File switch: sets selected format as default for that file
6. Click on Save button
7. Type in summary info
        Options:
        Title:
        Subject:
        Author:
        Version:
        Keywords:
8. Click on OK button
        Option:
        Cancel button: returns to editing display without saving

Task name: describes the feature in performance-oriented language.

Starting State and Goal: sets boundaries for the task and helps identify it as independent and modular.

Steps: tells the sequence of actions needed to perform the task. Steps form the basis of tutorial and procedural documentation.

Options: identify interface elements available but not used in the task. Often these get covered in tables as part of procedures and reference.

Screen: serves as reference point when writing the manual or help module.

Figure 3.2

Task Name: Saving an Untitled Document

This example shows an elaborate version of an individual task description.

1   DETERMINE THE RIGHT LEVEL OF DETAIL

The issue of level of detail in your task analysis arises when you consider that all planning tools require some judgment on your part. Too much or too little planning can cost you time and wasted effort later. What exactly, then, do we mean by level of detail in a task analysis? Notice the differences in Table 3.2 between the four levels of detail in the task list. Clearly, each level examines the same task, but each contains different kinds and

Table 3.2

Four Levels of Detail in a Task List

Level	Description and Use
1. Task Names (Basic for all projects)	List only for organizing the project, categorizing tasks, assigning tasks, assessing new release documentation, contents for help systems
2. Steps (Basic for most projects)	Routine procedures, larger programs, revisions of documentation
3. Options	Smaller programs, complex interfaces, parallel input methods (keyboard *and* mouse)
4. Screens	Smaller programs, first-release manuals, complex interfaces

Example

Task: Transferring a File

Steps
{
1 Select Transfer from the File menu
2 Select the desired file
3 Click the Transfer button
}

Options
{
Options:
Eject: ejects the selected disk
Drive: switches to another drive
Cancel: cancels the transfer operation
Filebox: shows path to the selected file
Scroll bar: scross through the file list
}

Screen
{
TRANSFER
}

1. Determine the right level of detail.

2. Categorize the program tasks.

3. Link the tasks with menu features.

4. Write steps as actions.

5. Break up long tasks into subtasks.

6. Don't list options as steps.

7. Test your task list.

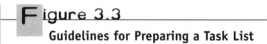

Figure 3.3

Guidelines for Preparing a Task List

different amounts of information. Each level requires more effort in preparation and has different functions in the planning process. You decide for yourself what level fits best. Until you have accumulated experience in documentation planning, you may find the following discussion of levels of detail useful.

Who Will Write the Documents?

If you plan to write the entire documentation set for your program, then you might get away with a level 1 or level 2 task list. Why so? As the solitary writer, you can go back to the program during the writing of the documents and check the steps, examine the screens, try out the options, and so forth. So why bother recording them here? One reason to record them is that a simple list of task names will get you started on your project. During the writing you can tick them off after you complete each one.

On the other hand, if you share writing responsibilities with a team, a supervisor, or programmers, you may want to go into greater detail, so that all the members of the writing/editing/revising team read from the same task list. This helps you ensure consistency in your final documents. Often, the publications manager distributes the task list in segments to the writers and keeps a complete copy. In this case, more detail pays off in greater consistency.

How Much Experience Do the Writers Have?

Clearly no two documentation projects will require the same degree of planning on your part. Consider these examples:

> **Less detail needed:** Laura has documented four previous releases of an operating system program, and, on the 5.0 release, plans just to update new functions. Laura would probably not require great detail in her task list, because she knows the system and she can rely on task lists done in the past. She also knows that her company has set standards as to what level of detail task lists need.

> **More detail needed:** Rex just joined a writing team and must face a few weeks of planning and writing the first-release manual for a financial market analysis program for the insurance company where he works. Rex would need greater detail in his task plan, to make accurate and consistent first-time plans. Also, since Rex's company has not developed computer programs before, they are likely to want greater detail in

order to make policy decisions about future projects. Because Rex has to justify his budget, a longer, more detailed task list will help strengthen his requests for time and resources.

In each situation writers face different deadlines, use different production tools, have different amounts of experience, must use documentation resources differently, and are constrained by different company policies.

What Kind of Interface Do You Have?

Accuracy and consistency result from greater detail in a task list when the writing is shared by various authors. But regardless of who you write with on your project, the project's size, or its complexity, the subject software itself may dictate how much detail you need in the task list. For example, imagine you need to document a graphics generation program that plots mathematical formulas in complex, 3-D grids. When your user has created a grid (a plot of a formula), he or she can expand or generally reshape the grid by pointing and clicking on the corners of the grid display. Each corner behaves differently depending on which view mode the user has selected. Retracing different views requires use of the function keys.

In this hypothetical example, you can see that the interface gets complex. The user needs extra support for the tasks of shrinking an image and turning an image, using keystrokes and mouse clicks unique to a particular system. This interface is not very *intuitive*; there's a low probability that the user will figure it out by trial and error. As an analyst, you fail if you do not record each option carefully and know exactly what each option does to the screen. Your task list needs greater detail in this case, where you have a system-unique, hard-to-use interface.

Also, different tasks of the program might require more detail than others. For example, your installation might require advance planning and a complicated installation interface. In this case, you might decide to make that part of the task list more detailed, anticipating that you will eventually need to pass these details on to your users. Look over your program and see where the application of functions in the workplace looks like it would provide specific problems, and then consider carefully whether you should include special options in the task list—options you will want to document in greater detail later.

What's the Stress Level of Your Project?

Different documentation projects impose different constraints on the documentation designer. Do you plan to test your documentation extensively or will you just spot check it? Testing and reviewing your work later may produce better results if you base them on an extensive task list. Do you need to produce the documentation set quickly? You may only have time to perform a level 1 list, for the sake of planning, and then fill in the steps later. Has a team of engineers and writers already described the functions of your program in *program specifications*? Acquire a copy of the "specs" document and follow its conventions; you may need to adjust its level of detail only slightly, although it's more likely the program has diverged significantly from the specifications written months before.

As you may see from the examples, adding more information to the task list gives it more detail. Table 3.3 can give you some guidance in choosing levels of detail for your list.

Table 3.3

Choosing Levels of Detail for the Task List

Level of Detail	Suggestions for When to Use It
Less detail: task list only	Larger programs (over 100 functions)
	Single writer
	Used as planning tool only
	General-purpose programs
Moderate detail: task list and steps	More than one project at a time
	Writing team
Exhaustive detail	Small, specialized program
	Individualistic interface
	Special, difficult interface items
	Large writing team: product family

2   CATEGORIZE THE PROGRAM TASKS

Not all program tasks fall into the same category. Most of them have to do with using the software but some have to do with installing and setting it up. Information developers at IBM Corporation pioneered the idea of identifying the program tasks and have compiled an extensive description of task categories and information about tasks in *Information Development Guideline: Task-Oriented Information.*[1] They describe a number of task categories that have to do with systems documentation, which has an audience of programmers, administrators, software developers, terminal operators, and end users. The information in this guideline is based partly on the task descriptions used at IBM, with particular attention to the task categories that apply to end users.

As you familiarize yourself with your documentation project and the software, identify tasks that fall into specialized categories and separate them from the typical use tasks. As a rule you will document them in separate sections of the document. Mirroring this separation in your task list will help you plan your documents.

End Use: Tasks That Put the Software to Work

Most of the tasks of a program fall under the category of use: starting the program, retrieving data, processing, storing data, communicating, calculating, quitting. The person who performs these tasks is the user or *end-user,* someone who applies the program to a work situation. Most users today fall into this category. Task orientation works best for this user, who needs to apply the program to solutions in the workplace. Identifying and naming use tasks may be your most important job next to analyzing the user, and for this

Table 3.4

Kinds of Program Tasks

Task Type	Description
Use tasks	*Use* means operating the features of the program and applying it to work situations. Most tasks are use tasks and most of them follow the menu or interface structure of a program. Examples: "Open a file" (word processing software), "Search for a record" (database software), "Use the pencil tool" (drawing software).
Installation tasks	*Installing* means copying or transferring the program from the disks to the user's computer. Installing can require a few simple steps or running a separate program. Examples: "Copying the [program x] files onto your Hard Disk," "Running the [program x] installation program."
Configuration tasks	*Configuring* means setting up the program to run once it has been installed. Some programs combine installing and configuring, but with most larger systems they occur separately. Once installed, a program may get reconfigured if the user adds new hardware or software.

reason you will find a separate discussion of use tasks under the guideline "Identify and Name the Program Tasks." This discussion focuses on installation and configuration tasks.

Installation: Tasks That Get the Software onto the User's System

Installation refers to the series of steps involved in transferring or copying the program from the ***distribution media*** to the user's hard drive. The distribution media simply means the media on which the software arrives for use. Some programs are distributed on 3.5-inch disks, others on CD Roms. Still other programs may arrive for use over transmission wires, as in shareware programs from networks and bulletin boards. Installing can merely require copying the programs onto the user's hard drive, or may require running installation programs. Some companies offer *compacted programs* that have been compressed to fit on disks. Installing these programs requires uncompacting them. Installing gets further complicated when the user works on a network, because, for most programs, installation on a network requires special installation procedures. With smaller programs, the user installs the program. With larger programs such as Novelle Netware, a system administrator or consultant might install the program. Figure 3.4 suggests the complexity.

Installation tasks almost always appear at the beginning of a manual or in a separate section or document (especially when the user must also install hardware such as circuit boards or drives). Furthermore, installation guides are almost always printed, even when the primary documentation consists of an online help system. The user needs hard-copy instructions for installing because, until the system gets installed and the user can get to the help system, there will be nothing to read.

Overview of the Contents

The following is a summary of this document's contents:

Chapter 1 — Installation Overview

Describes the prerequisites for installing VINES for HP-UX including serial numbers and activation keys, hardware requirements, sizes of the various filesets, the software, and the LAN drivers.

Chapter 2 — Installing VINES for HP-UX

Contains information for installing the base VINES product and VINES options, installing updates and patches, and removing VINES.

Chapter 3 — System Parameters

Describes some of the HP-UX system parameters that should be considered in the operation of a VINES for HP-UX network.

Chapter 4 — Initializing VINES for HP-UX

Contains information for initializing those VINES products requiring initialization. It discusses the procedure for initializing **vinesadmsh** and VINES, what initialization does, and items created by services initialization.

Chapter 5 — Installing VINES Patches

Explains how to install VINES for HP-UX patches on one or more servers, using the VINES Patch utility. This information is applicable to native VINES servers and to VINES for UNIX servers.

Figure 3.4

Example of a Page from an Installation Manual

This page gives an overview of the installation topics covered in the manual. It shows how complex installation can get with a large program.

Further Categorizing Installation Tasks

Table 3.5 explains the various kinds of tasks users may perform as part of installation. This table represents an overview of the potential tasks you may need to include in your task list. Some programs require more installation tasks than others; you should choose from this list for each individual project.

Configuration: Tasks that Get the Software Set Up Right

Once a program resides in the correct place on the user's hard drive, the user (or, again, a consultant or administrator) may need to configure it. *Configuration* refers to setting up

Table 3.5

Kinds of Installation Tasks

Task	Explanation
Running an installation program	Installation programs (sometimes called **batch programs**) handle the unpacking, copying, verifying, and other installation tasks for the user. In any case the user only has to give the command to run the program and then follow the instructions (supply the installation information) as prompted by the program.
Copying program files to the user's disk	Copying may require a number of steps whereby the user gives a command (e.g. "copy program.exe c:") or drags program folders to transfer a copy of the program off of the distribution disk.
Making backup copies	Often installation requires that the user make backup copies of the distribution disks and install from them instead of the originals. This process protects the originals.
Checking for disk space	You may have to instruct the user on how to check to see if the hard disk contains enough space (megabytes or Kbytes) for the installation. Users need to know what to do in case they need more space than they have available.
Checking for system compatibility	You may have to instruct the user on how to check to see if they have the right kinds of operating systems (e.g. the correct version numbers).
Completing registration cards	Installation provides a convenient time for users to complete their product registration cards, cards that, sent back to the software company, link the user's name and address with the specific serial number of the program (as well as providing useful purchase and use information).
Verifying the installation	Often you will want to provide information that can help the user tell whether the installation has succeeded. This may require procedures for examining directories.
Reviewing last minute "read me" information	Many programs have accompanying "read me" files containing last-minute information about installation, system compatibility, or file sizes. You may need to write procedures telling the user how and where to find these files.
Reviewing the license agreement	Installation often constitutes breaking the seals on the distribution copies of the program, which often commits the user to keeping the software. Installation tasks should inform the user of these commitments and remind the user of compliance with the agreement.
Network vs. hard disk installing	Installing on a different kind of system (network vs. hard disk) can require separate tasks. Additionally, you may have to remind the user of special copyright restrictions involved with network installation.
Hardware installing	Installing may require telling the system the kinds of printers, boards, or monitors. Some programs handle hardware as part of configuring (see Table 3.6).

the software so it will work in the user's hardware environment. For example, most PC programs today can operate on monochrome screens or on various kinds of color screens. To configure the program, the user must tell the program what kind of screen he or she uses before the program will work.

Configuration Plays an Important Role in Task Orientation

In terms of task orientation, configuring plays an important role. Configuring allows the user to record individual preferences about a program: where to store information, how an interface will look on a screen, what formats to use for reports and documents. Because of this, configuration tasks relate very closely to the user's ideas of information storage and communication with other persons in the workplace. For example, a user will more likely use a program if he or she can easily set the page format to match that of others working in the company or to match that of preferred reports. Doing so can give a user a sense of control over what a program does, and how the program will aid in performing workplace tasks. It can foster user control of the program (see Chapter 1) and help a user get a sense of the software program as a useful and beneficial tool.

Unfortunately, configuration elements of programs often do not get the kind of attention that they should in user documentation. This results from a number of causes: Configuration requires understanding the abstract elements of a program; configuration requires use of cumbersome utility programs (such as text editors to change set-up files); or configuration is poorly programmed and thus hard for the user (and documenter) to figure out, much less master. Thus, you face a challenge in making these features of the program accessible to the user.

In too many situations, writers of manuals and online help ignore or slight the topics of setting preferences and configuring the program or otherwise tailoring the program to the individual user. By relegating it to an appendix in the reference documentation or otherwise burying it, they give this message to the reader: "You have little control over this software." If you wish the user to fully integrate the program into the workplace, then the message should be: "You have control over how this software works, and here is how to exercise that control." Figure 3.5 shows an instance where such information was provided to users.

How Can You Identify Configuration Tasks?

You should study the ways that users can configure the software systems you document. Some names for configuration include *customizing, setting up, setting options,* or *setting preferences.* In some software programs, configuration or setup occurs during installation. The distinction between installation and configuration lies in the fact that installation only happens once, but configuration can occur often during the use of a program as the user changes hardware elements or decides to customize the program in different ways.

Configuration procedures involve telling the program what kind of video monitor, printer, and keyboard the user has. Configuration also refers to "tailorable" information—things like the company logo or name on the first screen, or the number of users and levels of security allowed. Often users store configuration information in setup files (special

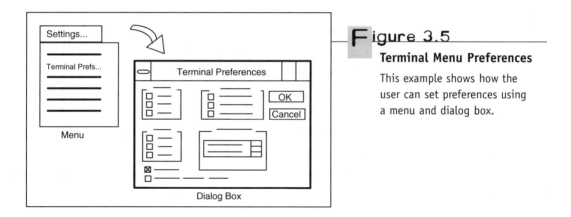

Figure 3.5

Terminal Menu Preferences

This example shows how the user can set preferences using a menu and dialog box.

files containing information specific to the way a user wants a program to operate). For example, communication programs often store *protocols* (information about the kinds of data sent over phone lines) in special setup files. Whenever the user calls up the program, the program uses the information in the setup files to run the way the user wants it to run.

Programs often come with default settings. Default settings consist of settings made at the factory or by the programmer that allow a program to run on first use. For example, the default settings for most people's video cassette recorder's clocks is 12:00 A.M. For another example, a word processor program might have one inch as the default top margin setting for pages. Users could change that to another setting if they wished. In doing so, they would be configuring the program.

Further Categorizing Configuration Tasks

In general, a program can contain configuration procedures in any or all of the categories shown in Table 3.6. Table 3.7 lists characteristics that help you identify tasks.

A user may configure his or her own program; however, in larger organizations these tasks may fall to consultants or computer professionals. Usually, procedures and tables of data are appropriate for these tasks, as opposed to tutorials intended to teach, because the user needs only to perform such operations once or intermittently and has no need to internalize or memorize them.

3   LINK THE TASKS WITH MENU FEATURES

As a way of understanding tasks, consider that *task* refers to a well-defined effort of short duration. Hanging a picture, starting the car, retrieving a record from a database—each represents a well-defined effort of short duration. Often a task has an objective, as in getting the picture on the wall, the motor running, or the record from the database and displayed on the computer screen. Because of their well-defined nature, tasks are *independent* of one another. They stand alone, have starting points and ending points. Because they occur in time, the intervals between these starting and ending points fall into steps.

Table 3.6

Kinds of Configuration Tasks

Task	Explanation
Personalizing	Configuring often requires that the user type in a personal name or a company name that appears on the first screen of a program. This can happen during installation, but can be changed later.
Screen Contents	Many programs allow users to configure the number of menus or other items that appear on screens of programs. Microsoft Excel, for example, allows users to customize the appearance of rulers, toolbars, ribbons and other elements using the "View" menu.
Security Restrictions	Large programs like Novelle Netware devote whole manuals to setting up security restrictions (who can gain access to what programs and directories) while smaller programs often have passwords for individual users.
Printers	You may have to instruct your user in how to set up printers for your system. Printers represent a key element in communicating for your users, so you should take special care in detailing these often complicated procedures.
Network Types	Programs that run on networks need to know the kind of network used, and many require special configuration in order for more than one user to access the program simultaneously.
Communication Protocols	*Communication protocols* refers to the format of data transmitted over modems and phone lines. You should take extra care in recording this important but complicated and often highly technical information.
Storage Addresses	Users need to record the locations of various files, utility programs, and other elements that programs use to run efficiently. For example, a word processor needs to know the storage address of the spell checker program. Configuration may involve recording where the user locates this program.
Special Commands and Macros	Special commands include keyboard shortcuts, customizable commands, and interface preferences (such as the mouse or the keyboard). Macros are strings of commands that users invent on their own. Configuration involves procedures for setting up these elements.

Seldom Rely on a Task List from the Project Manager's Desk

When you are working with other members of a software development team, program design documents (sometimes called *program specs*) contain lists of the program's functions. Should you have access to these documents (the project manager or program designer would have them) use them to help identify tasks but don't depend on them.

Table 3.7

Characteristics of a Task

- Independent of other tasks
- Short duration (usually under twelve steps)
- Goal-oriented
- Has starting and ending points
- Made up of steps
- Often relates to a menu function

Carefully double-check these documents against the actual program; often, in the programming, the functions (in both name and goal) may diverge from the definitions given them in the program design documents. This divergence, though natural, can really frustrate everybody on the project, and can lead to inaccuracy. This advice, of course, does not apply to you if you happen to *be* the project manager.

Identify All the Tasks That Your Program Can Perform

At the simplest level, try to describe the most obvious program functions using the most usual keys or mouse clicks for each task. You can check your tasks by seeing if they overlap, or seem to do the same things. Often you can begin to identify these tasks by looking at the menu structure. As Figure 3.6 shows, you should identify tasks according to *what the user would do with the program.*

Figure 3.6 illustrates how you can use the menu structure to derive task names. The program in this example tracks the user's progress in exercising. The intended users include exercisers, fitness counselors, and coaches. The *Main Menu* contains six choices, including Print Aerobic History. If you choose Print Aerobic History you get three choices on the Print Menu. The first choice on the Print Menu (printing detail/summary reports) results in two further options: printing detail reports (which show exercise information for a specific individual or day) and printing summary reports (which show exercise information for a group of individuals or days). You can also choose the second option under the Print Menu: president sports awards. In this case you can identify three printing tasks the user could perform, two based on the kinds of reports ("detail" or "summary"), and one based on "president sports awards". You would not make a task out of the third Print Menu option, Return to Main Menu, because it's not really a task but an option.

How Do You Name Tasks?

Observe certain conventions in naming tasks. You can always use the program-oriented naming convention, as in "The Sort Function" or "The Calendar Settings Dialog Box." This terminology may alienate the user because it expresses the task from the program's

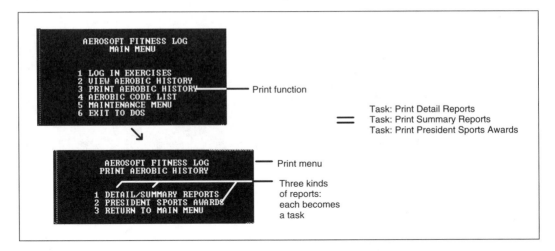

Figure 3.6

Deriving Tasks from the Menu Functions

The Print function on the Main Menu results in three tasks.

point of view instead of the user's. But you have options. As you can see in Figure 3.1 (page 88), tasks often use "ing" terms, as in "Sorting Your Data," or "Setting the Calendar." The advantage here lies in the performance orientation of the language: It suggests things *people* do in the workplace. Logically, users might understand this terminology more easily than the program-oriented convention.

On the other hand, you may also name tasks using "how to" terms as in "How to Sort Your Data," or "How to Set the Calendar." "How to" task names further strengthen performance orientation of the language. With some levels of task support, such as guidance, you will want to stress the actual "how to" nature of the task, especially if it contains important steps you don't want your user to miss. The sooner you can build this strong "how to" orientation into your procedures, the better. Table 3.8 indicates when you should use each of these naming conventions.

There are a number of ways to embellish your task list so it contains greater detail. As discussed above, you may want to include these details in your actual written list if you determine that the type of program, writing situation, or kind of interface requires it. The next guideline gives some examples of how to include greater detail in task lists.

4   WRITE STEPS AS ACTIONS

When you identify the steps in each task you break them down into discrete actions. Tasks break down into steps, each in chronological order, expressing the keystrokes and mouse clicks that the user has to make. The key to identifying steps lies in the words "break down." When you have broken the actions of a task down to their smallest *sensible* units, you have found the steps. However, as we shall see below, the process of identifying steps can get complex. You can always break steps down to smaller units. Consider the following example.

Too Much Detail	Appropriate Detail
1. Point the mouse to the **File** menu	1. Use the mouse to select **Open** from the **File** menu
2. Click and hold the mouse button to open the menu	
3. Move the mouse down to highlight the **Open** function	*or even more compact:*
4. Release the mouse button to select the open function	2. Select **Open** from the **File** menu

Can you see how the example of too much detail goes into too much depth and fails to identify the discrete action the user would take? Unless your purpose calls for explicit teaching of basic mouse handling techniques, use the level of detail suggested by the example of *appropriate* detail.

Follow these guidelines for numbering and wording steps:

■ Some tasks may only have one step, many have four or five, and a few have as many as twelve.

■ You can subdivide tasks with over twelve steps into groups of subtasks (see guideline 5 for a discussion of subtasks) but avoid the unnecessary complication of substeps.

■ If the task requires a tool (such as the keyboard, mouse, light pen, digitizer pen) indicate it, as in "Use the light pen to . . . ".

■ Use numbers, or have a good reason to deviate (later, while writing, you can use bullets, finger counters, or other step identifiers).

■ Use the command form of the verb for steps. Examples: "Click . . . ," "Press . . . ," "Choose . . . ," "Type . . . ".

Table 3.8

Naming Conventions for Tasks

Convention	Use	Example	Evaluation
Program-Oriented	Very seldom: only in reference material, lists of program functions	"Using the Open Function" "Using the Calendar Setting Function"	Weak: emphasis on program features
Performance-Oriented	User guides, tutorials	"Opening a File" "Setting the Calendar"	Strong: suggests action
How-To	Tutorials	"How to Open a File" "How to Set the Calendar"	Strong: suggests action

Remember that most of your users will look for tasks and numbered steps in procedures you put in manuals and online help. If you deviate from this pattern you risk thwarting their expectation and frustrating them.

5   BREAK LONG TASKS INTO SUBTASKS

Subtasks represent groups of steps within a larger task. You should use them when you have long tasks (over twelve steps, usually.) They help you plan because they add to the logical structure. For example, consider the list of steps in Table 3.9 for stitching two images scanned by a hand scanner. This example comes from a manual for a program called Picture Publisher. (Don't worry if you don't understand the specific steps in this example; focus on the idea of the structure of the task instead.) In this example the task would still work without the subtasks. The task records the steps just as accurately without them. However, the long list of steps on the left doesn't represent a user orientation, because the user could easily get bogged down in following nineteen steps. To overcome this difficulty, record the task as a series of stages toward completion, and give each stage a performance-oriented name. The subtasks add a level of hierarchy to the task that makes it easier to follow. To maintain the integrity of the task, keep the same numbering (from 1 to 19), rather than starting the numbering again with each subtask.

6   DON'T LIST OPTIONS AS STEPS

In your task list, as in the documentation you will write based on it, you want the focus to fall on the steps needed to perform tasks. This doesn't happen if you include two sets of steps both using command verbs in the task. For this reason, list options in terms of the *interface object* used to activate the the option. Interface objects include things like check boxes and buttons. Consider the example in Table 3.10 for how to word options in a task list.

Why Include Options in Task Descriptions?

In special cases, such as when a program has a complicated interface, you will want to include interface options along the way. What constitutes a complicated interface? Well, parallel interfaces make a good example. Many of today's personal computer programs operate using command keys on the keyboard but also allow for mouse clicks on pulldown menus. The user has two ways of doing everything; in the final manual or online help system you need to make sure that those ways get stated clearly and accurately. What better time to record those parallel interfaces than in your task list?

Generally speaking, options fall into the following three categories.

■ **Keyboard options.** Keystrokes or keystroke combinations that could change the state of the program but do not appear on the screen. Special hot keys, macro key combinations, special help keys, and the like make up this kind of option. Example: in a list of addresses the user may use the Page Up and Page Down keys, but the program does not list these keys in a menu.

Table 3.9

Use Subtask Categories to Break Up Tasks with Twelve or More Steps

Long Task without Subtasks (Weak)	Long Task with Subtasks (Better)
TASK NAME: STITCHING SCANNED IMAGES	*TASK NAME: STITCHING SCANNED IMAGES*
Starting state: user has scanned 2 images and saved them in a file. Goal state: 2 scanned images are stitched	Starting state: user has scanned 2 images and saved them in a file. Goal state: 2 scanned images are stitched

1. Open the File menu and choose the Open command. 2. Locate the first file in the dialog box and double-click the filename. 3. Open the File menu and choose the Open command. 4. Locate the second file in the dialog box and double-click the filename. 5. Click the Filter tool in the toolbox. 6. Click the Stitch tool. 7. Click the title bar of the first image to make it the active image, if necessary. 8. Move the cursor to an overlapping point located in the upper part of the image. 9. Click Button 1. 10. Move the cursor to an overlapping point that is located in the lower part of the image. 11. Click Button 2. 12. Click the title bar of the second image to make it the active image. 13. Move the cursor to the point that corresponds to the circular marker in the first image. 14. Click Button 1. 15. Move the cursor to the point that corresponds to the square marker in the first image. 16. Click Button 2. 17. Click Stitch. 18. Select the options in the dialog box. 19. Click Stitch.	**Open the files to stitch.** 1. Open the File menu and choose the Open command. 2. Locate the first file in the dialog box and double-click the filename. 3. Open the File menu and choose the Open command. 4. Locate the second file in the dialog box and double-click the filename. **Select the Stitch tool.** 5. Click the Filter tool in the toolbox. 6. Click the Stitch tool. **Prepare the first image.** 7. Click the title bar of the first image to make it the active image, if necessary. 8. Move the cursor to an overlapping point located in the upper part of the image. 9. Click Button 1. 10. Move the cursor to an overlapping point that is located in the lower part of the image. 11. Click Button 2. **Prepare the second image.** 12. Click the title bar of the second image to make it the active image. 13. Move the cursor to the point that corresponds to the circular marker in the first image. 14. Click Button 1. 15. Move the cursor to the point that corresponds to the square marker in the first image. 16. Click Button 2. **Complete the stitching operation.** 17. Click Stitch. 18. Select the options in the dialog box. 19. Click Stitch.

Table 3.10

How to Word Options in Task Descriptions—Weak and Strong Versions

Worded As an Action (Weaker)	Worded As an Interface Object (Stronger)
Task Name: Opening Ear Trainer	*Task Name: Opening Ear Trainer*
1. Double-click the Ear Trainer application icon.	1. Double-click the Ear Trainer application icon.
2. Click the OK button.	2. Click the OK button.
Option:	Option:
Click the Help button.	Help button: Starts the on-line manual.

- **Menu options.** Alternatives present as menu items, often at the bottom of the screen or in a dialog box. As you study programs you will see that these kinds of menu options change from one part of a program to another, depending on what navigational tools the program presents at one time or another. In this class we also find button alternatives: those present in dialog boxes that offer actions the user could take at any given time. Examples: "Cancel," "Return to the Main Menu."
- **Mouse options**. Alternatives that the user can perform using a mouse (or sometimes a light pen, a finger on the screen, a roller ball, or a joy stick). Mouse options often parallel keyboard options. When you write your task list, you should experiment with the mouse options (or other hardware alternatives) to see what they can do. In your documentation you will have to describe how they work.

A warning about options: you can easily go overboard in specifying interface options in a task list. This can bog down your efforts at clarity. Use discretion; indicate only those alternatives that you think should get recorded—that you think the user would need.

7   TEST YOUR TASK LIST

The goals of a task list include accuracy, comprehensiveness, and having the appropriate level of detail. Often you will find testing for these goals referred to as *validation,* or the testing of each task against the software. Before you can rely on your task list as a useful tool for further development of your manuals and help systems, you should put the list through a series of tests and reviews to make sure it meets these goals.

A Major Issue: Is the Program Finished?

Software documenters face a perennial problem of having to work with unfinished software. You have a choice of seeing this either as a blessing or a curse. Count yourself blessed if you find yourself writing manuals for a finished program. This happens when you have a software product that developers want to package for a wider audience, or when a developer has finished a program thinking it didn't need documentation, but realizes the marketing value of a manual after the fact. You can rely on your task list in this case, because the program won't change or will change very little. On the other hand, count yourself cursed because you have no say in the interface. You cannot make suggestions to the programmer about better ways to restructure the menus or make other interface improvements that make your job and the user's job easier.

More likely than not, you will write for an unfinished product, in which case you will have the chance to suggest improvements and find program bugs but you will also face the fact that your task list becomes less reliable as features get added and removed from the program and the menus grow and shrink. Developers have been known to find a task list so inspiring that they directed the programmers to add one or two tasks they hadn't thought of before.

In the case of a changing, evolving product, use the task list as a form of communication with the other members of the development team. Show programmers what their features look like when described in detail. But remember to get them to sign off on the tasks before you actually transform them into user's guides, help modules, and reference volumes. Also, remember that new features may appear on the menus of the program during the writing of the manuals; schedule the time to write up task descriptions for these tasks and add them to the formal task list.

Task Lists Are for Writers, Not for Users

You may want to show your task list to your users, but remember that users can give you only limited information about the task list. If you don't inform them of the specific goals of the task list—to record accurately in user-oriented phrasing the features of the program—they may recoil at the accumulation of detail and the non-user-friendly format. However, users can give you insight into useful groupings of tasks—by degrees of difficulty, job-related topics, or assignment of tasks to different user groups—so you may want to get their review.

Your most productive testing of the task list, however, will involve sitting down with another writer or member of the development team and checking the list for accuracy against the actual program. Ask the following kinds of questions:

- Does the task list cover all the tasks?
- Do all the tasks contain the right steps in the correct order?
- If the description contains options, are they all present and recorded accurately?
- Do the steps, as recorded, get the user from the starting state to the goal state?

If you have the time you should double-check each task; if not, you should spot-check, especially those tasks that involve complex procedures.

The development of any set of manuals and online help should involve the whole team. The task list gives you the opportunity to do this. Send copies to the programmers, developers, clients, sponsors, testing experts, and managers. The task list, as a tool of the software documenter, allows you to assert your presence on the development team as a person who uses professional tools to further the aims of the whole team. It can help you make a very good impression on others. Your review should ask for their sign-off on the list as an accurate and valid representation of the program you will document.

iscussion

This section of the chapter explores how the task list relates to planning the final document set. A later chapter on user analysis explores the *user tasks* and methods for studying the kinds of work users do. Together these two analyses form the basis for a thorough, useful task-oriented design. Table 3.11 lists phases in the manual production process.

The Task List As Part of the Overall Process

The task list forms part of the process of developing a manual or help system. The process followed in this book goes like this: First, compile a task list to list the features of the program and create a conceptual model for use in planning. Work on the task list simultaneously with your interviews and other research activities with the software users. Be-

Table 3.11

Phases in the Manual Production Process

Production Phase	What Happens
1. Perform the User Analysis	Analyze the user's application of the program in a work or performance environment, specifying the user's experience level and support needs. Pay particular attention to information transfer and communication.
2. Create the Task List	Prepare a task list, identifying and classifying all the functions the program can perform and converting them into task descriptions in user-oriented language.
3. Design the Documents	Determine the levels of support (tutorial, guidance, reference) and the specific form and media of the documentation (hard-copy, online, training, etc.).
4. Write the Project Plan	Write a description and outline of the documentation.
5. Write the Alpha Draft	Write the manuals and help modules.
6. Conduct Reviews and Tests	Submit the documents to development team members and users for rigorous examination for accuracy and format.
7. Revise and Edit	Incorporate the feedback gained during the review and testing phase. Edit for consistency of language and format.
8. Write a Final Draft	Prepare the final, camera-ready or disk-ready version of the documents.
9. Conduct a Field Evaluation	Survey the users to determine the usability and ease of use of the documentation and plan for maintaining the documents.

sides forming part of the overall manual production process, a task list gets you involved with the program and how it works. You can use it as an analytical tool to help organize your overall project; you will also refer to it while writing many forms of documentation.

You Become the Expert

For the documenter, specifying tasks constitutes the first step in producing task-oriented documentation products for a software system. The task list process also helps to familiarize you with the program. You use it to explore the program, get to know what it can do, how it is designed, what keys it uses, and what shortcuts it offers. During the writing of the task list, you learn what data goes into the program and what reports or other products the program can produce. When you have completed the task list, at least in a draft version, you should have become something of an expert in the use of the program and will have a record of your learning (often by trial and error) that can help as a resource document in the preparation of the manuals.

As stated above, the task list concentrates on the general uses of the program. The task list contains all the functions of the program, every little thing it can do, down to the smallest keystroke. Back during the program's design phase, the programmers or sponsors of the program decided what they wanted it to do. These are the *features* or *functions* of the program: we call them tasks, and need to pass them along to the users. The very concept of task orientation involves making these functions (tasks) available to the user in specific work environments in ways the user can identify with and put to productive use.

Why Do You Need a Task List?

All programs do things, and users need to know what they do. If, for example, pressing the F5 key on the keyboard turns off some display item—perhaps it hides a menu—then the user needs to be able to look up that function or somehow get to it at the appropriate time. We call this *point-of-need support*. Often users will not need all the functions of a program—certainly not all at once, nor all at first. In fact, most users employ less than 10 to 15 percent of a program's overall features. But at some point (in the context of their specific work) the users *may* need to know that they can hide these menus. At that point, the documentation set needs to provide the answer: "Press F5." If the documenter has written the manual or help system well, then the manual or help system will include that seemingly insignificant keystroke somewhere, with instructions on how to use it and, possibly, recommendations for its use.

A complete task list leads to a complete manual or help system. For help projects, as indicated in Chapter 13, "Writing to Guide" and Chapter 14, "Writing to Support," program tasks may become the beginnings of the list of help topics. With the sophisticated document conversion programs available today, you can take the raw material of your task list and use it as the basis for print, help, html (Internet-based) help, and other forms. The section on p. 111, "Program Tasks and Document Forms" explores this idea in detail.

How to Get Task Information from Programmers

Meetings, discussions, and interviews with programmers are a fact of life for software documenters. In some situations, with incomplete programs, you have to ask for elaboration about program tasks from programmers. In others you work very closely with programmers in designing and testing the program interface. You should try to create a good working relationship with these development partners. They, too, benefit from the user's efficient application of the program to workplace tasks.

The following remarks about communicating focus on programmers, but the information here could relate to other persons from whom the writer needs to get technical information such as marketers, trainers, support personnel, or subject-matter experts. It can include persons who engineer, program, or test software. Some writers refer to them as "development personnel."

Difficulties in Communicating with Programmers

You have to use skill in talking with programmers because often they see your work as secondary or outdated. Why do they see things this way? The answer to this question lies often in the management philosophy of the project, and the importance (or lack of it) placed on the documentation. Without going into the complexity of this issue, let's examine the following two reasons why programmers often misunderstand documentation.

1. **They may not understand writing and see it as secondary.** The correct impression sees technical writing as adding value to the product and the technical writer playing an equal role in the acceptance and usability of the product. Try to foster this notion among programmers and analysts.

2. **They may have moved on to other projects and don't care about this project anymore.** This misunderstanding occurs when documenters don't enter the development team at the very start and write while programmers program. Try to help the programmers define projects in a larger time-frame. Remind them of their commitment to their code and your commitment to making it as usable as possible.

Guidelines for Interviewing Programmers

Technical communicators have developed ways of dealing with programmers to make the interview situation more fruitful for all concerned. In general, follow these guidelines in dealing with programmers:

1. **Emphasize teamwork and team responsibilities.** In a group situation, programmers realize they have to cooperate with others to produce a usable product. Emphasize how their cooperation can help the group meet its goals. Show them how their input can improve the product. Say things like "Your ideas will show up in the book," or "May I quote you in the user's guide?" or "This information will *make* the help system!"

2. **Ask the right questions.** Programmers and engineers respect hard work and brains. Avoid asking questions that you can get answers to by simply working the software. For instance, to the question "Do *chgnm* and *reset_name* do the same thing?" a programmer may respond "Why haven't you tried this out?" A better question: "I have found that *chgnm* and *reset_name* appear to do the same thing. Can you help me clarify the distinction between these two commands?"

3. **Prove your technical knowhow or ability to understand their explanations.** Developers don't willingly give out information about their systems, and they want you "up to speed" on technical aspects. Do your homework so you don't waste their time uncovering the obvious. On the other hand, don't back off from getting something clear if you don't understand it. This approach also gains you respect.

4. **Use your interviewing skills.** Warn programmers that your job requires you to benefit from their expertise. Show up on time, and keep interviews to less than an hour. Show unconditional, positive regard for your interviewees. Don't grumble or put down other members of the team and always try to finesse your way out of arguments. Thank them for their time, in writing if possible.

Program Tasks and Document Forms

Earlier in this chapter we examined the way to prepare a task list that would help you in your document design. Now let's examine some of the ways the information in the task list can help you determine the kinds of document form you want to create for your users. The following discussion shows how the task list applies to the three main forms of support: tutorials (Chapter 12, "Writing to Teach"), procedures (Chapter 13, "Writing to Guide"), and reference (Chapter 14, "Writing to Support").

Use the Task List for Writing Tutorials

Because tutorial, or teaching, documentation relies heavily on simple steps (often no more than three or four at a time) with plenty of accompanying explanation, the task list can help here. Tested thoroughly, the task list can tell the tutorial designer what steps the user might need in order to perform the specific tutorial example. Because the task list includes optional keystrokes and mouse options, the writer can select from the information in it to build the strictly directed kind of instruction known as a tutorial.

Table 3.12, from a Microsoft Chart tutorial, illustrates how you can select elements from a task description to include in a tutorial. Underlined elements indicate parts used in the tutorial.

Figure 3.7 shows the same task transformed into a tutorial lesson from the Microsoft Chart manual. As you can see, the task of setting up a chart in Microsoft Chart takes on different form in the tutorial than it does in the task description.

DIFFERENCES AND SIMILARITIES BETWEEN THE TASK DESCRIPTION AND THE TUTORIAL. As you can see, the tutorial version of the task follows roughly the same step-by-step structure, in the same order. It begins with the starting state and ends with plotting the graph. The task description helped the writer stay on track. Because the tutorial version followed a scenario for building a specific graph (which the task description did not) the writer had to include some new steps, for example: "Type *Thousands.*" But the tutorial version differs significantly from the task description in the following ways:

■ **The tutorial contains information not used in the task description.** The screen in the tutorial version has the fields filled out, but the task description omits the

Table 3.12

Example of a Task Description from Microsoft Chart Used for a Tutorial

Task: setting up a chart
User: end user
Starting state: MS Chart is open, the user has created a spreadsheet document
Goal State: the parameters of the chart are set and it has plotted

Steps:

1. Choose the chart type.

    Options:

    line chart icon: selects the line chart
    bar chart icon: selects the bar chart
    stack chart icon: selects the stack chart
    combo chart icon: selects the combo chart

2. Type the Chart Title.

3. Type the Vertical Scale Title.

4. Type the Horizontal Scale Title.

5. Choose the Values to Be Plotted.

    Options:

    1st row: sets value for first row
    2nd row: sets value for second row
    3rd row: sets value for third row
    4th row: sets value for fourth row
    From Column: sets the beginning column
    To Column: sets the ending column
    Data Legends In Column: sets the column for data legends
    Horizontal titles in row: sets the row for horizontal titles

6. Set the Vertical Scale.

    Options:

    Numeric radio button: sets the v. scale to numeric
    Semi-Logarithmic radio button: sets the v. scale to semi-logarithmic

7. Set the maximum value for the vertical scale.

8. Set the minimum value for the vertical scale.

9. Select the Draw Grid option.

10. Select the Label Chart option.

11. Click the Plot!!! button.

    Option:

    Cancel button: returns to the spreadsheet document

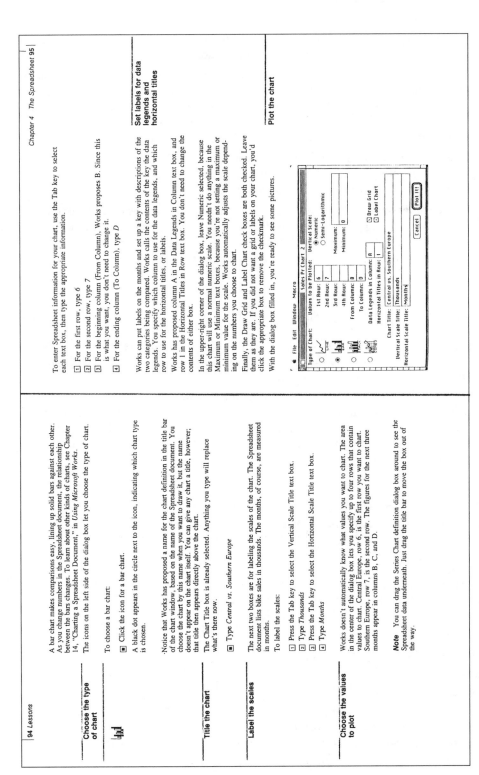

Figure 3.7

Example of a Tutorial Lesson from a Microsoft Chart Manual

This tutorial shows how a task description gets adapted to the needs of users seeking to learn the features of a program.

screen. And the tutorial version contains more explanation of what the options do, whereas the task description simply lists the options.

■ **The task description contains information not used in the tutorial.** Some of the options listed in the task description appear in the tutorial, others do not. For example, the third and fourth row values were not needed in the tutorial scenario but were included in the task description for the sake of comprehensiveness. The writer only selected options that fit the user's needs for the specific tutorial scenario.

■ **The tutorial contains a different tone and language.** The tutorial speaks directly to the user ("Notice . . .", "You . . .") but the task description doesn't. The task description speaks to the writer; the tutorial speaks to the user.

■ **The page layout and format differs.** The tutorial uses various page layout tools—indentation, putting steps in the outside columns for easy viewing, and different type styles—to facilitate easy reading by the user learning the program features. The task description uses a functional format for recording steps and options only.

Use the Task List for Writing Procedures

Another common form of documentation, the procedure or walk-through, depends heavily on guiding the reader through steps to achieve a goal. One such procedure might involve the installation of the software on a hard drive; another would require setting the search parameters in a word processing program. Procedures often include all the options as well as shortcuts, warnings, and tips for avoiding common errors.

A thorough task list includes all these elements and makes them available to the writer. When you write specialized procedures of a program—installation tasks, configuration tasks—you rely very heavily on the information in the task list. Consider the example of a task description adapted to a procedure that is shown in Table 3.13. Because

Table 3.13

Example of a Task from Microsoft Record Utility Used for a Procedure

Task: Deciding what to record
    User: end user
    Starting state: Windows accessory Recorder is running
    Goal State: The user has chosen what to record in a macro

Steps:

1. Choose Record from the Macro Menu.

2. Click on the Record Mouse list box.

3. Select an option.

    Options:

    Clicks and Drags: records keystrokes and all mouse actions with button pressed
    Ignore Mouse: records only keystrokes
    Everything: records keystrokes and mouse actions with button pressed and not pressed

of the complexity of the dialog box, the writer created a number of tasks to describe it. Compare this relatively brief and uncomplicated description of the task to the procedure in Figure 3.8. You can see a number of differences between the procedure version of this task and the task description. The procedure takes up much more space than the original procedure because it contains more information in a different format.

Deciding What to Record

When you record a macro, Recorder records all keystrokes and only mouse clicks and drags. You can choose, however, to record as much or as little mouse movement as you want.

Although you can record as many mouse actions as you want, it is best to keep the mouse actions to a minimum. Macros that record keystrokes are generally more reliable. This is because mouse actions that you record in one window might not be appropriate for the window in which you later want to replay the macro, particularly if the windows are not the same size or at the same location on the computer screen.

▲ **To specify the mouse actions you want to record.**

1. From the Macro menu, choose Record.

   The Record Macro dialog box appears.

2. Open the Record Mouse list to display its options.

3. Select the option you want to use.

   The option that appears as the setting in the Record Mouse box.

4. Choose the OK button.

   The following table describes the options available in the Record Mouse box.

Use	To
Clicks & Drags	Record keystrokes and all mouse actions while a mouse button is pressed. This is the default setting. It allows you to record most drawing and editing sequences in a program like Windows Paintbrush.
Ignore Mouse	Record only keystrokes. It is best to use this option when you want to record a macro to be used on more than one computer. Macros containing mouse actions will work properly only on machines using a display adapter identical to the one used when the macro was recorded.
Everything	Record keystrokes and all mouse actions even when a mouse button is not pressed. You should use this option sparingly.

Caution   If you use the Everything option to record keystrokes and all mouse actions, you should press CTRL+BREAK when you want to stop recording your macro. If you use the mouse to stop recording, the movement of the mouse to the Recorder icon can cause the macro to perform incorrectly when played back. For example, the Recorder icon could be in a different location, or the Window could be a different size.

Figure 3.8

A Procedure from the *Microsoft Windows User's Guide*

This example shows how a procedure uses information from a task description.

THE PROCEDURE CONTAINS MORE INFORMATION THAN THE TASK DESCRIPTION. The increased information in the procedure takes the form of *elaboration:* including details to help the user apply the feature to specific tasks. In later chapters we will look at the role of elaborations more carefully, but here, let's summarize some of the things that elaborations do.

■ **Elaborations emphasize user choice.** In the first paragraph, the sentence beginning "You can choose . . ." alerts the user to a choice and reinforces the user's control over the program. Further conditions of use are indicated with the phrase "If you use the Everything option . . ." and "If you use the mouse . . .".

■ **Elaborations give reasons for choices.** In the second paragraph, the sentence beginning "This is because . . ." tells the user why something operates the way it does. This increases the user's conceptual awareness of how the program works.

■ **Elaborations apply the feature to specific environments.** In the paragraph describing the "Ignore Mouse" option, the writer mentions a specific computer environment in the following way: "It is best to use this option when you want to record a macro to be used on more than one computer." This acknowledges the user's user community and gives useful advice for applying the feature in it.

■ **Elaborations give useful advice.** In the paragraph describing the "Everything" option, the writer mentions that "You should use this option sparingly." This useful advice passed along to the user helps apply the program feature.

■ **Elaborations give illustrative examples.** In the paragraph describing the "Click and Drag" option the writer includes a useful example of a program, "Windows Paintbrush," that the user might also use in conjunction with this procedure. This example helps the user integrate the program feature with other programs.

■ **Elaborations give the results of screens.** In the example above you can see that the writer included statements telling what happened after a user action: for example, "The Record Macro dialog box appears." Results don't appear in the task description, but in the procedure description make up an essential part of the step. Including the results of user actions reinforces the instrumentality of user interaction with the program. It tells what the user has done, not what the computer does.

THE *CAUTION* SHARES EXPERIENCE WITH THE USER. The example above also includes a caution giving advice on how to stop the recorder when choosing the "Everything" option. This caution represents a significant addition of information to the original task description. In it, the writer helps the user figure out what to do to avoid a potential problem with the feature. This increases the user's sense of control over the program, and helps the user make a wise choice of options. Furthermore, it shares valuable experience with the user. Clearly, the writer has tried the procedure and perhaps has experienced the difficulty of stopping the macro recording by using the mouse. Good documentation should pass this information along to the user in procedures, but only record the bare bones of the procedure in the task description.

THE FORMAT FACILITATES READING AND INTEGRATION. Rather than merely listing the options as in the task description, the procedure formats the options into a table with the headings "Use," and "To" to help the user relate the specific feature to the workplace task.

Tables like this, used consistently in procedures, facilitate reading by allowing the user to scan options easily and pick the one that best fits the work situation. The table headings reinforce the idea of a workplace context for the program features.

For more information on using tables to reinforce the workplace context, see Chapter 11, "Using Graphics Effectively," in the Discussion section under the heading "Types of Graphics in Software Manuals and Help." You can also get information on laying out tables as elements of screen design in Chapter 9, "Laying Out Pages and Screens," in the Discussion of "Elements of Page Design" and "Elements of Screen Design."

Use the Task List for Writing Reference Documents

The task list provides a basis for designing reference documents: documents that provide data to enable experienced users of the program to find specific pieces of information. Reference provides help at the *support* level, meaning that much of the motivation to use the information comes from the user, not from the manual telling the user what to do. Reference documents in "bare bones" format often list the name of a task and give brief steps. Reference documentation relates to the task list and task descriptions in two ways: as quick reference cards and as help.

The example in Figure 3.9 from a *Task Reference Guide* illustrates how task descriptions can inform the creation of this form of reference material.

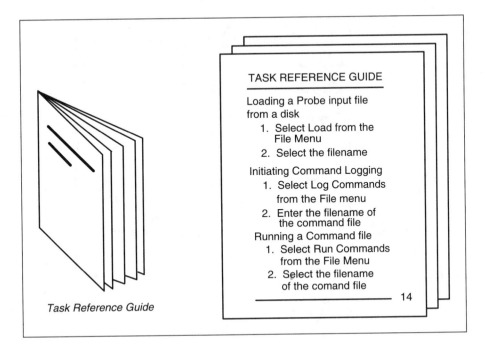

Task Reference Guide

TASK REFERENCE GUIDE

Loading a Probe input file
from a disk
   1. Select Load from the
      File Menu
   2. Select the filename

Initiating Command Logging
   1. Select Log Commands
      from the File menu
   2. Enter the filename of
      the command file
Running a Command file
   1. Select Run Commands
      from the File Menu
   2. Select the filename
      of the comand file
                               14

Figure 3.9
A Task Reference Guide

This example shows how task reference guides only contain steps for performing procedures.

Most of your reference material will consist of lists of commands and short explanations, definitions of key terms, tables of keyboard shortcuts, error numbers, switch settings, and similar items. However, many companies use the form of task reference illustrated above. Unlike the two previous examples of tasks in actual documentation, this reference contains *less* information than the task descriptions. You would use this kind of reference where you have:

- Complicated procedures requiring unconventional use of program features
- Users who use the system intermittently and need reminding of the steps to perform a task

Task Lists As Part of Help Systems

You also find task lists used as raw material for help systems. Often the command reference screen of a help system will use a hypertext link to connect to a procedure showing steps for using the command. The example in Figure 3.10 illustrates how task descriptions link with help information. In this example, we see the linking of two kinds of information: definitions (characteristic of reference documents) and procedures (characteristic of guidance or procedural documentation). Tasks from your task list will contain primarily procedural information. In this system the user can move from the conceptual

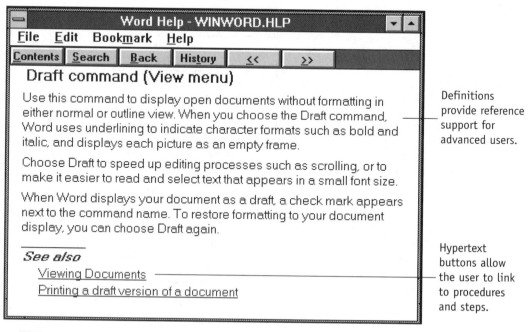

Figure 3.10

Help for Microsoft Word

This module shows how to link procedures to help modules.

level of definitions to the doing or acting level of procedures. This kind of linking, here facilitated through the Microsoft Windows WinHelp, facilitates both an understanding of the program and the application of the program to work.

ONLINE HELP PROVIDES FLEXIBILITY IN PRESENTING TASKS. You have the opportunity to integrate the information into your online system by the use of the *hypertext buttons* and other linking technology available through most *help drivers*. In the illustration above, the definition of the Draft Command contains the reference information. The hypertext buttons contain the procedural information contained in the task description. After reading the overview of the function, the user can see procedures by clicking on the two hypertext buttons "Viewing Documents" and "Printing a draft version of a document."

Relating the Task List to the Overall Project

As we have seen, the task list models the entire computer program and also gets you involved with the system by recording all its elements. Using it, you record the steps that form the basis for tutorials, user guides, and reference documents. But the task list's usefulness goes beyond that. In fact, the task list can inform the entire manual project—from planning which manuals to write, to setting up page and time estimates.

For a full discussion of the place of tasks in the overall project process you should consult Chapter 4, "Planning and Writing Your Documents," which shows you how to manage all the efforts it takes to plan and actually produce a manual or help system. The number of tasks and their complexity or simplicity determine the scope of your entire project. So you may want to browse Chapter 4 in conjunction with reading this section on estimating total hours. You will use the total hours number you derive from the formulas below in the documentation plan and estimating plan you write following the Guidelines in Chapter 4.

Planning Which Manuals to Write

You can see the usefulness of the task list in planning when you use it in conjunction with the other model prepared by the writer: the user analysis. The user analysis (described elsewhere) specifies who uses the program (novice users, experienced users, or power users) and what the users will do with the program (draw architectural plans, look up recipes, store addresses, etc.). The writer defines these user tasks in scenarios: stories of the actions taken by the user in typical operation of the program. Scenarios allow you to group tasks from the task list around categories that make sense for the user. Some categories for organizing tasks include the following: the degree of difficulty, sequence of job-related use of tasks, specific job titles, and the people who perform the jobs.

DIFFERENT USERS NEED DIFFERENT PROGRAM FEATURES. In many situations you will see clearly that not all users will perform all the tasks on your list. Take, for example, an educational program that teaches math facts to kids. Most likely you will identify two users of this program: the teacher and the pupil. But these users will not do the same things with the program: the teacher will install the program and set it up for the pupil to practice division; the pupil will run the drill, record a score, and quit the program.

To the casual observer this seems like an uncomplicated scene. But to the writer this hypothetical situation looks very different. The writer, in the role of document planner, might express the scene in the following way: the teacher (advanced user) will need all four of the program's installation tasks and two of its seven configuration tasks. Thus, the teacher will require *guidance documentation* consisting of six procedures. The student (novice user) will need to learn six of the programs use tasks. Thus, the student will require *tutorial documentation* consisting of six lessons. The rest of the procedures might get converted into *reference documentation* (probably a help system) containing command definitions and overviews of all tasks.

The writer sees the situation in terms of how the task list and the user groups *combine* to help define the required documentation. Other programs—network programs, office automation systems, database programs—involve specific user groups.

Put the Tasks and Users into a Matrix

One way to relate the task list to specific user groups is the *task matrix*. Figure 3.11 illustrates how you can coordinate different user groups and tasks using a matrix or grid format. You list the tasks down the left side, and then, picking a user, move down the list of tasks inserting an "x" for each task that the user would need.

A matrix such as this can ensure, as Scott Hubbard points out, that the writers write the correct manuals—that is, manuals that contain information for specific readers.[2] These manuals or sections of manuals evolve from the patterns of x's on the grid.

Page and Time Estimates

Good planning of any documentation project requires that you come up with two key estimates:

1. How many pages the project will take
2. How long it will take to write the documents

To the extent that the task list is complete and accurate and the user analysis detailed and probable, you can use the task list to help predict these two key elements.

A FORMULA FOR ESTIMATING PRELIMINARY PAGE COUNT. The principle of estimating page count relies on the fact that a task in the task list will get used in one or more document types: perhaps in a procedure, perhaps in a tutorial module. In that use, it will expand into a predictable number of pages, given the number of steps it contains and the overall complexity of the program. The formulas in Table 3.14 can help in converting the task list into preliminary page estimates.

Consider an example. Suppose you have a procedure that takes up one page in the task list. If you wanted to convert that task into a rich tutorial module or lesson, you could expect it to take three pages (one page multiplied by 300 percent). On the other hand, if you wanted to convert the task into a sparsely detailed procedure such as you find in most users guides, you could expect it to take two pages (one page multiplied by 200 percent). Finally, if you wanted to convert that one-page task into a help module that just named the task and gave the steps, you could expect it to take a half page. After you consider the kind of documents you will create and the amount of detail you will need, you can calculate an *estimated* total number of pages you will need all together.

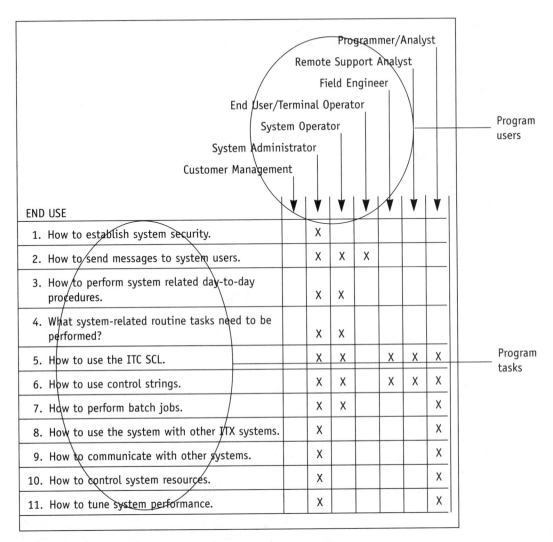

END USE	Customer Management	System Administrator	System Operator	End User/Terminal Operator	Field Engineer	Remote Support Analyst	Programmer/Analyst
1. How to establish system security.		X					
2. How to send messages to system users.		X	X	X			
3. How to perform system related day-to-day procedures.		X	X				
4. What system-related routine tasks need to be performed?		X	X				
5. How to use the ITC SCL.		X	X		X	X	X
6. How to use control strings.		X	X		X	X	X
7. How to perform batch jobs.		X	X				X
8. How to use the system with other ITX systems.		X					X
9. How to communicate with other systems.		X					X
10. How to control system resources.		X					X
11. How to tune system performance.		X					X

Program users — Program tasks

Figure 3.11

Task Matrix

The task matrix helps you identify the kinds of documents needed for different users.

Of course, a number of other factors can influence the *actual* total number of pages: user experience, page layout, and the amount of command summaries (descriptions of program features and their uses) you have. Clearly, however, the manager needs other information than just the task list to come up with these estimates. As you will see in subsequent chapters, good managers keep accurate records of how many pages it requires to turn, say, a medium-sized task into a tutorial module, a procedure, or a reference entry. Generally, tutorial modules take more space in a document than a procedure would. Reference entries often take fewer pages than either the tutorial module or procedure. But documentation is

Table 3.14

Formula for Estimating Approximate Page Count

To create this document format . . .	Multiply the number of pages of each task by
Tutorial: following a scenario to teach program features	200%
Tutorial with rich detail: lots of coaching, lots of screens to show user actions and results	300%
Procedures: guiding the user through the steps, pointing out options	150%
Procedures with rich detail: lots of tables of options, screens to show detailed screen results	200%
Sparse Reference: "bare bones" procedures telling just the name and the steps for each	50%

not an exact science: the accuracy of the estimate depends on the accuracy of your records and they are, still, only estimates.

FORMULA FOR ESTIMATING TIME TO WRITE. Time estimates, on the other hand, require the manager to dig up records of a different nature. To estimate time needed to create documentation products, you need to know how long it has taken in the past. Do writers keep accurate records? Rarely. The pressure to finish a project often means that the extra effort to record time spent gets channeled into actual writing and editing tasks. One could rely on "industry guidelines," which state that it takes about 2.9 hours of overall effort to produce a page of documentation. Using this number, you can **multiply the total estimated page count by 2.9** to derive a rough estimate of the total number of hours needed to write the document.

You can easily see where such estimates could be misleading: some document types take longer to produce, some don't. If you anticipate doing a lot of testing, then you need a higher factor because testing takes a lot of time. But if you have a fairly accurate task list matrix, then you can make other important calculations, namely, page and time estimates. From these two cornerstone estimates you can plan other important project elements: who will do the writing of the pages, and what resources—writers, artists, funds, equipment—they will require. What other tool, this early on in a project, allows you to make these estimates with such reliability?

You can find all these topics, and more, relating to planning your documentation project in Chapter 4, "Planning and Writing Your Documents."

Glossary

batch programs: a kind of program that runs other commands and, thus, get a lot of work done at once, automatically. You don't necessarily have to understand the technical side of these programs; however, you need to know that programmers use them to install programs, or to copy disk contents from the disk the user buys onto the user's hard drive.

command summaries: a kind of reference documentation that lists the commands of a program and gives a brief definition of each.

configuration: relates to those program tasks that get the software adjusted or set up so that it runs appropriately in the user's computer. Usually these tasks get done through menu commands such as "Setup" or "Preferences," or "Setting Preferences." Some configuration occurs during installation (copying the program into the user's computer), but in most programs the user can change the configuration later when the need arises.

dialog boxes: parts of a computer's interface that ask you to set the terms on which a chosen command should be carried out. For example, if you ask a program to save a document, you would get a dialog box asking you to tell which folder to store the file in. Dialog boxes usually contain a number of options and can give the user back information needed about the chosen task.

distribution media: the form of the software in the box it is shipped in. The most common distribution media today is the 3.5-inch high-density diskette or CD-ROM.

end-user: the person who uses a program for the intended purpose of that program.

guidance documentation: designed primarily to lead (hence "guide") the user through a series of steps. Unlike *tutorial* documentation, guidance documentation doesn't intend to teach the procedure, just help the user along. Unlike *reference* documentation, it gives steps and contains elaborations to help the user apply the procedure to workplace goals.

help drivers: software programs that present online help information to the user. They make up the software that runs online help systems. The help driver that comes with Microsoft Windows is called Windows Help. Other help drivers include RoboHelp and Doc-To-Help. These programs allow you to format text and graphics, and include hypertext buttons and other forms of links (electronic cross-references) among related information. They enable you to link procedural information with command summaries and definitions of key terms.

hypertext buttons: part of an online help document that links or cross-references information. For example, in the explanation of the "Open" command, you might insert a hypertext button that would allow the user to cross-reference related commands, procedures for using the command, or key definitions of terms related to using the command.

installation: software tasks that transfer the program onto the user's computer system. Installation may require simply copying programs from a disk to the user's hard drive, or may require complicated initial setting up of directories, filenames, user preferences, and many other elements associated with configuration. You can distinguish installation from configuration in this way: installation usually only occurs once, but configuration may occur more than once, often frequently, as the need arises.

interface descriptions: a kind of explanation that points out the main features of a program's screens, windows, and menu layout. Typical interface descriptions contain definitions of buttons, borders, title areas, help windows, tool ribbons, rulers, dialog boxes, and other elements of the screen. Often they include a labeled diagram.

interface object: all the menus, scroll bars, buttons, fields, arrows, rulers, progress markers, and other things you see when you look at a program. Programmers use the term to refer to these elements when they design and create programs. Documenters have to create information about them for the user who needs to understand how to use them to make the program work. Task descriptions should, if they go beyond the level of task names and steps, record the interface objects associated with each task.

intuitive: an adjective used to describe the interface of a software program that is so easy to learn that users don't need special training. They just learn it by *intuition*. The term has become a buzzword in software programing and technical communication. Some writers contend that such a thing doesn't really exist, and that all programs require training of some sort. Still, users of programs that are easy to learn often describe the interface as intuitive. A programmer might choose one way of programming an interface over another because it seems more *intuitive*.

output devices: include all the machines that connect to the computer and to which it sends information. Examples include printers, external speakers, and disk drives. Suppose you had a program that created financial reports. After creating one, you would have to specify what output device you wanted to send it to: the printer or the disk drive.

program specifications: also known as *component specifications, engineering specs* or just *specs,* program specifications refers to the planning document written by the software developer prior to the programming. Specs embody statements of what the software is intended to do, what functions it will perform, and how it will be programmed, managed, and documented. These documents vary from company to company and may represent various levels of complexity from rough to highly detailed.

program specs: a document or documents written by programmers or developers that specifies (hence the abbreviation "specs") the features of a program. Such documents tell the features of programs and function as plans for programmers to follow in actual coding.

processing parameters: the specific instructions given to a program in command form that limit or somehow guide the way it operates. In the example of the command "dir /w," the "/w" processing parameter tells the program to display the directory in a wide format.

reference documentation: documentation, usually for advanced users, that provides data to support a task. Usually consisting of tables of numbers or commands, it offers little direction in how to apply the information. Unlike *tutorial* documentation, it does not intend to teach, and therefore contains much less elaboration and explanation. Unlike *guidance* documentation, reference documentation focuses on definitions and commands instead of tasks, steps, and options.

task list: a planning tool used by software documenters that lists the features of a program in task-oriented language that represents the uses of the program by the intended users. Examples of task names: "Testing a loop before execution," "Creating or modifying distribution lists," "Opening an existing document in Word."

task matrix: a table format listing the tasks in the left column and the groups of users of the program across the top row. A task matrix provides an overview of the tasks and users and allows the writer or documentation planner to identify and record which tasks each type of user needs. It provides a basis for sound documentation design.

tutorial documentation: documentation containing steps, elaborations, and examples intended to teach a procedure to a user so the user can perform it from memory. Tutorial documentation focuses on a subset of tasks that the efficient user of a program would need to know from memory. It differs from *guidance* documentation because it limits the user to a practice scenario instead of dwelling on program options. It differs from *reference* documentation because it contains steps, overviews, and summaries intended to reinforce learning.

validation: testing each step of each procedure against the software program to make sure the task list is correct. In some companies, this kind of testing occurs in the quality assurance department and may require an elaborate lab for recording the test. Validation may occur in informal environments, such as the writer's office.

Use the following checklist as a way to evaluate the efficiency of your task descriptions and task list. Depending on the level of detail you choose for your list, some of these items may not apply.

Task Analysis Checklist
The Overall Task List

- [ ] The task descriptions contain the appropriate level of detail for the writers, program, and project.
- [ ] The task list describes all the programs menus and dialog boxes.
- [ ] The task list includes installation and configuration tasks.

Task Descriptions

- [ ] Task names follow a consistent pattern: program oriented, performance oriented, or how-to.
- [ ] The task descriptions contain concrete, recognizable starting states and goal states.
- [ ] Where appropriate, descriptions of options specify those for the mouse, keyboard, and menus.
- [ ] Wording of options follows the "object: function" pattern.
- [ ] Abbreviations for menu names are used consistently.
- [ ] Subtasks use continuous numbering.
- [ ] The step descriptions avoid direct address to the user.
- [ ] Steps contain discrete, identifiable, and logical actions.

Testing the Task List

The task list has met the following tests with other project members and users:

- ☐ It covers all the tasks.
- ☐ All the steps are in the right order.
- ☐ All the options are included and accurate.
- ☐ The steps reliably get the user from the starting state to the goal state.

Practice/Problem Solving

1. Compare How Different Manuals Describe Steps

Examine a selection of software manuals for methods of articulating steps. Categorize the kinds of step statements you find. Analyze them for their effectiveness in stating actions, tools, and results clearly. How could the writers have written them better? Write a short report on your findings.

2. Practice Writing Tasks for Non-Computer Technology

Write a task list for a relatively simple electronic appliance or device at your disposal: a telephone, a coffee maker, an automatic bread maker. Use the exercise as a way to practice identifying tasks and articulating steps.

3. Prepare a Task List for Your Class Project

Construct a task list for your class project. This could be for an entire program or one or two tasks for a tutorial or *Getting Started* booklet. Determine how detailed you should make your list, and write a brief justification for it. The justification should tell why you chose the level of detail you did, and how the task list will assist you in creating your manuals.

4. Reverse-Software Engineering: Go from the Manual to the Task Description

Mock up a task list of a procedure in a software users guide at your disposal. Analyze and discuss, in a short report, the differences between the finished procedure and the hypothetical task list you created. Identify and describe the user of the procedure how the elaboration on the finished product would meet the user's needs.

5. Match Tasks and Users

Study the following task matrix for an electronic gradebook program called GRADES. The program has two users: the teacher who sets up the program, records grades, and creates grade reports; and a student assistant user who helps by recording student grades for the teacher. Imagine you have decided to create a special section of the manual for this program that just supports the tasks needed by the student assistant. Using x-marks, fill in the elements of the matrix below for the student assistant user.

Tip: Your challenge is to identify the tasks the student user would need just to do the limited, routine work of recording grades. The object is to provide documentation for just the right amount of tasks. Too many would confuse; too few would deprive.

Task Name	Teacher User	Student Assistant User
1. Entering a student's name	X	
2. Saving a new gradesheet	X	
3. Entering a new assignment	X	
4. Entering a new set of grades	X	
5. Sorting grades by name	X	
6. Sorting grades by average	X	
7. Displaying statistics	X	
8. Displaying record numbers	X	
9. Displaying student aliases	X	
10. Displaying letter grades	X	
11. Displaying averages	X	
12. Setting preferences	X	
13. Selecting grades for averaging	X	
14. Changing a student's name/grade	X	
15. Locking grade records	X	
16. Adjusting type size	X	
17. Cutting information from the gradesheet	X	
18. Adjusting column size on the gradesheet	X	
19. Closing a class file	X	
20. Saving a previously filed grade sheet	X	
21. Printing the gradesheet	X	
22. Quitting the program	X	
23. Starting the program	X	

6. Practice Writing a Task Description

For the following dialog box associated with the command Font . . . on the Character menu of the Microsoft Write program, write a fully detailed task description (omitting the screen). Create a task name using whatever format you like and include the starting state, goal state, steps, and options.

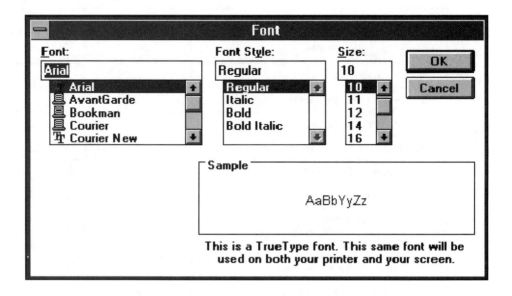

4

Planning and Writing Your Documents

This chapter explains the documentation process as a series of nine phases; a production task list for all nine phases is included. The chapter also examines some special considerations for developing online help systems. Examples show project plans for a documentation project, and the chapter gives guidelines for developing a documentation plan, including plans for designing the documentation set and managing the project. Each phase reflects user involvement.

How to Read this Chapter

Both project-oriented users and beginners should read and study the Example section in this chapter. It covers just about everything anyone needs to know as far as planning and writing. Then:

- If you've working on a project, you should read the entire chapter because it will become your bible. You will refer to many other chapters in reading this one, because you have to make decisions—planning decisions—based on what's in them, even though you may not have read them entirely yet.

- If you're reading to understand, then you should look in this chapter for ways to articulate document designs. Begin by reading about "The Documentation Process" in the Discussion section.

xample

Figure 4.1 shows plans for an online documentation project using HyperCard as the *authoring tool*. The project required that the writing group gather and assemble style

guidelines for company publications and put them online for the employees to access while writing. The plan shows how the members of the development team arranged the elements in the documentation process into a coordinated effort.

ONLINE NETWORK REFERENCE SYSTEM (ONRS)
Tentative Schedule

W = Writer   G = Graphics/Interface Designer
E = Editor   T = Tester
M = Manager   C = Client Contact

Week	Tasks	People Involved
1st	Study existing documents	ALL
	Visit user site	assigned by M, C
	Learn HyperCard	ALL (coordinated by W)
	Research	ALL, C
2nd	Meeting to compare information	ALL
	Prepare survey for users	W, E, M
	Deliver surveys to users	assigned by M
	Outline information meeting	ALL
	Design document/interface	W, E, M, G
3rd	Initial writing of document	W, E
	Get back survey from users	M
	Revise written document	W, E
4th	Edit document	W, E
	Put document online	G
	Troubleshoot online document	G
	Choose test subjects	T
	Schedule tests	T, M
5th	Test document	T
	Review test results meeting	ALL
	Revise document	W, E, G
	Final writing and editing	W, E
6th	Select evaluation group	T, E, M
	Evaluation	T
	Study evaluation results	ALL
	Write up evaluation results	M
	Prepare maintenance guide	W, E, G

Figure 4.1

Task List and Schedule for Developing a Documentation Project

This schedule arranges personnel, tasks, and time. The table makes a useful way to communicate project plans.

uidelines

1   Create a Task Sheet

You may not routinely think in terms of tasks, but for a documentation project, especially one involving a team, a list of tasks can save your life. The tasks that you decide on early in the project can help you identify the discrete activities for team members. As when you identify *user* tasks, try to find writing tasks that have beginnings and endings, things that you have to "do" in order to get from point A to point B. Figure 4.2 lists the tasks in the planning phase.

When you start thinking about tasks, you'll probably go through a process of saying, "Well, we're going to have to do this, and this," until you get rolling and the whole project starts to take shape in front of you. And after you've done it once, the stages of a project will make more sense and you'll have the chance to refine and, I hope, not make the same mistakes twice. I always underestimate the problems I'll encounter with a project. Sometimes I have to learn a new system, or change formats along the way, or bring on new personnel. For this reason, I've learned to anticipate the constraints of the technology, set up styles that I can change readily, and save my documentation plans to share with other writers.

The main advantage of the task sheet lies in the ability it gives you to tick off your accomplishments as you work. This always gives me a great deal of satisfaction when I'm stalled, waiting for a client to return a draft, or side-tracked making an index that takes twice as long as it should.

As you look over the suggested tasks in the list in Table 4.1, realize that not all of them will apply to your project. Use those that do, and invent ones you foresee that don't appear here. After you have your list together, share it with the other people in the project and get their approval. You'll thank yourself for this planning hassle later.

In thinking about tasks, I'd like to share a task sheet I found in the preface to an Ashton Tate manual for a product called RapidFile. Clearly, the team that developed this product worked together well, not only to do the documentation, but to design the program too. And it appears that the tasks they performed during the process brought the team together. Their preface read this way:

> Designed, developed, programmed, researched, planned, budgeted, forecasted, consumer tested, interface tested, product tested, written, edited, typeset, graphically designed, illustrated, proofed, quality assured, procured, photographed, copyrighted,

---

1. Create a task list.
2. Work backwards from delivery date.
3. Assign people to tasks.
4. Work in the drop-dead mode.
5. Make the documentation plan persuasive.

igure 4.2

**Guidelines for Planning a
Documentation Project**

Table 4.1

Tasks Corresponding to the Phases of Document Production

Document Production Phase	Corresponding Tasks
1. Perform the User Analysis	Identify and make contact with potential users.
	Design user interview materials and documents.
	Perform user interviews and observations.
	Identify and arrange for user test sites.
	Draft and review user scenarios.
2. Create the Task List	Obtain working copies of the program/s.
	Circulate and get approval for the initial task list.
	Contact programmers for technical walkthroughs.
	Set up meeting times with programmers.
	Organize testing of the task list.
	Produce the final task list.
3. Design the Documents	Identify suitable drafting and desktop publishing resources.
	Check document objectives for suitability to users' needs.
	Create mockups of all documents.
	Get user feedback/reality check on design prototypes.
	Arrange for meeting with design team.
4. Write the Project Plan	Check outlines for appropriate task organization.
	Identify and assemble the writing team.
	Identify and negotiate for project resources.
	Arrange for design testing and reviewing.
	Check list of hypertext links for help structures.
	Check outlines for completeness of information.
5. Write the Alpha Draft	Assign writing tasks.
	Test prototype designs with users.
	Set up the style sheet for the project.
	Refine publishing software styles.
	Arrange for transfer of text among team members.

Table 4.1

(Continued)

Document Production Phase	Corresponding Tasks
6. Conduct Reviews and Tests	Get user reviews for suitability, accuracy, completeness.
	Arrange for technical reviews and review meetings.
	Contact users and others for tests.
	Make final arrangements for the usability lab.
	Use users in usability testing of users guides and tutorials.
	Write a review and/or test report for the project meeting.
7. Revise and Edit	Reconfirm changes with users.
	Schedule the edits.
	Schedule the review meetings.
	Assemble and manage all the graphics.
	Review graphics/tables/figures for accuracy.
8. Write a Final Draft	Confirm vocabulary decisions with users.
	Maintain the file transfer system.
	Elicit user input on terminology used for indexing.
	Review definitions with users.
9. Conduct a Field Evaluation	Survey actual users for reactions, needed improvements.
	Contact customer support for records of user questions.
	Write an evaluation report on the project.
	Maintain project records and archives.

legally reviewed, approved, staffed, produced, maintained, cleaned up after, assembled, packed, readied for shipment, shipped, publicly related, advertised, promoted, secured, accounted for, marketed, sold, supported, trained for, prepared, and managed by: . . . The "RapidFile Team." (Ashton-Tate, 1986)

2   ## Work Backwards from the Delivery Date

Once you have a task sheet you should try to estimate how long each task will take. How well you do this depends on your degree of experience and, sometimes, luck. For instance,

I once estimated at least three or four hours of scanning illustrations for a project but found out later that the client had them already scanned and ready for me. I was lucky on that one; usually it works the other way and I spend much longer doing things like getting pages to fit or researching subject matter background. As a general rule, tasks that depend on coordinating events with others, such as reviewing documents, take longer than you think.

You can estimate the times it will take for the separate phases of the development project by adding up the total times for tasks for each stage. Estimating times for phases gives you an additional perspective on the events and can help you identify areas where you might over- or underestimate times.

After you have a general idea of how long you will take on each task (remembering that some of them overlap, as you will see later in this chapter), arrange the tasks in order from the last task to the first task. This allows you to find the *milestones* of your project, those happy days when things get recognized as "done." This list of milestone dates helps you coordinate with sponsors or others concerned with product development because it allows you to schedule demonstrations, meetings, and hand-offs (points at which a form of a document, such as a draft, gets passed from member to member, such as from a writer to an editor).

Once you have arranged the tasks starting with the due date, you may notice that, to get the project done, you needed to have started some months ago—or worse. When this happens you have to compromise on tasks. Discuss the list with your team members to see what can take less time, where you overestimated, or what tasks you may have included that you actually don't have to do. This process of compromising and setting priorities for tasks helps you fit all the tasks neatly into the space between the beginning date and the ending date. On the whole, scheduling often becomes an exercise in which you juggle, debate, negotiate, argue, compromise, give, take, project, guess wildly, anticipate delays, remember past mistakes, and cross your fingers.

3   Assign People to Tasks

You should determine the roles team members will play: manager, writer, editor, tester, graphics designer, review coordinator. Most of the tasks will fall into these categories. It then becomes a matter of assigning people to fill these roles.

The Discussion section of this chapter details the kinds of people involved in writing and development projects, but as a matter of planning you should try to assign people to tasks as early as possible. Assigning tasks means deciding who will take responsibility for making sure a task gets completed. This person becomes accountable for that task. Others may help the person with the task but usually one person reports on its completion.

As a manager you should know the talents and experience of your team members. When assigning tasks, keep in mind the following characteristics:

- Writing skills
- Editing skills

- Software tool skills
- Experience with the subject matter of the program
- Knowledge of the user and the user's workplace
- Familiarity with the development environment.

4   Work in the Drop-Dead Mode

"Drop dead mode" means that if you dropped dead one day, someone else could walk in and take over the project. It also means creating the structure of the documents and then filling them in. In this way you work top down. You always have something to show at meetings, and get very used to the overall commitments you made for the project. This helps keep the team unified.

Here are some ways to maintain a project:

- **Progress reports/project diary.** Keep a list of the hours you spend on a project and the types of activities you do such as researching, repairing old files, going to meetings, designing, writing, and such. This helps you in a lot of ways but, primarily, it gives you a professional perspective on your work. It gives you something to report at meetings.

- **Work record sheets.** Work record sheets take the idea of a project diary a step further and make it into an actual log. You can create a separate document outlining your tasks and then keep track of the times you take on each task. If you have a team to coordinate, you can give team members copies of work record sheets and get them to fill them out. I've done this in two ways: provided team members with blank calendars to record their work on, and kept a log file on my computer where I recorded every hour I spent on a project.

- **Librarianship.** Data librarians on software development projects have the responsibility of keeping track of all the program files and making lists of files for participants. They also create directories and assign them to team members. Often managers of documentation projects perform such tasks. I always set up directories for original files (the ones I get from a client containing earlier versions of documentation or research sources), newly created files (containing the .doc files I'm creating with new documents in them), graphics (containing bitmaps, gifs, screens, logos, icons, and the like), and management files (documentation plans, style sheets, time logs, standards, record sheets, invoices, letters, and memos). It takes time to set up these kinds of directories, but that pays off in better organization as the project goes on.

- **Project databases.** After you've completed the process a few times, you may want to consider setting up a fully automated database of times to completion and actual costs versus estimated costs. With this information in a database, you can assemble project plans that automatically calculate milestone dates and costs. To anticipate this kind of database, consider setting up your tasks in a spreadsheet so that as you complete a task you can enter in the actual time it took to complete the task, then automatically calculate the impact on the delivery date.

5   Make the Documentation Plan Persuasive

This bit of advice relates to the need to communicate with others not familiar with the documentation process. Sponsors, clients, and others working with clients have other responsibilities, and often don't have time to read your documentation plan carefully. Later, when it comes time for them to review or participate in testing, you don't want them surprised and swamped with other work—this can put a sudden slowdown in your work. To counteract this, use a clear executive summary in your plan that explains people's obligations. You might even create separate documents to deliver to these persons when the time comes, to make sure they become willing and informed allies.

Your documentation plan doesn't just set out what you want to do—it can be what gets you the contract or project. In other words, it functions as a pitch as well as a managerial document. Both of these roles are shown in Table 4.2.

Usually a documentation plan fails because the writer emphasizes one of these functions at the expense of the other. Your documentation plan has to pass muster with the developers and others involved in the software team. You can't expect nonwriters to understand the needs of writers as well as you and your writing group do. They know engineering, or programming, or graphics, or public relations, but don't understand document design, writing, editing, and the importance of user analysis. So justify your claims, refer to past records of performance, and present yourself as a team member.

Table 4.2

Functions of the Documentation Plan

Function of the Plan	Characteristics
Managerial	Schedule tasks and people
	Handle and keep track of the budget
	Keep track of documents and files
	Record and anticipate important meetings and other events
	Monitor progress and make concessions where necessary
Persuasive	Present a sensible design
	Show a willingness to cooperate
	Show good sense in planning
	Appear frugal and economical
	Indicate talents and capabilities convincingly
	Appear dependable and resourceful

 **iscussion**

The processes that you need to follow in arranging the workload of a documentation project basically follow the nine-step list you will find below. However, designing and managing an online help project includes some extra steps because of the intricacies of organizing help topics. This discussion of documentation planning looks briefly at the documentation process as a whole, to remind you of the process elaborated on and mentioned in earlier chapters. The discussion then turns to choosing online media and the special considerations you should know for developing help systems.

The Documentation Process

The documentation process for manuals and online help aims to tailor documentation products to the user's needs with great precision. To achieve this aim you use models to see the interaction of variables in print and online document design. The model of the system—the program task list—and the model of the user—the user analysis—combine to give you clear direction in the design of manuals. The final element of the models scheme—the levels of support—allows you to adjust the documentation forms accurately to meet the user's needs. The levels of support link the user and the system through appropriate print and online documentation.

The documentation process follows nine phases, each building on the previous one, and each implying testing procedures and management checkpoints. But above all, the steps of the task-oriented documentation process involve building all the documentation products around workplace tasks you specify in the user analysis and user scenarios. Below, you will find each of the stages of the process briefly described.

1. Perform the User Analysis

During this stage you research two aspects of prospective users: their professional responsibilities and their knowledge of computer programs. To perform the analysis you determine what level of support your users need, their user type, learning preferences, and other elements described in Chapter 2, "Analyzing Your Users." The user analysis results in scenarios of use for each of the primary users of the programs. User scenarios allow you to identify which of the tasks or functions of the program the user would need for various job tasks.

2. Develop the Program Task List

During this stage you familiarize yourself with the program and systematize all its functions in a logical way, as described in Chapter 3, "Constructing a Task List." Each task the user can perform with the program gets described in terms of who does it, what it accomplishes, and what steps it requires. This stage allows you to lay out the initial uses of the program in a way that you can later incorporate into document forms for different users. You write the program task list, including illustrative screens, and use it to help determine project milestones, budgets, and time/page estimates.

3. Design the Documents

During the design phase you apply the three types of document forms—tutorial, procedures, and reference—to your user's needs. The design phase also means that you outline the documents and decide about their layout: pages, text style, size, font, and language, as discussed in Chapter 4, "Planning and Writing Your Documents." At this stage you write the titles of your documents, indicating the level of support they offer.

For online help, you need to decide on the types of products you will produce (help, training, guided tour, templates, messages, tips, etc.), make a detailed list of help topics (as described in the section titled "Determine the Help Topics"), and determine their layout. During your work in this stage of the development process you should consult the chapters in "Part 2: The Document Design Handbook" as necessary to gain the right background information for making design decisions.

4. Write the Project Plan

The project (or documentation) plan allows you to specify the manuals and online help you identified during the design phase, and add information about the entire project. In writing the project plan, you must describe the management aspects of your work: schedules of drafts and tests, people and hardware resources, and time/page estimates. The project plan culminates your research and design work on a project. You can review and test the project plan before going on to the next stage in order to ensure appropriate document and project guidelines.

You will find a detailed outline of the documentation plan on page 168.

5. Write the Alpha Draft

The alpha draft represents your first complete document, including all the front matter, text, graphics, appendixes, indexes and associated documentation set materials. As a written document, the alpha draft is tested, reviewed, and edited—all according to the specifications laid out in the documentation plan. It's a good idea to make up an alpha draft checklist, showing all the elements you need in the complete document.

6. Conduct Reviews and Tests

Because your alpha draft contains all the elements of your product, you can send it out for review by clients, executives, and managers, as well as users. At the same time, you can design usability tests using the original documentation objectives, to test for elements such as accuracy, task orientation, and so on. Information from reviews and tests provides feedback for the next draft of the set. For information on these topics, consult Chapter 5, "Getting Useful Reviews," and Chapter 6, "Conducting Usability Tests."

7. Revise and Edit

While the reviews and tests provide feedback from external sources (managers, users, clients, and so on), revising and editing also allow you to submit your work to an editor or edit your own document, applying an editor's skills in reorganizing and checking for accuracy on many levels. Consult Chapter 7, "Editing and Fine Tuning" for information not only in what to look for in editing, but in ways to structure the editing process to make it efficient.

8. Write a Final Draft

The final draft revision contains information gathered from the activities in the two previous steps. If you do them thoroughly, you will find that your document improves greatly at this stage. Incorporating feedback into your document will result in a camera-ready copy that you can hand to the printer or, in the case of help systems and other online support, deliver ready for distribution with the program.

9. Conduct a Field Evaluation

After the user has installed and operated the program, the last stage of the development process happens: the field evaluation. This special kind of test enables you to gauge how well your manual met the task needs of the intended user. Information from this evaluation usually ends up in an evaluation report and provides input for your next project.

Because of the differences between the print and online media, these phases will grow and shrink in proportion to one another. But when you develop complex electronic documents, help systems included, you face technological and managerial challenges that you can weather if you anticipate and plan well for them. The following section focuses on the impact that developing a help component in your documentation set can have on your schedules.

Chapter 6, "Conducting Usability Tests," gives advice on testing that you can follow for evaluating the success of your project; see Guideline 1 in that chapter, "Decide When to Test."

Considerations for Planning Online Help Systems

Turn now to the process of developing online help systems and the many kinds of documentation you find under that heading. The nine-stage process described in the section above should sound pretty familiar to you, and you can find variants of it in other sources, although not so specifically tailored to writing for information-oriented work. But the process for developing online help, as you will see below, involves steps that require you to organize information into smaller chunks and carefully plan how the user will access them. These extra steps merit a detailed discussion.

Let's begin with a brief discussion of the choice to use online media in terms of the benefits to users and writers of the online media, and then discuss a sequence of steps you can use to pattern your help development.

Why Use Online Media?

Online documentation comes in many forms, getting very complicated, once you consider *multimedia*. While the technology and skill to design sophisticated multimedia training and instructional materials grows almost daily, often the process of developing this material follows the standard one, illustrated and adapted below. Help systems are the most widespread form of online writing done by software documenters—though for most software documenters, online documentation boils down to "Help," the series of indexes and topics contained in a special program and displayed for the user who clicks on the help menu in the upper right of the screen.

As you will notice in the process described below, help systems use indexes (cross-references among topics, search keywords, and so on) as the main access element to the information. How many kinds of indexes can you think of? Here the designer has the opportunity to address concerns of the user—to build paths to information that reflect the user's motivation for efficiency, information management, and communication. You can use groupings, called *topic categories,* to help the user get from a problem with, for example, the interface of the program, or the application of the program, to a satisfied solution contained in an online help topic. So help systems allow you to build a significant task orientation into your documentation system.

Online information also presents a number of benefits and drawbacks both for the user and for you, the writer. To help you make the decision between print and online media, consider the following discussion of the benefits and drawbacks of online help.

Benefits of Online Help for the User

- **Provides fast access to information.** Often the user has to look up the index, thumb to the page and so on. With an online help system, the user just has to click on the help menu or help button to get to the table of contents and can browse easily among related topics. This saves considerable time—a savings appreciated by busy computer users.

- **Offers more affordances than print.** With an online help system you get the usual affordances common to a book, such as communication areas (screens), text, and pictures, but you also get many affordances—such as hypertext links, buttons, automatic keyword searches, and so on—that you don't get with a book. These added affordances enable the user to structure information in ways that fit his or her professional needs. How many books can "remember" previous pages you consulted and retrace your browsing for you? How many books will automatically open themselves up to the correct page to reflect the context of your problem? A well-designed online help system, using the history tracking function and context sensitivity, can do this easily and quickly.

- **Provides greater convenience than books.** Despite our efforts to make books easy to use, they often don't fit on user's computer desks, don't stay open to the right page, and weigh too much. Online help systems work quietly, instantly, and efficiently. They don't lose pages and they don't take the user away from work to walk to a bookshelf. Help systems don't get lost or get coffee spilled on them. They don't use up forests.

- **Avoids the preconceptions of books.** Whether software documenters like it or not, computer manuals have had a bad reputation in the past. Inaccuracies, overly technical diction, and general user unfriendliness have caused most users to reject the manual, not read it, not consult it for help. While online help systems share some of that bad reputation, they do at least bypass the prejudice some users have toward manuals, and in that way, allow the user to approach them with fewer misgivings.

■ **Allows interaction with the document.** One of the biggest advantages of the online help system lies in the way it allows users to create their own paths. Their search paths and their methods of finding information allow them to interact with the document in ways that give them greater control of the information. This increased sense of control can affect their use of the program, adding to their sense of its usefulness..

Drawbacks of Online Help, for the User

■ **Requires more learning.** With any new system, the user has to learn it. That learning can get complicated: It means figuring out what categories of tasks you have set up, learning a vocabulary for the specific program, and so on. It also requires that the user become familiar with the kinds of buttons, pop-ups, links, and other affordances of your specific system. This increases the learning curve.

■ **Intimidates novice users.** An online help system can add to the amount of "program" that confronts the user, intimidating some novices. Those with problems navigating the program may also have problems navigating the online help system.

■ **Looks strange.** While users complain about print manuals, print manuals nevertheless have a familiarity about them that reassures some users. Many users haven't much experience with electronic books and have difficulty understanding the concept of an online help system. Electronic documents don't have weight, bulk, the feel of paper, so users have the added burden of getting the information and becoming familiar with the media. This burden gets lighter each year, as more users come to expect online help with their software. But for the present, many users have not yet developed a familiarity with electronic documents and still may resist using them.

■ **Has limited uses.** By their very nature, online help systems can't do some things. Take installation, for example. The user can't access the help system for information before installing the program. To overcome this limitation you need to provide print documentation for installation, and perhaps some maintenance and troubleshooting if the program crashes and takes the online help system with it.

Using an online help system also has benefits and drawbacks for the writer/developer, as you will see below.

Benefits of Online Help, for the Writer

■ **Saves paper.** Because the online help system exists in electronic form as a file on a diskette, the savings in paper can represent a significant advantage over print. Not only do online documents reduce paper usage, they reduce the cost of printing and distributing books. Usually companies distribute help files by copying them to the program's distribution disk—an easy way to distribute them.

■ **Updates easily.** Writers can benefit from online documents because these documents cost a lot less to update than print manuals. Whereas a change in a print manual requires that you reprint the page, and sometimes other pages if the change alters the pagination, changes to an online help system only require that you recompile the help file and transfer it to a disk. This makes it easy to make editing changes right up to the last minute before release.

Drawbacks of Online Help, for the Writer

■ **Takes up disk space.** A large help file can require up to one or two megabytes of disk space, sometimes more than you can fit onto a distribution disk. In fact, until storage capabilities of personal computers grew, many computers could not store a large enough online help system. Whether you will have problems with disk space will depend on your own system and the size of the user's space.

■ **Requires reformatting of print.** If you already have a print manual, you cannot simply use the same document online. Some programs do exist for displaying text online in the form of online books. Called "readers," these programs allow users to page forward and backward just as in a book. But for the most part, you will have to reformat your hard copy documentation to make it suitable for online. In some cases this will require more work for the writer.

Overview of the Online Help Development Process

Because of the tools and sometimes the personnel required to produce online help, you need to plan the project phases to include extra time. Creating a document seems relatively quick and easy compared to the authoring software you have to learn and the complication of creating files that the help software can handle consistently. Testing, in particular, takes much more time because you have to see to it that all the links work and you have to troubleshoot the ones that don't. The following brief overview of the process of developing online help can get you started and show ways you will need to adjust your plans for producing in this type of media.

1. Identify and List the Online Help Topics

At the heart of any online help system you will find topics, which can be defined as follows:

Topic: an identifiable body of usable information

Examples of topics include the following:

■ *Steps* for performing a specific procedure, such as opening a file or selecting a database to search

■ Definition of a *command* with an example of how to use it

■ Definition of a *term* relating to a program

■ A labeled *screen* with explanations of its interface elements

You have seen, in previous chapters, examples of topics: procedures, tutorial modules, reference entries. The *information* you use in a help system doesn't change from these print counterparts. The difference between print and online lies in how you present this information and how the user gets to the information.

From the user's point of view, the topic represents the final destination. It tells the user what key to press, what steps to follow, or what a term means. It provides the information the user needs to get back to the task of putting the program to productive work. To start designing a help system, you need to identify topics. If you have done the research needed for a print manual, you have half the battle won because you already know the topics and know your users. Topics come from a number of your research efforts. Table 4.3 can help you identify where to get information for topics.

You can find a number of topics by reviewing the information you collected during your construction of the program task list and your user analysis. Once you have identified the topics, list them under categories such as the following:

- **Procedures:** step-by-step sequences. You can further break this category into basic or advanced procedures, or you can organize procedures around user tasks: "Setting up a database," "Entering addresses," "Searching for addresses," and so on.

- **Shortcuts:** key combinations that save the user time. You can further break this category into groups of shortcuts by menu or by topic.

- **Background:** overview topics explaining the way a program operates.

- **Glossary terms:** terms that require definitions.

- **Menu commands:** explanations of items on the program menus.

- **Frequently asked questions (FAQs):** questions gathered through interviews with support technicians.

Once you have identified your topics and classified them into topic groups, you can move to the next step in designing online help: determining how they relate to one another.

2. Determine the Interconnected Elements

As you identified and classified topics, you no doubt began to see that they related to one another, or interconnected. Those interconnections make up the heart of a help system.

Table 4.3

Where to Find Topics

Topic Source	Topic Type	Description
Program Task List	Guidance	Steps for performing program tasks, in either elaborate or sparse format
Menus	Reference	Names of commands, lists of shortcut keys, definitions of menus, dialog box names
Tech Support	Reference	Frequently asked questions
User Analysis	Reference	Glossary terms, subject matter terms

In fact, you can see an online help system as one that allows you to identify interconnections and provide ways for the user to make the most of them.

The organization of modules in online documentation stays flexible because of the user's ability to leap from topic to topic using hypertext links. The diagram in Figure 4.3 outlines some of the components of a typical online help system.

You can identify a number of kinds of interconnections between information. Consider this example. In a system called AccountMaster, the user had the ability to create custom reports about clients in a database. To set up these reports, the user had to insert

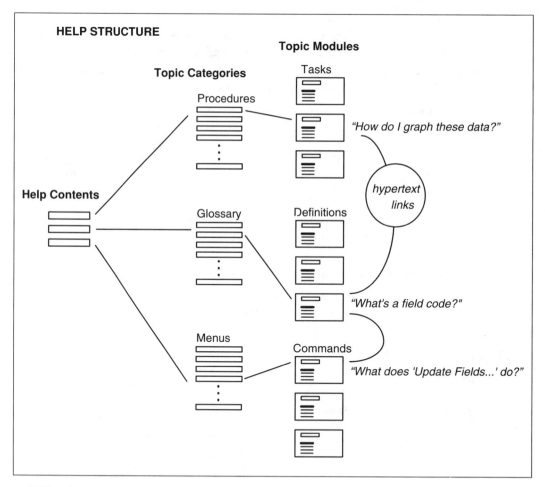

Figure 4.3

The Structure of Help

Decide on the categories of topics for your online document and explain them in your design plan.

electronic tags called *field codes* into a screen. The field codes corresponded to the information about each account, called an *Account Record.* After putting in the field codes the user had to use a "Make Report" command, located on the Reports menu. While working with the program task list and user analysis for this program, I identified a number of interconnections of information related to field codes, reports, the Reports menu, and so on. The following topics embodied this interconnection:

- Procedure for creating a custom report
- Definition of the term *field code*
- Overview of the items on the Reports menu
- Explanation of the command "Make Reports"
- Definition of "field" in an Account Record
- Glossary entry for Account Record

I reasoned that the user could, at any point in encountering any one of these topics, want to examine information contained in other, related topics. For instance, the user might look up the procedure for setting up a custom report and encounter the term "field code" for the first time. The user might then wish to look up field code and so on, jumping from one interconnected topic to the next.

The diagram in Figure 4.3 illustrates how topics could be linked in a help system. Let's say a user asked the question: "How do I graph these data?" In this case, he or she would ultimately have to find the procedural topic "How to Create a Graph" to answer this question. The user could find this topic in more than one way. Consider the following two such ways as an example. One way to get to "How to Create a Graph" would be to follow the top-down structure of the help system. The user would first select Procedures from the Help Contents list, and then select "How to Create a Graph" from the list of procedures. Voila! There's the procedure, and the user can get right to work. On the other hand, the user could get to the "How to Create a Graph" procedure by selecting Menus from the Help Contents list, then selecting Reports from the list of topics pertaining to menus, and then selecting the Update Fields command from the list of command topics listed under Reports. The command topic "Update Fields," which explains the Update Fields command, would contain a hypertext link (put there by a savvy information designer) to the topic "How to Create a Graph." The user would select that link and arrive at the desired procedural topic, "How to Create a Graph." You can see, of course, that because of the interconnected links in the topics the user has not just these two ways to get at the information, but has, in fact, multiple ways to do so.

This example illustrates how you can interconnect the parts of your online help system to create a system that allows for multiple access to information. You can see such a system in Figure 4.4. This diagram of the help system from the PowerPlay 4.0 Reporter program contains a number of topics arranged in groups (e.g. Glossary, Commands, Step by Step, etc.). The user can select from the lists presented in each of these categories and eventually get to the appropriate help topic. On the other hand, as in the example in Figure 4.3, the user who has arrived at a topic via another route can use the hypertext links that connect the topics (represented by the curved lines on the right) to navigate among related topics.

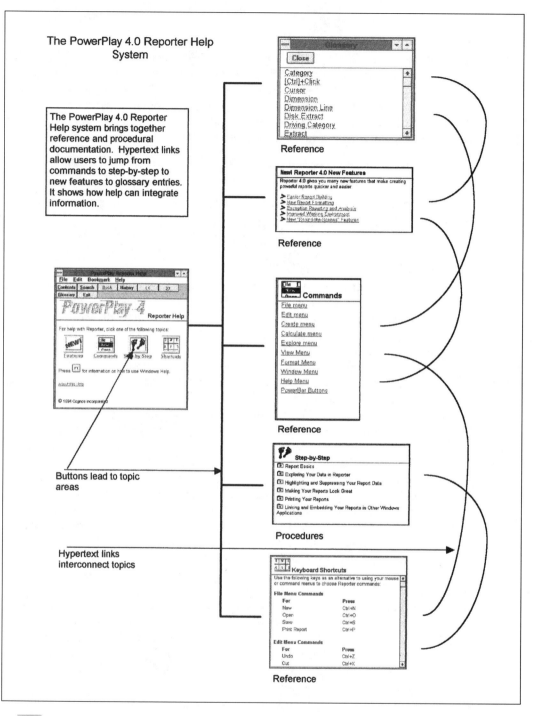

The PowerPlay 4.0 Reporter Help System

The PowerPlay 4.0 Reporter Help system brings together reference and procedural documentation. Hypertext links allow users to jump from commands to step-by-step to new features to glossary entries. It shows how help can integrate information.

Buttons lead to topic areas

Hypertext links interconnect topics

Reference

Reference

Reference

Procedures

Reference

Figure 4.4

A Well-Designed Help System Allows Users Multiple Access to Information

This example of the PowerPlay Reporter 4.0 help system shows how topics get organized by a table of contents and also through hypertext links. The user just needs to click on the links to move from one interconnected topic to another.

For the document designer, the challenge lies in discovering the related topics within a help system and then making them available to the user through hypertext links. But keeping track of related or interconnected topics can get complicated. So to help systematize your planning for the kinds of relationships among topics, I constructed the Topic Design Sheet (Figure 4.5). This sheet provides a handy way to keep track of how a topic relates to other topics. Figure 4.6 shows how the topic design sheet would look filled out for the procedure for creating a custom report. Later when writing the help system, I could refer to this sheet to see which other topics related to the task of creating a report. The related topics recorded on this sheet will appear later as the familiar hypertext links or pop-up glossary definitions that make up the connections in a help system. Depending on the system you design, you can make up your own design sheet.

3. Decide What Affordances to Use

As used in this book, the term *affordance* means the software capabilities that you can build into a help system that allow the user to find and use the information it contains. Explore the idea of affordances a little farther. Author Donald Norman defines affordances as "those fundamental properties that determine just how [a] thing could possibly be used."[1] Door knobs, shoe laces, handles, buckles make up the affordances of many kinds of everyday objects. Similarly, indexes, tables of contents, headers, and so on, make up the affordances of print manuals. One of the main differences between print manuals and help lies in the number of affordances you get with the online media. Whereas the print man-

Topic Name:	Type:	
Category:		
Related Glossary Terms:		
Search Keywords:	Index Terms:	Related Topic Names:
Browse Sequences:		

Figure 4.5

Topic Design Sheet

Use this form to help you keep track of the interrelationships among topics.

Topic Name: *Creating a report*	Type: *procedure*

Category: *step by step*

Related Glossary Terms: *account record, field, field code*

Search Keywords: *reports* *custom* *create*	Index Terms: *reports create* *custom open* *fields*	Related Topic Names: *deleting a report* *formatting a report* *printing a report* *report overview*

Browse Sequences: *report overview, [creating a report,] formatting, printing*

Figure 4.6

A Completed Topic Design Sheet

Keep track of your topics by filling out this sheet.

ual affords linear reading of pages and the table of contents affords searching for topics, the online system affords getting at the information in many more ways. Table 4.4 lists and explains the affordances of a help system. Use it to help you determine what affordances you want to use in your system.

4. Select a Development Method

Once you have selected the information for topics and decided on what technical affordances to use to present it to the user, you have to turn to the construction of the system. As you know, a help system uses screens and software rather than pages to present information. Using software can get complicated, so this guideline will give you an overview of the process to get you started.

The technical complications of setting up a help system really lie beyond the scope of this book. For one thing, you have a number of systems to choose from and they change all the time. Plus, when you consider the many kinds of online information—help, multimedia, computer-based tutorials, online books, animated demonstrations, electronically distributed documentation—you can see that going into each in detail would require additional books. In fact, you can get books on designing online help that cover many of the details not included in this one. (For further information on the technical aspects of setting up a Windows help system, see *Developing Online Help for Windows,* by Boggan, Farkas, and Welinske. This book covers the many technical details you will have to master and also helps you obtain the programs you need to do the work.) On the other hand, you can construct your help system using programs that handle many of the technical de-

Table 4.4

Affordances of a Help System

Affordance	Explanation
Hypertext Links	Embedded codes that take the user to another help topic. Usually hypertext links appear in green, and the cursor changes to a pointing hand when over it. Usually users need only click once on a hypertext link to jump to new information.
Button	A feature of the help interface that causes the program to display another topic, a search dialog box, a history of topics examined, or other element of the help system. Buttons usually look like buttons—have raised edges and depress when you click on them. Like hypertext links buttons
Hot Areas	Portions of an image (a screen or a diagram) that the user can click on to see more information. Usually the cursor changes to a pointing hand when the user moves it over the hot areas. Hot areas resemble labels on diagrams, only they operate electronically and on demand.
Browse Controllers	Forward and backward buttons that allow the user to follow a pre-determined sequence of linked topics. The sequence may cover procedures in a sequence, or sequences of background information.
Pop-ups	Small screens usually containing definitions that the user can view and then click anywhere to close.
Context Sensitivity	The ability to get help on the user's current screen or menu simply by pressing a designated help key, usually F1. The help program knows which screen to present by tags put into the program, indicating which screen or menu the user currently has displayed on the screen.
Balloons	A kind of help that displays, in a cartoon-like balloon, information about screen elements. The user selects balloon help from a menu or a button, and then moves the cursor to whatever part of the screen he or she wishes to learn about.
System Affordances	A range of buttons and capabilities provided by the help program. With Winhelp, for example, the help program used with Windows products, you can use a back button (to take you back to a previous screen), a history button (to show you the topics you've viewed in the current session), a search screen (to search the help system for keywords), an on-top button (to keep the window on the screen while the user performs the procedure), and an index (an electronic index system). Other help programs, such as HyperCard or Apple Guide offer a different set of system affordances.

tails for you. The following two programs are very useful in simplifying the overall process of setting up an online help system.

FOREHELP, ForeFront, Inc., 5171 Eldorado Springs Drive, Boulder, CO 80303 (303) 499-9181

RoboHELP, Blue Sky Software, 7486 La Jolla Blvd., Suite 3, La Jolla, CA 92037-9583

However, you should know how the process works in general terms so you can understand how interconnected topics get put into an electronic systems.

Process Example

The following description covers the process used in constructing a help system for a Windows product.

- **Design the documentation system.** If you have followed the advice above, you have pretty much designed the system. You know what topics you want to include and how they relate to one another. You have a list of keywords and glossary terms that you want to include in your help system (for more on preparing a list of keywords, see Chapter 15, "Building Indexes and Keyword Searches"). Finally, you should have a table of content topics that indicates the types of topics you have in the document: commands, step-by-step, etc. Assemble the topics into a single topic file that will contain all the information you want to present to the user through your help system.

- **Write the project file.** The project help file contains information about the help system you want to design. It contains a number of specifications you set up for your system, such as the title, the locations of your topic file and your image files, the appearance of help windows, fonts and colors, and so on. Basically, it determines the content and appearance of the help system. You have to follow a special format to construct this file, so you should consult the documentation that comes with the help compiler in order to make the right kinds of decisions as to what to include in it and how to get it right.

- **Compile the help file.** The third step in the process of constructing your help system requires that you use a special program called a help *compiler* to read the topic file and the project file and create a third file, the actual help document. Basically, the compiler reads the project file, follows the instructions it contains as to how to set up the help system, reads the topic file, and creates the system. Usually you will encounter errors in your topic files such as unresolved cross-references or missing information. You will have to correct these errors and compile the help system again. Once the compiler creates this third document with no errors, you can read and test your system.

- **Test the help system.** Testing the system occurs after the compiler has successfully created the help system. The problems here relate not to the technical aspects of creating the system, but to the information in it. Aside from the usual errors in spelling, punctuation, and mechanics, you may have hypertext links that go to the wrong topics or pop-ups that don't contain the right kind of information. Your task now consists of clicking on all the links and pops in order to make sure they do what you intended them to do.

Organizing Your Writing Team

A lot of documentation gets done by the lone writer in a company or by a contract writer working on his or her own. But with larger companies like Computer Associates, Inc., CONVEX Computer Corporation, or Microsoft Corporation, the writing, like most other efforts in business today, gets done by teams. Teamwork requires different skills than individual work. You have to communicate much more, and you have to respect leaders and followers. In fact, much of what it takes to make it on a team involves psychology.

What It Takes to Make It on a Team

A fellow member of the Society for Technical Communication, Debbie Rosenquist, gave a talk on good team behavior in which she mentioned the elements listed below. I've expanded on each of them to help give you a feel for your work on teams.

- **Attending meetings on time and prepared.** Teams mean meetings. As the project progresses you will have to attend meetings and possibly lead them when they concern your areas of responsibilities. Always try to get to the meeting a little ahead of time and always bring the relevant documents and a note pad. If you're running the meeting or are on the agenda, bring handouts for the others. If you're not prepared, tell the meeting leader at the beginning of the meeting so you can be taken off the agenda before the meeting begins.

- **Prompt response to requests from team members.** Teamwork requires you to pass a lot of things around—reports, drafts, test results, forms. When this happens, you need to put the team work first so the other members get the point that you're there for them, committed to the team over your other obligations. Keeping them waiting gives the impression that you have better things to do.

- **Straightforward communication of problems: no whining.** Members of teams need to feel that everyone does their share of the work. If you have a much heavier team workload than others do, say so and get some help. Your getting help will help the team and benefit all. Complaining doesn't get the team anywhere and isolates you from the earnest concerns of the group. I have a rule: No excuses. It's not always easy to keep, but I practice on small issues, like, "Dang, Kathy, I plain forgot about that footnote. I'll get right on it." This makes it easier to own up to big issues, like "Dang, Kathy, I forgot to tell the subjects about your test this afternoon."

- **Addressing issues to the appropriate persons: No "hall talk" or gossip.** It's professional to show respect for the persons on your team and expect them to give the team goals top priority. Gossip undermines this sense of respect because it gives the impression that you're unwilling to trust team members with the truth.

- **A sense of humor.** A sense of humor in teamwork means you see the team as very important but you don't let seriousness warp your vision of what's going on. You need to take criticism willingly and not always respond with hurt feelings.

You may find yourself on one of two kinds of teams: the development team—in charge of the development of the software and the documentation, or the writing team—in charge of the documentation only.

The Development Team

A development team develops the entire product: software and documentation. It assembles members usually from varied professional backgrounds and varied skills. The development team tends to define the team roles more distinctly because of the varied backgrounds of its heterogeneous members and therefore has a greater danger of fragmenting than the writing team.

You may find yourself on teams with different kinds of professionals than those described here, but for the most part, when you're on a development team you can expect some mix of the following persons.

- **Market/systems analyst.** The systems analyst studies the user situation and models the activities that the program will automate. The market/systems analyst often has a background in psychology, marketing, or information science.

- **Product developer.** The product developer designs the software program and often originates the project team. In software development, the product developer often knows the subject matter (medicine, accounting, science education, etc.) well and has done research into the area.

- **Project manager.** The project manager organizes the project, assigns tasks, and keeps the project on track. Often this person has a background in business management or organizational strategies.

- **Technical specialist/programmer.** The programmer knows the operating system well, and the language used for programming. This person actually writes and tests the program. He or she will have a background in programming or computer science.

- **Documentation specialist.** The documentation specialist handles all the writing of the manuals and help for the project. This person has a background in technical communication (or in English) and has considerable editing skills.

The Writing Team

Unlike the development team, the writing team develops just the documents. Working in the publications department of a company, the writing team may develop documents for more than one project at a time. On a writing team, especially one with a history of working on various projects, you will find fewer drastic distinctions among the roles. Writing teams show more cohesiveness because of the similarities of their backgrounds and the fact that they usually report to the same supervisor. Members of a writing team have to deal with developers, programmers, and others involved in the whole project, but these persons serve as subject matter experts and not members of the immediate work group.

- **Manager.** The manager takes charge of the overall project and keeps it on track by creating and maintaining a schedule; meeting with the developer, client, or project supervisor; assigning tasks; tracking progress; and handling meetings. The manager usually writes and maintains the documentation plan.

- **Lead Writer.** The writer conducts the user analysis and writes up the program task list and the drafts of documents and topics. While all the members of the team do some writing, this person develops the research information into actual drafts. The lead writer may or may not have other writers on the project, but he or she takes the initiative in assigning writing projects.

- **Editor.** The editor edits the documents produced by the writer and also sets up the standards for consistency among the documents. This person creates a style guide for the team members to follow and edits the documents to make sure they do. The editor also takes charge of production duties for the team.

- **Graphics Designer.** The graphics designer handles the technical aspects of screen captures and creating the illustration and artwork for the team. This person creates rough and final versions of all drawings and illustrations and tests them with users.

- **Tester.** The tester maintains quality in the documentation set by designing and conducting tests. This person contacts test subjects and communicates with them, sets up the test area, produces the test materials, and does the follow-up testing. This person may also, along with the manager, coordinate all the reviewing of the manuals and communicate the review information to the writer and editor.

The Documentation Plan

When you begin documentation planning you should set for yourself a number of goals, among them efficiency and logic in the whole process. Often you will have to meet with other persons involved in a software development effort (clients, executives, managers, programmers, and so on). Lay your ideas out for them as to how you will go about producing a user-friendly manual on time, using your staff to its fullest—and at a minimum cost. You may achieve these goals through the sheer power of your personality, your charismatic leadership, your gift for higher math, and your financial savvy. If you're like me, on the other hand, you need some help. I think of management plans as what we have instead of genius. For me, a solid, time-honored documentation management plan—reasonably thrifty and sensible—has to do.

Why Write a Plan?

If clients, managers, and programmers accept task orientation as a basic principle, you have half the battle won. They will understand that defining menu items does not necessarily constitute useful "how-to documentation." They will understand the distinction between teaching the system and teaching how to use the system. They will more than likely understand and accept the logic behind your plans for audience analysis and document testing. To them, your plans will make good management sense. Your plans should use personnel, computer resources, and budgets efficiently—maintaining close records of performance and a flexible and pleasant work environment. As a final element—probably most important—your plans should involve users in crucial development phases.

PLAN ENSURES STRATEGIC USE. To plan documentation for a computer program, you need to follow a process (such as the nine-part one described above that has a series of stages) from the start of the project to its end. This process needs to meet some pretty severe requirements to make it in today's competitive business world: you will need to defend it in meetings, explain it clearly to colleagues and clients, adjust it to fit just about any documentation project, and, finally, research and refine it in discussions in professional journals. But most of all, you should justify your process by the realization that you have based it on thorough audience analysis which guarantees its ability to help the user apply the program effectively in pursuit of larger professional and organizational goals. In other words, your process should encourage strategic, information-oriented use of software programs.

PLAN SAVES MONEY IN THE LONG RUN. It doesn't hurt to point out that not only should your plan encourage strategic use but it should do so because the developer makes more money that way. The ultimate payoff in efficient and effective use lies in the savings in time and money reflected by such use. Users have to make fewer support calls (estimated at around $50 per call); they waste less time searching through resource documents; they make fewer mistakes; they perform their jobs more efficiently. And for clients and developers, the investment they make in manuals and online help pays off by saving them and their users this expense. Manuals and help systems have to pay for themselves in this way.

No matter what justification for the planning strategy you use, you must create another model: a model that describes not the program or the user, but the documentation that you will produce. This model we call the ***documentation plan***. Other writers and editors refer to it as *document specifications* or *document specs* or *a document development plan*. In it, you create a model of your manuals and help systems *and* your project using sample pages, thumbnail sketches, lists of specifications, and statements of purpose. If you do it correctly and creatively, you can test this model, let users see your sample pages, mocked-up lessons, and so on, and let managers see your projected budgets, resource requirements, and schedules. You can review, test, evaluate, and reconsider these elements you express in the documentation plan so that you can better track them and have greater confidence in their ultimate on-time completion. I use a documentation plan on each project I undertake, and I never complete a project late. (If you believe that. . . .) Probably it's closer to the truth to say that I use documentation plans and that they save me from completing projects *really* late.

As you will see below, the documentation plan primarily describes your project, but it also argues for it. It has a persuasive purpose because you can use it to justify your budget, get approval for a project, and convince others involved in it to follow your design lead. In this regard, you should remember to reinforce the goals of your managers, sponsors, or clients in the document. Make sure to point out how your design meets their criteria—explicit or implicit—of efficiency, cost effectiveness, and usability. To the extent you find it necessary in your situation, make your documentation plan something of a proposal, employing strategies to make it persuasive.

Strategies to Make a Documentation Plan Persuasive

A persuasive documentation plan will cause your reader—a client, a sponsor, a writing team, a development team—to believe that the project will fulfill its purposes and that they should invest their time and resources in it. The suggestions below can help you polish and refine this persuasive purpose.

- ■ **Use an executive summary.** Give the bottom line up-front to help the users decide in favor of your project.

- ■ **Have a goal orientation.** Set out objectives the reader (client, developer, programmer, executive) can identify with.

- **Do the math.** Go over budget figures carefully so detractors can't argue over them.

- **Show a team orientation.** Emphasize the contributions you will make to the overall value of the project.

Strategies to Make a Documentation Plan Easy to Follow

You should keep in mind that these plans—the design plan and the project plan—all make up significant progress toward a successful manual. Write them with enough care and completeness that another writer could use them to produce the manual set as you envision it. In fact, that scenario often happens in the software industry: A consultant will design a manual or help system and then other writers will follow the design—like builders follow an architect's blueprints—to produce the final product.

I did a job like this for a local communications company. The company had installed a new accounting system for its expanding long-distance clientele and needed documentation of their custom-designed system. As it turned out, they needed various manuals: a front office manual, a user's guide for data entry clerks, a management user's guide, and a comprehensive reference for maintenance programmers. The resulting document plan indicated all the design and management aspects of the project in enough detail so that writers hired by the programming company could complete the manuals. Whether you will complete the project yourself or others will complete it, you should still write documentation plans as if others would complete it.

Below you will find a selection of strategies that you can employ in writing the design plan so as to make it "a piece of cake" for another writer to complete.

- **Standardize your terminology.** Keep the same names and titles for separate sections and documents. This way you don't confuse the writer, who sees projects in terms of filenames and titles.

- **Clarify the interconnectivity of information units.** You will realize that you can deal information out of your program task list like you can deal out cards to poker players. Each documentation type gets these or those tasks. Because the program task list contains electronic components, you can "deal" the cards more than once. You can include some tasks in the tutorial *and* in the user's guide, and possibly elsewhere too. Make this information sharing clear to the writer, who can cut and paste the program tasks into various documents. This ensures consistency, the writer's friend.

- **Include sample pages.** Clarity in exactly what you want the pages to look like can help any writer who has to follow your plans. To this end, sample pages work better than brain-numbing lists of fonts and point sizes. Also, if you know the production tools (graphics programs, spreadsheets, assembler programs like FrameMaker), you can specify the styles in the conventions of those production tools.

- **Don't stint on detail in the outlines.** Put as much well-considered detail into your outlines as you can so the logic of the document sections appears clearly to the writer. That will help the writer in deciding what to include in the sections you specify.

Two Parts of a Documentation Plan

Overall, the documentation plan does two things: first, it describes the manuals and second, it describes the documentation project. In the first part, the *design plan,* you tell what your manuals will contain (content) and what they will look like (forms, layout, language, graphics, etc.). In the second part, the *project plan,* tell *how* you will produce your manuals: the schedule, resources, and time/page estimates. The documentation plan may also contain appendixes about the users and the program. Thus, the project plan represents a culmination of your research work so far on the documentation project.

What Goes in the Design Plan?

In the design plan, you specify what the actual documentation products will contain and what they will look like. Use the skills you developed in your study of software document design earlier in this book. Also, pay attention to design elements in manuals you see and use. These can give you good ideas—solutions to problematic areas of design such as working around program bugs and other inconsistencies, or describing new interface elements that you have never seen before. Finally, use your creativity in coming up with variations of designs you see. Ideas in this book can suggest or recommend solutions, but your manual should look and function uniquely for your user and your program. Don't fear trying something different: you might stumble on a design that will work just right for your users and give your work the edge it needs to function well. Above all, use reviews and testing to make sure that your manual fulfills the user's need to accomplish real tasks in the work environment. The design plan contains three main parts: the description of the users, the description of the goals of the manuals, and the description of their content (outlines and layout).

DESCRIBE THE USERS. In the users section of your design plan, summarize the results of your research and analysis efforts. Specifically, describe your user or users in terms that indicate the kinds of tasks they perform and their level of computer expertise. A typical description would first name the user, in terms of job title, followed by a discussion of the user's job related responsibilities (Figure 4.7).

The Documentation Users

This section describes the two types of users and the ways that they would use The Runner's Log.

Runners: Runners would need to use this program to keep track of their progress, to determine needed levels of effort to reach their performance goals, and to compare their efforts with other runners.

Trainers: Trainers would need this program to keep track of their runners' progress, to evaluate runners' performance, to help design running and fitness programs, to inform runners of progress, and to compare the efforts of all the runners being trained.

Figure 4.7

A Sample Descriptions of Users

This description outlines the uses of a fitness database program by athletes and trainers.

You can get this user information from the descriptions you prepared in your user analysis. But you must remember that here you need to stay fairly brief and make it clear that you have done your research well. If you think that your manager, sponsor, or client would require a justification of your choice of users, include that. Often your interviews with potential users earlier on in the project will support points made here.

After you have introduced your user, introduce the user's types and learning curves—again, relying on your work in the user analysis. Specify and justify your reasoning as to the users' learning preferences, indicating special cases or variations that you must take into account. Also discuss the levels of task support each user should have, making it clear why these levels suit these particular users.

The description of users should weave in information from the user analysis relevant to your specific design. Rehearsing all the details of the analysis would bore your readers and not help you meet your persuasive purpose. So select those details that justify your plans. Table 4.5 briefly explains ways you can use elements of the user analysis in the documentation plan.

SET OUT THE DOCUMENTATION OBJECTIVES. Having discussed the users of your manuals, you should, in the next section, say what documents your project will produce. If you have separate documents, some longer, some shorter, you should list the titles of each. If you have a longer, continuously bound document containing sections for different users

Table 4.5

How the User Analysis Informs the Documentation Plan

Element of User Analysis	Use in Documentation Plan
Tasks	Useful to justify user's guide, special job performance aids, organization of the user's guide
Information Needs	Provides support for including information about transfer and storage capabilities of the program
Computer Experience	Explains why you used the level of technical detail specified in the design
Subject Matter	Explains the amount of background information you have included in the manuals
User Community	Explains special sections reinforcing organizational support and support from various user communities
Learning Preference	Helps justify your choice of training media, inclusion of instructor's material, computer-based training, or traditional manual tutorials
Usage Pattern	Helps justify the organization of the entire documentation set, manuals and online, helps explain elaborate routing schemes

(such as a tutorial, and a user's guide, etc.), you should treat each section separately, listing its title. Table 4.6 describes some frequently used titles. Most of the titles would include the program title, as in *AccountMaster User's Guide,* or *NetHog Reference Guide.*

By the time you write the design plan you should have an idea of what objectives each document type or section will achieve. You cannot design documents without objectives because the act of stating a design implies that your document will have to accomplish some task. For example, the installation procedures for a program fulfill the objective of allowing the user to successfully install the program. The same holds true for other task areas: configuration, use, maintenance, and upgrading. All have, at different levels, objectives they fulfill.

Table 4.6

Sample Titles for Software Manuals and Help Systems

Titles	Description	Support Level
User's Guide	Contains procedures for most program functions. Most titles with Guide in them contain mostly procedures, as in *Installation Guide.*	Guidance
Manual	Contains various sections including user's guide, installation section, reference section, and so forth. A good title for the all-inclusive manual.	All levels
Tutorial	A special book or booklet containing lessons that cover the basic and/or advanced features of a program	Teaching
User's Manual	Like *Manual,* this title indicates an all-inclusive manual for a specific user. Alternatives include: *System Operator's Manual, Teacher's Manual, Administrator's Manual.*	All levels
Help	The title for most online help systems. The help system usually contains an index and jumps to online tutorials and procedural documentation.	All levels
Quick Reference Card	This title indicates a brief overview of the commands, menus, tools, or other interface objects in the program. Usually printed on card stock.	Support
Pocket Reference	This title refers to a small brochure containing essential program and background information.	Support
Getting Started	This title indicates that the document will contain an overview, or perhaps a walk-through of some basic program features, using examples.	Guidance
Reference Guide	This title often gets used for manuals that include all three levels of documentation support. Technically it should just include reference or support-level documentation.	Support

COMPONENTS OF AN OBJECTIVE. Objectives for task-oriented documentation usually contain three things: the user of the manual, the task the user performs, and the level of task support. For example, a tutorial for a word processing program might have as its goal the following: the user will learn how to create a file, edit it, and save it on a disk. We can also add to that objective statement some indication of how well the person will do the task: "within an hour," or "easily, without mistakes," or some other kind of measure. Study the objectives statements below.

> The manual will introduce the user to the functions and the uses of the program, and will cross-reference advanced functions with the reference guide.

> The user will use the manual to learn basic program skills, and also use it later as a reference book.

> The help system will provide support for experienced users who need recall support at the point of need.

> The document will provide step-by-step instructions in using the program for file management, reporting, and writing form letters. The document will also work along with a booklet, a disk, and a procedural guide.

> The manual will provide mastery of the following five concepts of the program: how to draw paths, add shading and stroking, layer paths, use type, and transform paths.

As you can see, these statements contain specific goals of the documents. You cannot underestimate their importance. For one thing, they allow you to set goals for your work and provide, thus, a motivation to make the document functional for your users. Second, they allow you to determine measurable levels of achievement that you can test during development. You should build in a clear connection between your statement of objectives and your test plan, (discussed later in this chapter). Depending, for example, on how the writer defines *mastery* in the five areas of the manual (in the last example above), the writer can test for success in learning on the user's part. In fact, one should even test the objectives for suitability and acceptability, as we shall presently see in our discussion of the project plan.

INCLUDE DIFFERENT KINDS OF GOALS. Often you will set out documentation goals in general and then in more specific terms. Remember that the documentation plan primarily aims to convince your readers (clients and developers) of the sensibleness of your design; therefore, clarify just what you want your documents to do. Consider including the goals identified in Table 4.7.

Finally, your statements of objectives provide guidance for the work of writing. No matter how carefully you write your document specifications, you cannot outline every detail of the document at this stage. Writing always involves compromise, adaptation to new understandings of the material and the user, and new ideas about how to present material. Without the guidance of clearly defined goals, the along-the-way-decisions may tend to take the project off the path so that the elements of the manual and online help do not lead toward a single point. Stating goals ensures, to some extent, that we identify that point, that purpose. So we write objectives as a way of shaping our thoughts.

Table 4.7

Kinds of Documentation Goals

Kind of Goal	Purpose
Overall Goals	Explain the degree of usability in terms of ease of use and applicability to a specific job
Goals for Specific Users	Explain how documents will function for different users in different environments
Goals for Special Documents or Sections	Explain the purpose of installation guides, reference cards
Empowerment Goals	Explain the specific communication, information storage, and information transfer tasks the documentation will support

DESCRIBE THE MANUAL TYPES. The section describing the documentation types should describe in detail the content and layout of the documents (document, card, brochure, box, disk label, etc.), and tie the design clearly to goals and user descriptions that preceded it. For each document you should state specific goals, including levels of support and where you use them. If your reader may not see your reasoning perfectly clearly, spell it out. Don't forget to convince as well as explain. Present a detailed outline of the document followed by the details of the layout of each document.

DETERMINE THE HELP TOPICS. Because of the requirement of screen display and the problems with having users scrolling through online text, you have to modularize your online help information into topics. A topic contains the essential definition, steps, illustrations, or whatever information you want to display for the user. Table 4.8 describes kinds of topics and their use.

PROVIDE OUTLINES OF INDIVIDUAL DOCUMENTS. You should include one section for each of your individual documents. Each section includes the name of the document and the estimated number of pages. The outline should include complete section titles and other divisions of information in the document, down to the level of the individual task. An outline starts with the title page and ends with the index, and lists all sections and headings in between.

For online documents you need to describe the organization of topics. Like tasks and other content elements of hard-copy documents, online documents require organization according to a number of schemes—almost all the same ones described in Chapter 12, "Writing to Teach," Chapter 13, "Writing to Guide," and Chapter 14, "Writing to Support."

Even though you can display help topics in alphabetical order, a more useful arrangement follows task-oriented reader concerns that you discovered during your user analysis. In fact, online documentation allows you to incorporate any number of organizational

Table 4.8

Kinds of Help Topics

Kinds of Help Topics	Level of Support	Description
Topics	Reference	Reference description based on topic areas for program tasks
Command Descriptions	Reference	Lists of all the program's commands and what they do
How To	Guidance	Procedures for accomplishing program tasks
Tutorial	Teaching	Basic elements of the program interface and application
Toolbox	Reference	List of program tools and explanations of each
Examples	Guidance	Examples of command lines that perform common user tasks, also examples of use of compiler commands
Background Information	Reference	Explanations of subject matter topics the user needs to know to perform a task or use a program function
Glossary Entry	Reference	A list of terms and definitions. May use hypertext links to commands and procedures

strategies at the same time, thus accommodating a diverse user population. Some possible topic categories for help include the following:

- Daily tips
- Shortcuts
- Macro hints
- Most frequently asked questions
- Advanced keyboard skills
- Creative adaptations
- Use of software in work groups

LAY OUT INDIVIDUAL DOCUMENTS. Describe the layout for each of your individual documents with reference to thumbnail sketches and sample pages that you include in the appendices. The layout should contain enough detail so that if someone were to read your plan he or she could complete the documentation set exactly as you planned it and it would meet your documentation objectives. In other words, view the documentation plan from the viewpoint of its reader, and don't leave out information that you know already.

How much detail should you include? When in doubt, spell it out. Consult Chapter 11, "Using Graphics Effectively," which contains the most examples of sample formats of any chapter. Find a format that you think would appeal to your user and study the level of detail it contains. Then include enough detail in your plan so that the user could reproduce that page.

To specify the layout for your documents include the following information for each document:

- Page size
- Column specifications (for all page types)
- Table specifications (for all table types)
- Body text style, size, font
- Style specifications for:
  - Section and other headings
  - Task names
  - Steps
- Cuing patterns
- Notational conventions
- Binding and boxing specifications
- Any special formatting or page layout instructions

What Goes in the Project Plan?

The project plan section should detail the tasks and schedule you intend to follow to complete your project. The introduction should give an overview to the section and should introduce the main phases of document production. In addition, it should mention the final delivery date (just in case the reader misses it in the executive summary or the schedule section). The project plan consists of the following three main parts:

- Schedule of events for completion of your project
- Plans for using resources
- Time/page estimates

Each of these should follow a specific heading. You should introduce these subsections as you do all sections, with a brief, even one- or two-line overview.

ESTIMATE HOW LONG THINGS WILL TAKE. No two projects take the same time, and depending on how many persons you have working on a specific system, you can shorten or lengthen the overall time. Nor do the development phases always take the same time. Your user analysis may take less time if you already know a good deal about your user from writing previous releases of a product. Similarly, your editing time may shrink if you have more than one editor to work on your text. Your project will definitely take less time if you can get reviewers to return drafts on time. If you're writing online help you will need to schedule extra time for coding, compiling, and testing (see Chapter 6, "Conducting Usability Tests"), and for involvement of programmers and extra reviewers (see Chapter 5, "Getting

Useful Reviews"). Figure 4.8 illustrates the times that the development phases take in a typical project. Of course, when you schedule the phases of the document development process, they don't always come out in a neat, linear form. In fact, they always overlap one another and get spread out at various times over the total duration of the project. For example, my students at Texas Tech University usually find it advantageous to start the user analysis during the preparation of the task list. That way they get to know the users and the program at the same time. Testing goes on throughout the project, overlapping with other tasks. Finally, revising and editing usually occur during the preparation of the final draft. Figure 4.9 depicts the overlapping of phases during a typical project.

CALCULATE TIME/PAGE ESTIMATES. You can roughly estimate the number of pages in your final documentation set by calculating the number of overall tasks multiplied by the average page length for each task. (Remember that enriched guidance takes more space than sparse guidance does.) Add in extra pages for front matter (introductions, overviews, license agreements, etc.), and count cover pages and *all* other pages.

Multiply the grand total of all pages that you will produce by the industry standard of 2.9 hours per page to arrive at an overall estimate of the number of hours required to produce your documentation set. The figures here should appear accurate, and should convince your sponsor or client that you can actually carry out the task. If your estimates seem widely off the mark, reconsider your design plan.

DECIDE WHAT TO SCHEDULE. When scheduling a documentation project, you need to schedule the overall phases of document development and specific events, such as meetings and deadlines, that occur within the overall phases.

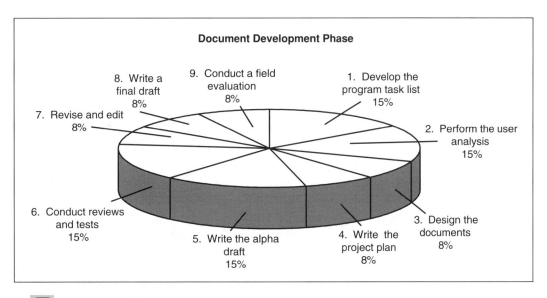

Figure 4.8

Time Estimates for Project Phases

Writing takes up less of the development process than you might think.

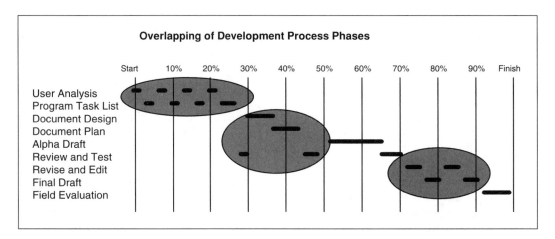

Figure 4.9

Overlapping Development Process Phases

Rarely do you complete one phase of development before starting another. This figure shows areas that usually overlap.

Aside from identifying the overall phases, your schedule should include dates for the following six kinds of events:

- Meetings
- Deadlines for drafts
- Project report due dates
- Test completion
- Review deadlines
- Edits

You should introduce your schedule, telling its purpose. Then you should create a table or tables to present the names of the events, known as project milestones, and their completion dates as illustrated in Figure 4.9. Your reader will examine your schedule for its completeness and its good sense. Don't, for example, expect a schedule of two days for a document review to get accepted—they take longer than that. In Figure 4.10 you will find explanations of the events you should schedule.

SCHEDULE MEETINGS. Meetings usually fall into two types: regularly scheduled ones to go over progress and problems with development or writing team members, and special meetings that occur at project milestones. Both types of meetings usually take about an hour. Agree on and include regular meetings in your schedule.

Special meetings involve other personnel associated with your project such as sponsors, programmers, and users. In scheduling special meetings, consider both the people who attend (and their possible schedule conflicts) and the purpose of the meeting. Usually the manager or supervisor will attend most meetings; Table 4.9 indicates attendees

Event	Start Date	End Date	Personnel
complete user analysis	*4/15*	*5/1*	*manager, writer, user group*
progress report		*5/15 (due)*	*manager*
write draft	*6/21*	*7/7*	*writer*
do user walkthrough (print) (meeting)	*7/12*	*7/12*	*user group, writer, editor*
do user walkthrough (online) (meeting)	*7/14*	*7/14*	*user group, writer, editor, test coordinator*
user walkthrough report		*7/16*	*manager*
technical review (meeting)	*7/15*	*7/15*	*programmer*
editing	*8/9*	*8/25*	*writer, editor*
. . .	. . .	. . .	. . .

Figure 4.10

A Table Shows the Schedule for a Project

Use a table similar to this one to help organize the events in your schedule.

whose input to the documentation process comprises the main reason for the meeting. In addition, all meetings should aim to increase communication generally and foster a team spirit. The "purpose" indicated in Table 4.9 tells what specific new information or chore the meeting focuses on.

SET DEADLINES FOR DRAFTS. Set the dates for your alpha draft and any other drafts for all documents. (Note: The day you will "complete" them is usually counted as the date when you will put them in the recipient's hands.)

SET PROJECT REPORT DUE DATES. Any development project requires some reports so others involved in the process can keep track of it. You, as a writer, benefit from this because those involved can see your work and approve it along the way. Report types (see Table 4.10) include the following: evaluation reports, progress reports, oral briefings, and test reports.

SET TESTS COMPLETION DATES. Tests fall into three categories: predictive tests, developmental tests, and evaluative tests. Predictive tests cover your design plans and documentation plans. They occur early in the process. Developmental tests cover elements of your document as you work on them. These occur while you write and the information feeds back into your continuing work. Evaluative tests occur after you have completed the document. Information from evaluative tests gets used in planning your next project.

Table 4.9

Kinds of Meetings Associated with the Documentation Process

Type	Attendees	Purpose
Review meetings	All persons who reviewed a draft	Go over the review information and resolve conflicts
User walkthroughs	Selected users	Go over the documentation design plans for suitability, ease of use, and usability
Technical walkthroughs	Programmers	Go over the program task list for inaccuracies, omissions, logic

Table 4.10

Kinds of Reports Associated with the Documentation Process

Report	Writer	Reader	Description
Evaluation	Team leader	Supervisor/ sponsor	Describes and evaluates work of team members
Progress	Writer/team leader	Manager/ client	Describes work to date and plans for completion
Test	Writer/tester	Manager/ writer	Describes the results of tests and recommends revisions
Oral briefings	Writer/team leader	Manager/ development team	Present new tasks, review progress, discuss team business

Depending on your documentation objectives, you may do more testing than this or less. Some solutions you design to meet objectives may end up more problematic than others. So if it appears that you may have some problematic elements in your design, your reader will want to see that you acknowledge this and have developed tests to assure that your designs will work.

ANTICIPATE REVIEW SCHEDULES. Reviews need special attention for scheduling because they take more time than other events. You have to really plan ahead for these. Depending on whom you choose to do your reviewing, you may have to set up times for the following: managers, users, technical personnel, attorneys, or clients/sponsors. Indicate on your schedule when you will put the documents in the reviewers' hands and when they will put the documents back in your hands.

If your program has more than one type of user (say both novice and experienced, or managers and technicians), you will probably want to get reviews from all types of users. The reader of your documentation plan will expect you to have anticipated this and scheduled it. Make your logic clear.

SCHEDULE EDITS. Edits focus specifically on your text. Usually you would edit after the alpha draft. If you arrange to have your work edited by someone else (a good idea), you should schedule this event carefully. Depending on the level of edit that your work requires, an edit may require more or less time.

JUSTIFY HUMAN AND MATERIAL RESOURCES. No project can move forward without human and material resources; you should plan yours carefully. When you present descriptions of what resources you will use to complete the project, consider that the sponsor or client who reads your documentation plan needs convincing that you have carefully planned and that the resources you specify will actually allow you to meet your documentation objectives.

- **Human resources.** Of course, your work makes up the main resource of a small project. Convince your reader that you realize this and have examined your human resources carefully, and that you know who you will have to involve in the project. Consider the efforts of the sponsors, users, testers, reviewers, and editors. They value their time, and their time adds to the value of your product. Plan wisely for their time on your project.

- **Material resources (computers and equipment).** Think through what machines you will use in a way that will benefit you and your reader. Assure yourself that the technology you will need will work and that you know how to use it. Consider and discuss what computers, printer(s), software, and "other" equipment (scanners, plotters, copiers) you will use. Explain your choices in a way that lets your reader know you have a valid plan.

Reviewing the Documentation Plan

Your documentation plan should undergo thorough testing and review by managers, clients, and users. Your coordinating editor, if you have one, should also examine your document plan. The design plan requires a much more extensive review than your user analysis received. The design plan review should cover the actual design of the document (pages, text, language, and other features) and the project plan (allocation of computer and human resources and scheduling of drafts and other production activities).

The documentation plan gives you the opportunity to hold a user *walkthrough* (going over the important design elements of your document) and a technical walkthrough (going over the accuracy and completeness of the program task list).

An Outline for a Documentation Plan

This chapter has presented many elements that could go into a documentation plan. Given the details of your project you may include all of them, invent some of your own, or only use a portion of them. The following outline will give you a start in putting together your documentation plan.

THE EXECUTIVE SUMMARY

■ One-sentence Purpose statement

■ List of primary users and user categories

■ List of the main elements of the documentation set

■ List of the deadlines for the alpha and final draft (and any other important dates)

OVERVIEW

■ Overview of the rest of the document

■ Overall goals of the documentation set: what kind of work will you support

THE DESIGN PLAN

■ Introduce the section

■ The Documentation Users. Describe users of the documents: one brief paragraph each, telling the following:
  1. Professional role
  2. User type
  3. Primary tasks
  4. Salient characteristics relating to:
     - Information needs
     - Computer experience
     - Subject matter knowledge
     - Workplace environment
     - Learning preferences
     - Usage patterns

■ Documentation Types. List each document giving the following:
  1. Title
  2. Kind of document (tutorial, guidance, reference)
  3. Media (print/online)

■ Outlines of Individual Documents. Give outlines of each individual document, including the following:
  1. Title
  2. Sections from cover/title page to index and all sections in between
  3. Estimated page length for each section

■ Layout of Individual Documents. List the following information for each individual document:
  1. Page size
  2. Column sizes
  3. Table sizes and styles
  4. Body text size, style, font
  5. Styles for sections, task names, steps
  6. Cuing patterns and notational conventions
  7. Binding and box specifications
  8. Special format or layout

THE PROJECT PLAN

Introduce the project plan, previewing its contents and sections: schedule, resources, time/page estimates, costs.

- Schedule. Paragraphs or a table detailing each of the following:
  1. Drafts: types and delivery dates
  2. Reports: types and delivery dates
     Report types may include: progress, evaluation, team briefings, walkthroughs, test reports.
  3. Tests: types and dates
     Types may include: predictive, developmental, or evaluative (see Chapter 11 for details on these types of reports.)
  4. Reviews: types and dates
     Types may include: managerial, user, technical, legal, sponsor/client (see Chapter 12 for details on these types of reports.)
  5. Edits: types and dates
- Resources. A paragraph or paragraphs detailing each of the following:
  1. Personnel resources: consider the efforts of all involved. Personnel include: sponsors, users, testers, reviewers, and editors.
  2. Computers and other equipment: think through the machines and software you'll need. Equipment resources include: printers, scanners, plotters, copiers, paper, ink, and software.
- Time/Page Estimates. A table or paragraph detailing the following:
  1. Total number of tasks and topics in each document
  2. Estimated average number of hours per task
  3. Grand total of hours for the project
  4. Total cost for the project

CONCLUSION

The conclusion usually summarizes and gives you a chance to reiterate that, given approval, you're ready to begin.

APPENDIXES

Put the following kinds of elements in the appendix:

- Pertaining to the program: The program task list
- Pertaining to the user:
  1. The transcript or report of the user analysis
  2. Task/user matrixes
  3. User scenarios
- Pertaining to the documents:
  1. Thumbnail sketches of pages and screens
  2. Sample pages
  3. Sample layout elements: tables, lists, etc.

Glossary

affordance: a capability of a program, or other technological device, to enable the user to take advantage of its functions. Examples of affordances of software programs include menus, toolbars, the cursor, and so forth.

authoring tool: a computer program that allows you to create a help system. Example: Hyper-Card or RoboHelp.

compiler: a type of program that creates other programs. Compilers read files of commands created by programmers and transform them into programs that users can run on their computers. If compiler programs can't create the program from the data files, they give a compiler error message, then the programmer has to fix the commands in the original file. Compiler programs contain many kinds of commands and other highly technical elements that need explaining in reference documentation.

documentation plan: a written document describing a manual or help system for a software program containing specifications for the document and a plan for creating it.

milestones: events in a project that indicate you have completed a phase. Often a milestone requires a written product, such as a report, and will entail a change in personnel (e.g., the project gets handed off to the editors).

multimedia: refers to a way of presenting information to a user, reader, or viewer that uses more than one method. This presentation method usually consists of video pictures, sound, text, and animation. Usually multimedia gets distributed on CD Rom disks because of the amount of space needed.

slippage: what happens to project schedules when programs and documents don't get done on time and everything gets delayed.

topic: in help systems, the basic unit of information. The topic can contain a step-by-step procedure, a definition, an explanation, or other useful information.

walkthrough: a kind of meeting where you step through a document or part of a document for the purpose of examining its design elements.

Checklist ✔

Use the following checklist as a way to evaluate the efficiency of your task descriptions and task list. Depending on the level of detail you choose for your list, some of these items may not apply.

Documentation Plan Checklist

The Overall Plan

☐ Does the documentation plan contain elements to ensure its persuasiveness? (executive summary, goal orientation, persuasive figures, team orientation)

The Design Plan

- ☐ Adequate user descriptions
- ☐ Objectives for the documentation set
- ☐ Descriptions of hard-copy and online documentation types
- ☐ Outlines of individual documents (task and topic groupings)

Specifies layout clearly for the following elements:

- ☐ page size
- ☐ columns
- ☐ tables
- ☐ body text style, size, font

- ☐ sections and headings
- ☐ task and topic names
- ☐ steps
- ☐ cuing patterns

- ☐ notational convention
- ☐ binding and packaging
- ☐ special layout

The Project Plan

Schedule includes all events occurring during the development process:

- ☐ Meetings
- ☐ Deadlines for drafts
- ☐ Project report due dates

- ☐ Test completion date
- ☐ Review deadlines
- ☐ Editing deadlines

Schedule includes the list of resources.

- ☐ Personnel
- ☐ Budgets
- ☐ Computers and other equipment

- ☐ Facilities
- ☐ Software
- ☐ Time/page estimates

Practice/Problem Solving

1. Reverse Engineering a Project

Reverse engineering means you take a product—a manual or help system—and examine the way the authors constructed it. You can do this with a manual for a program you work with. What user needs drove the design? What problematic stages would have presented themselves, and how did the writer overcome them?

To begin your study, imagine that your documentation department underwent a massive disk crash and lost the only backup copy of the documentation plan for the new accounting system. One morning you find a message on your email asking you to supply information about the documentation process on the new accounting system to make up a preliminary quality control inventory that's going on in your company. This means that they want the schedule and the project plan—resources, people, meetings—pronto. But the plan for the accounting system documentation went to bit-heaven last week when the disk went down. To make matters worse, you didn't work on the new accounting system, and as luck would have it, the person who did just left for a skiing vacation. Your only hope is to make it up!

Your first step in this practice exercise will be to select a manual to "reverse-engineer." You don't have to choose an accounting program manual as in the example. Any manual will do. Review the information about scheduling and project planning in this book, study the manual you have selected, and come up with reasonable answers to the following questions:

■ How long is the document?

■ How long did it take to create it from start to finish?

■ How much did the manual cost to produce?

■ What user needs drove the design of the document?

■ How many people worked on the document?

■ What testing or reviewing problems did the document offer?

■ What kinds of equipment did the writing team use?

■ What kinds of management reports, if any, did the writing team have to produce?

■ What kinds of meetings did the team hold?

2. Adapt Production Tasks to a Specific Solution

Study the list of tasks in Table 4.1 (pages 132–133). These tasks cover the design and production of a document set from scratch. However, many documents don't start this way, but from existing manuals that have become outdated because of revisions in the program or a need to be re-designed for greater task orientation.

Find a manual that you think could undergo this kind of revision. Maybe you would turn a system-oriented manual into a task-oriented manual. Or you might want to create a tutorial section that the previous document didn't contain. Perhaps you think the re-vised document should contain more graphics. Write out one or two goals you would have for your revision.

Then, try to imagine the production tasks that would be required for you imaginary revision project. You would follow the same nine phases as in Table 4.1, but you might add or change specific tasks within each phase. For example, under "Perform the User Analysis" you might want to add the task "Review the user evaluations of the previous release of the document."

Go over the list of tasks in Table 4.1, selecting those that would be appropriate to the revision project outlined above. Consider what tasks the revision project would en-tail, and add them to the list. Write a brief paragraph explaining and justifying the changes you made to the project task list.

chapter 5

Getting Useful Reviews

To review documentation, you send it out to get the reactions of other people. This chapter covers review procedures designed to provide information relating to the task orientation of your documents as well as to ensure their technical accuracy and conformance with company policy. It shows a page from a reviewed manual and an example of a review form you would use as a cover sheet for review copies. It details steps for planning and conducting reviews by users, managers, programmers, subject-matter professionals, and clients. It focuses on the review walkthrough as a way to gain specific information about the task issues your users face and to assess how well your document meets the needs of task-oriented employees.

How to Read This Chapter

All readers should study the examples and concentrate on Guideline 1: Review throughout the documentation process. No other technique ensures product success. Ongoing review keeps you on track and keeps managers, clients, and users informed and on board.

■ If you're working on a project, you should read the entire chapter. You may want to skim it in the early stages of a project, to get a sense of what's ahead, then read it in more detail later in the project when you have a first ("alpha") draft.

■ If you're reading to understand, you should study the Discussion section first in order to get a broad understanding of the process and its issues, then read the Guidelines as necessary.

Example

The *document review form* in Figure 5.1 illustrates a typical transmittal letter for reviews used at the Documentation and Training Center of Excellence (DTCE) at Texas Instruments

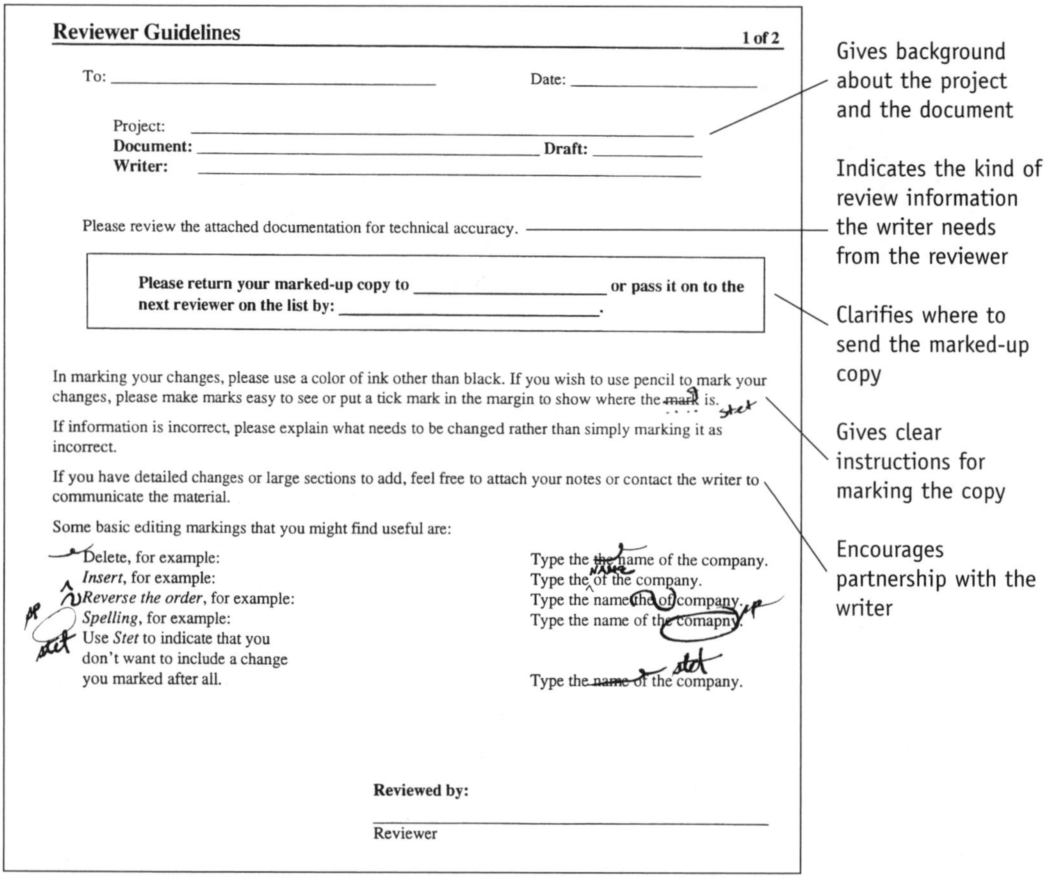

Reviewer Guidelines 1 of 2

To: _____ Date: _____

Project: _____
Document: _____ Draft: _____
Writer: _____

Please review the attached documentation for technical accuracy. ————

> Please return your marked-up copy to _____ or pass it on to the
> next reviewer on the list by: _____ .

In marking your changes, please use a color of ink other than black. If you wish to use pencil to mark your changes, please make marks easy to see or put a tick mark in the margin to show where the mark is.

If information is incorrect, please explain what needs to be changed rather than simply marking it as incorrect.

If you have detailed changes or large sections to add, feel free to attach your notes or contact the writer to communicate the material.

Some basic editing markings that you might find useful are:

Delete, for example: | Type the the name of the company.
Insert, for example: | Type the of the company.
Reverse the order, for example: | Type the name the of company.
Spelling, for example: | Type the name of the comapny.
Use *Stet* to indicate that you don't want to include a change you marked after all. | Type the name of the company.

Reviewed by:

_____
Reviewer

Annotations on form (right margin):
- Gives background about the project and the document
- Indicates the kind of review information the writer needs from the reviewer
- Clarifies where to send the marked-up copy
- Gives clear instructions for marking the copy
- Encourages partnership with the writer

Figure 5.1

The DTCE Review Form

This form from the Documentation and Training Center of Excellence at Texas Instruments, Inc. helps ensure accurate and consistent review information.

in Dallas, Texas. It represents one of a number of checklists and forms that managers at DTCE use to control their documentation process. The document review form in Figure 5.1 illustrates a number of factors that contribute to successful reviews. While technically you don't expect reviewers to edit a document the way a staff editor might, you realize that they will want to add, delete, and mark text. The form includes basic editing marks as a way of helping reviewers mark text consistently. Also, a reviewer's list (shown later in the chapter) accompanies the form. Forms like this are useful because they encourage accurate and specific information from reviewers. They indicate, through their professionalism, that the writer takes the reviewer's comments seriously as an added value to the documentation product.

Guidelines

Of all the activities associated with document production, reviewing may take more of your time and require more careful planning than any other. To make the most of your investment, approach the review stage with great care and with the attitude that the review can really increase the usability of your document. When you have to rely on users, managers, and technical experts to read your documents, you need to plan carefully how you will use their time. Following the steps shown in Figure 5.2 can help you get the most out of your review cycles.

1   Review throughout the Documentation Process

Often we think of reviewing as occurring only during the later stages of a project, after you have finished a complete alpha draft. In fact, that alpha draft can have fewer troubles along its way to becoming a final draft if you have taken time to have it reviewed at earlier stages. Reviewing as a part of the documentation process requires that you have some kind of document to send out. The earlier the stage of the process the more explanation you will have to provide about the background of the program and the project. You can find out about scheduling reviews and the place this schedule plays in your documentation plan by consulting the topic "Anticipate Review Schedules" in Chapter 4, "Planning and Writing Your Documents." Usually you can count on getting reviews at four key stages of the development process: after conducting the user analysis, after determining the task list, after designing the documentation set, and after writing drafts.

- **User analysis review.** If you have written up your audience analysis as a set of parameters, you should show them to your managers, clients, and users as a way of checking their validity and accuracy.

---

1. Review throughout the documentation process.

2. Write the review plan.

3. Review the document objectives from the documentation plan.

4. Determine the type of review needed.

5. Write a cover letter with questions for the reviewers.

6. Establish a review schedule.

7. Prepare feedback materials for reviewers.

8. See reviewers as partners.

9. Handle conflict diplomatically.

Figure 5.2
Guidelines for Managing Document Reviews

■ **Technical walkthrough.** Early in your development process you should validate the accuracy of your task list. A technical review with programmers, or a technical walkthrough (meeting to validate accuracy) can assure that you will get lighter markups on later technical reviews.

■ **Design review.** Your documentation plan should undergo thorough testing and review by managers, clients, and users. Your coordinating editor, if you have one, should also examine your document plan. The design plan requires a much more extensive review than you got for your user analysis. It should cover the actual design of the document (pages, text, language, and other features), and the project plan (allocation of computer and human resources and scheduling of drafts and other production activities).

■ **Draft review.** As opposed to a formal, scheduled review of your alpha draft of a document, you may want to schedule and implement draft reviews of parts of a document that have reached some milestone of completion: such as a portion of a tutorial, or an early draft of a quick-start section of a user's guide. Make sure you indicate in your cover letter what stage your document is in. Reviewers may take issue with some things (say the lack of adequate running headers and footers) if they don't understand that these elements won't get put in until a later draft.

2   Write the Review Plan

Your reviews will go more smoothly and produce better results if you plan them carefully and write up your plan. A well-articulated review plan has a number of advantages. It:

■ Encourages you think the process through by making it a goal-driven process

■ Acts as a communication device for review meetings: opens up the process to colleagues

■ Provides background material to help reviewers respond more productively

While it's not entirely linear, the process of setting up and executing specific reviews follows a fairly standard procedure. You can't fail if you follow the one suggested below.

1. Review the document objectives from the documentation plan.

2. Determine the type of review needed.

3. Write a cover letter with questions for the reviewers.

4. Establish a review schedule.

5. Prepare feedback materials for reviewers.

You will find more on how to follow this procedure in the guidelines below.

3   Review the Document Objectives from the Documentation Plan

As with all elements of document design for information-oriented work, you, like your users, should consider document objectives. Each kind of document you have (tutorial, user's guide, etc.) and each feature it has (elaborate background information, layered presentation of material, etc.) and its text and page design (columns, screen size defaults, etc.) result from a specifically articulated purpose. Your development team should have arrived at the purpose for your documentation set during the planning stage, and you should easily find those objectives in the documentation plan.

"Ha, ha, ha," you say, "We've flown on our seatpants the past few weeks, and we could probably find last month's pizza box before we'd find the documentation plan." You may experience this "let the documentation plan float over the falls" mentality. Fine. Here's what you do. You *make up* the documentation goals (remembering as much as you can from the original meetings about the product and extrapolating from the draft you have on your desk or in your computer). Goals become more readily apparent as the project progresses anyway, so don't pass up this opportunity to re-conceptualize. Besides, you need a set of objectives, as you will see below, to drive your design of your reviews.

Consider this example of document objectives and the questions they would pose to reviewers. The program Grabber captures screens and converts them into a variety of formats (GIF, TIF, BIF, BMP, PCX, etc.). The documentation plan for the Grabber *User's Guide* identified a number of objectives, listed in Table 5.1, with an explanation of how you would address them in reviews.

Document objectives also play a role as part of managerial review. Managers and supervisors review your documentation to make sure that it meets company policy and reflects well on the company. But they also have other responsibilities that relate to the documentation. Managers and supervisors need to review the existing documentation to verify that the features it implements carry out the objectives stated in the documentation plan. For these reasons, you should include those objectives in the review materials for them.

4   Determine the Type of Review Needed

The kinds of reviews you design will depend, in part, on the kinds of persons who have a stake in the documentation. These will include other members of the development team, or, in the case of technical writers doing independent contracting, programmers and clients. Each person on a team and persons sponsoring or paying for documentation represent a concern for the quality of the overall software product. Carefully planned reviews, like those described in Table 5.2, capitalize on the help you can get from these reviewers.

All reviews offer challenges and problems, because not all of the persons whom you need to do the reviewing may be at your job site, or they may lack familiarity with your project. All reviews challenge you because you need to focus the reviewers on the specific questions you want them to answer. But beyond that, the reviews present logistical problems that you must surmount. In Table 5.3 you will find some of the problems you might face with each type of review.

No two review situations present the same problems; however, you can bet that careful scheduling and planning will go a long way toward productivity in this stage of the documentation process. On the other hand, a haphazard approach can cost you your profit on a project.

5   Write a Cover Letter with Questions for the Reviewers

The key to getting useful information back from your reviewers lies in directing their efforts. If you just hand them a manuscript and ask them to read it over, you may get back a careful, studious review based on their responsibilities and expertise, but more likely

Table 5.1

Tie Document Objectives to Reviews

Examples of Objectives	Review Type	Questions Answered
Provide task-oriented examples of processed images	User	Do the examples reflect real-world tasks?
Encourage use of online help	User	Does the online help facility look usable or resemble others you have used?
Provide guidance to facilitate the easy translation of graphic file formats to desktop publishing programs	Technical	Do the translation procedures cover all supported formats?
Provide task-oriented guidance support for all program functions	User	Do the task names reflect workplace tasks?
Provide tutorial support for basic graphics conversion and basic screen capture	User	Do the tutorial lessons take up too much time for the normal user?
Provide extensive reference support for expert users in: 1) graphics file formats, 2) error messages, 3) frequently encountered image formats	Technical	Does the reference section cover all existing error messages and image formats?
Provide background information about graphic files and types	Subject Matter	Does the background section sufficiently explain graphics files?
Encourage efficient choices of file formats and conversion techniques	User	Do the examples of file formats match those you use in your work?
Support data transfer to programs users use most frequently	User	Does the manual need to cover data transfer to programs *not* mentioned in the manual?

you will get back a shallow reading focusing on idiosyncratic, arcane grammar rules the readers remember from college and doing you no real good. Garbage in, garbage out. Put clear directions for users in; get relevant information out.

To get relevant information out of your reviewers you should provide them with a cover sheet specifying the kinds of things you want them to examine and acquainting them with your project and your schedules. This letter has a huge job to do and should sound as professional as possible. The more you can convince your readers of the importance of the review and their contribution to it, the better their response. Compose your cover letter using the following guidelines:

■ **Indicate document objectives and benefits to the reviewer.** Tell the reviewers the objectives of the overall document; what specific kinds of work you want to sup-

Table 5.2

Types of Reviews

Type of Review	Persons Involved	Concern
Managerial review	Managers, supervisors, team leaders	Staying in budget, meeting document objectives, quality control
User review	Users, operators, system supervisors	Ease of use, applicability to task needs of empowered workers
Technical review	Programmers	Technical accuracy of procedures, coverage of functions
Subject-matter review	Professionals in a certain field	Accuracy of background information
Editorial review	In-house editors, team editor, writer in editor's role	Meeting standards of grammar, organization, format
Sponsor review	Client, sponsor	Meeting diverse user needs, getting value for money

Table 5.3

Problems Encountered with Reviews

Type of Review	Problem You Must Surmount
Managerial review	Making sure they review the document objectives, and see the document in the context of the whole software project
User review	Making sure reviewers represent the target users of the system
Technical review	Getting programmers to pay attention to a program they have stopped thinking about; getting them to care about something outside the technical area
Subject-matter review	Finding the experts in specialized fields willing to do the review
Editorial review	Making sure editors have a clear understanding of user needs
Sponsor review	Scheduling time with busy professionals

port; how the document and program will get used. Use a statement like "The overall objectives of this document include. . . ." Also, point out the benefits of the reader's participation in the review process. Your reviewer may enjoy specific benefits, but you can always point out these general ones to reviewers:

■ *Reviewers benefit from increased quality:* their work helps ensure quality documentation products. Reviewers need to know that their efforts add real value to your product.

- *Reviewers benefit from increased communication among company members:* their participation helps the company grow by departments sharing information. Reviewers need to know how the information they learn about your product can reflect on their own management concerns.
- *Reviewers benefit from increased visibility as team players:* employees like to create an image of themselves as cooperative and supportive. They need to know that you will alert their superiors as to their cooperation and the value they add to your document.

■ **Ask for specific advice/comments.** Tell the reviewer exactly what you want them to do: read the document and look at specific aspects of it pertaining to their expertise. This will forestall their focusing on editing details inappropriately. If you ask specific questions of your reviewers, you get usable answers. Examples include those indicated in Table 5.4.

■ **Provide the necessary background.** Where necessary, provide the appropriate background for your users so that they can respond better. Background can include a number of items, such as the following:

- Background about the *user:* review the user's task demands, computer proficiency level and user type, amount of subject matter knowledge the user has, other programs the user knows
- Background about the *project:* remind the user of the version and draft numbers, what department(s) and what people have committed to the project, the writer, the editor, the other reviewers
- Background about the *product:* list the main features of the product, platforms it runs on, relevant revision history of the product, current versions, how the product relates to other company products
- Background about the *subject matter* of the program: include definitions of key terms, brief overviews of the topic areas where necessary (how *project tracking* works, why do we want to model escaping gas from a chemical plant, etc.)

■ **Tell reviewers how to mark or comment.** Usually you only have to remind reviewers to make marks in the margins, and because you don't expect them to edit the document, you don't have to tell them how to make editing marks, such as insertion carets and delete marks. If you do, you might give a brief list of marks such as indicated in Figure 5.1. If you do a *sequential circulation,* you might want to ask the reviewers to use a certain color of ink to help you distinguish their comments from those of others. If they do their reviews online, ask them to include their initials with their comments so you will know who said what.

■ **Give dates and places for return.** You want your reviewers to get the document back to you on schedule, so tell them when you want or need their comments. Use a simple reminder like "To include your comments in the next draft I will need them back by. . . ." In some cases, with reviewers you know will put off reviewing or perhaps have difficulty meeting deadlines, you might offer to drop by their office to pick up the document. Tell them, "I'll be by next week to pick up the manual." This strategy helps them get ready in time and offers you a chance to discuss any troublesome areas that their review might have uncovered. Include the draft number and other details pertinent to the project.

Table 5.4

Sample Questions for Different Types of Reviews

Type of Review	Sample Questions
User	Does the table of contents reflect the order of tasks as you would perform them?
	Can you understand the example on page (n)?
	Does the binding and format make the document easy to use in your workplace?
	Do you think you will use the list of figures and list of tables, or do you think they could get left out?
	Take a look at the index: does it contain terms you would use in your daily work?
Managerial	In your view, does the document meet the objectives set out in the documentation plan?
	Does the document reflect the company and product favorably?
	Does the document meet all legal commitments required by our company?
	Does the binding and presentation of the document meet the standards for our other company publications?
Subject Matter	Does the document reflect the subject matter (e. g. accounting, statistics, geology) accurately?
	Does the glossary contain adequate and correct definitions of key terms? Can you add new ones?
	Do the examples used in the tutorial reflect realistic professional problems in the subject matter area?
Technical	Does the document reflect the functions of the program accurately?
	Does the *User's Guide* cover all the existing program functions?
	Have you added any new commands to the program since the release used to write this document?
	Have the installation steps changed since this version?
Sponsor	Does this document look like you thought it would look when you commissioned it?
	Do you think your managers and supervisors can use this document easily?
	Does the document present an accurate and acceptable representation of your company?

■ **Thank your reviewers.** Thank your reviewers for the time they have put into reading your document. Mention, in an email or written memo, the contribution they have made to your document's success.

Figure 5.3 shows a review sheet incorporating some of the guidelines in the previous paragraphs, but adapted to a specific situation.

6   Establish a Review Schedule

Scheduling a review means that you have to give your reviewers enough time to prepare their response, and you have to decide on the right circulation strategy. Make sure you give your reviewers enough time to fit the reading into their schedule of other projects. Reviewers may have to read all or parts of documents, and that takes time. A careful review takes about one hour per fifteen to twenty pages. When reviewers need to write extensive comments, that figure reduces drastically, to about five or eight pages per hour. Some reviewers may not need to read the whole document carefully: Managers, for instance, may only need to examine license agreements, and subject-matter professionals may only need to focus on certain parts containing overviews of topics.

Determine a Circulation Strategy

Circulation strategy refers to the way you circulate copies of your document to reviewers. You can choose one of two methods of circulating documents: *sequential,* where you send one copy to multiple reviewers, or *simultaneous,* where you send multiple copies to multiple reviewers.

Sequential Circulation

Sequential circulation entails making one copy of the document for each category of reviewer, then scheduling reviews for each reviewer in turn. Figure 5.4 shows an example of a cover sheet for a sequential review. Each reviewer reads the document and then either gives it back to you for you to give to the next person, or passes it to the next person for you.

ADVANTAGES OF SEQUENTIAL CIRCULATION

1. **Low cost.** The primary advantage of circulating sequentially lies in the cost. You only have to make one copy of a document, which can represent a significant savings on larger documents. At 5 cents per page, a 200-page manual costs $10 per document: a lot for a small project.

2. **Less hassle.** Sequential circulation may also save you by leveraging the reviewer's time and resources to circulate the document; they put it in the mail to the next person. Usually, with this method you attach a circulation list for each reviewer to check off his or her name in turn. This method works best when reviewers are near one another, such as in the same department.

3. **Encourages team spirit.** Sequential circulation requires each reviewer to see himself or herself as part of a team, as indicated by the list of other reviewers in the project. It's up to each person to contact the next reviewer or send it along, which may cultivate communication among the reviewers that ultimately could benefit the project.

REVIEW SHEETS
Document: *A Simple Introduction to PowerPlay Models*

These review sheets will make sure we agree on the design at this stage. It helps us both because it clarifies our understandings and assumptions. Important: the following represents rough material; please ignore typos but point out flaws in wording or concepts (such as if I call a "cat" a "dog").

Date sent: _____

Date I need your comments by: _____

Total sheets: _____

Background
Based on my notes of our last meeting, we agreed on the following:
  1 installation task
  3 program tasks involving opening and exploring 3 of the 6 models (other suggested and mentioned but not explored)
  • Two program tasks in graph format, one program task in cross-tab format
  • Each program task with different content:
      how to drill down to the SKU level
      how to use the add categories dialog box
      how to drag from the dimension line to the legend box.

My question: Do the tasks below cover these constraints, or do I go back to the drawing board?

  1. How to install the models

  2. Open, and explore a *2-year value trend* **graph** by dragging from the dimension bar to the legend box

  3. Open and explore a *2-year variance trend* **graph** by dragging and using the add categories dialog box

  4. Open and explore a *year-to-date sub-category report* in **cross-tab** by drilling down to the SKU level in a cross-tab format.

Reviewer Input
☐ Looks good to me
    Suggestions to guide the refinement of these basic ideas:

☐ Wrong track here
    (Specific revisions that require another review)

Figure 5.3

A Review Sheet Giving Specific Guidelines to the Reviewer

This document encourages the cooperation of reviewers.

<u>**List of Reviewers**</u>

When you have finished your review, please pass the attached document to the next person on the
review list.

Reviewer: _____
Date to complete review: _____
Date passed on: _____

Reviewer: _____
Date to complete review: _____
Date passed on: _____

Reviewer: _____
Date to complete review: _____
Date passed on: _____

Reviewer: _____
Date to complete review: _____
Date passed on: _____

Reviewer: _____
Date to complete review: _____
Date passed on: _____

Figure 5.4

Example of a Reviewers List for Sequential Circulation

This sequential circulation list from DTCE at Texas Instruments, Inc., a companion form to
the reviewer's guidelines form in Figure 5.1, tells readers where to send the document after
reviewing it.

DISADVANTAGES OF SEQUENTIAL CIRCULATION

1. **Spawns margin arguments.** Your document may spark arguments in the margins
   over certain features the reviewers encounter. While these arguments can enlighten
   you about the content, they can cause reviewers to ignore other important points.

2. **Early reviewers affect later reviewers.** One person's review may have an effect on
   subsequent reviewers. Say the first reviewer trashes your manual for an irrelevant reason (or because he or she hates your boss). That may cause remaining readers to lose
   their objectivity and result in a waste of time for you.

3. **Causes political problems.** It's often hard to say who gets the document first and
   who gets it later. The person last on the list may take offense at this, which may affect the outcome of the review.

4. **Hard to control.** When you depend on the reviewers to circulate the document, you
   are relying on the weak link in the chain. If one person lets your document sit on
   the desk for an extra week it can hurt your schedule.

5. **Takes extra time.** Circulating from one person to another means that some readers have to wait to get the document, and by the time it gets to them it may show signs of shop wear. Both of these facts can affect the reader's response.

Simultaneous Circulation

Simultaneous circulation entails making multiple copies of a document, one for each reviewer. Under this circulation method each reviewer gets a fresh copy, reads and records, and then gives it back to you.

ADVANTAGES OF SIMULTANEOUS CIRCULATION

1. **Fast.** With each person commenting on his or her own copy the process goes faster. You don't have to wait for the document to crawl from one office or cubicle to another or get lost in interoffice mail.

2. **Good for geographically diverse reviewers.** This method works well for circulating documents to reviewers at far-flung sites who would have to use the mail to send the document on.

3. **Fosters a one-on-one relationship.** This method makes reviewers feel special. Each person gets a fresh copy of the document and gives an individual reply that is unaffected by that of other users.

4. **Easy to control.** With simultaneous circulation you can track each document separately, and easily spot a review that is late. You can intervene by investigating and making adjustments (reminder memos, offers to help, reassignment of the review to someone with more time, etc.) to keep the whole schedule on track.

5. **Easy, when online.** Online documents can easily get circulated to more than one reviewer at a time because of the low cost of copying a document. Caution: Make sure the version you circulate doesn't get lost on someone's hard drive, only to crop up later and cause confusion with a later version.

DISADVANTAGES OF SIMULTANEOUS CIRCULATION

1. **Expensive.** With print documents you have to have a budget for duplicating in order to create the copies to circulate. Plus, you have to pay for mailing and duplicating cover letters. Bound documents add even more to the cost.

2. **Takes more of your time.** You may find yourself investing more time in duplicating and circulating documents simultaneously because you have to run the copy machine, make trips to the mail room, and dun your reviewers with reminders of deadlines.

3. **Fosters redundant comments.** With simultaneous circulation you may find all the reviewers spending time on one problematic element of a document. Had a previous reviewer already dealt with a problem and provided a suggested solution, the reviewer would know to move on to something the previous reviewer missed.

4. **Causes version mix-ups with online.** Unless you can control the access to your simultaneously circulated online help system, you may have trouble making sure that

reviewers read the most current version, and that all previous versions (containing potentially embarrassing mistakes) get deleted from people's hard drives.

7 ## Prepare Feedback Materials for Reviewers

Reviewers need to know that they count as partners in your documentation process. To foster this, show them that you read their comments and paid attention to them by making the required changes in the document. You won't and can't change everything a reviewer finds objectionable in a document. But a professional job of review management will certainly yield much useful information. Try to give some credit for that to each person on your review team. Let each person know the effect of his or her work on your project.

Memos and thank you letters work well for getting feedback to your reviewers. Refer specifically to items reviewers mentioned. You might not want to send them a whole new version of the document reflecting their comments, but you can photocopy the pages they marked significantly and attach them to revised pages, so the reviewers can see how you interpreted and acted on their comments. Remember that in most cases, as with user reviews or reviews by subject-matter professionals, you may not want their "approval" of your changes, as you might with a managerial or sponsor review. But it doesn't hurt to share your revisions with them.

8 ## See Reviewers as Partners

Good reviewing has to do with attitude: Reviewers can provide real help to your project. Imagine reviewing not as a chore, but as an opportunity to learn and get feedback and subsequently improve the task-orientation of your document. With the well-coordinated help of a series of reviews from users, managers, programmers, subject-matter professionals, and sponsors, you can't help but turn out a very high-quality, usable document. The first step in developing that attitude toward reviews comes with encouraging a sense of partnership among your reviewers. The following list outlines some techniques for fostering this kind of productive partnership.

1. **Tell them the benefits of participation.** Make sure your reviewers understand that they not only benefit you by reading your documents, but they also benefit themselves. A mutual benefit results in a win-win situation.

2. **Don't abuse the privilege.** Avoid going back again and again to a favorite reviewer because of his or her thoroughness. Make sure you get his or her permission before sending the document. Handle the whole process professionally because the offended or abused reviewer may have a long memory.

3. **Show them revisions.** Sharing revisions with reviewers can help them see themselves as co-writers or co-designers. If you have managed to get good feedback from reviewers, let them know how you used it.

4. **Hold review meetings or walkthroughs.** To encourage partnership with reviewers, call them together in a meeting and let them meet the other partners in the reviewing team. Plan the meeting well in order to foster a cooperative team spirit. Go

over the document, focusing on areas where you have questions about reviewers' responses or areas where you got conflicting feedback. This method works especially well for detecting technical errors early in the documentation process.

5. **Keep contact over time.** Keep in touch with good reviewers by keeping a file of information about the work they have done for you. This file can help you avoid over-using reviewers and help you establish long-term contacts.

6. **Return the favor.** Reviewing means often that you ask someone to read something without compensating them, as a favor to you. It's good business practice to return these courtesies in meaningful ways, like reviewing *their* documents or participating in activities that they sponsor within your organization, such as voluntary management meetings or focus groups.

7. **Thank them in print.** We have all seen passages at the prefaces of books where authors thank those who contributed to their manual. When you have the opportunity, list the names of those who reviewed for you. It doesn't take much room, and it demonstrates that you recognize the document reflects the best thinking of many thoughtful people.

9   Handle Conflict Diplomatically

Very often you will find yourself confronted with a conflict between reviewers and no easy way to satisfy both. For example, despite your document style guidelines, your reviewers may disagree over hyphenation in the word *online,* about the suitability of your examples, over the size of your page numbers or your style of numbering. In these situations you risk diminishing the productivity of your reviews if the conflict spirals. Keep in mind your goal of obtaining usable input from reviewers when reading the following example.

Example: We Don't Need Advertising in Documentation

You've just started in a new area of the company and have a draft of a *User's Guide* for a program that displays and plots scientific data. The users include scientists and engineers from various disciplines. You get the bright idea of supporting this diversity by including a list of the various disciplines with examples of how each could use the program. You circulate the document for review with special instructions for users to examine the list, and they all react favorably except one, who opposes the inclusion of all such information on the grounds that it represents "advertising." The argument she makes goes like this: "The user has already bought the software, so why include information to support the purchase? Get on to describing the program features." You have, unbeknownst to the reviewer, discussed the objection with your supervisor, who agrees with the other five reviewers that the information should stay in the document. What do you do?

One easy way out would simply require you to point out to this person that management approves the inclusion of the information and that's that. You can see that this won't work, because going over someone's head often leads to resentment and you need this person to review for you in the future. You could tone down the objectionable information, shortening the list of potential fields of application for the program, in an effort to appease the reviewer. But this option won't work either: You put a lot of research into the list, and it really does help potential users see how to apply the program (it meets one of your usability goals). Ignoring the problem won't make it go away: You meet with this person in weekly planning meetings and the issue will surely come up again. Force won't work: Not only do you need this person's buy-in to your design feature, you need this person to welcome the inclusion of this kind of information in the future.

Whenever you encounter conflicting views among your reviewers, you need to know, in detail, the substance of the conflict. Often one may have misunderstood the purpose of a design feature, and you can resolve the conflict by providing a clearer explanation. In the case above, schedule a one-on-one meeting with the reviewer, take the copy with the objection indicated, and get as detailed an explanation as you can.

Conflict also arises when more than one person disagrees over shared mutual goals. In the example described above, you both share the goal of producing usable documentation, but the reviewer's comments put you in a dilemma, caught between the document style guidelines and her disagreement. It's your problem, not hers. So describe your dilemma to her, and see if she has some ideas about how you should proceed. If you describe your options well, you may discover a solution you didn't think of before and one that satisfies both of you. Base the solution on shared goals you can both identify with. When you find yourself confronted with conflicting reviews that you cannot easily resolve, keep these principles in mind:

- Keep discussion focused on the document. Don't try to resolve existing political battles on your pages.

- Don't talk about reviewers to other reviewers. Treat each one as an individual with unique and valuable points of view.

- Avoid going over reviewers' heads. Forcing reviewers to adopt or assent to a strategy or design feature fosters resentment.

Discussion

All three functions of reviewing, testing, and editing represent the formal management procedures that constitute the quality control activities of your documentation project. In all three functions, your work gets scrutinized in specific ways for specific reasons, with the goal of improving the product.

Reviewing Defined

When you review, you send documents to other persons with cover sheets asking them to read or examine your materials and respond to issues in their area of expertise. Usually you do the following four types of reviews:

- **User reviews.** Reviews by the actual intended users of the document.
- **Management reviews.** Reviews by managers and supervisors associated with your documentation project.

- **Technical reviews.** Reviews by programmers and developers of the software.
- **Client reviews.** Reviews by the people or department paying for the software and documentation.
- **Subject-matter expert reviews.** Reviews by experts in the professional field represented in the software.

Some organizations include editors as reviewers and so would include an editorial review in the above list. In this book, editing is treated in Chapter 7, "Editing and Fine Tuning," and therefore is not included here, but you should realize that for many professional documenters the word *review* refers to editing as well as gaining comments from others on a draft.

Reviews can be classified according to when they occur in the documentation process. Thus we have the ***design review*** that asks managers, users, programmers, and others to respond to the documentation plan as a statement of the design of the document and the plan for producing it. We also have the ***document review*** that asks the same people to respond to the document as a whole, answering questions geared to their area of expertise and the documentation goals.

Reviewing Differs from Testing

The fact that reviews require comments from the array of persons listed above indicates one way they differ from testing (see Chapter 6, "Conducting Usability Tests"). Testing tends to concentrate on users and issues of usability. Reviews, on the other hand, develop information about conformance of a product to management schedules and company policy. Additionally, reviews don't produce evaluative data about a document. Reviews don't provide you with statistics about how accurately a procedure describes a function or how long it takes users to perform the function. Reviews produce comments, reflections from users about issues such as the suitability of an example or whether or not a task sequence matches a user's expectations. A test might tell you whether the access elements of a document (the index, the table of contents, and so on) helped users find specific information in a certain period of time. A review would provide you with a number of users' reactions to the format of the index or table of contents, from which you would make decisions on possible design changes. Finally, reviews don't occur in laboratories under controlled conditions. Reviews occur in offices and workshops of reviewers and usually take the week or so it takes to look over a whole document.

Reviewing Differs from Editing

When you circulate drafts for reviewing, you can expect to get information different from that you would get from an editor. Editors bring their training in editing to bear on your document, often using professional procedures such as the levels and types of edit described in Chapter 7. Reviewers, on the other hand, bring their professional training as managers, subject-matter experts, and programmers to bear on your document. Usually you submit a document once to a single editor; you may submit the same document to a number of reviewers, expecting to get different information back from each. With reviewing, you get more specialized kinds of information: on accuracy, suitability of information, compliance with management policies. While you may get some details of editing during your review process, usually you get responses and reactions to questions of suitability of an element or the usability of a specific feature.

The Purpose of Reviews

Reviews can serve a number of purposes in your project:

- **Communication function.** Reviews help you communicate with people associated with your project. If you work on a development team, reviews will reinforce the communication already set up and working among the other writers, the software developers and programmers, and the editors. If you work more or less on your own, reviews provide you with a way to share your work with others, to let them know what you're doing and to get their contribution.

- **Management function.** Reviews help you manage your project. Reviewing allows you to touch base with everyone's schedule and helps you keep your own production on track.

- **Quality assurance function.** Reviews help you maintain the quality of your product. Reviews offer you the opportunity to benefit from the insights of others concerned with usable documentation. Careful planning and preparation for reviews will reward you in helping you produce a better document than you could have without the review.

As you approach the task of having your documents reviewed, remember the main purpose of the process: to benefit from the reactions of others, with the aim of improving your work. Thus, when you plan your reviews, approach the job with the right attitude: that what users say about your document can help you shape it to meet the two goals of ease of use and usability. Reviewers represent workplace perspectives: those of clients, of subject-matter professionals and especially of users. Use their knowledge and energies to help make the document better. Empower your reviewers by telling them your shared organizational and professional goals and letting them benefit from helping you achieve them.

Do a User Walkthrough

Of all the reviews you do, the user review will contribute most to helping you meet the task needs of employees. Technical and management reviews focus mainly on accuracy and conformance with company publications and other policy. The kinds of information illustrated in the following list can only come from actual users.

- Does the document reflect recognizable workplace tasks?
- Does the background information support users' actual tasks?
- In what order do you think you would use the parts of the document?
- Are any important tasks omitted or treated inadequately?
- What tasks does the document not focus on that you find important?

■ Does the document accurately reflect your workplace goals?

■ Does the tone of the document suit your reading preferences?

■ Does the document support your information processing?

A Walkthrough Integrates the Documentation Team

To get this kind of information in a brief and very effective way, consider a user walkthrough. In a user walkthrough, you summon and meet with a group of your users for the purpose of going over the document from front to back, asking questions like those listed above, recording responses, and making changes on the spot. The concept of a walkthrough meeting developed out of writers' needs to keep technical reviewers focused on technical accuracy rather than editorial elements (spelling and punctuation), and from the need to resolve technical issues quickly and definitively. Writers who have used technical walkthroughs find that they give their users a sense of participation in the writing process, and they constitute an efficient way to obtain a large amount of information quickly. They report that, after a technical walkthrough, their conventional reviews turned up many fewer errors in the documents.[1]

As in the case of a technical walkthrough, a user walkthrough can keep users focused on the important issues of ease of use and task orientation. Also, a technical walkthrough allows you to get a lot of information in short amount of time about how well your document meets user needs. And because individually-circulated reviews often take so much time and present such scheduling challenges, you should consider the user walkthrough as an efficient way to bypass the hassles of circulation and still increase the task-orientation of your design.

How to Set Up a User Walkthrough

To set up and conduct a user walkthrough requires some planning. Overall, you should follow this process:

1. **Decide on the issues you want to examine.** You want to make sure you have the correct task orientation in your manual or help system. Look over your documentation plan and identify questionable areas. Prepare a meeting agenda based on these; prepare specific passages or document sections to present for user approval.

2. **Choose the attendees.** Select your meeting attendees carefully so they represent your actual users. Contact the users you discovered during the user analysis (see Chapter 2, Guideline 1 "Chose Reviewers Carefully"). You may also want to invite development sponsors or clients, who often have insights into workplace applications. Often these people represent your users' executives or managers, who have a concern for the user's workplace objectives. When you have distinct user groups, such as a teacher group and a student group, you may want to hold separate meetings.

3. **Make copies for all attendees.** During the walkthrough, you want all your attendees to have their own copy of the document, and preferably to have looked it over ahead of time. However, if you have clearly focused questions and representative sections to examine, you can probably conduct the meeting without requiring attendees to read ahead of time.

4. **Run the walkthrough.** The writer leads the walkthrough. Begin by announcing the agenda, which will keep the group focused on the issues you need to try to resolve. Make it clear that you welcome editorial comments (on spelling and punctuation) on later drafts and that attendees will have a chance to comment on that later. Go through the document section by section or part by part, focusing on key examples, page designs, cuing patterns, and user scenarios that you want your users to comment on. Record comments on a master copy of the document and remind attendees that they will receive a copy of it later. Allow attendees to discuss and try to resolve issues that come up.

5. **Do a follow-up review.** After the meeting, send copies with the suggested changes to users after the meeting. Again, remind them of the key issues you want to resolve in your document, and solicit comments.

The user walkthrough takes extra effort, but offers a number of advantages for writers and users. It allows users to have a say in the development of the documentation, and it allows you to gain valuable insights into the workplace usability of your document. Carefully planned and conducted, user walkthroughs can result in fewer negative comments on subsequent reviews.

Glossary

design review: a review that focuses on planning the design specifications for the document. It covers preliminary layout and overall document set design.

document review: a review that focuses on a draft of the finished product and whether or not it met the design goals set for it.

document review form: a transmittal document that you attach to the front of review copies, providing guidelines for the reviewer to follow.

sequential circulation: sending documents for review by giving it first to one reviewer, then another, then another through a sequence until all reviewers have read the same document.

simultaneous circulation: sending documents for review by giving each reviewer his or her own copy and having all the reviews done at once.

Checklists

Review Planning Checklist

Use the following checklist to help you plan for your reviews.

Document Objectives

☐ List the objectives from the documentation plan that you need to validate through your review.

☐ Review product specifications from the client or sponsor for objectives.

☐ List management or policy objectives your document must meet.

Stage of the Document Process

☐ User analysis review: Review user descriptions and scenarios for use in tutorials and as user role models.
☐ Technical walkthrough: Review the task list.
☐ Design review: Review or walkthrough design principles for the project.
☐ Draft review (draft 1, draft 2, etc.)

Type of Review Needed

☐ Managerial review (managers, supervisors, team leaders)
☐ User review (users, operators, system supervisors)
☐ Technical review (programmers, developers)
☐ Subject matter review (professionals from representative fields)
☐ Editorial review (staff editors, editorial department, team editor)
☐ Sponsor review (client, sponsor)
☐ Identify any special issues to address or problems encountered with any of the above reviews.

Cover Letter with Questions for the Reviewers

☐ Indicate document objectives and benefits to the reviewer (increased quality, increased communication, increased visibility as team players).
☐ Ask for specific advice and comments.
☐ Provide the necessary background (user, project, product, subject matter).
☐ Tell reviewers how to mark or comment.
☐ Give dates and places for return.
☐ Thank your reviewers.

Set Up a Review Schedule

☐ Sequential circulation (one copy: each reviewer passes the document to the next)
☐ Simultaneous circulation (multiple copies: each reviewer returns the document to you)

Feedback Materials for Reviewers

☐ Clean copies showing revisions with specific pages indicated (smaller projects)
☐ Copies of pages containing revisions stapled to copies of pages with reviewer's marks (larger projects)

User Walkthrough Planning Checklist

Use the following checklist to help you plan for your user walkthroughs.

☐ Decide on the issues you want to examine (write the agenda).
☐ Choose the attendees.
☐ Make copies for all attendees.
☐ Run the walkthrough.
☐ Do a follow-up review.

Practice/Problem Solving

1. How Would You Design a Review Questionnaire?

Recently I came across this message from a technical communicator discussing the review program at one organization. The message suggests some of the things documenters can do in conducting field evaluations.

> Date: Wed, 23 Nov 1994 08:47:20-0800
> From: Trevor Grayling <TREVOR@MDLI.COM>
> Subject: Re: Measuring Doc. Quality?
>
> Karen:
>
> RE your message (appended below):
>
> My company has a simple approach to measuring documentation quality: Quality is defined by our customers. That is, if our documentation end-users say that the documentation is good, then it is good.
>
> This requires us to ask our end-users for their feedback, for which we conduct phone surveys. We get an in-house statistician to tell us what a statistically-significant sample size would be, and then we phone that number of end users.
>
> The documents we last surveyed were a Tutorial and a task-oriented Reference for a Windows-based drawing program for drawing chemical structures. The goal of the documents, as defined in the doc plan, was to get the average user "up and running" and able to draw the chemical structures they were interested in with only occasional reference to the Reference manual for those more obscure functions not covered in the Tutorial.
>
> Trevor Grayling
> Manager, ISIS End-User Documentation
> MDL Information Systems, Inc.
> trevor@mdli.com   (used with permission)

Given these goals, what questions would you want to ask users about the tutorial and the reference? Make up your version of a short questionnaire. What tasks would the team have to undergo in doing the review? Write a brief, one-page report about your ideas.

2. Associate Types of Feedback

As you know, testing, reviewing, and editing address different aspects of a document's quality as a tool designed for access to information. For practice in managing this kind of information, consider a manual that you know well, such as one you did for a previous project or one you might currently have on the drawing board. Or, find a manual off a shelf of manuals and consider it for this exercise.

Look the manual over and put yourself in the manager's position. Undoubtedly the nature of the software and the software's users—needs, experience, and so on—will result in some quality issues. For instance, the program might require writing for two audiences simultaneously, or the program may deal with arcane and complicated subject matter.

Consider this example: a program that manages a stamp collection called "Stamp-Master." This program logs, tracks, and calculates the value of stamp collections. It also contains reference information about stamps and stamp collecting for beginners.

Here's a list of problems and issues that the program raises:

- How much background information about stamps should the program give the user?

- How many examples should the sample database contain?

- Does the user's guide comply with the company image of a trendy, specialty producer?

- Should the manual contain a list of Web sites pertaining to stamp collecting?

- Should the documents contain methods of using the program for unintended purposes (such as for a coin collection, or butterfly collection)?

- Is the manual technically accurate?

- What terminology should the document use in referring to the technical aspects of stamp collecting?

Which of these problems pertain to your testing efforts, your reviewing efforts, and your editing efforts? Which method of assessment would help you solve which problems?

chapter

6 Conducting Usability Tests

Testing documentation consists of procedures for gaining empirical data about the usability of documentation products. This chapter covers three basic types of tests: tests for task performance, tests for understanding, and tests for access to information. It recommends a ten-step test plan covering the main tasks you will need to perform when conducting usability tests for both small and large projects. The guidelines and discussion focus on the importance of user testing and emphasize three types of field testing to ensure task orientation. Additionally, the chapter discusses ways of interpreting user test data.

How to Read This Chapter

- If you're working on a project, you can adapt the procedure test form in Figure 6.1 to your immediate needs. If you plan to conduct extensive testing, you should read the whole chapter. Guideline 1, in particular, can help you plan extensive tests.

- If you're reading to understand, you should study the procedure test form in Figure 6.1, and then refer back to it as you read the Discussion section. This will provide the needed overview of the process so that you can use the Guidelines effectively.

Although this chapter discusses a variety of test forms, the one in Figure 6.1 covers many of the points you want to look for when evaluating procedures (or other step-by-step documentation.) As this chapter suggests, you should adapt this form, and others, to the specific needs of your documentation project. I would like to thank Mr. Mac Katzin, author and technical communicator, for the inspiration for this form.

 **Guidelines**

Figure 6.2 lists guidelines for testing documentation.

1 FOLLOW A TEN-STEP TEST PLAN

Your tests will go more smoothly and produce better results if you plan them carefully. While not entirely linear, the process of setting up and executing specific tests follows a fairly standard procedure. You can't fail if you follow the one suggested on page 198.

Procedure Test Form

Part 1: Information about the procedure and document being tested

Document title:

Procedure name:	Section #:	Page #:

Part 2: Information about the evaluator

Your name (or evaluator number):

Exact start time (hour/minute/second):	Exact end time (hour/minute/second):

Thank you for helping to find out how well this procedure works. Follow the steps as carefully and as far as you can, and then record your experience. Take your time. When you're ready, fill out Part 3.

Part 3: Evaluation of the procedure

Progress

☐ got to the end	☐ got to step #:

Steps

☐ OK	☐ out of order	☐ inconsistent	☐ incomplete

Indicate which steps need correcting:

Graphics/screens

☐ OK	☐ showed the wrong thing	☐ too small	☐ confusing

Indicate which graphics/screens need correcting:

Explanations

☐ OK	☐ incorrect	☐ not clear	☐ not relevant	☐ not enough detail

Indicate which explanations need re-writing:

Terms

☐ OK	☐ not clear	☐ too technical	☐ too simplistic	☐ too cute

Indicate which terms you had problems with:

Comments that might clarify your experience/reaction to doing the procedure:

Figure 6.1

A Procedure Test Form

You can use a form like this to test procedures. It helps the evaluator focus on the document rather than his or her performance.

1. Decide when to test.

2. Select the test points.

3. Choose the type of test.

4. Set performance objectives.

5. Select testers and evaluators.

6. Prepare the test materials.

7. Set up the test environment.

8. Record information accurately.

9. Interpret the data.

10. Incorporate the feedback.

Decide When to Test

You can test at any time during the nine stages of the documentation development process, even though stage six (review and test) focuses on testing (see Chapter 4, "Planning and Writing Your Documents"). Usually you test after you have a draft finished, can see areas that need testing, and can still make changes. But, as Table 6.1 shows, you can test at roughly three stages: during design, during writing or development, and after the document set goes to the customer.

Select the Test Points

Test points fall into three areas: procedures (tasks), terminology, and document design.

Select Tasks

To select tasks, follow the guidelines below. Identify what tasks you want to test by looking at the points in your documentation set where you perceive either a high *chance* of user failure, or a high *cost* of user failure.

HIGH CHANCE OF USER FAILURE.   There may be a high chance of user failure. When the procedure falls into one of the following categories, seriously consider taking the advice offered below:

■ **Complex.** Test tasks involving large number of steps and many subtasks.

■ **One-of-a-kind.** Test installation and configuration tasks that persons might only do once or might have done and forgotten.

1. Follow a ten-step test plan.
2. Tie testing to document goals.
3. Do some pilot testing.
4. Make the test *objective*.

Figure 6.2

Guidelines for Testing Documentation

Table 6.1

Decide When to Test

Development Phase	Kind of Test	Description
Phase 3: Design	Predictive	Done at the design stage to test the suitability of design specifications and production goals. High degree of flexibility in making changes based on results.
Phase 5: Writing/Drafting	Remedial	Done while drafting or writing. Corrections made immediately and re-tested. Moderate degree of flexibility in making changes based on results.
Phase 9: Field Evaluation	Evaluative	Done after finishing and shipping a product. No chance to change the existing product. Changes have to wait for the next release.

- **Highly abstract or technical.** Test difficult tasks, such as higher-level programming functions, advanced graphics processing, and importing files from other applications.

HIGH COST OF USER FAILURE. A user failure may be costly; in the following situations, the advice offered is based on much experience:

- **History of support needs.** Test the procedures for certain tasks that seem to provoke a large number of expensive support calls. Check with technicians and phone support personnel to identify these.[1]
- **User runs a risk of damage to data or data loss.** Test all procedures involving file deletion, maintenance of data files, and storage. User mistakes in this area could cost time and money.

Look for specific places in your documents where a mistake on the user's part could cost time (by causing other errors) and reduce efficiency (by forcing the user to do it the hard way). Here you want to review your document goals and any important, information-oriented tasks. For example, a documentation system that supports information transfer and storage should be tested to ensure that procedures for those information-related tasks contain no errors. Such tasks include:

- Importing information from other programs
- Creating, naming, and formatting files
- Exporting information to other programs or other program formats
- Creating printouts and reports

Test Terminology

Identify what terminology you want to test by looking at the points in your documentation set where you perceive the following:

- **Novice users.** Test all technical terms (computer terms) to make sure they are clearly defined.

- **Users needing subject matter support/background.** Test all subject-matter terms to make sure they are clearly defined.

Test Your Document Design Strategies

Identify what document design strategies you want to test by looking at the points in your documentation set where you perceive the following:

- **An index.** Test an index for consistent, recognizable terminology

- **Cuing patterns.** Test icons and labeling graphics that might confuse; or test potential graphical items for recognizability

- **Headings/layout.** Test for headings too small to see, layout that hides key information

- **Navigation.** Test for navigation that doesn't match the user's usage pattern

- **Extraordinary document formats.** Test for special conditions. Waterproof, fireproof, or childproof documentation should be subjected to these conditions for testing navigational aids.

Choose the Type of Test

The three types of tests indicated in Table 6.2 relate to the test points you identified in the previous stage.

Set Performance Objectives

Because you want your tests to measure actual behavior, you must come up with numbers that correlate with the kind of performance you want from your users. Performance objectives simply put numbers on that behavior. Often called *operational definitions*, performance objectives state, in clear terms, how long or what frequency of correctness we

Table 6.2

Match Types of Tests with Test Points

Test Point	Type of Test	Description
Tasks	Can-They-Do-It Test	Often called a *performance test,* this test requires users to perform a procedure.
Terminology	Can-They-Understand-It Test	Often called an *understandability test,* this test requires users to provide a summary of material they have read, or provide definitions of key terms.
Document Design Strategies	Can-They-Find-It Test	Often called a *read-and-locate test,* this test requires users to use mocked-up portions of a manual—the index or table of contents—to find information on key topics.

can expect users to perform software tasks. Often testers refer to performance objectives as *exit criteria* because performance objectives specify the criteria that a task must meet to exit from the testing situation.

A number of methods exist for coming up with performance objectives. With performance tests, you can simply measure your own speed or pace in actually performing procedures. Then, given what you know about your user, compare the time he or she would take to the time you take. This little exercise can help you establish the rate of performance to specify in the performance objective. Other methods of setting performance objectives include surveying potential users to determine how long they would take to do a task, or piloting the test with actual user. But the trial and error method works for most cases. Above all, you want to arrive at numbers that you can measure and compare. Table 6.3 illustrates some types of performance objectives.

Select Testers And Evaluators

Selecting *testers* may boil down to selecting yourself. On the other hand, you may increase your objectivity if you devise test materials for someone else to administer. That way you help eliminate the bias you will probably have for the test to come out positive for your materials. Often you can trade favors with other writers or development team members to obtain unbiased testers.

Selecting *evaluators* poses some interesting problems. If you began incorporating your users into the development process back when you did the user analysis (Chapter 2, "Analyzing Your Users"), then you have already lined up some potential evaluators among those you interviewed then. Let's be practical. You may not have actual users, or even potential users at your disposal—ready to spend one to five hours helping *you* do *your* job—

Table 6.3

Ways to Set Performance Objectives

Kind of Objective	Description	Example
Time-related	Time taken to perform a procedure	The user can install the program in under five minutes.
	Time taken to find a topic	The user can locate the import function in under one minute.
Error-related	Number of errors made during a procedure	The user can perform the procedure with a 20 percent error rate.
	Number of times a passage gets re-read before comprehending	The user can paraphrase the meaning of *field variables* after one reading.
	Number of tries in the index	The user can find the **Remove** function in under three tries.

so you will have to compromise. In Table 6.4, you will find an overview of potential situations and some suggestions for coping with them.

Prepare the Test Materials

Depending on the complexity of your test the written and other materials you supply for testers and evaluators can get very complicated. You will probably not use all these materials for your test, unless you plan to set up a testing lab, or temporary testing lab. For an informal field evaluation you would only use some of the test materials. In Table 6.5, you will find a list of kinds of test materials and definitions indicating when you might want to use them.

Along with written test materials, you need also to pay attention to the location of the test and the kinds of hardware and software equipment you require. Table 6.6 lists and describes most of the materials needed for testing.

Set Up the Test Environment

The environment for your test may range from the user's work environment (the field) or a controlled laboratory. Your best chance to learn about actual use in the context of the user's

Table 6.4

Ways to Compromise on Evaluators

Evaluator	Characteristics	Suggestions
Actual users	A given user type (novice, experienced, or expert)	No compromise necessary.
	A given degree of subject-matter knowledge	
Similar to your actual users	Same user type but lacking in subject-matter knowledge	Acquaint the evaluators with the major uses of the software.
		Have the evaluators read your user scenarios for background.
Not similar to your actual users	Different user type and lacking in subject-matter knowledge	Acquaint the evaluators with the basics of the software if they need to test advanced tasks.
		Remind them that they should assume the role of novice if they need to test basic tasks.
		Acquaint the evaluators with the major uses of the software.
		Have the evaluators read your user scenarios for background.

Table 6.5

Kinds of Written Test Materials

Test Material	Description and Use
Evaluator selection survey	A brief list of questions that potential evaluators fill out to ensure that they meet your profile as typical users. The selection survey should include a user *Permission To Participate Form,* with provisions for permission from the user's employer when needed.
Instructions for evaluators	A one-page list of instructions to help evaluators understand their role and what they should do during and after the test.
Test schedule	A schedule of testing times and locations for testers and evaluators to follow.
Instructions for testers	A set of instructions telling the test monitors how to conduct the test and how to record information. May also include operational definitions of key terms such as "error," or "success."
Test lab procedures	A set of instructions for operating the testing facility that expresses its purpose and policy of fair treatment of evaluators.
Pilot tests	Mock-up versions of test forms to try out as a way of determining how well the test works and the suitability of the performance objectives.
Test forms	Actual tests written up as test scenarios (suggesting job-roles for evaluators) task descriptions (telling evaluators what to do) and/or procedures (portions of hard-copy and online documentation products).
Test subject materials	Actual copies of documentation—hard-copy and online tutorials, procedures, and reference manuals—that the test intends to evaluate.
Software overviews	Marketing or overview information that informs evaluators of the main uses and features of the documentation they will use.
Test results records form	Charts and tables with spaces for testers to record results of task performance times, error rates, location names.
Exit interview questions	A brief schedule of interview questions for evaluators after the test, designed to gather incidental but potentially important information.

work and information environment comes from field testing. But, if you have one available, the laboratory offers you a greater degree of control and you may find it more convenient. Assuming you have a choice, Table 6.7 will help you decide where to perform your tests.

Researchers with experience in usability testing often recommend a combination of testing methods as a part of a complete usability program.[2] Using different methods independent of one another can help ensure a clear understanding of usability. Besides

Table 6.6

Kinds of Hardware and Software Test Materials

Material	Description And Use
Tape recorder	A portable mini-recorder used to record the evaluator's spoken comments during the test procedure.
Notebooks	Regular letter-sized notebooks for taking notes on the evaluator's behavior during the test and interview after the test.
Evaluator face camera	A VHS camera used to record and time the evaluator's eye movements from the manual or help screen, to the keyboard, to the screen, etc.
Evaluator keyboard camera	A VHS camera used to record and time the evaluator's use of the keyboard, mouse, light pen, digitizer, or other input device.
Screen camera	A VHS camera used to record and time the state of the evaluator's computer screen and use of online help.
Intercom	A portable walkie talkie or AC-Line intercom used to communicate with the evaluator during the test, if necessary, from an observation room.
Tables/chairs	Office furniture used to simulate the user's work environment.
Computer(s)	PCs, terminals, printers, modems, phone and network connections needed to simulate the user's computing environment.
Sample data files	Software-related files containing mocked-up data for use during the test.
Timing clock	A stop-watch or specialized clock for recording start, stop, and elapsed times for evaluator's test performance.

providing information about tasks for a specific product, you can use field testing to help establish test points: features that you want to examine more closely in the lab. Conversely, field testing can help to validate results that you discover after having done strict lab research.[3]

Record Information Accurately

As you conduct the test, you need to use accurate methods of recording what you see and hear. Your observations serve to flesh out what the cameras and other equipment records. For this reason, you should observe some guidelines in recording information. Synchronize your timing with the recorders so that you know when an event happened. That way, if the voice recorder, say, indicates a pause in the tape, you can go back to the same place in your notes and see what you recorded the user as doing at that time. Take copious notes, even of things that don't seem, at the time, to pertain to the evaluator's performance. Later these details can help you relive the event and interpret the results. Unless

Table 6.7

Advantages and Disadvantages of Various Testing Environments

Environment	Advantages (Lead to Clear Results)	Disadvantages (Lead to Mixed or Ambiguous Results)
Field (user's workplace)	Irreplaceable similarity to actual work demands	Intrusive in the user's workplace Less control over interruptions
Lab (documentation, software, hardware usability lab)	Controlled and consistent testing Better recording equipment Trained testing personnel	Lacks similarity to actual user's environment More expensive
Combination	Pilot testing done in lab can lead to better field results	Requires setting up two test events (expensive)

it would crowd the scene, invite disinterested observers to watch your tests. Their perspective can help you by reinforcing what you saw or filling in the gaps you missed.

Interpret the Data

Interpretation requires you to take into account all the elements that can go wrong with testing so that you get clear results. Seasoned document tester from IBM Roger Grice points out a number of variables that can have the effect of clouding the data. Table 6.8 summarizes those variables.[4]

Interpretation requires, of course, more than just calculating the data and making the changes that you can justify by the numbers. It requires that you make commonsense decisions about your manual design, so that the changes make sense to you and to others involved in development. In fact, most of the results that require a change in the design—changing a cuing pattern, adjusting the format of a table of contents—should appear clear from the test. A good test shows you what you should have seen anyway, and what makes sense after the numbers direct your attention to it. It should reveal something about your users, a missing piece of the puzzle of their usage and application of the program that you didn't know, that helps you make an intelligent design choice.

On the other hand, numbers can have great persuasive force with some technical audiences. A software usability specialist once confessed that he liked to record a problem with a program interface at least ten times, so that he could show it to the programmers. In this case, the sheer numbers of persons having difficulty with a part of their design helped convince them of the need to change. You may find yourself in a meeting with development team members for whom a satisfying flourish of numbers can help support your case.

Table 6.8

Variables Affecting Test Results

Variable	Description	Example
Halo effect	One detail of the testing procedure affects the entire test	In testing at the CIA you discover that the presence of cameras makes evaluators nervous. Tester's disdainful attitude causes evaluators to screw up intentionally.
Results not clear cut	Widely varying results	All three evaluators use different methods of finding a key term.
Wrong performance objectives	Evaluators perform a flawed procedure flawlessly	Evaluators take one minute to perform a procedure you thought would take two minutes but which actually should only take half a minute.
Unexpected factors	Chance details about the evaluators cause difficulty in performing otherwise easy procedures	Users are used to having color in manuals and yours are black and white. The evaluators you picked have an emergency meeting so the department sends you three substitutes named Larry, Curly, and Moe.

Incorporate the Feedback

No testing does you any good unless you incorporate the information into the design of the documentation product. Ideally, your testing produced such useful results that you could make the suggested change, and then re-test a few times with consistently positive results. However, you may only obtain partial results, in which case you analyze them reasonably, make the changes you think they imply, and get on with the project.

2   TIE TESTING TO DOCUMENT GOALS

In testing your documents, you'll have to find what parts you want to test. The sad fact that you can't test all your procedures leads you to this conclusion. You don't have time, and not all of your procedures, tutorials, and references need testing. As you have seen in the previous guideline, the objectives you set for your manuals and online help can guide you to test points. Your document objectives state how a manual or help system applies the program to the user's work environment. Focusing on objectives can help you maintain a view of the program in the user's workplace and give parameters for your test efforts. Also, the document features that you identified during the user analysis probably need testing. In general, whatever you try out as new, as innovative, or as different—which should make up a lot of your efforts—should get tested.

What drives you to design different formats or incorporate different strategies? Often you have to support more than one user of a program, and that leads you to try out innovative formats. Sometimes you realize that users of your program need more background material than you've given them, and you need to find out just what terms your target audience does and does not understand. Whenever you go out on a limb with your designs—set challenging objectives for yourself—you need to test.

3 DO SOME PILOT TESTING

Pilot testing means that you test the test. It's a way of reviewing your test, trying it out in a kind of dry run, to see if your testing materials will gather the kind of information you want them to. When you consider the ways that a misunderstood term or the omission of a detail can ruin the data you get, it just makes sense to administer a draft of your test to one or two representative users and then revise it.

Pilot testing doesn't require a lot of extra effort, and it provides a wealth of information to help your final version work better. For one thing, you can try the test out on a very small population and get their response. Suppose you're asking users to record information on a form. Do a dry run to find out if the kinds of tasks you ask about actually get performed by your users. Or you can make sure that you have given clear instructions to your evaluators. In general, pilot testing can help you in the following areas:

- **Instructions.** Do the guidelines you give to evaluators allow them to perform the test correctly?

- **Terminology.** Do you use any terms the user can't understand?

- **Timing.** Can the user perform the test in the time you have allotted.

4 MAKE THE TEST *OBJECTIVE*

Objectivity in testing means that you try to set up the test in such a way that you don't prejudice the outcome too much, so that the procedures don't "pass" automatically or the document doesn't come out with flying colors to let you get on with the project. While no test can be 100 percent objective, pilot testing can help you avoid slanting the test in one direction or another, but first you should understand where a lack of objectivity can come from. A bias can creep into your test from a number of areas, mostly unintentional. Consider the following scenarios:

- **Work pressure.** You got the project late, you lost personnel during the work, other members of the development team sigh and turn away when you announce that you're going to need a week to test before you can sign off on the document. So you shorten, simplify, expedite in order to conform to everyone else's schedule and production values.

- **Pro-forma testing.** Your department always "tests" procedures, but you pretty much know how the results will turn out because you don't put a lot of originality into the documents in the first place. You use the same forms you've always used and don't really pay attention to the "results" because you know that nobody else will pay attention to them either. They only care about getting the test form signed and getting back to work.

■ **Caring too much.** You have gone out on a limb with a new design of a fold-out, 3D, multicolor layout and you don't want to go back to the drawing board to come up with yet another killer design for your information. This one shows how original you *really* can get; it reflects the reason you should get a raise or a promotion. No way do you want the document to fail the usability test.

You may fall victim to these or other situations that cause bias to creep into your test. You cannot avoid these totally, but you can recognize them and pilot test first to make sure the test forms and situations don't provide you with only the evaluation you want. Also, rely as much as you can on numbers—calculations of frequencies, performance statistics, and such—to keep yourself "honest." Of course, you do have to interpret, but postponing your interpretation until you have some reliable data can help ensure objectivity. Also watch out for leading questions, such as "Don't you think this procedure makes you more efficient?" Such questions lean the user in the direction you want as opposed to the direction dictated by the usability of the information.

Above all, objectivity results from a right attitude on your part toward testing: it will help you improve your design. If you see testing in this positive light, you will want to make your tests as objective as possible so you will end up with better documentation.

 **iscussion**

In this chapter we study the usability testing of documentation products, which is a subset of usability testing of software and of products in general. A way of involving users in the documentation process, documentation testing consists of a series of structured inquiries that attempt to measure the effectiveness of various elements of manuals and online documentation. Testing of manuals differs from testing of online products in that when you test an online product you follow procedures for testing an actual software program.[5]

What Is Testing?

Testing usually requires a tester, an evaluator, and the subject material (a manual or online system). Figure 6.3 shows the necessary components.

Testing resembles reviewing; it generates information about a draft of a manual or online system. But it differs in the kind of information it creates. Testing generates statistical information—data in the form of numbers about user performance tasks or use of document features. Consider this list of questions you might have about a manual or online system:

■ How well do installation procedures work for a program?

■ Does the index contain sufficient cross-reference information to enable novice users to find information they need?

■ How clear are the definitions of the concepts in this manual?

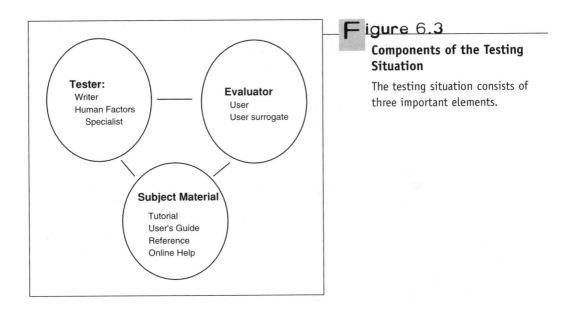

Figure 6.3

Components of the Testing Situation

The testing situation consists of three important elements.

Testing, done correctly, can provide answers to these and other questions. First, in testing you set the performance criteria by using an operational definition, (e.g., "*work well* means can be performed with 100 percent accuracy at least 90 percent of the time"). In testing, you get real people to actually try the procedures out. It puts your document "to the test." Your proficiency in doing usability tests lies in your ability to construct a reasonable test situation and to interpret the results intelligently. It fits in with the approach supported by this book, because it constitutes another way of building your design around software users.

The Importance of User Testing As Part of User-Driven Design

User-driven design follows the idea that the technology should adapt to the person, rather than the person adapt to the technology. Software documents enable that adaptation. They show the user how the program can perform useful work as a tool in various environments, something the user might not see or appreciate without the documentation, and something the software product cannot usually do on its own. You can't have user-driven design for your documents unless you first study the user, then test to find ways to make the documentation adapt to the user's needs. User testing also supports task orientation because it helps the documenter build a clear picture of the user's work environment and encourages a broader view of software use than mere learning of functions. From a practical standpoint, testing can occur in a variety of forms as a part of your documentation project.

Example of a Minimal Test

Many students use informal user preference tests of document design features as a regular part of designing manuals for software programs.[6] One student, Stacie, wanted to do a test at the design stage of her work on a desktop calendar program for the Macintosh. She identified the following test points for evaluation:

- Body text size (9, 10, or 12 point)
- Heading size (bold or plain)
- Cropped screens (versus whole screens)
- Cues for steps (italics, bold, plain)
- Page orientation (right/right or right/left)

To study these items she made up nine different mock pages with examples of different options she considered in her initial design. Her performance objective consisted of 100 percent, that is, a design feature had to get acceptance by 100 percent of her users before she would incorporate it into the document. In Stacie's test she assumed the role of tester, and she used three potential users as evaluators: a manager of an agricultural services company, a fellow student, and a features writer for the campus newspaper. These users represented the range of user type she had identified for the program (novice to experienced) and each possessed roughly the same amount of subject-matter knowledge of the program (using personal information management programs). Materials for this test took the form of a set of interview questions for the users, mocked-up pages showing the features, and a brief overview of the program's capabilities.

The tests took place in the user's workplace. After explaining the nature of her project to the evaluators, Stacie simply gave the three sheets to the users and asked them a series of questions about the page design features. Her results, when tabulated, showed that some of the test points won unanimous approval by her evaluators (thus passing the performance objective), while others did not. Interpreting her results, Stacie found that some of her original ideas (such as using italics to indicate steps in procedures) did not work for these users because they distracted or confused the users. The results allowed her to adjust the original design and taught her a lot about her users.

Example of an Elaborate Test

Recently I had the opportunity to visit an IBM usability lab near Dallas, Texas and to watch some usability testing of documents and interfaces for office automation products developed at the site. The lab consisted of two large rooms, one for the testers and one for the evaluators. The director of the lab had dual Ph.D.s in human factors and behavioral psychology. The assistant had training and experience in usability testing.

The test room consisted of a number of computers in office-like settings with video cameras strategically placed. One camera focused on the user's face, another on the screen, and another on the keyboard. The evaluator, a woman, sat at the computer and also spoke into a microphone connected to recording equipment in the observation room. She used manuals beside her on the table. A one-way mirror separated the test room from the observation room.

The observation room held a wealth of recording and processing equipment. The VCR cameras in the testing room fed into a bank of VCR recording equipment. The evaluator's face appeared on a number of display screens, above the digital timer. In fact, the tester showed how images of the evaluator's screen, keyboard, and face could all be imposed on one screen for a total view of the testing event. Microphones allowed the testers to communicate with the evaluator in case she needed help. The test director told me he often invited writers and programmers to visit the lab (and sit in the row of observation seats provided) or he would record the testing events for replay for product developers. Usually testing involved performing tests designed by documentation and software developers, and then preparing reports based on the results. An elaborate testing facility looks something like the one illustrated in Figure 6.4.

Clearly the two situations described above differ in a number of ways, ways that reflect the nature of commitment to testing within an organization or with a given project. Below we examine the two primary variables pertaining to the elaborateness of a testing effort.

Testing as a Corporate Priority

You may work for a company that places testing high on its priority list. Such institutions, research and development organizations, or companies used to producing high-tech computer and other products, see the value of testing as a way of involving the user, client, or customer in the production loop. In many situations, however, technical communicators

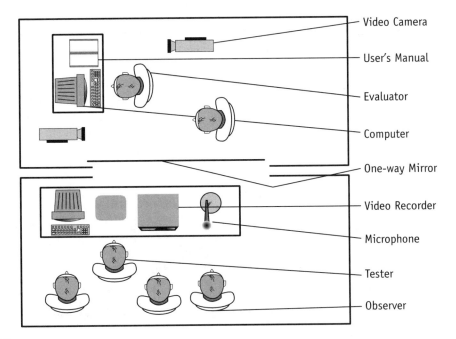

Figure 6.4

A Layout for a Usability Lab

Usability labs for software and documentation require equipment for viewing and recording user interaction with manuals and help products.

find themselves having to argue for the value and benefit of testing. Often, documenters who take on the challenge of instituting usability testing programs in corporations find themselves faced with organizational cultures that resist a user-centered design of products and the shift in development processes it might take to begin regular testing. Those working to develop a testing facility may find it difficult to obtain authorization to bring in the human factors professionals it often takes to start a usability testing program.

Testing As a High-Cost Endeavor

As you can imagine from the description above, setting up a testing lab requires a large initial investment. Not only does the recording equipment cost, but you have to include costs for room renovation, maintenance, and salaries for trained personnel to act as test monitors, testers, and evaluators. While testing on a limited scale can happen for smaller projects, once you think about labs the cost goes up dramatically and you begin to need the buy-in of other important departments within your organization. Testing, at least the type described above, requires resources in time and equipment that many companies just cannot commit.

The Advantages of Field Testing

Because of the high cost of testing and the resistance to user-centered design often encountered by technical communicators in traditional corporate cultures, many software documenters turn to field testing as a way to gain valuable information about the use of their documentation products. Field testing can make up a part of your ongoing, managerial attempt to discover and test ideas with actual users or can constitute a more modest step in your regular documentation process. Researchers have identified a number of things that a documenter can learn by conducting field research. Table 6.9 identifies some of them.[7]

Table 6.9

Things You Can Learn from Field Testing

Topic	Explanation
Demographics	Information about age, gender, years in the profession, job titles, educational levels, specific individuals in fields
Environments	Office design, network designs, team structures, reporting structures
Information Access	Corporate information channels, sources of documentation/computer support, user communities
Information Use	Sharing, storing behavior, information systems
Software Use	Tasks, applications, training, upgrading, purchasing
User Satisfaction	Effectiveness of written and online documents, support

Remember that field research poses issues of time, politics, budgets, ethics, and legality that require you to proceed carefully. While most users will welcome you into their workplace, they will most likely do so only if you approach them with full authorization, treat them with respect, and conduct yourself professionally. Researchers who have done extensive field testing recommend that you follow the guidelines below.

- **Do preliminary research into the company and users you want to test.** You can study the history of user feedback from technical support personnel, or examine the trade literature for reviews of products like yours to get a sense of the kinds of companies you're investigating and their use of software. Contact any persons you know in the company to find out the ideal employees to contact and how to do it.

- **Construct a sensible field testing plan.** A well-designed field test should have a plan that includes the following: a schedule, list of resource personnel, questions that will guide the test, objectives of the test, and the authorization to conduct the test. A plan like this, in writing, gives you something to send to managers and supervisors who need to approve your testing activities.

- **Prepare to compromise.** Unless you have developed a track record with a certain company or group of users, you will find that your actual site testing will involve fewer people, or you will have less time than you thought you had, or you won't get the exact users you wanted. Flexibility in your plans and good research ahead of time can help accommodate some of these inevitable shortfalls.

Field testing should be a part of your ongoing involvement of users in your project. It helps build rapport and sends a message to users that you care about their software support needs. Additionally, because you focus on the users' environments, field testing enables you to support critical workplace tasks.

Methods of Field Testing That Emphasize Task Issues

While almost all of your work in field testing contributes to the user's ability to do tasks productively and proficiently, some methods specifically allow you to target information and communication behavior and thus give you specific insight into how to help users meet their work goals. Below you will find some of these tests described.

Modified Q-Sort Tests

Task efficiency relates in some ways to how people process information. In fact, people process more and more each day, especially those who work with information systems or manage and store their own information. The more we know about their thought processes and can support them, the more we can facilitate their information tasks with a given piece of software. To perform their information tasks, users employ patterns or group their work into categories. To identify these categories, psychologists have devised methods called *q-sorts:* These operate like surveys by asking users to rank their preferences for items.[8] Q-sorts can help you identify users' patterns for the information tasks they perform in their work.

Q-sorts require users to respond based on a scale, but instead of ordering preferences on a single sheet of paper, users receive a set of index cards with one preference listed on each. They only have to sort the cards in the order of their individual preferences. For example, you could put real-world tasks on the sort cards and ask users to rank them in order of performance or order of *frequency* of performance. The cards can contain statements such as "I transfer a document to a work-group storage area" or "I download information from the main office." The actual test asks users to sort the statements into categories, such as the following:

- Perform every time the software is used
- Perform sometimes, but not every time the software is used
- Perform seldom, or only under special circumstances
- Never perform.[9]

When you administer the test, you can present these guidelines to the user:

1. Take as long as you like to sort the cards.
2. Look at all the cards before sorting them.
3. Make a list of the card numbers in the pile after sorting.

Analysis of the results consists of calculating the frequency that certain cards fall into certain categories, as illustrated in Figure 6.5.

Results from q-sorts can help you establish users' general patterns in using a particular piece of software, or with regard to their perceptions of their tasks. Tasks that receive a high percentage of frequency (i.e., are used often by many users) should be included in your documentation.

Q-sorts not only work for establishing what tasks belong in the user's schema for using the software, but for establishing the importance of other elements of the user's psychology and work environment. You can modify this technique to measure the kinds of information indicated in the following list.

- **Work motivations.** Create statements of internal, external, and environmental motivation to perform tasks and have users arrange them in categories of importance.

Categories of Frequency	Task types
Perform every time the software is used	Task A, Task Y, Task C
Perform sometimes, but not every time	Task D, Task F
Perform seldom, or under special circumstances	Task L
Perform never	Task B, Task M, Task O

Figure 6.5

A Way to Record Results of Q-Sorts

Organizing responses can help you see how to incorporate results into your document.

■ **Task Categories.** Use task names from the task list and have users arrange them according to perceived difficulty, centrality to their job success, relationship to group or team activities.

■ **Documentation types.** Create statements of use of various documentation media and types and have users arrange them according to categories of frequency of use or attitudes.

■ **Document sections.** Present names of existing document sections (tables of contents, index, chapters, quick reference cards) and have users categorize them according to their perceptions of how frequently they think they would use them.

■ **Tutorial lessons.** Present titles of existing tutorial lessons on cards and have users arrange them by task sequence, perceived usefulness, or perceived difficulty.

Vocabulary Tests Tap the User's Viewpoint

The language you use in the manual provides the key to the usability of the manual. Language evokes the schema or mental patterns in your users and allows them to read more easily and process instructions more efficiently. If you use the right kind of vocabulary in your manual you have a better chance to evoke divergent thinking, suggest information-related usage of a program, and achieve your goals of efficiency and effectiveness. Based on these observations, it makes sense for you to test the users' vocabulary extensively.

You begin identifying your user's vocabulary during the user analysis phase of the project (although you will learn new terms all along). If you have different user sets or groups, they will probably distinguish themselves by their different vocabularies. As you build lists of these vocabularies you should consider ways to test the user's knowledge of them. You really have two kinds of vocabularies to consider with users:

■ **Subject-matter terms:** Subject-matter terms relate to the area of expertise reflected by the program. Professionals in engineering, accounting, physics, genetics, medicine, retail, and many other fields rely on the jargon of their profession to communicate with each other and to build their sense of professional identity. Because you want to evoke that sense of professionalism in the use of the software product, you will want to use the terminology to do it. Thus in retailing you'll refer to "cumulative monthly" figures in regards to business data or "skus" when you're referring to data items in a program.

■ **Computer terms:** Computer terms refer to those terms associated with the software and hardware that the user has to manipulate in the use of the program: all the terms relating to processors, printers, interface cables, network protocols, hard drives, modems, keyboards, screens, files, operating systems, desktops, and windows. As with subject-matter terms: Use the wrong ones at your peril. Incorrectly using terms like "jumper-wires" or "register tables" can get you into trouble with users.

Create vocabulary tests to make sure that users understand any problematic terms, or that you can get away with using jargon in your information products. A couple of simple vocabulary tests you can employ are listed below.

- **Match definitions with terms.** Providing a scrambled list of terms and a list of definitions to match can help you see which terms users understand. This test has the advantage of putting the terms in a context of other terms so that the user doesn't have to rely on the active vocabulary, but can take cues from the context of usage as he or she would in a workplace context.

- **Ask for definitions.** Ask your users to provide short definitions for terms. This kind of test allows you to see how the user defines a term, so it can also help you find terms that the user just doesn't know and doesn't have the chance to guess at.

Scenarios Trigger Problem Solving

Scenario-based testing differs from the forms above because it allows the user to explore a product and documentation on his or her own, guided by goals set in a scenario. Scenarios—brief narratives of realistic work situations—suggest a situation to the user as a way of guiding the testing activity. As author Donald Norman points out, scenarios evoke a specifically human perspective to thinking.[10] According to Norman, human thinking differs from strict, logical, machine-type thinking in approaching problem solving from a story perspective, detailing how a person did one thing and then another, sometimes failing, sometimes succeeding, until achieving an acceptable solution. For example, when a person gets lost driving in a strange city, logical thinking might suggest that the driver should ask a pedestrian for directions. But people often will drive around trying first one street then another, until they arrive at the destination. Such trial and error characterizes human thinking.

In testing, you can easily end up with results that diverge from reality if you encourage too much logic, or machine-like methods of problem solving. Your carefully planned task sequence for setting up a spreadsheet, for example, might not appear logical to the user, who can easily see alternative sequences. And additionally, using stories in testing allows your user to bring in human emotions and biases, to consider personalities and human informational needs and preferences—something of the rich context of realistic workplace problem solving.

Depending on your knowledge of the user's informational or organizational background, you can focus these scenarios on information tasks, or on more routine tasks. The example in Figure 6.6 represents a commonly used scenario.[11]

In the test associated with this scenario, the tester provided the user with a prototype of the software and the documentation and appointed an unbiased test administrator to observe the test. The administrator recorded how long the user took to perform the test and

---

It is Monday morning, and you find a new computer on your desk. Your boss has left you a memo, asking you to set up the computer and enter product forecast data (provided on the attached sheet). Set up the spreadsheet and get a printout for your boss.

Figure 6.6

A Typical Scenario

This scenario allows the tester to observe the user applying the software to workplace tasks.

the errors the user made during the test. After the test, the writer and program developer interviewed the user to gain information about reasons for the user's specific performance.

This kind of test can provide a large amount of information about all aspects of a document and product, including the following:

- **Task selection.** What tasks did the user choose to perform the task?
- **Access methods.** What access elements (table of contents, index, running heads, etc.) did the user rely on in performing the task?
- **Time to perform.** How long did the user take to perform specific tasks? the overall task? to recover from errors? to read background information?
- **Success rates.** How often did the user achieve the desired results? how often did the user fail or get sidetracked into necessary but non-relevant tasks?
- **Assistance needs.** What elements (user's guide, quick reference cards, online help) of the documentation set did the user depend on for help?

As you can see, a scenario-based test can reflect on many parts of a manual, encourage the kind of divergent thinking you want to encourage among users, and give a wealth of information about your document.

How to Interpret Test Data

The question of interpretation of test data relates to the difficulties of understanding numerical representations of survey results. Interpreting data of any type presents a challenge. For one thing, you have constructed operational definitions of things, and, by definition, these definitions contain flaws. For example: you can say that a good cup of coffee would contain 1 teaspoon of sugar, 1.5 oz. of cream, and be served at 109° Fahrenheit. Many coffee-drinkers would agree that a cup of coffee with those characteristics would classify as "good." But what kinds of bias would cause us to suspect such a generalization? Regional, for one thing: Many drinkers in the southern United States drink their coffee black. Age, for another: many younger drinkers of coffee require much more sugar. Test bias, for yet another: the test may not have been given to enough subjects. Tester bias, for another: the test may have been administered by representatives of the dairy industry, known to favor the inclusion of milk products in coffee.

Whenever we make generalizations about data, we assume that what some specific examples show as true necessarily represents the whole. Thus, if nine out of ten of our procedures meet the acceptable performance objectives, then we assume that the tenth one will also meet acceptable performance objectives, or that our documentation will lead to efficient and effective use. But the problem stems from the fact that we have given a number to something (operational definitions) that is innumerable, and such generalizations necessarily contain flaws.

Interpreting test results means converting the data you obtained into document design changes. Often if you just naively make changes based on the data, you may overlook a bias you had in your test that would invalidate the results. For this reason you need to stay aware of biases, and make sure that any changes to the documentation reflect what you, your other team members, and often your users see as reasonable and based on common sense.

Remember the Testing Paradox

The other problem with interpretation has to do with the testing paradox, stated as follows:

> *The earlier you test the weaker the results but the easier it is to make changes; the later you test the better the results but the harder it is to make changes.*

Consider the design stage of your documentation, when you can make vast, sweeping changes in all aspects of the document design: page layout, type size, style, and font. You can include or exclude tasks, specify all kinds of special job performance aids, design or delete innovative formats. Even as your project progresses, you can make changes to task formats and other elements with little cost. Changes this early in the project might cost you $10 to $12 each. But as your project progresses, those changes begin to get much harder to make, because one change in design principle means changes in many instances of that design in the documentation set. Sure, your word processing technology can mitigate the difficulty of making such changes. But you still have to consider the labor and time it will take to make even slight changes. The cost for each change may escalate to $45 to $50 per change. By the time your project has reached the later stages, where you have whole sections completed, edited, and ready for review, the cost for even slight changes may reach $100 or more.

Now consider the quality of the information that your testing reveals. When you did your design testing you obtained pretty good results, but you had to use mocked-up pages to do it. To what extent did those mocked-up pages affect the validity of the results? Often you can't even get good results until you have the entire book or online system completed. You certainly can't really check the comprehensiveness until that stage. Consider the example of a 350-page manual. You really can't check whether the gutter margin is too narrow until you print the whole book. And by the time you print the whole book, the cost for changing the binding seam has gone through the roof. The situation with testing resembles that of performers: there are some things that you just can't rehearse until you get on the stage. But by the time you get on the stage the cost of messing up has increased because of the presence of the audience.

The testing paradox puts extra stress on you as a tester. Design your early tests as carefully as possible to ensure that you can make changes while the cost remains low. Detect major flaws early in development before you build them in and can't remove them easily.

Distinguish between Problems with the Documentation and Problems with the Product

Documentation has a special relationship to the software product itself: it helps make the product usable. But what about products with inherently bad or poorly designed interfaces? Can documentation make up for bad system design? And if it can, to what extent should documenters feel obliged to make up for bad system design?

Your first obligation lies in distinguishing between product deficiencies and documentation deficiencies. Baker identifies three characteristics of testing that seem to indicate a problem with the usability of a product rather than the documentation. These include:

1. An expert can do the task in much less time than the neophyte
2. Documentation has been debugged, yet users still struggle with tasks
3. Subjects understand instructions but object to the procedure itself[12]

Often the problem will lie with the documentation, but sometimes users left alone with just the product experience difficulties. Usually, Baker points out, users can figure out how to use a feature after a few tries without documentation, but if they continue having difficulty, then the problem may lie with the product.

In many development situations you will simply have to make the best of the system because you can't change it. This situation presents an advantage: With a set interface you don't have to play catch-up with last minute product changes. But most documenters consider themselves experts in adapting technology to human users and so welcome the opportunity to contribute their expertise both in document design and interface design. Where possible, you should offer your expertise in interface design as part of the overall development team's attempt to make the technology usable.

Glossary

evaluator: the person taking the test.

exit criteria: the performance standards that you set, so that when the procedure meets these standards you can leave the test situation for that procedure.

operational definitions: a quantified definition of something that you can't otherwise quantify because of its inherent vagueness. Defining "efficiency" in terms of time (under ten seconds) and effectiveness (fifty units per hour) means you have a definition with which you can operate.

tester: the person conducting the test.

test points: specific elements in the documentation that you want to learn about such as problems with specific procedures, specific terminology, or special elements of document design.

Checklist ✔

Use the following checklist to remind yourself of the important elements.

Test Plan Checklist
- [ ] What document or section are you testing? Describe briefly.
- [ ] What is the overall objective or purpose of the document or section?
- [ ] Describe the phase of development for this test (design, development, field evaluation).
- [ ] What elements of the test (test point) will you be testing (tasks, terminology, design features)?
- [ ] Describe the test type (performance, understanding, read and locate).

- ☐ Describe the performance objectives for the user tasks.
- ☐ Name and describe the evaluators. In particular, tell how closely your evaluator resembles your actual users and what compromises you will make in using him or her instead. What extra background will you need to supply for these evaluators?
- ☐ Name and describe the testers. Tell what materials you need to provide for conducting the test.
- ☐ What gathering methods will work best for this test (talk-aloud protocol, unobtrusive observation, interviews, watch and take notes).
- ☐ Describe any special test materials you will have to write for this test (instructions, authorization forms, performance record sheets, product information, scenarios).
- ☐ Describe the test environment (user's site, neutral site, testing lab, other).
- ☐ Narrative: tell what will happen, step-by-step, during the test. Try to envision it.
- ☐ Explain what you intend to do with the results, especially naming who will take responsibility for reworking the documentation.

Practice/Problem Solving

1. Discuss the Effect of Testing Online Documentation on the Project Estimates

In reading the Internet list for technical writers, TECHWR-L, I encountered the following exchange pertinent to this discussion of testing. Use it to discuss what you see as the effect of online or other kinds of testing on overall project estimates.

Looking through an old issue of the STC Intercom, I found the following figures for calculating documentation hours:

Writing new text:	*3–5 hours per page*
Revising Existing Text:	*1–3 hours per page*
Editing:	*6–8 pages per hour*
Indexing:	*5 pages per hour*
Production:	*5 percent of all other activities*
Project Management:	*15 percent of all other activities*

Do you think these figures are still accurate? If not, why?

More or less. But one important task is left out: testing. And the testing of online information takes more time than the testing of printed information. (That's all fine and good if you're using a standard writing paradigm, but what if you're doing something like writing your online information first, then creating print docs. Or having to code tags into text (ugh!). Makes a mess of simple estimates.)

Chuck Martin
Techwriter@aol.com   (used with permission)

Notice that Martin observes that the per-hour estimates for these development tasks are accurate, except that he suggests that testing, especially testing of online documents, adds time. Given the discussion of testing in this chapter, decide how many hours you think it might take to test the following documents, both for minimal, quick testing and for extensive testing:

- A two-page installation guide
- A quick-reference page showing commands and menus
- A tutorial on three basic program tasks
- An online tutorial on three basic program tasks

Note that Martin suggests that testing online documents may take more time than the testing of printed documents. What technical elements associated with writing online documents do you think might make this so?

2. Test Report

Find a manual or help system that you think could use some improvements in its procedures or step-by-step documentation. Select a relatively simple task, such as changing the date and time display in Windows or Creating a New Folder on a Macintosh.

Performing the role of both tester and evaluator, use the Procedure Test Form on page 197 to test a procedure from the manual, and then write a brief, one-page report telling the results. Discuss these topics in your test report:

- Objectives of the test
- Expected performance of the procedure
- Test structure and activities
- Results of the test
- Recommendations for improving the procedure

3. Deciding on Kinds of Tests

Considering the advice in this chapter, what methods would you use to test the following kinds of documents or sections. Can you test them in more than one way?

- Reference page containing images of all the menus of a program (to accompany an engineering drawing program)
- Three-part quick setup and installation fold-out card (to accompany a program to teach students principles of microbiology)
- Brochure giving an overview of how to use color in documents (to accompany a desktop publishing program)
- Online index (as part of a help system for a financial analysis package)

Editing and Fine Tuning

Editing, like reviewing and testing, challenges you to create an attitude conducive to productivity. The examples show how to apply proofreading marks to a page and how to use style sheets to maintain editing consistency. Like other elements affecting document design, editing requires you address the needs of knowledge workers in a high-tech workplace. The guidelines help you develop good editing attitudes and adapt the levels of edit to the needs of your project. The discussion links editing tasks with users' information-task concerns and covers editing as a management concern.

How to Read This Chapter

- If you're working on a project, here you need to change gears and approach your document from a different angle, that of the writer. Read the Discussion section first to put some distance between your mind and the project. Then edit, using the symbols in Figure 7.2.

- If you're reading to understand, it doesn't make that much difference which order you follow here. The Guidelines in this chapter offer practical tips rather than a specific sequence, and they offer an interesting overview of the function of editing in the information workplace. The Guidelines and the Examples will give you the information you need to complete a documentation plan.

 xamples

A Page with Editing Marks

Figure 7.1 shows two versions of a page that illustrate the use of proofreading marks in a manuscript. As you can see, the editor has made the corrections clearly and has made them easy to find. To facilitate ease of reading, editors often use red, blue, and green pens.

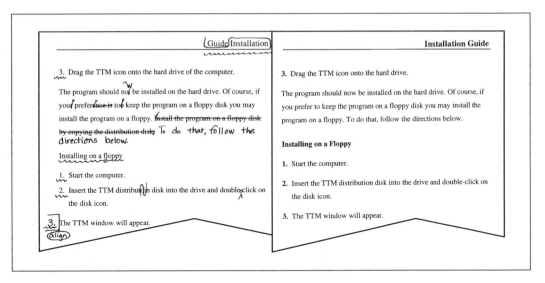

Installation Guide

3. Drag the TTM icon onto the hard drive.

The program should now be installed on the hard drive. Of course, if you prefer to keep the program on a floppy disk you may install the program on a floppy. To do that, follow the directions below.

Installing on a Floppy

1. Start the computer.

2. Insert the TTM distribution disk into the drive and double-click on the disk icon.

3. The TTM window will appear.

Figure 7.1

Sample Marked-Up Page and the Corrected Page

This example shows how editors use proofreading marks to include instructions to the writer in a document.

You might have to draw some lines or use both margins to avoid clutter on the page, or you might have to rewrite certain passages and paste them into the manuscript or print them on separate pages and attach them. If you're editing a help system, you might have to print it and edit the hard copy or use an electronic annotating feature to put notes into the manuscript.

The symbols in Figure 7.2 represent standard ones used throughout the industry. The example shows how you use them on a draft of a print manual or a printed version of an online help system. As you will see in other parts of the chapter, you base decisions about changes on a variety of authorities: standard style guides, in-house style guides, specifications for a specific document, and, more often than not, common sense.

Style Guide for a Software Company

The example in Figure 7.3 shows a sample page from an in-house style guide for a software company, or for any computer hardware and software manufacturer. Such a company would employ a staff of about twelve writers and editors, perhaps even a full-time indexer. For these writers, the style guide provides general information about documentation at the company, tells how to write and format procedural tables, and gives other typical pages. The document itself demonstrates the overall format it describes, and it also refers to an online version of the document so writers and editors can see what commands to use to achieve the exact same format.

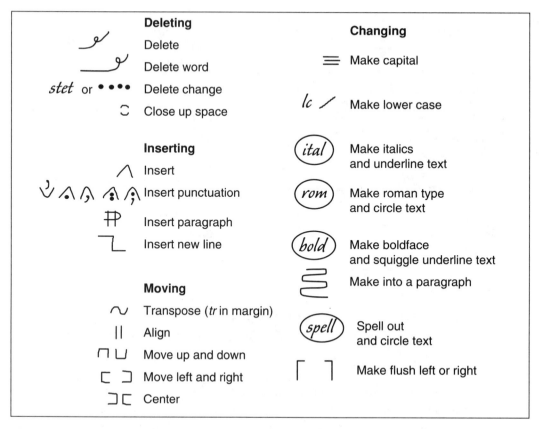

Proofreader's Marks

These proofreaders marks help you standardize the instructions you give to writers about text.

Guidelines

The steps involved in editing and fine tuning are shown in Figure 7.4.

1 Know Your User

Like all activities associated with tailoring technology to users, editing begins with a clear idea of the needs of the people who will put the manual or help system to productive work. Commonly, novice editors see their work as making documents conform to style guidelines or hunting for mistakes in grammar and mechanics. True, editors rely on the *Chicago Manual of Style* or their company style guide, but they inform their best decisions as to level of detail, sentence structure, and language by reviewing information about the software user.

460-006-000   General Guidelines
Issue 1, April 1992   Page 2-1

ACRONYMS

General   The following information applies to acronyms and their usage:
- Acronyms can be used in section names, sideheads, table titles, bulleted lists, etc., if they are already coined or are coined in the text after the first appearance.
- Coin acronyms upon first usage each time they appear in a table or figure, or use a legend.
- An acronym list is required and should always be the last subsection in the first section or the introduction of a document.
- Always index acronyms or abbreviations that are defined in the document's acronym list under their fully spelled-out form.

Placement   The standard header for an acronym list is as follows:
- All Caps
- Bold
- In the right column
- Preceded and followed by short nonbold lines

Rulers   The ruler for the acronym list is as follows:

```
              19          35                    70
              |           |                     |
       10......1.......W2.........3....W....4.........5.........6........R
              |           |
       Acronym begins   Meaning of Acronym begins
```

Lines   The acronym list header is preceded and followed by a short nonbold line. There are no other lines associated with acronyms.

Figure 7.3

A Page from an In-House Style Guide

These instructions to writers tell how to format and handle acronyms for company manuals. Style guides help maintain consistency among writing staff members.

Here the thorough job you did in Chapter 2, "Analyzing Your Users," will serve you well. In particular, you should pay attention to the tone of language the user employs and the level of formality he or she expects. All the elements of language that you use require validation in some aspect of the user's characteristics, as Table 7.1 illustrates.

1. Know your user.

2. Take a constructive attitude.

3. Don't edit your own on your own.

4. Use editing forms.

5. Edit strategically.

6. Develop an editor's reading skills.

7. Consult standard style guides.

8. Don't confuse editing tasks with other tasks.

Figure 7.4

Guidelines for Editing Software Documentation

Editing encompasses more than finding mistakes. The good editor should see his or her job as molding all the details of document design, from pages and binding down to punctuation and mechanics, as the fine tuning of communication guided by user characteristics. Table 7.1 indicates how some of the areas of editing relate to user characteristics.

2   Take a Constructive Attitude

Editors have to deal with other people, often in a relationship fraught with problems from the start. Consider the quips people make about editing: "A person's greatest urge is to edit someone else's writing," or "Commit random acts of editing." Tell someone you work as an editor and see how long it takes them to make a joke about watching their language.

Table 7.1

Editorial Areas Reflect User Characteristics

Editorial Area	User Characteristic
Tone	User type: novice, experienced, expert
Level Of Detail	User's knowledge of computers
Vocabulary	Level of subject-matter knowledge, user type: novice, experienced, expert
Sentence Structure	User's education/demographics, learning preference
Examples	Learning preference, subject-matter knowledge
Graphics	Learning preference
Organization	Usage pattern
Content	Information and task needs

Table 7.2

Ways to Take a Constructive Attitude toward Editing

Editorial Relationship	Problematic View	Enlightened View
Editor and Writer	Editor as grammar police: "Make me bleed."	Editor as partner: "Help me communicate better with users."
	Editor as outsider: "When the document's done I'll send it to the editor."	Editor as team member: "The editor and I will work together on this document."
Editor and Subject Matter Expert	Editor as window dresser: "Make it look pretty," or "Dot the i's and cross the t's.	Editor as adder of value: "Help me avoid embarrassing technical flaws and inaccuracies and improve the document."
Editor and Self	Editor as writer: "I can see all the mistakes because I wrote it."	Editor as alter ego: "I've got to shift roles to see my blind spots as a writer."

Like it or not, people often see editors as grammar police. (I tell them I'm a vampire after "*type*-o" blood.)

So take an enlightened view. See yourself not as an adversary, but as a partner sharing the goals of good communication with the writer. Table 7.2 summarizes the kinds of relationships editors can have with others, and indicates the way the tenor of certain relationships depends on how you interpret them.

Seeing yourself as a partner with the writer can take you a long way toward having a satisfying experience as an editor. Roger Masse, among others, has examined the relationship between editors and writers and suggests that we see it as a dialog rather than a confrontation. He suggests that working to achieve the components of a dialog, shown in Table 7.3, can ameliorate some of the problematic elements of the editorial relationship.[1]

3   Don't Edit Your Own on Your Own

We all have blind spots. Among others, my blind spots include the spelling of certain words ("ballance," "recieve," "proceedure"). Also, because we created a document, we tend to feel protective of it, or we want it completed without extra effort, or we want it to reflect our view of the user. For these reasons, seasoned writers know that you can't edit your own work. It resembles the quip of lawyers: "A lawyer who defends herself has a fool for a client." An editor who edits her own work has a client who doesn't believe editing will do any good.

Besides the issue of blind spots, you also have fatigue to worry about. Editing requires hard, often tedious work. Often when editing you will read the first part of a page

Table 7.3

Elements of a Constructive Editorial Dialog

Quality	Description	Technique
Genuineness	Being yourself and expressing what you think and feel, not what you think you ought to express	"We have a problem with the style guidelines here." (not *"You* have a problem. . . .")
Accurate, empathetic understanding	Comprehending and understanding the other person in a relationship	"You've done a lot of work here."
Unconditional positive regard	Affirming the other person as a partner in dialog.	"Thank you for working with me on this document."
Presentness	Being consciously and actively present in a dialog and concentrating on the other person.	"Explain what you want to do with this passage." "Let's convert your verbal explanation into prose."
Spirit of mutual equality	Seeing the other person as an equal	"I like what you've done here." [Find areas you really admire in the document and say so at the start.] "What do you think?"
Supportive psychological climate	Communicating without preconceptions.	"So what I hear you saying is . . . [accurate reflection mirroring of the other person's ideas]"

and then, after not finding many challenging mistakes or points of consideration, continue reading without really comprehending the text—just moving your eyes over the page. I have done this many times. It's hard to remain attentive while editing.

To mitigate the effects of your own biases and human weaknesses in editing, consider two techniques that help ensure productive editing of one's own work.

- ■ **Edit with a partner.** Ask another member of your documentation team to help you with proofreading. Typically you would use two versions of a manuscript, with one person reading aloud and the other person reading along. Professional copyeditors use this technique to ensure against tediousness and to balance their blind spots.

- ■ **Shorten editing sessions.** Don't try to do a whole document at once. Do a task at a time, or section at a time, so that you pace yourself, and shift tasks frequently. First read for sentence coherence, then for mechanics, then double-check the format, then move on to the next task or section. This shifting of tasks helps you keep attentive.

4   Use Editing Forms

Because editing requires you to establish relationships with other persons on the documentation team or in your organization, you will find that creating editing forms, or using existing forms, can help you regularize your procedures and communicate with others more clearly. Table 7.4 summarizes the main kinds of forms you might use as part of your work in the role of the editor.

When you planned your documents, you should have planned what styles you would follow during the writing. Thus, when you make up any editing forms for a project, it's a good idea to consult your documentation plan (Chapter 4, "Planning and Writing Your Documents") first, to update the project plan, and more important, identify the styles it specifies and reuse as much of the original information as possible.

5   Edit Strategically

As indicated above, editing requires a lot of very hard work, partly because of the overall abstractness of the task. For this reason, you should pace yourself in the job, and edit

Table 7.4

Forms Used in Editing

Editing Form	Description	Purpose
Editing cover sheet	A cover sheet to attach to documents you edit, containing names, titles, schedules, and specifying the level of edit preferred.	Allows you and your client to easily see the terms of the edit. Acts as an informal editing contract.
Editing checklists	Lists of items with check boxes at the left.	Act as reminders of elements to examine in editing.
Editing review form	Contains information about the document and editing activities. Asks questions about the writer's agreement with editing suggestions and elicits constructive criticism about editing.	Allows writers to critique editing practice. Adds to quality control of editing groups. Gathers constructive criticism.
Policy document	Overall policy statement regarding scheduling, style guidelines followed.[1]	Helps your client understand the editing relationship and accept suggestions. Contributes to your professional image.
Style sheet	A single page divided into 9 alphabetized squares where you record conventions for a specific document.	Helps you remember the changes you made at other places in a document. Enables you to maintain consistency within a document.

for only one document feature at a time. Fortunately, the industry has a kind of standard to follow known as the nine levels of edit. Formalized by Mary Fran Buehler and Robert Van Buren at the Jet Propulsion Laboratory at the California Institute of Technology, the levels of edit constitute a way of specifying the kinds of editing done on a specific manuscript.[2] They contribute to your doing a valuable job as an editor because they allow you to segregate the kinds of things you look for in a document. They free you from the sit-down-and-do-it-all-at-once approach. Table 7.5 explains briefly the nine levels of edit.

Clearly, all documents require these edits, regardless of whether they get done by the writer or a designated editor. Notice, too, that the higher the number of the edit, the more the edit deals with the information in the document. The lower numbers concern themselves more with the management and production of documents, whereas the higher numbers concern themselves with text and the expression of ideas.

In some organizations people edit their own work; in others they don't. You may find yourself in one of three situations:

- **Writer and editor's roles combined.** In this situation you would perform all these edits yourself, preferably systematically so as to counterbalance your tendencies to overlook your own document's weaknesses. Knowing which levels to perform helps you organize your editing work.

- **Writer submitting to an editor.** In this situation you would specify the kind of editing you want done on your manuscript. Depending on your efforts and skill as a writer, you may not require the "deeper" language and substantive edits. Knowing which levels to perform helps you give the right instructions to the editor.

Table 7.5

The Nine Levels of Edit

Level	Explanation
1. Coordination edit	Planning, estimating, monitoring the production process
2. Policy edit	Making sure the document reflects company policy
3. Integrity edit	Making sure all the parts match each other
4. Screening edit	Making sure the document meets minimum editorial standards (spelling, etc.)
5. Copy clarification edit	Clarifying all the parts of a manuscript for typesetters and illustrators
6. Format edit	Making sure all the parts conform with acceptable format
7. Mechanical style edit	Making sure all the mechanics (capitalization, abbreviations, etc.) are consistent with a specified, often in-house, style
8. Language edit	Clarifying the expression of ideas in a document
9. Substantive edit	Ensuring that all the information elements of a report work together

■ **Editor of the work of another writer.** In this situation you would ask the author to specify what level of edit the work requires, and then perform just that edit. You would only perform the required edits, or you might examine a manuscript and let the writer know how many levels a document requires. Knowing which levels to perform helps you estimate how long you will take and how much it will cost.

I find it useful to use three categories of editing, each applying the kinds of edits described above, but each providing a different kind of service to a document. Below I describe each kind or level of editing. These levels can help you both in planning your editing and in clarifying the kinds of editing services you may offer to a client. In some ways you will perform these kinds of tasks on your own documents if you have control of the production process. Most likely you will work in a development team with specific responsibilities for the documentation that may include your editing work done by subject-matter experts. In that case, a clear idea of the kind of editing you will provide helps all team members understand and appreciate your contribution.

The Managerial Edit

Managerial editing concerns itself with edit levels 1 through 5: coordination, policy, integrity, and screening. This kind of editing doesn't relate specifically to the language of the document, but more to how the document gets produced. To do this edit you track and coordinate all the production processes, and the relationships with other documents. A managerial edit requires involvement all during the documentation process, from the documentation plan onward. Often writers call it a coordination edit, because it coordinates schedules, reviews, and other edits.

DOCUMENTS NEEDING A MANAGERIAL EDIT. A managerial edit, sometimes called a policy edit, gets done by managers and editors from an editing group or working with writers on a team. This kind of edit gives you an overview of the document's production and allows you assurance that you don't release anything politically embarrassing or downright wrong. It also allows editors to oversee and catch potential problems that might require a deeper-level edit. A managerial edit ensures that rewritten documents—documents based on previous releases and documents that contain material basically changed from previous releases—will get the required attention. The edit involves integrity edits and basic screening that will ensure that new material fits with previous material. Because this depth of edit requires involvement of editors in all aspects of the document's production and planning, it assures maximum quality. Managerial editing usually adds between 15 to 20 percent to the cost of a project.

The Copy Edit

The copy edit concerns itself with editing types 6 and 7: format and mechanical style. In this level you pay attention to all the surface-level elements of the words, sentences, paragraphs, pages, and books. The copy edit can range from very light to very heavy: essentially, you address details of prescribed style and convention. Basically, when you copy edit you ensure conformity with style guides for usage, list and table format, footnote formatting and placement, page layout, and other visible elements of the document.

DOCUMENTS NEEDING A COPY EDIT. Do this kind of edit on documents that writers have already tested and subjected to user and other reviews. Copy edits occur also in organizations with set practices and forms for documents, where you can pretty much assume coherence among the document parts. This kind of edit should represent the basic level for all documents, because to perform it you don't need to know a great deal about the reader of a specific document. You do, however, need to know a lot about users in general to do this edit. An experienced editor can usually copy edit eight to ten pages per hour.

The Substantive Edit

Substantive editing concerns itself with editing types 8 and 9: language and information. To do this level of edit you address the clarity of ideas. Sometimes writers call this level a developmental edit, because you do it early in the development process and use it as a pass to get all the information elements together and in an effective order. During the substantive edit, you examine the sentences as expressions of the information in the document, making sure that each expresses ideas clearly and forcefully.

DOCUMENTS NEEDING A SUBSTANTIVE EDIT. All documents should receive a substantive edit in some form or another. Less skilled writers or writers just beginning in software documentation need this kind of edit. Often documentation gets written or sketched out by subject matter experts such as programmers, engineers, or managers. In case these persons have little training in software documentation, you will want to require or suggest this kind of edit; the editor gets highly involved in all aspects of the document's structure and ideas. An experienced editor can usually substantively edit two to three pages an hour.

Editing Levels of and for Online Help Documents

The application of the levels of edit to editing online documents depends on whether you will write your online screens and topics first using a word processor, or create them directly on the screen. Usually, when you write your topics first and then convert the files to screens, you have the chance to print them. In that case you would edit them as paper documents.

Editing online information also poses significant challenges in the area of format because of the reader's ability to vary the size of the display. The capability to vary the size of the display creates difficulties with line lengths wrapping improperly and tables losing their formatting when the user "scrunches" a screen. Additionally, when the user changes the size of a screen, it often changes the relationship of the text with the graphic. The expert editor will establish a style that allows for these variations in user display.

For example, you can construct your tables using tabs instead of worksheet cells, as you might do using a word processor like Microsoft Word. The advantage of this technique, of course, is in the flexibility of the tabbed text when the information has to appear in a 5- by 3-inch window. Tabs can allow your tables to retain their row and column structure, even in these cramped communication spaces.

You also should edit for consistency in aspects of help screens that don't exist for paper documents. For instance, make at least one editing pass over an online document just to make sure the context-sensitive tags in the document all conform to the list of tags in the program.

6 Develop an Editor's Reading Skills

The kind of reading you do as an editor differs from reading you do as a user or a writer. Often it means not reading at all, but *looking,* stifling the urge to understand in order to pay attention to editorial details. Untrained editors often lack these skills. Judith Tarutz recommends developing the kinds of reading skills that help you find typos and other mistakes quickly.[3] You might identify some methods such as those listed below:

- **Flip test** (ten seconds per manual): get the overall organization and layout of pages, check for glaring inconsistencies
- **Skimming** (six to ten pages per minute): spelling, mechanics, punctuation
- **Reading selectively** (two to three minutes per page): spot-checking for tone, grammar, complete sentences, transitions, parallel sections
- **Reading analytically** (five pages per hour): missing information, technical inaccuracies, paragraph organization and unity
- **The long look** (one to two minutes per page; errors will not appear until *after* the first minute): omissions in title pages, tables of contents, indexes, headers and rules out of place, misaligned graphics, tiny extra spaces in front of some words, double spaces between words (like this), stupid mistakes

You can use these techniques selectively, or apply them all to the same document at different times. I find, for example, that when I read selectively I often find patterns of mistakes I can then catch by skimming through the rest of the document.

You can use these estimates of pages per minute in planning your documentation project. Chapter 4, "Planning and Writing Your Documents," discusses where you can use this kind of estimating information.

7 Consult Standard Style Guides

You will find yourself needing to check general ***style guides*** and reference materials from time to time, especially when controversies occur over points of mechanics or style. The following list presents examples of style guides you may have at your disposal.

- **General style guides and dictionaries.** Guides that give broad ranges of information on mechanics, punctuation, and usage, especially technical terminology. Examples include the following:
  - *The Chicago Manual of Style,* 14th ed. Chicago: University of Chicago Press, 1997
  - *Technical Writing Style,* Dan Jones. Boston: Allyn & Bacon, 1998

- *Publication Manual of the American Psychological Association,* 4th ed. Washington, DC: APA, 1994
- *Scientific Style and Format: The CBE Manual for Authors, Editors, and Publishers,* 6th ed. Chicago: Council of Biology Editors
- *Technical Editing,* 2nd ed. Carolyn Rude. Boston: Allyn & Bacon, 1998
- *Science and Technical Writing: A Manual of Style.* Philip Rubens. New York: Henry Holt, 1994
- *The GPO Style Manual,* 28th ed., Washington, DC: U. S. Government Printing Office, 1984

■ **In-house style guides.** Guides that embody the specific conventions for text and format, and all the style elements for a specific company. Examples include:
  - *The Digital Style Guide* of Digital Equipment Corporation, Burlington, MA: Digital Press, 1993
  - *Convex Style Manual,* Richardson, TX: Convex Computer Corporation, 1991
  - *Style Guide for Procedural Documents,* Dallas, TX: DSC Communications Corporation, 1992

■ **Specialized reference works.** Reference books that contain specific conventions for publishing and documentation in specialized technical areas cover broad conventions within fairly narrow definitions of fields. You will find specialized guides like those listed below of great value in establishing project conventions.
  - *IEEE Standard Dictionary of Electronic Terms*
  - *Electronic Computer Glossary,* Alan Freedman, The Computer Language Company, 1995.
  - *The Computer Glossary,* ed. Alan Freedman, 6th edition, 1993
  - *IBM Dictionary of Computing,* 10th edition (August 1993), McGraw-Hill
  - *IEEE Encyclopedia of Computer Science,* 3d edition (1993), IEEE Press
  - *McGraw-Hill Dictionary of Scientific and Technical Terms.* 5th edition, 1994
  - *Galaxy,* a guide to Internet-based reference materials and dictionaries, http://galaxy.einet.net
  - *The Free Online Dictionary of Computing,* http://www.instantweb.com/~foldoc/

8   Don't Confuse Editing Tasks with Other Tasks

While you edit you should try to see your editing tasks as separate from your writing tasks. This allows for greater efficiency in the process. Also, if you edit the work of others, you should identify tasks that you don't have to do. The tasks listed below don't really fall into the editing category.

■ **Don't supply missing material: procedures, definitions, explanations.** Editors do the work of forming and shaping a document, not the research that provides the information in the document. As an editor, you will find many areas during the substantive edit that require more information, especially if you have the readers' informational needs in mind. Mark these for the writer to address.

■ **Don't supply missing screen captures.** If you think a procedure needs a screen, indicate so, but don't capture it yourself. Screens require careful planning, in most cases, and the right software.

■ **Don't write more than short passages.** Often you will write short passages because the original sounds so garbled or misdirected that you just can't stand it. Often it will not fulfill the purpose of the heading. But editors don't write longer passages.

■ **Don't edit a manuscript more than once.** Theoretically, you should only edit a document for one level of editing once. That should catch most mistakes. Of course, on the flip side, you need to catch all the errors and problems the first time. With a particularly needy manuscript you will want to spot-check it afterwards.

Discussion

Writers and editors share a lot of the same characteristics: they work on development teams and work in the same environments. They may work in the same publications department or work group and often have the same reporting structures. They concern themselves with the same documents and share the same goals: to produce usable documents to support work. But to do good editing you also need to know the differences between editors and writers.

Writing versus Editing

Usually you write first, then you edit or get edited. Some writers edit while writing, stopping to fix a typographical error or dress up a table before writing more sentences. I do it as a way of lingering over a passage, of slowing down writing so the words that appear on the screen have time to sink in. But this kind of fiddling with text while you write doesn't pass for systematic editing, which can't really happen until you complete the whole document. Writing also differs from editing because editing requires you to form a different relationship with the text than you had as a writer. You need a distance from text when editing, so you should approach it "coldly," after a period of time. Similarly, if you edit someone else's work, you approach it with a different attitude from the one the writer had. Even though you may have editors helping the development team from the start and you consider matters of style all through the early stages of writing, you can't escape the feeling that when you write you *make* the document and when you edit you *shape* something already made. When you turn from writing to editing, you turn from issues of content to issues of consistency, integrity, shape, and form.

Table 7.6 gives you a broad overview of the differences between writing and editing. For writers who have to turn from one activity to another, such a comparison can help you avoid a confusion of roles that can lead to unproductive work and, ultimately, to missing your documentation goals.[4]

Editing in Desktop Publishing Environments

Before desktop publishing, editors formed important links between the writer and the document and the production personnel (illustrators, typists, typesetters, printers). The editor read the text and gave instructions to these persons on how to manipulate—reformat, set, draw—the information according to the author's intentions. With desktop

Table 7.6

A Comparison of Writing versus Editing

As a Writer You . . .	As an Editor You . . .
Concentrate on generating, collecting, testing useful information	Concentrate on document standards, production processes, printing, schedules
Become expert in a specific program, interview experts, learn all the features	Become expert in writing standards, company policies, stylistic guidelines
Work on one project at a time	Work on multiple projects at a time
Compose	Correct, check, compare
Maintain direct contact with readers	Maintain indirect contact with readers through writers and document specifications
Work on one kind of document: user documentation	Work on many kinds of documents: internal publications, style guides, brochures,
Are very familiar with a specific product or technology	Are very familiar with the company and a variety of products
Start with a product and produce a document	Start with a document and produce an information product

publishing, the editor's role often changes to giving those instructions back to the writer who often, in the role of typesetter or illustrator, will make the changes.

Problems with Editing Manuals and Online Systems

When you edit online help systems you face essentially the same concerns as you face when editing print: consistency, clarity, and integrity. But you have to deal with the different medium. I've made a list of some of those differences for you here.

1. **Heavy emphasis on editing the index.** Users don't know online systems as well as they do books, so you have to edit *search keywords* and navigational aids carefully.[5]

2. **Different production process for planning and scheduling.** Your online help system will usually be built long before your manual will, and you have to coordinate with programmers for much of it.

3. **Format of material: multimedia, hypertext.** Because you're dealing with electronically presented text, you can't scribble on it in the same ways as you do on paper. You can't distribute it as easily, in some cases, because of the equipment that readers need to view the draft material. Sometimes you end up printing and editing the draft.

4. **Editing for completeness and accuracy of topics given the initial topic list.** In online help systems you should have an updated topic list to work from, so you can make sure all topics have been written and that they all meet their original specifications.

5. **Print screens, then edit them, but also edit on the screen.** Customarily you print your help topics and then work off the paper version. While you can see the same words this way, you don't see the words the same (through a screen). You can't get their impact as electronic text, can't scroll them, can't see the same colors or highlighting as on a screen. These subtle differences can affect your editing.

How Do You Know What's Correct?

People expect the editor to know the correct spelling, usage, grammar, punctuation, and capitalization of all matters of language. For example, should you tell users of a network to "*Login* to the system," or "*Log in* to the system," or something entirely different? Try as they might, editors have yet to disabuse the general public, especially writers, of the myth that somehow *they* know the correct usage in this and many other cases. In truth, language, especially the language of high-tech computers, changes daily, and often you have difficulty finding standards of usage, spelling, and other matters. As an editor, you need to know where to look to find answers to questions like this.

Answers to questions of correctness depend, in large part, on how widely a particular spelling or usage has gained acceptance. To find correct answers to these matters you should start at the top of the hierarchy of authorities and work your way down. Clearly, the higher an authority you can cite, the better your chances of gaining acceptance among those you wish to convince. Basically, you can consult the five levels of authority illustrated in Table 7.7.

Editing and Task Orientation

All types of editing support task orientation because, when editing, you aim to produce a document that meets the needs of users in the workplace, particularly in the information-intensive workplace. But the issues raised in substantive editing perhaps have a more evident bearing on helping users communicate and manage information. The paragraphs below attempt to explain the types of editing as they pertain specifically to print and online documentation and to show how each one helps you meet your users' task goals.

Coordination Edit

In the coordination edit, your job is one of managing and planning, to shepherd the document and writer through the production process. This kind of edit requires you to manage the scheduling of drafts, tests, reviews, edits, printing, and production. You attend planning meetings and gather cost estimates to match the specifications in the document plan.

TASK CONCERN. Here you have the opportunity to help maintain a productive relationship between the writer and the user and between the writer and other support groups. In fact, in this kind of edit, you help maintain a focus on user concerns among all the persons and departments associated with a particular document.

By setting dates and helping to schedule user reviews and tests, you make sure that the user's job needs and usability perspective get heeded during the production process. You can clarify user input and make sure that it is reflected in the revised document

Table 7.7

Levels of Authority in Editorial Decisions

Level from Highest to Lowest	Description	Example
General Style Guides: *Chicago Manual of Style* *The American Heritage Dictionary*	All elements of punctuation, mechanics, grammar, spelling, and style.	"Use a hyphen to join multiple-word unit modifiers: 'easy-to-learn software.' "
In-house Style Guides: *CONVEX Style Manual*	Standards unique to a company, the subject matter, kind of product, and controversial matters where style is adopted for consistency.	"Always place CONVEX in all caps. The exceptions are those specific product names that use the word otherwise. Examples: ConvexOS, ConvexAVX, ConvexRTX."
Document Specifications for a Specific Document	Standards unique to a specific document or product.	"Refer to the product as 'DOANE On Disk.' "
Common Sense	Standards used because they appear logical.	"Use *online* rather than *on-line* as a spelling because the word gets used so frequently the unhyphenated spelling will make it easier to type."
Consistency	Standards used in order to achieve consistency.	"Use *on* instead of *upon* consistently for no particular reason other than to avoid arguments."

through careful coordination of the writer's responsibilities in fixing the document. Often we call these responsibilities *rework commitments*.

Policy Edit

Policy editing requires you to make sure the document conforms to the policy of your organization or department. Here you relate the document to the policies specified in your company's style guide and other expressions of policy of the company, such as conformance with regulations or governmental standards. You have to follow the style guide for the presence and proper format of the following:

- Document elements: front matter, table of contents, index
- Special pages: title, copyright, revision history
- Page layout elements: titles, headings, headers, footers, page numbers
- Format of special elements: tables, figures, special lists (trademarks, measurements, etc.)

A policy edit also requires you to make sure that you don't advertise for competing products or make statements that reflect negatively on your company or your software.

TASK CONCERNS. These specifications exist to give your manual a consistency among other publications done by your company. You and your users benefit from this consistency because it fosters transfer of reading and information access skills your users develop from one manual to another. All these elements perform the function of making the document usable. If your company encourages user input, make sure you acknowledge that. Clarifying previous versions of a document can help users transfer their familiarity from previous manuals. Citing trademarks and measurements clearly reinforces the context of software use.

Integrity Edit

The integrity edit ensures that the parts of a document match one another. When you edit for integrity, you make sure, for example, that if in Section 3 you refer the user to related information in Section 8, the information actually exists at that location. The integrity edit examines manual elements for these criteria:

- Table of contents matches the text pages and page numbers.
- List of tables and figures matches the tables, figures, and screens in the text.
- Routing sequences specify the correct location within the document of the necessary information.
- Cross-referencing of tutorial lessons, user's guide, reference, and online support is consistent.
- Screen captions and figure numbers are unique and consecutive.
- Numbered or lettered sequences, as in steps, are correctly labeled.
- Spine copy, bleed tabs, and index pages are consistent.

TASK CONCERNS. When you perform the integrity edit, you examine one of the most important elements of any documentation product: the navigational structure. This structure ensures that your user learns the way of finding information you set up within your manual or online system. Mistakes in the integrity of this system can cost the user time and drastically reduce the document's effectiveness. Consider how low an online system will plummet in user esteem the first time a link from a definition to a procedure winds up taking the user to the wrong procedure. What happens when you send the user to Section 8 for a glossary definition but have forgotten to include it at that point? When your document contains these kinds of mistakes, you take what the industry refers to as "high level shots." Such mistakes appear on your user response cards and can even get quoted in your performance evaluations.

Elements of consistency in format and text references encourage cognitive processing; users quickly learn how to get information from the document. Even users who don't quite fit your user profile are especially likely to follow these elements. They may even temporarily assume the user profile you provide them, reflected through your examples and cross-references, as a way of paralleling their own occupational pattern. They use the lists of figures and screens as ways of finding information. So you can see how crucial the integrity edit is to the task orientation of your manual.

Screening Edit

The screening edit consists of making sure the document meets basic standards for any document. It identifies and corrects errors in the text and visuals. When doing a screening edit, you look for the following elements:

- Correct spelling
- Subject/verb agreement
- Complete sentences
- Incomprehensible statements due to missing information
- Suitability of screen captures for publication (clarity, no site-specific information, etc.)

TASK CONCERNS. Mistakes in a document that render it substandard erode user confidence in that document. And users need to have confidence in your manual or help system because it has to compete against other forms of information in their work environment that also intend to make them productive workers. A satisfied user places trust in a good document.

Satisfied users perceive their documentation as supportive and of good quality. They see the value of it because it helps them in their work, but to value it they have to see it as a quality document. Trokzadeh and Doll have explored the place and value of documentation in end-use computing and found a number of simple measures of documentation quality that you would expect to catch and pay attention to while doing a screening edit.[7] Users perceive quality user documentation to have the following characteristics:

- Complete
- Easy to read
- Accurate
- Well-written

Proper care during the screening edit can help assure that users will give the documentation "high marks" for quality.

Copy Clarification Edit

The copy clarification edit involves reworking illegible text and artwork so that persons involved in production (illustrators, printers, typists, typesetters) will not make mistakes. You need to clarify whether the printer can or can't reduce screen size; you need to make sure the callouts on illustrations read legibly so that the illustrator does them right.

TASK CONCERNS. Copy clarification relates to task orientation of users in subtle ways. The user's preferences for screen size, or for legibility of callouts, should determine the kind of clarification of the manuscript needed. Printers, illustrators, and typesetters will adjust text and visuals to the lowest common denominator when rearranging your words and layout to fit the requirements of publication. If your user requires special consideration in these areas, then the copy clarification editing process will make sure that distortions of text and graphics don't creep into the document after it has left the writer's hands.

Format Edit

The format edit ensures that all instances of typography, style, and page layout conform to the style guidelines for the document. In particular, the format edit examines elements that transcend a specific document. To do a format edit you look at the following:

- Typography: type styles, leading, column widths, headings, indentations
- Style: continuity instructions (so users don't get lost between pages), positioning of figures and tables
- Progress indicators and navigational aids
- Running headers and footers
- Margins, spacing, rules, fonts, page numbers, binding, tabs

TASK CONCERNS. Format elements help adapt the technology to the user's human nature, help with problem solving, mirror cognitive ways of reading/scanning, facilitate workplace usage, and reinforce the structure of a page. Many of these features relate not just to your specific document, but to documentation in general: how manuals can be used by various kinds of users. To do an effective format edit you should draw on your knowledge of computer users in general, attempting in your examination of the document to help the document do its job effectively.

Mechanical Style Edit

In the mechanical style edit you make sure that the document mechanics conform to whatever style specifications you use, whether a company style guide or the document specifications done in the document plan. An edit for mechanical style ensures conformity in the following areas:

- Capitalization related to content ("CPU" versus "cpu")
- Spelling ("disk" versus "disc")
- Word compounding ("online" versus "on-line")
- Form and construction of numerals and terms ("drive A:" versus "A:-drive")
- Form and use of acronyms and abbreviations
- Use of cuing patterns (bold, script, color, etc.) for specific words or content.

TASK CONCERNS. The edit for mechanical style makes sure that the document's details of style match those set in your house style guide or the style set up for a specific document. In the case of an in-house style guide, you need to make sure the document conforms with the user preferences that the style guide represents. Some of the information in that guide will bind the editor and author to one alternative, but style guides frequently allow for leeway. So you may have both the in-house style guide and the specs for a specific document to guide decisions about mechanical style. Style guidelines set for a specific document usually get articulated in document specifications or *style sheets* prepared by the writer.

    As in the previous kinds of editing, the mechanical style edit helps the specific writer and document conform to standards designed to ensure that documents present information in usable form to users. They assure that users can read documents easily and quickly to find the information they need.

Language Edit

The language edit has to do with the way writers express thoughts through language, regardless of format. Unlike the previous kinds of edits, it goes further into how clearly and precisely the sentences express explanations, steps, definitions, elaborations, and other language elements of a document. On one level, the language edit concerns itself with spelling, grammar, syntax, punctuation, and word usage. Because the language edit relies on standards beyond those of personal preference of the editor and writer, editors often rely on standard reference guides in case of disputes over specific cases. These guides include *Webster's Third New International Dictionary* and Fowler's *Modern American Usage.*

When doing a language edit, you will also examine elements of writing that will call forth your skill in crafting economical, concise sentences. These include:

- Ensuring fluency of one sentence to another within paragraphs
- Crafting parallelism in steps and lists
- Deleting for conciseness in sentences
- Ensuring proper use of description, elaboration, examples, screen-focusing statements
- Clarifying definitions of abbreviations, acronyms, and symbols

TASK CONCERNS. Because one of the main impediments to efficient and effective use of software lies in the user's lack of familiarity with the computer-mediated tool, language becomes the most important link between user and software. The user brings a knowledge of language to an otherwise abstract and confusing situation and relies on it to uncover what to do and what to understand. The language edit makes sure that words, sentences, and paragraphs convey accurate and concise information about a program and its use to the user.

Substantive Edit

When doing a substantive edit, you pay close attention to the meaningful content of a document. The introduction, procedures, definitions, and other parts should accurately and consistently reflect one another. A substantive edit examines these elements of meaningful content in the following ways:

- Make sure all elements are in the right order.
- Ensure that titles, introduction, and appendices contain the right information.
- Check divisions of information are logical and consistent.
- Maintain the correct emphasis on certain elements, such as information-related tasks.
- Minimize redundancy and repetition.
- Omit irrelevant or inappropriate material.
- Find instances of missing information.

TASK CONCERNS. Because it deals with information the user needs, the substantive edit addresses task-orientation concerns directly. The information needed in a document set depends on the user's task demands and needs for subject matter knowledge (background). A document set acts as a whole: tutorial, procedures, reference, and online parts should work together in a concise, coordinated unit to adapt the software to the designated user. The need to keep print manuals short and economical and to tailor information products to users means that manual sets have no extra room. Elements that contain inappropriate information, lack needed information, or skew the emphasis of information are a waste of space.

Glossary

rework commitments: the responsibilities of a writer or writing team to make sure that problems found in editing or reviewing get fixed in a document.

search keywords: terms associated with topics in help systems that allow the user of the help system to find information.

style guide: a book or booklet-length collection of conventions of grammar, punctuation, spelling, format and other matters associated with written and online text.

style sheet: a page or document divided into alphabetical sections and used to keep track of conventions used for a specific document.

Checklist ✔

The conventions covered in this checklist cover general conventions rather than specific guidelines for a company. Also, I could not include every convention in the book, nor would I want to here, because you can find them in standard reference guides.

Editing Checklist
Mechanics and Punctuation

☐ Abbreviations: Follow style guidelines, use consistently, explain clearly. Example (if this is what you had decided): "3.5 in." rather than "3.5-inch" or "3.5"."

☐ Acronyms: Check for consistent use, explain unusual terms used for the first time. Example: use "DOS" but spell out newer terms to avoid confusion, as in "Virtual instruments (VIs) have three main parts. . . . The front panel specifies the inputs and outputs of the VI."[7]

☐ Capitalization: Check all trademarks and product names for consistency and conformity to style guidelines ("RoboHELP," "WordPerfect Corp.").

☐ Cues: Check all cues such as glossary terms, keypress sequences, and menu choices for consistency and conformity to style guidelines.

☐ Hyphens: Check all compound adjectives preceding the word modified for proper hyphenation. Example: "end user documentation" should be "end-user documentation," but "documentation for the end user" is correct.

☐ In-text definitions: Follow style guidelines for use of bold and/or italics, and (possibly) explanations in parentheses.

- ☐ Quotation marks: follow style guidelines for usage around terms (possibly) or Chapter titles, to name two possibilities. Example: . . . see Chapter 3, "Program Manager."[8]
- ☐ Spelling: Use a spell checker, spell special terms according to style guidelines.
- ☐ Steps: Number/bullets consistently and consecutively.
- ☐ Trademarks: Check with the trademark "owner" for legal restrictions on use of trademarks and names. Always say "Use the Excel spreadsheet program to . . ." rather than "Use Excel to . . ."

Language and Usage

- ☐ Consistency of voice: Use active and passive voice consistently. Example: "You need to check the results of this step to be sure the stream network has been thinned to one pixel width. Once this has been accomplished, continue to the next step." The second sentence should begin "Once you have accomplished this" to keep it parallel with the active voice in the first sentence.
- ☐ Fragments. Check for sentence fragments where they would be inappropriate.
- ☐ Paragraph length: Check for unusually long paragraphs. You can probably subdivide any paragraph longer than 1.5 inches into subtopics.
- ☐ Parallelism: Check for parallel grammatical structures in all lists. Example:

  The options described below allow you to do the following:
  - Choose a logarithmic scale.
  - Scale limits defined. [Should be "Define the scale limits."]
  - Set the minimum step of the scale to be an integer.

- ☐ Performance orientation: Make sure all instructions and explanations indicate performance of a task in the workplace. Example: "Grass 4.0 has a number of tools provided to help find and solve problems that can occur in digitizing." [should be "Grass 4.0 provides you with a number of tools to help you find and solve problems . . ." or "Grass 4.0 provides a number of tools to help you find and solve problems . . ."].[9]
- ☐ Unbiased gender references: Check for appropriate gender representation in language and examples. If names are used, for example, include women's names and men's names in approximately equal proportion, even if the activity has traditionally been performed more commonly by one gender than the other.
- ☐ Precision of diction: Check for precise technical terms. Don't say "use" when you mean "install." Don't say "boot" when "start" would be clearer to the uninitiated user. Whenever you use jargon you should do so with proper explanation. Other jargon terms include "download," "site," "hub," "black box," "tower," "fiber," "backbone," and "log."
- ☐ Sentence Length. Check for unusually long sentences and re-write as two or more sentences.
- ☐ Unclutter cluttered sentences. Example: "Do not install other desk accessories either in the System file in the Server Folder on the startup volume or in the System file in the System folder on the *AppleShare Server Installation* disk." This should be rewritten as more than one sentence to separate similar-sounding terms.
- ☐ Usage: Use precise, simple, descriptive terms. Example: "Idealiner enables [should be "helps"] you to control the appearance of characters."

Organization

☐ Completeness: Check for the following parts (does not all apply to all manuals):

☐ Title page   ☐ Acknowledgments   ☐ Notetaking page(s)
☐ Copyright page   ☐ Trademark list   ☐ Revision history page
☐ License   ☐ List of Tables   ☐ Index
☐ Table of Contents   ☐ List of Figures   ☐ Appendices
☐ Foreword   ☐ List of Screens   ☐ Advertising insert

☐ Organization: Check for the following overall organizational schemes for manuals and sections:

- Degree of difficulty (beginning, intermediate, advanced)
- Sequence of use (starting, processing, analyzing, printing)
- Tasks (task a, task b, task c)
- Job-related topics (topic a, topic b, topic c)
- User types (novice, experienced, expert)
- Program areas (area a, area b, area c)
- Alphabetical (a, b, c)
- Order of menus (menu a, menu b, menu c)

Format

☐ Lists: Follow style guidelines established for the project. Example: "Colon preceding list, no periods for fragments; square 10-pt. filled 'bullets' align with left text margin; ¼" indent to text; text returns wrap to same ¼" point."

☐ Tables: Follow table guidelines established for the project. Example: numbered titles above in bold, rules above and below first column heads, column heads left-justified, rule below last row, initial caps in row heads.

☐ Page consistency: Check that pages have the same top, right, bottom, and left margins.

☐ Margins: Check that top, right, bottom, and left margins conform to the document specifications.

☐ Headers and footers: check that headers and footers reflect the information in the sections and contain the correct text.

☐ Pagination and page breaks: Check for correct right/left pagination and page breaks above individual tasks and sections.

☐ Page numbering: Check front material ("i, ii, iii," etc.) and main section pages for consistency, correct sequences, and format.

☐ Vertical spacing: Check for correct spaces between lines and paragraphs, and between rows in tables.

☐ Horizontal spacing: Check for correct spacing before lines, between words; check centering of figures and lateral alignment of headings and marginal icons.

☐ Type styles and fonts: Check for the correct type styles and fonts for: body text, cued text, user-typed information, figure and table titles, callouts, header and footer text, and headings.

☐ Orphans and widows: Check for orphans (abandoned at the bottom of a page) and widows (isolated at the tops of pages).

☐ Rules: Check line thickness and length of rules in tables, headers, footers, columns, and section breaks.

Visuals

☐ General: Check for presence of all titles.
☐ Unneeded elements: Check for clutter in screens, items in directories in screens that don't relate to the user's environment.
☐ References to visuals: Check for clear, consistent references to visuals in the text.
☐ Appropriateness: Check that screens and cropped screens reflect the appropriate elements discussed in the text.

Tables

☐ Units of measurement in column heads
☐ Placement appropriately in the text
☐ Accurate table numbers
☐ Punctuation of elements consistent

Figures

☐ Elements correctly identified
☐ Aligned correctly with text
☐ Accurate figure numbers
☐ Accurate and complete captions

Screens

☐ Accurate labels
☐ Clear relationship to the text
☐ Cropped appropriately
☐ Legible
☐ Correct sizing and alignment

Practice/Problem Solving

1. A Style Guide for Editing Online Help

Editing online help requires attention to individual topic modules, examining them for elements that we know make online help work. These might include:

■ Information access
■ Navigation
■ Overall help design
■ Keywords (equivalent to index)
■ Completeness/accuracy of topics
■ Image fit, orientation

Imagine that you have just started as a publications manager of a software firm looking to expand its staff of writers and to begin shifting to more online documentation. You realize the value of a style guide for an expanded staff, many of whom haven't written help before, so you start taking notes. Considering the challenge of editing online material, make a list of the kinds of topics you want to address in your style guide and how you will create consensus in the guide.

2. Study the Work Habits of an Editor

Find the editor in your company or an editor of software documentation at your university. Set up an interview with him or her and see what you can find out about the editing habits discussed in this chapter. If you have access to email and the Internet, you may find a cooperative editor willing to answer a brief series of questions in an email message. Consider exploring these questions:

- How does the editor's work differ from that of writers of the documents?
- What forms, such as style sheets and checklists, does the editor use?
- What different demands do different media, such as print, online, and multimedia put on the editor?
- How much say does the editor have in establishing guidelines for his or her own organization?
- What kind of training does the editor see as most helpful for preparing editors?

3. Resolving Controversial Usage

Often technical editors get drawn into discussions of editing specific controversial usage. Often you have to refer to different authorities to resolve the discussion. Consider the lists below. How would you resolve the controversy, and what authorities would you refer to for help?

The user *who* initiates the first search procedure on the network.	The user *that* initiates. . . .
Upon opening the file, you will see table headers.	*On* opening the file. . . .
You will find tables of commands in the Appendixes.	. . . in the Appendices.
Procedures are found in the "User's Guide."	. . . in the *User's Guide.*

4. Create a Mock Style Sheet

Study a manual or help system with which you're familiar for the conventions it follows. Mock up a style sheet for the document following the example in Figure 7.3. What elements of the style of the document would you want to record as you wrote it? Can you find any inconsistencies in the document?

8

Designing for Task Orientation

This chapter presents tools and techniques for responding to the characteristics of software users. The chapter suggests a problem-solving approach to design of documents, allowing the writer or designer to apply those techniques that adapt technology to human use through a manual or help system. The chapter covers guidelines for designing to meet user needs, and then explores techniques for responding to each of the elements in the user analysis checklist. Next it presents a document designer's toolbox in a discussion of each element.

How to Read this Chapter

All readers should read this chapter from start to finish. Along with Chapter 9, "Laying Out Pages and Screens," it functions as a key statement of how I articulate the relevance of design concepts to task orientation. These represent just the beginning. With the ever-broadening definition of the page and the book—including things like htmlHelp and other hypertext technologies—the technical writer in the software industry needs to know a growing number of page and book *affordances*. This chapter gives you the basics of *book* design, and Chapter 9, "Laying Out Pages and Screens," gives you the basics of *page* design.

■ To those working on a project and anxious to get started, practical tips for design are discussed in Guideline 5: "Review the User Analysis," p. 254.

■ Those readers interested in broadening their understanding will appreciate the psychological discussion of users under the heading "The Design Problem," p. 261. And if you are in the midst of planning a project, the "Solutions to the Design Problem" for print and online help systems acts as a handy resource, a gallery of features of manuals and online help systems.

Figures 8.1 and 8.2 present some elements of document and screen design.

Chapter 10   Compiling, Testing, and Eliminating Errors in Projects

Using the Error Location Agent

RoboHELP's intelligent error location agent can augment your intellect with some automated error location features.

Locating an Error in a Help Topic

The error location agent can track down most errors that occur within a Help file. If the Help compiler gives a location for the error, the agent can track it down.

To locate an error in a Help topic

1. Do *one* of the following:

   MOUSE Click the Errors button from the RoboHELP tool palette.

   KEYBOARD Choose View Errors from the Word 6.0 Project menu (ALT, P, V).
   [In *Word 2.0*: Choose 'Help Compiler Errors' from the View menu.]

   The Errors button

   -Or-

   • Choose the Errors button from the Quick Check or Make progress dialog box.

2. Select an error from the list of errors. Do *one* of the following:

   • With the mouse, double-click on the error.

   -Or-

   • Choose the Locate button.

   The RoboHELP intelligent error agent determines the exact location of the error and does one of the following:

   • If the error occurred in a Help topic, it moves the Microsoft Word insertion point to the start of the topic where the error occurred.

   • If the error occurred in the project or context string mapping file, it pops-up the exact file and line number where the error occurred.

3. To obtain hints about hidden paragraph errors and other errors in topic text, do the following:

315

Headers help users locate the information within the context of the entire manual

Introductions help users see the workplace application of functions

Headings help users see the hierarchical structure of information

Icons help users recognize key information

Cuing patterns (bold, italics, etc.) help users recognize key information

Lists and tables help users decide how to apply program functions to workplace tasks and give users a sense of control

Page numbers help users navigate among abstract concepts

Figure 8.1

Elements of Document Design

This page from the RoboHELP *User's Manual,* Version 2.6 shows how elements of document design help users gain access to and manage information.

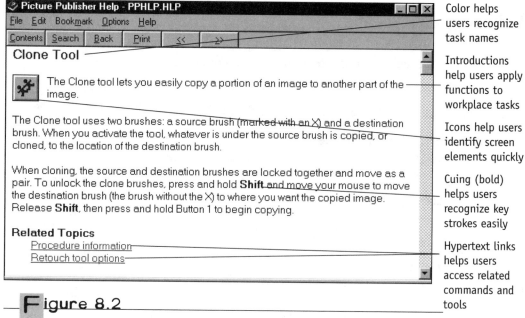

Color helps users recognize task names

Introductions help users apply functions to workplace tasks

Icons help users identify screen elements quickly

Cuing (bold) helps users recognize key strokes easily

Hypertext links helps users access related commands and tools

Figure 8.2

Elements of Online Help Design

This screen from Picture Publisher *Help* shows some design features used in online documentation that enable users to access and manage their information.

Guidelines

Guidelines for designing documents are listed in Figure 8.3, and described in the paragraphs that follow.

1 FOLLOW A PROBLEM-SOLVING PROCESS

Think of document design as a sequence of steps beginning with a problem (meeting users' needs) and ending with a solution (a manual and/or help).

- **Set goals for your documents based on the user analysis.** What levels of usability and support for information-related work do you want to see in your users? What do they need to understand and how do they need to perform?

- **Identify a number of techniques that would meet the goals.** Start with a blank page or screen determine what elements (see Figures 8.1 and 8.2 for examples) you need to help meet those goals.

- **Mock up examples of one or two potentially useful designs.** Create one or two prototypes of pages or screens you want to use, representing two "looks." Use prototypes derived from successful models on competing or related products.

1. Follow a problem-solving process.

2. Meet task needs.

3. Try out ideas on users.

4. Examine existing documentation.

5. Review user analysis

6. Acknowledge production constraints.

7. Design the documentation as a system.

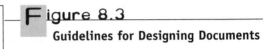

Figure 8.3

Guidelines for Designing Documents

- ■ **Test and review.** Evaluate through reviews by clients and sponsors. Test problematic areas in a lab or field test.

- ■ **Decide on a design.** Decide on a design with confidence, having followed a process based on logic and experimentation.

2 MEET TASK NEEDS

At the heart of any task-oriented documentation you will find step-by-step procedures called tasks that your user can follow to perform useful work. In terms of the design of your book or help system, you'll have the job of organizing those tasks so that they match the pattern of activity your user will understand as logical. And what's logical for some users won't appear too logical for others, precisely because they do different kinds of work.

Table 8.1 can help you find ways to organize your tasks, and in turn, provide a basis for organizing your manual or help system. It covers eight recognized methods of organizing tasks that you can use for individual documents or for sections of documents.

3 TRY OUT IDEAS ON USERS

Involve users in the process of designing documentation because it will allow you to eliminate a number of alternatives that would not work for your users. For example, one manual puts the index at the beginning of the document. This idea seems like a good one because users claim that they use the index more than any other part of a document to find information. Had the designers of the document tested its organization with users ahead of time, they would have realized that the "index in the front" needed some kind of explanation and justification. As it turned out, users rejected the document because it didn't fit their "expectations" of having an index in the back.

- ■ **Mock up pages with access elements on them and field test them.** Give users sample pages and find out which one they prefer. Preferences mean a lot in manual design. Find out your users' definition of "cluttered" pages, and avoid them.

- ■ **Consult the chapter on testing for ways to do quick usability tests.** Many field testing techniques, like summary tests and vocabulary tests, can yield data to help you decide between one design and another.

Table 8.1

Typical Ways to Organize to Meet Users' Task Needs

Method	Structures	Used For . . .	Examples
Degree of Difficulty	Beginning Intermediate Advanced	Tutorials	From *HBOOK Reference Manual:* (Makes histograms based on scientific data from particle physics experiments) *"1 and 2-D Histograms—Basics"* *"Advanced features for Booking and Editing Operations"*
Sequence of Use	Starting Processing Analyzing Printing	Tutorials Standardized usage software: word processors and spreadsheets	From *Getting Started with PV-Wave:* (Allows scientists and engineers to visualize and analyze technical data) *"Importing ASCII Data"* *"Creating a Date/Time Variable"* *"Using Mathematical Functions"* *"Reformatting Datasets"* *"Displaying Data as an Image"* *"Creating 3-D Surface Plots"* *"Printing Your Results"*
Jobs or Tasks	Job a Job b Job c	Programs with distinct users: administrators, clerks, executives	From *Municipal Court System Ref. Manual:* (Describes parts of the citation entry system for a city court system) *"Entering Citations"* *"Processing Receipts"* *"Setting Trials and Hearings"* *"Performing Batch Runs"* *"Handling Warrants and Capes"*
Job-Related Topics	Topic a Topic b Topic c	Large systems Fewer user types Identifiable topics	From *DELPHI: The Official Guide:* (Software to connect to an online information service) *"Business and Finance"* *"Computing"* *"Entertainment and Games"* *"Groups and Clubs"*

Table 8.1

(Continued)

Method	Structures	Used For . . .	Examples
User Groups	Group a Group b Group c	Educational programs Networks Groupware	From *Ear Trainer:* (Software to teach note and interval recognition to voice students) *"Teacher's Guide"* *"Student's Guide"*
Major Program Areas	Area a Area b Area c	Distinct program elements	From *MSGRAPH:* (Software to draw graphs from table data as part of a word processing program) *"Working with a Datasheet"* *"Working with a Graph"*
Alphabet	Task a Task b Task c	Experienced users Expert users	From *WordPerfect:* (Word processor) *"Align"* *"Append"*
Order of Menus	Menu a Menu b Menu c	Special menus	From *Pegasus Mail: Assistance Features* (Electronic mail system) *"Context-sensitive help (<F1>)"* *"Listing users on a server (<F2>)"*

4   EXAMINE EXISTING DOCUMENTATION

You can learn a lot by examining existing documentation for computer programs. You can find documentation in a number of places.

- **Software stores that carry used copies of programs.** Users have opened these programs so you don't have to break the shrink wrap.

- **Bookstores.** Bookstores always have one or more shelves containing books on computers. Many of these represent very well-designed books written by professionals about popular programs. You should spend time at these shelves when you visit the bookstore.

- **The user's workplace.** Ask to see the documents they like. Sometimes you can find shelves of programs and documents, often containing older versions of programs. Use caution in examining older versions of the manuals for these programs because the field of document design has progressed rapidly in the past five years or so. You may find yourself learning from others' mistakes.

■ **University computer centers.** Often these centers check out programs for students and other users, and they check out manuals with them.

■ **Public libraries.** Libraries have software available for you to use on site, and some may check programs out to patrons.

■ **Offices of friends.** All kinds of businesses and offices contain software that you can browse through and examine if you work there or know someone who works there.

■ **Programming shops.** Programmers and other high-tech professionals immerse themselves in software and use manuals a lot.

■ **Shareware programs.** Shareware comes with manuals in text files and help systems. You can find these on various archives on the Internet. Helpful sites include the "Woo Archive" (wuarchive.wustl.edu) and the Stanford Archive (sumex-aim.stanford.edu.) You can also get shareware programs on most network services (America Online, GEnie, Prodigy) and local bulletin boards. Like other sources of help systems, you will get the well-designed systems as well as those less well designed. Again, learn from others' mistakes.

5   REVIEW THE USER ANALYSIS

The following suggestions are from the user analysis checklist presented in Chapter 2. These questions give you a way of summarizing the important characteristics of your users. Specific design suggestions follow each element of the checklist. You should remember, however, that designing to meet user characteristics requires creativity and a willingness to test new ideas.

Design for Different Groups

> Possible Users of the Program
>
> ☐ What recognizable groups (teacher/student, system administrator/end user) will your users compose? Describe each group briefly.
> ☐ Provide a brief scenario of use by representative professions in order to show how the program will serve different professional user groups.

As you design for different groups, consider including all of the following elements:

■ Navigational aids to make sure groups get to the information pertinent to their needs

■ Scenarios to give each group a role model

■ Icons to identify information for each group

■ Metaphors (stadium, showroom, floorplan, schoolroom) for different users

Design for Specific Program Issues

> ### Primary Issues Raised by the Program
>
> ☐ What learning difficulties, motivational problems, technical difficulties will your users face?

To help your users meet the difficulties you identified, design your documentation to include:

- Job performance aids that cover technically difficult tasks
- Extra background information to meet special needs

Meet the User's Task Needs

> ### The User's Tasks
>
> ☐ What workplace jobs will the user do with the program?
> ☐ What important sequences will the user follow that can help you organize your program tasks?
> ☐ What tasks can you use as examples in your help and print manuals?

A lot of complaints are passed along by developers from their customers, but the most common complaint is that the documentation doesn't tell the users how to do things. It just describes the system and defines the terms and fields on the screen. Follow the suggestions here and in the rest of this book to make sure you don't get that complaint about your manuals.

- Show photographs, drawings, or clip art of users performing familiar tasks.
- Follow the eight methods of organizing tasks described in Guideline 2.
- Make the document fit the user's desktop.
- Include scenarios in *sidebars* explaining examples of use of the program.
- Provide a "getting started" section with three or four useful examples.
- Include performance-oriented elaborations and introductions.
- Have a special section showing users in various professional settings.

Meet the User's Information Needs

> ### The User's Information Needs
>
> ☐ What important kinds and forms of information does the user need in order to use the program?
> ☐ Whom does the user communicate with, and in what forms and media?
> ☐ What internal and external motivations affect the user?

Meeting the user's information needs requires you to understand how users manage information within a job setting. Then you "simply" write a manual that tells him or her how to use your program to support that work. The following strategies work well for meeting these needs.

- **Explanations.** Certain functions can lead to storage and re-use of information, but only if the user understands their use and their importance. Explain why file naming and directory structuring of program files can help retrieve reports and files.

- **Examples.** Examples that illustrate workplace uses of information the program generates can help users see how to manage their own work. Show program data imported into a word processing or database program.

- **Meet efficiency goals/command summaries for efficiency.** Both keyboard and mouse users appreciate avoiding irregular and time-consuming behaviors, so you should provide shortcuts, quick-key combinations, and pre-existing macros liberally. Unfortunately, many users may not see the relevance to their own goals, so include an introduction that explains the use of these shortcuts.

- **Problem solving.** Workers see themselves as problem solvers. Figure 8.4 shows how a writer's knowledge of examples of problems faced by a variety of user types allowed for an emphasis on problem solving with the program. Encourage problem solving by suggesting options, encouraging creative solutions and thought-provoking suggestions, and generally letting the users know that the writer has anticipated their problems and can show them how to use the program to solve them.

- **Emphasis on information management and communication work.** Identify functions that relate to information management and communication: file naming, saving files under other names, configuration of the program output, translating files to other formats, importing information from other programs, printing, report generation.

Match the User's Computer Experience

> ### The User's Computer Experience
>
> ☐ Describe the kinds of novice, experienced, and expert behavior exhibited by the user.

To suit the predominant type of user, consider the following characterizations and how you can incorporate them:

- **Novice.** Tutorial covering basic functions, definitions, full screens, sample files and templates, keyboard templates, automatic installation, humorous and reassuring tone, second (elaborate) table of contents

- **Experienced.** Problem solving support, transfer learning by references to commands in other programs, short-cuts, special section on "Ways to Use the Program Efficiently," error recovery techniques, full index

- **Expert.** Highly structured reference, troubleshooting support, command reference, quick reference card, full three-level index

PV-WAVE P&C is well suited for a variety of engineering and scientific tasks. The following table summarizes PV-WAVE P&C's capabilities.

Application	Capabilities
Test Engineering	Visualizing and analyzing data from analytical instruments.
	Evaluating results from quantitative experiments in fields such as cryogenics and materials testing.
	Visualizing vibration, heat transfer, stress, and emissions test data.
Space Exploration and Astrophysics	Studying geodynamics and seismology of planets.
	Analyzing data from satellites.
	Determining the composition of comets, meteorites, and other celestial bodies.
Computational Fluid Dynamics	Identifying flow patterns such as shock waves, vortices, shear layers, and wakes.
	Applying CFD research to aeronautics, automotive design, weather forecasting, and oceanography.
	Analyzing data from thermal dynamics, fluid dynamics, and nuclear reactions.
Medical Imaging	Displaying and analyzing bio-science imagery, including NMR/MRI, X-ray, CAT, and electron microscopy.
	Planning medical treatments, such as targeting areas for radiation therapy.
Earth Sciences	Simulating meteorological conditions and making predictions.
	Analyzing well logs to locate mineral deposits.

6   Getting Started with PV-WAVE Point & Click

Figure 8.4

A Way to Support Task-Oriented Work

This example from *Getting Started with PV-Wave* enables the user to see how the functions of the program support critical decision making and professional goals for a variety of user fields.

Enhance the User's Subject-Matter Background

> ### The User's Knowledge of the Subject Matter of the Program
>
> ☐   What kinds of vocabulary reinforcement and subject-matter background will the documentation have to provide?

Take advantage of the user's knowledge of the subject in your documentation, to enhance the usability of the software.

- **Special glossary of background terms.** Learn this by studying the user's job and workplace. What terms do they use to indicate what? Put these in a special glossary. It doesn't have to take up a whole section, but just a part of a page. In online help you can allow users to jump to definitions.
- **Index entries linking background terminology to program functions.** Identify the users' terms for special workplace concepts and include these in the index, along with mention of the relevant program functions.
- **Special booklets/sections describing background concepts.** PageMaker software now comes with a booklet explaining the elements of page design for desktop publishers. This may have reduced the frequency of "over-designed" documents that were being produced by those new to desktop publishing.
- **Elaborate examples with explanations of key concepts.** In the program Glider Design, the documentation includes a section on the theory of flight.

Leverage the User's Workplace

> ### The User's Workplace
>
> ☐   What other computer programs are used at the user's job site?
> ☐   What user's groups does the user belong to or have available?
> ☐   Describe the degree of organizational support for computer use in your user's organization.

Your documentation can help the new user build the necessary sense of community. Try to incorporate the following:

- Introductory passages/scenarios suggesting help from other users
- Special sections on in-house users groups or in-house technical support
- Encouragement of group use of the program
- Descriptions of network use

Meet The User's Learning Preferences

> ### The User's Learning Preferences
>
> ☐   Describe the user's preferences for instructor, manual, or computer-based learning.

Meeting learning preferences has to do with your choice of *media* and the design of documents for those media. The characteristics of the three predominant media vary; the following list includes some of the most usual ones.

- **Instructor learning.** For the *instructor:* lesson plan, overheads, sample files, quizzes, background information, equipment list, schedule/sign up sheet, video tape; For the *learner:* workbook, diskette, notes pages
- **Manual learning.** Tutorial manual, or elaborate "Getting Started" section, list of learning objectives, sample files
- **Computer-based learning.** Programmed computer-based training modules, sample files

Meet the User's Usage Pattern

> ### The User's Usage Pattern
>
> ☐   Describe the patterns users will exhibit in using the software in terms of regular, intermittent, and casual usage.

To meet the user's usage patterns, first determine which category is most appropriate:

- **Regular usage.** "About This Manual" section, interrelated examples to support incremental learning, organization around beginning, intermediate, advanced functions
- **Intermittent usage.** Troubleshooting to help with error recovery, fully detailed procedures to support on-demand learning, help systems, reminders of the interrelationships among program features, support for problem solving (tips, scenarios)
- **Casual usage.** Quick cards, keyboard templates, scenarios suggesting mental models of program usage and application

Your user analysis will also contain suggested document features that you should try out with potential users as part of the design process.

6   ACKNOWLEDGE PRODUCTION CONSTRAINTS

In each situation, whether involving a corporation with a large publications department or a smaller company with one or two people writing the documents, the environment in which we work poses constraints on the design choices we make. In Table 8.2 you will find some of these constraints posed as questions one should ask as part of the design effort.

7   DESIGN THE DOCUMENTATION AS A SYSTEM

A well-designed manual approaches these design variables systematically, so that each element of the design contributes to the overall user effectiveness, whether through teaching, guiding, or supporting user tasks. As a system, it uses the many solutions or tools described below, but it does so with a sense of unity, so that separate sections support one another: They assist one another in a way that makes the various parts of the manual usable to each respective audience. This unity of overall design makes a manual especially usable. If the document relies heavily on graphics, then it should use them throughout, so the user gets used to them. If the manual has a colorful style, then that style should be

Table 8.2

Production Constraints

Type of Constraint	Description
Writing Tools	What design capabilities does your word processing or publishing programs offer?
	How can we optimize the design of documents by using a computer network?
	What graphic programs or other graphic technologies (such as scanners, plotters, and printers) can we use?
Production Tools	What type styles and fonts does the laser printer support?
	Can we use color reproduction?
	How can different binding methods make manuals more accessible?
Human Resources	How much do members of the writing team know about user- or task-oriented design?
	How can we use management know-how to achieve the most usable design?
	Do we have clerical or other basic help available to allow for more complicated design solutions?
	What testing facilities can we use to try out new design ideas?
Budgets	How can we fit all the design ideas into the existing budget?
	What neat design ideas will we have to sacrifice or work around to meet cost and printing constraints?
	What design ideas will work when we have limited testing and review budgets?
External Considerations	How do other departments in the company design their documents and to what extent should we design like each other?
	What legal constraints—in terms of copyright/trademark protection and adequate warnings—should we build into the design?
	How do competing software products design their documents?

followed throughout. If you have established a pattern of steps and explanations, stick to it when confronted with a function that does not fit easily into the system. If you establish a pattern of describing error messages that might occur when you run certain procedures, make sure that you use that pattern for all relevant procedures. Build this kind of consistency into your manual, and you will have gone a long way toward successful user task orientation.

Let me describe briefly an example of a high degree of consistency and unity within a manual system. I examine all documentation with a critical eye, trying to see whether it would really help users. I came across the documentation for a product called Power-Play, a program that allows businesses to explore, analyze, and graph statistical information relating to business. It has uses in virtually all areas of business. At first the documentation disappointed me because the "manual" covered basic concepts, and a booklet accompanying it gave great examples of use, but nowhere could I find the kind of step-by-step documentation that I suspected users would want. It did, in fact, exist, but in the help system. After I familiarized myself with all the elements of the documentation system—the tutorial in the "manual," the examples, and the very extensive, task-oriented help system, I realized the efficiency of the design of the entire documentation set. The parts worked together very efficiently to teach, guide, and support the program's users. I liked the help system so much that I got permission to use it as the example in Chapter 8 on designing help. You can see it described there. The point, however, remains that for the various parts of a documentation set to work well they should not overlap and they should support each other.

Discussion

We live in an age of accommodation of writing to readers. All functional documents—not only those supporting software—require and allow a great deal more reader involvement than before. Readers no longer have to follow a strict linear form in reading. Consider *hypertext* documents, in which readers determine the order in which they read: The electronic form allows them to restructure the document according to their needs. In software documents, users also need this kind of freedom. They need to select parts of a manual that fit their needs, that help them perform their tasks. The manual should reflect a design that matches their needs and tasks. Because computer support comes in pages and screens—a linear format—many readers have a problem finding information and mentally restructuring it according to their task needs. Documentation designers call this the design problem.

The Design Problem

The design problem of software documentation resembles that for instructional materials in general. It has to do with the user's needs for support versus the document's organization and content. Essentially the problem results from each reader needing to apply the computer system to a multitude of tasks. And because of the linear bias in most information presentation—pages or screens in a row—users expect information organized linearly. One book, many users. To meet the goals of efficiency and effectiveness we need to accommodate the one to the many.

The Difficulty with Printed Books

Consider this example: An attorney writing a brief needs to shift a quoted passage to the right five spaces. The user might ask, "What do I do to make the text shift to the right with this word processor?" The user has a whole manual to search through to find an answer. She may not know what terminology to use to start: Is it an "indentation" problem, a "tabs" problem, a "page layout" problem, or a "margin" problem? As a rule, she will start looking in the wrong place, or at a random place in the book. Many users will simply open a book and thumb through it, looking for an answer. Others will use the table of contents or the index. She might try exploring the help facility, looking under "indent" or "margin" or "page layout." She might ignore the documentation altogether and use the space bar to force the text to the right, thus avoiding using the books at all. In fact, the information exists under the heading of "temporary indentation."

In terms of the design problem, the manual needs to accommodate her dilemma: The answer occurs in only one place in the manual, but there are many ways she might try to find that answer.

What Does *Guide* Mean?

What does *guide* mean? It can mean a lot of things. Does it mean that the manual will guide the user to the answer? In this sense the user sees the *manual* itself as a kind of jungle to be navigated, using tools like the table of contents, running headers, and index in order to find the page that has the right information. Does it mean that the manual will guide the user through the program? In this sense the user sees the *program* as a jungle, with a tangle of menu bayous and dialog box dead ends that the user has to search through to find the right function. Finally, does it mean that the manual will guide the user through the many ways to use the program? In this sense the user sees the *job* as a jungle, with many tasks to accomplish and goals to realize; the manual helps the user find productivity in the workplace.

You can see the idea of guiding in the three ways above: You guide the user to the manual, to the program, and to the job. In this chapter we look at ways to guide the user to the manual. In the example above, of the attorney trying to find out how to indent a paragraph, the manual itself represents a kind of jungle. Assuming the attorney does turn to the manual as a last resort, it needs to get her on track to an answer as soon as possible. In that way the manual is a "guide," in the sense that it must guide her to an answer in the manual. It has to educate her as to what term this particular program uses to describe her problem, tell her what page or screen to see, tell her what steps to follow to solve it, show her what indented text looks like, and offer help in case she gets off track. Doing these things well means that the manual has solved the design problem.

Documentation that overcomes the design problem depends in part, as we have seen in this example, on the *vocabulary* that users bring to their computing tasks. But the problem really involves more than vocabulary. In fact, it represents one of the most complicated and least understood aspects of software document design. So before discussing some of the design, let's examine the problem further.

Variable: Types of Users

You must constantly consider the degrees of experience among types of users. Each type of user will react to your manual or help system differently. This variety means that you cannot just write one manual; you have to write two or three manuals in one book, sometimes satisfying two or three sets of expectations and needs on the same page. You may categorize users in many ways, as we will study further in subsequent chapters, but the two ways we will take up here have to do with categories based on users' degrees of experience with computers (novice, experienced, expert) and users' professional roles (installers, managers, operators).

A common way to define users distinguishes between those just beginning to use computers and those who have either intermediate or advanced experience. Below we will examine how these groups' psychological differences and their informational needs pose challenges to manual designers.

PSYCHOLOGICAL DIFFERENCES: THE READINESS TO REJECT. The experienced user often has more patience with a program, more confidence than a novice user. The novice user will often blame a difficulty on the program ("This word processor doesn't allow you to move text to the right . . . imagine that!"). A more experienced user, on the other hand, will show more persistence ("This word processor must have a way of moving text to the right; they all do, I just haven't found it yet."). In this example, the novice user would perceive the software design as weak, whereas the experienced user would give the design more slack.

Novices have less experience with documentation—both manuals and online help. They don't know conventions of documentation (such as *tutorial, guidance, reference*) and can get lost looking for things in the wrong sections. They don't know terms manuals use, such as *routing systems,* don't know how to use help, can't identify their level of knowledge, and don't know where to go to look. Experienced and expert users know many manual and help conventions and can use them with confidence.

DIFFERENT INFORMATIONAL NEEDS: THE FACTOR OF PREVIOUS EXPERIENCE. In our example of shifting text to the right, the novice user would more than likely see the problem as one of margins, because of the similarity of the word processor to the typewriter. In this way, previous experience would cause her to look under "margins"—a mistake, because for the task of shifting text to the right, most word processors have an "indent" feature. In fact, only when one has a degree of experience with word processors does one know to look under "indent." The experienced user would recall the different terms for the task, and look in both, or other places, until finding the right term. The document designer needs to use a variety of features such as glossaries, cuing, graphics, and type styles to catch users of limited experience and get them on track.

Variable: Role-Based Types

Another variable regarding user types has to do with what we call role-based user types. To determine role-based user categories, we need to know what kinds of jobs the user performs with the software. Examples of role-based types include installers, operators, evaluators, decision makers, troubleshooters, and so on. Unlike the types based on degree of experience that we examined earlier, here the types describe the users' jobs and their relationship to the software. The manual set for the Convex operating system, for example, segregates users into role-based user categories: users, system managers, and programmers. Each of these categories of users needs to use different functions of the program and requires different levels of support. The writer, in this case, should segregate the information into the appropriate sections and then use adequate cuing to make sure each user type doesn't wander into the wrong section, like a hotel guest lost in the kitchen.

What defines performance, achievement, productivity, or efficiency for computer users in the professional workplace? You need to know what motivates professional employees, then tap into that motivation as a stimulus for the user to learn to use the program.

Variable: How People Solve Problems Using Computers

Another variable affecting the design problem concerns how people solve problems using computers. The more we know about how people get the program to do what they want, the better we can make their use efficient. Consider the way beginning artists typically solve the problem of drawing the human face. A common error among art students is to draw the eyes in the upper portion of the face, because people tend to see the eyes at this position, above the nose, above the cheek bones, above the mouth. In fact, the eyes fall about in the middle of the face. Knowing that people perceive the face the way they do, mentally putting the eyes in the upper half, the good art teacher will caution students about this, will watch for this common difficulty, and will design the instruction to counteract it (by having students actually measure the placement of the eyes, and so on). So it is with the designers of text instruction systems we call software documentation. The more we know about the common errors people make using computers, the more we can anticipate those errors, and design documentation that will counteract them.

In this regard, the current research into software use can help. Areas like *cognitive science* and *human factors* research have, during the last ten years, looked at how people use computers to find ways of making computers more usable, of making people more productive in using them. What do they have to say that might relate to the design problem?

Cognitive scientists show us patterns that people follow in solving problems with using manuals. Sullivan and Flower, two researchers at Carnegie Mellon University, used a *protocol method* to study manual users: they recorded all the keystrokes, pauses, and reading times of manual users to determine not how people read, but how they use manuals.[1] Their research led them to the following five conclusions. Each of their conclusions is presented below, followed by some design advice you can use to help anticipate and overcome the design problems involved.

1. No one carefully reads more than two sentences at a time. Busy professionals just don't have time for more than this. They value work time more than computer time.

   Design Advice:
   - Keep paragraphs short.
   - Arrange information into tables and lists wherever possible.
   - Put important information at the beginning of each paragraph.

2. Most of the users begin to use the table of contents before they read the manual. Professionals learn early in their careers that planning ahead, even for short tasks, pays off.

   Design Advice:
   - Make the table of contents complete.
   - Use both an abbreviated and an elaborate table of contents for complex material.
   - Use chapter-by-chapter tables of contents.

- Make table of contents headings task-oriented: "Setting up a schedule" rather than "Schedule."

3. Most users go to the manual or help only after they have failed to perform a task. At this point you will find them hasty, stressed, and impatient.

Design Advice:

- Be sensitive to a user's state of mind after failure.
- Make descriptions of error recovery clear and complete.
- Emphasize getting back to real-world tasks.

4. Most readers do not read the introduction first, nor do they generally read all of it, even if the introduction is only three short paragraphs. Most professionals consider introductions "useless information" and want to skip directly to the steps for doing.

Design Advice:

- Replace the "introduction" with useful information about user needs, special document features, or helpful routing information.
- Replace the "introduction" with material designed to get them applying the system right away.

5. Most readers do not read any section in its entirety. Reading by professionals almost always connects with some real-world task that helps them filter information.

Design Advice:

- Avoid the injunction to "Read this manual before proceeding." Instead tell them which sections to go to for particular tasks or problems.
- Make sure that all descriptions of tasks and functions contain complete information for performing that task.
- Don't expect users to remember on page 50 what they read on page 33. Repeat important information if necessary.

Another researcher, Judith Ramey, studied how people use manuals by giving carefully designed questionnaires to computer users in a *usability lab*. She also taped them describing their use of the manuals and did follow-up interviews. Her results corroborated much of the work of Sullivan and Flower, but she makes another important point: Users of computer systems use *mental models* to understand the computer's functioning. Let's examine the idea of mental models further to see how it affects the design problem.

How Mental Models Work

Reading a manual that talks about a system of which you have no prior knowledge is like listening to a traffic report about a city where you don't live. You understand the idea of the traffic report, but it doesn't match the city map in your mind. Mental models are pre-existing maps, or frameworks, that people see in their minds as they strive to understand the world. For example, we identify a classroom by seeing elements of the "model classroom" in our mind: desks, chalkboard, lectern. Our prior knowledge of classrooms allows us to build the mental model. We have mental models for many things; according to theories of cognitive science (the study of how we recognize and think) these models comprise our basic tools for understanding the world.

Documentation readers use mental models to understand computer systems. The problem with computer manuals occurs when the manual contains a framework or design of the system that does not coincide with the one the user has in mind. This situation creates a gap in understanding. For example, imagine a manual for an office automation system that contained examples from a manufacturing automation system. These examples would not correspond with an office manager's mental model. That understanding gap costs time and money and leads to frustration for the user. A good manual, in that case, should bridge the gap between the computer program's "point of view" or model and that of the user. It would contain examples that relate to the environment most familiar to the user.

Design Advice:

- Include graphic overviews of the software system.
- Use analogies to the user's experience.
- Evoke the user's goal and achievement models.
- Use the same terminology as the user.
- Identify tasks the user recognizes and performs.
- Frequently suggest ways a function can help the user.
- Avoid elaborate, overly technical explanations with novice users.[2]

Another cognitive scientist, John Carroll, has done research at IBM on the way users learn—how they approach material specifically designed for teaching. While we will study the difficulties of teaching in subsequent chapters, here we will look at some of the characteristics of manual users that Carroll discovered and see how we can design manuals with these characteristics in mind.

Carroll observed many of the things discussed above: Novices get lost; readers skip around; users need task-related examples and instructions. But he found something that we have not discussed yet—that successful users of computers got to be so only after making an unusual number of mistakes. This makes sense when you think about it: We reason and learn by taking the wrong track and starting again. Imagine a keyboard without a backspace key. Unforgiving! And because users make so many errors, much of their frustration with learning and using computer systems comes from the fact that document designers failed to realize this and failed to build in adequate instructions for what to do when they get lost, press the wrong key, or click in the wrong box.

Carroll offers this simple advice: Expect errors, and make sure you tell the reader how to get out of trouble. Also, let the user direct his or her own learning; this way the user feels less overwhelmed by the tasks at hand, perhaps makes fewer errors, and when mistakes occur can back out without getting frustrated and giving up.

Design Advice:

- Focus on real tasks and activities that the user understands and has some degree of control over. Avoid "made up" examples, and replace them with examples derived from extensive user analysis.
- Slash the verbiage that does not relate directly to what the user needs to do. Do not present information that the reader does not need.

- Support error recognition and error recovery. Let the user know how to recognize when a mistake has occurred, and explain how to get out of trouble.
- Use guided exploration. From time to time encourage the user to try out a function, to experiment, to play.[3]

Solutions to the Design Problem for Printed Documentation

So far we have examined the elements of the design problem, investigating how variables such as user experience, user problem-solving strategies, and production constraints can alter the nature of the design of documents. Now turn to some of the solutions to that problem: ways you can design user task orientation into your products, while still recognizing the constraints of users and production tools.

Navigation

Navigational aids are elements of a document that tell the reader where to go next for what kind of information. Typically, you would place a navigational statement or section at the beginning of a manual, listing the types of users and indicating what parts of the manual you have designed for each. This section, usually under the heading of "About this manual . . ." distinguishes between levels of expertise (novice, expert, or power users) or users' professional roles (system administrators, terminal operators, sales persons, etc.). It tells them what portions of the manual contain information specifically for them.

Navigational aids helps you overcome the design problem in a number of ways. First, it allows you to accommodate both experience-based types and role-based types of users. Consider the experience-based types first. Often the levels of support—teaching, guidance, reference—correspond to levels of user experience with computers in general. In this case, you can direct novice users to sections containing tutorials, experienced users to sections containing procedures, and expert users to sections containing reference.

Usually, however, your specific users and program will not fall together quite so neatly. You may have a program of fairly specific application that would require you to design a tutorial for expert users. In this case, you should route these users to the appropriate sections of the manual, explaining what they will learn, how long it will take them, and why they should learn it.

You may also need to accommodate the user's learning curve with the specific system. Depending on your user analysis, you may identify some program tasks that users need first, and other program tasks they will need later. In this case, you should design your document accordingly, with "learn these first" functions in one section and "learn these later" functions in another. For example, with a database program that looks up information about agricultural markets, you may have some functions that support the user task of "getting data about farmers in the Texas panhandle." You would describe the program tasks needed to accomplish this in a section on basic functions. However, you also need to support the user task of "producing a written report to accompany a proposal." This user task requires more advanced program tasks than just looking up the data, and so you would describe these program tasks in a section on advanced functions.

Figure 8.5 shows how you can help users navigate to specific topics of interest to them. You will need navigational statements like this one to direct traffic to sections of your print documents. You will also need to describe the user tasks that these sections support.

How This Guide Is Organized

This guide is divided into five chapters, followed by appendices, a glossary, and an index. Use the following table as a general guide to find the information you need in the Wisconsin Package documentation.

If you're interested in	Turn to
An overview of the VMS operating system	Chapter 1, Getting Started
Starting the Wisconsin Package	Chapter 1, Getting Started
Specifics about using sequences	Chapter 2, Using Sequences
Databases	Chapter 2, Using Sequences
Learning about the basic concepts you will need to use the programs of the Wisconsin Package	Chapter 3, Basic Concepts: Using Programs
Learning how to run specific programs	**Program Manual**
Finding out about different data files, for example scoring matrices and restriction enzymes	Chapter 4, Using Data Files **Data Files** manual
Learning more about Wisconsin Package programs that produce graphic output, how you can use and manipulate that output, and what graphics configuration languages are available	Chapter 5, Using Graphics Appendix C, Graphics
Printing ASCII or graphic files	Chapter 3, Basic Concepts: Using Programs Chapter 5, Using Graphics
An alphabetical list of GCG commands and programs	Appendix A, Short Descriptions
Basic guidelines for using the text editor EDT	Appendix B, Text Editor Basics
Differences between VMS and UNIX	Appendix D, Command and Keystroke Differences Between VMS and UNIX
Definitions of some terms found in this guide	Glossary

xiv   Before You Begin   Wisconsin Sequence Analysis Package

Figure 8.5

Navigation Statements

These instructions from the Wisconsin Sequence Analysis Package *User's Guide* help the user understand where to go to find the right information for specific uses or experience levels.

In large computer systems, role-based user types often need specific manuals of their own, describing the program tasks needed to fulfill their roles. In this case, a separate section in the main manual performs the navigational function. For example, the Novell NetWare's manual set contains separate manuals for supervisors, users, system administrators, and so on. The "Guide to the Manuals" contains elaborate definitions of user types, under the heading of "What Type of User Are You?" These definitions help the user determine whether he or she is a "Novice, Experienced User, Supervisor, or Installer." The user who is a "User (Novice or Experienced)" is directed to manuals specifically designed for a user's needs (and conveniently marked with a "U" on the spine). The supervisor's manuals have an "S" on the spine, and the installer's manuals have an "I" on the spine. This navigational system helps the user make the most of a very complicated six-manual document set (a documentation set not made for the casual reader).

Systems for navigating manuals pose significant problems as well as solutions for document designers. The statements themselves make a manual more cumbersome. It sections off parts of manuals, segregating some users from others. Can the user possibly get lost in the wrong section? Yes. What's more, having a navigational system gives you another thing to *teach* the user: the system you use in the manual. This adds another level of complexity. And every time you add a level of complexity, you increase the distance between the material in the book and the relevance to the user's task. You build a layer of difficulty between the program and its task application. An office worker, for example, who needs to figure out how to create a spreadsheet for a project budget will not appreciate having to learn an overly complex system of navigating in a manual. Learning the system only relates tangentially to his or her task. Little of that task energy, that desire on the user's part to do well on the job, will carry over into learning the navigational system.

What can you do to be sure, first, that you really need a navigational system, and, second, that it will work? For one thing, you should make your decision to include navigating as an organizing feature only after you have examined your user's tasks carefully. These tasks will show you what jobs the user will need to perform, and in what environments. In later chapters we will study how to construct a "pattern of use" for your manual. A pattern of use tells how you imagine your users applying your manual in the optimum work situation. This pattern of use can help you decide whether or not to use navigational directions as a method of overcoming the design problem and increasing the access to information. The clearer you can see a definite pattern of use among a majority of users, the more likely that a navigational system will work.

Cross-References

Cross-references point to other sections or chapters containing related information. For example, in a procedure where you give guidance support on how to print a document, you would include a cross-reference to the section of the manual containing procedures for setting up the printer. That way, if the user needs to adjust the printer settings, or hasn't set the printer up yet, he or she can easily flip to the appropriate page.

The difficulty lies in the hassle of including page numbers of all your cross-references. Most word processors, such as Microsoft Word, can handle these page references automatically. When you create a reference, you insert a field at the point of cross-reference that points to a bookmark in the target section. Then every time you update the fields of the document, the program automatically updates the cross-reference, inserting the new page number of the target section or information. So much for the mechanics.

In some cases, however, writers use an easier solution to this problem, by inserting *generic* references to items in the task list that the user knows will occur in the table of contents or index. Thus a reference like "See the section on Setting Up a Printer in this manual for more information" does not require a specific page on which the target information resides. The trade-off, of course, requires that the user take an extra step by looking the page number up in the table of contents.

Given the specific constraints on your project, consider that to a user the best approach means you include the information they need at the point they need it. When you can't do this, consider the ease-of-use scale in Table 8.3 in deciding how much trouble you want you user to go through.

Running Headers and Footers

Running headers and footers such as those shown in Figure 8.6 consist of the page numbers and text information that occupy the top and bottom lines of a page. These may include any number of the following elements:

- Chapter and section names and numbers
- Book titles
- Graphic cues and icons
- Task names
- Color to indicate sections

The following paragraphs discuss these elements.

Table 8.3

Scale of Ease of Use of Types of Cross-References

Scale of Ease of Use	Reference Type	Example
Easiest	References to specific pages	"(For more information on setting margins see Page Setup, page 7-32.)"
	References to near-by information	"(Make sure to read the Tip for Efficient Use that follows this procedure.)"
	References to sections/chapters in the same book	"(For definitions of commands see **Chapter 4: Command Reference.**)"
	References to other books in the documentation set	"(For help understanding error messages consult the *System Error Messages Reference Manual,* vol. 6 of your Novell documentation set.)"
	References to manuals for other programs the user uses	"(See "Configuring Your System" in the manual that came with your operating system.)"
Most difficult	References to other sources of information (recognized professional handbooks, standards books, phone books, etc.)	"(See the *IRS Tax Schedule for 19XX* for information about tax rates.)"

Chapter 5   *Case and Sequence Structures and the Formula Node*

1. Open the Diagram window.

2. Place the Sequence structure (**Structs & Constants** menu) in the
    Diagram window.

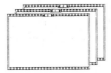

The Sequence structure, which looks like frames of film, executes
diagrams sequentially. In conventional text-based languages, the
program statements execute in the order in which they appear. In data
flow programming, a node executes when data is available at all of the
node inputs, although sometimes it is necessary to execute one node
before another. The Sequence structure is the LabVIEW way of
controlling the order in which nodes execute. The diagram that the VI
executes first is placed inside the border of Frame 0, the diagram to be
executed second is placed inside the border of Frame 1, and so on. As
with the Case structure, only one frame is visible at a time.

3. Enlarge the structure by dragging one corner with the Positioning
    tool. To create a new frame, pop up on the frame border and choose
    Add Frame After from the pop-up menu.

Frame 0 in the previous illustration contains a small box with an arrow
in it. That box is a sequence local variable which passes data between
frames of a Sequence structure. You can create sequence locals on the
border of a frame. The data wired to a frame sequence local is then
available in subsequent frames. The data, however, is not available in
frames preceding the frame in which you created the sequence local.

4. Create the sequence local by popping up on the bottom border of
    Frame 0 and choosing **Add Sequence Local** from the pop-up menu

The sequence local appears as an empty square. The arrow inside the
square appears automatically when you wire to the sequence local.

5. Finish the diagram as shown in the opening illustration of the *Block
    Diagram* section.

Tick Count (ms) function (**Dialog & Date/Time** menu). Returns the
number of milliseconds that have elapsed since power on.

Random Number (0-1) function (**Arithmetic** menu). Returns a random
number between 0 and 1.

Multiply function (**Arithmetic** menu). In this exercise, multiplies the
random number by 100. In other words, the function returns a random
number between 0.0 and 100.0.

© National Instruments Corporation   5-9   *LabVIEW for Windows Tutorial*

Figure 8.6

Headers and Footers Help Users Navigate

These headers and footers from the *LabVIEW for Windows Tutorial* contain elaborate information to help users keep track of their location within a manual.

CHAPTER AND SECTION NAMES AND NUMBERS. Chapter and section names and numbers help the user locate a specific page within the overall scheme of a manual. Because they occur at the head or foot of each two-page spread, they are always at the user's disposal. Names of chapters and sections should correspond to levels of support, such as "Beginning Tutorial" for teaching support, or "User's Guide" for guidance support. Generally, names work better than numbers because they describe tasks more accurately. Numbers, however, can correspond with the index and table of contents as points of reference. With chapters or sections you will usually use sequential numbering and restart numbering with each section. The number "5-1" refers to the first page of Chapter 5; the number "6-1" refers to the first page of Chapter 6, and so on.

BOOK TITLES. Book titles, like chapter and section titles, allow the user to see quickly where the current page falls within the entire scheme of the documentation set. Again, like chapter titles, book titles can refer to levels of support (e.g. *Tutorial* or *Learning System X*) or to role-based user types (e.g. *Supervisor's Manual, User's Manual*). Book titles also can contain the title of the program, as in *MS-DOS User's Guide* or *Pocket Guide to Microsoft Word.*

GRAPHIC CUES AND ICONS. Graphic cues consist of icons, product logos, company logos, and other images that help orient the user to the overall design of the documentation. Figure 8.7 shows how you can include them in headers and footers as a way of increasing the user's awareness of design on the particular page, so that he or she does not have to search around, or, worse, keep a finger in the table of contents while examining specific pages. Graphic cues have the advantage of showing with pictures. This means that

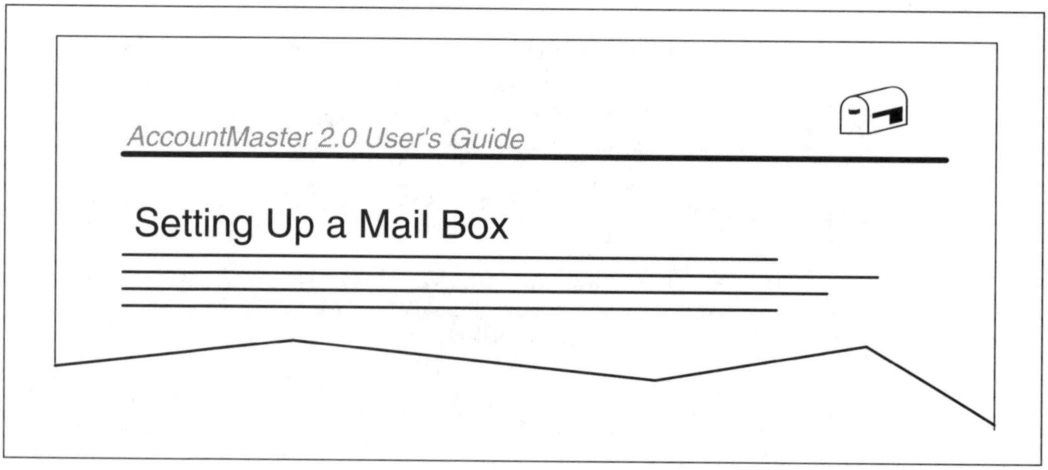

Figure 8.7

An Icon Used in a Header

Icons used in the header allow users to identify important information easily.

they can use the rich evocativeness of pictures to refer to things like program tasks, user types, sections, and other manual design elements. They make great labels.

Only your imagination limits the styles of graphic cues that you can include in headers and footers. Often programs and companies have logos that you can include in headers and footers. On a more specific level, you can put generic icons for teaching (lectern), guiding (pointing hand), and reference (open book) to reflect levels of support. Another form of graphic cue, the progress indicator, tells the user how far along in the section he or she has come (see Figure 8.8). Progress indicators consist of timelines representing the total length of the section and markers separating the portion already covered and the portion remaining. In tutorial documentation, for example, a progress indicator would show graphically the lessons completed and those left to go.

TASK NAMES. Often in user's guides you will find the tasks that the pages describe indicated in the header or footer, as shown in Figure 8.9. For instance, "Using the File Management Function" or "Saving a Document" would appear in the header. The advantage here lies in the way this technique accommodates the user's technique to read quickly, scanning among pages to find a function. As we saw earlier in this chapter, many computer users become impatient with tables of contents and indexes, preferring to scan the manual searching for information to perform some real-world tasks. Putting names of program tasks, user tasks, tutorial lessons, or data tables (in reference sections) can help such users make sense of the overall manual structure at the same time as they relate to information on separate pages.

COLOR TO INDICATE SECTIONS. You may also indicate sections by color bars in the headers and footers. Like graphic cues discussed above, these show sections using primarily visual

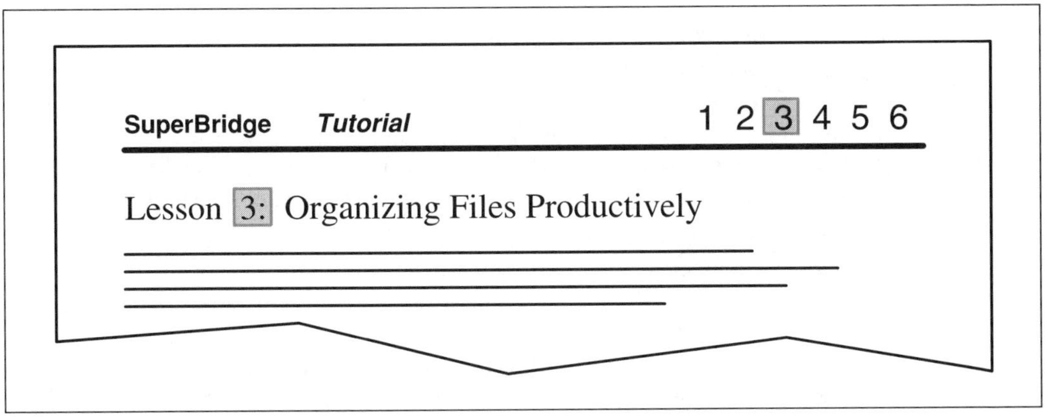

SuperBridge *Tutorial*   1 2 3 4 5 6

Lesson 3: Organizing Files Productively

Figure 8.8

A Header Using a Progress Indicator

Progress indicators help users keep track of their location within a larger structure of a document.

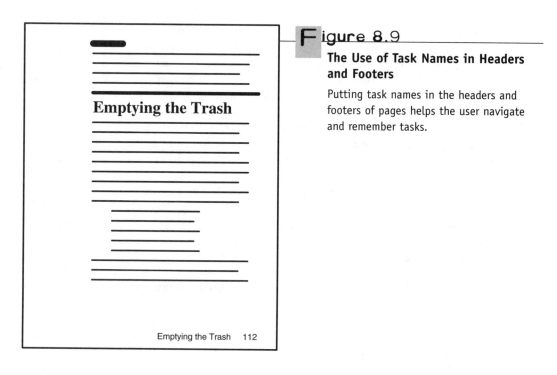

Emptying the Trash

Emptying the Trash   112

Figure 8.9

The Use of Task Names in Headers and Footers

Putting task names in the headers and footers of pages helps the user navigate and remember tasks.

information. They help reinforce the pattern of use of your manual because they tell the user where a certain page or section falls within the big picture.

Color can unify your documentation system and allow users to key on specific information. Below you will find some ways you can use color in your document design.

- ■ **To identify specific sections of a document.** Color used in *rules, bleeds,* and as a highlight to section names can help users remember where they saw what kind of information. It's easy to do this in an online system because it's easy to use color in the non-scrolling region as a background for sections, such as yellow for step-by-step, green for command reference, blue for glossary, and so forth. The advantage here lies in not having to use a lot of color but still getting the benefit of identification.

- ■ **To match pocket guides with user's guides.** If you have pocket guides associated with various documents, you can use the same color highlights for the pocket guide as for the document. The Thomas-Conrad Corporation's writers featured this kind of color linking in their award-winning four-volume set of installation guides for computer network adapters and cards. Each pocket guide has the same color scheme as its corresponding installation guide, even down to the colored spiral binding of the installation guides.

- ■ **To cue specific kinds of information.** Color can work very well for identifying specific types of information within your document layout. You can cue tips in blue or cautions in yellow. You can set the background color of all your demonstrations the same or box your elaborations in an eye-catching color. As with the other aspects of color use, cuing relies on color not as a decoration or to give a realistic feel to images, but to link to the structure of information in your document.

Layering

Layering refers to having two versions of information on the page at once, to satisfy more than one type of reader. For example, if you have elaborate steps for the novice user, you might also include on the same page an abbreviated version of the steps for the experienced user. Follow these suggestions for layering:

- Put keyboard equivalents next to mouse instructions (or vice versa).
- Put commands in the table of contents along with the terms.
- Put advanced instructions or definitions in tables alongside instructions for intermediate users.
- Use one column of instructions for beginners and one for advanced users.

At Texas Tech University we found ourselves faced with the need to provide layered information to support both the new and experienced users of our Technical Communication Production Lab. We wanted the new users to learn a number of basic word processing functions, and we wanted the experienced users to refresh their memories when they returned at the beginning of the semester. The solution that one of our design project teams came up with involved a specially designed manual with a layered, two-column format.

We put the steps in the left-hand column and the explanations in the right-hand column. At the top of the left-hand column we put a hare and at the top of the right-hand column we put a tortoise. The users actually figured it out. Experienced users just had to follow the steps at the left to complete their editing exercise. Beginning users could follow the explanations in the right-hand column to figure out how to follow the steps and to get help if they got stuck. Both users ended up with a completed real-world task (the edited document) that met the objective of preparing them for the start of a semester's work in the facility. The page made a good example of how you can layer information for users on the same page.

Special Devices for Layering: Speed Boxes

There are a number of special patterns of presenting text that the software documenter can use as solutions to design problems. One, the speed box, allows some readers to get information about dialog boxes, control panel settings, and other interface elements quickly. In the HiJaak manual, shown in Figure 8.10, speed boxes show tables of commands and screens. They act like summaries on the same page as the explanation.

Headings

All manuals use headings, and all users expect them. Not all headings work equally well. In the example of the tortoise and hare tracks described above, the heading work fell to the icon. Icons make good heading elements, because of their visual nature. But most of us use text headings: short phrases indicating, at a glance, the contents of a section. Often we make headings too short: "Margins" or "Save." The problem here lies not in the intrinsic arrangement of the information: You can have a task-oriented organization, but still

Destination

3.6 Destination File Dialog Box

After you have specified the necessary information about the files you wish to convert, you must supply some information about the files HiJaak is to produce. The Destination File dialog box is for picking your file type, specifying the directory where the files are to be put, and renaming your images during the conversion process. You can also access an options screen with image processing features before converting the files.

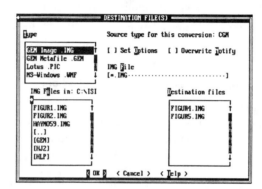

Speed Box for Destination File Dialog Box

Purpose: To select the file type to be created.

Location: Second dialog box (or third if you've set Source Options) under Convert.

How to Proceed:

1. Select the File Type.
2. Check the File extension in the File edit field. You may edit the field to alter the file filter or to specify an alternate drive or path.
3. Check the Path shown above the Existing Files list box. Select the desired directory from the list box. (Drives and subdirectories come after any listed files in the list box.)
4. If you wish to rename any files, select the file to be renamed in the Destination Files list box. Its full file specification will appear in the File edit field. Use the arrow keys to move to the part of the edit field you wish to change. Characters are deleted with the delete and backspace keys and inserted by typing them.
5. If you need to set output options before proceeding to the destination screen, turn on the Set Options check box. The Options boxes allow you to specify application specific information and provide access to image processing functions.
6. Click on < OK> or Press Enter to proceed with the conversions or, if selected in #5, the Destinations Options specification.

Figure 8.10

A Speed Box

Speed boxes like this one from Inset Systems' _HiJaak User's Manual_ allow you to layer information for both experienced and expert users on the same page.

diffuse the usability potential by not focusing the information clearly. The problem here lies in the fact that the writer failed to make the headings part of the manual's system. Better headings would read "Setting Margins" or "Saving a file."

Don't forget that headings, besides focusing on workplace objectives, also make up part of the visual nature of pages. Below we discuss the way all text elements contribute to the look of a page. Headings do this. Usually we print them in larger, darker type so they catch the reader's eye. Good design of headings, like those in Figure 8.11, should support this function and make them fitting and easy to see. Easy-to-see often means less complex in font and style.

Follow these guidelines for including headings in computer manuals:

- Support workplace applications with elaborate headings: "How to Use Advanced Functions."
- Use a consistent font and style for headings.
- Use a *sans serif* (plain) font, in bold.
- Make headings task-oriented, as in "Promoting Arrays," or "Using Loops with Function Calls."
- Use appropriate graphical cues in headings, such as check marks, pointing hands, warning triangles, or note pencils.
- Make headings parallel in grammar.

Advance Organizers

Advance organizers tell the user the structure and organization of the information that will follow. In tutorial documentation we see them in the form of statements that describe a

Chapter Heading	18 pt. bold non-serif	Use to indicate chapters.
Section Heading	14 pt. bold non-serif	Use to indicate sections that relate to groups of tasks.
Topic Heading	12 pt. bold non-serif	Use to indicate subgroups of tasks.
Task Name	10 pt. bold non-serif	Use to indicate task names.
Subtask name	10 pt. non-serif	Use to indicate groups of steps within tasks.

Figure 8.11

Headings Show Hierarchies

Headings indicate the organization and structure of information within a manual.

lesson's structure. When expressed in terms of skills, these statements let readers know what kinds of activities they will encounter and their relevance to real-world tasks. In procedures and reference documentation advance organizers consist of introductory passages showing the organization of sections and telling how the user should read them for best advantage.

The following example of an advance organizer appeared in the RoboHELP *User's Manual*:

> *This chapter is organized by task. That is, each section describes a common task which you will, from time to time, need to perform as you work with RoboHELP, creating, editing, and reorganizing topics on your way to a perfect Help system. (p. 163)*

This advance organizer helps users anticipate what will occur in the chapter. Advance organizers can do any number of the following things:

- Introduce the user to the layout of the pages
- Suggest real-world uses of the tutorial lesson
- Introduce the focus example of the lesson
- Tell approximate time commitments
- Tell ways the user can structure the tutorial
- Explain previous knowledge needed for the tutorial
- Refer users to other documents.

A common and very effective type of advance organizer is the **graphic overview**. Often cartoon-like in design, the graphic overview uses images, arrows, menus, and icons to create an image in the reader's mind of how the elements of the program fit together.

Follow these guidelines for creating advance organizers:

- Put them in front of the information they reflect.
- Use them consistently: Users will look for them if they know they exist.
- Make them relate to user's work/task.
- Make them fit with other advanced organizers in style or design.
- Keep them short: People may not read them anyway.
- Make them functionally redundant: Don't include information readers won't get elsewhere.

Document Overview

When users open a document for the first time, they need to be introduced to its setup and how to use it to find information. Usually you perform this task using a section explaining "How to Use This Manual." Below you will find a list of the kinds of information you can include in this section.

- **Audience.** What kinds of users the manual is designed for and how it can help them use the software system.
- **Content.** What kinds of information (technical, instructional, reference, etc.) is contained and how it can be used.

- **Organization.** What comes first, second, third, and so on in a document, and how the sections can be used.
- **Scope.** What hardware and software the program works on, and what kinds of computer systems or peripheral devices (printers, monitors, etc.) are required.
- **Navigational information.** Where various user types need to go to get the information they need.

Parallel Structures

A good software manual contains useful patterns to help the user identify information easily. It repeats itself in a way that does two important things for the user. First, parallelism reassures the user that the writer has sorted out the important information. Second, it creates patterns of expectation so the reader learns how to use the document. Parallelism puts similar things into the same grammatical or spatial relationship. You can use many techniques for structuring information in parallel ways. Figure 8.12 shows examples of these from the smaller elements to larger elements:

Patterns of Redundancy

You can detect patterns of redundancy in almost all software documents once you know what to look for. You may not want redundancy in some writing, because you should always try to say things clearly the first time. But in instructional materials, repeating information, and doing so in repeating structures, helps users remember. It serves the purpose of a backup strategy for information. If the user doesn't get the point in one way, he or she will get it in another.

REDUNDANCY IN TABLES OF CONTENTS. You can usually include commands in the table of contents that help the user realize that each task or topic has an associated command. Figure 8.13 shows one way to do it.

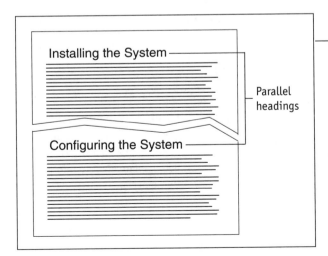

Figure 8.12

Parallel Headings

Parallel headings reinforce users' recognition of information structures. These are parallel in terms of the document structure, and they "match" in typographic style and grammar (both verbs end in "ing").

Process Insurance Claims	(INS01)	8-1
Prepare Insurance Claims	(INS02)	8-3
Claim Print Order Listing	(IN02A)	8-4
Print Insurance Claim Forms	(INS02B)	8-7

Figure 8.13

Redundancy in Tables of Contents

This example illustrates how you can use redundancy in table of contents pages.

The column on the left contains task names and the center column contains file names. The user may use these file names as shortcuts around the menu system of the interface, thus saving time. The example shows how parallel types of information ("task names" and "file names") can work together to improve the efficiency of Table of Contents pages.

Cuing

Cuing refers to the technique of including visual patterns to make a certain kind of information memorable. We respond to visual cues often when driving: An octagonal sign means stop, triangles mean caution, and so forth. Your reader needs the same cues when navigating your document. The psychology of doing this is pretty straightforward: If you always include warning signals in a double box, then the reader will know to pay attention to them without having to dig the warning out of the rubble of text.

Software documenters can use many elements as cuing devices in manuals: icons, rules, fonts, styles, and others described below. The many cuing devices in software manuals include what we call "notational conventions": styles of type, use of brackets, boxes, highlighting, and so on for certain kinds of information (commands, keys, input text, etc.). On the one hand, notational conventions make up the pattern of text the document uses; on the other hand, from a cognitive point of view, they add to the schema of a manual and greatly increase its usability.

CUING WITH ICONS. Figure 8.14 shows simple icons that can lead readers to the information they need.

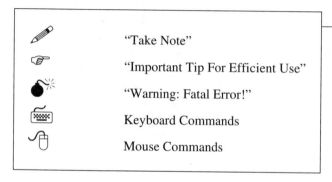

	"Take Note"
	"Important Tip For Efficient Use"
	"Warning: Fatal Error!"
	Keyboard Commands
	Mouse Commands

Figure 8.14

Cuing with Icons

Simple icons like this abound in software documentation to help readers identify information quickly.

> 1. To open a file, choose **Open...** from the **File** menu
> 2. To give the name of the file type `test.doc` and press \<Enter\>

Figure 8.15

Cuing with Fonts

Changing to a different font for types of information creates easy patterns of recognition for users.

CUING WITH RULES. Cuing with rules means using solid or gray-valued lines to indicate the hierarchical structure of information in a manual. As shown in Figure 8.16, usually the thicker lines indicate higher—more general—information. You can use rules with headings to indicate hierarchies.

Headers and footers can also contain rules that indicate, by their relative width of line, the hierarchy of the entire document. The thinner the line, the more detailed the information. Rules also help with layout, as we will see in Chapter 9, by helping the reader's eye define the page.

CUING WITH FONTS. In the example in Figure 8.15, the menu commands appear in bold and the information the user should type appears in Courier font.

CUING WITH CAPS. The use of capitalization styles is an important way to build parallel cuing structures into a document. In fact, you can choose from a number of capitalization styles which, when combined with bold letters, larger type sizes, and color, can give you a wide range of possible patterns. But don't overdo it. The best cuing scheme is one that does the job elegantly and simply.

Writers and companies use capital letters in many innovative ways in the software industry. Often you see capital letters in the middle of names of programs, like WordPerfect,

MAIN HEADING OF CHAPTER

Second Level Heading

Third level heading

Figure 8.16

Cuing with Rules

Varying the thickness and style of rules adds to the ease of understanding document structure.

WordStar, or ConvexAVS. While you may not have the opportunity to take these kinds of liberties with capitalization, you can follow these conventions:

- **All caps**   CHAPTER OVERVIEW
- **Initial caps**   Using Bookmarks, Cross-Referencing
- **Down-style caps**   Bookmark text, Bookmark names

In many manuals you will find initial caps used in first-level headings and down caps in second- and third-level headings. This arrangement is logical because the number of capital letters diminishes as the user moves into the lower levels of the text. Figure 8.17 shows an example from a manual illustrating how you might explain the notational conventions that make up the cuing pattern you decide on for a page or screen.

Indexes and Tables of Contents

Indexes and tables of contents make up the two most important user tracking and navigational devices in any manual. Users consult them more than any other part of the manual. The table of contents describes the contents of the document from a task perspective: It is often arranged in order of typical use, and often task by task. The index, besides being the collection place for all the important terms used in a document, also contains abbreviations, synonyms, slang terms, substitute words, and user questions: all the terms the user might use, along with the terms the user should use to get at the right functions of a program.

Often a manual will present the table of contents in more than one form: an extended form including a great deal of detail for the uninitiated, and an abbreviated form for the advanced user. You can also include a table of contents at each section or chapter to remind the reader of the contents without sending him or her back to the front of the book. Its layout, as we shall see in the next chapter, uses dots or "leaders" to make it easier for the user to follow from the terms on the left to the page numbers on the right. Some newer formats for tables of contents put the page numbers next to the entries, allowing readers to connect page numbers and topics easily.

The index provides a meeting place of all the users of a program. It includes all the synonyms for program terminology that users would employ in their workplace and, through "see" and "see also" references, can put users in touch with the right information in the manuals. Users who migrate from one system to another, as in switching from one word processor to another, find the index especially useful because in a well-designed index they can find *terms they know* with references to terms they *need to know*. The index also presents a number of opportunities for the writer to use some of the cuing and parallelism tools discussed earlier in this chapter. The well-done index will contain lists of keystrokes and lists of commands and will present them in the font and type style used elsewhere in the manual. You can find out much more about building an index in the section on indexing in Chapter 12.

Lists of Figures and Tables

You may think that lists of figures and lists of tables exist in software manuals as a matter of convention. In fact, they make up a main element in the usability of a document.

Notational conventions	This section discusses notational conventions used in this book.

Bold monospace

In command examples, text shown in **bold monospace** identifies user input that must be typed exactly as shown.

Monospace

In paragraph text, monospace identifies command names, system calls, and data structures and types.

In command examples, monospace identifies command output, including error messages.

In command syntax diagrams, text shown in monospace must be typed exactly as shown.

Italic

In paragraph text, *italic* identifies new and important terms and titles of documents.

In command syntax diagrams, *italic* identifies variables that must be supplied by the user.

{ }

In command syntax diagrams, text surrounded by curly brackets indicate a choice. The choices available are shown inside the curly brackets and separated by the pipe (|) sign.

The following command example indicates that you can enter either a or b:

command {a | b}

[ ]

In command syntax diagrams, square brackets indicate optional data.

The following command example indicates that the variable *output_file* is optional:

command *input_file* [*output_file*]

...

In command syntax, horizontal ellipsis shows repetition of the preceding item(s).

The following command example indicates you can optionally specify more than one *input_file* on the command line.

command *input_file* [*input_file* ...]

xvi   SPP-UX System Administration Guide

Figure 8.17

Notation Conventions

This example shows how a manual announces the cuing patterns in the front matter of a manual under the heading "Notational Conventions."

Lists of figures and tables allow users to see quickly if they can find an example of a screen in a figure (see Figure 8.18). Similarly, many users expect to find lists of commands, syntax conventions, and procedures in tabular form (for easy reading). The list of tables, in this case, can direct users to the right information.

Lists of Screens

In some cases you should include a list of screens in your manual as an access tool for users. This list works when you have a program with easily recognizable screens. For example, university administrators use programs to track and register students. These programs contain a "student information screen," a "transcript screen," an "enrollment history screen" and so forth. Computer operators routinely call up these screens using acronyms and numbers, such as "SIS" for the student information screen. They relate to the system through these screens, as in "That program has 120 screens; dang!" Most of an operator's time gets spent calling up screens and filling out or updating fields. Where screens make up a prominent feature of a program's interface, users expect to scan a list to find a screen and information about it.

The list of screens should appear early in a manual or in the primary index screen of a help system. Format it like the table of contents or other lists, including the chapter and page numbers.

Interrelated Examples

You use interrelated examples when you follow the same example from one procedure to another. Doing so builds continuity into your document design. In documents where you use a lot of procedures, the use of interrelated examples becomes increasingly important. You should always use examples in a manual or help system because examples allow the reader to view the use of the program in terms he or she can understand. When the examples work this way we say they "contextualize" the information of the program—put it in the user's work context.

The best way to uncover realistic examples is to look for them during the process of user analysis discussed in Chapter 3. The earlier you can find them, the more valuable they can be because they increase understanding. Using interrelated examples provides the following benefits to the user and to the writer.

- **Creates a *learning curve*.** When you use aspects of the same example throughout the document, you allow the user to build on previous learning. The user doesn't have to remember the details of the example each time.

- **Ties the document together.** Using interrelated examples helps give unity to your document. Depending on the kind of program you're working on, you may have a set of data for a business or work environment that you can use from one procedure or lesson to another. You can re-use images, forms, names, and so on, to give the same reference point to different parts of the document.

- **Makes the writer's job easier.** If you follow through with the same example in the whole document, you don't have to think up new examples each time you need one.

FIGURES

Figure 8.18

A List of Figures Helps Users Find Information

This list of figures, from the TC8215 Sectra Management System for Windows *User's Guide,* illustrates the use of detail in a figure list to help users find the right information.

Solutions to the Design Problem for Online Documentation

With an online help system you face the same objective as you do with print: getting the user to the right information. But you don't face the same constraints as you do with a book. While topics bear some resemblance to pages, the system for delivering topics to users differs significantly. Help systems provide a much larger array of *affordances*—tools for use—that the user can employ for finding information. Whereas books provide headers, tables of contents, and so on, help systems provide these *plus* jumps, hypertext links, history displays, and many more tools for the user. When you design a help system, you should familiarize yourself with the access tools it provides your user. Below are descriptions of some of these tools common to help systems and how help systems differ from print documents. You'll find a more elaborate explanation of these affordances in Chapters 12, 13, and 14. Figure 8.19 shows a thumbnail sketch for a help topic.

Non-Scrolling Regions

Headings differ in online documentation because you can keep them in a region of the help page that doesn't scroll. These non-scrolling regions appear at the top of the screen and stay there while the user scrolls through the procedure or topic. This ability to stay in the user's view represents an advantage over print documents because the user doesn't lose sight of the topic and thus can keep a clearer focus on the task while performing it.

Keyword and Whole Text Searches

Keyword searches refer to the ability of a help system to electronically find topics that the user types into a keyword search box. The system looks through all the topics and finds those that were pre-set in the system. *Whole-text searches* refer to the ability of a help sys-

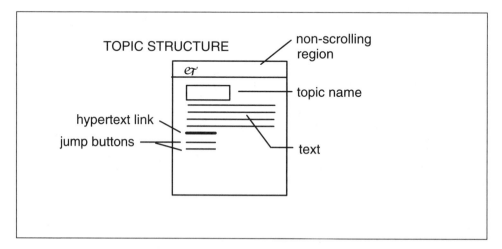

Figure 8.19

Use Thumbnail Sketches to Design Help Topics

Consider the elements of a help topic when specifying the structure of the help system.

tem to find topics containing any word or combination of words the user types. You don't have to pre-set words with whole-text searches. The ***help driver*** (program) does the searching. This kind of search resembles the searching done in a library, where you indicate the subject or subject identifiers and the system coughs up the resulting topics.

How does this differ from a print index? Print indexes can contain the same information as keyword indexes, but the user has to turn pages to get from the locator in the index entry to the resulting page or procedure. Keyword searches have the advantage of ease of use over print indexes. As for whole-text searches, print documents have nothing parallel. But whole-text searches of online documents can pose problems for users unfamiliar with doing them. If the user can't tailor the search in the right ways, the result may be a flood of irrelevant information.

Links and Jumps

Links and jumps in a help system allow users to go directly from one topic to a related topic. With a book you can make these references (called cross-references), but the user can only get there by turning pages. Here, online help systems have a definite advantage. Not only can you link topics as part of the design of a system, but you can allow users to go back and forth between topics.

Popups

Popups provide a way to handle glossaries in an online system. With a book you can highlight your glossary entries in the text with bolding or some other cuing technique. But to get to the glossary, the user has to turn to the page or to the glossary section in the book. In an online system the user just has to click on the term in the topic to see a window containing the definition. Another click of the mouse closes the popup window.

Context Sensitivity

With a print manual, the user goes through a chain of events between identifying a problem and finding the solution. He or she has to name the problem, then consult the table of contents or the index or thumb through the book to find the right procedure or explanation. With *context sensitivity,* the ability of a help system to present information based on the current state of the program, the user goes directly from a problem with a screen or a field to an appropriate help topic containing a solution. The user doesn't have to identify or name the problem because you, the writer, have already done it. You put the tags into the program (probably with the help of the programmer) that tell the program which topic to get when.

Of course, you have to put the tags into the program, using up more time in development. And after you recompile, test, edit, review, and revise, you can't guarantee that the user will get the right information after all. If the user has a question about *format,* and presses the help key while the *print* box is on the screen, the system will provide the wrong advice consistently. This example shows how the randomness of user questions limits the usefulness of context sensitivity as an online affordance. Nevertheless, context sensitivity gives you a powerful and flexible tool to tailor information to the user's tasks.

Histories

History buttons allow users to trace their steps. They can pull down the history list and easily go back to a previous topic. They can even save histories and refer to them later. Users can't do this with a book, unless they make notes or leave bookmarks to retrace steps. And given that people solve problems by trial and error, using a path like this, and having the option to retrace steps, might encourage more exploration and enhance their problem solving.

Browse Sequences

When you identify a series of related topics, such as those relating to printing or to formatting, you can easily include the relationship in the form of browse sequences. When the user clicks on a topic that's part of a browse sequence, the system displays forward and backward arrows to facilitate moving from topic to topic. Unless you group your procedures or other print topics, you can't set up this kind of sequence easily with a book. Nor can you set up as many of them as you could with an online system.

Bookmarks/Annotation

With a book the user can easily mark a place in the book and then return to it—possibly using sticky notes, pieces of paper, dog-eared pages, and so forth. With early help systems you didn't have this advantage. You can't put a mark on a screen. However, newer help systems have elaborate ways to incorporate bookmarks. This is an example of online documents mimicking an affordance of print documents.

The same goes for writing on pages. Books have a marvelous surface for marking on that screens don't. However, you can also do this with online systems, using annotation features. Not only can you annotate online systems, you can do other things, like collect your annotations, print them, revise and delete them, or share them with colleagues.

Using the Task Analysis for Design Planning

As you construct your task analysis, look for features of the program that might require special design solutions. For example, if you have a number of complicated dialog boxes, you might use speed boxes to explain them. Or, if you have complicated procedures for installing or configuring a system, you might need special walk-through sections. As you do your task analysis, try to develop an interrelated example to unify your documents. The more integrated your elements, the more retention of information your user will have. Also, the simpler the document, the greater the clarity.

Glossary

affordance: a feature of an item—a document or other technology—that enables its use. For instance: guitars have affordances that allow for adjusting the pitch of the strings, called *tuning keys.*

advance organizer: a paragraph at the beginning of a section of a document that tells the user the structure and organization of the information to follow.

bleeds: illustrations or graphic elements (lines, shaded boxes) that extend to the edges of the page and remain slightly visible when the book is closed.

cognitive science: a branch of science that studies how people think and solve problems.

graphic overview: a drawing using symbols to represent the parts of a document or a program.

human factors: an area of research that studies the design of tools to fit human physical and psychological needs in the workplace.

hypertext: documents stored electronically with the capability to move from one topic to another automatically using pre-set links. The user of a hypertext document uses the mouse pointer to click on special areas of a document, which results in the system presenting another part of the document.

learning curve: the plot of progress of a user's learning, with time on the x-axis and skills on the y-axis.

media: the technology you choose to deliver instruction or other information to the user. Media usually includes print or online, but may include "multimedia," which uses sound, images, and animation on the computer screen to deliver instruction.

protocol method: a method of researching that records and then analyzes the actions a computer user makes when using a program or a manual. Sometimes the researcher asks the user to talk aloud while using the program, telling about decisions and reasons for actions. The record of these comments helps researchers understand user behavior.

rule: a horizontal or vertical line used to indicate column widths or to separate vertical columns.

sidebar: a boxed text area on a page containing relating but different information than that on the page.

usability lab: a room equipped with cameras and recording equipment used to study the behavior of software users.

Checklist ✔

Use the Document Design Planning Guide on the next page to plan and analyze your document design. In the column on the left, jot down important characteristics of your users, based on the user analysis. Then in the columns on the right, make notes to yourself about the kinds of design features you think would meet the users' special needs. The planning guide allows you to compare your users' characteristics, which you write in the left-most column, with the document design features discussed in this chapter, which are summarized for you in the three right-hand column headings. This planning guide groups the document design features into three categories: visual elements, textual elements, and structural elements. The example, in the first row, shows how you might use the planning guide for a grade calculation program. In this example, the program has two very distinct user groups (teacher users and teachers' aides). The designer has considered creating a special job performance aid to cover the teachers' aides' three basic tasks: opening the

DOCUMENT DESIGN PLANNING GUIDE

User Characteristics	Design Solutions		
	Visual Elements	**Textual Elements**	**Structural Elements**
	(Cues, rules, headings, labels, icons, illustrations, progress indicators, color)	*(Layering, advance organizers, scenarios, parallel structures, hierarchies, document overviews, examples, explanations)*	*(Job performance aids, organizational strategy, lists of figures, tables, screens, table of contents, index, links, browse sequences)*
User groups: *I have two groups: teachers and teachers' aides*	—	*—Overview of how program works for teachers*	*—Use job performance aid for teachers' aides. Do 3 basic tasks.*
Learning, Motivational, Technical Problems:			
Information Needs:			
Workplace Tasks:			
Experience Categories:			
Subject-Matter Knowledge:			
Workplace Characteristics:			
Learning Preferences:			
Usage Pattern:			

program, entering the daily grades, and closing the program. The example also shows that the user also plans an overview of how the program works to explain it to teachers unfamiliar with computerizing grade books.

Like all planning guides, this one aims to help you think. Use a pencil. Expect to revise it as you progress toward achieving just the right mix of features to tailor your document to the user's needs.

Practice/Problem Solving

1. Inventory Page and Screen Affordances

According to author Donald Norman, the function of a machine, tool, or even household object gets communicated to us through its switches, buttons, and handles. In *The Psychology of Everyday Things,* Norman points out how affordances of doors (handles) give clues as to how the door opens (right or left.)

Norman defines affordances as "strong clues to the operation of things." A phone has affordances. For instance, mine has a "talk" button that allows me to use the phone by switching it on. All technology, even prehistoric, has affordances. Spears had handles to suggest throwing.

Affordances should give right clues for the right kind of uses. In page design we use all visible print marks, white space, page numbers, and many other affordances that give clues to the page's system of arranging information.

THE PROBLEM. Imagine you have a sheet of 8.5 × 11 paper that contains the solution to the biggest problem on the globe: war. Your sheet of paper can tell us how to achieve world peace. Because that information carries so much informative value for people, you want to take a careful look at the design of the document that contains it. Hopefully you'll get widely read; beyond the manufacturing department, at least.

So take a good look at your page. Decide what affordances (clues to operation of the page) you want to use on this page, and start a list. Write an explanation of how each affordance (even the smallest of them) would contribute to making that important and significant information available to the waiting world.

After you have done this exercise with a page, imagine the blank screen of a help topic. What affordances would an ideal space contain, and how can you make it easy for all users to get this important topic? Again, make a list and try to think of ways to use them in projects.

2. File Manager Blues

A number of functions in a help system go under different names. When you use the Windows file manager program, it keeps coming back to the same directory each time you click on the C: drive button. The solution could lie under a number of names: window, display, view. Actually the problem lies in something a new user of the program would not know: the "Save settings on exit" option on the Options menu. Devise a way to help users of the system solve this problem more efficiently and write up your design solution.

3. Explore Design Problems

Find a computer user who uses manuals daily, who knows a lot of programs, and seems to be a "computer person." Also, find a computer user who is just beginning or who isn't a "computer person." Discuss their use of computer documentation, and prepare a short report comparing how they differ. How do their different experiences affect the way they see and use documentation? What design problems/implications does this have for the software documenter?

4. Compare the Design Solutions in this Chapter to the Real Thing

Report on the design elements of a software manual. Analyze the manual specifically for the design elements described in this chapter. Which solutions to the design problem do you find in the document? Write a short report in which you describe some of the features you have found, telling which ones you think work well, and which ones you would design differently.

9 Laying Out Pages and Screens

In this chapter we examine the two main elements of document layout: the design of the screens and pages and the design of type. Seeing pages and screens from the designer's point of view, as *communication spaces,* means that you acknowledge the degrees of modularity and structure in pages and screens, and you learn how to look at their density, balance, legibility and lookability. Common page formats—one-, two-, and three-column—use page design in different ways to achieve usability goals. We also see how to use many elements of design—the parts that make up the structure of a page—to help the user find information quickly. Practice using two designer's tools, the page grid and the thumbnail sketch, can help you become a good page and screen designer.

Designing the type for manuals and online help means determining the size, font, and style of the letters used to make words. The goals of the designer in using type consist of helping readers recognize words and building a pattern of information that allows readers to understand and navigate the document easily.

How to Read This Chapter

All readers will benefit from a study of the differences between the examples in this chapter and those in Chapter 8, "Designing for Task Orientation." These two chapters complement one another and contain important principles on which to build a successful task-oriented document. Guideline 4 gives specific advice for planners, and the Discussion section contains many examples on which to base further discussion or design decisions.

Examples

The examples in Figures 9.1, 9.2, and 9.3 offer you, in different ways, overviews of major trends in page and screen design. Figure 9.1 uses thumbnail sketches to outline five basic manual page layouts and one Windows-based help screen format. Figure 9.2 focuses on

Figure 9.1

Thumbnail Sketches

These sketches illustrate the variety of formats available for page and screen design.

an example of the two-column format, showing how the physical elements of the page combine to ease the reading experience and lead to workplace solutions with the software. You may want to compare this example to the one in Figure 8.1 (page 249). Both figures show the same page, but the callouts in Figure 9.2 draw attention to elements of *page* design instead of document design. Figure 9.3 carries the concepts of page design into screen design, showing points of similarity and difference in basic guidance documentation.

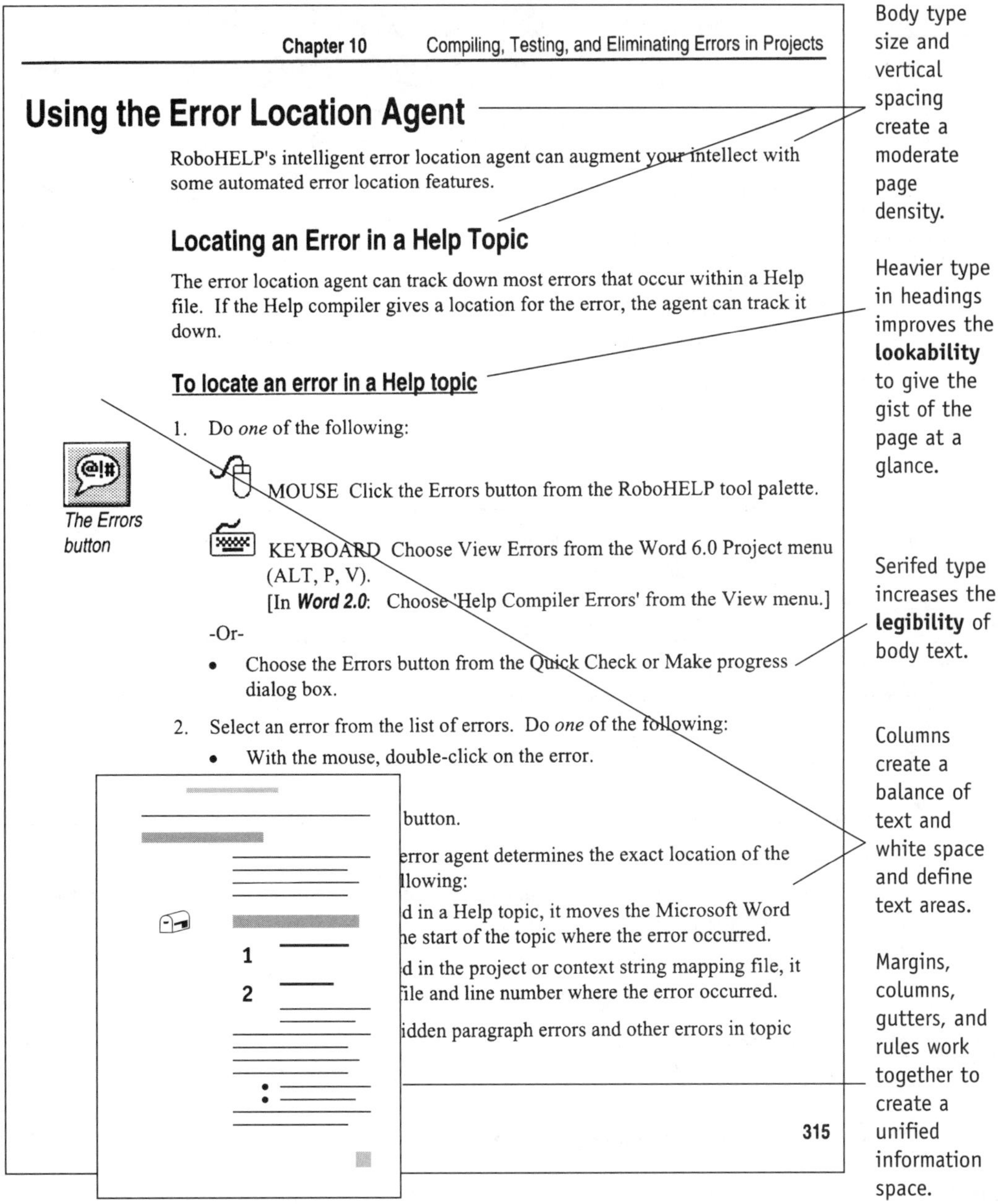

Chapter 10 Compiling, Testing, and Eliminating Errors in Projects

Using the Error Location Agent

RoboHELP's intelligent error location agent can augment your intellect with some automated error location features.

Locating an Error in a Help Topic

The error location agent can track down most errors that occur within a Help file. If the Help compiler gives a location for the error, the agent can track it down.

To locate an error in a Help topic

The Errors button

1. Do *one* of the following:

   MOUSE Click the Errors button from the RoboHELP tool palette.

   KEYBOARD Choose View Errors from the Word 6.0 Project menu (ALT, P, V).
   [In ***Word 2.0***: Choose 'Help Compiler Errors' from the View menu.]

   -Or-

   - Choose the Errors button from the Quick Check or Make progress dialog box.

2. Select an error from the list of errors. Do *one* of the following:
   - With the mouse, double-click on the error.

button.

rror agent determines the exact location of the
llowing:

d in a Help topic, it moves the Microsoft Word
e start of the topic where the error occurred.

d in the project or context string mapping file, it
ile and line number where the error occurred.

idden paragraph errors and other errors in topic

315

Body type size and vertical spacing create a moderate page density.
Heavier type in headings improves the **lookability** to give the gist of the page at a glance.
Serifed type increases the **legibility** of body text.
Columns create a balance of text and white space and define text areas.
Margins, columns, gutters, and rules work together to create a unified information space.
1
2

Figure 9.2

A Well-Designed Page

This page from the RoboHELP *User's Manual* shows how elements of page layout lead to a unified communication space.

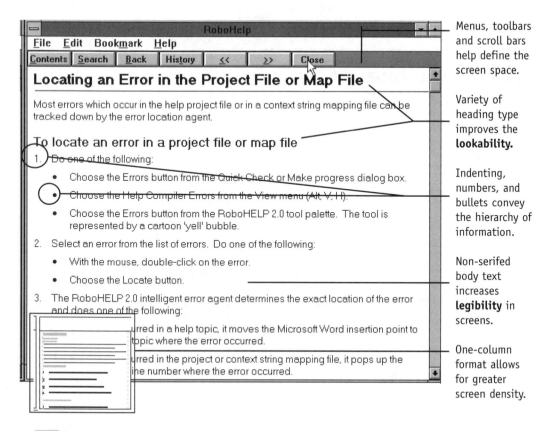

Callouts around the figure:

Menus, toolbars and scroll bars help define the screen space.

Variety of heading type improves the **lookability.**

Indenting, numbers, and bullets convey the hierarchy of information.

Non-serifed body text increases **legibility** in screens.

One-column format allows for greater screen density.

A Well-Designed Screen

This screen from the RoboHELP *User's Manual* shows how elements of screen layout lead to a unified communication space.

Guidelines

Figure 9.4 lists the guidelines for designing pages and screens.

1   CREATE PAGE GRIDS

We model a software system in a program task analysis, and the user in a user analysis; we model a page using a ***page grid***. Page grids define space by drawing invisible fences among the areas of a page. A page grid also acts like a scaffold or framework onto which you put text and graphics. The grid resembles a rack, a kind of shoe tree for words and pictures, or a word and picture parking lot with the spaces falling within the invisible grid

1. Create page grids.

2. Draw thumbnail sketches.

3. Define styles for pages and screens.

4. Set up pages and styles in your word processor.

5. Online help can repeat printed information, as appropriate.

Figure 9.4
Guidelines for Designing Pages and Screens

lines. To design a page well you need to know about grid lines and the other parts of page grid:

■ **Grid lines.** Lines drawn where the page and column margins would fall

■ **Margins.** Areas of actual space between the text and paper's edge

■ **Columns.** Spaces between the grid lines marking columns

■ **Gutters.** Space between columns

■ **White space.** Space, inside the margins, where no text or pictures may go

■ **Baseline.** Grid line at the bottom of the text and graphics area that defines the bottom margin

Making a page grid forces you to see the page in abstract terms. Page grids show us columns, text areas, graphics areas, margins, and heading areas—but only in a general way. When you compare one page grid design to another, you can see how some are better suited for highly structured pages, others not. When you create a page grid for a manual, you see the arrangement of the page more clearly, and in advance. If you want to get good at seeing the underlying page grids of all pages, practice drawing thumbnail sketches.

2   DRAW THUMBNAIL SKETCHES

Like a diagram of a building or a football field, a thumbnail sketch uses lines and spaces to show how pages get organized. You would make *thumbnail sketches* as part of your planning effort for your publications department or to experiment with different plans for your company's style manual. As a student of software documentation, making thumbnail sketches helps you sharpen your eye for effective page designs that encourage usability. The following section will guide you through the process of making your first sketch.

Pick a page that you think exhibits good page design. Does it have just the right balance for you, or just the right degree of formality you like? Did you find it in a manual that clearly succeeds in helping readers use a system? Once you have chosen a representative page to draw, follow the steps below to draw a sketch of it. At the end, compare your page to the original to see if it has the same balance and look as your sketch. These instructions focus on drawing on a section of a regular page, but you can use a draw program for this exercise if you want.

1. Fold a piece of paper in half, then into quarters.

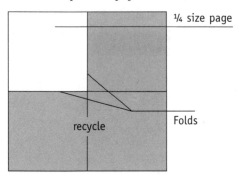

Keep the page proportions the same when you reduce the page size. Reducing the page proportionally forces you to draw a more economical composition. Smaller also works better for doing thumbnail sketches, because the well-done sketch *abstracts* and *shrinks* the original. You should try to spot the general elements of page design and represent them in your diagram. So look for the forest, not the trees.

2. Draw lightly around one quarter to mark the edges of the quarter-size page.

    You actually have four smaller pages. Pick any one you want to draw in. If you make a mess out of the first square, start again in a different one.

3. Based on the original page you chose as your model, draw grid lines for the margins.

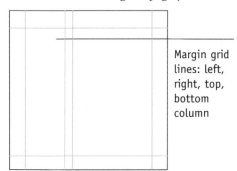

Grid lines should be accurate but light, so hold your pencil a little away from the tip and don't bear down. Keep the lines straight. Draw them all the way to the edge of the paper, so that they cross one another. The space defined by the top and bottom margins should be the same proportion as the original.

4. Using the original as a guide, draw grid lines for columns.

    Again, draw these lines lightly but accurately. They too go all the way to the edge of the paper. If you have a two-column format, one column would be the graphics column, another the text column.

5. Sketch in the page features.

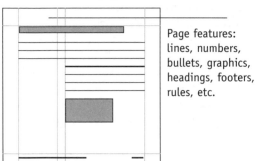

As you sketch in the page features, you should try to dither them. *Dithering* means replacing each and every page element with some symbol: a line or a box, or a shaded area. A landscape seen at a distance by a near-sighted person will get dithered by the eye's inability to focus. If you imagine seeing your page from, say, twenty feet away, the length of a room, you can imagine what it would look like dithered. Try to make your thumbnail sketch look like the page seen from twenty feet away.

Sketch the page features using the guidelines below:

- **Text.** Draw straight lines for all body text lines. Use a ruler if you want, but if you don't have one, learn to draw lines *sketch-straight:* Put your pencil on the starting point, look at the ending point and, using short, straight pencil movements (about ½ inch each), work your pencil across the page to the ending point. The resulting line will look straight and will not have a tendency to drift up or down. This technique takes practice.

- **Graphics.** Draw all the graphics using shadows, abstract sketches, and circles and lines. Draw tables and lists using lines to represent text. Give the scribbles in your thumbnail graphics the same relative darkness or lightness that they have in the original.

- **Headings.** Headings usually appear in larger fonts than body text, so draw them as shaded rectangles, again using their relative size in the original as your guide.

- **Rules, boxes, other features.** In your sketch, you may need to draw rectangles around rules to give them the same value on your sketch as they have on the page. Make sure you include all the graphics and text in the headers and footers.

TIPS FOR DRAWING THUMBNAIL SKETCHES

1. Drawing a thumbnail sketch may take from ten to twenty minutes. Slow down, and make it accurate.

2. Keep the page items in proportion while trying to include everything that is in the original.

3. Keep the values of darkness, density, lightness, and spaciousness the same in your sketch as in the original.

Drawing thumbnail sketches will help you identify the layout of your pages and screens. You should identify grids for all the kinds of pages you want to use in your document.

3 DEFINE STYLES FOR PAGES AND SCREENS

When you have identified a grid for your pages and screens, you've identified the basic pattern you will follow throughout your manuals and online help systems. Some pages will look different from the grid pages: Tables of contents pages and index pages, for instance, may not stick to the columns you define for other pages. But they will stay the same size and use the same header and footer scheme you identify in your page grid. Remember that a page grid provides the road map for almost all your pages.

Once you have decided on the grid for your pages, you should identify the styles you want to use to set up the pages. As a rule, your styles for page and screen components should include all the components listed in Table 9.1.

Notice that for screen presentations you don't identify margins in a one-column format because the margins (usually about ⅛") get set by the variable-sized window in which

Table 9.1

Styles for Page and Screen Components

Component	Unit(s) of Measurement	Example: RoboHELP 2.0 *User's Manual* and *Help*
Page:		
Top and bottom margins	Inches from the edge of the page	Top 1", bottom 3.5"
Left and right margins	Inches from the edge of the page	Left .5", right 2"
Column margins	Width in inches	Left .75", right 4.75"
Gutters between columns	Width in inches	.25"
Line spacing above	Points	6 points
Line spacing below	Points	None
Icon caption	Font, size, style, capitalization	Arial, 10pt, italics, title case
Page numbers	Font, size, style, justification	Arial, 12pt, bold, right justified
Tabs	Inches	.25 inch
Body text	Font, size, style, justification	Times Roman, 10pt, plain, left justified
Headings	Font, size, style, capitalization	Main: Arial, 14pt, bold, upcaps
		Second: Arial, 12pt, bold, upcaps
		Third: Arial, 10pt, bold/underlined, sentence caps
Rules	Color, point size, length	Black, 1.5 pt, 5.5"
Bullets	Symbol, point size, indentation	Circled numbers, 12pt, .25" indent
Numbers	Style, point size, punctuation	Arabic, 12pt, followed by a period
Step	Font, size, style, punctuation	Times Roman, 10pt, plain, sentence caps
Screen:		
Columns	Width in inches	One-column, variable
Headings	Font, size, style, capitalization	Main: Arial, 14pt, bold, upcaps
		Second: Arial, 14pt, plain, sentence caps
Step	Font, size, style, punctuation, justification	Arial, 12pt, plain, sentence caps, flush left
Body text	Font, size, style, justification	Arial, 12pt, plain, left justified
Bullets	Symbol, point size, indentation	Solid, 12pt, .5" indentation
Line spacing above	Points	6 points

the help screen appears. Notice also that the font for the body text is a serifed font (Times Roman) for printed documentation and a non-serifed font (Arial) for screen presentation, because the non-serifed font is more easily read on a screen. The rest of this chapter discusses these and other concerns in the difference between print and online text.

4   SET UP PAGES AND STYLES IN YOUR WORD PROCESSOR

Once you have identified your styles and written them down, you can set them up in your word processor or desktop publishing program. You handle the *specifications* for pages in two ways: styles for the text and page setup. Depending on your word processor, you will do these either together or separately. Most programs do the layout of the pages with one function and set text styles with another. When laying out pages, you tell the program the margin dimensions, orientation of the pages (landscape or portrait), and the number of columns. Most page setup functions allow you to arrange your pages in a *mirrored page* or two-page spread fashion, each pair of pages having a right-hand and left-hand page. Figure 9.5 shows the page layout dialog box used in the Microsoft Publisher program.

You should set up your page as you did in your planning with Guideline 3, with the columns and margins identified and set on the page as you want them in your manual. Usually you will use a different word processing function to set up the styles that define your text. Find whatever function in your word processor that defines styles and use it. A style defines the format you specify for a page or screen element (such as body text, headings, etc.), stores your choices, and applies them when you want to any text you type. You might ask yourself, "Why should I go to all this trouble and not just set the styles as I type in the words?" Good question. Basically, setting styles saves you time in the long run for two reasons.

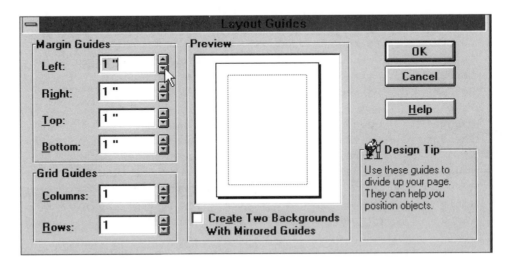

Figure 9.5

A Page Layout Dialog Box

Use a dialog box like this one from Microsoft Publisher to set up your page grid.

1. You can change the styles later, and you don't have to change each instance of a certain text. Thus, if you get into the project and decide that you want all your steps to print in boldface, you only have to change the definition of the step style. *Voila:* all the steps you have formatted using the step style change to boldface.

2. Setting up styles insures consistency in your document. Unless you have a perfect memory, you will end up with a patchwork of formats by the time you get to the end of the document. I learned (repeatedly) the hard way by setting different formats throughout a document because I forgot how I did it in earlier pages. The result costs money later in editing for consistency, and making a lot of changes to get things straight.

Figure 9.6 shows a list of styles I defined once for a manual for a database program. I used WordPerfect as the word processor. Each style contained the point size, margin dimensions, and other information to set the pages up just as I wanted them. Once you've got your styles set up in your word processor, you should use them to write up a few procedures and have them reviewed by the development team or your client. These pages will show the layout and allow the other team members to suggest changes or improvements. Make these changes at this stage to avoid having to make them later.

5   ONLINE HELP CAN REPEAT PRINTED INFORMATION

Usually, as indicated in Chapter 8, you do not want to repeat the same information (basic steps from your task list) in more than one document in your documentation set. But sometimes you may want to include the same steps from the pages of a tutorial in the screens of

```
Body text     Open        All body text paragraphs
Bullet        Open        Used for all bulleted lists
Chapter       Paired      Used for all chapter titles
Defs          Paired      Used for all definitions of terms
Footer        Paired      Used with alternating footers
Header        Paired      Used in all L/R headers
Indent        Open        Sets indented portions of text
Margins       Open        Sets T, B, L, R, margins
Scenario      Paired      Used for scenario headings
Step          Paired      Used for all steps
Task          Paired      Used for all tasks in the tutorial
Text box      Open        Used for all screen shots
Title         Paired      Used for the main title of the guide
Topic         Paired      Used for reference topics


1 On; 2 Off; 3 Create; 4 Edit; 5 Delete; 6 Save; 7 Retrieve; 8 Update:
```

Figure 9.6

A List of Styles for a Manual

This list of styles, done in a word processor, controls the layout of the page and the text.

your online help system in order to make it complete. You may find yourself using the same information in more than one format, and for different purposes. You would write the tutorial version of the steps in tutorial style and write the help version in a reference style. (When you do this, make sure to use your computer to import procedures from the task list as a way to ensure that the same words and steps get used in both places.)

But you also need to consider the differences between layouts of pages and screens when you have this kind of information overlap. The constraints of pages and screens result from the various sizes of pages and print capabilities, the user's type of display, and other technical elements. So you have to examine these limitations to determine the differences between putting the same steps in different formats. To help you overcome some of these limitations, consider the list of layout elements for pages and screens shown in Table 9.2.

Table 9.2

Differences in Layout Elements for Pages versus Screens

Element	Page	Screen
Headings	Horizontal spacing by line proportions	Horizontal spacing by blank lines
Fonts: general	More flexibility in using fancy fonts with wide stroke variations	Less flexibility: simple and bold work best
Body type size	Smallest type size: 8 point	Smallest type size: 10 point
Body text	Unlimited range of fonts	Font range limited by the user's computer
Page length	Limited to the edges of the paper	Unlimited because of scrolling ability
White space	Use to balance text, create "soft" boundaries	Use to decrease clutter
Indentation	More because of larger communication space: more hierarchies	Less and for smaller increments because of the smaller communication space: fewer hierarchies
Cuing	Greater detail in small cuing graphics like icons and dingbats	Detail limited by the graininess and decreased legibility on the screen
Lists	Use as much as possible	Use as much as possible, but limit their length
Graphics	Greater detail	Less detail
Icons	Greater detail	Less detail
Line length	Between 4" and 4.5"	Variable by re-sizing the help window
Rules	Wide variety possible	Less variety possible
Margins	Larger, up to 1" all around	Smaller, usually ¼"

iscussion

Document layout basically falls into two kinds of activities: designing page layout and designing type. *Designing page layout* means determining the best arrangement of words and images on a page or screen to achieve maximum usability. *Designing type* means determining the proper font, size, and style of characters as well as determining the format for tables, lists, and paragraphs. As in the overall design of the document discussed in the previous chapter, constraints complicate the design process: constraints of user types and experience, of the user's problem-solving techniques, and of the documenter's resources. You must account for these constraints in any intelligent design of page and screen layout to achieve your design goals.

The Goals of Page and Screen Layout

The goals of layout, again, resemble those of document design in general. For one thing, the layout should *allow the user to overcome the design problem;* the layout should meet dynamic needs with a static document. (And even though a help document seems less static than a page, it differs from the manual only in *degree* of being static.) The document should support task orientation by helping the user perform information-related tasks efficiently and productively. The well-designed page or screen should lead users to the right kinds of information. This doesn't just mean helping them not get lost; it means making it easy for them to move from a problem in their work to a solution in the manual or help.

For its second goal, then, good page and screen layout should *support overall task orientation.* In some manuals, for instance, this means that the *task* becomes the primary unit of information, as opposed to the older style of making the function or command (a system-oriented element) the main unit of information. In addition, the well-dressed page or screen should bear some consistency with the interface of the program itself. This means using screens and icons to help the user make the connection between page or screen and program.

Finally, the layout should *accommodate the visual needs* of the user, the need to learn and do through images rather than words. Our knowledge of how people perform real tasks tells us that speed increases when the reader can see the steps and see the results of steps, instead of reading about them. While words insure accuracy, more and more the *look* of a page or a screen—the overall impression created by the size and placement of text and images—determines its effectiveness.

Designing Communication Spaces

The documenter needs to decide two important things: the degree of modularity pages need, and the degree of structure they need. These two elements will determine the overall look of the communication space, regardless of the pattern of columns and words (discussed below) you choose. Follow these important principles because they bear directly on how well one puts a task orientation into layout.

Degree of Modularity

Modularity means breaking information into chunks of text and graphic units and fitting them onto a one- or two-page spread. Using a modular format, the writer would follow the one-task-per-page idea, being sure to include at least one image per task. Usually the graphic consists of a ***result screen*** (showing what happens when the user follows the steps). Chapters and sections do little to make a page or screen modular. Modules, stand-alone elements of information, each contain just the information needed to complete the task, no more no less.

MODULARITY AND PAGES. You can gauge the degree of modularity of a page or screen by asking this question: Does this communication space contain all the information the user needs to perform the task and understand the concepts in the task? For instance, a task that presents steps on one page but refers to screen captures on another page (or in a list of figures) does not give all the information needed at the time. Keeping tasks self-contained increases modularity. Often this means doing the following.

■ Repeat background information where necessary.

■ Repeat screens when necessary.

■ Include orienting information about the relationship of a task to other tasks.

■ Keep all relevant steps on the same page.

■ Minimize cross-references.

Edmond Weiss, in his book *How to Write Usable User Documentation,* champions the cause of modularity.[1] He points out that modules are functional (based on tasks the user performs), independent (don't rely on the reader having read previous modules), and small (fit on a page and are easy for the user to hold in short-term memory). Weiss uses compelling logic in promoting the modular concept. He sees the following advantages of the modular-format idea:

1. Text is kept with images so the user avoids having to turn the page to see the screen that relates to what is being read.

2. The act of designing modules helps the writer structure the writing process, from the research phase to the editing phase.

3. The modular concept is task-oriented and thus helps the user in the work environment.

You can easily see why modular design would help address the documentation problem. Greater ease of access unlocks the information. Theoretically, modularity accommodates both the experienced and advanced user because each may select only those modules that solve a particular problem. Similarly, different user role types—managers, system administrators, users—can easily choose the modules they need. But beyond these advantages, the modular document provides the writer with the ideal format for working with elements of the task analysis. Whether the writer creates documentation to teach, to guide, or to support the reader, the tasks identified in the task analysis seem naturally to fall into the modular format.

The tradeoffs of modularity lie in the costs associated with producing modular documents. Because some modules can take less than two pages, the resulting manual often has empty spaces; the next task starts on the next page. To publications managers or project sponsors the bottom line is often the total page count and the cost per page. Their main concern is keeping the manual production costs within budget. A writer working under these constraints may need to modify the modular design, keeping the concept of task orientation, but filling pages as much as possible.

MODULARITY AND SCREENS.   You should also note that modularity has less and less to do with online help systems. Because of the physical constraints of a page, you have to put all the necessary information in one space; otherwise the user has to go to another page. With a help system, however, you can overcome this problem with things like popup windows. For example, in a page telling how to put interactive fields into a form you would have to define the term *field* for the user. In a help system, you would simply include a link to the glossary entry, and the user who didn't know the term could simply click on it to get a popup window defining *field*. Because of online help's ability to link information together, help documents can segregate information more clearly. For this reason you see help systems with many different parts. The parts simply represent information categories, not physical locations.

Degree of Structure

Structure in page design means that we place the information on the page according to patterns, with certain kinds of information only in certain places. This process reserves certain areas of the page or screen for certain kinds of information. As an example, imagine a section of farm land: Some parts are used for grazing cattle, some for growing wheat, some for the farmhouse and barn, some left alone for woods and a pond. Similarly, the structured page has certain areas for headings, certain areas for overviews, others for screens. Highly structured pages use gardens of bulleted lists, tables of commands, and indented margins for steps, cautions, warnings. Highly structured pages also use fence-like vertical and horizontal lines, called *rules,* to separate and help the reader keep track of information on the page.

When you structure writing on a page, you must develop the knack of breaking down information into types. Often called *chunking,* this technique helps the reader identify what kinds of information the page presents. Helped by headings the user (ideally) can quickly learn where to look on a page to get what. This idea makes sense from the point of view of information processing. Researchers have determined that readers locate information in computer manuals (in fact in all documents) by remembering the physical location of information on the page, rather than the more abstract terms of chapter or section numbers. Additionally, the use of lists and tables gives the user the option to look over a list to select the appropriate function. In this way, the dynamic needs of the user may mesh more often with the static organization of a manual or help.

How much structure you build into your pages and screens depends on the degree of clutter you will allow and on the amount of white space you will need in order to balance the text items. Indeed, as Figure 9.7 shows, the structured method packs a lot of usable informa-

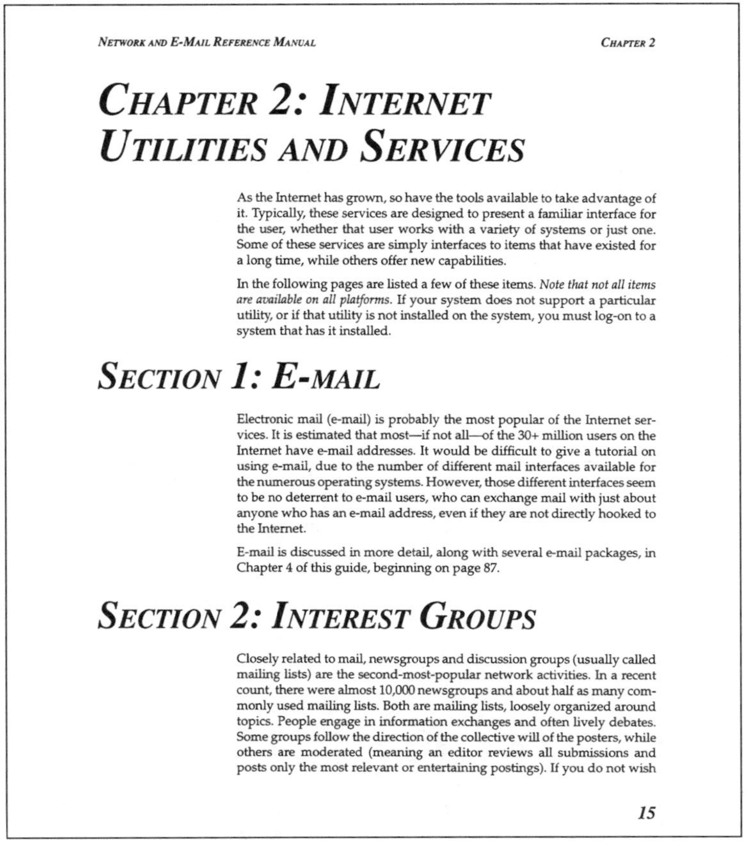

NETWORK AND E-MAIL REFERENCE MANUAL — CHAPTER 2

CHAPTER 2: INTERNET UTILITIES AND SERVICES

As the Internet has grown, so have the tools available to take advantage of it. Typically, these services are designed to present a familiar interface for the user, whether that user works with a variety of systems or just one. Some of these services are simply interfaces to items that have existed for a long time, while others offer new capabilities.

In the following pages are listed a few of these items. *Note that not all items are available on all platforms.* If your system does not support a particular utility, or if that utility is not installed on the system, you must log-on to a system that has it installed.

SECTION 1: E-MAIL

Electronic mail (e-mail) is probably the most popular of the Internet services. It is estimated that most—if not all—of the 30+ million users on the Internet have e-mail addresses. It would be difficult to give a tutorial on using e-mail, due to the number of different mail interfaces available for the numerous operating systems. However, those different interfaces seem to be no deterrent to e-mail users, who can exchange mail with just about anyone who has an e-mail address, even if they are not directly hooked to the Internet.

E-mail is discussed in more detail, along with several e-mail packages, in Chapter 4 of this guide, beginning on page 87.

SECTION 2: INTEREST GROUPS

Closely related to mail, newsgroups and discussion groups (usually called mailing lists) are the second-most-popular network activities. In a recent count, there were almost 10,000 newsgroups and about half as many commonly used mailing lists. Both are mailing lists, loosely organized around topics. People engage in information exchanges and often lively debates. Some groups follow the direction of the collective will of the posters, while others are moderated (meaning an editor reviews all submissions and posts only the most relevant or entertaining postings). If you do not wish

15

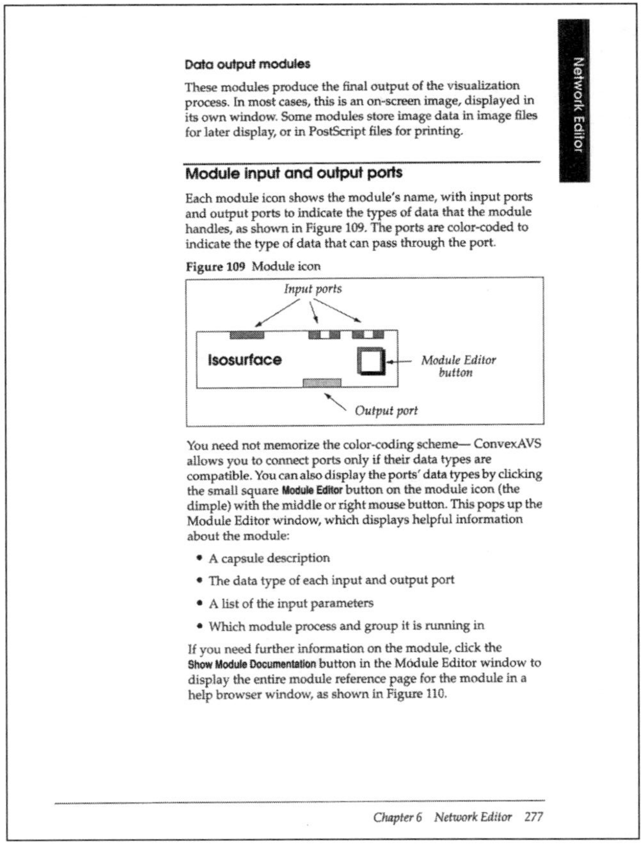

Network Editor

Data output modules

These modules produce the final output of the visualization process. In most cases, this is an on-screen image, displayed in its own window. Some modules store image data in image files for later display, or in PostScript files for printing.

Module input and output ports

Each module icon shows the module's name, with input ports and output ports to indicate the types of data that the module handles, as shown in Figure 109. The ports are color-coded to indicate the type of data that can pass through the port.

Figure 109 Module icon

You need not memorize the color-coding scheme— ConvexAVS allows you to connect ports only if their data types are compatible. You can also display the ports' data types by clicking the small square **Module Editor** button on the module icon (the dimple) with the middle or right mouse button. This pops up the Module Editor window, which displays helpful information about the module:

- A capsule description
- The data type of each input and output port
- A list of the input parameters
- Which module process and group it is running in

If you need further information on the module, click the **Show Module Documentation** button in the Module Editor window to display the entire module reference page for the module in a help browser window, as shown in Figure 110.

Chapter 6 Network Editor 277

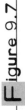

Figure 9.7

Effective Pages Showing Less and More Structure

The page on the left from the Texas Tech University *Network and E-Mail Reference Guide* has less structure, to accommodate reading of background information. The page on the right from the Convex AVS Operating System *User's Guide* has more structure, to accommodate scanning and selective reading.

tion into a small space, because all the format conventions help keep things in order. As Figure 9.7 also shows, a less-structured page, illustrated on the left, also shows efficiencies for its purpose. Uninterrupted paragraphs make a suitable format for reading background information. Elements that contribute to structure in your pages include the following:

- **Rules.** Various lengths and thicknesses help the user tell the reading area from the heading or scanning area

- **White space** (or quiet space in screens). Helps the user focus on page elements such as graphics without having to process impinging information. Helps create a balanced page or screen.

- **Bullets.** Help the user identify the kind and organization of information at a glance

- **Chunks.** Help the user identify reading information in overviews and elaborations.

How to Look at Pages and Screens

To learn how to design pages for a software manual, you must first learn how to look at pages. You should always give a manual the flip test and register an impression of the overall layout of the book. The arrangement of pages in software manuals does not follow any predictable forms. In your study of page layout you should make a point to browse through computer manuals found at computer stores or program libraries. The best place to get a good idea of different page layouts is a software company because often these companies purchase and use a wide variety of software. Many businesses that use software keep shelves of program packages that you can learn from. In studying layout, try to develop an eye for the following elements of page design.

- **Page density.** Comparing the pages of one manual to another, which seems darker, or heavier, or more crowded with text? Which seems lighter, using white space as a soft barrier between kinds of information?

- **Balance.** Compare how one manual balances white space and text space with one another. Do some pages seem top-heavy, bottom-heavy, right- or left-heavy? Well-balanced pages have a unified effect.

- **Legibility.** Compare the ease of reading of the type font and style among manuals which you think read clearly. Some combinations of fonts seem to work well together; others don't.

- **Lookability.** Perhaps the hardest element of page design to define, the lookability of a page has to do with how easily you can get, at a glance, the gist of a page. A key element in lookability is the collective impression made by the graphics (icons, diagrams, cartoons, drawings, rules). These elements should complement text to help the reader find information easily.

Experience will help you develop a feel for pages; you should also try to develop a sense of how the values listed above—density, balance, legibility, and lookability—get determined by and controlled by page elements like margins, columns, and images (screens, rules, and icons). The next section will discuss how these elements contribute to the overall design of pages.

Common Page Designs

Many designs used in software manuals incorporate the concepts of modularity and structure to varying degrees. Often we discuss pages in terms of the two-page spread: the left, or even, page and the right, or odd page. Talking about and viewing pages in this way helps the designer get a feel for the binding, which joins the pages in the middle. All designs leave about one-half inch on the binding edge to accommodate spirals and loose-leaf rings. Page layout also has to do with the number of columns.

Screen design needs to accommodate many of the same elements as pages: columns, headings, text, and graphics. But screens also need to arrange space for the non-scrolling region of the screen: the part that contains the topic name. The page designs described below by no means make up all the designs you can have for the page. But they do represent some very popular ones, and studying them can get you started on the design of pages for your projects.

Two-Column Format

Most software manuals today display a two-column format, shown in Figure 9.8. Most two-column formats have a graphics column (an area reserved for screens, icons, diagrams, and headings) and a text column (an area reserved for explanations, steps, notes, cautions, tables, and screens). Most patterns follow this basic design. Many such pages contain *rules* that either separate the graphics from the text column, or separate task names or other headings in the text column.

The graphics column contains *icons* and headings: the signposts for the user to the explanation of the task he or she needs to perform. The text column contains the explanation, in the form of steps, lists, definitions, explanations, and lower-order headings. The writer arranges the words in *bulleted* lists or numbers (for steps) and keeps the text width to about 4½ inches (or one and a half alphabets). Some variations of this format have the graphics column very narrow, and others have it wider in order to include features such as tips or illustrations.

ADVANTAGES AND DISADVANTAGES OF THE TWO-COLUMN FORMAT. The two-column format allows the reader to distinguish easily between guidance information and support information. Guidance consists of those elements on a more general level—icons, headings—with which to navigate the document. At points where the user needs more precise information—steps for actual performance, explanations of commands—he or she may stop browsing and read carefully in the text column. The impatient reader can easily pick up the pattern of general to specific—the most common and preferred pattern of all information.

The two-column format works best with guidance-level documentation: procedures, step-by-step, installation, getting started. It does a good job where readers read selectively, when they read to *do*. But on a space-to-unit of information ratio, the two-column format uses more space per information unit than dense one-column format. For sustained reading, say of background information, use a one-column format.

Quotes and Portfolio

The Financial Information folder in the Services Window includes two services that enable you to obtain current stock quote reports and portfolio evaluation reports. Both Quotes and Portfolio get data from BASICQUOTES, which is one of the basic services that you can access for your flat monthly rate without incurring connect-time charges.

The "current" stock price data retrieved by Quotes and Portfolio are delayed at least 15 minutes, in compliance with the regulations of the various stock exchanges.

Be sure to use ticker symbols

To identify securities you must provide their ticker symbols. Neither Quotes nor Portfolio work with CUSIP numbers, CINS numbers, or company names.

Navigator maintains only one list of ticker symbols for Quotes and only one list of portfolio entries for Portfolio. You can access these same lists in as many different scripts as you want.

Quotes

How to add Quotes

When you add CompuServe Quotes to the Script Editor window, Navigator displays the **Stock Quotes** task. Click the adjacent ▸▸▸ to display the Stock Quotes dialog:

To add a ticker symbol to the Tickers list, type the ticker and then click <<Add. Once you create your list, you can Copy All>> the tickers to the Get Request list, or Copy>> selected tickers one at a time. The Get Request list tells Navigator which stocks to report next time you run your script.

Portfolio

How to add Portfolio

When you add CompuServe Portfolio to the Script Editor window, Navigator displays the **Stock Portfolio** task. Click the adjacent ▸▸▸ to display the Stock Portfolio dialog:

To add information about a stock to your portfolio, fill in all the blanks in the Add Portfolio Entry box and click Add. When you have finished adding entries, click OK.

C R E A T I N G

37

Figure 9.8

A Two-Column Format

The two-column format, illustrated here in the CompuServe Navigator Windows Version *User's Guide,* allows users to navigate by topics and icons in the left column and then read details in the right column. Note also the use of prose-style instructions, discussed in Chapter 13.

One-Column Format

The one-column formatted page, shown in Figure 9.9, arranges both graphics and text in the middle of the page, in effect filling the page. Smaller page size on manuals using this design allows for the text lines to be kept at around the 4½-inch optimum for reader comprehension (optimum line length is discussed below). This format can help pack plenty of information into smaller pages of reference manuals for large systems, but it might impede the progress of the user trying to learn material for the first time.

In the one-column format, all graphics, icons, headings, and text obey a strong vertical left margin. Some text items—like notes, cautions, syntax examples, examples of commands to type in, and messages from the program—get indented. Because this page layout fills up the main portion of the page with text, it has a less dynamic look than pages with space reserved for cartoons and icons on which to rest the eyes.

ADVANTAGES AND DISADVANTAGES OF THE ONE-COLUMN FORMAT. In some ways the one-column format helps a writer modularize a document because it makes it easy to keep task information together in a linear form. The task or module just keeps on going until the next one starts, sometimes spanning pages. But because it does not have the large guidance column presented by the two-column format, the one-column format forces the reader to rely more heavily on other guidance elements, such as main headings that start new pages or tasks, and section, chapter, or topic notices contained in headers and footers. With a one-page format, I always find myself consulting page numbers to keep track of my progress.

In this regard, writers have used the one-column, full-page format for tutorials— which tend to have longer passages of prose—because they think that they can get away with cramming information on the page. Uncorrected, this mistake leads to the tutorial section not being read at all, or read complainingly. The one-column format works best for procedures and reference manuals and in documents where the margins are large and numerous graphics and other visual aids help the reader follow along.

The Elements of Page Design

We have seen how page design can contribute to overcoming the design problem. The writer's decisions about the degree of modularity and of structure, and choice of one- or two-column format, will determine how well a given audience can use the manual. Pages consist of the arrangement of many complex elements. But by mastering a few of these, you will begin to understand the building blocks of pages. The following paragraphs describe these elements.

The Left Margin

Text and graphics (the edges of boxed graphics, screens, or the imaginary "soft" edges of icons surrounded by white space) align according to various margins, but most important, they align according to the left margin. The indent margin, the right, top, and bottom margins all play their part, but the left margin rules the page, so to speak. This makes sense, because most of the items on the page use the left margin as a starting place and

---

USING A BOOT ROM WITH THE DOS ODI DRIVER

If your adapter uses a boot ROM, you must install the program RPLODI.COM (written by Novell) before you install the Thomas-Conrad driver. RPLODI.COM is available from the same sources as LSL.COM.

To install RPLODI.COM, install it between LSL.COM and TCNSW.COM. For example, enter the following commands from the DOS command line, or put them in the AUTOEXEC.BAT file:

LSL
RPLODI
TCNSW

CREATE NET.CFG IF NECESSARY

The NET.CFG file includes configuration information about the network adapters in your workstation. If you are not using any of the options listed in this section, you do not have to create NET.CFG.

❑   You will need a NET.CFG file,

❑   If you do not use IRQ2.

❑   If you do not use memory address D0000.

❑   If you want to include additional shell commands.

❑   If you want to add additional protocol stacks.

If either of these conditions applies to your workstation, take the following steps. Otherwise, you are finished installing the workstation driver.

STEP	ACTION
1	Create the NET.CFG file.

NET.CFG resides in the root directory of the workstation's boot drive. If NET.CFG does not already exist, use your text editor or the **COPY CON** command to create the file.

Insert the following statement into the NET.CFG:

LINK DRIVER TCNSW

Page 6-4   DOS ODI Workstation Driver

Figure 9.9

A One-Column Format

The one-column format, illustrated here in the Thomas-Conrad Corporation's award-winning manual TC3045 TCNS ADAPTER/AT *Installation Guide,* shows how you can present a lot of information in a small space and still allow for easy use. Note the innovative style for introducing steps that reinforces a sequence–action pattern.

are defined relative to it. In a two-column format the left margin has the extra importance of dividing two kinds of information: images and headings for tracking, and text for close reading.

Columns

Most software will set up columns for you easily. When your desktop system or word processing system does this, it reveals them to you in the form of grid lines (imaginary lines where the margins lie). Grid lines help you see the page or screen before you fill it with words and pictures, and they show the spaces between the columns, called **gutters**. Columns can work in two ways: as newspaper columns and table columns.

Newspaper columns fill the page by snaking text from the bottom of one column to the top of the next. The effect is to fill one column before the next one gets any text. Table columns, on the other hand, treat the columns on the page as discrete items, and will move text lines from the bottom of one column onto the top of that column on the next page. For most manual projects, table columns work best, because they give you the option of not filling up the bottom of the column before the next one gets filled. For two-column formats, this helps, because each column does indeed contain different information: one with graphics, one with text. Table columns make this arrangement easier to manage.

Headers and Footers

No manual page will work unless it has headers and footers to help the reader keep track of sections, topics, and page numbers. Additionally, these text areas also contain product names, version numbers, company or program identification icons, and rules (lines) to help define the page space. For taking up such a small part of the page, they do a big job. How much stress you place on your headers and footers depends on the kinds of user support your specific pages need to give and the kinds of page design you choose. As we saw earlier, the one-column format places a heavy burden on headers and footers to help the reader navigate the information. The two-column pages shift some of the navigational burden onto the text and graphic elements of the page.

Icons and Diagrams

Increasingly, the easy-to-use page or screen contains many visual elements. These include **icons,** screens, diagrams, pictures, and **rules**. Subsequent chapters will treat these elements in detail; here we will see how they contribute in a general way to overall page design. Icons and diagrams function mostly to help the reader identify the needed information, to move from one section to another. They support the cuing system used in a manual. If the page designer has done the job well, they will fit, have adequate white space around them, and occur often in the document.

Screens

No documenter can avoid including screens in a manual and to do it well you need to know their types. These include the following:

- Full screens (showing the entire computer display)

- Partial screens (showing usually half of the display or an important part such as command lines)

- Menus showing just the pull-down type menu, or the objects (buttons, sliders, check boxes) that a user can choose from

Because the user needs to refer to these screens during careful reading, design them so that they have accurate details in large-enough type. You will often need to compromise legibility of these screens with the size needed. Bigger usually works; better might mean smaller, to save space. Also, don't forget that screens need captions and labels, which increase the amount of space the screens take up.

Rules

Rules consist of lines of varying width and length that you place on a page to help line up columns or to distinguish types of information. Rules come in thick or thin, tones of gray, double, hairline, color, and other types of border artwork. As a visual element, they present a wide variety of options for the software manual writer. More often than not, rules get used to separate levels and thus help the user keep track of the depth of information. The user will seldom read highly technical material unless he or she knows that it contains the right information.

No matter how many columns on the page, rules used along with headings (rules that are often the same length as the heading) help signify levels of detail. In highly structured documents, rules play a crucial role in keeping page areas distinct and defining columns. When used in headers and/or footers, rules help the reader maintain a sense of the size of the page and thus aid in recall of information locations.

Pagination

While it may seem like a simple concept, how you paginate a manual can greatly affect its usability. If you paginate a document from front to back, starting with page one, then the manual has sequential pagination. If you paginate a document chapter by chapter, with each chapter starting again at page one, then the manual has modular pagination.

Sequential pagination works best with documentation sets where different user's needs are met in different books. When you have a supervisor's guide, a user's guide, and an installer's guide, then use sequential pagination in each one to help give each a sense of unity. When your tutorial reference section fills its own book, you can get away with sequential numbering because it encourages the reader to keep reading.

Modular pagination has the advantage of making the reader more aware of chapters and their contents. It works well in user's guides that contain tutorial and reference documents all under the same cover. Because each chapter starts with page one again, you can easily maintain this pagination scheme. When you add to a chapter, simply reprint that chapter, not the whole book.

Like the modular scheme, sequential pagination works with other user navigational elements like headers and footers. Headers and footers contain names and numbers for sections, parts, and chapters. Working with your pagination method, these add to the degree of structuring each page has. You should also use care in designing pagination for appendices, indexes, and front matter pages (usually they just have lower-case roman numerals). Make it clear that these sections of the manual differ from the body portion; also make clear what these sections contain.

Common Screen Designs

You will find a lot of variation in help screens among software programs, especially in interactive tables of contents screens and index screens. The following paragraphs discuss some of the common screen formats.

Windows Screen Format

The windows screen format, shown in Figure 9.10, contains the usual system affordances of a window: It contains a non-scrolling region (or regions) that can help the user keep track of his or her position in the levels of information. It usually uses a one-column design with hot areas that take users to related topics. In some variations of this screen design you can divide the screen into two columns, with the index entries in the left column and the selected topic in the right column. In this way the user can move among the help topics on the left, select from the list, and see the topic on the right. This design has the advantage of always letting the user see the table of contents—to navigate the system with it always in view.

You can also set up screens using this format to illustrate the functions of a program as they relate to the interface. In Figure 9.11 the dialog box contains hot areas. When the

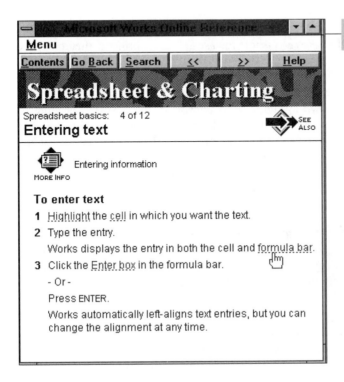

Figure 9.10

A Procedure in Windows Screen Format

This format from the Microsoft Works *Online Reference* shows a one-column screen with the task name and other information in the non-scrolling region at the top.

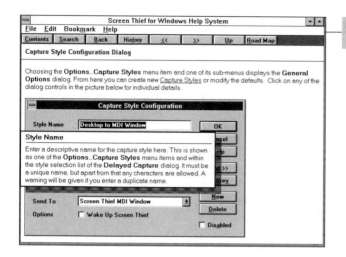

Figure 9.11

A Screen Topic Showing Parts of a Dialog Box

This screen from the Screen Thief *Help* shows a common format: a dialog box or other interface item with pop-up explanations.

user clicks on a hot area, a popup window explains that function. Another click closes the popup window. You can use this format for illustrating screens, toolbars, menus, and other interface elements. You can also include links to procedural documentation on this topic. In this example the layout has the title in the non-scrolling region, the definition of the dialog box, and then a bitmap of the dialog box with the hot areas pre-defined by the system designer.

Man Pages Format

Many users will recognize the *man pages* (short for *manual pages*) format if they have any experience with operating systems like VMS or UNIX. It basically consists of a handy format for dumping print documentation online. It has no left margin or other niceties of a windows-like bitmapped screen.

The man pages format, shown in Figure 9.12, consists of three parts: a heading or title area, a text area, and a navigation area. The title area usually falls at the top, and in it you find the title of the topic or command. The text area falls in the middle of the screen, and it contains definitions, examples, and references to associated commands. The navigation area at the bottom of the screen contains a prompt. Variations of this format can contain other help system commands such as to print or search the help system.

The Elements of Screen Design

Designing screens can get very complex because screens get easier to read as new technology emerges. The following paragraphs discuss some of the design challenges you face and offer advice for writing highly usable screens.

A Changeable Space

The idea of a communication space changes when you compare pages and screens. With pages you have a static space, the same with each page; with screens the user can re-size, scroll, and in other ways change the communication space. How can you design infor-

```
HELP

    Enables you to obtain information about the Mail utility.

    To obtain information about all of the Mail commands,
    enter the following command:

        MAIL>HELP

    To obtain information about individual commands or topics, enter
    the HELP command followed by the command or topic name.

    Format

        HELP [topic]

Additional information available:

ANSWER   ATTACH   BACK   COMPRESS   COPY   CURRENT   DEFINE
DELETE   DIRECTORY   EDIT   ERASE   EXIT   EXTRACT   FILE
Files   FIRST   Folders   FORWARD   Getting_Started   HELP
Keypad   LAST   MAIL   MAIL_Commands   MARK   MOVE
NEXT   Overview   PRINT   PURGE   QUIT   READ   REMOVE
REPLY   SEARCH   SELECT   SEND   SET-SHOW   SHOW   SPAWN
Usage_Summary

Topic?
```

Figure 9.12

A Topic in Man Pages Format

This format, common to mainframe operating systems and other large systems, presents information in an easy-to-use format compatible with just about any screen.

mation effectively for this space? As a starting place, I find it useful to see the space as a frame, one of many in front of the user at any given time. The document you're presenting to the user shows through the frame. So design for the document, so that when the frame changes, the user can still read it effectively. Consider following these guidelines to design for help screen frames:

- **Forget line length.** Don't bother adjusting the line length as you might in a column of a page because the user can bring the right screen border in and change the shape. In most cases you only have to design for the left and other indent margins.

- **Avoid lots of scrolling.** You can expect the user to do a degree of scrolling to get to the end of a long procedure of explanation. But too much scrolling can disorient just about anyone, especially if the text doesn't contain cues like numbers or characters of the alphabet (as in the case of an index) to give a sense of location. You should make your topics no longer than two screens, 3½ inches, in length. Break up longer topics.

- **Indicate the extent of the topic.** If the topic contains more than one screen and you move screen by screen, indicate so with a "More" button, or a "1 of 3" progress indicator.

Multiple Window Management

You have to determine how and whether users can manage information in help windows. The help system program that you use will provide you with a number of tools for doing this. When making decisions about how to manage the help windows, you might want to follow these guidelines.

■ **Don't obliterate the user's work.** Some help systems splash over the entire screen when you call them up. But this can disorient users because suddenly their existing application vanishes. Allowing the help screen to cover only part of the screen reassures users that their application didn't go anywhere.

■ **Avoid window clutter.** Try not to let too many windows clutter the screen. A window within a window within a window can confuse users because they loose a sense of the levels of topics. Of course, with some systems you can't avoid the clutter the user might create. With WinHelp you can implement an "On Top" button that allows users to keep a topic (usually a procedure) on the screen to read while performing the procedure. You can't stop users from leaving a number of these topics open, but you can try to minimize the number of windows the system itself presents.

■ **Give the user control over frames.** Some windows will close automatically when the user presses a key or clicks with the mouse. Others can close automatically in a pre-set time. But you should make sure that when it's up to the user to close the window, you make it clear how to do it.

Color

Use color to cue important elements. Color provides you with a powerful tool for helping users manage the help system. You can use it to indicate sections of the screen and to help identify important kinds of information like navigational tools, tips, interface tools, and so forth.

Graphics

Use simple graphics. On most systems graphics appear grainy and may not allow you the kind of detail you get when you print them on a page. Overall, you find fewer graphics in help, for this reason, and because of the space they take up and the limitations of some systems in reading and displaying them. In general, use simplified images that don't rely on details to communicate: cartoons, simple icons, screens.

Screen Grids

As discussed above, the grid you use for the screen differs from the one you use for a page. Most of the differences result from the differences in the lower legibility of screens and the flexibility of the screen frame. Consider these differences when setting up screen grids:

■ **Use narrower margins.** On a page you would use a 1" left margin, whereas on a screen you only need about ⅛" to ¼" margin. You don't need the passive white space of a margin to define the communication space; the plastic edge of the computer monitor does that for you.

■ **Use less indentation.** Indent only about ¼" rather than the standard ½" you would indent on a page. For one thing, you don't want to waste the space, and for another, you don't need as much indentation with the larger fonts used on screens.

■ **Define the grid for single pages only.** It may seem obvious, but you don't have left-hand and right-hand pages online. Similarly, you don't need to plan for a binding offset.

■ **Use rules sparingly.** With screens you tend to define topics as whole units and don't need as many rules to segregate information and establish hierarchies.

Line Spacing

In general, when you're setting up screens, you put your lines closer together or at least almost always single spaced. And because of the overall reduced legibility of screens, you use larger type in headings to make them more visible.

Designing Type

The second major component of document layout, type design, challenges you to use the complex writing tools at your disposal to overcome the design problem: getting users linked up with information. Years ago, small-budget documentation projects had few tools to work with. Now, powerful desktop publishing systems, and even low-cost PCs with page design software, allow writers many possibilities for designing type.

A study of type design should begin with what we know about how users recognize words, from a researcher's point of view. Then we will apply some of that knowledge to the specific job of building task orientation into software manuals.

Helping People Recognize Words

Much of what we already know about users becomes important when we consider ways to help them use the text portions of the pages to their maximum capacity. We know that the user's experience with computers, with other programs, and with the subject matter of the program will play great parts in our determination of type size, font, and style. Designing type means accounting for as many idiosyncrasies as possible. But beyond that, type designers need to understand some fundamental principles of how readers get meaning from words and how readers process words on a page into ideas.

One of the things we have learned about the way people recognize words reinforces the idea we have discussed earlier: that people prefer a visual orientation. Manuals that support a visual orientation consistently test higher in usability evaluations. For this reason, we should focus our attention on the shape of words, researchers tell us, as well as the fact that they consist of letters.

Software documenters need also to acknowledge the shape of words. For evidence of this, remember the times you have heard someone read a sentence like this: "Don't forget to store the disk accessory in the startup folder," substituting the incorrect word *disk* for the correct, look-alike word *desk*. Words that look like one another confuse us at times, because we read by shape. For simple words like *the* and *and* we may not even see more than the vague outline or part of the shape before we have already understood the word and gone on to fit it into the overall meaning of the sentence. Long, tall, short, mixed: Words speak to us by their shape, as well as their letters.

The serifs on type characters add to the shape of the word. Serifed type has little strokes at the ends of the letters that almost connect the letter to its neighbor. *Sans serif* fonts—Helvetica, the "modern" fonts—don't have these little connectors. (The *sans* part of the phrase comes from French—the word for *without*.) The difference between serif fonts and sans serif fonts resembles that between hand-printing and cursive, or script. Script letters, similar to serif characters, have lines that connect one letter to the next. Hand-printed characters, like sans serif characters, consist only of straight-ended strokes.

The distinction between serif and sans-serif type means a lot to the software documenter. Because close reading by users occurs so infrequently, the design of the type should support scanning, make it as easy as possible. In addition, reading should take place in as small a space as possible. Serifed fonts work well for this because those little strokes on the ends of the letters contribute to the shape of the word and contribute to legibility. The serifs help the eye move quickly across the page. Non-serif fonts, on the other hand, work best when the font size makes up for any loss of legibility. The smaller the type, the more important the serifs.

Design Advice

- **Choose a type face the user knows well.** Reserve exotic type faces like Albuquerque or NASA for the cover or title page.

- **Choose a font with definite ascenders and descenders for small-sized type.** Ascenders are the part above the line in "b" and "d"; descenders are the part below the line in "p" and "y."

- **Choose a type style familiar to the user.** These include Times Roman and Courier (for input information).

- **Avoid long passages in italics or all caps.** Both italic and all caps make the shape of a word more difficult to recognize. Using all caps, because all letters stand at the same height, blurs the distinction between one word and the next and slows down comprehension.

- **Keep headings short.** Use the *implied* "you" as in "Installing the Program" instead of "Here's How You Install the Program."

- **Use serif for body text, sans serif for headings.** Headings speak most boldly when they stand out and stay short.

Building Patterns with Type

As we discussed earlier, the main way you help the reader overcome the design problem consists of giving your manual a recognizable pattern (the cognitive scientists call it a *schema*). Just as you would use a schema for finding your car in a parking lot ("big antenna, rack on top") to help you distinguish your car from the others that resemble it closely, so you want to show your user how to use a schema for recognizing important information in your manual. In our study of software document design so far we have seen a number of ways to do this: using cuing techniques, page structures, headings, rules, and other layout elements.

Type design also contributes to the pattern of a manual because you can use it to signal kinds of information for the reader and to assist the reader in getting the needed information from closely read passages. Table 9.3 shows the differences between these three elements. As a designer of type you face three important questions: what size, what style, and what font.

Table 9.3

Type: Style, Size, and Font

Type Characteristic	Examples	Used to . . .
Style	plain **bold** *italics* <u>underline</u>	add special emphasis, distinguish foreign terms, identify titles, and make headings stand out.
Size	very small small medium large	label callouts, present warranty information, identify body text, identify headings, and identify document title pages.
Font	Times New Roman Courier New **Arial** *Caliban*	distinguish body text from headings, represent "typed" text, and add emphasis.

Design Advice

Keep it simple. If you have doubts as to which font, size, or style to use, change them in this order: first the style, then the size, then the font. Thus, if you decided that you wanted to give, say, glossary terms a special look, make them bold, or italics, first. If this does not make them recognizable to the user, then, keeping the same font, make the type bigger by two or four points. After that, as a last resort, change the font to make them stand out better.

- **Arrange for no more than three levels of information, preferably two.** If you limit the number of major hierarchies on the page, you limit the number of times you might have to change size, style, and font.
- **Use a sensible cuing pattern.** Don't overdo your pages with three or four kinds of cuing devices (usually based on size and style of type) because it makes the page look cluttered and adds to the user's cognitive load.
- **Use type design consistently.** Throughout the manual and help system, use the same design in associated documents.
- **Think in terms of styles.** Decide what you want your paragraphs to look like and specify your type style, font, and size, along with your indentation and margin

specifications. Most word processors work in this way: They allow you to set the way you want paragraphs to look (their layout and type) so that you can determine the look of the text by evoking the style from a saved style guide. When you work like this, you help ensure consistency in the whole document. Later, when we discuss document planning, we will again see the importance of designing type in terms of styles.

The Idea of Body Text

When you select type style, font, and size for the main text portion of your document, you make one of the most important choices in document design: You determine body text. Body text fills the pages and screens of your documents. Explanations, introductions, advance organizers, glossary definitions, index entries—all these convey their information to the user through variations on the type style, font, and size that you selected for body text. You can modify body text in size and style (but not font) to achieve different effects without introducing significantly different elements onto the page or screen. While the general consensus on body text dictates that readers like a plain style, serifed font, between 10 and 12 points in size, many constraints affect the actual choice of body text style. Your main constraints follow, in descending order of importance:

- **Page size.** Generally, the smaller the page, the smaller the size and the less dense the font. On smaller pages you need a smaller size in order to economize. When you reduce the size of the type from 12 to 10 points, you gain an additional 20 percent of space. This gain can allow you to modularize more effectively and to keep manual size to a minimum. As for a less dense font, such as Times (less dense) instead of Schoolbook (more dense), the smaller page looks less crowded with a font with slimmer lines. And the reader has less ink to process.

- **Media.** Pages allow you to use much smaller, more detailed fonts for body text, whereas screens allow a more limited range of fonts. Some help programs come with their own fonts, recommended by the help developer. Usually these consist of sans serif fonts of slightly larger size, say 12 or 14 points. You want a font that defines the character clearly (and from the distance between eye and screen) but that doesn't include fine details (like serifs) to confuse the recognition. Sometimes a combination font (such as Chicago or Geneva) works best online.

- **User expectations.** The document designer should pay attention to what kinds of type users see regularly in software documents. For the most part, you can predict what the type design for body text will look like before you open a new manual. However, in some manuals you will find sans serif fonts (Helvetica, etc.) used for body text, and you will also find it used as body text in other documents people read regularly: books, newsletters, journals. If you decide to set body text in one of these fonts, make sure you have a good printer and the manuals get reproduced on high-quality copiers. This way you offset any loss of legibility due to sans serif fonts.

Non-Body Text

A manual or help system consists of more than just body text. Once you determine the style, font, and size of body text, you next have to deal with the variations of body text that will make up the rest of your pages and screens. Readers need to have information other than explanations and introductions set apart—given a distinctive look—so they can remember them, look forward to them, and relearn them. What other kinds of information require such fancy treatment? Many of them found their way into the discussion of basic document design above: headings, cautions, warnings, notes, input instructions, and computer messages. Below you will find discussions of these elements and suggestions for selecting type for them.

Headings

Headings function to help the reader locate important information, and they do their job best when the reader can easily distinguish them from body text. For this reason we put them on separate lines, in special columns, and in larger, attention-grabbing type. Try to make the different levels of headings (chapter titles, section titles, tasks, etc.) consistent in type design.

Conventional wisdom dictates that they should look larger, use a sans serif font, and use a bold style. This choice makes sense when we consider the lookability of type. The size catches the user's eye; the size also makes up for the lack of word-shape cues in the sans serif font; and the bold style gives the heading a distinctive density, apart from that of the body text.

Other possibilities for heading type design include keeping the same font as the body text but varying the size and style of different levels of headings proportionately. So you would end up with small, medium, and large versions of basically the same font. The users of the document get their navigational needs met, and the writer's task stays a little simpler.

In choosing the type for headings, designers should also remember that such elements as the use of rules can significantly affect one's decisions. Again, the manual's type design should conform to an overall vision of the manual as a system. All the parts need to work together.

Hints, Notes, and Cautions

Like the other informational elements of manuals, hints, notes, and cautions give the user extra, or special, information. Some writers call these "asides." They, too, must read easily and use visual cues to catch the reader's eye. Thus, you will format them using headings, indentation, boxes, icons, and color to make sure the user gets the message.

With all these other visual cues helping the user, the type design decision often amounts to this: Should the writer adjust the type size, font, and style, too? Often these messages occur in the type used for body text because, unlike some features discussed below, they consist of information from the writer to the user. You decide to include one of them as a way of saying, "Pay attention to this information" or "Note the variation possible here." You may, thus, choose to leave them in body text type because, after all, you want the reader to see them as body text, but body text of a special kind.

If anything, change the type characteristics of the heading or cuing word for the note or caution. You will see many of these elements set in larger, sans serif font, bolded italics style. This way the word itself catches the reader's eye and identifies the information. The rest of the processing event gets managed by indentation and rules or boxes.

User Input, Computer Output

Unlike the features discussed above, software documentation also consists of information that the user has to type in, and that the computer program displays. The writer does not write this information; the interface of the program dictates it. Commands and displays make up the substance of computer interaction, whether the user gives commands with a keyboard or mouse, or whether the computer displays, by means of the screen, the speaker or the printer.

For these reasons, then, writers usually change the font of input and output messages from that of body text. For input, most users expect the `Courier font`, because it resembles typewriter text, and the analogy of the keyboard to the typewriter helps them understand that they should now use the keys to enter a command or a file name, or whatever. For output, warnings and other messages may catch the reader's eye better in a small-sized sans serif font like Helvetica. A font like this allows the message to resemble body text but still look distinctive.

Tables and Lists

As with hints and notes, discussed above, your main decision with tables and lists will revolve around how to do the headings: The substance of the tables and lists—words—works best set in the type size, font, and style used for body text. Don't change type elements just for tables; instead make the tables differ in indentation and column layout. That way, you emphasize that they resemble text but have been reformatted and condensed for greater clarity. You can also call attention to tables and lists by altering the style of headings and adding rules.

Glossary

ASCII: plain unformatted text and numbers in computer files.

bullet: a heavy dot, filled square, or other graphic device that calls attention to important points.

communication spaces: in document design, any area within both print and online media containing text and images designed for viewing and communicating information. The communication space of print usually consists of pages in a relatively fixed one- or two-page spread and presents the best space ever invented to communicate highly detailed information. The communication space of online media consists of the screen, a relatively flexible and dynamic space presenting one of the worst spaces to communicate highly detailed information.

gutter: space between columns; also, the page margin on the inside (binding) edge.

icon: a graphic element that cues the reader to a function of the program, such as a wastebasket to signify file deletion.

mirrored pages: pages making up a two-page layout, with page numbers located on the outside edge of each facing page.

modularity: a page design in which the page contains all the information required about a particular topic so that understanding the topic or task doesn't depend on the information that appears in previous topics or tasks.

page grid: a device for designing pages that uses lines and boxes to identify page margins and to mark the main communication spaces of a page and used as a pattern.

rule: a horizontal or vertical line used to indicate column widths or to separate vertical columns.

sketch-straight: a line made by short pencil movements that looks straight but doesn't require a ruler to draw.

specifications: statements of the requirements of page design that tell the dimensions of pages and columns, size, font, and style of text and other details. You write up specifications for page layout in the documentation plan.

thumbnail sketch: a miniature sketch of a page showing the placement of text and graphics, used in page design.

Checklist ✔

Use the following checklist as a way to keep you on track when making the many decisions involved with page and screen layout.

Document Layout Checklist
Overall

☐ Has the client, sponsor, and/or user reviewed your selection of page or screen design?
☐ Do all elements of your manual and online help set contain parallel information for consistency and efficiency?

Layout Goals

☐ Include elements to help the user overcome the documentation problem.
☐ Include support for overall task orientation.
☐ Accommodate the user's visual needs.

Modularity

☐ Repeat background information where necessary.
☐ Repeat screens when necessary.
☐ Include orienting information about the relationship of a task to other tasks.
☐ Keep all relevant steps on the same page.
☐ Minimize cross references.

Structure

☐ Rules   ☐ Bullets
☐ White/quiet space   ☐ Chunks

Page and Screen Designs

Page: **Screen:**

☐ Two-column format   ☐ Windows help format
☐ One-column format   ☐ Man-page format
☐ Multiple-column format

Determine the Following Layout Elements

Page: **Screen:**

☐ Left margin   ☐ Sizing and Scrolling
☐ Columns   ☐ Multiple window management
☐ Headers and Footers   ☐ Cuing and Highlighting
☐ Icons and Diagrams   ☐ Icons and Buttons
☐ Screens   ☐ Margins and Columns
☐ Rules   ☐ Line spacing
☐ Pagination

Determine the Following Text Elements

	Size	Style	Font
Body Text			
Headings			
Hints			
Notes			
Cautions			
Warnings			
User input			
Computer output			
Tables			
Lists			

Practice/Problem Solving

1. Learn from the Competition

Elements of page layout should accommodate different kinds of documentation. Analyze the design of two or three manuals for the following elements, explaining how you think the writer did or did not adjust them for the appropriate:

- Page density
- Balance
- Legibility
- Lookability

2. Practice Drawing

Draw thumbnail sketches of three different page designs in computer manuals that address user's needs at the same level (e.g., three different designs for procedures, three different designs for tutorials, etc.). Submit these sketches, along with a brief, one-page report analyzing how each design met the user's task needs. Which one do you think worked best, and why? How much of the success or failure of a document can you attribute to its design as revealed in the thumbnail sketch? What elements of page composition do you think affect the document the most? What would an ideal page design look like?

3. Analyze Flyer Pages for New Ideas

Often software packages come with flyers, telling the main features of the program and showing sample screens. Often these documents contain support information for decision-making: "Should I buy this program or not?" Examine some of these flyers—available at a software or computer store—for ideas about how to construct such a document. Create a list of page layout options and styles that you find. Discuss how you can take some of the basic ideas in this text and apply them to the variety of layouts you find in software flyers.

4. Use Thumbnail Sketches in the Design Process

Prepare a series of thumbnail sketches for the program for which you are currently writing documentation. Get these designs approved by your sponsor or client. Revise the sketches and create a final, mock-up version. You may want to do this with your word processor or page-design program.

5. Go on a Scavenger Hunt

Sometimes you can learn a lot by examining as many elements as you can think of at once, just to find representative examples of the kinds of features discussed in Chapter 5, and, to some extent, Chapter 4. If you have a bookshelf of documentation nearby, go through it and leave a trail of post-it notes showing examples you found of the features in the list. Identify, in a list, some that would apply to your current documentation project.

6. Design for the Page and the Screen

Study the task illustrated in Figure 3.2. How would the layout of the information differ if you developed it 1) to teach a clerk the basics of the word processing program, or 2) to guide a marketing executive who knows the word processing program well enough to use the online help when writing letters to clients? You might include more elaboration for one user, and include the procedure as a task in a help system for the other. Create page designs for the layout and text for two different pages or screens, and list differences in the two screens as they pertain to the two users.

10
Getting the
Language Right

In this chapter we study the role language plays in helping the manual and help system attain the goal of supporting information-oriented work. You have to think about the users of the software and say things in a way that has value to them. Following the guidelines of performance-oriented, structured writing can help ensure that your language supports the overall task-orientation of the manual. Our study of language and style needs to start with what research tells us about how we process language and how we remember and learn. We process language by providing a task context for the words, by bringing meaning *to* the words and not getting meaning *from* them. We learn and remember easily when we have patterns and structures in language and when the language in manuals and help does not violate the structures we expect. We will also see that many problems in the language of software documentation all revolve around two central difficulties: failure to write so that the user can perform the task easily, and failure to write as if we were speaking to real human beings.

How to Read This Chapter

You should study the Example and read the Discussion section first, and then the Guidelines, because in this case you can see a clear logical connection between the psychology of language processing—even though only the basic concepts are presented—and injunctions like "Focus on Functionality Rather Than Functions."

- If your project or the work of other writers places you in the role of editor, you may appreciate the discussion of "Style Problems in Software Documentation."

- For those readers reading to *understand,* the entire chapter is focused on problems specific to software documentation and not other forms of writing in the computer industry.

The example in Figure 10.1 comes from an award-winning software manual that uses style to its best advantage. Written for scientists, this passage embodies important background

---

What are Data Files?

By now you've learned the basics of how to use GCG programs to analyze the nucleic acid or protein sequences that are stored in the sequence databases or in your own personal sequence files. Additionally, many programs require nonsequence information, or *data files*, which they use to analyze the sequences. For example, one of the nucleic acid mapping programs, Map, requires two data files: Enzyme.Dat, which contains restriction enzyme names and corresponding recognition sites; and Translate.Txt, which associates codons with their corresponding amino acids.

Default vs. Local Data Files

All programs that require a data file have a default file they use, so as a new user, you don't need to worry about supplying one. These default files are public in that they are available to everyone who uses the Package. Default data files are located in the public directory with the logical name GenRunData and may be accessed by everyone who uses the Package. When you run a program that requires a data file, it automatically finds the appropriate default file in this directory; this means you don't have to specify the directory and filename.

GCG also supplies alternative data files you can have a program use instead of the default. These files are located in the directory with the logical name GenMoreData. There may be times when you want to use one of these alternative data files rather than the default data file. For example, if you're using the CodonPreference program to analyze a Drosophila sequence, you may want to use the alternative codon frequency table Drosophila_High.Cod rather than the default table, Eco_High.Cod, which is more appropriate for bacterial sequences.

You also can create your own data files or copy a default or alternative public data file to your local directory and modify it. These files are known as *local data files*. For instance, let's say you're working with the FindPatterns program and you create a data file of patterns specific to your research. This personal data file, then, would be available only to you. When you have a local data file a program can use, it tells you so as you are running the program. For example, it displays a message similar to "*** I read your "data" file. ***" to remind you that you have a data file in your directory which the program is using instead of the default.

This operational overview emphasizes program use instead of technical details.

The paragraph ties in clearly with the heading.

Sentences focus on user actions instead of program functions.

Use of the active voice enhances clarity.

Paragraphs are kept at a reasonable length.

Informal diction increases ease of reading.

Word choice emphasizes the program rather than the computer.

Figure 10.1

Effective Writing Style

This example from the Wisconsin Sequence Analysis Package *User's Guide* shows some of the features of good writing that help users gain a sense of control over the program and understand how it will do work for them.

information and leans toward the reading-to-understand user—hence the lack of a lot of page structure in order to maximize the number of words on the page. But when you write in this compact way, the style needs enough strength and clarity to encourage the user to read and understand.

 **uidelines**

Figure 10.2 lists guidelines for ensuring that your style is oriented to users' needs.

1 FOCUS ON ACTIONS RATHER THAN FUNCTIONS

One of the main differences between system-oriented manuals and help- and task-oriented manuals and online help lies in their language. With every menu item you describe you have the opportunity to tell users the name of the function and what results from its use (*system* orientation) or to tell users the name of the function and what workplace task it will perform (*task* orientation). The first kind of statement puts the users at odds with the program—as something apart from them that they will have to learn to use; the second, and preferred, kind of statement, puts the program on the users' side—as a set of tools designed to help them do their work. The more you focus on actions rather than on functions, the greater the likelihood that your users will recognize that usefulness and pay attention to your manual or help.

To write effective performance-based sentences you should create direct sentences that focus on user actions, such as those in Table 10.1. Tags like "You can . . ." or "X function helps you to . . ." work well when used frequently.

2 USE THE ACTIVE VOICE

The active voice puts a *subject* at the beginning of each sentence, a *verb* in the middle, and a *receiver* of the action at the end. "You can use the File menu to . . ." uses the active voice. "The File menu is used to . . ." uses the passive voice. The negative results of the passive voice abound: Your sentences will fill up with noun words (*functionality, usefulness, motion*) instead of verbs (*function, use, move*). Nouns clutter things up; verbs get things done.

You can force yourself to write in the active voice easily if you write in **e-prime,** but you can also write in passive voice using e-prime. E-prime writing resembles normal writing in English with one difference: Any forms of the *be* verb (*is, are, am, was, were*) get left

1. Focus on actions rather than functions.
2. Use the active voice.
3. Keep writing simple.
4. Build parallel structures.
5. Use operational overviews.

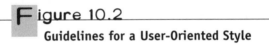 **igure 10.2**

Guidelines for a User-Oriented Style

Table 10.1

Examples of Statements That Emphasize Actions

Focus on Functions	Focus on Actions (Preferred)
"The Apple Menu has four main functions."	"The Apple Menu indicates the four main tasks you can perform."
"The tutorial is organized in a step-by-step manner so that the user will gain a basic understanding of the program and be able to create readme files."	"The tutorial is organized in a step-by-step manner, so that you can understand the program and create readme files."
"The greatest speed in List Box scrolling is achieved from the keyboard by typing one character to get the part of the list where the entries begin with that character."	"You can scroll quickly in the List Box by using the keyboard to type one character to get the part of the list where the entries begin with that character."
"The main function of the Calendar menu is to make changes or set-ups to the existing calendar."	"The main function of the Calendar menu is to help you with any changes or set-ups you want to make to the existing calendar."
	or
	"You can use the Calendar menu to change the set-ups for the existing calendar."

out. Rather than writing a first draft and then editing out *to be* verbs, the writer in e-prime simply omits them from the very start. The discipline comes easily after a little practice.

You will not see drastic changes in your writing when you write in e-prime, except that your sentences will contain an energy they lacked before. And the performance orientation of your prose will increase substantially. What e-prime forces you to do—omit *be* verbs—causes you to seek out actors for each of your sentences. And who does most of the action in computer use? The user, of course. You can clearly see this user emphasis in the examples in Table 10.2 under the heading e-prime prose. As a result, task orientation pervades all your actions, explanations, hints, and examples.

3   KEEP WRITING SIMPLE

Simplicity helps every aspect of software manual writing; You should strive for simplicity in each sentence. Often you will find sentences that suffer from the reading difficulty of the following one:

"Warning: Do not install other desk accessories in either the System file in the Server Folder on the startup volume, or in the System file in the System Folder on the AppleShare Server disk." (From a computer manual)

Table 10.2

Passage in Normal Prose, Same Passage in E-Prime

Normal Prose	E-Prime Prose
The draw program must be running for you to add color to your document.	Run the draw program before you try to add color to your document.
If you are using Windows 3.1 in enhanced mode, DataMaster will be run in a window. If you are using standard mode, DataMaster will be run as a DOS application in full screen.	If you use Windows 3.1 in enhanced mode, DataMaster runs in a window. If you use standard mode, DataMaster runs as a DOS application in full screen.

The preceding sentence makes perfectly good sense. But what price must the reader pay to get at that sense? For one thing, the writer has crammed it with look-alike words (*System file, Server Folder, startup volume*). Consider the burden these words put on the reader trying to get the point the first time. Without *first-reading clarity* the reader must waste twice the time rereading and pondering. Not good. Break sentences like the one above into more than one sentence. Separate out or find acceptable substitute phrasing so sound-alike words don't bombard the reader. Consider something like the following: "Warning: Do not install other desk accessories in the System file in the Server Folder on the startup volume. Do not install other desk accessories in the System file on the AppleShare Server Installer disk."

The next example shows how separating the subject from the verb creates a sentence which forces the user to put understanding on hold while the sentence presents related data.

Subject

"An example of a program that was the first to implement a Windows capability and has demonstrated a high rate of speed is Netscape." (From a help system)

Verb

In this case, you should revise the sentence to keep the subject and verb together. Something like "Netscape implemented a high-speed Windows interface long before any other program" might work.

4   BUILD PARALLEL STRUCTURES

Of all the solutions to the problem of using the user's short term memory effectively, none works as well as *parallelism*. Parallel items acknowledge the similarities between concepts and express that similarity in matching grammatical structures. Headings that *all* end in *-ing* follow the principle of parallelism. So do steps that *all* begin with a command verb and so do sequences of results described from the user's perspective. Parallelism helps readers remember even though they may not recognize the pattern.

Such subtle patterns should abound in your writing. In Table 10.3 you will find some examples of ways to use them in all aspects of manuals and help.

Table 10.3

Types of Parallelism in Software Documentation

Type of Parallelism	Example of Use
. . . ing	Task Names
	Opening a file
	Saving a file
	Closing a file
Noun First	Lists of options
	Options for setting the display
	Options for setting the transfer directory
	Options for specifying file types
Parallel Sentences	Giving overviews of commands, or suggesting alternatives:
	To get a closer _view_ of the drawing object, use the Zoom+ command; _to get a_ farther _view_ of the drawing object, use the Zoom–command.
Imperative Voice	Steps
	Select File from the Draw menu.
	Type in the filename.
	Click on the OK button.

5   USE OPERATIONAL OVERVIEWS

The way you present conceptual information makes a huge difference in documentation because of the highly abstract nature of software work. Often users react negatively to manuals and help because they do not have the necessary theoretical and technical background to understand the vocabulary and ideas. Primarily, users want to use a program and thus care mostly about how it operates and how it can make them efficient. Your manual is like a bathroom key: People want to get their hands on it not because of its intrinsic properties but because it lets them do what they need to do. That motivation to do can lead users into reading carefully for meaning or it may lead users into scanning the text before reading, depending on how important the program is to them.

Because users often read for meaning, you should provide prose passages (paragraphs) containing clear overviews of concepts as well as straight procedures (steps); users appreciate learning the conceptual model of the program and how the program does its processing. Of course, your well-crafted examples and accurate metaphors should point out the benefit of the model to the user. Notice how the following passage points out the benefit to the user of storing the location of project files.

> Aside from the fundamental organizational benefits of keeping things structured beneath the Project Directory, RoboHELP provides some additional affordances for this organization. As you might guess, RoboHELP needs to keep track of the files which make up your Help Project. RoboHELP stores the location of these files (in HAPPY.HPJ and HAPPY.RBH) as 'relative' paths based on the Project Directory. The main benefit of this technique is that it allows you to move the entire Help Project to another drive, computer or directory (or all three), without confusing RoboHELP or the Microsoft Help Compiler. For instance, if you've maintained this organizational hierarchy beneath the Project Directory and you're suddenly called to move your project onto a laptop computer in order that you might complete the project while sipping piña colada under the Caribbean sun, you are free to do so. Once the files are transferred to the laptop, you can immediately open the Project Document in your word processor and at once be productive." (From an online help topic: RoboHELP's Model of a Help Project)

You can choose how to emphasize your explanations of abstract concepts, but writers primarily use three: the theoretical (emphasizing the theories behind the working of a program), the technical (emphasizing the technical functioning of the program), and the operational (emphasizing the application of the program.) Overall, for end users interested in productivity, the operational emphasis works best. Consider the examples of these three kinds of overviews in Table 10.4.

Table 10.4

Ways to Present Conceptual Information

Emphasis	Example	Use
Operational	"Word allows you to write documents easily, and also lets you communicate numbers using graphs and ideas in pictures and drawings."	Novice and experienced end users in business and other professional fields
Theoretical	"Word attempts to combine word processing with other communication domains, such as presentation of numerical data and visual symbols."	Experienced and expert users; linguists; computer professionals
Technical	"Word is a DOS-based text editor and page design program using a point and click interface with embedded draw and graphics functions."	Expert users in the computer industry with a high degree of technical background

In the previous chapter we looked at ways the physical layout of pages can help the manual overcome the design problem. In this chapter we examine the part language plays. We look at how word choice can affect how a user applies the program to information work. First, we have to concern ourselves with how language creates meaning and how the skillful writer can craft sentences that convey useful ideas. Most important, the practical advice you will find in this part of the chapter bears directly on the writing of software manuals. As in previous chapters, the primary focus of using language effectively will fall on building task orientation into the document.

In software documentation, you will often use different writing styles and different tones to support different user tasks. Tutorial documentation, for example, involves a much closer relationship between the writer and the user and thus uses more words and contains more familiar diction, even humor. Reference documentation, on the other hand, involves a very distant relationship between the writer and the user, requiring a more formal, businesslike tone. Other levels of user support require stylistic adjustments that are treated in Chapter 8. Here you will find general advice that you can apply to most writing in software documents.

How Do We Process Language?

To set goals of language use to support task orientation, first look at how readers process language. For most people, the words in the document take a second place in their experience. They might have a problem using a computer, head for the manual, look up the task in the manual, return to work, and try it out. This simple scenario, however, gets more complex the more you examine it. The "looking up" part requires that the user scan the index, scan the chapter, pick a task description that sounds good, read one or two sentences of the introduction, scan the steps quickly to get the gist of the procedure, and return to work. This act of reading requires that the concept in the user's mind bond with words on the page and that the words register as significant. Significance is meaning. And you don't have it unless the word connects with the user. So in this way, we say that the words don't convey meaning to the reader, but the reader brings meaning to the words.

We should also factor in other variables, such as the fact that the motivation to consult the manual in the first place comes from subtle elements of the task context. The person using the computer might want to effect change in his or her organization. He or she might want to improve job performance, fulfill personal goals, increase job visibility, generate or express power. Moreover, the person has specific searching behavior (which some information scientists study) or problem-solving strategies (which cognitive scientists study). These elements of the job context give complexity to the created meaning of the words. The language of the document should help appropriate the energy the person puts into the task. It should fit into the dynamic psychological pattern of effort and reward, exertion and satisfaction.

The examples above are simple models of the act of processing language. While these models lack the complexity of some of those constructed by linguists to interpret how users make meaning, you probably get the point. Meaning, according to these researchers, depends on the context of the whole reading event, not just the context of the sentence. Instead of our words containing meaning, they say, we should think of words as getting meaning from our readers. Not only does meaning come from the user and the user's job context, the amount of meaning a text has—something finally impossible to measure—depends on the demands of the user's current task. The more clearly writers can anticipate that task—in layout as we saw earlier, or in language, as we see in this chapter—the more task-oriented the manual.

Performance-Oriented Language

Clearly the user's guide or manual could benefit from clear explanations of how to perform using the software system. In software documentation I call this making the language *performance oriented*. The bet that the reader will slog through extended passages for simple information has not paid off for many documenters. Using the active voice, using the *you* pronoun, and using the imperative verb add to the performance orientation of the style. In a larger sense, too, the skillful documenter will write as if writing to a real human being. So often computer-related language sounds cold and alien to the novice user and probably bores the experienced user too. Written as if to an imaginary person, software language does not have to be stuffy, formal, or robot-like.

For example, consider this passage from the TC8215 SECTR Management System for Windows *User's Guide*. While most of the manual contains very technical information, this section, called a "Guided Tour of Sectra," uses relaxed diction to emphasize performance.

> An address search can find a lot of objects, but you can stay active while the search is underway. For example, you can create objects by clicking on them and then clicking the **Create Object(s)** button. Another good move would then be to click on the **Hide Dialog** button so you don't have the Address Search dialog box in your face while you do other things. (TC8215 SECTR Management System for Windows *User's Guide*, p. 2–5)

Notice the diction: *a lot of, another good move,* and *in your face.* We would speak to real people using words like this, so why shouldn't we use "real" words like this in a manual? Of course, this kind of writing would flop in a reference section, where users don't expect to dally on ideas. But it does work in a tutorial section, where readers temporarily give control to the guiding voice of the manual writer.

How Do We Remember and Learn?

So, good writing in manuals and online help leverages the users' need to do work. But what happens, exactly, when users finally come across an idea they can employ: a procedure, a command, a technique? They have to remember the idea until they get back to work.

When you read technical information—documents, guides, manuals—you have to rely on both short-term and long-term memory. Your ability to understand depends on words triggering memories you have of stored information. Some writing requires you to search extensively through your memory databases to find something to connect with the words on the page. Some writing seems to trigger these memories much more easily, so you don't have to put out so much effort in understanding. As a rule of thumb, the writing that requires a lot of effort in connecting words to meaning will not work as well as writing that makes the connecting seem effortless.

Structured Language

The requirement of putting as few demands on the user's memory as possible means that the software documenter needs a thorough knowledge of how to structure information clearly in sentences. For one thing, the degree of structure in sentences will not necessarily show up as fewer words. More likely, it will show up as patterned, highly parallel sentences, balanced sentences, and sentences that end in three rhythmic clauses like this one. Well-structured language also requires that sentences stay simple (using easy-to-understand language) and short (so as not to overburden the user's short-term memory). Below, we will explore many ways to build structures into the language of software manuals, with the intention of controlling the amount of structure in the style and thus adapting to the job needs of the user.

Style Problems in Software Documentation

Problems with style in software documentation relate directly to your overall goal of making software easy to use. Like it or not, users have to read, actually read, a passage once all the access features of the document or help system have gotten them to the correct nugget of information. And that information, as you know, can take many forms: not just steps, but explanations, encouragements, overviews, interpretations, and other forms of sophisticated and well-designed language.

The next section details some of the problems that befall instruction writing in software documentation. It may help you to study the overview of some of the ways style hinders the use of software for productive work.

Table 10.5 gives you some idea of just how the very words you use and the way you arrange them in a document can affect the key goals of your manual. The following discussions of these and other maladies in language and style can help you target areas where your style can benefit by careful adjustment to achieve maximum ease of use.

Acronyms and Abbreviations

Most computer users have learned the more familiar acronyms used in programs: **DOS** for *disk operating system,* **RAM** for *random access memory.* They have learned these even though they may not know their meaning completely. Anyone beyond a novice knows these terms, but that does not guarantee that their use leads to task orientation. Users often can understand common acronyms like these, but the difficulty comes when some of the terms constructed as part of the computer program or system appear in the document. This results in writing that emphasizes the system and its construction, rather than the user and the user's work.

Usually these uncommon acronyms consist of contractive acronyms, like *txt* for text, and *dcmnt* for document. The difficulty increases when these contractive acronyms refer

Table 10.5

Problems with Style

Ways Style Goes Wrong	Explanation
High Level of Abstraction Users confronted with terms that don't connect directly and immediately to daily work situations.	Acronyms: shortened versions of words: *DOS, MAC, UNIX*
	Synonyms: words that mean the same thing: *hit, press, push*
	System orientation: an emphasis on using commands rather than doing work: *"Using the File command."*
	No analogies/poor transfer leaning: poorly developed mental model of the system: *"The program runs efficiently in batch mode."*
No Performance Support Users confronted with the need to do work, but a language that emphasizes passivity and acceptance.	Passive voice: cluttered language based on helping verbs and nouns, *"The file was displayed by the program."*
	Definitional emphasis: language that tries to define rather than instruct, *"F1 is a function key used to open the context-sensitive help module."*
	Ambiguous task/step names: terms that name commands rather than giving steps, *"Printer."*
	Formal tone: language that ignores the way other users talk in the workplace and that discourages help from the user community, *"Entering data into the data-entry window of BossPro is quite intuitive."*
Overly Complex Syntax Users confronted with complex sentences that diverge greatly from the simple meaning.	Faulty parallelism: nouns, . . . ings, and verb phrases not in grammatical alignment: *"Saving a File, Open a file, . . ."*
	Lack of fluency: paragraphs don't develop the intended subject in the heading (*under the heading*) **Overview of the Program** *"Printing is very easy to do with BossPro."*
	Noun addiction: using nouns in front of words to define them, causing intense cognitive overload in the user: *"The advanced processor playback allocation file stabilizing fault-anticipator bit should be set to 'on.' "*
	Contorted syntax: overly complex sentences that block first-reading clarity, *"The Enter key, which causes the data-entry screen to disappear entirely without saving changes, should be hit."*
	Confusing sequences: instructions that don't clarify steps properly, *"Before you open the file you should first have set up the file directory."*
	Sentences/paragraphs too long: unnecessary length where shorter, well-focused paragraphs would work better, *a "brief overview" that takes more than one or two short paragraphs.*

to parts of programs and don't make intuitive sense, as with *INSCOMP* or *PROC.* Throw in some numbers and the problem gets out of control—as in the following example:

> The AFC17 is a flexible, high performance, multi-channel analog-to-digital (A/D) converter. Under program control the AFC17 performs a 13-bit A/D conversion at a rate of 200 channels per second.

Consider the kinds of *acronyms* and *abbreviations* illustrated in Table 10.6. You can't avoid them, but try to use only a few of these in a sentence at a time.

You can easily see that these acronyms need to appear in documents because software systems contain hundreds of them. They function very well for programmers because they allow for easy naming of program parts (called *routines*) that get generated during program development. Acronyms save time. But the trade-off for the saved space in text costs the reader in lost usability. Every acronym that you use should be shadowed by its meaning, either in parentheses or in the context of the sentence.

Synonyms

Some of the most common tasks in software use go by some of the most diverse names. What terms can we use to convey the idea of doing something as simple as pressing a key? A partial list would include the following: *hit, depress, punch, push, touch,* and *strike*. I like *mash*, myself, as in "*Mash* on the Enter key." Some of these terms seem to come from slang usage, such as those for starting programs: *open, boot, start, run, call up, load, bootstrap*. Some of these terms have special meanings that distinguish them from one another, but in the common vocabulary of the computer user, some of whom have no computer vocabulary at all, they all mean about the same thing. Some terms for computer tasks even

Table 10.6

Acronyms and Abbreviations Abound in Manuals and Help

Type of Acronym or Abbreviation	Example
Abbreviation	Win, demo, doc, exec
Acronym	I/O, TEDIUM,, BASIC
Three Letter Acronyms (TLA's)	IBM, VAX, DOS, RAM
Contractive Acronym	dcmnt = document
	dbms = database management system
	txt = text
	hlp = help
Command Contractions	autonum = automatic numbering
	fldsrch = field search

evoke disgusting metaphors, as in *purge* or *depress* or *dump.* Others sound violent: *kill, terminate, abort.* Some terms evoke paradoxes. My favorites include "Press Enter to Exit" and "Press Return to Continue Quitting."

Along with these synonyms, you also find terms that change meaning from program to program. For example, take the concept of saving a document to a disk file. Some call the process *saving* and see the document as saved. Others call the process *transferring* and see the document as transferred (to the disk). One program puts numbers in *boxes,* others put numbers in *cells,* or *fields.* What should the documenter do when faced with a program that uses a variation of one of these terms (some of which you see illustrated in Table 10.7) and the user knows other programs that use different terms?

Usually these terms have developed as ways to describe overall tasks, but you should always use them consistently, and as accurately as possible. You should anticipate those terms that your readers most likely will recognize and build in crossover techniques, such as using synonyms in parentheses, in the index, in tables, or just in text. Some have suggested that the prudent writer will index terms and even commands from competitive products.

Paragraphs and Sentences Too Long

Another typical problem we find in software manuals stems from overly long paragraphs and sentences. Some writers see their mission in life as initiating the user into all the intricacies of computers in one manual. The length of their paragraphs and sentences attests to this. Ideally, paragraphs should focus on explanations, not performance, and not on steps telling the reader what to do. Paragraphs work best when they support a simple concept, such as definitions for terms, or distinguish between functions or elements of the program. They help explain what happens after a step, and, because the user will not usually tackle paragraphs unless he or she must, they should read as quickly and easily as possible. It would probably be good for the documenter to forget about paragraphs altogether and just think in terms of lists and chunks of no more than three sentences.

Table 10.7

Confusing Synonyms

User Question	Synonyms
"I want to start my program."	Open, boot, start, run, call up, load
"I want my program to work."	Install, setup, configure
"I want to stop my program."	Quit, exit, terminate, kill, abort
"I want to use a key."	Hit, press, depress, mash, punch, push, strike
"What kind of program do I have?"	Software, shareware, netware, freeware, dareware, beggarware, bread-on-the-waters ware

Emphasizing the Computer Instead of the Program

When you think about computerized work, you realize that it involves basically three components: the user, the program, and the computer. The computer makes the work happen by taking the input from the user and processing it into output. But from the standpoint of the software manual, everything that happens results from what the program does, not what the computer does. We interact with the program, not the computer.

In conversation we often speak as if the computer does the interacting. Clerks enter data "into the computer," or "computers make the cartoon images on TV," or "computer simulations show how molecules attach." In reality, all these computer effects result from specific programs, but the computer gets all the credit.

The software documenter should try very carefully not to fall into the trap of ascribing the actions of the program to those of the computer. For sure, the computer does a lot of things: It starts up, it shuts down. But for the most part, it follows the instructions from the program. Besides, often the documenter wants to promote the program name as part of helping the reader identify these functions with this program. Besides clarifying who does what, keeping this focus helps the user with learning, which translates into more doing. The following sentences emphasize the program, not the computer:

"The **Edit I** will store your document in the folder you specify."

"When you press Return, **HyperCard** looks for text that starts with the letters you typed into the Message box, starting with the card you're looking at."

No Connection between the Heading and the Topic

Often you will read a passage from a manual or readme file that contains headings followed by sometimes interminably long paragraphs explaining a program. They tell how it works, what computers it runs on, and other stuff. The problem with these passages is that often the paragraph doesn't contain the information announced in the heading. Instead, the writer has included one or two relevant details about the program, which get presented in highly technical language. Details like this require topic sentences, elaborations, examples, and other information elements to help the reader put the particular piece of data into some meaningful—work-related—context. An example:

How BeyondHelp Operates

Special care has been taken to adjust the BeyondHelp graphics filtering file format so that it processes files in half the time it did in previous versions. This change allows BeyondHelp to handle much larger files.

If you get right down to specific details, you miss the point of the heading. The reader of this example probably expected an explanation organized from general to specific that explained the basic principle of the program. The paragraph should have followed the heading with specific explanations of how the program operates, as in these two examples: "AccountMaster uses Excel spreadsheets to maintain bookkeeping information for small businesses" or "PagePro translates page formats among a large number of word processing and desktop publishing programs."

Too Formal Tone

Software documentation that you write for real people using the program in their work should sound conversational, not too formal. This example shows that the writer needed to relax: "A blank disk has been provided for you. It would be to your benefit to make a back-up copy so that you may always have an extra copy of the program if one should fail." Part of the formality here ("It would be to your benefit to . . .") comes from the writer not realizing that sentences must communicate with another real person. So often, the writer only thinks about getting the idea out.

But the idea really only counts if it makes contact with the motivation of the user, which usually means getting some job done. A well-intentioned writer might offer this hint: "Now that you know how to add an occasion to the file, may I suggest that you add some occasions of your own, such as your birthday." In a less formal tone, that sentence might read as follows: "Now that you know how to add an occasion to the file, try adding some occasions of your own, like your birthday." Speaking in an informal tone—without being overly familiar or presumptuous—makes contact more quickly and evokes the user's desire to do well on the job. You can identify an informal tone by incorporating the following characteristics into your style:

- **Use of contractions.** "Once you've set the parameters, you can use Alt+M to return to the main menu."

- **Reference to other users.** "Most people use the Home stack as their base of operations."

- **Humorous aside.** "Note: Only the left mouse button has function. (Even on the rare fifteen-button mouse found only in the Australian outback.)"

When to Use Humor

The topic of humor relates to that of tone in software documentation. In manual writing, humor sparks as much controversy as it does good feeling. Glaringly inappropriate when it fails, bad humor can cause the user to reject a manual. Common sense tells us that humor will not work in all kinds of documentation, especially in support sections (reference, appendices, etc.) where the user simply looks up information and expects it to come sliding across the countertop without a lot of extra posturing on the manual's or writer's part. The psychology of the reference situation complicates the problem of humor because often the urge to insert a wry comment occurs when you describe errors or the results of errors. If the joke does not work, then the user will in no way appreciate the fun at his or her expense.

It makes sense to write reference documentation in a cooler tone. The relationship between the writer and the user takes on a more distant feel, not one conducive to back patting or rib tickling. Also, experienced users, for whom reference sections function best, tend to value accuracy over an open, more intimate style. Finally, not every writer has the talent to see the little quirks of computer interactions that give rise to humorous remarks. Even writers who do have that talent should consider what their manual will sound like in later editions when updated by a new writer who may not have a talent for humor.

When humor works, it works because it breaks some rule of formality. An early Word-Star manual showed a picture of a little granny being escorted away by two huge, uniformed police officers; the picture had the caption: "What happens if you press the wrong key." Humor takes a risk that many writers do not want to take, fearing that the joke will fall flat. Another difficulty lies in the exclusiveness of humor. Humor almost always leaves *someone* out of the joke—a powerful argument for a businesslike tone at all times.

So when should you use humor? Never in reference documentation, seldom in procedures, from time to time in tutorials and background information when a lighter, more familiar tone seems desirable. Never overdo it, and always edit carefully so you don't offend anyone. Always test drive passages that have jokes or puns in them, to gauge users' reactions.

Ambiguous Task Names

Part of the problem of weak language in documentation comes from some writers' tendency to refer to tasks vaguely. In task-oriented documentation you should name tasks clearly, with a sense of planning for the user's new vocabulary. A task name like *Remove Applications* does not convey the idea clearly. Remove applications from what? Or does it mean applications that remove? *Removing Applications* or *How to Remove Applications* does a better job. You should try to make task names into headings or short sentences that predicate the user's action. Table 10.8 gives examples of headings.

The name of the task, in performance-oriented phrasing, should appear frequently in the text of the manual. Task names help steady the user on the right task, and they help focus on usability by allowing you to keep track of just what needs explanation. Because task names occur in headings, you may hesitate to repeat the task names in the text, fearing redundancy. Not repeating task names, however, leads to an overuse of the relative pronoun *this,* as in:

> Click the Speedo Icon to start the program. This will cause the icon to flicker and the program will display the main screen.

or as in

> Whetstone: This classic benchmark is primarily a test of floating point math with a heavy emphasis on transcendental functions.

Table 10.8

Examples of Headings

System Oriented	Performance Oriented
The Mouse	Using the Mouse
Curve Quality	Adjusting Curve Quality
Pragmass	How to Use Pragmass
Open Documents	To Open Documents

The problem here relates to vague pronoun reference, but it also signifies a lost opportunity for the writer to reinforce the task orientation of the manual. Revised, the second example above would read "Whetstone: Using the Whetstone test (see page xx) allows you to examine. . . ." The result makes better sense as good syntax and reinforces the idea that the whetstone test can help the user.

Step Not a Step

Very often the beginning documenter will not clearly understand the nature of a step in software documentation. As we saw in Chapter 2, the step constitutes the basic element of human–computer interaction. As such, you should articulate the action element of a step very carefully. Where does the following step fail? "Step 2: You will be prompted with a dialog box that will ask you the name of the file." This step fails because it does not express an action. Actions come in the form of a command, so the step should read: "Step 2: Type in the name of the file when the dialog box appears." To avoid this problem you should always examine your steps to make sure they contain a clearly stated action, often using an imperative form of the verb.

Omitted Articles

It's very common in documentation to fall into the telegram style of writing. Telegram style refers to the time when people paid per word to send messages, and so they left out articles like *the* and *an* to save a buck. Telegram style writing sounds like this:

> "Use **doclst** only when existing doctor or referring doctor treats patient at other hospital or not at office site."

In fact, we don't have to pay per word anymore for our messages, and such attempts to sound official fall flat. Why not communicate with real people, using something like this:

> "Use *the* **doclst** function only when *an* existing doctor or referring doctor treats *the* patient at *an*other hospital or not at *the* office site."

ⒼLossary

abbreviation: a shortened form of a word, used to save space and avoid repeating long names.

acronym: a shortened form of a word or group of words that uses the first initial of each word in the phrase.

e-prime: a method of writing that, for the sake of creating energy in sentences, omits any form of the *to be* verb: *is, are, am, were, was, been, being.*

first-reading clarity: a kind of clarity in writing that allows the user to understand on the first reading.

parallelism: the technique in writing characterized by repeated structures of grammar, syntax, or other sentence elements for the sake of emphasis and easy learning by repetition.

performance orientation: a way of using language based on the premise that the user will more readily understand if explanations are put in terms of performing useful workplace actions.

Checklist ✓

Use the following checklist as a way to analyze your writing style for usable task orientation.

Style Checklist

☐ Do your sentences emphasize actions the user can take rather than functions of the program?

☐ Do your sentences use the active voice predominantly?

☐ Have you reviewed your sentences to make sure they have first-reading clarity?

☐ Have you avoided overly long and complicated sentences?

☐ Do your sentences contain easy-to-use parallel structures?

☐ Have you included clarifying operational overviews in your documents?

☐ Do your sentences reflect a performance orientation?

Analyze your style to make sure you avoid the following problems:

☐ Overused and unexplained acronyms and abbreviations

☐ Confusing synonyms

☐ Overlong paragraphs and sentences

☐ Emphasis on the computer rather than the program

☐ Lack of connection between headings and topics

☐ Too formal tone

☐ Inappropriate humor

☐ Ambiguous task names

☐ Confusing statements of steps

☐ Omitted articles

Practice/Problem Solving

1. Analyze Writing Style

Analyze the style in two comparable manuals or help systems according to the principles expressed in this chapter. Given the differences you find between them, which do you think contributes more to the task orientation of the document?

2. Learn from Others' Mistakes

Find an example of weak language and style in a procedural manual (a user's guide or other document designed to lead the user through steps). You may want to review examples of in-house manuals written by persons not adequately trained in performance-based writing. Determine whether the language reflects a system or performance orientation. Use specific sentences and phrases from the manual that, to you, indicate opportunities for stronger guidance. Practice by rewriting the passage so that you think it reflects a performance orientation.

3. What's Wrong Here?

The 752 controller may satisfy a read request via data in the read ahead buffer. If a read IOPB is satisfied by data already in the FIFO rather than a traditional disk access, the IOPB will be updated with the RAIBPB bit set (bit 0) in the 752 internal status byte (byte3). This bit has been added as a performance analysis tool to accurately measure the hit-rate of the read-ahead offered by the 752.

How would you revise this passage to make it more understandable?

4. Revise for an Emphasis on Actions

Revise the following sentences to shift them from a focus on functions to a focus on actions.

1. The speed bar simplifies a number of functions.
2. The following section will explain the use of the List menu.
3. In order for these instructions to be used effectively, the user must have a working knowledge of WordPerfect.
4. The Reporting sub program provides a number of features, including print setup, multiple report printing, fax printing, and a selection of full color or greyscale.

5. Revise for the Active Voice

Revise the following sentences putting them in the active voice.

1. The following examples are to be used as a reference guide.
2. Check to see if the data are entered correctly.
3. The prompt will be shown as a dollar sign.
4. Events do not need to be all entered at once and can be modified accordingly.

6. Revise for Correct Parallelism

Revise the following sets of lists and put them in grammatically parallel format.

- IBM-compatible PC with a 486DX2 CPU running at 100 MHz or better
- Available 16-bit ISA AT-bus slot
- Windows-compatible color VGA or Super VGA
- The program requires 16 megabytes (MB) system memory

Message	Description
mailbox open	You have new faxes in your New Faxes log.
mailbox flag up	Your New Messages log has a new voice message.
mailbox flag up	
door open	Look in the logs for both new voice messages and new faxes.
mailbox flag down	
door closed	No new messages or faxes.

1. Press Esc.

2. When the program asks, "Are you finished," press Y to answer.

3. Saving changes is then done by pressing Enter.

4. You do not want to start a new database, so press Enter when the program asks you to.

7. Revise to Simplify

Revise the following sentence to make the grammar and style as simple as the idea they express.

1. Before you start using ModemMaster you should have set up your computer by plugging it into a power source, attaching the keyboard and mouse, and connecting any peripheral devices, such as printers, which are described in Section 4: Printer Setup.

2. For each event you are asked to enter planned, revised, and actual event start dates and event end dates.

3. If at any point during the entry of the maximization function and the constraints the data are entered incorrectly the following may be done at any point during the program to edit the data.

8. Write Operational Overviews

Rewrite the following paragraphs shifting the focus from the technical to the operational.

1. Sending mail is controlled with QuickMail's message windows, toolbars, and icons. Message composition occurs offline, reducing the amount of connect time. Composing offline represents a significantly cost-effective approach for users.

2. In the first place, there is only one official version of FlagMaster and changes to the basic program are discouraged. A "file change" mechanism allows the program to be compiled differently as dictated by the hardware and system software constraints that exist at any particular computer installation, but these changes should not modify FlagMaster's formatting capabilities.

9. Relax the Diction

Rewrite the following passages in a more conversational style that encourages performance among users.

1. Before you can begin using the Party Planner program, you should have set up and configured your computer. Setting up involves plugging it into a power source, attaching the keyboard and mouse, and connecting any peripheral devices, such as printer or fax machines. Instructions for setting up the computer are in the owner's guide.

2. If the user is printing a large database, the command prompt "Press any key to abort print" appears. Pressing a key will eventually result in the "printing process abort confirmation" prompt.

3. As the user progresses in the comprehension of the software application program, facility in executing and customizing the utility of the Analyze features will increase substantially.

10. Make the Diction Less Abstract

Examine the following sentences that demonstrate the difficulty of understanding abstract terms. Rewrite them to make them more concrete.

1. As soon as the chart data form appears on your screen, press F9/Options and select Option #6, Bullet Options. Use the SPACE bar to cycle through the cycle through the selections until the word "None" appears (or use the F3/Choices function key to display a complete listing of bullet types.)

2. All the programs included here use 286-specific instructions and therefore will not run on 8088/8086 even if a fast enough one could be found. The routines RVOI_INIT and PVOIKIT.DOC and VPMED.DOC) test for CPU type before doing anything else, and return an error code of 2 if an 8088 or 8086 is detected.

3. If you hit auto-configure on boot you may set up the wrong file table, so you should press Esc to terminate the load.

11. Eliminate the Clutter

The following sentences don't support workplace tasks because of their wordiness. Revise them using fewer words and making clearer sentences.

1. You are prompted to enter a chapter name when you use the Create Chapter function to create a new chapter. You may also change the current chapter name at any time while running the program by selecting the Rename Chapter function under the Chapters menu.

2. The following page shows a photocopy of the model that is produced by this set of instructions. This copy may be used as a reference to ensure that the program has been correctly completed.

3. Installing the Race Sheet program on a hard drive requires that the software program is on a non-copy protected program distribution disk. The user of the program must insert the program distribution disk into the floppy disk drive of the computer.

12. Reduce the Number of Acronyms and Abbreviations

Rewrite the following passages to reduce the use of acronyms and abbreviations.

1. There are several reasons to name BNN files, not only to use them with the RETRF and RENAM functions, but to avoid confusing with DOS or UNIX filenames.

2. To round out our discussion of \def, we will note that there exists a \let primitive that is somewhat analogous to \def but differs from \def in timing. The difference can be explained by noting that \let\b=\a sets \b to \a at the time when \let\b=\a is read by MegaForm.
    (Hint: \b and \a are "values" and \let\b=\a is an "expression.")

3. Use .ip, .ep, .sp, and .lp to set VARS for paragraph and chunk sizing in SETUP or REDO modes when running in DOS.

13. Create Real Steps

Rewrite the following sequence of steps, eliminating the nonsteps, and organizing the information in an action/result pattern.

---

1. Enter the maximization function at the colon prompt:

    `:MAX  3x+2y`

2. Press ↵

3. Note: At this point, a ? prompt will appear.

4. Type the following at the ? prompt: Note: This command stands for "subject to" which signals the computer that the next set of data entered will be the constraints.

    `?S.T.`

5. The program will display the ? prompt.

6. Press ↵, the program will display the ? prompt.

7. Type `?END` at the ? prompt. The program will respond by asking you to enter a disk in drive A:

---

14. Add Articles

Revise the following sentences to include articles and make them sound more human.

1. If insurance company found in list, then type in number of carrier. Press Return.

2. Turn on computer and monitor.

3. If doctor is not in history file or has changed diagnosis data but not updated patient record, then do 1-main menu, 1-update patient record to update patient record.

4. Find data and resource files in cabinet next to computer.

15. Add Humor

Imagine you're working with a scientific calculation program that displays some irregularities in its overall operation. This program, DigiDoc, displays the odd feature of requiring the user to input the same information (a date parameter) twice in the same sequence of steps, once at the beginning of the sequence and again at the end. If the user doesn't enter the date in the exact same format as the original date, the program assumes the user has given a "nul" date variable and stops the operation, returning the user to the system prompt. Other than that, the program runs pretty straightforwardly.

Your task: write a paragraph or so about this behavior, informing and warning the user. The description will go in the introduction to a chapter called *Inputting Calculation Variables*. Use the technical description above as the starting place, but put the experience in terms of the user's point of view.

16. Shift the Focus from the Computer to the Program

In the following examples, revise the sentences to emphasize the program and its functions rather than the computer.

1. When you ask for an inquiry, the computer searches the hard disk for the file containing the account records for that vendor.

2. The computerized version of the document will appear on the screen, and you may edit it using the draw functions.

3. To choose a control code, click in the box next to the number one (the first column) and type in a code. The screen shows the code you entered.

4. When you press Tab the computer automatically records the default data for that field and moves to the next field.

11

Using Graphics Effectively

This chapter covers the use of visuals in manuals and online help. Examples of graphics in manuals reinforce the key role images play in helping the user access information. The chapter offers guidelines for selecting and designing types of graphics that are essential to software documentation. It discusses the functions of graphics and presents an overview of the types of graphics and graphic elements.

How to Read This Chapter

You should read this chapter in conjunction with the previous chapter. This chapter on visual elements complements Chapter 10, "Getting the Language Right," just as text and images complement one another on the page and screen. Both the project-oriented reader and the reader for study and understanding should study the examples and eventually read the entire chapter.

■ Those planning a project or involved in a project will want to consult the section on "Types of Graphics in Software Manuals and Help" (p. 378) for a quick overview of the main options available in these media. In creating graphics, the section on "Elements of Graphics" (p. 388) and the Checklist at the end of the chapter can aid in double-checking work.

■ For the reader wishing to master the basics of graphic design in manuals and online help, the Discussion section provides a clear overview; you should probably read it, then the Guidelines.

The two figures provided in this Examples section show you two ways you can support task orientation by using graphics. Figure 11.1 illustrates how graphics can present printing options to the user in a way that makes selecting the correct printing paper easy and efficient. This example uses graphics to support user decision making. As you'll see from this chapter, printing options present just one of many opportunities to use graphics. You can also use

352

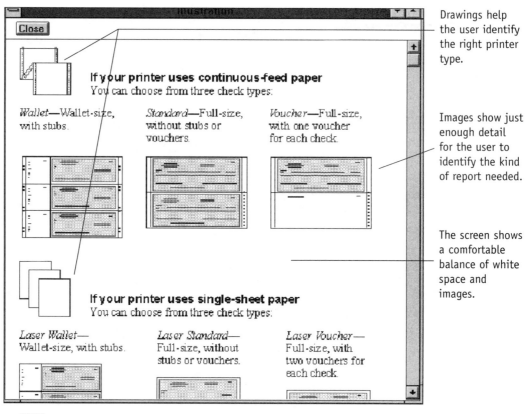

Drawings help the user identify the right printer type.

Images show just enough detail for the user to identify the kind of report needed.

The screen shows a comfortable balance of white space and images.

igure 11.1

Graphics That Support Decision Making

These graphics from the Microsoft Money Help system assist the user in making decisions about how to apply the program features to the workplace.

graphics to indicate the interface elements of a program's main screen, as shown in Figure 11.2. This reference-type documentation is a staple of manuals and online help, and one that you should prepare carefully, with close attention to the user's task needs.

Guidelines

Figure 11.3 lists guidelines for using graphics effectively.

1   ANSWER USERS' QUESTIONS

As with all elements of a well-constructed manual or online help, the graphics should support user questions: "How can I use the program easily?" and "How can I put the program to work?" To meet the first need, use graphics to help the user *locate* and *act:* to get

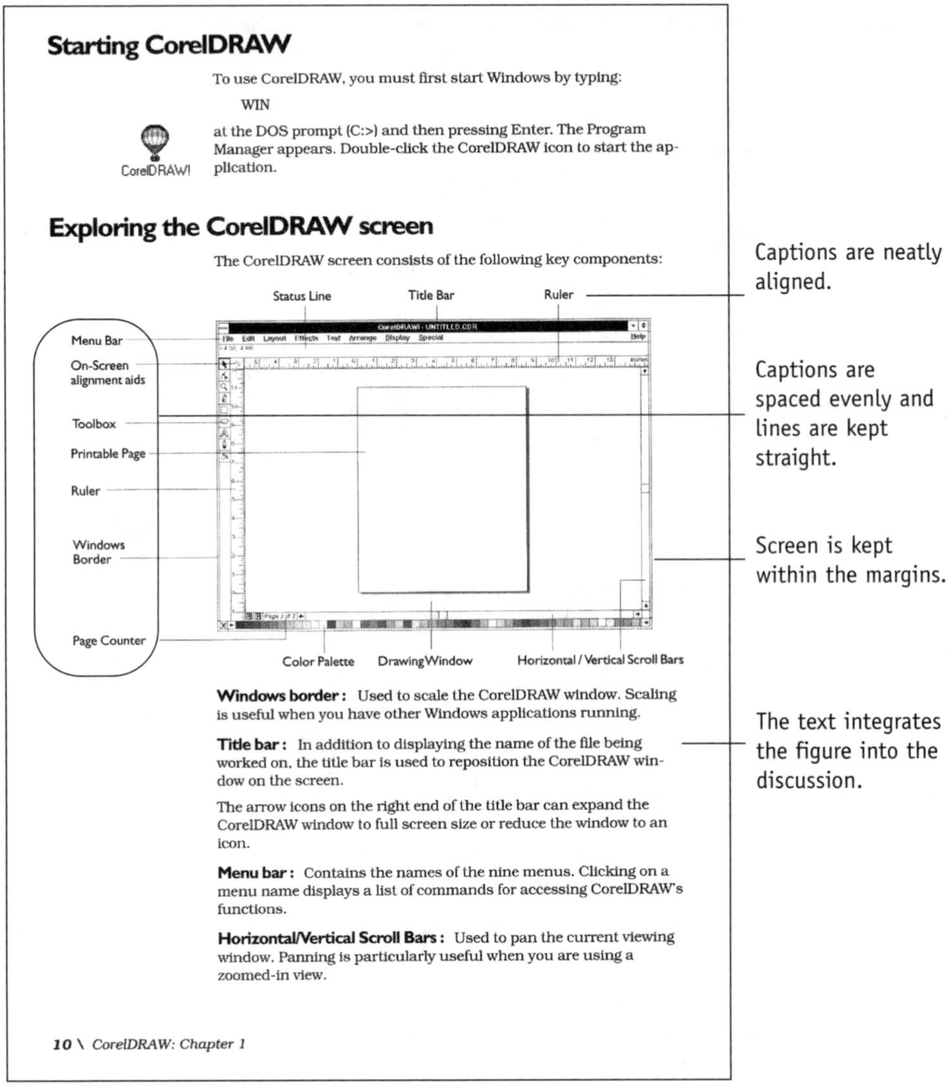

Starting CorelDRAW

To use CorelDRAW, you must first start Windows by typing:

WIN

at the DOS prompt (C:>) and then pressing Enter. The Program Manager appears. Double-click the CorelDRAW icon to start the application.

CorelDRAW!

Exploring the CorelDRAW screen

The CorelDRAW screen consists of the following key components:

Status Line
Title Bar
Ruler
Menu Bar
On-Screen alignment aids
Toolbox
Printable Page
Ruler
Windows Border
Page Counter
Color Palette
DrawingWindow
Horizontal / Vertical Scroll Bars
Captions are neatly aligned.
Captions are spaced evenly and lines are kept straight.
Screen is kept within the margins.
The text integrates the figure into the discussion.

Windows border: Used to scale the CorelDRAW window. Scaling is useful when you have other Windows applications running.

Title bar: In addition to displaying the name of the file being worked on, the title bar is used to reposition the CorelDRAW window on the screen.

The arrow icons on the right end of the title bar can expand the CorelDRAW window to full screen size or reduce the window to an icon.

Menu bar: Contains the names of the nine menus. Clicking on a menu name displays a list of commands for accessing CorelDRAW's functions.

Horizontal/Vertical Scroll Bars: Used to pan the current viewing window. Panning is particularly useful when you are using a zoomed-in view.

10 \ CorelDRAW: Chapter 1

Figure 11.2

A Fully Labeled Screen

This example from the CorelDRAW *User's Guide* shows how to do one of the basic graphic elements in your manual: the screen shot.

to and operate the actual features of the program. To meet the second need, use graphics to help the user *understand:* provide images that encourage education, guidance, and support for workplace tasks. Thus, instead of using graphics for decoration, you use graphics strategically to locate and direct user actions in using the program, and you also use them to explain concepts and illustrate examples.

1. Answer user's questions.

2. Make it visible.

3. Keep graphic styles consistent.

4. Don't overdo graphics.

5. Label consistently.

6. Use typographic techniques.

7. Size the image correctly.

Figure 11.3

Guidelines for Using Graphics Effectively

You can meet the user's needs by following an easy process of first identifying user questions and then choosing graphics that respond to those questions. Go back over your user analysis and sift through the observations it makes about specific difficulties your user has. Generally, use more cartoons and animation with novice to experienced users and technically-oriented charts and diagrams with experienced to expert users. Respond to the questions you think your user would have about a task by designing graphics to support those questions. Some typical user questions are discussed next.

Where Is It?

Use graphics to help the user locate buttons, rulers, sliders, check boxes, menu commands, and other *interface elements* on the screen. Table 11.1 indicates some of the things users need to find and suggests ways to signal locations.

What Is It?

Use graphics to help define concepts unfamiliar to the user. These needs often fall into the area of subject-matter knowledge or background information the user needs about a program or idea. User testing and interviews can help you identify those concepts that you need to define. Graphics that are used to reinforce concept understanding fall into two types: examples and metaphors.

Examples show documents, reports, printouts. Examples also, as in the example in Figure 11.4, show sample code, helping the user identify the various aspects of a routine. Mind you, inserting an example doesn't make it a graphic in the sense that it communicates visually. But examples benefit greatly when you box them and label them as in Figure 11.4. You should use examples liberally, especially in highly technical, *command-driven* programs. Such programs include compilers, scientific graphing and analysis software, and operating systems.

Metaphors show the basic nature of an idea by relating it to something the user already knows. Common metaphors that abound in software manuals and online help are shown in Table 11.2. Metaphors work because they allow the user to know something without having to learn it from scratch. Users can rely on their previous experience in the world to do some of the explaining for them. Metaphors act as workarounds for the

Table 11.1

Help Users Find Things

Elements User Needs to Locate	Ways to Signal Locations
Screens	Arrow
Buttons	
Menus	
Checkboxes	
Scroll bars	
Sliders	Circle
Toolbars	
Message/Status boxes	
Page/Section numbers	
	Highlighting

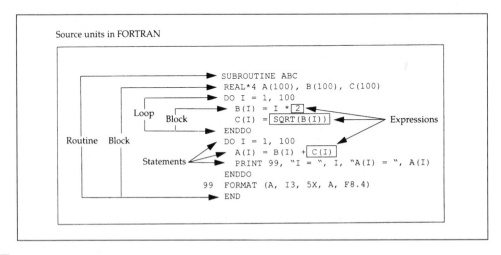

```
Source units in FORTRAN

                              SUBROUTINE ABC
                              REAL*4 A(100), B(100), C(100)
                              DO I = 1, 100
                                 B(I) = I * 2
                     Loop        C(I) = SQRT(B(I))          Expressions
                           Block
                              ENDDO
                              DO I = 1, 100
          Routine   Block       A(I) = B(I) + C(I)
                    Statements   PRINT 99, "I = ", I, "A(I) = ", A(I)
                              ENDDO
                         99   FORMAT (A, I3, 5X, A, F8.4)
                              END
```

Figure 11.4

Graphic Showing an Example

This labeled routine shows how you can incorporate graphics into examples to illustrate parts of things.

Table 11.2

Graphics Help Users See Metaphors

Concept	Metaphor
Typing	Courier font (typewriter):
	`Type the filename.`
Work area on a screen	Desktop:
Fill areas in draw programs	Paint bucket:
Email	Mailbox:

general abstractness of computer terminology. They compare two things: the abstract or hard-to-understand technical concept, and a concrete object or idea known to the user but in another domain. For example, novices can understand the abstract concept of the workspace of a computer by relating it to a concrete workspace they know well: the desktop. Metaphors abound in the kinds of interface elements in programs: radio buttons, sliders, pull-down menus. To help us understand the program's capabilities, designers have portrayed them using pictures of familiar objects. This familiarity increases the likelihood of successful interaction with the processing capabilities of a program. Figure 11.5 illustrates the power that graphics have to make the abstract concrete through metaphors.

You could argue that metaphors belong under the subject of language because we usually use words to convey them: "The program has three levels" or "Take the MS-DOS 5-minute workout." But such metaphors of language, where we compare two things (a program and a level, a lesson and a workout), gain strength when we support them with the actual images suggested by the words. Thus, the MS-DOS five-minute workout booklet contains an abundance of runners, rope skippers, and images of tennis shoes and gym equipment to help create and extend the metaphor.

How Do I Do It?

Users wanting to know how to perform a procedure will welcome graphics that demonstrate and support sequential actions. These kind of images use drawings to introduce the step-by-step procedural work done in most computer work. Graphics that answer the question "How do I do it?" give overviews of procedures as a way of introducing the user

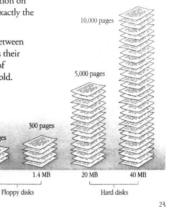

Prepare Disks for Use

Understanding hard and floppy disks

Both hard and floppy disks store information so you and your computer can have access to it.

Hard disks are sealed inside a disk drive (which in turn may be sealed inside your computer).

Floppy disks can be inserted into and ejected from a disk drive.

Both hard disks and floppy disks show up as icons on your desktop. You look at, work with, and add to the information on both kinds of disks in exactly the same way.

The major difference between hard and floppy disks is their *capacity*—the amount of information they can hold.

The basic unit for measuring information is the *byte.* A byte, like an ounce or a second, is a very small unit, and not convenient for describing how much information fits on a disk. Disk capacity is measured in two larger units:

- A *kilobyte* is 1024 bytes, and is represented by the abbreviation KB—or just K.

- A *megabyte* is 1024 kilobytes, and is represented by the abbreviation MB.

A convenient rule of thumb is that a full page of text takes up roughly four kilobytes (4K).

10,000 pages

5,000 pages

300 pages

200 pages

1 page

| 4K | 800K | 1.4 MB | 20 MB | 40 MB |

Floppy disks   Hard disks

23

Figure 11.5

Metaphor Helps Define an Abstract Concept

In this page from the Macintosh *User's Guide,* the metaphor compares the capacity of disk drives to stacks of paper. The *familiarity* of the concept of stacks of paper to measure storage capacity helps the user understand the *unfamiliarity* of the concept of bytes to measure storage capacity.

to the steps that follow. In their simplest form overviews of procedures can consist of words inside boxes connected by arrows.

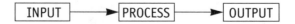

Get the picture? Because they use flowcharts in designing computer programs, many people working in the computer industry see these kinds of process charts frequently. Overviews, like the one in Figure 11.6, help the user build a mental model of the process

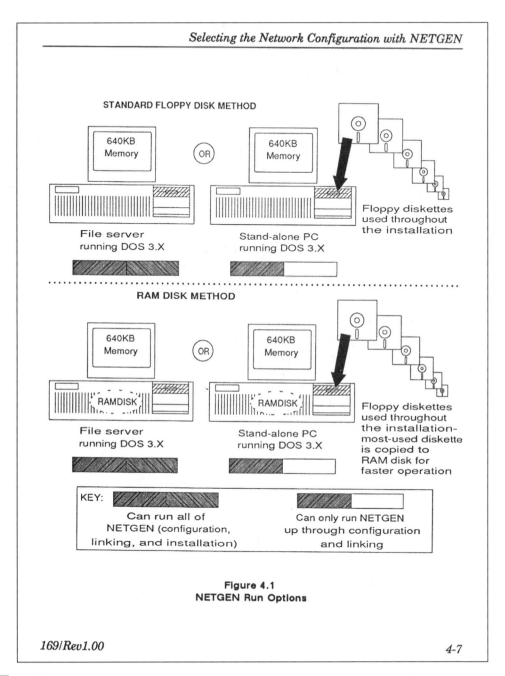

Selecting the Network Configuration with NETGEN

STANDARD FLOPPY DISK METHOD

640KB Memory

OR

640KB Memory

File server running DOS 3.X

Stand-alone PC running DOS 3.X

Floppy diskettes used throughout the installation

RAM DISK METHOD

640KB Memory

OR

640KB Memory

RAMDISK

RAMDISK

File server running DOS 3.X

Stand-alone PC running DOS 3.X

Floppy diskettes used throughout the installation—most-used diskette is copied to RAM disk for faster operation

KEY:

Can run all of NETGEN (configuration, linking, and installation)

Can only run NETGEN up through configuration and linking

Figure 4.1
NETGEN Run Options

169/Rev1.00

4-7

▟igure 11.6

Diagrams of Processes Help Users Understand Steps

These diagrams from the Novell Network *Installation Guide* give the user an overview of the run options for a particular software installation. They not only help the user see the process in advance, but they also help the user decide what kind of installation to use.

before performing it. They also, in the case of the Network installation in Figure 11.6, help the user decide which installation procedure to use. You can only do this with graphics: can you imagine having to read these installation procedures—or boring descriptions of them—in order to pick one?

Where Am I?

It's a better idea to *show* users their location in a manual or online help system than to tell them. Called **access indicators,** graphics like this tell users where the information they have before them fits into the organized whole. As indicated in Figure 11.7, you can reproduce a small-sized map of the document structure in the margin of your chapter title pages, and at other points, to keep your user from feeling lost. Access indicators consist of structure diagrams showing current location, history maps, and header and footer icons.

  Where pacing counts, as in tutorial documentation, you want to make sure the user can easily see progress through a number of pages or lessons. For this reason you might use a **progress indicator** in the header or footer to keep track of lessons, as shown in Figure 11.8.

What's the Big Picture?

People new to computing, or new to a program, need to know the structure of the program—how it's all assembled. Beginners need this because they can't draw on a store of knowledge of computer systems to help them operate efficiently. Experienced users need reminders of how programs work. And expert users need this because they may never have worked with the program before, but their knowledge of computer systems in general leads them to expect that such a structure exists.

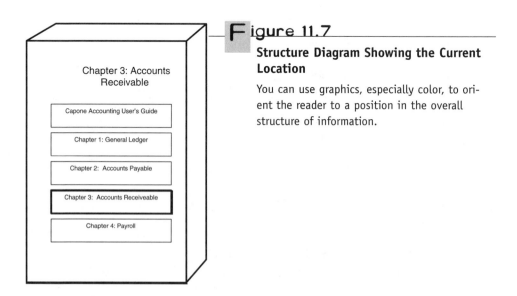

Figure 11.7

Structure Diagram Showing the Current Location

You can use graphics, especially color, to orient the reader to a position in the overall structure of information.

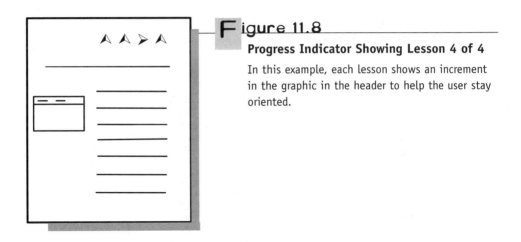

Figure 11.8

Progress Indicator Showing Lesson 4 of 4

In this example, each lesson shows an increment in the graphic in the header to help the user stay oriented.

Using a good printer and publication program, you can produce a very high quality overview graphic for your manual or online help system. I think one of the tricks involves keeping things as small as possible when you're drawing an overview graphic. You have the capability to make elements very small in these drawings so that the clarity of line available on laser printers can pay off by allowing you to present a fair amount of legible information. You can use icons from the program to help users make the connections between the things they see on the screen and their workplace demands to learn, process, communicate, and store information. You can also use color, to indicate levels and to separate elements of the program for easy recognition.

The following gallery illustrates some of the graphic elements you can use to give overviews.

Gallery of Examples

OVERALL PROGRAM DIAGRAMS. Overall program diagrams illustrate program system components so the user can see the flow of information. These comprise some of the most important kinds of information you can present and will result in greater dependability of user performance. Figure 11.9 shows an example.

MENU MAPS. Menu maps abound in software documentation. Essentially they consist of program menus arranged on the page in the same structure as they appear in the program interface. As reference documentation, they help the user maintain a sense of organization of the program's features. The user can relate any specific function to the whole picture of functions in the program. Figure 11.10 shows a menu map.

CONCEPTUAL OVERVIEWS. Unlike program structure overviews, conceptual overviews reinforce the ideas of how to use a program. These essential and economical kinds of graphics help users see how to put the program to meaningful work, often, as in Figure 11.11, through the sharing of information and resources. Graphics of this type strengthen the emphasis on using programs in the workplace.

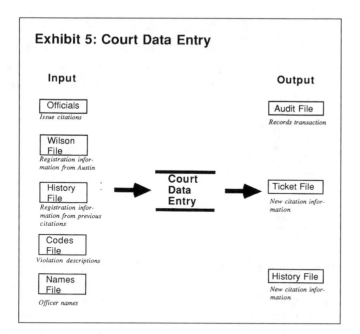

Figure 11.9

Overall Program Diagram

This diagram illustrates what occurs during processing. The diagram helps the user anticipate the process and fit unexpected events into the overall picture.

Follow these guidelines in designing conceptual overviews:

- Use generic figures. In all representations of the user, mix races, ages, and genders where appropriate (e.g., don't represent young persons in images of patients in nursing homes.) Reflect the users sampled in the user analysis. Find images that relate to the user's workplace. Use easy-to-identify images.

- Embody the *mental model* of use to predict successful user actions. Think of the mental model you want the user to have: working with a single file, storing in compressed format, dragging and dropping, filtering formats. Use a graphic that can be associated with the mental model.

- Simplify use concepts, but make the images visually interesting. Graphics don't work well for overly complicated ideas, and users like to rest their eyes on visually satisfying images. The more satisfying the image, the more the user pauses and thinks. That's good because it encourages the building of important *internal models* in the user.

HOW TO USE THE MANUAL. Often you have the opportunity to use graphics to reinforce the idea of the big picture of your manual and online help system. In such cases you can route users to the right book.

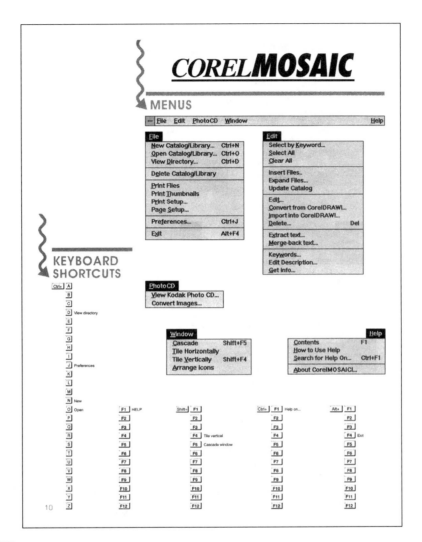

Figure 11.10

Menu Map Helps Users See Features

Menu maps like this one foster a sense of control over the program because they make all the features visible.

2   MAKE IT VISIBLE

Making things visible means three things:

- Show the user where to look to perform tasks (see Figure 11.12).
- Show concrete versions of abstract things.
- Make visuals clear.

Chapter 1   A Brief Overview of Microsoft Windows Networking   5

Exchanging Information

By using Windows for Workgroups, sharing information is easy. For example, although they work in different departments, John, Sue, and Mary can take turns working on the company's annual-report document without leaving their desks or passing around a floppy disk. They can even design the report so that each time someone updates it on one computer, the information is automatically updated on every computer that contains a copy of the report.

In this example, John, who works in the marketing department, writes the text for the annual report.

Sue, who works in the graphics department, opens the file and adds the illustrations.

Mary, who works in the finance department, opens the file and adds financial information. Then she prints a copy of the report, using Sue's printer.

Finally, John sends an electronic mail message notifying reviewers that the annual report is ready for them to see. John can even include the entire report within the mail message or use Windows for Workgroups to fax the report to reviewers who are not in the office.

Figure 11.11

Conceptual Overviews Illustrate Workplace Use

You can use graphics like this from the Microsoft *Windows for Workgroups User's Guide* to portray many kinds of concepts related to efficient and effective work.

Show the User Where to Look to Perform Tasks

Users of programs need to map their intention to perform a task (set a format, delete a drawing object, run a program) to the right interface object (button, ruler, icon, pointer, etc.). By showing the user the button rather than naming the button, you automatically encourage use. Also, the picture of a button requires less thought than the word "button."

About This Manual

This manual contains instructions for installing and configuring the National Instruments AT-GPIB/TNT or AT-GPIB interface board and the NI-488.2 software for DOS. The NI-488.2 software is intended for use with MS-DOS version 3.0 or higher (or equivalent).

This manual uses the term *AT-GPIB/TNT* to refer to a National Instruments GPIB board for the ISA (PC AT) bus equipped with the TNT4882C ASIC. The term *AT-GPIB* refers to a National Instruments GPIB board for the ISA (PC AT) bus equipped with the NAT4882 and Turbo488 ASICs. This manual also uses the term *GPIB board* in cases where the material can apply to either board.

This manual assumes that you are already familiar with DOS.

How to Use The Manual Set

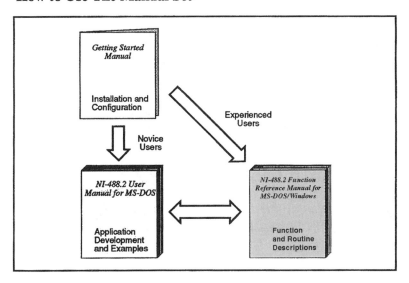

Use this getting started manual to install and configure your GPIB board and the NI-488.2 software for DOS.

© National Instruments Corp.   *ix*   *AT-GPIB/TNT for MS-DOS*

Figure 11.12

Graphics Show the Document's Structure

In this example from a manual called *Getting Started with Your AT-GPIB/TNT and the NI-488.2 Software for DOS,* the images convey what information users need from what documents. Users can identify their use class and react appropriately.

In simple terms, let the page reflect the screen. Use capture and art programs to bring elements off the screen and into manuals and online help. Usually, capturing a button takes little time or space. When you describe tasks involving choices from menus, show the menus, as in Figure 11.13.

Show Concrete Versions of Abstract Things

Making things visible means helping make the abstract concrete. We saw earlier how metaphors help define abstract concepts. Figure 11.14 helps users see the abstract concept of a relational database. The user is probably the biggest abstraction in your manual or help system. You should try to present images of your user in the manual to emphasize important points. Showing the user in images (as in Figure 11.11 explaining how the program works with a workgroup) provides a role model for the user. For novice users, such a role model can help them see the productive interaction of their work, themselves, and the program.

Make Visuals Clear

Make sure your users can see the things you want them to see. Avoid screen captures of buttons and keys that clutter the page or that you have had to reduce and squash to fit into the lines while sacrificing overall sharpness of the image. You will face the temptation to make your graphics smaller at times, to make them fit on the page, but you should remember that they do no good if the normal person can't distinguish details easily.

3   KEEP GRAPHIC STYLES CONSISTENT

You should use the same types and fonts, the same arrow styles, and box and frame styles throughout your document. Establish these standards for yourself early in the project, communicate them to your team members, and record them in the documentation plan.

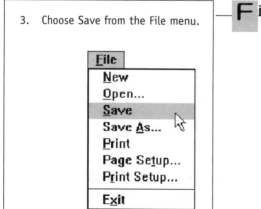

3. Choose Save from the File menu.

Figure 11.13

Area Captures Show the User Where to Look

These captures help users find the right place to click.

What Is a Relational Database?

A relational database like the Northwind database stores information in a collection of tables, each containing data about one subject. Because the tables are related, you can use information from more than one table at a time.

For example, you may want to combine information from an Employees table with an Orders table to create a report of total sales per employee for the past month. The two tables share one type of information (in this case, the employee ID number), but otherwise maintain unique data. Storing data in related tables is very efficient because you store a fact just once, which reduces disk storage requirements and makes updating and retrieving data much faster.

In a relational database, each table includes a field that is also included in another table so tables can share information.

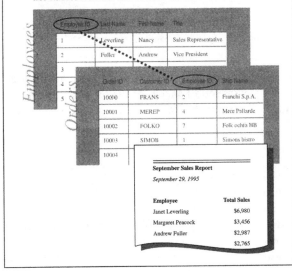

Figure 11.14

Make the Abstract Visible

Graphic examples such as this one from the Microsoft *Getting Results* guide enable the user to associate something visible with something abstract.

Update the standards as you encounter constraints of equipment or time and refine them as you go to your next project. Table 11.3 lists the elements of graphical styles.

Keeping styles consistent also has to do with the degree of realism you impart to your graphics. Depending on how much you want your images to reflect realistic details, you can gain some advantages by deleting details from your drawings and using more of a

Table 11.3

Elements of Graphical Styles

Elements	Examples and Uses
Lines	Thin for callouts
	Thicker for highlighting choices
Fonts	Elaborate for titles
	Bold for tasks
Arrow Styles	Match sizes with uses, don't cover up part of an image with an oversized arrow
Box Styles	Use simple boxes for structure charts
	Use shadowed boxes for examples and reports
Frame Styles	Use simple shapes for error messages
	Use ornate shapes for tips and anecdotes

cartoon or line drawing style. This not only helps you focus the user's attention on specific elements of a drawing, such as report shapes or dialog box choices, but it keeps the size of your drawings down. Photographic realism costs in hard disk or CD-ROM storage space.

4   DON'T OVER-DO GRAPHICS

Graphics, by their visual nature, present the user with the thing itself rather than the word for the thing. Because of this visual nature, they work best for recognition and retention in memory rather than for understanding. For this reason you should give your graphics a clear purpose—to support a task, to remind of an idea, to show use of a tool—so the visual element doesn't confuse the user. Software gives us the capability to make just about everything in a manual or online help system graphic. But should we use graphics as much as possible? Should we associate each task with an image?

I would answer no. Users have a craving for names: for the name of the thing (a word) rather than the thing itself (a picture). Words complete the user's sense of control over what the program does. Try to stick to the following limits when using graphics:

- Don't use the same graphic over and over again because it's easy to use. Users will catch on.

- Use screens and icons liberally, but restrict yourself to one *conceptual* image per chapter (often on the chapter title page) and one *cartoon* per procedure.

- Only use conceptual images in *getting-started* demonstrations and *tutorials,* and then only one conceptual image per main idea.

■ Explain most (or all) figures. A figure without explanation *sometimes* works: icons and other spot graphics that work as special eye catchers for users don't need explanation; they explain themselves. Other figures presented as examples require mention.

5 | LABEL CONSISTENTLY

Set styles for your graphics and the apparatus that presents them to the users. This means specifying a number of these issues in your documentation plan. If your company has prevailing means of doing these details, then follow them.

■ Use large enough arrows. Make sure the user can see them but that they don't hide essential details.

■ Use consistent capitalization. In general, the shorter your headings and labels, the more you should use all caps. In principle, identify a style and stick to it.

■ Place callouts outside the image or screen. Callouts should go in a line at the left or the right of the image but should not cover part of the object they identify. Break this rule when you don't have space outside the image to put the callout.

■ Keep lines straight and of the same value. Double-check to make sure you have the same size box for each item.

BAD:

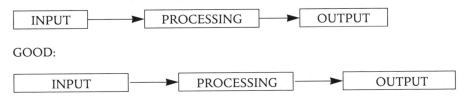

GOOD:

■ Position table and figure titles consistently. Usually you put table titles *above* the table and figure titles *below* the figures.

6 | USE TYPOGRAPHIC TECHNIQUES

Using *typographic* techniques means giving an arrangement to the images based on a logic. In words we use headings, margins, lists, and other devices to shape the information to the user's needs. When using images, you should arrange and design them so that they convey the structure of the meaning you intend.

Follow these guidelines to give the kind of emphasis on meaning, information, action, and productivity that a successful manual or online help system should have.

- **Make important things larger.** Sometimes you can adjust the scale of surrounding objects in a drawing to make one object larger than the other. When you have the opportunity, reserve the largest category for your most important element.

- **Make important things darker.** Darker elements on an otherwise homogeneous page will attract the viewer's attention. Often manuals use this typographical technique to show the screen in a lighter value (say, 40 percent) and the menu the user should select in full black. The contrasting effect works because it shows the user where to find the menu.

- **Make important things central.** The viewer's eye naturally gravitates to the center of a page or screen, so you have a better chance that the person will see what you want if you put it in this critical location. Of course, this doesn't apply to lists with graphic bullets, where the central focus falls on the text, with the graphics serving as access reminders.

- **Make important things sharper.** The viewer's eye will more likely settle on a sharp image than a fuzzy image. Using picture and photograph processing programs, you can adjust the focus of surrounding details to guide the reader's eye to the important part of the image.

- **Align related things.** Because of our preoccupation with lines of type as a major structure of communication, we tend to ascribe importance to things that are aligned. In structure charts, we naturally associate things adjacent to other things. For this reason you should use alignment to help convey your information structures.

- **Put first things left, later things right.** As we do with other patterned responses to visual and verbal information, we tend to associate chronology with left and right, at least in the western hemisphere. Many manuals use a left-right progress from step to step in designing procedures spanning two pages. Because we read left to right, we ascribe firstness with leftness; the reverse—putting the first step in a procedure at the right—just wouldn't feel right for many people in our culture.

7   SIZE THE IMAGE CORRECTLY

This guideline requires that you give some thought to planning and setting standards for how you want graphics to appear. You have to make them fit in the overall page design, as one of the elements that has its own area or rules that the user can count on. And the sooner you can decide on the major issues (size, type) the better.

Too much crowding of images and text creates an unattractive space, one the user has to work extra hard to get information from. Decide in advance on a look and then write down your decisions. Consider the following guidelines for setting standards about your graphics.

- **Give it enough white space/soft boundaries.** Usually you should have about ½ inch white space around figures. You have less space on screens: ⅛ to ¼ inch.

- **Make it large enough to show up.** You can make screens and figures wider than one column. Make screens about 3 to 5 inches wide.

■ **Keep it within the margins.** When you enlarge a screen to take up two columns, consider that its new margins consist of the left margin of column 1 and the right margin of column 2. Always put these limits on your images so they fit into the manual or online help system.

■ **The larger the better.** When in doubt, make screens larger. But avoid cluttering your pages or screens with over-large images.

Functions of Graphics

To operate a computer program, a user must take some kind of action. Press a key or click a button, and the program performs a calculation or prints a character on the screen. If the documenter has done the job well, the user will press or click the correct key or button. To convey such actions, the manual should focus on two things: the action itself and the result of the action. These two elements completed successfully and usefully will lead the user to the next action and so on. For this reason we say that the key to usability lies in describing actions. And with each action in the use of a system comes the opportunity to show, using graphics, two things: how to do the action and what happens next. The first shows the use of the software tools, the second shows the results of their use.

Show Use of Tools

One of the most common kinds of graphics in software documentation, showing the use of tools, relates directly to the concept of task orientation. At the point where you tell the user to press a key or use any of the many interface elements of the software, you instruct in the simplest sense. All these keys make up what we call software tools: objects that the user can manipulate to do work.

The interface of a computer contains many tools, often called *interface elements.* They include keys and key combinations, the mouse and its buttons, and the screen tools: scroll regions, radio buttons, data entry fields, check boxes, and so on. At times the devices for manipulating the software get complex, as in sophisticated control widgets and image sizers used on three-dimensional image processing computers. Using graphics in the documentation enables the user to see exactly which buttons and keys to press.

More often than not, you will show the use of tools in documentation for novice users: those new to computers and those who may not have used this particular interface type before. In fact, every software system usually has some starting place, a menu or a command line, from which the user will want to begin. Special keystroke combinations needed to manipulate this starting place should be recorded in your task analysis and should appear in your documentation.

Documentation for the novice usually requires a high degree of internalizing and remembering. It falls in the *teaching or guidance level* of task support. Writing for novices, you might find yourself in a very close relationship with the user, giving specific guidance for each step, including showing exactly where and how to click with the mouse.

You can support the operation of these tools—keystrokes, mouse clicks, and interface objects—in two ways: by using images of the actions taking place, or by using tables showing the commands, the objects, and their definitions. Support for keystrokes and other interface elements usually falls into getting started sections of manuals, or guided introductions to tasks. In special cases, where the user must manipulate complex interface items, you would put support for tools in reference guides. Figure 11.15 is an example of a graphic showing the use of a tool. Figure 11.16 illustrates a more abstract tool use.

Show Results of Actions

Nine out of ten images you will find in a software manual show the results of actions. Results of actions can come in various forms, but most commonly they show the screen that appears after the keystroke. Typically, showing results occurs on all three levels of task orientation—teaching, guidance, and reference. At the teaching level, it accompanies the illustration of the tool in use: In fact, the two work together to support the action/result movement found in tutorials. At the guidance level, it usually accompanies the most important step of a procedure, often the culmination or the goal state of the task. At the support level, it shows specific screens or other results the reader should see when the function is used. Figure 11.17 is a graphic that shows the result of an action.

Present Overviews

In all task-oriented documentation you will find introductions (described in Chapter 4) that help the user fit the procedures into his or her existing mental framework. Often images can do this job better than words (see Figure 11.18). The images we use to present

Moving the pointer by moving the mouse.

Figure 11.15

Graphic Showing the Use of a Tool

This example from a Macintosh *User's Guide* shows the user how to move the pointer (use) with a mouse (tool).

Figure 5-2
Rotating an Object with the
Virtual Trackball

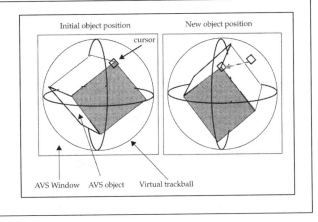

Initial object position   New object position

cursor

AVS Window   AVS object   Virtual trackball

Figure 11.16

Use Graphics for Special Cases of Tool Use

This illustration from the Convex AVS *User's Manual* helps expert users manage a particularly difficult interface.

overviews often consist of cartoons or drawings of various elements with process arrows (the arrows used to show "cause" between one image and another) to show how things fit together. They work particularly well with installation sections, showing the big picture of how the disks in the box will end up as the system on the hard disk.

You will find that help systems tend to have overviews built in because of the interactive nature of the screen. The first screen of a help document tends to have icons showing the different elements of the help system that the user can choose from. But with manuals

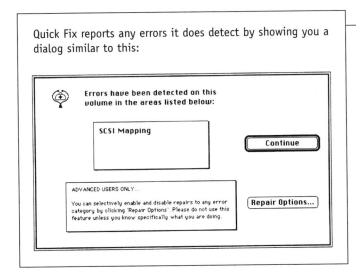

Quick Fix reports any errors it does detect by showing you a dialog similar to this:

Errors have been detected on this
volume in the areas listed below:

SCSI Mapping

Continue

ADVANCED USERS ONLY...

You can selectively enable and disable repairs to any error
category by clicking 'Repair Options'. Please do not use this
feature unless you know specifically what you are doing.

Repair Options...

Figure 11.17

Graphic Showing the Result of an Action

Here the text in a manual for a computer security program introduces the dialog box that resulted from the selection of a command.

you need to explain the access elements more explicitly, so users will understand how you have designed the manual system. In large programs manual systems may require a number of books; in smaller programs manuals may consist of chapters or special sections of a single book. Graphics also help explain how users should read pages: what the headings look like, where to find the step-by-step parts. In particular, graphic overviews of procedures can greatly increase the usability of manuals because they reinforce the task orientation. Used wisely—consistently with other task descriptions and well-designed—graphic overviews can make the difference between a usable manual and a boring one.

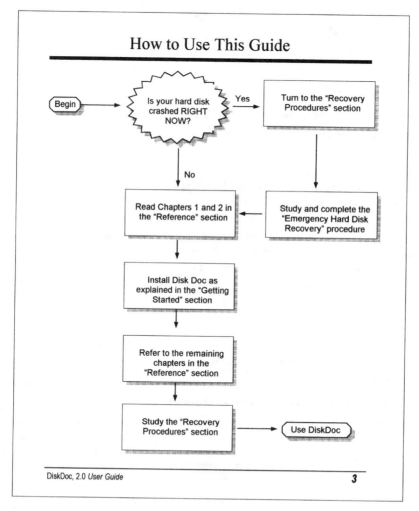

Figure 11.18

A Graphic to Give an Overview of Manual Use

This example shows how the graphic style (flowchart) fits the user—in this case, experienced users familiar with programming symbols.

Suggesting Functions and Uses

Software manuals often contain graphics to illustrate problem-solving situations or work environments. These images fall into the category of graphics to suggest functions and uses. These images include pictures of desktops or pictures of kinds of reports a program will produce. They often highlight the strongest, most dramatic feats a program can perform, like drawing 3-D graphs or plotting fancy maps. Documenters often use photographs, stylized drawings, or screens here. Photographs may include users at the keyboard. Usually these graphics are found in "Getting Started" sections that operate at the guidance level of task support.

Pictures or diagrams showing suggested uses should present something familiar and pleasant to the user. It helps if the writer has visited the user's office or other work environment. This realism does more than just make the images look familiar; it can reinforce the task orientation of the manual. Visual images carry a power that words cannot, and that power works directly on the user's ideas about what to do with the program and manual. Unlike other devices in manuals that convey specific information about tasks, the graphics suggesting functions and uses also work on the level of the user's imagination.

In a more specific way, though, you can key suggestions of functions and uses to the task analysis by designing them so that they capture a *typical-use scenario.* The typical-use scenario outlines the most common use of the program, often the one described in the program planning document. A well-designed program will revolve around some typical use, or often around a number of them. Also, higher-level tasks, such as installation, configuration, and operation make good material for suggesting uses. If you have the resources to produce pictures in your manual (and many systems can do that pretty easily using a camera and a scanner as well as other high-tech image sampling techniques), you should take care to make them as professional as possible. Study the images you see used as cover art on manuals or (and here you will find them most often) study the images adorning the section and chapter dividers in manuals that you admire. Remember to make the suggestion of function or use a pleasant place for the reader to rest the eyes, and in doing so, see a clear message about the use of the software product. Figure 11.19 is a good example.

Make the Abstract Concrete

Think of the first time you used a computer. Fortunately, I recorded my first experience using the TECO editor on a terminal at The University of Texas in 1981. The recording survived a couple of desk and office changes and still knocks around in one of my drawers. Among the many puzzles it records me having, it shows my faltering attempts to grasp the idea that a program would work on one "level" but not on other "levels." Actually, I struggled with the extremely basic, fundamental idea of running programs but did not know it. For me the idea of *programs* and *running* them presented a particular hurdle, something I couldn't grasp because of its complexity and its abstractness. No motor? No pen? To me using a machine or a writing tool meant having something physical to manipulate, and the computer seems so physically non-physical.

What does this tell us about how to use graphics in manuals? It tells us that users often have to make the transition from analog or by-hand methods of doing tasks to computer-based methods of performing the same tasks.

CHAPTER 2

Inside the Macintosh IIci

IF YOU USED THE TOUR DISK, *YOUR APPLE Tour of the Macintosh IIci*, or went through the tutorial in the *Macintosh System Software User's Guide*, you've already learned the basic skills you'll use to work with your Macintosh IIci computer. The next two chapters expand on what you've learned.

This chapter briefly introduces you to the more important parts of the Macintosh IIci—the basic hardware components of your computer system. Chapter 3 descirbes how they work together with software.

You don't need to know the material in this chapter or in Chapter 3 to use your Macintosh IIci. But a basic familiarity with how a Macintosh works will help you understand advanced concepts that you may encounter in using system software and applications. It may also come in handy when considering hardware options and peripheral devices for your computer.

Figure 11.19

Photograph Suggesting Uses

This photograph from *Macintosh IIci Owner's Guide* illustrates how to suggest the uses of software and computers to users. Showing the user's environment like this can provide a powerful image in documentation because of its direct relationship to productive work.

Graphics that convey abstract concepts perform a basic task for the user: They help him or her see the invisible. They work well alongside words or in place of them. You will find them in places where the writer of manuals needs to convey a concept, especially an abstract one. Scrolling a text on a screen, merging two files into a third, connecting over phone lines, finding a card in a HyperCard stack: These concepts do not come easy to many users without graphics to help out. Figure 11.20 shows a graphic depicting a very basic abstract concept: that of the desktop in a PC environment.

Often images conveying abstract concepts portray a central metaphor of a program: the idea of communication using images of phone lines, the idea of capturing a screen using images of butterflies and nets. However, they most often show up in manuals for programs that produce graphic output: image processing software, desktop publishing programs, clip art programs, drawing programs. In these manuals, images of abstract concepts function as examples of the output of the program and often get put in special reference sections.

Explain Processes

Images that convey processes directly enhance the task orientation of the manual. They allow the user to see how elements of the program fit together to accomplish real results.

Page layout defined

Putting it all together

Simply defined, desktop publishing is the process of laying out and printing text and graphics using a desktop computer and printer. One of the reasons why PageMaker is the most popular desktop-publishing package is that PageMaker uses a simple and intuitive electronic pasteboard to lay out text and graphics on a page quickly, easily, and precisely.

Anyone familiar with traditional publishing knows the importance of the pasteboard: the work surface on which you position the text and graphics that become your publication.

PageMaker's on-screen pasteboard is very similar, both visually and functionally, to the traditional pasteboard—it's just on your screen. The pasteboard provides a convenient work area where layout and pasteup tools are within easy reach.

If you're new to page layout and design, you will appreciate how easy PageMaker is to use. This is because PageMaker's layout view displays all the elements on the page as "what you see is what you get" (WYSIWYG) so you can immediately see how everything looks on the page. And when you use PageMaker's ruler guides and underlying grid, the elements you position will be precisely aligned to each other.

To help you get started with PageMaker and laying out your publications, we have included several templates, or pre-designed publications, that you can use as is or modify for your own use.

■ **For more information**, refer to these entries in the *Aldus PageMaker 4.0 Reference Manual*: Layout grid, Master pages, Setting up your pages, Templates.

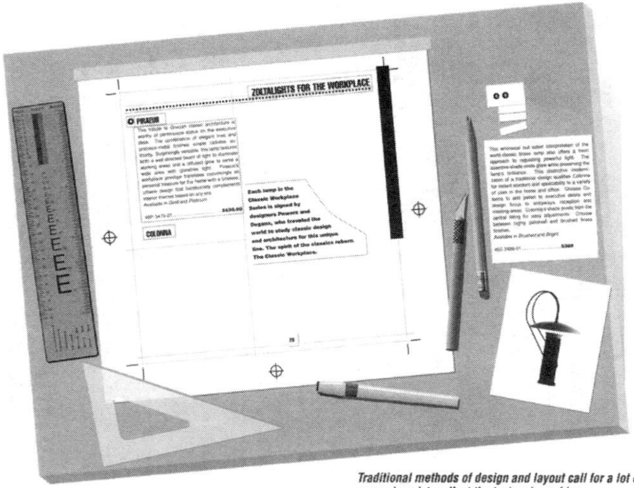

Traditional methods of design and layout call for a lot of manual work to adjust the text and graphics

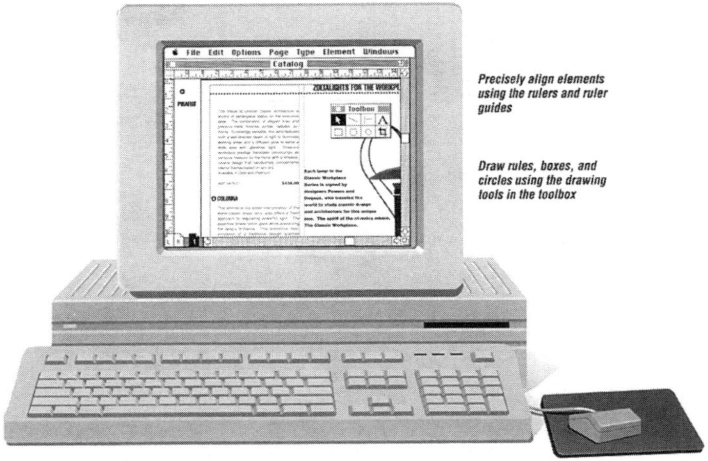

In PageMaker, you can move text and graphics from the on-screen pasteboard onto the pages of your publication simply by selecting and dragging them with the mouse

Precisely align elements using the rulers and ruler guides

Draw rules, boxes, and circles using the drawing tools in the toolbox

Page 2 • Introduction to PageMaker

PageMaker and desktop publishing • Page 3

Figure 11.20

Graphic Depicting the Abstract Concept of the Desktop

Here the images portray the idea of the document designer's workspace in Adobe PageMaker's *Introduction to PageMaker.*

These might include the printing programs associated with a word processor or utility programs used in an operating system. Often such images use the techniques of the flowchart with simple lines, boxes to represent processes, and arrows to show the flow of events. They demonstrate the values of neatness, simplicity, and concentration on one process at a time.

Software documenters can learn about how to convey processes with images or diagrams from hardware documenters who write wordless instructions. Wordless instructions show hands, hardware, and arrows and use color to help highlight important relationships between parts of machines. Wordless instructions grew out of our need to communicate often with non-native speakers or customers in foreign countries. How do you say "Press the Enter key" in Japanese? You show it.

Images (usually drawings or diagrams) showing processes should focus the user's eye on the specific process described. They may use color or contrasts to do this, and the caption and labels on the diagram should reflect the terms used in the text. List images of this type in a list of figures so that the user can look them up easily.

Support Text Explanations

Use labeled drawings of keyboards and screens to reinforce explanations in the text. These kinds of things, illustrated in Figure 11.21, work in two ways: They accommodate the (possibly impatient) experienced user because they are easy to scan, and they help the (possibly uncertain) less experienced user determine whether to stop and read the text.

Types of Graphics in Software Manuals and Online Help

This section discusses the types of graphics you can use in your manuals and online help. It includes brief discussions of these types, with examples, to give you some pointers on how to design graphics and help you select which ones to use.

Screens

Screens represent the most common form of graphics in software manuals. They perform all the functions of graphics described above. They work particularly well with text in describing tools and results. But they also can show menus, reports, steps, errors, computer messages, command lines, windows, help screens, desktops, dialog boxes, examples—anything that the user could possibly see on the computer screen. Because screens work well with text, supplementing or repeating what the text presents, screens aid the reader in remembering task-related information. You will find screens useful in all levels of task support for teaching, guiding, and reference.

Usually you capture screens with a program that reads the content of the computer screen and saves it in a file or on the clipboard. Most producers of word processing programs recognize the need for screen capture programs and provide them with their software.

Screen representations sometimes have borders, either a simple box with rounded edges, or a more complicated drawing of the outline of a computer monitor. The border serves to distinguish the screen image from the surrounding text. To help the user read screen images effectively, you should keep their format consistent and simple. Screens usu-

Delete

Deleting Messages from a Thread

Clicking the Delete button while you're viewing a forum message within a thread takes you to the Thread Editor dialog, which looks like the sample below.

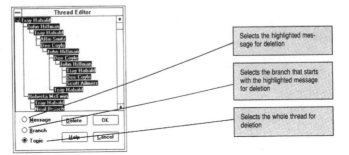

The group of forum messages stemming from any one forum message is called a branch. A branch can be a single message (a 'leaf' on another branch), a small 'shoot' like the adjacent sample, a stem with several shoots, or an entire thread.

Once you've selected a forum message or a branch, click the Delete button. This grays the selected message or branch. When you've selected everything you want to delete, click the OK button. (If you decide not to delete any of the selected items, click Cancel.)

Fast deletions

You can delete the current message or the current thread quickly, without stopping at the Thread Editor, by pressing one of the following key combinations while you're viewing a message:

* `Shift`+`Delete` deletes the current message.

* `Control`+`Shift`+`Delete` deletes the current thread.

Figure 11.21

Labeled Screen That Supports Text Explanations

In this example from the Compuserve Navigator *User's Guide,* the labeled screen reinforces the explanation of the task.

ally require captions and labels to identify their contents and to make the association with the relevant text and tasks clear. However, current designs often keep the screen quite near the relevant text, so a caption or label is not needed.

Screens should only contain information pertinent to the task: no "chart junk" or extra details to interfere with the user's perceptions. The user needs to get the relevant information quickly. The problem is that computer screens often do contain irrelevant information: options that the user might not want to take at this time or might not relate to the task being performed by the system. Screens can also contain lists of files that the user would not find on his or her directory. Such extra information on the screen only confuses or detracts from the screen's effectiveness.

The problem of irrelevant information on screens, whether caused by the complexity of the program's interface or overwork by the writer, will not disappear without careful planning. Often you can use partial screens to limit the amount of information in the image to only that needed by the user and demanded by the task. Partial screens work well with command interface programs such as DOS or UNIX where the user has to type commands to run programs and look for files. Command lines and other elements of screens, called interface objects, can easily fit into smaller boxes with or without borders. You also save space, obviously, when you use partial screens.

The example from the CorelDRAW *User's Manual* (Figure 11.2) provides an excellent example of how to do screens.

Reports

Many programs produce output to printers, other programs, or storage. These we call *reports*. A report represents work done by the program and by the user working with the program. In documentation you will find numerous examples of reports that have resulted from calculations on data provided by the software designer for the sake of demonstrating the program. Use such reports (with permission) liberally in your work to reinforce the notion that quality work can result from this sometimes uncooperative machine.

Anything that gets sent by the program to the printer we consider a report. These items include pages from word processing and desktop systems, tables of statistical data, analyses of oil revenues, and spreadsheets with financial plans. Technically, anything that the program sends to the printer you would classify as a report, but you can also include as reports those written to the disk storage or sent over fax equipment. A report that the program presents on the screen technically qualifies as a screen, and in using them you should follow the guidelines for screens described above.

In general, when you need to incorporate reports in your documentation, you should follow some simple guidelines. Scan reports to get a realistic look and to give the reports the authenticity you need to reinforce the task orientation of your manual. So show the perforated holes in the borders around the reports in your manual. Besides, taking time to produce reports well might pay off if you can recycle some of the images into promotional material for the program.

In the example in Figure 11.22 the illustration used in the document shows the screen that generated the report and the final report itself.

Photographs and Drawings

Photographs and drawings resemble one another in that they both show physical things: images of hands assembling parts, inserting disks, moving mice. Photographs, as we saw above, can add an important task-oriented dimension to your work, catching the reader's eye and focusing it on task-related material. However, photographs and drawings also differ. You need to try to balance the visually rich nature of photographs and the visually sparse nature of drawings. You may find that the drawing or the cartoon might work better to help the user orient to a task, because the visually sparse drawing may closely imitate the kind of image stored in the user's brain. Above all, pictures and drawings both

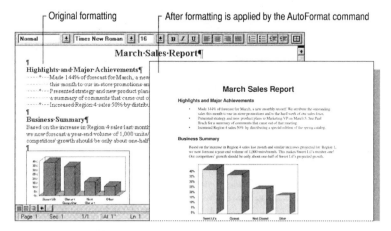

AutoFormat analyzes a document and applies formatting for you

AutoFormat combines styles and templates in a powerful new way. AutoFormat analyzes and polishes a document for you. You can quickly reformat all or part of a document and approve the changes AutoFormat makes.

⌐ Original formatting   ⌐ After formatting is applied by the AutoFormat command

The AutoFormat command formats a document by applying styles to headings and other text.

The Table Wizard helps you create and format a table quickly

If you need to organize data in a table, try the new Table Wizard. It helps you create and format a table and adjusts each column to accommodate its contents.

	Dallas	Hong Kong	Madrid	Paris
Dallas		8370	4965	4936
Hong Kong	8370		6554	6204
Madrid	4965	6554		649
Paris	4936	6204	649	
Rio de Janeiro	5218	11136	5064	5697

The Table Wizard helps you arrange data, text, and graphics in tables like this.

You can also use the Table AutoFormat dialog box to format a table quickly. Click anywhere inside a table and choose the Table AutoFormat command from the Table menu. Then select the look you want.

Figure 11.22

Graphic Showing a Report

This page from the Microsoft Word *Quick Results* booklet shows how you can present a report and the screen that created it, to help the user make the connection.

have a dramatic effect. They impress the user and give a manual a classy look. Unfortunately, their cost prohibits them from widespread use in manuals. Nevertheless, you should know how to use them.

With pictures and with drawings, the user's context of the image will determine its meaning, or its significance. Like words, pictures can evoke an image from memory, but they do a much better job than words. You should take care in using photographs to assure that they include information about the user's task needs.

Crop and size photographs to focus them on the task the manual describes. Only use photographs if you have a high quality reproduction system; low-quality photographs are not memorable in a positive sense. Also, researchers tell us certain spatial relationships may not be clear when presented in photographs, especially fuzzy ones.[1] When arranging a photograph, you should cast the composer's eye on all the items you plan to include in the shot. With photographs, the details on the edge carry as much weight—potential to spark the user's memory—as the middles. Use words with your photographs to take advantage of the association, and make sure you list your photographs in the list of figures.

Drawings also require a high degree of skill in their preparation. You may not think of yourself as a cartoonist or artist, but care and the use of precise tools (like drawing programs) can make you look very good. Besides, many writers have banks of clip art images to use in manuals and online help. With drawings, you have the chance to control carefully the amount of detail in a picture (Figure 11.23). And while the amount of detail may not determine whether the user will use your drawing to, say, remember the relationship between the compiler and the debugger, you can bet that if your drawing contains irrelevant details that they will increase the user's cognitive load. If you can, get a professional to do your drawings for you, then use them wisely to support your manual's task orientation.

Charts and Diagrams

Because charts and diagrams, sometimes called schematics, show components of systems or phases of the software and documentation development effort, the documenter should know how and when to use them. Different types of charts you might create include the hierarchical diagrams, often called *structure charts,* of system components. Everyone involved in software development uses these charts to keep track of the work effort in producing software. Such charts represent the bare bones of a system, whereas the emphasis in documentation will more likely fall on the task orientation: the *use* of the system, not

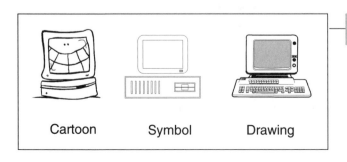

Cartoon   Symbol   Drawing

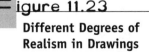

Figure 11.23

Different Degrees of Realism in Drawings

These drawings represent the different degrees of realism you can use in adapting drawings to your user's needs.

its makeup. Nevertheless, you should understand the function of structure charts in the whole development effort and at the same time realize that you can turn them into useful, task-oriented parts of your documentation project.

Diagrams help the user see how abstract ideas fit together to perform the work done or assisted by the software. As such, they offer the writer the chance to build graphic-oriented advance organizers to help the user grasp the cognitive framework of processes. Charts can show the relationship of one task to another, even though they primarily function as analytical maps of program elements. For instance, they can lay out how different files (input files, help files, control files) fit together in systems. They can plot how different subprograms (training, installation, communication) share data or otherwise interrelate. Figure 11.24 is a good example of an atrractive and informative chart.

As mentioned earlier, you can create drawings by using draw programs or by using clip art. You can plan them depending on the degree of abstractness you think you can get away with, given your users. For example, chart elements can look a little like the

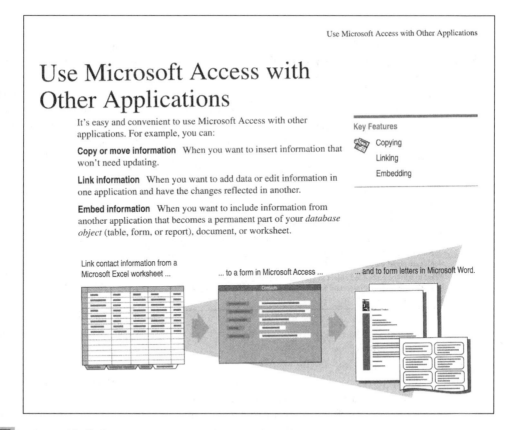

Figure 11.24

A Chart Showing an Information Task

This chart from Microsoft's *Getting Results with Microsoft Access* emphasizes the flow of information from a worksheet to documents.

thing they describe: printer symbols look like little printers, tape storage symbols look like tape canisters. On the more abstract level, you only use boxes or circles to depict the elements of the system or steps. The graphic design in Figure 11.24 shows abstract, cartoon-like drawings to represent pages, giving emphasis to the task and not the details of the images. This more abstract approach has the advantage of emphasizing the concept; the more realistic approach has the advantage of providing useful visual cues.

Good charts and diagrams should look balanced on the page. Try to pick out the main element you want the user to see, and place it centrally in the overall page layout. If the image has a circular arrangement, make it really circular, to get the idea across. If you have a balanced hierarchical arrangement, avoid making it look lopsided; arrange the branches symmetrically on the page. You can also confuse the task orientation of a diagram if you do not keep the flow of action normal (left to right). Use directional arrows sparingly in order to clarify what direction the user's eyes should go. Use these sequences to show how things should get done: left to right, first to last, input to output, problem to solution.

Icons

Icons stand for actions or components of a computer system, especially its interface. Icons have received much attention during the last few years because of their prevalence in computer interface systems. Many researchers have investigated why they work so well in helping users make the best of systems. Part of the answer to why those little pictures work in computer interfaces lies in their relevance to the idea of language itself. When we study them, says Robert Krull, we learn that they work much like words, and that they stem, in practice, from early forms of languages, such as cuneiform and hieroglyphs.[2] Asian languages today still contain elements of their roots as picture-based communication systems. Icons were used in the middle ages on knights' shields and on shops to identify guild members, and to suggest to the potential customer the nature of the goods. Today, you can see icons everywhere, especially in airports and on interstate highways, where instant recognition of a concept requires the use of these graphic elements.

Software documenters can learn much from studying the way icons work as pictures and also as words. Software manuals can benefit when icons are included as pathfinders for users, especially if the icons fit the scheme of task orientation in your manual. By crossing language boundaries, icons can help users who know other, similar systems, relate to the way things work.

You can use icons of your own design in all levels of task support. Integrate them into the cuing scheme of your manual to guide the user to task information or simply to signal the beginnings and endings of tasks. The chart in Figure 11.25 shows one way to incorporate icons into a task matrix.

You can also use icons that you find in the program's interface. As objects that your user will manipulate to use the program, they are a ready-made tool for directing the user to task information. Because of the role icons play in a graphic interface, such as on a personal computer, you should use them liberally in your manual. They have the advantage of suggesting uses, and as such can help the instructional purpose of your documentation. Use them in the navigational columns of a page to assist the user in finding the right in-

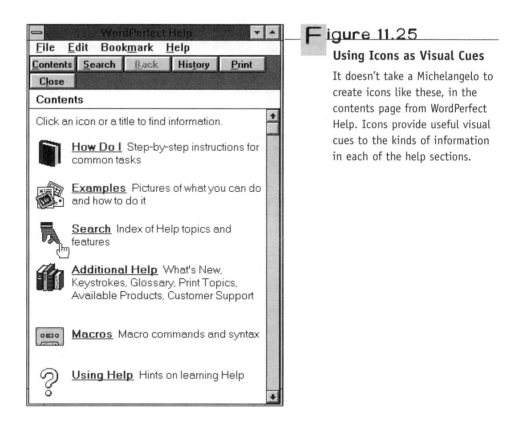

Figure 11.25

Using Icons as Visual Cues

It doesn't take a Michelangelo to create icons like these, in the contents page from WordPerfect Help. Icons provide useful visual cues to the kinds of information in each of the help sections.

formation. In the example in Figure 11.24 the icons cue the kinds of information in each of the sections of the help document.

Matrices That Show Interrelationships

Matrices compare related sets of information. Mostly they function to help users decide how to apply the program, or choose what features apply to what tasks. You might find one, for example, at the start of a manual, showing, in one list on the left, the various manuals in a documentation set, and, in a second list on the right, a list of possible or targeted users. In the intersection of these two lists, in the boxes made by their intersecting lines, you would find dots or x's indicating which of the documentation products would suit which user. Figure 11.26 shows one such matrix. Such matrices may also help experienced users of a system trouble-shoot. Trouble-shooting charts compare or relate error messages with software remedies for problems. Most experienced users would gladly look over a trouble-shooting matrix instead of dictionary-like reference pages. The user needs the detailed information in the pages, but at many stages of the problem-solving process—with many programs—a matrixed overview of choices gives just the right kind of task guidance.

Getting the most from your NetHog+ manuals and help...

	New to NetHog+	Experienced with NetHog+	NetHog+ Power User
What's New with NetHog+		✘	✘
Getting Started with NetHog+	✘		
NetHog+ *User's Guide*	✘	✘	✘
NetHog+ *Technical Reference*		✘	
NetHog+ *in the Workplace: Suggested Uses*	✘	✘	

Figure 11.26

Matrix Chart Links Users with the Right Documents

A matrix like this one can guide your users to the documents that pertain to their needs.

And finally, Figure 11.27 shows how you can combine a chart with another graphic for an element that is informative as well as visually pleasing.

Tables

One of the most versatile forms of illustrations, tables enable you to assemble information in an easy-to-use format that readers of manuals have come to expect. Tables arrange information in a highly structured form, using rules, columns, and titles. Tables may serve as overviews of commands or listings of keystrokes and explanations of their use. Whatever you use them for, they should conform to the system of task orientation that you have built into your manual.

Tables function in all levels of task orientation, from teaching to reference. Whenever you want to show your users all the available options in one place, do it with a table. Designing tables also forces the writer to see the information in groups and thus can help in the planning of documentation products.

Generally, tables contain lists of things such as interface objects or commands, that the user would need to scan and pick from. Often a computer program includes special parameters that the user can attach to commands, each with some explanation. These items go into tables, with a column designating the command ("Use this command . . .") and a column designating the result ("To do this . . .").

Tables range in degree of structure, depending on the writer's use of lines or other design elements. Some tables require only one rule at the top and one at the bottom, to set the columns off from the surrounding text and margin areas. These more informal tables resemble formatted lists as opposed to tables, really. More structured tables, on the other hand, require a grid of lines forming boxes containing explanations, commands, keystrokes, and other items. As a general rule, you want to keep the columns straight and in line with their associated headings. Users read tables from left to right, top to bottom,

BEYOND THE BASICS

Dashed Line Effects

You can create various borders and lines by layering copies of dashed lines and painting them differently. The chart shows some possibilities. Layer 1 is the top layer. To apply an offset amount, select the specified line (layer), and use the Move command or the arrow keys to move the line by the given amount. To create similar effects using patterns on lines, see "Path Patterns" on page 66.

Preview		Layer	Stroke Color	Stroke Weight	Stroke Options		Offset amount
••••••••••••	————	1	Color	2 pts	⊙—⊙	Dash 0; Gap 4	
☐☐☐☐☐☐☐☐☐☐☐	————	1	Color	3 pts	⊡—⊡	Dash 0; Gap 4	
		2	White	2 pts	⊡—⊡	Dash 0; Gap 4	
ccccccccccc	————	1	Color	3 pts	⊙—⊙	Dash 0; Gap 4	Move 2nd line .5 pts down and right
		2	White	2 pts	⊙—⊙	Dash 0; Gap 4	
∿∿∿∿∿∿∿∿	————	1	Color	5 pts	⊙—⊙	Dash 0; Gap 4.5	Move 2nd line 1.5 pts up
		2	White	5 pts	⊙—⊙	Dash 0; Gap 4.5	
▬ ∙ ▬ ∙ ▬ ∙	▬ ∙—∙ ▬	1	Color	2 pts	⊡—⊡	Dash 3; Gap 8	Move 2nd line 7 pts right
		2	Color	2.5 pts	⊙—⊙	Dash 0; Gap 11	
o—o—o—o—o—o—o	————	1	100% Color	3 pts	⊙—⊙	Dash 0; Gap 7; Dash 0; Gap 4.5	
		2	50% Color	1.5 pts	⊙—⊙	Dash 7; Gap 4.5	
⌇⌇⌇	⌇	1	Color	4.5 pts	▤	Solid line	
		2	White	3 pts	▤	Solid line	
⊚⊚⊚⊚⊚⊚⊚⊚	————	1	Color	8.5 pts	⊙—⊙	Dash 0; Gap 6	
		2	Color	6.5 pts	⊙—⊙	Dash 0; Gap 6	
		3	Color	2 pts	⊙—⊙	Dash 0; Gap 6	
▮▮▮▮▮▮▮▮	————	1	Color	12.0 pts	⊡—⊡	Solid line	
		2	Color	8.0 pts	⊡—⊡	Solid line	
		3	Color	4.0 pts	⊡—⊡	Dash 0; Gap 6	

Figure 11.27

Table Integrated with a Drawing

This example shows how you can integrate a table with a drawing for a striking effect.

so unless the material imposes some special order (like the order in which commands must follow one another in a syntactic arrangement) follow this natural order. Build task orientation into tables by putting the most logical (task-oriented) set of commands on the left and the others to the right and so on. Don't forget that tables need titles, headings (which should be bold), and captions explaining their relevance to the reader.

Elements of Graphics

The following section offers advice for the care and feeding of your graphic elements. Under each of the headings you will find practical advice that, coupled with common sense and a developed eye for images, will help you design a scheme of graphics and text that will enhance the task orientation of your document set.

Titles

Not all images or screens require titles. As a rule of thumb, the more complex, the more the need for a title. Also, if the user can't easily see the relationship between the image and the text, then you should use a title to clarify the function of the image. Follow the guidelines below in creating titles for your graphics.

- Number the titles sequentially.
- List numbers and titles in the front of the manual.
- Use boldface titles, sometimes enlarged, in body-text style.

Labels

As with other graphic elements, you don't need labels on all your images. Often called "callouts," labels point out the salient elements of a picture or drawing and direct the user to the correct and informative parts. If you label your graphics, follow these guidelines:

- Label components of screens used for presenting overviews and screen objects.
- Keep captions brief (don't try to say in a caption what you should say in the text).
- Make captions terminology consistent with the text.

Placement

Placement relates to where you put images on the page or screen. Follow these simple rules for placing graphics appropriately:

- When you can, obey the text margins; or set margins for illustrations and stick with them.
- Set aside a region for graphics (like a column) and always put them there.
- Always place graphics as close to and following the text they relate to.

Rules and Lines

Rules and lines help define the communication space and give your page structure. Use them consistently to help the user navigate your manuals and online help. Follow these guidelines in using rules and lines:

- Make rules and lines straight and neat.
- Make rules conform to the style of headers and other cues.
- Use rules to indicate hierarchies of information in your text.

■ Use greyscale rules when you don't want to waste ink and you need to save disk space.

■ Use rules sparingly in help screens, usually only thin ones across the top.

Size

Images that the user can't read clearly don't do you any good in a manual. You should not make them too large either, or else they take over the page. Follow these guidelines for sizing your visuals:

■ Try to keep your illustrations on one page (at least for larger ones).

■ Turn oversized illustrations 90 degrees.

■ Crop pictures for maximum impact.

■ Design a hierarchy of sizes of illustrations and stick to it.

Colors

Color can add to the appeal and impact of your manuals, especially your online help documents (where color is "cheap"). But these elements should relate clearly to the scheme of information you have designed. In particular, color can help you identify kinds of tasks, information, reference, and other elements of documents to help unify the document. Follow these guidelines in using color:

■ Relate color schemes to patterns of information.

■ Keep elements the same tones of gray or the same families of intensity: pastels, primaries, earth tones.

■ Use a single color for bars along the paper edge for cuing.

■ Avoid "reserved" colors: red for danger, yellow for caution.

Glossary

access indicators: special types of graphics that present overviews of programs or manuals with the intention of orienting the user to his or her place in the system.

command-driven: a type of computer program that relies primarily on the user typing commands to perform functions. MS-DOS is an example of a command-driven program. Other types of programs include menu-driven programs where the user selects from a menu.

interface elements: parts of a computer program that the user can manipulate to perform work. Examples include buttons, rulers, sliders, check boxes, menus, and commands.

internal model: the idea or thought that a user has of a task or activity that may come from past experience, or be triggered by the manual or help.

mental model: a conceptual structure of a task or activity that represents the kind of thinking needed to perform a task with a software program.

progress indicator: a kind of graphic that shows how far a user has come in a tutorial by showing the total lessons or pages, those already covered, and those still to come.

structure chart: a kind of graphic that illustrates the relationship between parts of a system, showing levels of hierarchies.

typography: the arrangement and appearance of images and text elements on a page.

typical-use scenario: a description in chronological format of the tasks that comprise the most frequent work done by users of a software program.

Use the following checklist as a way to evaluate your use of graphics on a project and to plan for incorporating graphics in your documents.

Graphics Checklist
Responding to User Questions

From your user analysis and program task list, find areas where users might have the following questions.

User Question	Option to Respond
☐ Where is it?	☐ Arrows ☐ Circles ☐ Highlighting
☐ What is it?	☐ Examples ☐ Metaphors
☐ How do I do it?	☐ Process overviews ☐ Diagrams
☐ Where am I?	☐ Access indicator ☐ Progress indicator
☐ What's the big picture?	☐ Overall program diagrams ☐ Menu maps ☐ Conceptual overviews ☐ How to use this manual

Making It Visible

☐ Do your screen captures clearly show the user where to look to perform tasks?
☐ Do you show concrete versions of abstract things?
☐ Have you made your graphics clear and easy to interpret?

Keeping Graphic Styles Consistent

In the area on the right, indicate what styles of graphics you plan for your manual or help project.

Graphic Element	Planned Styles
☐ Lines	*4-point grey for subheads*
☐ Fonts	
☐ Arrow styles	
☐ Box styles	
☐ Frame styles	
☐ Labels and callouts	

Typographic Techniques

☐ Identify elements that the user will see as important in the program or the workplace in your project that you can accommodate using typographic techniques.

Indicate how you will make these elements clear to the user by selecting from among the following techniques:

Technique	Element
☐ Make it larger than surrounding text and graphics	*Lassie (help) icon: ½-inch*
☐ Make it darker than surrounding text and graphics	
☐ Make it central on the page or in the figure	
☐ Make it sharper than surrounding text and/or graphics	
☐ Align it with related elements	
☐ Arrange elements in a left to right progression	

Identify the Function of Your Graphics

Which of the following functions will you emphasize in your design of graphics? Use the table below to help you plan.

Function	Type of Graphic to Support the Function					
Showing use of tools	☐ Screens	☐ Reports	☐ Photographs			
	☐ Drawings	☐ Charts	☐ Diagrams			
	☐ Icons	☐ Matrices	☐ Tables			
Showing results of actions	☐ Screens	☐ Reports	☐ Photographs			
	☐ Drawings	☐ Charts	☐ Diagrams			
	☐ Icons	☐ Matrices	☐ Tables			
Presenting overviews	☐ Screens	☐ Reports	☐ Photographs			
	☐ Drawings	☐ Charts	☐ Diagrams			
	☐ Icons	☐ Matrices	☐ Tables			
Suggesting functions and uses	☐ Screens	☐ Reports	☐ Photographs			
	☐ Drawings	☐ Charts	☐ Diagrams			
	☐ Icons	☐ Matrices	☐ Tables			
Making the abstract concrete	☐ Screens	☐ Reports	☐ Photographs			
	☐ Drawings	☐ Charts	☐ Diagrams			
	☐ Icons	☐ Matrices	☐ Tables			
Explaining processes	☐ Screens	☐ Reports	☐ Photographs			
	☐ Drawings	☐ Charts	☐ Diagrams			
	☐ Icons	☐ Matrices	☐ Tables			
Supporting text explanations	☐ Screens	☐ Reports	☐ Photographs			
	☐ Drawings	☐ Charts	☐ Diagrams			
	☐ Icons	☐ Matrices	☐ Tables			

Elements of Graphics

Use the list below to evaluate your designs for consistency and effectiveness.

Titles

☐ Titles numbered sequentially
☐ Numbers and titles listed in the front of the manual
☐ Titles cued by boldface or enlarging in the text

Labels

☐ Components of screens labeled to correspond with user tasks
☐ Captions kept brief
☐ Caption terminology consistent with the text

Placement

☐ Graphic frames obey the margins of the page grid

☐ Graphics assigned to a specific column or page region
☐ Graphics placed close to and following the text they relate to

Rules and Lines

☐ Rules and lines kept straight and neat
☐ Rules conform to the style of headers and other cues
☐ Rules clearly indicate hierarchies of information
☐ Greyscale rules used to save disk space and ink
☐ Rules used sparingly in help screens

Size

☐ Illustrations kept one page
☐ Oversized illustrations turned 90 degrees
☐ Pictures cropped for focus
☐ Illustrations organized around a clear hierarchy

Colors

☐ Colors related to patterns of information
☐ Colors kept in the same families of intensity: pastels, primaries, earth tones, etc.
☐ Single colors used for bleeders or cuing
☐ Reserved colors avoided

Practice/Problem Solving

1. Practice Using Different Kinds of Graphics

Find an example of a procedure in a manual or help system for a program you use. Rewrite the procedure using graphics. For example, you could choose the task of putting a disk in a computer and illustrate it in the following ways:

■ With process boxes
■ Using icons to represent the task
■ With drawings
■ With a scanned photograph

Follow the guidelines in the chapter for clear, focused graphics.

2. Make Up a Speed Box

A special form of table, the speed box accommodates the scheme of user tracking in your manual. A speed box contains definitions of special tasks or dialog boxes and abbreviated steps for using them. Speed boxes have developed out of the documenter's need to provide information for the advanced user and the novice user at the same time. Using speed boxes creates a layered effect, providing information for two kinds of user needs on the same page. Follow the example of the speed box in Chapter 8, Figure 8.10 (page 276), and create one for a task from a manual or help system you currently use.

12

Writing to Teach—
Tutorials

This chapter follows the organization of software documentation into three main levels, called *levels of support:* teaching, guidance, and reference. These levels tie in with recognized user behaviors, questions, and needs, and act as design tools. The chapter offers examples, guidelines, and discussion for design of teaching-level documents, or *tutorials.*

Like other elements of a documentation project, the form of a tutorial grows from the purpose of accommodating information to the needs of users at the ***teaching level*** of support, as opposed to the ***guidance level*** or the ***reference level.*** Remember: People tend to associate this level with novice users. But tutorials often serve as quick, first introductions to new software for experienced or advanced users. Tutorials follow principles of instruction that assume that users progress in skill and confidence with a program. With teaching, the intense contact between teacher and learner requires a different design of text and graphical information than the more distant contact in the guidance or reference forms of documentation.

This chapter covers the issue of how to select the right skills to teach and gives you an overview of some usual forms of tutorials that you will find popular among software documenters. It discusses two important ways to teach software—the elaborative and the minimalist approaches—and shows you how to design your teaching modules according to their principles.

How to Read This Chapter

As indicated earlier, this chapter forms a quartet with the last three chapters, each dealing with a prominent form of writing for task-oriented product support documents. All documentation writers need to know how to write tutorials, and, increasingly, online and demonstration-type tutorials.

■ For the project planner, this chapter can give you valuable information about tutorials as a part of the document set: how long they take, what resources they require. If you need to write a tutorial, you should at least skim the Discussion section and then follow the Guidelines. Then re-read the Discussion.

■ If you are reading for understanding, the Discussion characterizes the main trends in tutorial design and applies those trends to ways to meet user task needs.

xamples

The example in Figure 12.1 won an STC Distinguished Technical Communication Award in 1995. It illustrates the basic features of a document designed to teach software skills so that the user can perform them by memory. This chapter will show you the basics of design of this kind of documentation and also introduce you to a style of teaching that relies on principles of exploration of software.

Figure 12.2, also from the *HiQ Demonstration Guide,* illustrates the way overviews, steps, and graphics work together to help the user focus on the material of the lesson.

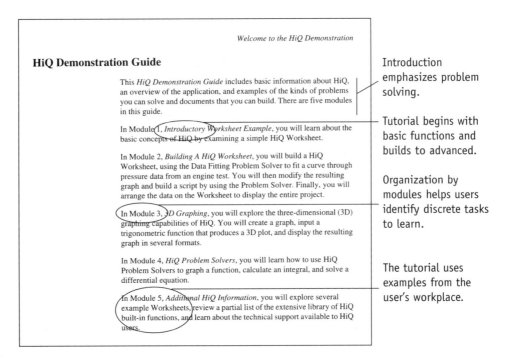

igure 12.1

Award-Winning Instructional Documentation

This award-winning example, from the HiQ *Demonstration Guide,* illustrates the organization of the direct instruction tutorial.

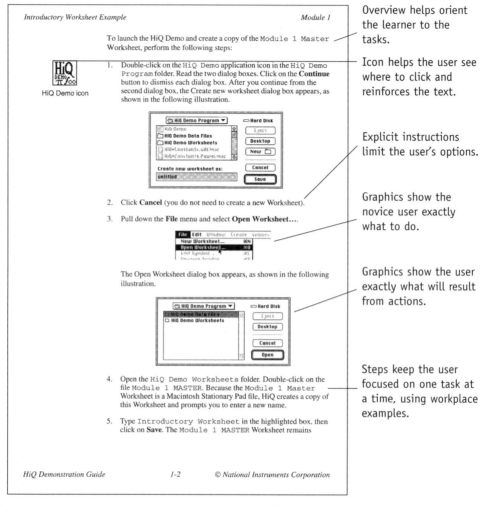

The figure contains the following annotations:

Overview helps orient the learner to the tasks.

Icon helps the user see where to click and reinforces the text.

Explicit instructions limit the user's options.

Graphics show the novice user exactly what to do.

Graphics show the user exactly what will result from actions.

Steps keep the user focused on one task at a time, using workplace examples.

The sample tutorial page reads:

Introductory Worksheet Example   *Module 1*

To launch the HiQ Demo and create a copy of the `Module 1 Master` Worksheet, perform the following steps:

HiQ Demo icon

1. Double-click on the `HiQ Demo` application icon in the `HiQ Demo Program` folder. Read the two dialog boxes. Click on the **Continue** button to dismiss each dialog box. After you continue from the second dialog box, the Create new worksheet dialog box appears, as shown in the following illustration.

2. Click **Cancel** (you do not need to create a new Worksheet).

3. Pull down the **File** menu and select **Open Worksheet...**.

The Open Worksheet dialog box appears, as shown in the following illustration.

4. Open the `HiQ Demo Worksheets` folder. Double-click on the file `Module 1 MASTER`. Because the `Module 1 Master` Worksheet is a Macintosh Stationary Pad file, HiQ creates a copy of this Worksheet and prompts you to enter a new name.

5. Type `Introductory Worksheet` in the highlighted box, then click on **Save**. The `Module 1 MASTER` Worksheet remains

HiQ Demonstration Guide   *1-2*   © *National Instruments Corporation*

Figure 12.2
Sample Tutorial Module

uidelines

Writing tutorials well takes a great deal of skill and experience with people and training situations. When trying to teach skills, you should rely on your memories of your own learning and the difficulties you had with new software, and then combine your memories with empirical observation. By following the guidelines in Figure 12.3, you can design tutorial documentation and be confident that your design follows the principles of task-oriented documentation.

1. Identify the skills you need to teach.
2. State objectives as real-world performance.
3. Choose the right type of tutorial.
4. Present skills in a logical, cumulative structure.
5. Offer highly specific instructions.
6. Give practice and feedback at each skill level.
7. Test your tutorial.

Figure 12.3

Guidelines for Designing Tutorials

1 IDENTIFY SKILLS YOU NEED TO TEACH

You should review your user analysis to help you identify what skills you need to teach. Usually you want to teach the basic features of the program, but really any of the tasks that you identify or any *scenarios* that your user would participate in make good problems for users in tutorials. Decide on what skills you want to teach. For a drawing program, for example, you might want to teach the user to operate the freehand drawing tool. With an accounting program, you might want to teach the user to post a transaction to the general ledger. Whatever tasks you select, each can only get accomplished if the user has mastered certain skills from the program: how to use menus, how to click the mouse, and how to combine program features meaningfully in the workplace.

Plan your tutorial around these tasks. For each task you will teach, list the program skills that the user needs. This list can serve as the basis of your lesson plans. Identify the commands that the user should associate with the skill and put workplace task and program skill together.

Tie Tasks to User Needs

Selecting tasks for a tutorial requires that you look over your task list (Chapter 3) and decide on which ones to treat in a tutorial. When selecting tasks, you can follow these guidelines:

- **Central to job performance.** Some tasks will relate more directly to the user's work. Look for tasks like reporting or printing, or tasks relating to your users' communication or information transfer needs. Users may also run some other key piece of software, such as a specific operating system, that they will need to integrate with your software. Users may care more and want to learn more about certain features that they perceive as essential to problem-solving on the job.

- **Essential for efficient software use.** Some tasks, like file management, security, or basic screen handling, must be taught. Teaching should acquaint users with basic concepts used in programs, such as tree structures or processing sequences.

■ **Frequency of performance.** Some tasks occur so frequently that you will want to teach them to your users. Which tasks get done hourly or daily? Also, some tasks occur within pre-set sequences, such as opening a file, entering data, processing data, printing data, and quitting the program. Users need to know tasks in these sequences by heart.

Let the Help System Detect Skill Needs

Some help programs allow the software to choose the tasks for tutorials. For example, in a drawing program, when the user moves one design object over another for the first time in the use of a piece of software, the program can detect the opportunity for a highly specific lesson. This program is *context sensitive.*

Context-sensitive programs present a task to the user reflecting some event that triggered the help driver. They should clearly show choices for the user, and keep the task simple and relevant. "Next" and "Done" buttons help the user select the pace of the tutorial, and to exit at any time. Users should also clearly see how to shut down or de-select the context-sensitive prompting for mini lessons. Users going through the learning process a second time, say, after re-installation, or who for whatever reason don't see the benefit of the help system, may not need the prompting. For the user, such an intrusion may not sit well, but, on the other hand, it offers a way to deliver highly specific information at the point of user's need.

Context-sensitive *tags* in a software program can trigger a number of help opportunities, including the following:

■ **Tips for Efficient Use.** Reminders of keyboard shortcuts, suggested filenames

■ **Cue Cards.** Brief explanations of buttons and fields, done in a memorable way

■ **Short, Animated Demonstrations.** User-paced procedures showing movement, as in the computer program performing a function for the user, who clicks on a "next" button or a "close" button when done.

■ **Trouble-shooting Tips.** Procedures offered when users perform the same, nonproductive keystrokes over and over

2 STATE OBJECTIVES AS REAL-WORLD PERFORMANCE

Write out the objectives you want your tutorial to achieve. Stating objectives in terms of performance by the user can help you plan your lessons by providing you with the bare outlines of your tutorial project. You should state the objectives of your tutorial in your documentation plan and then again in the actual lesson or tutorial help module.

Objectives should appear as skills that the user should learn as a result of the tutorial. Often objectives sound like "In Chapter X, you will learn the following skills. . . ." Tell the user what he or she will learn from the lesson. And put the objectives in measurable terms: "This lesson will teach you to create a drawing with three colors." Table 12.1 shows examples of objectives statements and corresponding summary statements.

At the end of the lesson, review the objectives and direct the user toward the next lesson. At this point, if you want, you can encourage exploration or some kind of practice.

Table 12.1

Examples of Objectives Statements

Document	Objectives Statements
HiQ Demonstration Guide	Overview Statement:

In this section you use another HiQ Problem Solver, the Ordinary Differential Equation Initial Value Problem Solver (ODEIVP), and HiQ Script to perform a dynamic system analysis. Users who are familiar with differential equations will benefit most from this section. p. 4–11

Summary Statement:

In the final section of Module 4 you used the Ordinary Differential Equation Initial Value Problem Solver to plot the oscillation patterns of a mass-spring-damper system. You also used HiQ-Script to define a forcing function to simulate an external force on the system. p. 4–20

PageMaker 4.0 Tutorial   Overview Statement:

In this session you will:

    Learn Macintosh Basics
        The Macintosh Desktop
        Windows
        Icons and File Names
        Desktop Menus
    Examine a PageMaker Document
        Open a Document
        PageMaker Menus
        Tools and Toolbox
        Revert and Close p. 1

Summary Statement:

In this session you learned to:

✓ Use the mouse and the Macintosh desktop commands to view the contents of your disks

✓ Start the PageMaker program and open a PageMaker document

✓ Use PageMaker's toolbox

✓ Use the Page menu's commands to change your view of a page

✓ Identify some of PageMaker's other commands

✓ Select a graphic object and move it

✓ Select a word within the text, type new text, delete text

✓ Use the grabber hand (option-drag) to move the page in the window

✓ Close a PageMaker file, p. 24

Always remember to get the user on track again for the next lesson: Usually you would do this by announcing "What's ahead. . . ." Notice, also, that in the examples in Table 12.1, the summary statements contain more detail than the overview statements, reflecting that the user has learned terminology in the lessons. It mentions the commands that the user learned.

To enable the user to apply the skill learned in the lesson to the workplace, you must clarify how it applies. Ensure that the objective statement clearly relates to a workplace task. Examine your user analysis for information, gathered from interviews and personal observation, about how the user would put the skills to work. You can also do this by including real-world examples, or examples that the user would understand readily. For accounting programs, for example, take the time to construct a fictional company; for office-related programs, invent a person who resembles the prototype of your user. Then, state objectives in terms of the kinds of work that this person would accomplish. For example: "This morning Deborah will use the *transrpt* command to review yesterday's transaction report and use the *newdb* command to post the debits to the general ledger."

3   CHOOSE THE RIGHT TYPE OF TUTORIAL

Tutorials come in many forms, from very brief ones to full-scale manuals, and they occur both in print and online media. I have found little consensus among writers as to terms that designate types of tutorials. Take demonstrations, for example. The example at the beginning of this section, called the *HiQ Demonstration Package,* takes over eighty pages and teaches both basic and advanced skills, whereas the demonstrations in my word processing program usually take only three or four simple screens each. The descriptions below try to follow the general trend. Use them to help you decide what kind of tutorial to develop for your program.

The Guided Tour

A guided tour presents an overview of the program features to a user unfamiliar with them. It focuses on the overall program capabilities and things like main screens and useful commands. The emphasis falls on introducing an overview of all the program can do, rather than just a few functions, as some other types of tutorials do. Usually the tour, online or print, will follow a made-up example but provide little user interaction. Like other brief forms of tutorial, the guided tour includes both information and persuasion: it tells the program features, and it also helps convince the user of the usefulness of the program.

In form, the guided tour can occur online and in print. Print guided tours consist of a booklet or section highlighting the program's prominent features. Online, the guided tour can consist of screens and message boxes explaining the prominent and useful features of the program. Some guided tours can include sound and animated figures superimposed on the screen that act as tour guides to the program.

Example of a Guided Tour: ClarisWorks **Possibilities for Business**

The six-page ClarisWorks *Possibilities for Business* booklet covers tasks users would frequently do using the ClarisWorks, spreadsheet, data analysis, word processing, and publishing package. The pages show examples of documents created by the package, and call-outs indicating the features. These call-outs tie in to the ClarisWorks manual, as in this example: "Use a line chart to show the changes in values over time" (page 5–44). This cross-referencing tells the user where to get more detailed information in the user's guide. The document covers five topics (each on a right-left, two-page spread), using the following headings:

1. Creating a Quarterly Report Is Easy
2. Maintain Up-to-Date Sales Information
3. Broadcast Product News to Your Customers
4. Publish Your Success
5. Wake Up Your Meetings

The document concludes with the following topic: "Get Going Quickly and Keep Up the Good Work," a section that highlights the other elements of the documentation set: a *Getting Started* booklet and a *Handbook* and two online documents, *ClarisWorks HyperTour* and the *ClarisWorks Help System.*

Example of a Guided Tour: MS-DOS 5-Minute Workout

The designers based MS-DOS 5-Minute Workout on the metaphor of physical exercise. The six-panel foldout contains images of a male in colorful exercise togs, a stopwatch, and exercise equipment, along with an image of a computer showing a MS-DOS screen. The five exercises include the following:

1. First put on something cool *(type dosshell at the c:\ prompt to see the new MS-DOS shell)*
2. Then stretch out *(notice that the new version allows more memory for programs)*
3. Do some jumping *(notice the task swapper allowing users to jump from one program to another)*
4. Pick up the pace *(save time using the full-screen editor)*
5. Last, warm down *(use the undelete and unformat options to secure information)*

The Demonstration

Design a demonstration when you want to illustrate some specific parts of a program, perhaps for a specific user considering a purchase, or a user wanting to learn advanced program features. Usually you use an example of the program, often a limited version of the program (one with some features locked out). Often with demonstrations the user observes passively but can choose which features to observe. Like the other shorter forms of tutorial, the demonstration both informs and persuades.

In form, the demonstration can consist of a limited version of the program and a brief print tutorial. The tutorial instructs the user in starting the program and tells the user what commands to use to perform the demonstrated procedure. Online, the demonstration shows you a procedure, allowing you to choose which procedures to see. You can link the demonstration to the help system via a button the user can press to see the command in action. This "watch while I do it for you" technique works best if you provide the user an "I've seen enough" button to allow an exit at any time. Such demonstrations represent a considerable cost in development time and disk space.

Example of a Demonstration: FrameMaker 5.0 Demonstration Disk

The FrameMaker 5.0 demonstration covers the following topics:

1. FrameMaker Demonstration

2. FrameMaker in Different Industries

3. User's and Expert's Evaluation

4. Key Features Summary (with capability to print summary)

5. How to Find Out More or Purchase FrameMaker Products

This demonstration consists of brief sentences in large type, scrolled on the screen in a text box. The screens, with example documents, appear in the background. The user can choose which features to see demonstrated and watch as the cursor does its work, formatting paragraphs and performing other tasks. Writing such a demonstration requires that you keep the text to a minimum and identify only key tasks to present. However, this kind of tutorial, as well as the guided tour, allows you to point out important workplace applications of your software. For example, in the FrameMaker demo, the second section, FrameMaker in Different Industries, contains application suggestions in a variety of settings, including education, finance, and manufacturing.

The Quick Start

Quick start tutorials differ from the previous two forms in important ways. Write quick start tutorials for experienced to advanced users who want to get going with a program, who want to explore. Quick start tutorials involve significant user interaction with the program itself, and rarely use examples. They help users get down to work without going into complicated configuration procedures. They cover basic and advanced procedures, kind of like a survival kit for impatient users.

In form, quick start tutorials consist of one-page or folded cards that explain how to start the program and list a sampling of commands. Often they will include a labeled main screen and tables of commands. They differ from command summary cards and quick reference cards because of the steps they include for starting the program and executing basic functions.

Example: CompuServe Navigator Windows Version Quick Start

This six-page tri-fold brochure instructs the user in the four basic steps in using Navigator:

1. Locate the CompuServe services to access.

2. Define the tasks to complete the specified services.

3. Run your Navigator script.

4. Review the information that was retrieved.

The brochure then folds out to show steps, tips, and labeled screens teaching the user these basic program functions.

Unlike the two previous forms of tutorial discussed above, the quick start expects the user to interact with the program, starting the operating system, inserting the disk, starting the program, and so forth. I particularly like the way this quick start brochure emphasizes information tasks, as in the following example: "Scripts can be saved and run again at later times for instant retrieval of the information that is important to you" (p. 4). The card ends on a last panel by offering "Navigator Assistance," telling the user where to get online help, documentation, and customer service.

The Guided Exploration

Guided explorations consist of a special, well-researched form of tutorial based on the idea that users need to control the learning experience. Like the demonstration, it may use a limited version of the program, but one with possible errors blocked so that the user can't make serious errors. Also, these kinds of explorations contain, as you might expect, instructions for the user to "try out" commands. Instructions like these encourage exploration of the program, but don't limit the user as to exactly what to do. Freedom from these limits helps give control over the learning experience to the user. To give the experience over to the user, the guided exploration contains little discussion. Omitting discussion helps relieve the user's fear of wasting time. For a further discussion of guided explorations, read the section on "minimalist tutorials" later in this chapter.

Guided explorations usually take the form of short tutorial manuals. They may or may not provide scenarios (examples for the user to follow). They may include objectives and summaries to help give the user direction, but do not constrain the user to learning specific commands. This lack of constraint allows the user to learn functions and commands that relate specifically to his or her needs.

Example of a Guided Exploration: HyperCard Basics Manual

This thirty-three-page tutorial follows the principles of guided explorations. In a way, I think this type of tutorial makes sense for a program like HyperCard because the program uses an intuitive interface. Such an interface encourages the user to navigate the program with little outside help. Designed to teach the user HyperCard, the tutorial covers the following topics:

- Install and start using HyperCard.
- Look through HyperCard stacks.
- Create places to hold new information.
- Edit text on *cards* (the HyperCard basic unit of information).
- Search for information.
- Print information.

The tutorial encourages users to explore with the program by using statements like this: "You'll probably find it just as easy to create new cards and then type the new information on them. Try it now and see how it works" (p. 9). It also contains statements like the following to help the user avoid errors while exploring: "Before you print: Make sure you've chosen a printer in the Chooser and have checked the settings in the Page Setup dialog box (the Page Setup command is in the File menu)" (page 16). By encouraging exploration, helping the user avoid errors, and keeping things brief, the manual provides a challenging learning experience for the user.

The Instruction Manual

The instructional manual focuses on users who intend to operate a program or expect to have to learn a number of complicated commands and functions. The most traditional type of tutorial, the instruction manual consists of lessons bounded by elaborate objective and summary statements. Each lesson focuses specifically on these objectives, usually tied in with specific command sets. This type of teaching also relies on the principle of accumulative learning: the idea that you have to learn one skill before you take on another, more advanced one. Like the other forms of tutorials, it focuses on basic program features, at least at first, and then advanced ones. Program features (from the program task list) take the form of lessons or modules, each about the same time length. This kind of tutorial contains a great deal of user interaction, but not as much as the guided exploration. Often modules or lessons will contain practice sessions and/or evaluations or tests to see if the user learned the material. You can find out more about direct instruction, the basic principle behind instruction manuals, by reading the section on elaborative tutorials later in this chapter.

In form, direct instruction tutorials take the form of a separate tutorial manual or section of a manual. Additionally, you may want to develop teacher's materials (overheads, lesson plans) and student's materials (worksheets, job sheets, notebooks, tests) for use in a classroom environment. The manual usually follows scenarios or presents problems for users to solve, so you may have to develop sample data sets, documents, templates, databases, or other elements the program requires for working. For instance, I once wrote a tutorial for an accounting program that used a fictitious company—ABC Lumber Co.— as an example. The learner took on the role of bookkeeper for the company.

Example: LabVIEW for Windows Tutorial

This unusually long, 190-page tutorial covers many of the features of this "feature-rich" program. Each chapter begins with a list in a box indicating what the user will learn. For instance, for the first chapter the tutorial announces the following objectives:

> **You Will Learn:**
>
> What LabVIEW is.
>
> What a Virtual Instrument (VI) is.
>
> How to use the LabVIEW environment (windows, menus, and tools).
>
> How to operate Virtual Instruments.
>
> How to edit Virtual Instruments.
>
> How to create Virtual Instruments. (page 1-1)

The steps instruct the user to call up example files and demonstration data sets that show the program functions on data that the tutorial designers included with the program. Each chapter ends with a summary that reiterates the knowledge covered in each chapter. The following excerpt comes from the summary for "Chapter 1, Introduction":

> Virtual instruments (VIs) have three main parts: the front panel, the block diagram, and the icon/connector. The front panel specifies the inputs and outputs of the VI.

The block diagram is the executable code that you create using notes, terminals, and wires. With the icon/connector, you can use a VI as a subVI in the block diagram of another VI. (page 1–27)

As you can see, this summary elaborates on the skills the user has learned, using concepts covered in the lessons. This kind of tutorial represents a full-blown effort to teach as much of the program as possible. It uses all the characteristics of direct instruction discussed below.

4   PRESENT SKILLS IN A LOGICAL, CUMULATIVE STRUCTURE

In Guidelines 1 and 2 you saw how you need to articulate the program features in the form of instructional objectives, and how to tie these to the relevant tasks in the program task list. However, the job of designing tutorials requires that you next assemble the tasks in a logical order of lessons.

The most important source for your decisions about structure will come from the typical-use scenario, or some other user activity that you think most likely resembles the task that most users would perform. This scenario you support with your tutorial. Examples of typical-use scenarios include a student typing a paper, a clerk calling up a record to check for payment of a bill, or a salesperson checking the computer for the availability of an inventory item. All of these scenarios require different tasks or features of their respective programs. For the word processing scenario, for example, you might need these tasks: opening a document file, typing in text, editing the text, saving the file, and printing the file. For the accounting program scenario you might need these tasks: looking up a record, checking the appropriate screen for payment, closing the screen, and printing an invoice for the customer.

Some logical or cumulative structures include the following: beginning to advanced, simple to complex, generalized to specialized, input/accumulating data to output/reporting data, starting a session to ending a session, using default options to using customized options, working with text to working with graphics.

After you have articulated the goals of the instruction and linked it to real-world task situations, you can proceed to select illustrations and write the instructions.

5   OFFER HIGHLY SPECIFIC INSTRUCTIONS

Your instructions or lessons should focus on a specific *scenario* or problem that the user would recognize. It should include details, such as what data to plot, or what names and addresses to type in or look for. This way you help the user stay focused on the task. During your user analysis, look out for examples that you can use as a mock-up for particular tutorials. You may find yourself tempted to use generic instructions, such as asking your user to "Enter a name" or "Enter a number." These don't work nearly as well as "Enter 'Zachary Poole' " or "Enter '11786'." These details give a realism to your instructions that work better than phony-sounding details like "Enter 'Any Person' " or "Enter '12345'."

Often learners of software programs feel insecure about the new program they're learning. They may think they will break some hardware or lose some data. They may feel anxiety because they see time spent learning software as time spent away from their job. They may feel that having to go to a class or learn a new system may make them look stupid or ignorant. Because of these anxieties surrounding learning new software, you want to do all you can to help users maintain focus. If you tell them to "type something" they may lose focus or may just get stuck trying to think of something to type. Keep them on track with specific instructions, such as the following:

- **Specific data.** Numbers, names, words, variables, formulas, search strings, customer names, client names, addresses, dates, filenames, directory names, times, printer names, printer port names, sizes, protocols, email addresses, IPX addresses, ISBN numbers.

- **Tools.** Mouse buttons, keyboard keys and key sequences, buttons, icons, check boxes, directional arrows, hot spots, hypertext links, radio buttons, toggles, list boxes, spin boxes.

- **Screens.** Mouse selection screens, result screens, icons, menu selections, highlighted areas, data fields.

- **Commands.** Control commands, alt commands, line commands, keyboard shortcuts, macro names, escape sequences, function keys.

Avoid distractions that could cause the learner to lose concentration. Make sure you carefully edit your screens to eliminate any extraneous images, extra files, extra menu items, other disk icons—all the stuff that can distract your user. Do what you can to not draw attention to details of page design.

You may want to review the prescriptions for designing illustrations for tutorials in Chapter 7. Depending on your user's skill level, you may want to include screens showing tool use and screens showing results. Omit tables of alternative keystroke options, as these may dissipate your user's attention span. Keep the illustrations close to the steps so the user can see the knotless connection between them.

6   GIVE PRACTICE AND FEEDBACK AT EACH SKILL LEVEL

Like all good teaching, the completion of a lesson by the student should result in praise and reward. Do this in a tone of what interviewers call an "unconditional positive regard." Imagine that the user always has patience, imagination, and a pleasant disposition. State goals positively, instead of negatively, and avoid controversial jargon. Remind the user of the reward for understanding and correct performance (a new skill or job capacity), or use the conclusion of the lesson to help you establish a feeling of goodwill. The TC8215 Sectra Management System for Windows *User's Guide* establishes a feeling of goodwill in the following way: "This is the end of the Console program guided tour. Thanks for coming and we hope you enjoy the rest of your trip!" (p. 2–18).

You may use the "we" pronoun—as well as the "you"—liberally, to reinforce the performance orientation. Also, contractions add a colloquial tone. They can help a novice user relax, and they give breathing room around difficult concepts the user encounters for the first time. Again, the TC8215 Sectra Management System for Windows *User's Guide* (explaining how to create program objects manually) states: "The advantage of this method is that it lets you create objects you know about (and that's your job, right?) so you can get started managing them right away" (p. 2–8).

Imagine you can lean over the user's shoulder and point to the screen. Say things like "Notice that the text has turned gray, indicating that you have already chosen it" or "See how the icon changes from open to closed when you click on the *close* box." Let this imaginary posture of helpful teacher help you find ways to guide the reader's attention on the screen as he or she follows the steps on the page or examines a screen to see if the steps worked.

Build a Pattern of Exposition

Remember, too, to build in a pattern of exposition, whereby you repeat the following rhythm (or something like it):

1. **Give the tool and the action.** "Use the mouse to select Open . . . from the file menu."

2. **Explain the result.** "The program will display an empty file."

Spend your time explaining the result, and avoid giving alternative advice, as in "You could have also used the keyboard to. . . ." Alternative advice, as an *elaboration* in software tutorials, tends to distract the user from the task. Key the user to the screen and where to look.

Sometimes you can give practice and feedback by including exercises in your lessons. These exercises, if you design them realistically, can give your user the kind of freedom to experiment that adult learners like. As for feedback, you might try including a quiz or question-and-answer list that reinforces the main points of the lesson. Don't forget, if you find yourself writing many lessons, to let the user know when to take a break.

Pace the Tutorial

When you put your tutorial together, consider that you don't want to waste your user's time. Neither do you want to waste yours, given the high cost of developing tutorials. Try not to take the user away from the job for more than an hour at a time, and expect that they won't have even that much time to give. Keep the lessons down to about ten to twelve minutes each. That enables the user to maintain concentration during a lesson. Also, consider that busy professionals may get called away during a training session or may only have a limited time to devote to learning each day. So give them a chance to quit during the tutorial and show them how to quit the program without losing data and having to restart later.

7   TEST YOUR TUTORIAL

Your tutorial, like other documentation products, should get a thorough session in the testing lab, whether you use a fancy, well-designed lab with recording equipment and a coffee machine, or simply the user's environment (where possible). You should base your testing on the objectives of the tutorial. (Chapter 6, "Conducting Usability Tests," has information on specific ways to design your test.) But you should keep testing in mind during your planning stages and watch out for points you will want to verify through testing.

Design your test by determining whether you will test the entire tutorial, or just parts. Probably you can only test parts: besides, you get diminishing returns if you spend too much hard work testing. Design the test, also, to focus, as much as possible, on the design elements: the *cuing system,* the effectiveness of the graphics, the pace, or style of writing steps. Get feedback on the tone if you allow yourself some humor. Above all, find out if you can count on your lessons to get the user from point A of ignorance to point B of skill mastery, in the allotted time using the instruction you provided. When you can, try out the tutorial and revise it based on results. If you don't have a real user of the program at your disposal, do your best to mock-up the situation with someone of similar background as the users.

Discussion

This section will present the elements of tutorials, followed by a close examination of two philosophies of teaching: the *elaborative approach* and the *minimalist approach*. Finally, we will examine design guidelines for each approach.

Designing Tutorials

When you set out to design and write tutorial documentation, you should start with the knowledge of how tutorials work and when your particular users need them. Because not all documentation sets contain tutorials, you should know when to use this form of documentation, and when to apply others. This section will help you make that decision by examining some of the basic elements of tutorials.

Intention to Teach

With tutorial documentation you should intend for the user to internalize certain skills or concepts about a program. You want the user not only to gain a familiarity with skills but also to remember them and perform them later from memory—a tall order. Documentation like this operates on the teaching level of task orientation, meaning that often you must create a close relationship between the *persona* of the writer and the reader.

But most of all, you try to limit the awareness of the user, so that he or she can focus only on the steps discussed in the lessons. In other forms of documentation, you try to expand the user's awareness—of options, alternatives, short cuts—but in tutorials you limit the user's awareness to one way, one option, one skill. This takes a great deal of control and structuring of the user's interaction with the material.

Selectivity in Choosing Material

Clearly you can not *teach* all the functions of a software program. To do so would take many books, given the fact that tutorial documentation takes up more space, usually, than documentation at other levels of task orientation. This need for selectivity means that you must know your users very well. You should know which essential tasks need learning and which don't. Usually you can only afford to teach the essential ones: the others, well, the user has to get them somewhere else.

To select material wisely, you should first do a thorough user analysis. The user analysis first narrows down the field of all users to potential users, then to user types, then to usual scenarios of use of the program, and finally to the *typical-use scenario*. The typical-use scenario represents the fundamental tasks of them all—the ones that probably would get performed most often. If you have done your user analysis well, then you can design a tutorial around these tasks.

Stand-Alone Design

Judith Crandall makes a point that all tutorial designers should remember: Often users only have the tutorial section to rely on to learn a program. They do not have teachers or other advisors: The documentation has to do the work of these. Such "self instructional" documentation, says Crandall, should take the place of teacher, textbook, workbook, lectures, question-and-answer session—all the usual elements of the teaching environment. The tutorial sections of the manual become the teaching environment.[2]

Tutorial Users Need Special Care and Feeding

A number of studies of tutorial users show us that they often require special considerations, mostly because, as adults, they have special learning styles. For example, most adult learners are oriented toward goals: They want to know why they have to learn something and what good it will do them. Also, they like to have control of their learning. Adults like to think of themselves as self-motivated and self-assured, not as ignorant bumblers. They do not like to make mistakes and often do not realize the value of making mistakes in the learning process.

The more we know about these styles, the better we can design effective documentation for them. This presents design challenges for the software documenter, because to build task analysis into tutorial documentation means that you have to accommodate the learning styles of a specific population. The designer needs to know how to build tutorial modules that avoid public display of a user's mistakes, limit the lesson times, give positive feedback and reinforcement, and also imbue a sense of self-direction in the steps. You can accomplish this by studying carefully how you learn programs, and how others do, and by applying the principles of task analysis to the documentation situation.

The first step in your study of tutorial design begins with an awareness of the two trends in tutorial design that have grown in the United States during the last decade: the elaborative approach and the minimalist approach. In the area of document design, these two approaches fall at opposite ends of a spectrum of information design ideas. In many ways, document design is a matter of determining more or less information in a document, and these two approaches represent major trends based on either of those poles. Each of the two approaches described below represents different philosophies of learning. The discussion attempts to bring out the task-oriented characteristics of each so you can make informed design decisions based on your user's characteristics and workplace tasks.

The Elaborative Approach

Research supporting the elaborative approach answers "yes" to the question "Does elaboration improve retention of skills in software manuals?" Elaboration includes summaries, explanations, examples, articulations of goals and objectives. Elaboration also includes elements of good storytelling, the ability to describe a scenario carefully, and the ability to pace, in measured steps, the user's progress through highly technical material and to make it stick.

The elaborative approach responds to the needs of the new-to-computers user: not the engineer who needed referential documentation, but the person from a noncomputer background who needs a highly structured, skill-oriented approach. Indeed, the skill orientation of the elaborative approach should make the designer pay attention to its principles. Task orientation, the emphasis taken in this book, highly values any structure that assists the designer in building performance elements into documentation. We have something to learn from the elaborative approach.

The elaborative approach borrows elements of instructional principles from the field of instructional design, as a way of approaching the problem of teaching foreign, often abstract and highly technical material. Other researchers have studied the effectiveness of the *direct instructional* or *elaborative approach* to manual design and have also discovered how computer manual users learn.

Among the foremost researchers of elaborations in tutorials, Davida Charney and Lynn Redder[1] have studied the effects of elaborative elements in software manuals and found that while sometimes summaries and overviews distract the user from focusing on information, these elaborative elements helped them *apply* their tasks to real-world situations. Elaborative elements help the readers see how the program could help them perform more efficiently in their jobs. They also found that people learn skills in complex ways. Some characteristics of their learning of skills, such as how they understand procedures versus how they understand concepts, makes summaries useful at certain times and not as useful at others.

Elaboration serves your purpose in tutorial documentation when you have abstract concepts to teach and the user is encountering a basic idea for the first time. Elaboration helps users learn to apply certain functions of the program. On the other hand, when you must concentrate on teaching procedures—steps for performance—elaborations in the form of examples and accurate *notational conventions* work best. In particular, research seems to indicate that when you use elaborations, lots of examples, tables of commands, and so forth, you should use them in conjunction with accurately designed steps.

Finally, you should always consider using the elaborative approach with novice users who know little about computers or your program. These users have a much more difficult time experimenting and need more guidance than more advanced users. Besides, they need specific guidance in applying tasks; they lack the experience to make the connections themselves.

The design of the elaborative manual follows the traditional principles of lesson design:

1. Instruction results in articulated skills.

2. Skills transfer capability to real-world performance.

3. Steps should present skills in a logical, cumulative structure.

4. Highly specific instructions work best.

5. Give practice and feedback at each skill level.

6. Master one skill before going on to the next.[2]

The Minimalist Approach

We noted earlier that the minimalist structure takes what some see as a *realistic* view of human behavior. In the research that supports this approach, we find this realistic view reflected in the kinds of sobering observations made about user behavior. Minimalist principles assert that people learn on a concrete plane. In this approach, less means more: out go the introductions and the reviews. Let's explore this approach more closely to see how minimalist ideas can contribute to the design of a task-oriented manual.

Observations of Software Users

Researcher John Carroll[3] explored the ways people learn software programs. He makes the following observations about user behavior:

1. **Users jump the gun.** From the work Carroll and others have done, it appears that users of computer manuals like to get started right away with a program and will resist reading information designed to introduce or orient. They want to see results from a new program, and will not read the manual first. They will use the program first.

2. **Users will skip information.** Users will rarely read the introduction to a manual. Carroll relates an interesting anecdote in which a researcher observed that a user flipped quickly through the first pages of a manual. The user decided that part could be skipped "because it's just information." Such a casual approach seems incongruous with life in the "information age." But on the other hand, we want relevant information and have learned to tell the useful from all the rest. So in that case, the casualness of the user makes sense.

3. **Users like to lead.** Users like to create their own perspectives on their training. Carroll found that when you ask learners of a word processing program, for example, to type whatever sample document they want, they may not always pick the job-related option of a memo. Instead, he found that many computer learners would prefer to write a letter to their mom. Users, adult learners most of the time, like to take charge of situations, they like the control and don't like manipulative instructional strategies.

The Principles of Minimalist Design

These and other observations about how users react to traditional learning materials makes common sense, and they present design challenges to software documenters. Rising to the occasion, Carroll has devised the minimalist approach, which grows in popularity among software documenters.

The minimalist manual teaches by following some basic principles: Slash the verbiage, encourage exploration, and support error recovery. The psychology dictates that these three principles will help the user focus better on information, allowing him or her to try out the program and get out of trouble when needed.

FOCUS ON REAL TASKS AND ACTIVITIES. The need to focus on real tasks and activities may seem obvious to you, having read some of the previous chapters of this book which emphasizes the task as the basic building block of successful documentation. But the reason for that focus comes partly from the observation that readers prefer to do something with a piece of software rather than learn about it. If they perceive that the tutorial focuses them on the system of teaching, the highly structured nature of the traditional elaboration, they often will try to subvert the tutorial. They want to type the letter to mom or supply their own example for the tutorial.

SLASH THE VERBIAGE. As far as the *minimalist* designer of tutorials cares, the elaborative manual resembles the long-haired recruit getting a haircut at the army induction station. The introductions, overviews, illustrative examples, statements of objectives, double-checks, exercises, and practice sessions get swept out like curls on the barber's floor. As far as language goes, the minimalist manual sounds lean and mean. But it may gain in brevity. Some have suggested that all introductions go, because the user doesn't read them anyway. A minimalist manual may have as few as three pages in a chapter. This extreme economy of language accommodates the often-impatient user.

ENCOURAGE EXPLORATION. People have a natural human tendency to want to try things out, so software use is unpredictable. Computer users, especially those who have to take time away from their jobs to learn a new program, like to go their own way. The minimalist model capitalizes on this explorative and unpredictable impulse. Minimalist tutorials, instead of having a practice session at the end of a lesson, encourage practice as the main way of learning all the way along. They suggest that the user "try it out." People often try out products before they read the manual anyway. "As a last resort," they say, "read the instructions." They want to know what's inside the box, what they can do with their new toy or tool, what happens if they press *this* key. To the extent that your users would feel this natural curiosity, this drive to try out the computer program, you should consider encouraging exploration with program features.

But the documenter must make sure that the exploration leads in the right direction. Real-world tasks can guide the user in this effort. The user analysis proves invaluable here, to the extent that it includes descriptions of what users really do in the workplace from a nonautomated perspective. The designer of tutorials should study the work which the program will eventually support. The tasks that make up this work also make up the goals, the direction, provided by guided exploration.

SUPPORT ERROR RECOVERY. It should come as no secret to you that we learn by making mistakes. The progress from ignorance and ineptitude to awareness and skill necessarily seems to involve trying out a solution, failing, and trying again. This happens no matter how carefully we plan our actions or choose a possible solution. The direct, elaborative approach to teaching accommodates this tendency to make mistakes by minimizing it. Directly instructional materials do not allow us to make mistakes. Instead they carefully guide the learner around the mistakes to the desired goal. The indirect method used in minimalist manuals, by following the strategy of exploration, leads to mistakes, almost encourages them. For many learners, exploration leads to a delightful serendipity—a learning of unexpected things. Learning like this sticks with the student. It also leads to mistakes: a necessary part of exploring.

If you design minimalist approaches to information, you need to make it easy for the user to get out of trouble. Study the user, and learn where mistakes can and probably will occur. Many mistakes arise from users trying to apply principles from their noncomputerized way of doing things (for instance, the fear that the computer will lose data permanently) or their application of techniques from other programs (for instance, pressing the F1 key for "help," only to find that it means "cancel the operation"). Sometimes users make errors because they simply lack practice with nonintuitive elements of systems, such as awkward header and footer commands in word processing programs. Whatever the cause of errors, in writing the minimalist tutorial, you should find out the kind of errors a user most likely will make (or which ones the procedure may lead to) and include information for recovering from mistakes. Turn the user loose, but give the steps to recover.

Carroll calls this technique the "training wheels" technique. On your first bike, the training wheels allowed you to take off down the street, but they caught you in case of a mistake. Usually you can catch and avert potential errors simply by including a statement like this: "If you make a mistake typing, use the backspace key." You can also give reassurance: "You can always restart the system without damaging the data."

Depending on your user's needs and learning preferences, you may decide to use either an elaborative or minimalist tutorial, or to create a hybrid of the two. Table 12.2 lists some of the issues you might consider in such a decision.

Table 12.2

Comparing the Elaborative and Minimalist Approaches

Criterion	Elaborative	Minimalist
Uses	Programs with highly abstract concepts, complicated procedures, large systems	Getting started booklets, guided tours, demos, programs with intuitive interfaces, programs requiring creativity by the user
Advantages	Good for users who like structure, first-time users, traditional	Cuts writing time, document length, interesting
Disadvantages	Limits documenter to one or two scenarios, boring	May frustrate the first-time user, may backfire, increases testing time

Glossary

context sensitive: refers to the capacity of a help system to detect what interface element (menu screen or dialog box) the program currently displays and to provide a help screen appropriate for that element. With this system the user doesn't have to ask for a specific topic, but is presented the topic appropriate to the current situation (hence "context").

cuing system: refers to the pattern you establish of formatting or other noticeable change to signal a specific type of information. Usually you use boldface, italics, or all caps to cue items such as steps, numbers, commands, menu items, and so forth. In this book, for example, glossary entries are cued with boldface italics (*like this*). When you see a word in boldface italics you know you can look it up in the glossary.

direct instruction: an approach very similar to the elaborative approach in teaching.

elaborative approach: a more-or-less traditional approach to teaching software skills relying on a strict focus on a mocked-up scenario and tight control over the user's actions. It contrasts with the minimalist approach that encourages exploration and user control of learning.

elaboration: refers to explanations of steps in procedures or tutorials. Usually one or two sentences in length, elaborations give further details, explanations of why things happen, results, and other information.

guidance level: a type of documentation designed to lead the user through a procedure one step at a time from a designated starting place (such as a certain menu) to an ending state (such as a printed report). Guidance level documentation (or procedures) defines the task for the user, but does not teach the task. See also **teaching level** and **support level.**

levels of support: categories of information supplied to users. Levels relate to the *teaching* level (tutorial), the *guidance* level (procedures) and the *reference* level (reference). Levels differ in terms of purpose: to teach, to walk through step-by-step, and to provide data. They also differ in the relationship of the writer to the user: from very close and controlling (with the teaching level), to distant and business-like (with the reference level).

minimalist approach: an approach to teaching software skills that relies on encouraging exploration and giving control of the learning to the user. It contrasts with the elaborative approach that emphasizes a focus on a mocked-up scenario and a tight control over the user's actions.

notational conventions: conventions relating to how terms, commands, menus, and other interface elements appear in a manual. For example, often manuals will use italics (as in *dir, copy*) as the notational convention for commands.

persona: the character of the writer as portrayed in the language and tone of the documentation. In teaching documentation the writer may assume the persona of a counselor or teacher. In guidance documentation the writer may assume the persona of a colleague. The writer often does not assume a persona in reference documentation, depending on it does on the orderly presentation of data more than a relationship between the writer and the reader.

scenario: a story or narrative describing the kinds of activities a user would undergo in using a program. Example: Sloane would open the word processor, open the daily report, edit it for new transaction, save the daily report, and print the daily report. These events make up a scenario.

reference level: a type of documentation intended to provide the user with a piece of information needed to perform a task. Reference documentation does not define the task for the user, but provides the necessary data the user needs to complete a task. See **guidance level** and **teaching level.**

teaching level: a type of documentation intended to instill a knowledge of how to use a program feature in the memory of the user. Teaching level documentation (tutorials) aims to enable the user to perform a task from memory. See **guidance level** and **support level.**

typical-use scenario: a description of the most usual task or tasks that a user would perform with a program. It often forms the core of a tutorial project. For example: a typical-use scenario for a word processing program would entail opening a file, typing, formatting, saving, and closing the file.

tags: tags refers to words or phrases inserted into a computer program that relate to specific help topics. When the user calls for help at a point within the program, the program reads the tag and presents the appropriate topic to the user as a help screen.

Checklist ✓

Use the following checklist as a way to evaluate your tutorial design. Depending on the kind of tutorial you have and your users, some of these items may not apply.

Tutorial Design Checklist
Identifying Skills to Teach

☐ Do the tasks you wish to teach relate closely to the users' critical job tasks?
☐ Do the tasks you wish to teach relate to efficient use of the program?
☐ Will the user perform the tutorial tasks frequently?
☐ Do you have the option of letting the help system detect skill needs through context sensitivity?

Identifying Objectives

☐ Do you state the teaching objectives in terms of real-world performance?

Choosing the Right Type of Tutorial

Which of the following types best fits your users needs for efficient and effective software use?

☐ The Guided Tour
☐ The Demonstration
☐ The Quick Start
☐ The Guided Exploration
☐ The Instruction Manual

Presenting Skills in a Logical, Cumulative Structure

Which of the following orders best suits your users?

- ☐ Beginning to advanced
- ☐ Simple to complex
- ☐ General to specific
- ☐ Input of data to output of data

- ☐ Starting to using to ending a session
- ☐ Using defaults to using custom options
- ☐ Working with [topic 1 of 2] to working with [topic 2 of 2]

Specificity of Instructions

Which of the following specific details do you intend to include in your tutorial exercises?

- ☐ Specific data
- ☐ Specific tools

- ☐ Screens
- ☐ Commands

Practice and Feedback

- ☐ Do you give practice and feedback, where appropriate, at each skill level?
- ☐ Have you paced the tutorial to match the users' concentration level and work requirements?

Testing

- ☐ Have you chosen a test site (lab, users' environment)?
- ☐ Have you decided on the most relevant test points for your tutorial?
- ☐ cuing system
- ☐ suitability of details (scenario, tools, screens, commands)
- ☐ pace
- ☐ users' familiarity with the form

Elaborative Tutorials

If you choose to design an elaborative tutorial, does it follow the principles of this type of teaching?

- ☐ Instruction results in articulated skills
- ☐ Skills transfer capability to real-world performance
- ☐ Steps should present skills in a logical, cumulative structure
- ☐ Highly specific instructions work best
- ☐ Give practice and feedback at each skill level
- ☐ Master one skill before going on to the next

Minimalist Tutorials

If you choose to design a minimalist tutorial, does it follow the principles of this type of teaching?

- ☐ Focus on real tasks and activities
- ☐ Slash the verbiage

- ☐ Encourage exploration
- ☐ Support error recovery

Practice/Problem Solving

1. Analyze a Tutorial

You work for a medical office that wants to buying a new word processor for use by secretaries, doctors, and nurses at the office. The committee working on the choice has a number of problems to face in choosing just the right system, including the problem of training. How will they learn the new system?

The committee has turned to you, the resident expert on training, for help. They would like you to analyze two word processing packages (you pick which two) in terms of their training. Analyze the tutorial material accompanying both programs. Compare the differences between the tutorials you find, and recommend the one that you think will provide the least difficulty of leaning. Remember: Justify your choice in terms of the tutorial, not the inherent ease of use of the program.

2. Analyze a Task List

Examine the following task list and identify three elements for each task: 1) importance to job performance, 2) importance to efficient software use, and 3) frequency of performance. Use the grid on page 418 to analyze the task list.

- Put a $\sqrt{}$ + for highly important to job performance, a $\sqrt{}$ for useful but not critical, and an ✗ for not important to job performance.
- Put a $\sqrt{}$ + for highly important to efficient software use, a $\sqrt{}$ for useful but not critical to efficient software use, and an ✗ for not important to efficient software use.
- Put a $\sqrt{}$ + for used very frequently, a $\sqrt{}$ for used frequently, and an ✗ for used infrequently.

Use your analysis to reorganize the list of tasks from most likely candidates for a tutorial to least likely candidates for a tutorial. In a brief report, describe the contents of the tutorial you would create for the program and justify your design. What tasks will you include, and which would you leave out? What purpose does your tutorial fulfill? What does it offer users that makes it worth their while to use it?

Program: *StampView*—a program to record, sort, and maintain large stamp collections for professional collectors and stamp store owners.

User: A manager/owner of a hobby store specializing in stamps and rare baseball cards. The owner the program to record new trades and purchases, to find specific stamps for customers, and to calculate the value of the total collection for tax purposes.

3. Analyze Elaborate versus Minimal Methods

Imagine that you work for a publications department in a software development organization called Software Associates. They have come out with a new line of intermediate

Task Name	Importance to Job Performance	Importance to Software Efficiency	Frequency of Performance
Create new file	✕	✓	✓ +
Open File	✕	✕	✓ +
Save File			
Update record			
Import data from a spreadsheet	✓	✓ +	✕
Add new record			
Find existing record			
Scroll through records			
Exit update			
Change record			
Print all records			
Print individual record			
Delete record			
Sort records			
Pack records			
List records			
Analyze records			
Set up customized search macros			
Customize StampView screen			
Exit StampView			

user software and they want to do some predevelopment thinking on how to handle training for the new programs. To this end, they have asked you, as a person who would possibly develop the materials, to do some thinking about one of the programs, and tell the committee what you think. Should they go elaborate or minimal?

Follow these directions to prepare your thinking, then put together a brief recommendation report based on your findings.

1. Identify three and *only* three job-critical tasks that you would support in tutorial for *one* of the following programs:
   - A modem/fax/voice-mail program called ModemMaster that operates on a business PC server. User: Traveling sales associates with laptops.

- A dialup tracking program for a national chain of rental trucks called RoadWarrior. User: Franchise customer representatives at remote offices.
- A program to manage timed and scored athletic events called RodeoBoss. User: Officials at collegiate and professional rodeo events.

2. Pick one of the programs and users and briefly write down your justification of your choice of tasks.

3. Then brainstorm how you would develop the tasks into a tutorial using both the elaborative approach and the minimalist approach. You may have to make up or imagine some of the details of the programs, their users, and the environments in which you want to make them effective.

You can use the worksheet provided to record your ideas.

Elaborate vs. Minimalist Analysis Worksheet

Program name:

Three most job-critical tasks:

Justification for picking these tasks:

Elaborate Method (intro. and lessons with mock data)

List the *program skills* the user will need to know to perform these tasks.

List the *objectives* of the lessons.

Evaluate the elaborate approach (for this case).
   Strengths: Weaknesses:

Minimalist (hands-on exploration)

List the skill objectives the user should attain.

List the points the tutorial would explore:

Evaluate the minimalist approach (for this case).
   Strengths: Weaknesses:

Recommendation

Which treatment (elaborate or minimal) do you think would work best in this case?

---

4. Revise the Objectives Statements

The following objective statement contains all the information required to introduce a tutorial lesson for the program PhotoBase, used by scientific users to record and analyze photographs of museum specimens. Rewrite it using a user orientation, emphasizing the terms the user should know by the end of the lesson, and the commands the user will master. Make whatever format and content revisions (you may have to make up some details) that you need in order to make an effective overview.

> THE PROGRAM REQUIRES FAMILIARITY WITH REGISTRATION, THRESHOLD, STABILITY POINTS, QUARTERTONE CALIBRATION, AND DITHER TABLES. THIS CHAPTER PRESENTS SEVERAL METHODS OF DATA INPUT FOR DEVELOPING A PHOTOBASE DATABASE. DATA DEVELOPMENT (MOSTLY DIGITIZING) REPRESENTS BETWEEN 75% AND 95% OF THE TIME SPENT USING PHOTOBASE. THE FIRST EXERCISE WILL BE FOCUSED ON DIGITIZING. FOR MAXIMUM DIGITIZATION ACCURACY SEVERAL DIGITIZING METHODS DISCUSSED IN THIS CHAPTER SHOULD BE USED. THE SUBPROGRAM *DDRIVER* MUST BE MASTERED. THE COMMANDS USED IN DIGITIZING ARE: PB.STAB, PB.QUART, PB.IMPORT, PB.EXPORT, PB.VECTORSET, AND THE COMBINATION OF P.DOT AND P.LASER.

5. Write Practice Problems for Users

Often you will have to describe problems that users would have to overcome as scenarios in tutorials. For example: with an accounting software program, the users would have to delete a transaction to a ledger after discovering a mistake, or a manager would have to extend an existing database by adding new entries. Each of these user tasks requires knowledge of certain program tasks that you can provide from your task list. Your skill is in writing the task in a way that reflects your analysis of the user.

Choose one of the following users and write a description of a task or problem suitable for the introduction to a tutorial. Then describe what software functions you would need to design the tutorial.

A business traveler in a hotel room	GlobCon connection software
A sales accountant	Client database software
A clerk in a Pack 'n' Mail Outlet	Client billing software at the point of sale
A city planner	Urban resources allocation tracking software

chapter 13

Writing to Guide—
Procedures

This chapter follows the organization of software documentation into three main levels, called *levels of support:* teaching, guidance, and reference. These levels tie in with recognized user behaviors, questions, and needs, and act as design tools. The chapter offers examples, guidelines, and discussion for design of guidance level documentation.

Guidance information, also known as step-by-step instructions, or how-to instructions, or the best-known term, *procedures,* makes up the heart of all task-oriented documentation systems. Much of the documentation you write will consist of procedures. Guidance documentation gets its name from the characteristic way that procedures lead the user from step to step through the task. Your program task list (Chapter 3) was designed to provide you with the raw material for formatting the various styles of procedures discussed in this chapter. But they all share the characteristic of leading the user, as opposed to teaching a task by memory (tutorial) or supporting a user-defined task (reference). *Guidance* means that the user temporarily forfeits a certain amount of control to the manual or help system in order to perform a discrete task. Then he or she resumes control again, possibly forgetting the actual steps, as one might do when following a guide to a hotel in a strange city.

Such procedures consist of a mix of explanations and steps, as you will see. That is, procedures consist of how-to-do-it explanations, but they also require how-it-works and why-it-works overviews. Your job as a designer of procedures is to balance these elements to meet users' informational needs and to make them efficient and effective software users in their workplace.

This chapter covers formats you will find among manuals and online help: standard, prose, parallel, and context sensitive. The chapter then discusses the elements of a procedure, breaking it down so that you can see how to combine information in ways to offer your user the maximum in usability and efficiency of use.

How to Read This Chapter

This chapter forms a quartet with the last three chapters, each dealing with a prominent form of writing for task-oriented product support documents.

- The Procedures Checklist and the Procedure Test Form in Chapter 6, "Conducting Usability Tests," can assist the project-oriented reader in managing the checking and testing of procedures.

- Those reading with a project in mind might skim the Guidelines first in reading this chapter, but for the most part all readers should read the Discussion section (containing an analysis of the parts of a procedure) before reading the Guidelines.

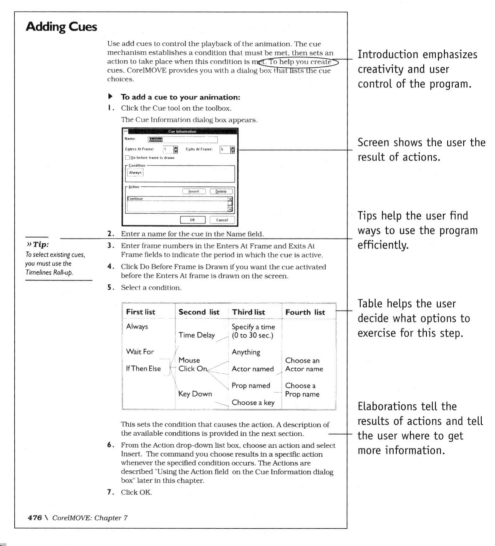

Figure 13.1

Example of an Effective Procedure

This procedure from the *CorelDRAW User's Manual, Version 4.0,* indicates the many kinds of information you need to provide in an effective procedure.

xample

Most task-oriented documentation takes the form of procedures, also known as stey-by-step or how-to documentation. Procedures work in practically all media and fall naturally into a chronological order. The procedure in Figure 13.1 follows this order, as indicated by the step numbers. It also indicates a number of other elements that you must carefully design to maximize the user's efficiency and effectiveness in the workplace.

uidelines

Figure 13.2 lists guidelines for writing at the appropriate level for your user's needs.

1 DETERMINE HOW MUCH INFORMATION YOUR USER NEEDS

You may design procedures to contain varying amounts of detail, sometimes rich with detail, at other times more sparse, depending on the difficulty of the task or the reader's experience. A rich procedure needs more visuals and a greater amount of explanation. It requires you to state more options and describe more results than a sparse procedure. Some rich (highly detailed) procedures will contain a note for each step, pointing out all the "what ifs" and all the other alternatives: basically, more information. Sparse (less detailed) procedures, on the other hand, because of the nature of the task and the reader's needs, often require only the repeating of the steps.

Figure 13.3 illustrates the difference between a step in a procedure with sparse detail and one with rich detail. Notice that the step with rich detail contains explanations of the following things:

- What happens when the user takes the action ("You will see . . . The program prompts you . . .")
- Suggested response to the program state ("We suggest that. . . .")

The richly detailed step also includes a *screen capture* to help focus the user on the events on the screen. The writer included these details because, with this installation, the novice or experienced user needed a great deal of guidance.

1. Determine how much information your user needs.

2. Choose the appropriate instructional format.

3. Follow a rhythm of exposition.

4. Test all procedures for accuracy.

igure 13.2

Guidelines for Writing Procedures

| 4. Type A:DZSETUP and then click on the OK button | 4. Type A:DZSETUP and then click on the OK button.

You will see the following introductory screen:

The install program will prompt you for the directory where you want to install Drag and Zip and Zip View.

We recommend you install Drag and Zip and Zip View into the default directory: C:\DZ. |

Figure 13.3

Sparsely Detailed Step versus a Richly Detailed Step

Other details you can include to enrich procedures include the following:

■ Screens showing where to point the mouse

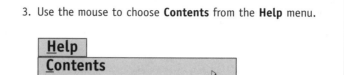

■ Cautions and warnings

Make sure you want to delete the patient's records because once you do they will vanish from the database for good.

■ Tips for efficient use

> ☞   You can become a powerhouse of productivity with MemoMaker by using the Ctrl-T command to import a ready-made memo template.

■ Tables showing options the user can take with a specific step

4. Choose one of the following options:

To do this . . .	Press . . .
Delete the image	Del
Copy the image	Ctrl-C
Cut the image	Ctrl-X

■ References to other sections of the manual

Procedures for organizing data into tables appear in the section on "Presenting Data in Tables" later in this chapter.

2   CHOOSE THE APPROPRIATE INSTRUCTIONAL FORMAT

The well-designed procedure should follow one or two accepted formats for instructions or a format of your own design. Whichever you choose, you should stick to one form or another in your manual, or in sections. It would work, say, to switch from one format to another, for example, if you wanted to include some steps in the Reference Section using the prose format, but use the standard format in your Installation Manual. At the same time, your Getting Started manual might use a playscript style, because more than one user might perform the tasks. But we would not advise you to change styles within a certain section, say, the Getting Started or the Reference sections. Doing so risks confusing the user. Some of the accepted formats are reviewed below.

Standard Format

So far we have described the standard format of instructions. The standard format consists of steps, notes, screens, and other elements aligned on the left margin and continuing in either one or two columns, in a numbered sequence, from first step to last. Figure 13.4 is a good illustration of this format.

The advantages of this format include the fact that the user will most likely recognize it. It follows the steps clearly to the end. The convention of putting each step on a separate line helps the user see the step and retain it in short term memory long enough to execute it on the computer.

Advantages of the Standard Format

The overall advantage of the standard format lies in its recognizability with users. They have seen it in software manuals and other instructional writing, and that transfer

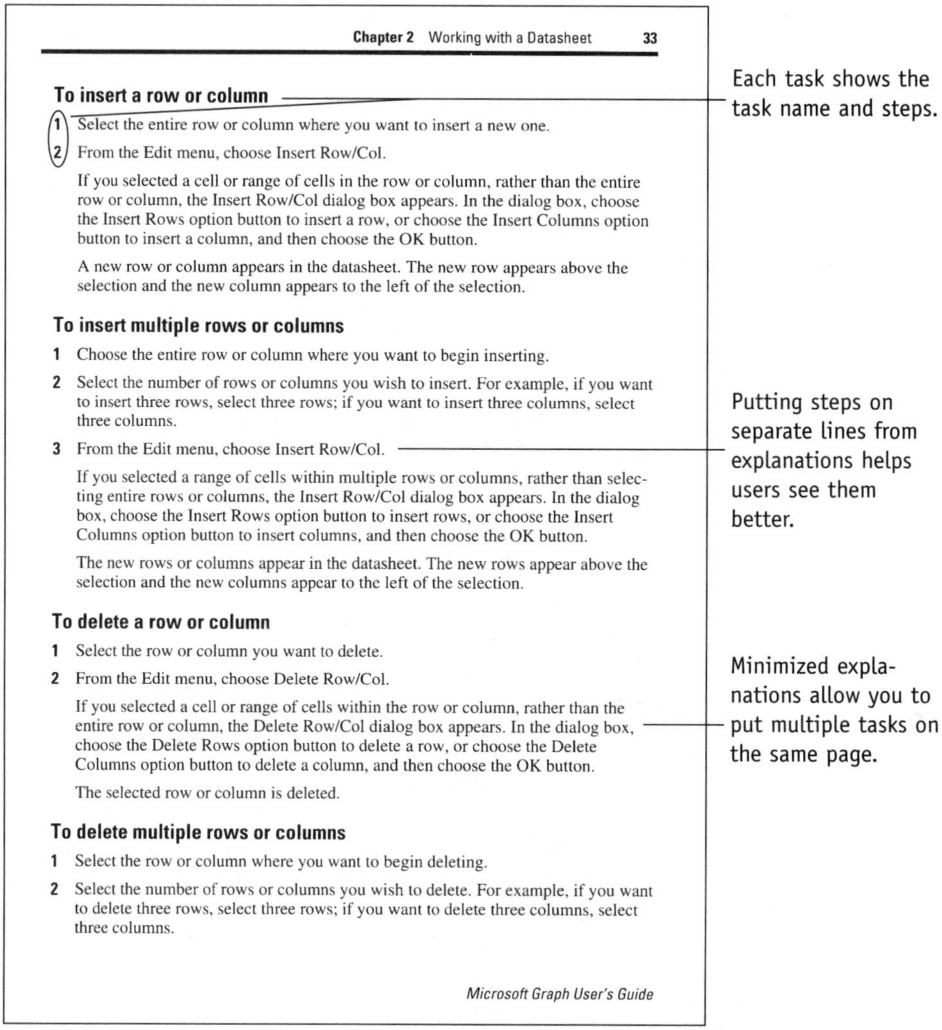

Chapter 2   Working with a Datasheet   **33**

To insert a row or column

① Select the entire row or column where you want to insert a new one.

② From the Edit menu, choose Insert Row/Col.

If you selected a cell or range of cells in the row or column, rather than the entire row or column, the Insert Row/Col dialog box appears. In the dialog box, choose the Insert Rows option button to insert a row, or choose the Insert Columns option button to insert a column, and then choose the OK button.

A new row or column appears in the datasheet. The new row appears above the selection and the new column appears to the left of the selection.

To insert multiple rows or columns

1   Choose the entire row or column where you want to begin inserting.

2   Select the number of rows or columns you wish to insert. For example, if you want to insert three rows, select three rows; if you want to insert three columns, select three columns.

3   From the Edit menu, choose Insert Row/Col.

If you selected a range of cells within multiple rows or columns, rather than selecting entire rows or columns, the Insert Row/Col dialog box appears. In the dialog box, choose the Insert Rows option button to insert rows, or choose the Insert Columns option button to insert columns, and then choose the OK button.

The new rows or columns appear in the datasheet. The new rows appear above the selection and the new columns appear to the left of the selection.

To delete a row or column

1   Select the row or column you want to delete.

2   From the Edit menu, choose Delete Row/Col.

If you selected a cell or range of cells within the row or column, rather than the entire row or column, the Delete Row/Col dialog box appears. In the dialog box, choose the Delete Rows option button to delete a row, or choose the Delete Columns option button to delete a column, and then choose the OK button.

The selected row or column is deleted.

To delete multiple rows or columns

1   Select the row or column where you want to begin deleting.

2   Select the number of rows or columns you wish to delete. For example, if you want to delete three rows, select three rows; if you want to delete three columns, select three columns.

Microsoft Graph User's Guide

Each task shows the task name and steps.

Putting steps on separate lines from explanations helps users see them better.

Minimized explanations allow you to put multiple tasks on the same page.

Figure 13.4

Page of Procedures in Standard Format

These procedures from the Microsoft Graph *User's Guide* follow the standard, left-margin format, using numbered steps and indented explanations.

of recognition carries a lot of weight. The advantages of this format follow in the list below:

■ Recognizable by users

■ Easy to flow from one page to another

■ Easy to re-number and test

- Hanging indent makes steps easy to see
- Easy to convert from the format of the program task list

Disadvantages of the Standard Format

The standard format works best when you don't have a variety in complexity from task to task, and your users become familiar with it. It has the following disadvantages:

- May take a lot of space for really simple, brief procedures.

- Confusing if you have to mix complex steps with simple steps. The user in this case can loose track of the chronology while handling a difficult interface item.

Prose Format

The prose format for instructions puts the steps in sentences and paragraph form. The prose format occurs fairly commonly in programs with simple tasks (no more than three or four steps per task) and a simple interface. Prose format instructions also work well in reference sections, where you want to include only abbreviated steps. Because many manuals use this form, the user will probably recognize it, especially the experienced user. Finally, it conserves precious space where you simply need to cover the basic steps. You might use it, for instance, in the cramped space of an error message box to give users a way to correct a problem. Figure 13.5 is a good example of prose format.

The prose format uses cuing schemes for command verbs, function keys, buttons, and input text—as you might imagine. Also, most prose instructions keep the sentences short (under twenty words) and the paragraphs short (less than five sentences). This brevity guarantees that the user will find it comfortable to transfer the instructions from the page

---

Adding an Address

You can add a single address or multiple addresses to your address book. When you add an address, the program automatically checks to see if you've already added it. This feature saves you time later, avoiding the need to clean out double addresses.

> Choose **Add Address** from the **Utility** menu. When you do, the program will display the message: "Address added." If you already have that address in your address book, the program will display the message: "Doubled Address," and ask you if you want to change or delete the current new address. Press **Cancel** if you want to keep the new address, or change it in the spaces in the dialog box.

Figure 13.5

Procedure in Prose Format

The prose format saves space when you write for experienced users.

to the keyboard or mouse. No rules exist for how many screens or other illustrations you may use with the prose format, but usually you would include no more than one screen per task, if that.

Advantages of the Prose Format

- Saves space
- Good for simple, basic steps
- Works best with experienced users

Disadvantages of the Prose Format

- Steps get lost in the paragraph
- Hard to include lengthy explanation of individual steps
- Can't include graphics for individual steps
- Doesn't offer much support for novice users

Parallel Format

The parallel format comes in handy when you have a program that uses complicated data fields or dialog boxes. Examples would include database programs, address or Rolodex type programs, invoice or order entry programs—in general, programs that require the user to move from one field on the screen to another, filling each one along the way. The parallel format shows the screen with the fields empty, and parallels the field names in the steps that follow. Each of the steps indicates to the user what kind of information to include in each field—characters or digits or both—gives examples, and cites special cases. There is one step for each field, usually. Figure 13.6 shows a procedure written in parallel format.

When you find yourself confronted with this kind of interface, the parallel format can help you and your users stay organized, as long as you keep the reference between the steps and the screen clear. The format helps keep the information centralized, and helps the reader see the filling out of the dialog box or screen as a single task. On the other hand, the parallel format can break down if the procedures get so long as to take up more than one page. In this case the user has to refer back to the illustration on a previous page—an awkward situation that allows for plenty of mistakes. Should you decide that your program and your users require the parallel format, you can set it up easily by following the directions below.

1. Keep the terminology consistent. If the screen uses the terms "Employee number" and "Employee name" then use the same terms in the explanatory steps. Slight variations, such as "Your Employee Number" or "An Employee Number" increase the user's cognitive load and thus should be avoided.

2. Cue the terms to the screen. Keep the same type font, size, and style in your steps as the screen shows. Even more efficiently, reproduce the screen element, showing the box, say around the field, or the line the user would write into, in the steps. This increases the user's ability to recognize what steps go with what screen elements.

Query on Patient Accounts Form

The Query on Patient Accounts Form allows you to systematically recall information about patient accounts.

To get to the Query on Patient Accounts Form follow these steps:

1. Press F2 from the Medical Menu
2. Press F1 from the Query and/or Recall Menu

The program will respond by displaying the following form.

Query on Patient Accounts Form

Query and/or Recall Fields on Patients

Patient no. : (. . . . .) to (Patient no.): (. . . . .)
Last Name: (. . . . .)   First Name: (. . . . .)
Balance Due: (. . . . .) to (value): (. . . . .)
Birth Date: (. . . . .)   SS#: (. . . . .)

Tab (to move among fields), F10 (done) Esc (exit),

Description of the fields in the Query on Patient Accounts Form.

Patient No. (8 digits)   Query on this field displays the patient number, name, home phone, family balance, last visit date, and check and credit status. You can enter a single patient number, or a range of patient numbers.

Last Name: (up to 18 chars)   Query on this field displays the same informaton as the patient number query field. Enter the name, and press the Enter key. The program will display the record of the first person with the name you entered.

First Name: (up to 18 chars)   Query on this field displays the same information as query on the patient number field. Enter the first name, and press the Enter key. The program will display the record of the first person with the name you entered.

Balance Due: Query on this field displays a list of patients whose balance falls under the specified range. For example, here you can get answers to questions such as "Show me all patients whose balance due is between $100 and $250." Enter $100 in the first space of this field and $250 in the second space in this field.

NOTE: You can get any range from $1 up by inquiring on this field. You must enter something, so if you don't want to use this field, enter $9999 to get all the patients.

2-5

Figure 13.6

Procedure in Parallel Format

Parallel format procedures work extremely well when the user needs to fill out an entire screen of data fields.

3. Discuss one screen item at a time. Usually when you set up parallel instructions you cover only one field at a time, even though two fields may be related. For example, your user may have to fill in the employee number before the employee name field will take any data. In this case, resist the temptation to discuss both fields at a time.

Simply make filling out the first field a prerequisite for filling out the second, and mention this in the discussion of the second field.

4. Use plenty of examples. Tell the user whether the fields require characters and digits, and give examples of each in your notes to the steps.

5. Make sure you explain to the user how the parallel format works. Introduce the idea, and, in complicated tasks, explain the cuing scheme and other conventions used.

Advantages of the Parallel Format

- Can help you and your users stay organized
- Works best with shorter procedures
- Good for filling out complicated screens and dialog boxes

Disadvantages of the Parallel Format

- Does not present information in a step-by-step, task-oriented manner
- Specialized: can't use it for all procedures
- User can get lost moving from steps to screen
- With large screens the user has to keep referring back to the screen shot

Context-Sensitive Procedures

Remember those times when you had a dialog box open, probably in a Windows program, and you just pressed the F1 key to call up a help message? The help program "knew" your location in the program through *context sensitivity:* No matter what menu or dialog box you have open, the help program will display information appropriate for that location. The help program showed sensitivity to the context in which you worked. Such kinds of responses occur because of information called *tags* that the writer, usually working with a programmer, put into the program.

In a variation of this scenario, some programs even present help when the user makes a mistake or tries something the first time, regardless of whether the user requested help. This has happened to me frequently (maybe because I make so many mistakes.) I get messages something like "You just tried to put a drawing object into a text box. Press Cancel to return to the program, or Press OK to receive a brief demonstration of how you *should* have done it." Of course, not all help systems use this much directness, and I may have exaggerated. The point: Some help just appears, whether you want it or not.

I see this kind of help as a cross between usual context sensitivity (where you press F1 anytime to get help on a specific *topic*) and error messages that appear unbidden when you do something the program doesn't like. You can identify those tasks that the experienced user would perform and present them as solutions to the current user's predicament. Usually when you present the help screen to the user, you give several display options: scroll the procedure, keep it on top for further reference, and so on. At this time you usually present straight step-by-step procedures. It looks complicated, but really you need only link the help screen to the usual procedures you have online, so that the error message allows access to the help system. Figure 13.7 illustrates an error message that shows context sensitivity.

Can only connect to a text frame.

The frame you have clicked is not a text frame.
When the mouse pointer changes to a cup it
means you can connect one text frame to
another. If you now click an empty text frame, it
will be connected to the current frame. You can
press ESC to cancel, or press F1 now if you
want more information on connecting text
frames.

OK

Figure 13.7

**Error Message Shows Context
Sensitivity**

This help screen from Microsoft
Publisher Help tells the user the
error and offers context sensitive
help for learning how to perform
the operation successfully.

3 FOLLOW A RHYTHM OF EXPOSITION

By *rhythm of exposition* we mean a pattern of step, note, and illustration. Think of your procedure as occurring in this way:

1. First I say what will happen.
2. Then I give the command for the first action.
3. Then I say how the program will respond.
4. Then I tell the next step.

The basic idea of a rhythm of exposition lies in the action/response pattern. Computer programs work in that way: Take an action, the system responds. These two events get repeated
over and over with incremental progress toward the goal of the whole procedure. Technically, then, each step should have a note to explain the result of the action. But not always.
Often, with simple steps, the results do not need explanation. Thus, with more sparse
procedures—depending on your users' information needs—you would just give the steps.

Whether your procedures contain lots of notes or few notes, they should be compact
enough so that the user doesn't get lost between steps. The eye needs to follow easily
from step to step. If your procedure contains extra information—other options, definitions of terms, or complicated interpretations of results—then put the extra information
after the steps, so that the reader gets less confused.

4 TEST ALL PROCEDURES FOR ACCURACY

During the developmental phase of your projects you will most likely test your procedures to gauge whether the pacing and the format conventions you follow have the desired effect. Once you settle on a format, however, the testing does not stop.

As a designer and writer of procedures, you must see that your descriptions accurately
reflect the program. To do this, you need to test every procedure you write. Tests of this
type we call evaluative tests, which means that after you finish the procedure, you have
an actual user, or a prototype of the user, or yourself as a last resort, perform the steps.

Get ready to have your eyes opened to all the conditions, alternatives, options, and other details you left out.

As part of your review of your procedures, you should double-check them, to make sure that the screens represent the program accurately, that all the options you need get included, that your statements of syntax, field content (digits versus characters), and field size are accurate and complete. (Chapter 13 gives further details on kinds of tests and test methods.)

Discussion

If you only write one kind of computer manual, make it a set of procedures based on a thorough task analysis and complete testing. You would call it a *User's Guide,* because, as opposed to system administrators or maintenance programmers, users perform most procedures. At the beginning you would announce that your manual provided "step-by-step instructions" on using the program. All your readers could identify the manual at once. And if they act the way typical users act, they may try to disregard it.

They would disregard it because most people only read procedures, or read "to do" as a last resort. So you will have to trade off *explanations,* for greater overall efficiency: the less you explain, the greater your efficiency. As you will see below, the decision as to how much information to include will often determine the style of your procedures and how well they work.

This section examines the structure of procedures to determine how you can design them to guide the reader effectively. We will look, first, at the user psychology regarding procedures, and how they need to focus heavily on tasks. In fact, of all the documentation forms you will design, those offering procedures will most closely resemble the bare bones tasks you identify in your program task list. Next, we will see how the parts of a procedure, examined analytically, can perform a special function in orienting the user to the right information. Finally, we will look at guidelines for writing effective procedures, including a discussion of different formats available for procedural information.

What Constitutes a Procedure?

The documenter should remember that procedures do not always simply describe the functions of the software system. The *functions* of the system can differ greatly from the *uses* of the system in the office or business. In fact, you should see the functions of the program—whether the program processes words, or creates graphic images, or calculates farm-listenership data—as constituting the tools that the program provides for the user to apply. Thus, the procedure you design might include one or more functions of the program. Nor do procedures stem from descriptions of the components of the software system. These components—programs, data files, resource forks, and so forth—do little (usually) to help the user because they work in the background. Procedures result directly from your thorough program task list, putting the functions of the program into usable sets of steps that do the user's work.

Most of your writing in software documentation consists of writing procedures. All procedural documentation answers the user's simple question "how do you use the program?" As such, it functions on the *guidance level*. The reader of procedures needs to know what keys to press, what reports and screens will look like, and how to get out of trouble. The reader of procedures also needs to know what options relate to the task and how to perform them. But mainly, the task of writing procedures consists of giving guidance, of leading by the hand, and not teaching. The *teaching level* of task orientation has as its goal the internalization of concepts: you try to get the user to remember the procedures after the lesson finishes. Procedures and lessons differ greatly. Procedures focus much more on options the user might take, whereas lessons focus on only those keys and actions needed to perform one highly limited task. A procedure expands the user's focus; a tutorial contracts it.

Guidance-level documentation also differs significantly from *support-level* documentation, in that when you guide the user the *documentation* defines the task: its beginnings and endings. You do this so the reader can follow unfamiliar steps to perform a task he or she does seldom, or now does for the first time. With support-level or reference documentation, the *user* defines the task and goes to the documentation to get an essential tidbit of information needed to perform the task. Probably this difference explains why reference entries (for example: error messages, ASCII codes, command summaries) usually consist of smaller units of information than procedures.

With what kinds of information would the user need guidance? With installation, for one thing, because installations vary from system to system, depending on the type of program and the kind of media or disks it comes in. Users also need guidance in maintaining and repairing systems: open this file, check this variable, close the file, and so on. But in the end use of the program you find the main bulk of procedural tasks. Usually, when you describe procedures you concentrate on the end-use tasks of the user in a workplace.

To help enhance the workplace application of a program, each procedure can contain a scenario—a brief description of how and why to use the procedure. And each scenario should indicate the user's role and needs, and the goal of the procedure. For example, you might point out the scenario in this way: "You perform these tasks every day after you have posted your last transaction and before you turn the computer off." User's roles might put things in terms of office roles—sales clerk, accountant, front office—or in terms of program roles—programmer, maintenance programmer, end user, installer. The goal of the procedure should indicate what task it performs: installing a printer, retrieving a record, dialing a phone number, setting a tab. Such a scenario makes a very useful introduction for the end user.

How Does a Procedure Work?

A procedure works, guides the user through a series of tasks to a designated end, because you design each of its parts to do a specific job. The sections below discuss how those parts each contribute to the overall task-orientation of the procedure.

Task Name

The task name identifies the program function in *performance-oriented* language. You can design most task names based on the following model: "Opening a file," or "Recalling a Record from the Client Database." Often you set off task names with a rule or special type font, style, or size. But remember this important point when naming tasks: the task name should describe what job the user performs, not what functions he or she uses. For example, the task name of "Using the Open . . . option" indicates the use of a program function. You should describe the task as "Opening a file." Other examples include the following:

Program-Oriented Task Name: Weak	Task-Oriented Task Name: Strong
Using the Print Function	Printing a Card
Selecting the List All command	Listing All the Disk Functions

Scenario

Technically, *scenario* means a small story or narrative in a setting. The scenario tells, or reminds, the reader what the task will allow him or her to accomplish in a work setting. As a reminder, the scenario has the dual function of introducing the task and suggesting workplace applications. It should indicate, using informal language, the starting state of the task and what goal the user should expect. Sometimes you might include two scenarios if more than one user type would perform the task or if the user could put the task to more than one use. Base the scenario on information you discovered while writing your program task list and analyzing your user.

The scenario should set the user up to perform the steps. If the user needs to have certain skills to perform the task, then mention them, as in "To perform this step you should be familiar with raster formatted images." Likewise, if the task has conditions for performance, mention them in the scenario, as in, "You should only perform the end-of-day posting after you have closed down the general ledger file."

Study the examples of scenarios and introductions to tasks, starting with the one shown in Table 13.1.

Steps

Steps make up the most important part of the procedure. However, often the user will skim the steps, either to avoid having to read the explanations, or to pick out the essential step and try it without reading further. Even so, you should take care to write them well.

Steps tell the user what to do, and in so doing, tell two things: the tools to use and the action to take with the tools. If you can rely on the program task list then you have half your work done for you when you formulate steps.

Steps can include both the tool and the action, as in: "Use the mouse to select 'Open . . .' from the file menu." However, you may include only the action, if the user can perform the step easily, as in: "Select 'Open . . .' from the file menu." In the first example, the writer included the tool or interface object ("Use the mouse to . . .") and in the second the writer omitted the tool. The decision to include the "use the . . ." part of a step depends on the user's familiarity with the task and the program. Often users will not read the notes and explanations that go along with steps, so you should make the steps as self sufficient as possible. Imagine that your user only read the steps: would they contain sufficient information to perform the task?

Table 13.1

Examples of Introductions to Tasks

Task Name	Introduction/Scenario
Changing Default Settings	"Picture Publisher lets you save defaults in the tool ribbons and in some dialog boxes. You will find these features extremely helpful when working with Picture Publisher." *Picture Publisher Reference Guide,* (1992), p. 4–11
Creating Groups	"*Groups* are containers; they can contain objects and/or other groups. A group window can also contain links to other groups to form a *group structure.* The group structure is useful to represent the structure of your network hierarchically or functionally." *TC8215 Sectra Management System for Windows User's Guide,* (1995), p. 4–9
Including Graphics in a Document	"When you prepare reports, manuscripts, or other types of technical documents, there may be times when you want to include GCG graphics. The Wisconsin Package lets you save files in Encapsulated Postscript (EPS) format, which you can include but not edit in most commercial document processing programs." *Wisconsin Sequence Analysis Package User's Guide,* (1994), p. 5–36
Controlling the Screen Display	You can use the Display command on the Options menu to change the colors in the MS-DOS Editor window, display or hide scroll bars, and set tabs. *Microsoft MS-DOS User's Guide and Reference* (1992), p. 221

Below are listed four versions of a "Step 1." Note how they increase in elaboration.

Step 1: Open a file.

Step 1: Select the **Open . . .** option in the **File** menu.

Step 1: Use the **Open . . .** in the **File** menu to open an existing file.

Step 1: Using the mouse, select the **Open . . .** option in the **File** menu to open an existing file.

Steps should always occur in chronological order. Putting them in sequence ensures that the user will not get lost, or get the sequence mixed up. For these reasons, we usually use numbers instead of bullets for steps, because numbers have a built-in sequence that bullets lack. You should also include the word "step" as in "Step 1 . . . , Step 2 . . ." to help the reader note the need to take action. If your procedure contains smaller actions, remember to keep all the main steps in one continuous sequence. In other words, do not renumber under the other actions required for a step because this can cause confusion as to which step to take next. Consider the following **BAD** example:

BAD EXAMPLE

Step 1.   Choose Groups from the Maintenance Menu.

Step 2.   Choose an action from the Groups dialog box.
1. Select a name for the group.
2. Select a directory name for the group.
3. Set the access code to either Open or Restricted.

Step 3.   Choose Close from the Groups dialog box.

This sequence of steps risks confusing the user because it contains two sequences of steps. In other words, you have two step 2s, and so on. You can avoid this confusion by trying a format like the following **GOOD** example:

GOOD EXAMPLE

Step 1.   Choose Groups from the Maintenance Menu.

Step 2.   Choose an action from the Groups dialog box.
Once you have opened the Groups dialog box, you need to select a name for the group, then select a directory name for the group, then set the access code to either Open or Restricted.

Step 3.   Choose Close from the Groups dialog box.

The second example puts the smaller actions in a paragraph and doesn't number them. This way the user runs less risk of confusing the step sequence. As indicated in the example, it's also a good idea to separate the smaller steps from the main steps by putting them in a paragraph on the next line.

Also, you should avoid giving commands in notes and explanations. Reserve commands for steps. Technically, if the user needs to perform an action and that action has some result, then the action should appear as a numbered step. Putting actions in explanatory notes that accompany your steps begs for the user to ignore them—which may happen.

Elaborations

Performing the steps will get the task completed, but not without explanations. Here, elaborations come in. They explain the steps, commenting on them *as they get performed*. You learned a lot about how to perform the procedures when you did your program task list, so share that experience with your users when you write the procedures. In elaborations you share the following kinds of things with your users:

- Possible mistakes and how to avoid them
- How to perform procedures efficiently
- Alternatives such as keystrokes, toolbars, or function keys
- Definitions of terms
- Ways to tell if a step has been performed correctly
- Where else to look for additional information

When you write elaborations, always try to use the active voice and refer to the program. For example, instead of saying "The control panel will come on the screen," say "MarketMaster will display the control panel."

Tables

Often when you describe a procedure you will have to include a list of commands or keys needed. Put these in an easy-to-read table. Tables in procedures give the user options and save time and space. Consider the following example:

3. Adjust the color of your image.

At this point you can adjust the color of your image by using the following commands.

To do this . . .	Use these keys . . .
Set colors to black and white	Ctrl-M
Revert to default colors	Ctrl-D
Adjust the brightness	Ctrl-B
Adjust the tones	Ctrl-T

You should follow the guidelines for tables presented in Chapter 7, but also observe some specific guidelines for using them in procedures:

- Keep tables simple. Start with columns and bold style headings for a simple table. For more complex tables, add a ruler under the headings. Next add a rule under the columns: the bottom rule. After this you could add a complete box around the table for more complexity. Next, add vertical rules separating the columns; next, add horizontal lines separating column entries, with the boxes sized to the largest entry. Whew! But a simple table works best.

- Cite the table in the text. Citing the table makes it clear when the user should consult it, and for what purpose.

- Use descriptive, performance-based column titles.

- Use visual cues for keys or commands, or menu selections presented in tables.

Screens

Include screens in your procedures when the user needs either to see the tool in use or the goal or results of an action. Rich procedures would include a screen for the starting state of the task, one or more screens illustrating how to use *interface tools,* and a screen indicating the result of the task. Depending on your constraints of time and budget, and depending on your user's level of expertise, you will include more or fewer of these screens. Use a box or active white space around your screens to make sure the user can distinguish them easily from the surrounding text. Finally, if you sense any chance that the user may not associate the screen to the appropriate step, give the screen a name, or descriptive caption.

Usually you will find yourself using screens to do the following:

- Show the **partial result** of a procedure (a stage in the process) to help the user keep on track.
- Show the **final result** of the procedure to let the user know where the procedure ends.
- Show **dialog boxes** where the user has to make choices.
- Show **toolbars** indicating which tools the user needs.
- Show **menus** indicating what commands the user needs.

Chapter 7 deals in greater length with the subject of screens and other graphics used in procedures.

Glossary

context sensitive: refers to the capacity of a help system to detect the location of the user in terms of what interface element (menu screen or dialog box) the program currently displays and to provide a help screen appropriate for that element. Using this system the user doesn't have to ask for a specific topic, but just gets the topic appropriate to the current situation (hence "context").

evaluative test: a test of a document's usability, done after releasing to the user.

guidance level: a type of documentation designed to lead the user through a procedure one step at a time from a designated starting place (such as a certain menu) to an ending state (such as a report printed.) Guidance level documentation (or procedures) defines the task for the user, but does not teach the task. See also **teaching level** and **support level.**

interface tools: refers to buttons, menu items, and other clickable or selectable elements of the display of a computer program that allow the user to perform tasks. In word processors you will often find a toolbar, containing a number of buttons (or interface tools) to do things like *copy text, cut text, paste text,* and so on. Draw programs have interface tools like the *draw tool,* or the *eraser tool.*

screen capture: an image of a screen from a computer program electronically recorded in the form of an image file that you can use in a manual or help system to illustrate what the screen looks like.

support level: documentation designed to provide reference information for a user.

performance-oriented: one of the "bla-oriented" adjectives (as in task-oriented, job-oriented, and so forth) in which I indulge myself in this book. It simply means focusing on or emphasizing performance of a task, as opposed to focusing on the features of the software system. All good documentation should focus first on using the program, then on the features of the software system.

teaching level: a type of documentation intended to instill a knowledge of how to use a program feature in the memory of the user. Teaching level documentation (tutorials) aims to enable the user to perform a task from memory. See **guidance level** and **support level.**

topic: in help systems, the basic unit of information. The topic can contain a step-by-step procedure, a definition, an explanation, or other useful information.

Checklist

Use the following checklist as a way to evaluate the efficiency of your design for procedures. Depending on your users and the level of detail you choose for your procedures, some of these items may not apply.

Procedures Checklist
Determining How Much Information the User Needs

Your users require what level of detail in the procedures?

☐ Sparse   ☐ Moderate   ☐ Rich

Specific details to meet your users' need include which of the following?

☐ Screens showing where to point the mouse
☐ Cautions and warnings
☐ Tips for efficient use
☐ Tables showing options related to specific steps
☐ References to other sections of the manual/help

Format

Which format suits your users best?

☐ Standard format (step after step)
☐ Prose format (steps in paragraph format)
☐ Parallel format (steps associated with screen fields)

Rhythm of Exposition

☐ Have you reviewed your task design so that each one follows a similar pattern?

Testing

Have you identified the appropriate test points for your procedures?

☐ Accuracy of steps
☐ Accuracy of details
☐ Pacing/rhythm
☐ Format conventions
☐ Inclusion of options/conditions/alternatives

Elements of Procedures

Have you double-checked your procedures for the suitability of the following elements?

☐ Performance-oriented task names
☐ Scenario relates to users' expectations

☐ Steps include tool, action, and result
☐ Steps only present one sequence of numbers
☐ Steps in the correct order
☐ Elaborations emphasize performance
☐ Tables used to conserve space and promote efficient use
☐ Screens focus the user's eye on the correct interface element

Practice/Problem Solving

1. Build a Procedure for Users with Different Skill Levels

The following task describes how to transfer a document file in a program called DocView to a separate disk drive using the transfer feature. The screen shows a thumbnail sketch of the transfer dialog box. The users of the program include novices, who use to examine help files for programs, and experience users, programmers who use it to document their programs. In a development project you would have to decide how much detail to include for these two users: one needing lots of details, the other probably needing less and getting it in the step-by-step help system.

Practice designing for users of different skill levels by developing this task in two ways: first for novice user, and second for experienced user. After you have created the two different versions of the procedure, try them out on a few test subjects. How has the experiment helped you determine how much detail to include in your procedure for this task?

TASK: TRANSFERRING A FILE (ALL-10)

Performer: the user, novice or experienced
Starting state: DocView is running
Goal state: the current document has been saved on a selected drive

Steps:

1. Use the mouse to select Transfer from the File menu
2. Use the mouse to select the desired file
3. Use the mouse to select the Transfer button

Options:

Eject: ejects the selected disk
Drive: switches to another drive Cancel: cancels the transfer operation
Transfer: saves the current document in the selected drive
Filebox: shows the path to the selected file
Scroll bar: scrolls up and down the file/folder list

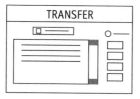

2. Rewrite Prose Format into Step Format

The following example shows a procedure done in prose format that probably should appear in step format. Rewrite it in the different format. Correct any errors you find and reorganize the passage.

Getting a Chart

To get a chart you should follow this procedure. Select Option #4, file from the Main Menu. Then, select Option #1, Get, from the File Menu. A listing of files in the default directory will appear. (If necessary, TAB to the DIRECTORY field to change the default directory.) Highlight the file you would like to retrieve and hit Enter. As an alternative you can use the CTRL+G speed keys to get a chart from any screen in ZQ. This allows you to get a chart without having to back out to the Main Menu.

chapter

14 Writing to Support— Reference

This chapter follows the organization of software documentation into three main levels, called *levels of support:* teaching, guidance, and reference. These levels tie in with recognized user behaviors, questions, and needs, and act as design tools. This chapter offers examples, guidelines, and discussion for design of print and online procedural information.

Reference documentation, also referred to occasionally as *support documentation,* includes all the look-up sections and elements of your manuals and help. It takes forms such as command descriptions, menu overviews, lists of definitions, function descriptions, and error messages.

So often, we think that these sections don't require design, or that they consist of merely alphabetized lists of commands. But, with the rapid growth of computer skills among all workers, we should study ways to design this information in a task-oriented way. To this end, this chapter covers how to select the right form of support documentation (online and print) by examining both usual and special forms of reference. The chapter also discusses the idea of parallel patterns in reference documentation, emphasizing methods of organizing: alphabetical, menu by menu, and context sensitivity. The chapter then offers you a discussion of why users consult support documentation, looking specifically at the psychology of the reference user and how reference entries parallel the user's informational needs.

How to Read This Chapter

- For the project-oriented reader, the examples in the figures will provide enough background to get you started on the design of your project as outlined in the Guidelines. But before you finish your project, you should familiarize yourself with the principles in the Discussion section.

- For the reader reading to understand, the Discussion section offers a basic background for which to read the Guidelines.

Example   443

Example

The example in Figure 14.1 shows a number of elements of a typical, structured reference entry, such as you would find accompanying a computer compiler or other computer language manual. The entry reflects the questions that reference users have about software, and it illustrates how to present answers to those questions in a highly accessible way.

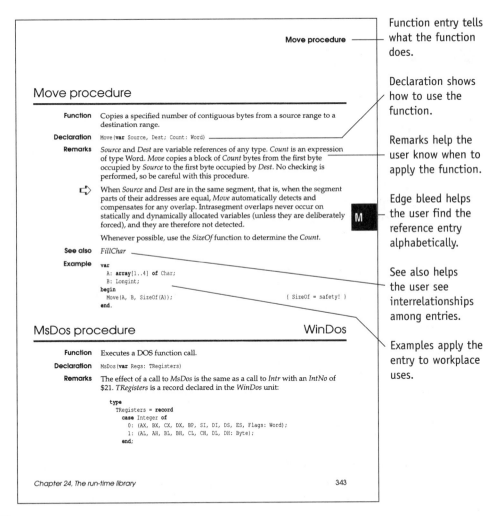

Function entry tells what the function does.

Declaration shows how to use the function.

Remarks help the user know when to apply the function.

Edge bleed helps the user find the reference entry alphabetically.

See also helps the user see interrelationships among entries.

Examples apply the entry to workplace uses.

Figure 14.1

A Structured Reference Entry

This reference entry from the Turbo Pascal for Windows *Programmer's Guide* shows how elements of a reference create a structure for explaining program functions.

1. Choose the right form of reference.
2. Decide what to include
3. establish a pattern.
4. Organize the reference section.
5. Show how to use the reference information.

Figure 14.2

Guidelines for Designing Support Documentation

uidelines

Figure 14.2 lists guidelines to follow as you design support documentation.

1 CHOOSE THE RIGHT FORM OF REFERENCE

Reference users probably don't come to the manual naive; they usually come looking for a specific piece of data to complete some task they themselves have defined and probably know how to do already. No how-to *here*! Usual forms of reference have evolved that you can follow, knowing that reference users will identify them. Later, some special forms of reference you may want to use to tailor your information to your users' work situation are covered.

The Usual Forms of Reference

With some programs you will design information in all three of the forms below. With still others you will just supply a quick reference, along with the procedures in a user's guide. When you design a documentation set with all three kinds (and others), you gain the advantage of using the same information in each form. Using the same information in each form helps you as a writer because you can see the consistency among the forms. Consistent information helps the user, who begins to learn how to cross-reference information in various elements of the documentation set. Additionally, these forms can go online, with appropriate adjustments for format, and with online documents your user gains the benefit of easy access through help buttons, *context-sensitivity,* and *keyword searching*.

Special Forms of Reference

Special forms of reference refer to sections of documents where you can put reference information without going to the trouble of creating a "reference section."

Appendices

As you know, most people see an appendix in books the same way they see an appendix in their bodies: as a useless structure. But, in fact, the appendix in a software manual often contains some of the most valuable information relating to the use of the program. Appendices allow documenters a place to put all the highly detailed, technical information

Table 14.1

Identify the Form or Forms for Your Reference Information

Type	User	Characteristics	Typical Programs
Reference Section	Expert: system administrators, programmers	Lots of technical details organized by menu or function, can take hundreds of pages or go in appendix programs: searched by topic in online, or context sensitive (F2)	Compilers: Turbo Pascal, COBOL, Think C operating systems: UNIX, VMS, OS/2 networking system: Novelle Netware Netware
Task	Experienced, intermittent users	Covers mostly steps, organized menu by menu or alphabetically, called step-by-step in online	Word Processors, accounting programs, programs requiring monthly maintenance, backup, file maintenance
Quick Reference	For expert, experienced, (or novices once they have learned the program)	Covers program interface: commands, keys, screens, organized by menu or function, often on a folding card or in a booklet-sized pocket guide, usually not online	PC operating systems: MS-DOS, MS-Windows word processing systems: MS-Word, WordPerfect

that highly detailed, technical persons would want and use in the workplace. Your users may perceive the appendix with the kind of incorrect attitude referred to, but you should do your best to convince them otherwise and make the appendix a valuable part of the document set.

The print appendix does bear some resemblance to its biological counterpart: It contains information that's relevant and useful, but not *essential,* to all users. Examine some appendices to software manuals and you will find the kinds of things listed below.

- Error messages and explanations of how to recover from them
- Filenames and extensions of files associated with the program
- Troubleshooting tips
- Matrixes of compatibility with other programs
- ASCII charts showing word processor program key-combinations
- Printer driver charts showing capabilities with various printer brands

Update Information Sections/Readme Files

Readme files consist of text files that accompany programs on the distribution disk. In a way they're a kind of primitive online documentation. Programmers love them and use them to pass along all kinds of information about their software. Sometimes a readme plays a very important part in a program, in which case you call it a *rdmefrst.doc* or something like that. Usually you name it *readme.txt* or *read.me,* and users can read them using a notepad or word processing program. In the Macintosh environment, you can use a variety of programs like TeachText that users can activate and read just by clicking on them.

Readme files contain the following kinds of information:

- Installation details

- Last-minute changes too late for the manual or online help system

- New features in a recent release of a program

- Revision histories

- Errata in manuals and online help

- File descriptions

- Contents of directories

- Installation tips

- Compatibility requirements with other programs

Keyboard Templates and Short Forms

Keyboard templates usually consist of very brief reminders that attach to the actual keyboard. Usually limited to defining keys, they can stick to the keyboard or overlap the keys. Once more popular than now, they help the user remember how a specific program uses the ten special function keys usually on the left-hand side of the keyboard, or what Shift-, Alt-, and Ctrl- keys the program uses. Microsoft Word and WordPerfect, to name just two, package keyboard templates with their programs.

Innovative Forms: The Cube

Innovative forms make up a special class of reference information. It's very easy to put command information on foldouts, posters, and the back covers of documents. But I only know of one example of a *cube* for conveying software documentation. This one received an award at a recent meeting of the Society for Technical Communication. Entitled the *System 4000 Quick Reference Cube,* it consists of a clear, six-sided plastic cube, three inches on a side. One panel tells the contents of each of the remaining five sides, each color coded with the table of contents. Each side gives tips and steps for performing a variety of tasks associated with a phone-based software system. The table of contents lists the following five main tasks:

- Making a Video Call (red)

- Moving a Camera (green)

- Sending Video and Graphics (purple)

- Making an Audio Call (brown)

- Making a Multipoint Call (blue)

What makes this an interesting and innovative form of short reference? Consider the following *affordances* of this format:

- **Easy to read.** You can turn the cube so that you can see the side you want to read.

- **Contains a surprising amount of information.** Because it has so many sides, it can cover a number of tasks. The *System 4000 Quick Reference Cube* gives steps for twenty-three tasks. Sure they're short, but they're complete.

- **Color coded.** Color coding of the table of contents and sides gives the users another way to recall information, as in "Ah, yes, that's on the *blue* side."

- **Unique and interesting.** The cube fits easily on a user's desktop and poses an interesting challenge when you try to figure out how to get into it.

- **Affords easy access to information.** You can easily get to information on the cube simply by turning it from one side to the other. It's always "open."

2   DECIDE WHAT TO INCLUDE

When you look over your program or program task list, you will want to begin identifying topic areas you want to cover as reference. Below, you will find an overview of the kinds of things to include in a reference section, categorized into three groups: commands, interface elements, and terminology.

Commands

In reference, *commands* refers to all the instructions that the user employs to put the program to work. Information about commands would include the following:

- **Meanings of special function groups.** These groups contain commands that the program assigns to specific function keys, such as CTRL-C or ALT-Shift.

- **Explanations of set commands.** In some programs you can set certain things at the prompt. For example, in the VMS operating system, you can use "set host" to identify another host for your computer to connect to. Users need to know what kinds of things they can use the set commands for.

- **Definitions and uses of format commands.** These groups contain commands or tags, such as one might find in an HTML document, like <fontsize=z>text</font> to set the font size. Postscript commands consist of embedded commands in a document that perform certain functions, such as the hidden commands in MS Word (ﬞﬞﬞﬞﬞ) that control tables of contents, indexes, and lists of figures.

- **Special procedures for using utilities.** Programs have utility functions that do things like transfer files to other programs or filter images from different draw programs. Usually you provide a list of these with definitions.

- **Explanations of toolbars.** Almost all Windows-based programs contain toolbars: a series of icon-based commands that the user can select by clicking on the mouse.

- **Definitions of macros.** *Macros* refers to preidentified and prewritten sets of commands that do certain things with programs that you need to list for the user. Most programs allow users to create sets of commands, but some provide them already and describe them in a reference section.

Interface Elements

Interface elements refer to the parts of the screen or ***command line*** that the user sees and has to read and manipulate in order to put the program to work. Information about interface elements would include the following:

■ **Explanations of menus.** Menus contain most of the commands of a program and most reference consists of detailing what the menu items do.

■ **Definitions of keys.** Here you define all the keys that the program assigns to special functions, like CTRL-S for save or ALT-T for tab, and so forth. With some programs, like large PC word processors, this group of interface elements gets very large, because they use the ALT, CTRL, SHIFT, ALT/SHIFT, CTRL/SHIFT, and ALT/CTRL key combinations along with letters, numbers, and symbols to allow keyboard input for just about every command in the program.

■ **Labels of screen regions.** These refer to things like toolbars or scrolling regions that you need to inform the reader of.

■ **Explanations of rulers.** Word processors and draw programs have different kinds of rulers to help the user measure and draw on the screen. These elements of the interface need referencing, often with a labeled screen.

Definitions of Terms (Glossary)

Glossaries contain definitions of terms that the user finds in the manual and needs to understand in order to work the program. Basically, you have two kinds of glossary items: concepts in the software, and concepts in the subject matter of the software.

■ **Concepts that underlie the software.** Examples include *masks, shells, routers,* and so forth. Some will get defined with the procedures they relate to, but you'll collect them all in the glossary.

■ **Terms relating to the subject matter of the software.** For example, *general ledger, connectivity, gutter.*

What to Include in a Single Reference Entry

Imagine that you have a reference section in a manual or help document that covers the commands of a program in alphabetical order. You will still have to answer the question of what to put in each command description. Clearly, the simplest response would involve simply listing the command and a brief definition. But you could go further. In fact, you will find a bewildering array of things to include in each reference entry. Consider the following list of possible elements of reference entries. For the sake of convenience, these information elements are divided into groupings relating to the kinds of information each presents to the user.

Conceptual information (emphasizing the idea of the command and its function)

■ The command itself

■ Definitions and descriptions of the command and what it does

■ Explanations of how the command affects the user's work

■ Notes to explain the command further

■ Sample reports showing what the command produces

Structural information (emphasizing the relationship of the command to other commands)

■ Access sequences to tell the user how to get to the prompt where the command works

■ Screens or menus showing where to find the command

■ Alternative commands (such as keyboard or mouse alternatives)

■ Cross references to tutorials, procedures, other entries where the command gets further explanations

■ Tables showing variations of the command and how it relates to other commands

How-to information (emphasizing the use of the command)

■ Steps for executing the command in tasks

■ Examples showing the command in a syntax statement

■ Tips for when and how to use the command efficiently

■ Error messages for when you use the command incorrectly

Technical information (emphasizing the software programming associated with the command)

■ File specifications for what files the command uses

■ Input requirements (characters, data, or both) telling what kind of data to use with the command

■ Warnings telling how not to lose data when using the command

■ Syntax diagrams telling how to use the command in statements

■ Switches that allow the user to tailor the command to various needs

Clearly, you cannot include all the items in the list above in each reference entry. Your task will be to include or omit items that match your particular user's characteristics and workplace needs. In fact, the task orientation of your reference section may depend on your ability to build a set of elements that meshes with your user's expectations and needs.

The next guideline demonstrates how you can select from the list of all possible reference elements to create a pattern for your reference entries.

3   ESTABLISH A PATTERN

The key to reference material lies in patterns: repeating the same set of elements over and over again so the user learns to identify what each element of an entry means. Like other methods of building patterns into reading material, you want this one to assist recognition through regularity, yet allow for enough flexibility to present variations in information effectively. The following selection works well as a recognizable yet flexible pattern for reference entries.

- **Definition:** Tell what the command or function does.
- **Explanation:** Tell how to apply the command or function.
- **Example/syntax:** Give an example of the command or function in use.
- **Step-by-step:** Present abbreviated steps for using the command or function.
- **Warnings/cautions:** Let the user know what problems might arise.

4   ORGANIZE THE REFERENCE SECTION

As part of your design of reference sections, you will have to decide on an organizing principle. Unlike documentation on the teaching and guidance level of task orientation, the reference does not come with a built-in sequential organizational scheme. You will have to decide on what comes first, what comes next, and so on. And you will have to make a decision that supports, overall, the task orientation of the manual.

In general, you have two basic choices for organizing your reference section: alphabetical or menu-by-menu. Both of these methods have certain advantages and disadvantages, as the following discussion will show. You should decide based on the kinds of information your user needs and the kinds of documentation your user expects.

Alphabetical Organization

As the name implies, when you set up the reference section alphabetically, you usually heap all the functions of the program together, regardless of the menu structure, and go through them one at a time, starting with the a's. The MS-DOS 5.0 *Reference Guide* follows this method, starting with the *append* command and ending with the *xcopy* command. Like other documents, it divides the commands into groups: MS-DOS commands, batch commands, *config.sys* commands, and so on. Each command grouping starts the alphabet again. Likewise, you can organize your reference section according to sections of like commands, like **command sets,** or other topic areas.

In the case of topic areas, or command sets, the question becomes how to organize the sections. You may, for example, put them in a simple-to-complex order, including the basic ones at the first and the advanced command sets at the end. Or you might choose to start with the more abstract, concept-oriented information and progress to greater and greater levels of concrete, procedural information. The Lotus Manuscript manual, for example, starts with "A View of Manuscript" and progresses to various categories of conventions, file names, interface conventions and other features. The Adobe Postscript Language *Reference Manual* begins with definitions of terms that are:

> essential to understanding the problems the PostScript language is designed to solve and the environment in which it is designed to operate. Terminology introduced here [in the second of eight chapters] appears throughout the manual. (p. 11)

Glossaries follow an alphabetical organization because of the great virtue of predictability. As long as your user knows the name of the function, he or she can find a description of it easily. Your index can help direct the user to the right function name. It also strongly emphasizes the features of the program over the functionality. It lets the user know what features the program contains, and so appears comprehensive. Indeed, organizing this way helps the writer by allowing you to make sure you explain all the features.

Drawbacks of Alphabetical Organization

But the drawbacks of the alphabetical method often outweigh its advantages. While it may reassure some users to see a familiar alphabetical list of features, it does little to support the task orientation of your manual. For instance, since the items appear alphabetically, you always have to include access information for each item, telling what menu it goes under or how to get there. The user could get this access information from the surrounding text, but not if the next item occurs on a menu from another part of the program.

Menu-by-Menu

In many ways, the alphabetical organizational structure does not enhance the task orientation of a manual as much as a menu-by-menu organization. Using this scheme, you set up your reference section by menu, according to how the user sees them in the program. You could alphabetize the menus, but it makes more sense to arrange them as they appear on the program's main menu or menu bar. Often such menu groupings reflect workplace tasks anyway. Using the menu-by-menu method, you start with the main menu, then secondary menus. Present each menu, and then, in the subsequent pages, describe each of the commands in the order they appear on the menu. Present each command in a standardized format, with categories if necessary. Also include dialog boxes, confirmation boxes, and other elements the user sees when using each command.

The very strong advantage of the menu-by-menu system lies in its reinforcement of the task orientation of your work. The user sees the information in the same shape as he or she does when using the program. Thus, the document and the screen reinforce one another. The user's experience with the program itself helps with the understanding of the manual, and vice versa.

Context-Sensitive

You can organize your help section according to the context within which the user asks for help. This way, your help doesn't depend on the user's knowing the alphabet of commands or the menu where a command resides. The organization of the work really doesn't make that much difference with context-sensitive reference, because the user only sees one or two screens at a time.

5   SHOW HOW TO USE THE REFERENCE INFORMATION

In many cases, your reference section or document will require no instructions. Maps of menus or one-page summaries of commands represent this kind of self-explanatory reference page. However, with reference entries containing multiple elements, you should tell the user what pattern you intend to follow. This establishes the pattern in the user's mind, sets up the right expectations, and serves as a handy reminder of how you organized each entry.

Usually you instruct your user in the organization of the reference information in an introduction. In some instances the introduction takes the form of a paragraph or so explaining each of the entries, along with other items. Such an introduction should explain the following:

- **Who should use the information.** Remind the user that the information will best serve the advanced user, or users with special tasks, such as supervisory tasks, or transferring data from other programs.

- **How you organized the information.** Point out whether you used alphabetical order or menu-by-menu order, or some other category.

- **Elements of each entry.** List the elements of each entry, telling what kind of information each contains.

- **Relations to other sections of the documentation.** Indicate cross-references to other parts of the documentation set, like the procedures or tutorial or help. This helps reinforce the idea of the documentation system in the user's mind.

Figure 14.3 illustrates this kind of simple introduction to a reference section.

AccountMaster User's Manual

Reference

This section contains information for users who have some familiarity with AccountMaster, and who want to look up specific commands.

Commands are arranged alphabetically, and each entry, where appropriate, will contain the following elements:

Name:	(the name of the command)
Access:	(the keystrokes for getting to the menu containing the command)
Usage:	(what the command does)
Exceptions:	(special qualifications in the way you use the command)
Notes and Tips:	(advice for increasing your efficiency using the command)
See Also:	(page and screen numbers of related AccountMaster commands.)

You can find additional information in the AccountMaster User's Guide and Help.

5-1

Figure 14.3

Introduction to a Reference Section

This section helps orient the user to the pattern used in the reference section.

```
Sample procedure                              Unit it occupies

   Function    What it does
  Declaration  How it's declared; italicized items are user-defined
 Result type   What it returns if it's a function
   Remarks     General information about the procedure or function
 Restrictions  Special requirements or items to watch for
   See also    Related procedures and functions
   Example     Here you'll find a sample program that shows the use of the procedure or
               function in that entry. All of the examples that produce output (Writeln)
               or require input (Readln) should use the WinCrt unit.
```

Format shows how each entry is laid out.

Definitions explain each entry.

Figure 14.4

Library Entry to Orient the Reference User

This example from the Turbo Pascal for Windows *Programmer's Guide* allows users who know the pattern to follow each entry more easily and make the best use of the information.

As an alternative to an introduction, many reference manuals and sections include a sample library entry showing categories and telling what each does. The advantage of using this technique lies in the capability to show an entry when you have a highly structured, visually-oriented format. You give the user a chance to see an entry, labeled clearly. In one example, the writers of the Codewright *Programmer's Reference* included a sample entry with numbers for each of the items (i.e., "Function Name," "Usage Syntax," "Icons," and so on). They then explained what each numbered entry meant in a list of definitions taking a few pages.

The example in Figure 14.4, from a Turbo Pascal *Programmer's Guide,* illustrates the use of a sample library lookup entry. Compare it to Figure 14.1, a reference entry in this same document.

Discussion

Reference documentation means those parts of your documentation product that you design for the reader to be able to look up information about the program. Almost all software documents contain reference sections describing details such as what printers the program supports, or what settings the program needs to perform certain functions. Ordinarily users do not read reference sections completely; they only go there for help.

Reference documentation functions on the support level of task orientation. By support, I mean that much of the motivation for success and guidance in the use of the program comes from the user, not from the document. So you don't really push the users, or constrain their focus to your carefully preselected path; instead, you try to respond on call and let the users take the initiative. Unlike in **teaching** or **guidance levels** of task orientation, the reference document contains very little "how to" information. If a reference entry does contain steps, they function merely to jump-start the user, who then can take off on his or her own power. The *reference level* entry contains primarily data (commands, key-stroke lists, menu item definitions), with well-designed but relatively limited access and tracking devices (such as elaborate headings or routing information).

Also, unlike documentation that functions on the other levels of task orientation, reference documentation establishes, through its style and tone, the least engaging relationship with the user. The relationship between the writer's persona and user stays formal, very businesslike. The businesslike nature of the reference section reflects the special needs of the reference user.

The Psychology of the Reference User

The reference user knows the program well, at least better than the novice or casual user. Put yourself in the reference user's place and consider the following scenario. You have been using a desktop publishing package for a few months and have done one or two projects with it. But you have never tried to import graphics files from, say, PC Paintbrush. Now, however, a client has some graphics done in PC Paintbrush and wants them in the manual. You have to consult your program to see what utility to use to import these specially formatted files. At the last minute, after you have already taken on the job and have much of the document put together, you turn to the reference manual that accompanies your desktop publishing program and start looking for the utility that will do the trick.

Given this description, what generalizations can we make about you as a reference user? You do not like to waste time looking things up. Probably, when the solution shows up, it will have to reside in your short-term memory only long enough to do the job of importing the files. The scenario above also indicates something of the psychology of the reference user: He or she hates to leave the screen, and often will hurry to get back to it. Thus, the well-designed reference section should cater to the values of efficiency but, above all, thoroughness. Usually, the reference user complains that manuals don't cover all the functions of the program. The user may not realize this until after having used the program for some time. However, when he or she does realize this, it only adds to the overall distrust of the manual as a support document.

Another important characteristic of reference sections relates to what we have discussed above: the structure of the page. In reference sections, structure, often parallel or repeated structures, abounds. To an extent, a reference entry resembles a card in the card catalog of a library or a record in a database. You fill in a form. Sometimes you structure entries with relatively simple headings, and sometimes you put information into tables and matrices. At the heart of it, you have to establish a pattern and then follow it, so the user quickly understands where to look. Generally, the more structure you can build into your reference entries without overdoing it, the more usable your reference entries. We will discuss the structuring of reference entries below.

Large systems, networks, *compilers,* operating systems—these have lots of look-up commands to make them work. These system get used by computer professionals whose needs differ from those of the novice or intermediate user. Learning how to use these programs depends on the user's experience outside the manual: as in a programming class or an accounting class. If your user analysis shows that you need to support mostly experienced users, then you would increase the proportion of reference material. You should also do this if you expect inexperienced users to become experienced as they progress.

If you need to support inexperienced users, on the other hand, you should, as a rule of thumb, reduce the proportion of reference material you include and cover the functions in your procedural manual. With a word processing program, for example, you could describe *procedures* for importing files from graphics programs instead of having a *reference section* listing programs and brief overviews of the process. Go for an oversized "Quick Reference" that doubles much of the information in the procedures. This approach, coupled with a well-done index, can make your manual more task oriented overall.

The Psychology of a Reference Entry

The psychology of the elements of your reference entries deserves some special consideration. By psychology, I mean the idea behind the repeated categories, column heads, or other user-oriented reference elements elements. These introduce, orient, inform, and direct the user in the search for a solution. But what exactly makes them work? They work because each one answers a question your user might have about a function or command. Figure 14.5 illustrates the psychology behind using structured reference entries.

Notice how the elements of a reference entry respond to the needs of the reference user. These elements come from a program called FormMaker, used by managers to attach multiple notes to forms during the review process for developing forms. The authors of the manual chose to alphabetize the functions—a strategy that bets that the user will know the right names for things or get set straight by the index. At any rate, each entry includes the following:

- **Access information.** Access information tells what menu contains the function, and shows the chain of commands the user needs to issue in order to get to the function.
- **Function definition.** The function definition tells what the function does and what it enables the user to do.
- **Associated commands.** Associated commands tell what other keys or commands the user needs to use the function effectively.
- **Qualifications/special cases.** Qualifications and special cases offer information about *field* lengths, maximum or minimum allowable inputs, time limits, or prerequisites (i.e., you can't save a file that you have not created). It also tells what to do in special cases, such as hardware limitations or dealing with earlier versions of the program.
- **Tips.** The tips section of the reference entry tells ways to use the function efficiently, plus shortcuts and potential problems. It represents software "wisdom": good advice from an old pro.

As you can see, even a simple, five-part structure of a reference entry contains plenty of useful information for the experienced user. To help see clearly how such an entry works, think of each of the items as answering some need or question of the reference user.

- **How do I get to the function?** Probably the experienced user needs to know simply how to find a function more than any other type of information. Many advanced

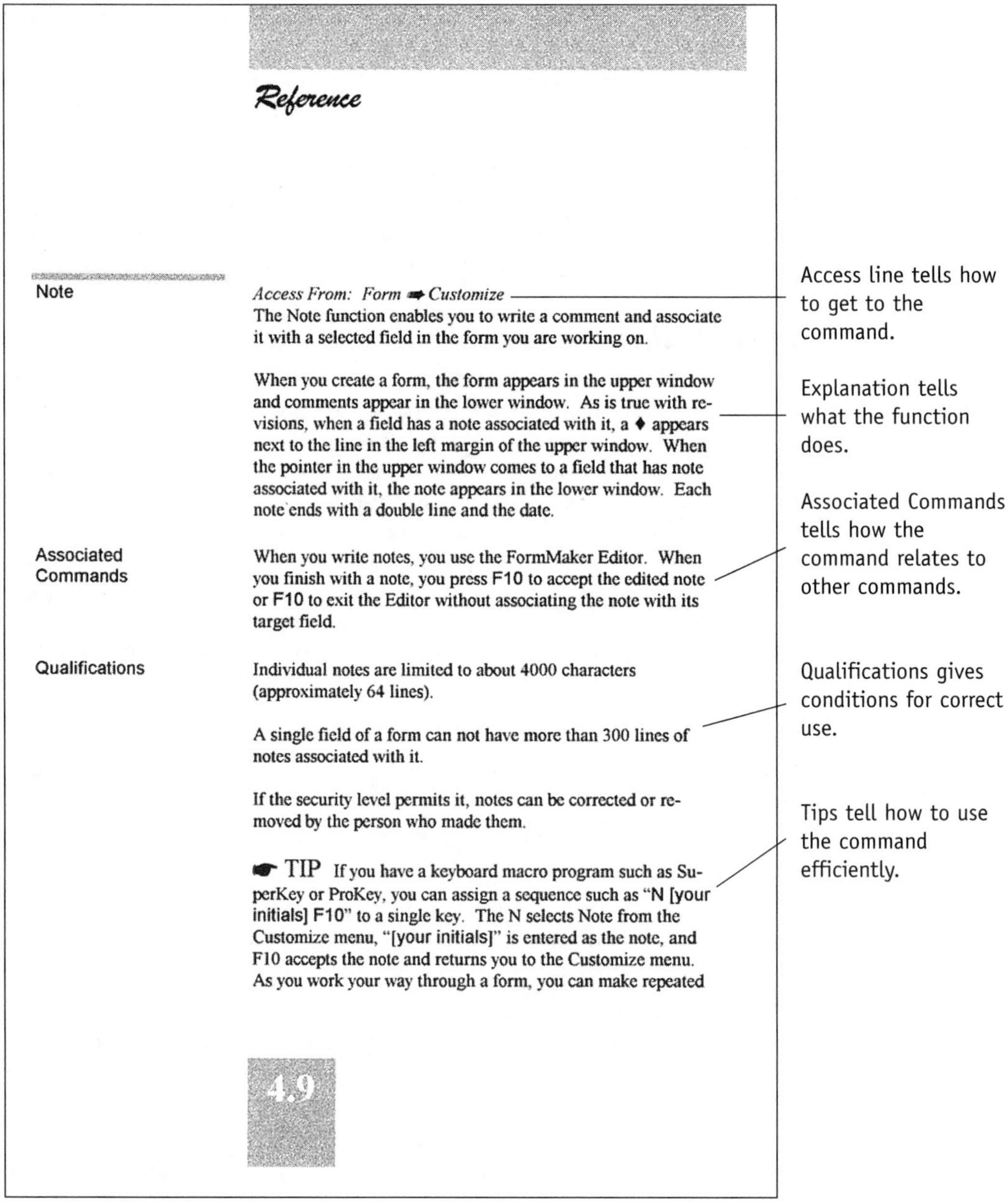

Reference

Note

Access From: Form ➡ Customize ————————
The Note function enables you to write a comment and associate it with a selected field in the form you are working on.

When you create a form, the form appears in the upper window and comments appear in the lower window. As is true with revisions, when a field has a note associated with it, a ♦ appears next to the line in the left margin of the upper window. When the pointer in the upper window comes to a field that has note associated with it, the note appears in the lower window. Each note ends with a double line and the date.

Associated Commands

When you write notes, you use the FormMaker Editor. When you finish with a note, you press F10 to accept the edited note or F10 to exit the Editor without associating the note with its target field.

Qualifications

Individual notes are limited to about 4000 characters (approximately 64 lines).

A single field of a form can not have more than 300 lines of notes associated with it.

If the security level permits it, notes can be corrected or removed by the person who made them.

☛ TIP If you have a keyboard macro program such as SuperKey or ProKey, you can assign a sequence such as "N [your initials] F10" to a single key. The N selects Note from the Customize menu, "[your initials]" is entered as the note, and F10 accepts the note and returns you to the Customize menu. As you work your way through a form, you can make repeated

4.9

Access line tells how to get to the command.

Explanation tells what the function does.

Associated Commands tells how the command relates to other commands.

Qualifications gives conditions for correct use.

Tips tell how to use the command efficiently.

Figure 14.5

Well-Structured Reference Entry

Each part of this entry from the FormMaker *Reference Manual* answers an important question posed by the reference user.

users need only this to get them going. Once they have the sequence of commands, many users will close the book and return to the program to try them out.

■ **What does the function do?** After checking the chain of commands to get to a function, the experienced user would want a very brief, performance-oriented explanation of what the function does. This allows him or her to double-check whether this or some other function really applies.

■ **What other commands do I need to know about?** The user wants to know how to use the command along with other commands, as well as how to get out of trouble. The reference entry should indicate what other commands to use and how to back out of trouble.

■ **When can I use the function?** In case the user had difficulty using the command, he or she needs to know that special conditions might exist, such as disk drive incompatibility or file size limits. Certain functions will not work unless the user has set the program up just right. Certain menu items stay dimmed until the user loads a file or creates an entry.

■ **How do I use the function well?** The experienced user wants to make the most out of the system and needs to know any short cuts or efficiency measures that apply. Here one might include an example of the function in use.

As we can see from the discussion above, the elements of a reference entry do much of the work of establishing the task orientation of your manual. They make up the structural elements that you use to analyze and present each reference entry—a command, a menu option, or a definition. In your study of reference documentation—look-up documentation on the support level of task orientation—make sure to study any reference sections you come across to see what elements the writer has used to help structure the entry information to the user's needs.

Glossary

affordance: a feature of an item—a document or other technology—that allows for its use. For instance: guitars have affordances called tuning keys that allow for adjusting the pitch of the strings.

command line: refers to that part of a software program that allows a user to enter commands. Example: with MS-DOS the command line displays a C:\> prompt. With other programs, the command line looks different. Often you want to show the command line in documentation to show the user where and how to enter commands.

command sets: refers to groups of commands that resemble one another, or use the same control keys on the keyboard. Example, "CTRL-S," "CTRL-Z," and "CTRL-Y," belong to a command set.

compiler: a type of program that creates other programs. Compilers read files of commands created by programmers and transform them into programs that users can run on their computers. If compiler programs can't create the program from the data files, they give a compiler error message and the programmer has to fix the commands in the original file. Compiler programs contain many kinds of commands and other highly technical elements that need explaining in reference documentation.

context sensitive: refers to the capacity of a help system to detect the location of the user in terms of what interface element (menu screen or dialog box) the program currently displays and to provide a help screen appropriate for that element. Using this system the user doesn't have to ask for a specific topic, but just gets the topic appropriate to the current situation (hence "context").

guidance level: a type of documentation designed to lead the user through a procedure one step at a time from a designated starting place (such as a certain menu) to an ending state (such as a report printed.) Guidance level documentation (or procedures) defines the task for the user, but does not teach the task. See also **teaching level** and **support level.**

keyword searches: electronic and automatic searches of the topics in a help system to find pre-identified words relating to certain topics. Example: the keyword "File" might call up the following topics: "opening files," "saving files," and "deleting files."

levels of support: categories of kinds of information supplied to users. Levels relate to the teaching level (tutorial), the guidance level (procedures) and the reference level (reference). Levels differ in terms of purpose: to teach, to walk through step-by-step, and to provide data. They also differ in the relationship of the writer to the user: from very close and controlling with the teaching level, to distant and businesslike with the reference level.

reference level: a type of documentation intended to provide the user with a piece of information needed to perform a task. Reference documentation does not define the task for the user, but provides the necessary data the user needs to complete a task. See **guidance level** and **teaching level.**

teaching level: a type of documentation intended to instill a knowledge of how to use a program feature in the memory of the user. Teaching level documentation (tutorials) aims to enable the user to perform a task from memory. See **guidance level** and **support level.**

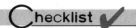

Checklist

Use the following checklist to evaluate the efficiency of your design for reference.

Reference Checklist
Choosing the Right Form of Reference

Have you chosen the right form of reference to match your users' needs?

☐ Reference section (tables of date, definitions, command descriptions)
☐ Task reference (sparse steps for all procedures)
☐ Quick reference (card, booklet, brochure)
☐ Appendix (tables, messages, troubleshooting, etc.)
☐ Update information/Readme (disk file containing update highlights)
☐ Keyboard templates and short forms
☐ Innovative forms (cube, poster, coffee mug, tattoo [just kidding!])

Deciding What to Include in the Reference Section

Which of the following elements meet your users' needs?

☐ Commands
☐ Interface elements
☐ Definitions
☐ Background

Deciding What to Include in Each Reference Entry

Identify which of the following elements you want or need to include in each reference entry to meet your user's support needs.

☐ The command itself
☐ Screens or menus showing where to find the command
☐ Definitions and descriptions of the command and what it does
☐ Steps for executing the command in tasks
☐ Contexts/overviews of what the command does
☐ Tables showing variations of the command and how it relates to other commands
☐ Error messages for when you use the command incorrectly
☐ Alternative commands (such as keyboard or mouse alternatives)
☐ Explanations of how the command affects the user's work
☐ Cross references to tutorials, procedures, other entries where the command gets further explanations
☐ File specifications for what files the command uses
☐ Input requirements (characters, data, or both) telling what kind of data to use with the command
☐ Notes to further explain the command
☐ Tips for when and how to use the command efficiently
☐ Sample reports showing what the command produces
☐ Examples showing the command in a syntax statement
☐ Warnings telling how not to loose data when using the command
☐ Syntax diagrams telling how to use the command in statements
☐ Switches that allow the user to tailor the command to various needs
☐ Access sequences to tell the user how to get to the prompt where the command works

Establishing a Pattern

☐ Have you established a pattern for each reference entry?

Organizing the Reference Section

Which of the following organizational patterns do you intend to use?

☐ Alphabetical
☐ Menu by menu
☐ Context sensitive
☐ Combination

Showing the User How to Use the Reference Information

Have you written a section that tells the user the following things?

- ☐ Who should use the information
- ☐ How you organized the information
- ☐ The elements of each entry
- ☐ The relation of the reference to other sections of the documentation
- ☐ Have you included a sample library entry to orient the reference user?

Practice/Problem Solving

1. Analyze a Reference Entry

Each of the elements of the reference entry below has a number next to it. For each number, explain what question the user (a programmer) might ask. Then describe briefly the answer that the reference entry supplies.

❶ TABCREATE

❷ Syntax	TABSET tabcreate(rw,string, . . . /cl,string, . . . /fm,var)
❸ Remarks	*TabCreate creates a table with the rows and columns specified, and formats it according to format variables supplied.*

Format Variable	Result
tr	traditional format with rules above and below headings
bx	a grid format with a ¾ pt border around each data cell
dd	a 3-D format, using greyscales to create an in-depth look

❹ Events triggered	checksp_anchor#set_errorlevel0
❺ See also	*tabdelete, tabcopy*

2. Design a Reference Entry

Often you have programs that produce special reports or special forms of documents and you want to catalog them for the user, so he or she can browse through the examples. Assume you have a program that creates special reports for financial analysis.

You would like to include a section in which you show each type of report and describe its use and other features of each report. Below you will find a description of a report from a program called "DollarDoctor." Users of the program include small business owners and instructors at a business college.

1. Follow the guidelines in this chapter decide what to include in each entry, establish a pattern for other entries, and organize the reference section.

2. Then create a sample of one entry, following the principles of layout in Chapter 5.

   When you create the pattern for your sample reference entry, consider the questions the users might like to know about each report and use those questions as a basis for your reference paradigm.

Kinds of Reports Produced by DollarDoctor:

Transaction Report	Capital Gains Report	Net Worth Report
Income Report	Market Value Report	Loan Payment Report
Expense Report	Performance Report	Tax Report
Portfolio Earnings Report	Price History Report	Depreciation Report
Summary Report	Insurance Report	Budget Report

chapter
15   Designing Indexes

Of all the *affordances* of software documentation that you can offer your user, the index ranks among one of the most valuable and most popular. It allows you to guide the user to information in your manual or help system. This chapter helps you decide what index methodology to use: manual or electronic. But the main focus of the chapter falls on deciding what to index and setting levels of detail, phrasing, and techniques for building and proofreading. The chapter discusses the function of indexes and examines the differences between manual and online indexes.

How to Read This Chapter

This chapter follows a straightforward approach to indexing and building keyword searches. Necessarily limited in scope, it nevertheless provides you with the basic ideas behind these valuable task-oriented tools.

- The project-oriented reader can begin with the Guidelines and then read the rest of the chapter.

- The reader seeking greater understanding of indexes should also start with the Guidelines because they proceed through a demonstration-type sequence that can help those uninitiated into the mysteries of indexing compare one element to another.

The index in Figure 15.1 exhibits many of the features of an index designed to support easy processing of information and to accommodate a variety of workplace uses. In particular, it demonstrates how you can orchestrate various kinds of information in the index.

Example **463**

Menu initials appear in brackets for easy identification.

Main headings and subheadings.

Entries sound like sentences, easy to read.

Locator numbers.

Error messages help famililarize users with the correct terminology.

F igure 15.1

A User-Oriented Index

This index page from the Norton Textra Writer word processing program illustrates standard features of a two-level outline.

1. Decide on the indexing methodology.
2. Decide what to index.
3. Identify the level of detail.
4. Decide on phrasing and format.
5. Build and proofread.

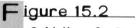

igure 15.2

Guidelines for Designing Indexes

Figure 15.2 lists guidelines for designing indexes, all of which will be discussed later in this chapter.

1 DECIDE ON THE INDEXING METHODOLOGY

Basically, you have two methods for making an index: manually or electronically. A manual index requires that you go through the document and write index entries on cards. An electronic index uses the indexing feature of your software program to accomplish the task. Below you will find a discussion of each of these methods to help you decide which best suits your project. Probably you will do an electronic index.

Manual Indexes

Most manual indexes require that you have essentially finished the document because you need to write down the page numbers on which the terms you index occur. After doing this, you organize the cards alphabetically and type up the index. You would use this method for indexing projects that others have done, where you don't have access to the automatic features of a word processor. Most writers use the automatic indexing capabilities of word processing software.

Electronic Indexes

Word processing software programs usually contain functions for indexing. These require that you identify a term on a specific page that you want to index, and then highlight it, along with the category it pertains to. You can use this method from the very beginning of working on a document, and then compile the index at the end of the project. The advantages of this method include the following:

- **Automatic alphabetizing.** You don't have to rely on your abc's.
- **Automatic formatting.** You don't have to bother with indenting by hand.
- **Ease of revision.** You can change the index at the last minute.

2 DECIDE WHAT TO INDEX

As you will see below, you can index a number of different types of information. You should try to match your choice of what to index with your user analysis. Consult your documentation plan for the specifications set up earlier in the project for the kind of index that you need for your users and your project. If you don't have an index specified in your documentation plan, make up some index specifications now and have the developer, users, and other writers review them.

Consider the following list of elements you could index, and determine the ones you need. Keep the list in front of you as you go through the document making your index. If you do your index electronically, enter these items into your style guide early in the project and refine the list as you go along. You probably will add to it or refine things as you go. Also, if you have others working on the project, make sure they know the elements to index and the categories they belong in.

Commands and Functions

Commands and command sets and functions consist of all the terms that you find on menus. It also includes Control or Alt key sequences. Usually you would format the commands differently in the index because they don't sound like parts of sentences. This helps the user identify them as commands and spot them while scanning the index. In the example below, the commands under one menu were included in a special section under the name of the menu. You would also cite the occurrence of the command or function at another place under the name of the function.

Commands and Functions

Occurrence in the Document	Result in the Index
Use the Make Report command (Report menu) to arrange your data into one of the many reports available in MarketMaster. (p. 48)	Make Report (Report Menu), **48**, *x*, 4 • • • Report Menu Make Report, **48**, *x*, 4 Delete Report, **51** Format Report, **52**, 8 Set Report Preferences, **55**, 38, 112

Concepts

Concepts refer to the ideas related to the subject matter of the program. All users have to understand these basic concepts in order to understand how the program works. Concepts make up an important element of your index because when the user encounters the term in various parts of the book, he or she will look the term up in the index.

Concepts

Occurrence in the Document	Result in the Index
AccountMaster uses the idea of client levels as a way of organizing your client database. Basically, a client level identifies the category in which the client's record information resides, Client levels. . . . (p. 15)	Client levels, *xi*, **15**, 24, 33–38, 111 • • • Levels, client,, *xi*, **15**, 24, 33–38, 111

User Terms and Questions

The index functions to connect words the user may know to synonyms or related words used in the program. For example the user may say "quit a program" but the program's function uses the term *Exit*. The index should list *quit* with an entry saying See *Exit, 23*. You can think of many examples of this type: *Blank line above a paragraph*, see *Line spacing; Start a program*, see *Load; Search,* see *Find.* Many of these terms come from users' experience with other software that uses parallel terms.

Users also have terms they use in their work that they need to correlate to the program. For example, the term *sku* (pronounced "skew") in retailing stands for *stock keeping unit* and represents an actual product (such as Sparkling Dawn Dish Detergent, 10 oz., lemon scent #5167443704). In a program that analyzes business data, let's say, the term *item* refers to the lowest level of a hierarchy of categories of data. A user would come to the index thinking "How do I display information at the sku level," and look under *s* for *sku.* A good index, in this case, would include the entry *Sku,* see *Item,* **45.** Such an entry would direct the user to the correct term and the correct page.

One experienced editor, Christine Hash, suggests indexing user questions: questions they might have about a procedure or terms in the program. For example, users who don't know about *justification* in a word processing program might ask the question "How do I align text with margins?" Hash suggests that this question justifies including an entry like *Margins, aligning text with* to help the user find the right information.[1]

When you do your user analysis, you should watch out for these kinds of terms. Begin making a list while you have access to your users so you can then incorporate these terms into your index. You need this list, because in the case of user terms you will index words that don't actually occur in your manual. So if you don't have a list of them, you won't find them while scanning the pages.

User Terms and Questions

Occurrence in the Document	Result in the Index
You can easily delete files from your directory by dragging the filename into the Recycling Bin. The recycling bin stores files you've deleted until you empty it using the **Shred** command. (p. 19)	The recycling bin is almost full, *see* Shred, 19, **50** • • • Trash can, *see* Recycling Bin, 19

Glossary Terms

Indexing glossary terms simply means that you include a reference in the index for all the terms in your glossary.

Glossary Terms

Occurrence in the Document	Result in the Index

Scratch sheet. A scratch sheet refers to a quick print of account details. It has a set format, and you can use it to quickly print out data about a client to use in an office visit. (p. 112)	Scratch sheet
	    printing, 67–68
	    deleting, 69
	    defined, 112

Proper Names of Products and Companies

With some programs you will find yourself documenting names of other programs or companies. Often your program will write files in formats usable by other programs, or you will refer to other companies that do business with your users. An manual that supports information-oriented work should do its best to acknowledge connections to the larger business environment surrounding the user's workplace. It should also acknowledge that users use other programs in their work. Users will consult the index with terms relating to this context and need to know where to get information about them.

Proper Names of Products and Companies

Occurrence in the Document	Result in the Index
If you run AccountMaster on a computer with an 8088 processor, such as an IBM PC-XT you need to install a Hercules graphics card. (p. 2)	Hercules graphics card, 2

Tasks and Procedures

You may want to have a special index for tasks and procedures, or you may want to include them in the main index. Often you will see tasks highlighted in some way to indicate to the user that this entry will lead them to guidance or step-by-step information.

You may want to include section names as part of the scheme for indexing tasks. Section names usually correspond to main areas or categories of tasks that the user would most likely look up in the manual or help system. You usually include them in an index to direct the user to the section containing these kinds of tasks.

Tasks and Procedures

Occurrence in the Document	Result in the Index

Deleting an Account
 	
You should delete accounts when you find that you have inadvertently created more than one account for a client, or a client goes out of business. It's a good practice to maintain your account lists in these ways.
 	
Follow the steps below to delete an account.
 	
1. Choose **Delete . . .** from the **Utilities** menu. (p. 37)
	Accounts
	   creating, 30, **22–25**
	   deleting, **37**
	   formatting records in, 20, **25–27**
	      •
	      •
	      •
	Delete
	   a report, 60
	   an account, **37**
	   a list record, 20, 22
	   a report field, **60,** 61

3   IDENTIFY THE LEVEL OF DETAIL

You can define the level of detail in two ways, one by the number of levels in the index (see Table 15.1), and the other by the number of items you index per page.

Levels of Detail

A very simple index will contain only one level and will probably only show the main headings within the text. Such an index, usually for a shorter document, basically puts

Table 15.1

Levels of Indexes

One Level	Two Levels	Three Levels
Getting Help, **3**	Getting Help, **3**	Getting Help, 3
Graphics, **30,** 32–35	Graphics	Graphics

Greeting, 12, 33, **51**	importing, 30, 32
	   in reports, 30, 32–35
		importing
		      bitmaps, 30
		      converting, 32

	Greeting	in reports
		      example, 30
		      inserting 32–35

	deleting, 33
	   example, 12
	   setting, 51
		Greeting

		deleting, 33
		   example, 12
		   setting, 51

the table of contents into alphabetical order and allows the user to access information in that way. A two-level index organizes terms by categories, where appropriate, and represents a more sophisticated organization of the material. The most extensive index usually goes to three or more levels and indicates a very complex way of organizing material.

Another way to describe the amount of detail in an index focuses on the number of indexable items per page. Of course, the number of items per page will vary from one part of a document to another, depending on the density of your pages, the number of figures, and the kinds of things you need to index, but basically you can rely on the following averages.

- Light index   two to three items per page
- Medium index   five to seven items per page
- Heavy index   eight to nine items per page

4   DECIDE ON PHRASING AND FORMAT

You should give some time to the planning of the phrasing and format of your index entries. You can consult your documentation plan and coordinate the cuing of commands and other items in the index with your overall *notational conventions*. The following list discusses the kinds of issues you will face in this regard.

- **Cue the primary locator numbers.** In some indexes you will find the *primary locator number* cued in some way, usually by bolding. Example: Greeting, 12, 33, **51,** where the main information for the entry occurs on page 51. This requires some decision making on your part as to the main entry. Usually you would use the primary locator to refer the user to the procedure related to the task, or to its definition.

- **Capitalize terms consistently.** In some indexes you capitalize all terms as a matter of editorial principle, and in others you don't. Consider these examples:

Capitalization

Uncapitalized terms	Capitalized terms
getting help, **3**	Getting Help, **3**

graphics
  importing, 30, 32
  in reports, 30, 32–35
	Graphics
	  Importing, 30, 32
	  In reports, 30, 32–35

greeting
  deleting, 33
  example, 12
  setting, 51
	Greeting
	  Deleting, 33
	  Example, 12
	  Setting, 51

- **Make entries sound like sentences.** You want to make your entries sound like sentences when you put them together with their heading. Consider the following examples of how and how not to do this.

Entries That Sound Like Sentences

Short Phrases (bad)	Complete Phrases (good)
Getting Help, **3**	Getting Help, **3**
Graphics	Graphics
Format, 36	Format of, 36
Import, 30, 32	Importing from other programs, 30, 32
Reports, 30, 32–35	Using in reports, 30, 32–35
Greeting	Greeting
Delete, 33	Deleting, 33
Example, 12	Example, 12
Set, 51	Setting, 51

■ **Cue special terms.** Identify a special format for commands, tasks, function keys, and other kinds of things beyond just words. In the example below, the toolbars appear in brackets and the command appears in bold face, followed by the menu it appears on.

Cuing Patterns for Commands and Other Special Entries

Toolbars
   [Accounts], 98
   [Format], 100
   [Utilities], 102

Tracing Activities
   Defined, 28
   Reasons for, 29
   Tracing Activities . . . Utilities menu, 102

5   BUILD AND PROOFREAD

If you're using an electronic editing feature of your word processor, the procedure for building the index entails that you tell the program where to put the index and then select the "compile the index" command. Your program will go through the document, collect the index entries you've made, and put the index where you told it to. You then have the job of formatting it, probably into columns, getting the page breaks just right, and putting in the alphabet indicators.

Once you have created your index, you should proofread it carefully for format mistakes. Check specifically for indentation problems if you have two or more levels. You should also spot-check the page references to make sure they take the user to the right pages. If you have a user available, you should test the index with the user. You can do this simply by having the user review it, or by asking specific questions about terms you included. Finally, check the index for inconsistencies of reference, things like:

Accounts, opening

Accounts, open

Accounts, to open

There is more about proofreading indexes in Chapter 7, "Editing and Fine Tuning."

You may look at indexing tasks as a hassle you have to take care of after you've done the manual. I certainly see this in some students, who, after printing out a shiny new manual breathe a sign of satisfaction at its crisp print and smooth pages. That sigh often turns to a growl when they remember that their documentation plan called for "a complete index." It's normal to feel this way about indexes, because they take a lot of time—sometimes up to three hours per index page—and they lack an intrinsic interest. Besides, you might say, the manual has a table of contents, why does it need an index?

Why an Index?

Seeing an index as a chore or as redundant shows that you don't have a correct understanding of the importance of this element of software documentation. In fact, you would do well to see the index as an integral part of the access system to your information. Consider the following justifications for indexes.

- **Performs a unique function.** The index does not just repeat the information in the table of contents. The table of contents expresses the organization of the document, but the index does something completely different. It accesses the document from the user's point of view, in the user's language. It directs the user straight to the material in the manual and, for this reason, forms one of the most important elements of the manual. In fact, some manuals even print the index in the front of the manual before the table of contents.

- **Meeting place of multiple users.** Almost all programs have users in various business areas or professions. These users bring a multifaceted vocabulary to their work with the program. Also, you may have both beginners and advanced users who know other kinds of programs relating to your application and who use different terms to refer to different functions. The index serves as the meeting place of the vocabulary used by all these kinds of users. If you design and build it right, all users will find the terms they use in it and it will direct them to the information they need.

Online Index versus Print Index versus Keywords

When you design your indexing system, you need to consider the three main forms of index material in a situation where you have manuals and online help. Your manual will contain an index, possibly at the front but usually at the back, and your help system will probably contain an online index and a capability to do a *keyword search*. Consider the following differences among these three forms of the index information.

- **Print index.** Contains the terms printed in two- or three-column format usually at the back of the manual, divided into sections by alphabet.

- **Online index.** Contains terms printed in a long, scrolling list with the alphabet displayed at the top of the page. The user can click on an alphabet entry to display the terms listed under that letter.

- **Keyword searches.** Consists of a list of terms and phrases that the user can scroll through or enter manually, after which the program, or *search engine,* will scan the list and find the closest related topic. The designer (you) has created *electronic links* to certain topics, a list of which appears for the user to choose from. The keyword search list differs from the index information because it limits terms to those relating to topics in the help system. The keyword search list usually doesn't contain user questions, user synonyms, or other material, and focuses strictly on the help topics.

The essential element here lies in the interchangeability of the information in all three of these lists. The words that trigger the keyword search among the topics should also appear in your print and online indexes. Careful planning on your part can help you achieve a high degree of consistency among these three forms of index information.

Glossary

affordance: a capability of a program, or other technological device, to allows the user to take advantage of its functions. Examples of affordances of software programs include: menus, toolbars, the cursor, etc.

electronic links: software functions within hypertext programs, such as Windows Help or HyperCard, that allow the user to jump to another designated position within a text. The position or *target* to which the user moves is highlighted in the text, usually with blue as on Web pages, or green as in Windows Help documents.

keyword searches: electronic and automatic searches of the topics in a help system to find pre-identified words relating to certain topics. Example: the keyword *File* might call up the following topics: *Opening files, Saving files,* and *Deleting files.*

notational conventions: conventions relating to how terms, commands, menus, and other interface elements appear in a manual. For example, often manuals will use italics (as in *dir, copy*) as the notational convention for commands.

primary locator number: the number in an index entry that tells the user which of the selection of numbers contains the main information about the entry.

search engine: a kind of computer program that searches an online document for words, parts of words, or search keywords provided by the writer.

Checklist ✔

Use the following checklist to evaluate your index.

Index Checklist
Decide on the Indexing Methodology

For your index, which methodology will you use?

☐ Manual ☐ Electronic

Decide What to Index

Which of the following elements will you include in your index?

☐ Commands and functions
☐ Concepts
☐ User terms and questions

☐ Glossary terms
☐ Proper names of products and companies
☐ Tasks and procedures

Identify the Level of Detail

How many levels do you plan to include in your index?

☐ One level   ☐ Two levels   ☐ Three levels

How many indexable items do you plan to do for each page (on the average)?

☐ Light index   2 to 3 items per page
☐ Medium index   5 to 7 items per page
☐ Heavy index   8 to 9 items per page

Decide on Phrasing and Format

Which of the following format options do you plan to use?

☐ Cues for primary locator numbers
☐ Capitalization of terms
☐ "Sentence-like" entries
☐ Cues for special terms

Build and Proofread

Proofread and check the index for the following items:

☐ Page references (spot check)
☐ Cross references (spot check)
☐ Review terms with users
☐ Inconsistency of references

Practice/Problem Solving

1. Practice Indexing a Page

Choose a page of a manual and write a set of index items for it. Make sure to include terms on other pages that would make references to your page. Use your judgment about what level of detail the user would need to guide your indexing. After you have written the index, check with the existing index and consider the differences between your index for that page and the existing one. How would your index differ?

2. Analyze an Index

Find an entry in an index to a computer manual with three or more locator numbers. Analyze each locator number (entry) for task orientation, rank, cross referencing, and accurateness. Copy the sentences and evaluate the index for overall usability.

Endnotes

Chapter 1

1. Norman, Donald A. 1993. *Things that make us smart: Defending human attributes in the age of the machine.* New York: Addison-Wesley Publishing Company.
2. Bell, Paula and Charlotte Evans. 1989. *Mastering documentation.* New York: John Wiley & Sons.
3. The ideas that underlie the approach described above come from work done by researchers in the areas of management, information management, a relatively new field called end-user computing, and a rapidly growing field called cognitive science. Much of the discussion below derives from the work of Shoshana Zuboff's article "New worlds of computer-mediated work," in *Harvard Business Review* 60, September-October, 1982, pp. 142–152, and Saul Wurman in his book *Information Anxiety,* New York: Doubleday, 1989.
4. Yaverbaum, Gayle. 1988. "Critical factors in the user environment: An experimental study of users, organizations and tasks." *MIS Quarterly* (March): 75–88.
5. Zuboff, Shoshana. 1988. *In the age of the smart machine: The Future of work and power.* New York: Basic Books.
6. Yaverbaum, p. 85.
7. Wurman, p. 34.
8. Yaverbaum, p. 79.
9. Bostrom, Robert P., Lorne Olfman, and Maung Sein. 1990. "The importance of learning style in end-user training." *MIS Quarterly* (March): 101–119.
10. Hellman, Ritta. 1992. "Comprehensive user education for successful end-user computing." *Information Technology & People* 6:1. 81.
11. Hellman, 75–76.
12. The idea of users performing a cost/benefit analysis occurs in Fred Davis, "Perceived usefulness, perceived ease of use, and user acceptance of information technology," *MIS Quarterly* (September, 1989): 319–339. The "cost" part of the user's argument addresses the ease of use of the program: *"How much time and effort will I have to invest to use this software tool?"* and the "benefit" part of the user's argument addresses the usefulness of the program: *"Will this software tool help me to perform my job better?"* p. 321.

Chapter 2

1. Karis, William and Stephen Doheny-Farina. 1991. "Collaborating with readers: Empower them and take the consequences." *Technical Communication* 38: 513–519.

2. Grice, Roger and Lenore Ridgeway. 1991. "Information product testing, An integral part of information development." in *Perspectives on software documentation: Inquiries and innovations.* Thomas T. Barker, ed. Amityville, NY: Baywood Publishing Company, Inc., 209–228.

3. Karis, 514.

4. Rosenbaum, Stephanie, L. 1992. "Collecting usability data: Alternatives to testing." In *Conference Record, IPPC,* pp. 248–253. Santa Fe, NM.

5. These steps and the tips that follow are adapted from Rosenbaum, pp. 251–253.

6. Meyers, Martha M. 1992. "Motivating high-tech workers." *Best's Review* 93:2. 86–92.

7. Honeyman, David S. and Warren J. White. 1987. "Computer anxiety in educators learning to use the computer: A preliminary report." *Journal of Research on Computing in Education* 20:2. 129–138.

8. Bracey, Gerald W. 1988. "Computers and anxiety in education: Round two." *Electronic Learning* 8:3. 26–28.

9. Foss, Donald J., Penny L. Smith-Kerker, and Mary Beth Rosson. 1987. "On comprehending a computer manual: Analysis of variables affecting performance." *International Journal of Man–Machine Studies* 26. 277–300.

10. Norman, Donald. 1988. *The psychology of everyday things.* New York: Harper Collins Press: 11.

11. Barfield, Woodrow. 1986. "Expert–Novice differences for software: Implications for problem-solving and knowledge acquisition." *Behavior and Information Technology* 5:1. 15–29.

12. Marchonini, Gary. 1989. "Information-seeking strategies of novices using a full-text electronic encyclopedia." *Journal of the American Society for Information Science* 40:1. 54–66.

13. Lee, Denis M. S. 1986. "Usage pattern and sources of assistance for personal computer users." *MIS Quarterly* December: 313–321.

14. Inglesby. 1992. "An interview with Ken Sharma." *Manufacturing Systems* 10: 54.

15. Vaske, Jerry J. and Charles E. Grantham. 1990. *Socializing the Human–Computer Environment.* Norwood, NJ: Ablex Publishing Corporation.

16. A. Rafaeli. 1986. "Employee attitudes toward working with computers." *Journal of Occupational Behavior* 7: 89–106.

17. Liqueur, J., M. Fleischer, and D. Arnsdorf. 1992. "Fulfilling the promises of CAD." *Sloane Management Review* 33: 74–86.

18. Czaja, Sara J., Katka Hammond, James J. Blascovich, and Helen Swede. 1986. "Learning to use a word processing system as a function of training strategy." *Behavior and Information Technology* 5:3. 203–216.

19. Czaja, op. cit.

20. Michael D. Cooper. 1991. "User skill acquisition in office information systems." *Journal of the American Society for Information Science* 42:10. 739.

21. Santhanam, Radhika and Susan Weidenbeck. "Modeling the intermittent user of word processing software." *Journal of the American Society of Information Science* 42:3. 185–196.

22. Santhanam, p. 194.

23. Marchonini, pp. 54–66.

Chapter 3

1. IBM Corporation. *Information development guideline: Task-oriented information.* Document Number ZZ27-1971-01, October, 1992.
2. Hubbard, Scott E. 1991. "Process implementation—The key to quality documentation." In *Perspectives on Software Documentation: Inquiries and Innovations.* Thomas T. Barker, ed. Amityville, NY: Baywood Publishing Co.

Chapter 4

1. Norman, Donald. 1988. *The Psychology of Everyday Things.* New York, Basic Books.

Chapter 5

1. Chatfield, Carl S. 1994. "Improving the Documentation Process through Structured Walkthroughs." *STC Proceedings:* 90–92.

Chapter 6

1. Masuda, Tadashi. 1994. "Using customer inquiries as a basis for revising and editing user manuals." In *Proceedings, 41st Annual Conference of the STC,* p. 83.
2. Gould, Emile and Stephen Doheny-Farina. 1988. "Studying usability in the field: Qualitative research techniques for technical communicators." In *Effective documentation: What we have learned from research,* Stephen Doheny-Farina, ed. Cambridge, MA: The MIT Press: 329–343.
3. Gould, p. 332.
4. Grice, Roger, and Lenore Ridgeway. 1991. "Information product testing: An integral part of information development." In *Perspectives on software documentation: Inquiries and innovations,* Thomas Barker, ed. Amityville, NY: Baywood Publishing Company, Inc. 209–228.
5. Boggan, Scott, David Farkas, and Joe Welinske. 1993. *Developing online help for Windows.* Carmel, IN: Sams Publishing.
6. You can find a more elaborate description of the user preference test in Michelle Corbin Nichols, "User preference tests: Show and tell for information design," in *1994 STC Proceedings,* pp. 321–322.
7. Some of these advantages are pointed out in Gould, p. 333.
8. The following description of Q-sorts adapts information in Claudia M. Hunter, "Pre-testing the usability and task orientation of computer documentation," in *Conference Record,* IPCC, Santa Fe, NM, 1992: 80–85.
9. Claudia M. Hunter. 1992. "Pre-testing the usability and task orientation of computer documentation." In *Conference Record,* IPCC, Santa Fe, NM: 82.
10. Donald A. Norman. *Things that make us smart.* New York: Addison-Wesley Publishing Company, p. 229.
11. Lauren Baker. 1988. "The relationship of product design to document design." In *Effective documentation: What we have learned from research,* Stephen Doheny-Farina, ed. pp. 317–328. Cambridge, MA: The MIT Press.
12. Baker, pp. 317–328.

Chapter 7

1. Masse, Roger E. 1985. "Theory and practice of editing processes in technical communication." *IEEE Transactions in Professional Communication,* 28: 1. 34–42.

2. Van Buren, Robert and Mary Fran Buehler. 1976. *The levels of edit.* Arlington, VA: The Society for Technical Communication.
3. Tarutz, Judith. 1992. *Technical editing.* New York: Addison-Wesley.
4. Restive, Katherine, and Phillip R. Shelton. 1994. "From editing to writing: Learning the write stuff." In *STC Proceedings,* pp. 70–72.
5. Berry, Robert, Falpy Earle, and Michelle Corbin Nichols. 1994. "Good online indexing: It doesn't happen automatically." In *STC Proceedings,* pp. 110–112.
6. Torkzadeh, Gholamreza, and William J. Doll. 1993. "The place and value of documentation in end-user computing." *Information & Management* 24: 147–158.
7. *LabVIEW for Windows Tutorial,* National Instruments Corporation, 1993.
8. *Microsoft Windows User's Guide,* Version 3.1, Microsoft Corporation, 1992.
9. Parks, John E. *Grass 4.0* (draft document). Center for Advanced Spatial Technologies, National Center for Resource Innovations, SW, University of Arkansas, Fayetteville, AR, November, 1991, p. 61

Chapter 8

1. Sullivan, Patricia, and Linda Flower. 1989. "How do users read computer manuals? Some protocol contributions to writers' knowledge." In B. T. Petersen, ed. *Convergences: Transactions in reading and writing.* Urbana, IL: National Council of Teachers of English: 163–178.
2. Ramey, Judith. 1988. "How people use computer documentation: Implications for book design." In Stephen Doheny-Farina, *Effective documentation: What we have learned from research.* Cambridge, MA: The MIT Press: 143–158.
3. Carroll, John M., Penny L. Smith Kerker, Jim R. Ford, and Sandra A. Mazur. "The minimal manual." In Doheny-Farina, pp. 73–102.

Chapter 9

1. Weiss, Edmund. 1991. *How to write usable user documentation.* Phoenix, AZ: Oryx Press.

Chapter 11

1. Lewis, Elaine. 1988. "Design principles for pictorial information." In *Effective documentation: What we have learned from the research,* ed. Stephen Doheny-Farina. Cambridge, MA: The MIT Press.
2. Krull, Robert. 1988. "If Icon, why can't you?" In Doheney-Farina.

Chapter 12

1. Charney, Davida, Lynne Reder, and Gail Wells. 1988. "Studies of elaboration in instructional texts." In *Effective documentation: What we have learned from the research,* ed. Stephen Doheny-Farina. Cambridge, MA: The MIT Press: 47–72.
2. Crandall, Judith A. 1987. *How to write tutorial documentation.* Englewood Cliffs, NJ: Prentice-Hall, p. xvi.
3. Caroll, John M., Penny L. Smith-Kerker, James R. Ford, and Sandra A. Aazur-Rimetz. 1988. "The minimal manual." *Human–Computer interaction,* 3:123–153.

Chapter 15

1. Hash, Christine Mulligan. "Indexing: A step-by-step workshop," in *1994 STC Proceedings,* p. 56.

Credits

This is a continuation of the copyright page.

Figures 1.1 and 8.4 are used with permission of Visual Numerics, Inc.

Figures 1.2, 1.6, 2.3, 2.8, 3.7, 3.8, 3.10, 9.5, 9.11, 11.1, 11.11, 11.14, 11.22, 13.4, and 13.7 are reprinted with permission from Microsoft Corporation.

Figure 1.4 © Ed Stein, reprinted by permission of Newspaper Enterprise Association, Inc.

Figure 2.4 is used with permission of Academic Computing, Texas Tech University.

Figures 2.5, 9.10, 11.5, 11.15, and 11.19 are used with permission of Apple Computer, Inc.

Figure 2.6 is used with permission of the PC Resource Center, Brookhaven National Laboratory.

Figure 3.4 is used with permission of Banyan Systems, Inc.

Figure 3.11 is used with permission of Symbios Logic.

Figure 4.4 © 1994 Cognos Incorporated. All rights reserved.

Figure 5.1 is reprinted by permission of Texas Instruments, Inc.

Material in Chapter 7 is used with permission from *The Levels of Edit,* published by the Society for Technical Communication, Arlington, Virginia.

Figures 8.1, 9.2, and 9.3 are used with permission of Blue Sky Software Corporation.

Figure 8.2 is licensed from and used with the permission of Micrografx, Inc. © 1991–1995. All rights reserved.

Figures 8.5 and 10.1 are used with permission of Genetics Computer Group, Inc.

Figures 8.6, 11.12, and 12.1 are used with permission of National Instruments Corporation.

Figure 8.10 is used with permission of Quarterdeck.

Figures 8.17, 9.7, 11.2, and 11.16 © 1995, Hewlett-Packard Company, Convex Division. Reproduced with permission. Hewlett-Packard makes no warranty as to the accuracy or completeness of the foregoing material and hereby disclaims any responsibility therefore.

Figures 8.18 and 9.9 are used with permission of the Thomas-Conrad Corporation.

Figures 9.8 and 11.21 are used with permission of CompuServe Incorporated.

Figure 9.12 is used with permission of Nildram Software.

Figures 11.2, 11.10, and 13.1 © Corel Corporation. Used with permission. Corel is a registered trademark and CorelDRAW is a trademark of Corel Corporation.

Figures 11.6 and 11.25 are from the Novell NetWare Installation Guide, © 1991, 1994 Novel, Inc. All rights reserved. Used with permission.

Figures 11.20 and 11.27 are reprinted with permission from Adobe Systems, Inc. PageMaker and Adobe Illustrator are trademarks of Adobe Systems, Inc.

Figures 14.1 and 14.4 are reprinted with permission of Borland International, Inc.

Figure 15.1 is used with permission of W. W. Norton and Company, Inc.

Index